Windows Server 2003 Security Infrastructures

Jan De Clercq

AMSTERDAM • BOSTON • HEIDELBERG • LONDON
NEW YORK • OXFORD PARIS • SAN DIEGO
SAN FRANCISCO • SINGAPORE • SYDNEY • TOKYO
Digital Press is an imprint of Elsevier

Digital Press is an imprint of Elsevier
200 Wheeler Road, Burlington, MA 01803, USA
Linacre House, Jordan Hill, Oxford OX2 8DP, UK

Recognizing the importance of preserving what has been written, Elsevier prints its books on acid-free paper whenever possible.

Library of Congress Cataloging-in-Publication Data
A catalog record for this book is available from the Library of Congress

ISBN: 1-55558-283-4

British Library Cataloguing-in-Publication Data
A catalog record for this book is available from the British Library.

For information on all Digital Press publications
visit our website at www.digitalpress.com and www.bh.com/digitalpress

Transferred to Digital Printing 2009

To my wife Katrien, my son Johannes, and my daughter Elise
for the hours I could not spend with them,
and for their continuous support
and loving care while writing this book.

Contents

Foreword

by Tony Redmond

There is no doubt that Windows has accumulated a bad reputation for security since Windows NT made its debut as Microsoft's enterprise operating system. Microsoft is partially to blame because its coding practices and development methodologies led to holes that hackers exploited. But perhaps the industry itself is also to blame because all of us have forgotten that computers are complex devices that need to be properly managed before they can provide reliable and secure service. To a large degree, PCs are easy to set up, and it takes only a few minutes to install and deploy software. The same is true of servers, so as Windows NT and later Windows 2000 took more market share, I think we were lured by ease of use and ignored best system management practices built over many years in mainframe and minicomputer environments.

Knowledge is key to developing best practice. If you don't know your subject inside out, you can't know how to best take advantage of the features of any tool. Computers are no different, and you cannot expect to approach any aspect of computer infrastructures without knowledge. Security is possibly one of the most difficult subjects to master, if only because it is so easy to make mistakes and end up with a computer that is insecure and data that is open to all. Windows is no different from other operating systems. It has features that allow you to secure computers, if you want to—and know how to.

Ever since I have known Jan, I've admired his dedication in mastering all aspects of Windows security. He has played a key role in educating his colleagues in HP Services through the programs we have to train our Windows technical community, especially in how to develop and implement best practices for security within large-scale corporate infrastructures. His experience is not just theoretical because Jan has had the opportunity to put his knowledge to the test in some of the largest deployments of Windows technology worldwide. He has taken his experience of teaching others and combined it with his knowledge of how things work in real life to produce this book, which I think is an extremely valuable contribution.

Windows 2003 is absolutely the best and most secure operating system Microsoft has released to date, but like anything else, it can always use some help to be even better. No book is ever perfect, but this is probably the best guide you can find to the essentials of securing a Windows infrastructure. It will certainly point you to where you need to do extra research or what you need to concentrate on to deploy best practices within your own infrastructure.

Enjoy!

Tony Redmond
Vice President and Chief Technology Officer
HP Consulting and Integration

Foreword

by Mark Mortimore

Security is a critical component in delivering on the vision of trustworthy computing. Understanding how to secure and manage access to systems, networks, and data is currently the most sought-after information for IT professionals managing connected infrastructures. For technical professionals, especially in recent years, security is repeatedly identified as the most important area for improvement in terms of how applications are designed, deployed, and maintained. There are several reasons for this need. Most important is the ubiquitous nature of technology in running businesses today. For most businesses, electronic communication, digital information, and technical infrastructure have become the foundation on which business processes are built.

Threats from malicious insiders, cyberterrorists, virus writers, and even unintentional misuse must be prevented to maintain the integrity of these systems. Threats from malicious sources are increasing in frequency and in sophistication. These threats are also being developed and released more rapidly after vulnerabilities are first discovered. Although in most cases remediation is available to counter the threat, the race to deploy these mitigations is producing a burden on IT professionals and unprotected systems that can expose key assets to malicious intent.

At the same time, our data center boundaries are expanding to include distributed servers, broad network accessibility, remote access, wireless networks, mobile and handheld devices, and interconnected business-to-business and business-to-consumer capabilities. In many cases, these distributed systems must have access to data and resources that used to sit safely inside isolated data center cores. I recently had a customer demonstrate a compelling application that allowed him to connect to sensitive customer data and inventory management systems via his mobile phone. Although opportunities for revolutionary advances in productivity, accessibility, and functionality are emerging, the security challenges these advances produce are formidable.

The days where IT professionals can achieve career success by stubbornly isolating data center resources has ended. Businesses require agility and accessibility to remain competitive. IT professionals must architect, deploy, and develop systems that support compelling new functionality and simultaneously safeguard critical systems and data.

Defense-in-Depth methodologies are built on the concept of layered defenses. This means designing systems that are resilient and protected at many levels. This balancing act between providing ever-increasing accessibility while simultaneously protecting critical assets requires considerable technical depth and a solid understanding of how systems work and how the connections between these systems function.

Bill Gates kicked off the Trustworthy Computing Initiative at Microsoft several years ago, and the industry has rallied around this commitment. Across the industry, and around the globe, no one can deny the breadth and importance of this effort. In Microsoft, this has produced waves of enlightenment and sustained growth in awareness and skill. This has resulted in development, deployment, and default configurations that are built around security. In Windows Server 2003, Microsoft has delivered tremendous new functionality enabling powerful new scenarios. For example, multifactor authentication scenarios are made easier than ever to deploy, and hardware and software advances are enabling business to authenticate users by who they are, what they know, and attributes or objects that only authorized personnel possess. Tremendous advances in the infrastructure to secure data and communications are built into the operating system. Another example of advanced functionality includes powerful advances in Active Directory that support more robust authentication and authorization scenarios.

In this book, IT professionals, advanced application developers, and security specialists will find a wealth of information about an array of key security topics. In particular, readers will find deep technical detail here regarding security administration and management, PKI and certificates, authentication, and access control. This information is based on the author's years of study and experience with leading-edge technologies. This experience is extended through engagements with Microsoft, customers, and an extended team made up of among the most experienced and technically capable specialists in the industry.

The details and specific implementations described here will be of keen interest to technical professionals. What makes this information especially valuable is the integration of technical detail with years of enterprise experience in managing secure infrastructures in the largest and most technically advanced deployments in the world. This real-world experience provides an insight into the practical reality of architecting, deploying, maintaining, integrating, and evolving systems so that these systems are as secure as possible, and stay secure over time.

The importance of deep technical knowledge, architectural depth, and real-world experience can not be overstated. Technical professionals must continue to invest in their education and training to effectively utilize and integrate new technology. This investment will result in an immediate payoff in specific solutions being developed now and deployed locally. Over time, the investment, attention, and diligence of technologists will result in infrastructures that will allow businesses and consumers to move forward with confidence and trust into an era of new opportunity.

Achieving this vision will require diligence and sustained effort. I encourage you to make the investment in developing practical skills, technical depth, and real-world experience. In making this effort we take important steps toward a shared goal.

Mark Mortimore
Senior Technologist
Security and Trustworthy Computing
Microsoft Corporation

Preface

Over the last four years, Microsoft has made security a top priority. This was first illustrated by the Windows 2000 operating system (OS), which includes major security enhancements. Windows 2000 supports several open security standards (e.g., Kerberos, IPsec). These standards are critical for security interoperability with other platforms and drive the operating system's open reputation—or the fact of not just being rooted on proprietary security protocols. Windows 2000 also included an important shift in the overall security manageability of the platform: Group Policy Objects (GPOs) were a big step forward.

After the release of Windows 2000, Microsoft, its flagship OS, and other MS applications were hit badly by the hacker community. These events forced Microsoft into a series of strategic security announcements, first of which was the Secure Windows Initiative, whose primary goal was to enhance the Windows base OS. Then came the Strategic Technology Protection Program (STTP), which provided a set of software tools and prescriptive guidance documents enabling customers to get secure and stay secure. Finally in 2002, Microsoft announced the Trustworthy Computing (TWC) initiative, which is about four principles: secure by default, by design, by deployment, and communications. Secure by design means that Microsoft takes the appropriate steps to make sure the overall design of their products is secure. This principle primarily affects the Microsoft development teams. The goal of secure by default is to ship products that are secure enough out of the box. Secure in deployment means the software is easily maintainable from a security point-of-view once the product has been installed. Communications means that Microsoft has become much more verbose in the IT security community and that they offer prescriptive security guidance to their customers to a maximum extent. A major TWC-related initiative for the years to come is the Microsoft Next Generation

Secure Computing Base (NGSCB), which is all about providing trustworthy computing platforms.

Windows Server 2003 is Microsoft's first enterprise OS resulting out of the TWC initiative. The main difference from its predecessor is that Windows Server 2003 is much more hardened by default. Instead of focusing on the security feature set of the OS, Microsoft now primarily stresses this default lockdown to the outside world. It is fair to say that Microsoft's efforts in the security space are truly impressive, but as with any security solution, technological advances are not enough. We should never forget the important role of people and processes. Security governance has become more important, and Microsoft also delivers solutions in this space: Good examples are the Microsoft Operations Framework (MOF) and security patch management initiatives.

I had the privilege to work with Windows Server 2003 (or Whistler, as it was codenamed back then) from a very early stage in the product's lifestyle. Hewlett-Packard was involved in the Whistler Joint Development Program (JDP). At HP we also created an internal test forest (codenamed QNet), starting with the Beta versions of the Whistler software. Perhaps the opportunity that helped me most with getting experienced with this new Microsoft OS was the development and delivery of the Windows Server 2003 Academies. This is a five-day learning event consisting of both lectures and hands-on labs focusing on Windows Server 2003. We delivered the academies successfully to both HP Services (HPS) consultants and HP customers. I also leveraged the experiences gained when writing my previous book *Mission-Critical Active Directory*, which I co-authored with Micky Balladelli.

This book focuses on the security infrastructure building blocks Microsoft provides as part of the Windows Server 2003 operating system. It covers authentication, authorization, key management, and security management infrastructures. The first chapters introduce general Windows security concepts. Special attention is given to single sign-on (SSO) and the account management and authentication integration between Windows and UNIX platforms. The book is based on years of experience with the Windows family of enterprise operating systems, both internally at HP and at customer sites. As such, the book also provides architectural guidance and best practices for the design of Windows-rooted security infrastructures.

The book does not cover the typical communications security infrastructure building blocks coming with the OS. For example, Microsoft's RADIUS solution—Internet Authentication Services (IAS)—is mentioned but is not covered in detail. Also, the book does not offer an introduction to general security and cryptographic terminology because it assumes that the reader is already familiar with these concepts. Finally, the book does not cover any of the security infrastructure building blocks Microsoft provides as part of their other product offerings: Good examples are the security infrastructure features of Systems Management Server (SMS) and Operations Manager (MOM).

If you discover inaccuracies or if you have general comments on the structure and/or content of the book, don't hesitate to send me your feedback. Your comments are very much appreciated! You can reach me at jan.declercq@hp.com.

Enjoy reading my book!

Jan De Clercq
December 2003

Acknowledgments

I would like to thank the following people for helping me create this book:

The technical reviewers: David Cross (Microsoft), Roland Schoenauen (Banque Gènèrale du Luxembourg), Kevin Laahs (HP), Guido Grillenmeier (HP), Alain Lissoir (HP), Janusz Gebusia (HP), and Olivier Blaise (HP).

The drivers on the Digital Press side: Theron R. Shreve and Pam Chester for keeping me rolling in hard times and Alan Rose for his incredible patience during the editing of this book.

The HP Windows Server 2003 Academy team: Guido Grillenmeier, Aric Bernard, Jeff Dunkelberger, and Alain Lissoir.

Tony Redmond for his mentorship and leadership, for his support in bootstrapping this book project, and for his efforts in getting the Windows Server 2003 Academy running.

The Microsoft-focused members of HP's Technology Leadership Group: Donald Livengood, Kieran McCorry, Aric Bernard, Kevin Laahs, Emer McKenna, Pierre Bijaoui, Dung Hoang Khac, Daragh Morrissey, Veli-Matti Vanamo, John Rhoton, and Todd Rooke.

Compaq's technical community of consultants, who are always willing to learn and share. Special thanks go to Ian Burgess, Gary Olsen, Ken Hendel, Joe Palermo, Henrik Damslund, Jeffrey Honeyman, Dirk De Bock, Marc Van Hooste, Els Thonnon, Rudy Schockaert, Kris Bosmans, Herman De Vloed, Susan McDonald, Vincent D'Haene, Eric Bidonnet, Martin Boller, Wayne Laflamme, Scott Hebner, Patrick Salmon, Patrick Lownds, Ebbe Jonsson, Patrick A. Dant, and Didier Lalli.

The following Microsoft people for their technical advice: Andreas Luther, Markus Vilcinskas, David Cross, Dave Mowers, Ronny Bjones, Marie Maxwell, Tony deFreitas, Mark Rankin, Jerry Cochran, Olivier d'Hose,

Mark Mortimore, Fred Baumhardt, Kyle Young, John Brezak, J. K. Jaganathan, Matt Hur, Sanjay Tandon, Eric Fitzgerald, Praerit Garg, Kirk Soluk, and Martin Hall.

My parents, my wife's parents, and the whole family (especially my little nieces and nephews, Johanna, Lucas, Charlotte, Clara, Astrid, Kato, and Anton), for the time I could not spend with them, for their interest in my writing this book, and for being a great family!

1

The Challenge of Trusted Security Infrastructures

This chapter introduces the concept of trusted security infrastructures (TSIs). The opening sections outline the different TSI services and their components and interactions. All services are illustrated with a set of security product offerings. Note that the list of software examples is nonexhaustive. The second part of the chapter looks at what Microsoft can provide in the TSI space and more specifically what TSI functions are bundled with the Windows Server 2003 operating system. Finally, the chapter also introduces other Microsoft software products offering TSI services.

1.1 Introduction

"Outsourcing" is a primarily economic concept that many other sciences have adopted. In information technology (IT) the outsourcing of processing functions was extremely popular during the mainframe era, but has become less common over the last two decades. With the rise of the personal computer (PC), everyone wanted more and more powerful client computing devices. Less powerful clients and the outsourcing of special functions to dedicated server machines have regained popularity only recently. For enterprises a major business driver behind the latter process was the need for reduced total cost of ownership (TCO).

For the IT security space, the use of outsourcing can be summarized as follows: Even though the outsourcing of specific and specialized security functions to trusted third party (TTP) servers has been used for many years in specific areas of IT security (e.g., authentication), it was only at the beginning of the 1990s that this outsourcing became accepted for a wider range of security functions (such as key management and access control). The reason why this took so long is mainly because of the perception of insecurity and the feeling of losing control when security services are outsourced and centralized at a TTP. The widespread use of strong cryptographic techniques and the adoption of open security standards have been important incubators for the rise of outsourcing in the IT security space.

Recent security incidents in the Internet world have also shown that it will take more than just outsourcing of security functions to dedicated TTP servers to make the IT world really secure. What are really needed are *pervasive* security services. These are security services that are omnipresent and that are implemented and used in a coherent and standardized way by different applications, platforms, and IT environments. Pervasive security services require a coherent security policy enforcement mechanism, which becomes easier in a centralized TTP environment.

The next few sections try to provide an overview of one of the latest trends in the outsourcing of security functionality: the creation of trusted security infrastructures (TSIs). These infrastructures provide the following core security services:

- Identification and authentication
- Key management
- Authorization
- Auditing and accounting
- Security-related administration, including identity and security policy management

In the context of TSIs, outsourcing tends to go as far as moving away all core security services from applications and making them infrastructure services, just as happened before for networking, file, print, and messaging services.

Trusted security infrastructures will allow applications to focus on their core business function. They will provide centralized security management and accounting, and thus much more accurate security data. Most importantly, they will facilitate the creation of pervasive security services for a wide range of applications. They will also facilitate single sign-on (SSO) and more rapid and more secure application development. Because of their central role, trusted security infrastructures must use open standards. They also must be implemented in a platform-, application-, vendor- and device-neutral way.

1.2 Positioning trusted security infrastructures

To position TSIs, we have to look not only at their logical positioning as part of the *security architecture* but also at their physical positioning as part of the *security design*. A security architecture is a high-level specification of security major components and how they relate to each other. A security design specifies the physical placement of components.

From a security architecture point of view, trusted security infrastructures introduce a new layer of security services that is sometimes referred to as the access layer, a concept that was first introduced by the Burton Group. The access layer is between the resource layer and the perimeter layer (as illustrated in Figure 1.1). The resource layer contains applications and data, or, in short, the information and application assets of an organization. The perimeter layer contains all elements that make up the perimeter security infrastructure of an organization. The perimeter layer contains security devices like firewalls, access routers, intrusion detection and prevention systems (IDS), and virtual private networking (VPN) tunnel endpoints.

In the context of this chapter, I will simply refer to the access layer as the trusted security infrastructures, or TSI, layer. The key role of this logical layer of security services is illustrated in Figure 1.2. The TSIs are built upon and used by a set of core infrastructure services like directory, database, messaging, and management services. In turn, the TSIs are—like all other core infrastructure services—used by a set of commercial off-the-shelf (COTS) or custom-built applications.

TSIs are created to provide a unified and universal security infrastructure for applications and services that are accessed in different environments and using different communication protocols: be it in a typical office setup

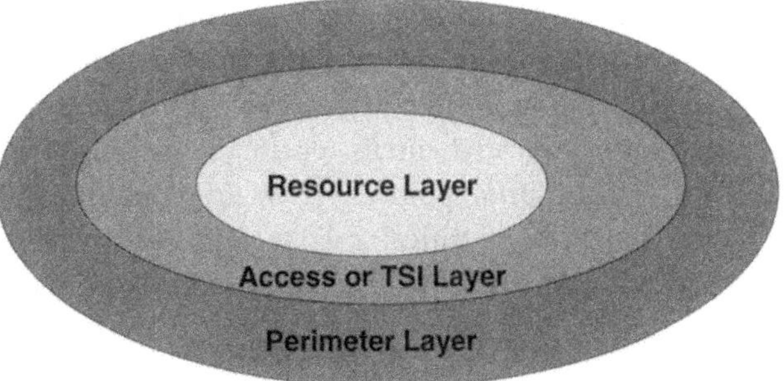

Figure 1.1 *The access or TSI layer.*

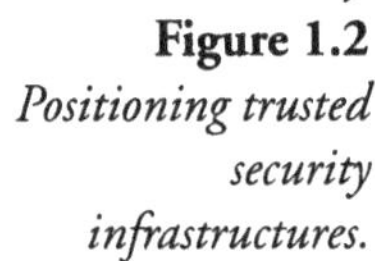

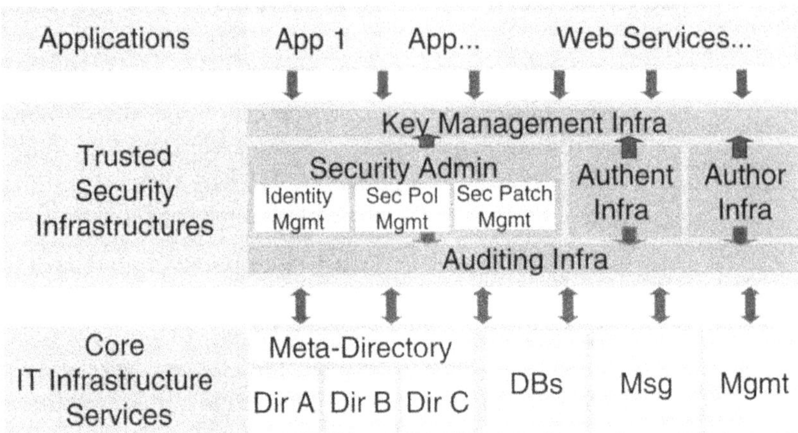

Figure 1.2 *Positioning trusted security infrastructures.*

(using RPC and SMB-like protocols), across the Web (using the HTTP protocol), in a remote access setup (RAS) (using the PPP protocol), or in a wireless environment (using WAP or any other wireless protocol). TSIs are created to also serve business-to-employee (BtoE), as business-to-consumer (BtoC) and business-to-business (BtoB) environments.

Looking at TSIs from a security design point of view and taking into account their critical security role, it is fair to say that they should be located in a separate security zone. This zone should be governed by a strong security policy. To shield the TSIs from the rest of the world one will typically use a set of perimeter security devices that enforce the appropriate security policies to let the right office, web, RAS, and wireless users in and keep the wrong ones out.

In the introduction I shortly mentioned the security services provided by TSIs. Figure 1.2 shows the key TSI components providing these services:

- *Security administration infrastructures,* or security management infrastructures, are the administrative engines of a TSI. A security administration infrastructure typically manages security identities, authentication credentials, entitlements, authorization intermediaries,[1] and security policies. A security administration infrastructure also takes care of critical tasks such as security patch and security policy management. Often the latter services are also provided by enter-

1. Authorization intermediaries are administrative entities that facilitate authorization administration. Examples are groups, rights, and roles.

prise management systems such as HP Openview, CA Unicenter, and BMC Patrol.

- *Authentication infrastructures* provide the entry points into a secured IT environment. They verify the identity of entities before they are allowed to use resources. To do so, the TTPs that are making up the authentication infrastructures support a set of authentication methods and protocols. To prove its identity, an entity provides the TTP with a set of authentication credentials.
- *Authorization infrastructures* are the next level of security guards following authentication infrastructures. Once an entity's identity has been verified, authorization infrastructures will decide which resources the entity is allowed to access and the level of access it has to those resources. Authorization infrastructures do not necessarily deal with the management of authorization–related objects such as groups, roles, and entitlements. The latter functionality is typically provided by security administration infrastructures.
- *Key management infrastructures* provide key life cycle management services. A good example of a key management infrastructure is a public key infrastructure (PKI).
- *Auditing and accounting systems* are keeping track of all events (security-related but also other ones) that occur in your infrastructure. Given the high degree of outsourcing in a TSI setup, auditing systems have an even more critical role. Auditing and accounting systems are not considered a separate infrastructure component. They are an integral part of the other TSI components: Every authentication, authorization, and security administration infrastructure includes an auditing and accounting system. Often they are also integrated with enterprise management systems.

Altogether these TSI components are also referred to as the AAAA security services: where the four A's stand for administration, authentication, authorization, and auditing (or accounting). In the following sections, we will explore the different TSI components in greater detail. We look at how they operate and interoperate. We will also give some examples of TSI software solutions for the different TSI categories. In this chapter we will not specifically focus on auditing and accounting systems because, as I mentioned earlier, these systems are normally bundled with other TSIs or with enterprise management systems.

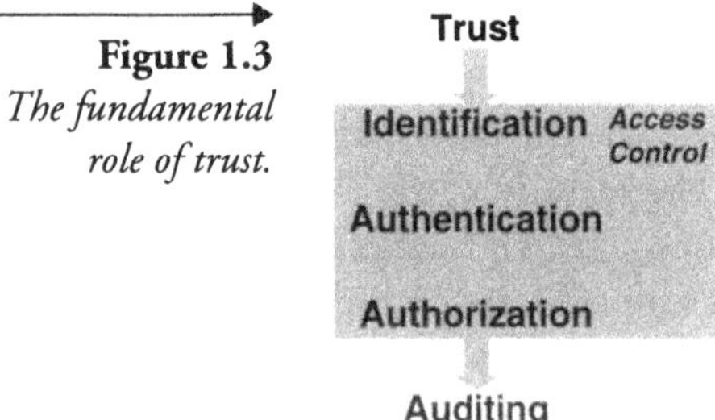

Figure 1.3 *The fundamental role of trust.*

1.3 The fundamental role of trust

All TSI services mentioned in the previous sections depend on the existence of a trust relationship between the users of the services and the service providers. As Figure 1.3 shows, all security services are built on trust. The figure also illustrates the link between access control, identification, authentication and authorization. Access control requires 3 security services: identification, authentication and authorization. Too many people use authorization and access control as synonyms.

Trust cannot be provided just by using technology solutions. A trust relationship also requires the presence of security policies and administrative procedures to provide an operational framework for the creation and maintenance of the trust relationship.

In most enterprises trust relationships between internal TSI users and the TSI service providers are relatively easy to put in place. Things become much more difficult when the TSIs must provide security services to external entities such as partners or customers. An even bigger challenge is to provide trustworthy TSI services on the Internet. The latter problem is discussed in James Essinger's book *Internet Trust and Security.*

Trust will be covered in more detail throughout this book when discussing the different Microsoft Windows Server 2003 TSI technologies.

1.4 TSI roles

The next sections focus on the four key TSI roles and their supporting infrastructures: authentication, key management, authorization, and security administration infrastructures.

1.4.1 Authentication infrastructures

Authentication infrastructures are a TSI component that has been around for many years. In computing environments with high scalability requirements, it is not cost-efficient from an implementation and an administration point of view to create a separate authentication system for every individual computer system, resource, or application server. It is much better to outsource this functionality to an authentication infrastructure. Outsourcing also enhances the enforcement of a consistent authentication policy throughout the enterprise. Another major driver behind the creation of authentication infrastructures is single sign-on (SSO). SSO is covered in greater detail in Chapter 9.

An authentication infrastructure is made up of one or several authentication servers. Authentication security policies can be managed by the authentication TSI itself or, depending on the degree of centralization, using tools that come with the security management infrastructure. The authentication infrastructure interacts with a repository (a database or directory) to store and validate user credentials. Authentication servers will obviously be linked to an auditing system and may have management agents from the corporate IT infrastructure management software installed. Finally, the authentication services provided by the infrastructure will be used by a set of applications.

The authentication infrastructure software products that are available on the market today can be categorized as follows:

- *Authentication infrastructures integrated with network operating systems.* They are typically used in enterprise environments to ease authentication for accessing internal enterprise resources.
- *Authentication infrastructures integrated with Web portal access management systems.* They focus on authentication and authorization enforcement for resources that are accessible using a Web interface. Their scope goes beyond enterprise intranets and extranets—they can also be used for authentication and authorization on Internet portals. Also, these systems are not just providing authentication; most of them are integrated "authentication-authorization-security management" infrastructures. They are covered in more detail in Sections 1.4.3 and 1.5.2.
- *Web authentication infrastructures.* These infrastructures focus on authenticating Internet users that are accessing Internet resources.

Table 1.1 *Authentication Infrastructure Solutions*

Vendor	Product	URL
Authentication infrastructure integrated with network operating systems		
Microsoft	Windows 2000	http://www.microsoft.com
Novell	Netware	http://www.novell.com
Authentication infrastructure integrated with Web portal access management systems		
Netegrity	Siteminder	http://www.netegrity.com
RSA	Securant	http://www.rsa.com
IBM/Tivoli	Access Manager	http://www.ibm.com
Web authentication infrastructures		
Microsoft	Passport	http://www.passport.com
OneName	OneName	http://www.onename.com
Novell	Digitalme	http://www.digitalme.com
Jamcracker	Jamcracker	http://www.jamcracker.com

Table 1.1 provides a list of sample authentication TSI solutions out of the different categories listed above. Note that this is a nonexhaustive list: It does not give a complete overview of the authentication infrastructure products available on the market today.

Web-based authentication infrastructures are specifically Internet-focused; extranet access management systems (EAMS) are intranet- and extranet-focused and mainly offer SSO solutions for corporate Web portals. An important difference between both product categories is the entities controlling the authentication infrastructures. In EAMS, an organization's IT department controls the authentication infrastructure. In most Web-based authentication infrastructures, control over the authentication infrastructure is outsourced to a commercial Internet authentication provider. The latter is not a rule, though: Novell's Digitalme currently focuses on extranet SSO; Microsoft's Passport currently focuses on Internet SSO, but may in the future also be extended to cover extranet SSO.

From this categorization it becomes clear that, to date, no universal authentication infrastructure is available that can provide SSO for Web-based Internet, intranet, and extranet resources, as well as for the resources in an enterprise environment. This may change as key management solutions such as PKIs gain wider acceptance and when some of the proven authentication protocols (e.g., "Kerberos") are supported across multiple communication protocols and applications.

1.4.2 Key management infrastructures

A key management infrastructure's primary reason for existence is, obviously, key management. Any security solution using cryptographic ciphers has to deal with cryptographic keys. When deploying these solutions in large environments, key management becomes a major issue. A scalable and easy-to-manage key management system is obviously of critical importance for authentication infrastructures used in large environments. The latter can be corporate intranets, extranets, or even the Internet. In such environments authentication keys would be hard to manage without using a centralized key management infrastructure. The use of TTPs makes authentication solutions scalable to very large environments.

Key management is certainly a big issue when using symmetric key ciphers. The use of symmetric key ciphers among many different entities poses important key distribution and key update problems. The problem is alleviated when using asymmetric key ciphers—but still it remains an important issue. Let me illustrate this using the following example: Setting up a symmetric key-based authentication solution between 10 people without using a TTP would require the creation and exchange of (10 * 9)/2 keys. This makes 45 keys total. When everyone trusts a TTP, only 10 keys would be needed. In the case of asymmetric keys the amount of keys needed remains the same, independent of the use of a TTP. However, the use of asymmetric keys has other advantages, as I will explain.

Based on the key material with which a key management infrastructure deals, we can differentiate between two different types of TTPs: key distribution centers (KDCs) and certification authorities (CAs). KDCs deal with symmetric keys—they can be linked together in multidomain or multirealm trust networks. CAs deal with asymmetric keys—they can be linked together in PKIs.

A key management infrastructure is made up of one or several TTP servers, whether CAs or KDCs. To enroll entities, key management infrastructures may use dedicated enrollment services (in PKI terminology, registration authorities). The registration authorities allow for a highly decentralized administration model. To provide access to these enrollment services to the widest possible range of users, most key management infra-

Table 1.2 *Public Key Infrastructure Solutions*

Vendor	Product	URL
Entrust	Authority	http://www.entrust.com
Baltimore (beTrusted)	UniCert	http://www.baltimore.com
Smarttrust	Security Center	http://www.smarttrust.com

structures provide a set of connectors. These usually include Web, wireless, and VPN connectors. Key management security policies can be managed by the key management TSI itself or, depending on the degree of centralization, using tools that come with the security management infrastructure. The authentication infrastructure interacts with a repository (database or directory) to store and validate user credentials. Key management servers are obviously linked to an auditing system and may have management agents from the corporate IT infrastructure management software installed. Finally, the key management services provided by the infrastructure will be used by a set of applications.

KDC-based key management infrastructures usually come bundled with network operating systems such as Netware, NT, or Windows 2000. They can also be purchased separately: A good example is CyberSafe's TrustBroker. TrustBroker is a Kerberos-based key management infrastructure product.

CA-based key management infrastructures can come as an add-on to a network operating system (NOS, e.g., Windows 2000 and Novell Netware), but generally high-end PKI products must be purchased as separate products. Big names in the PKI software space are Entrust, Baltimore, and Smarttrust PKI (as listed in Table 1.2).

1.4.3 Authorization infrastructures

Providing authorization services for employees to internal IT resources in a closed and homogeneous enterprise environment is relatively easy. Network operating systems such as Netware, NT, and Windows 2000 come with a set of built-in authorization management and enforcement features such as the ability to group resources in administrative domains, object models that support access control lists, security reference monitors (SRMs) bundled with the OS to evaluate and enforce authorization settings, and groups and rights to facilitate authorization management.

Things get much more complicated if the scope of the authorization infrastructure is broadened to cover not just internal users but also external users and if the resources can be accessed using different communication protocols and devices. Another complicating factor is the use of different applications that are using their proper authorization systems. Enforcing a single coherent authorization policy throughout an organization for all IT applications and services is an incredibly difficult task if every application and service maintains its proper authorization settings and makes its proper authorization decisions.

At this moment authorization infrastructures are certainly among the largest TSI challenges that many companies have ever faced. For TSI software vendors, they are also a very hot topic: It seems as if vendors' and customers' interest is shifting from PKI toward authorization infrastructures and PMIs, or from TSIs that can only provide authentication services toward TSIs that can provide both authentication and authorization services.

When discussing authorization in the context of TSIs, we must consider the following authorization services:

- *Authorization policy management* deals with the creation of resources to be protected, groups, roles, access rights, permissions, and special access rules. Most important, it links users, groups, and roles with resources, access rights, and access rules. The administrator responsible for authorization policy management decides on the level of access that users have to resources (e.g., can John just read a file, or can he also delete it?). The latter process is also known as the creation of "permissions." Resource, right, group, role and permission definitions are stored in an authorization policy repository.
- *Authorization decision making* is the real-time process of deciding on whether a user is allowed or disallowed to access a resource and the level at which he or she can access the resource. The input to this process is the information stored in the authorization repository.
- A resource manager is responsible for *authorization enforcement.* It makes sure that the authorization decision is executed correctly. In other words, he or she makes sure a user is allowed or denied access to a resource. Authorization infrastructures may enforce the authorization decisions themselves or delegate it to another trusted entity (e.g., an application).

In the early days of distributed client-server applications, every application maintained its proper authorization database, did its proper authorization decision making, and enforced authorization accordingly. There should be no need to explain that in such an environment, creating and maintaining a coherent authorization policy is a nightmare.

A first shift toward authorization service centralization came with first generation NOS, which centralized the definition of authorization intermediaries (objects like groups and rights) in a database. Because authorization enforcement is often very application-specific, applications kept on making their proper authorization decisions. Also, permissions remained to be stored in individual application authorization databases. Microsoft environments contain plenty of examples of this. The decision whether or not a user is allowed to access a particular NT workstation is always made by the workstation's local security authority; likewise, the decision to access a SQL Server database is made by the database server itself.

To ease the creation of application permissions and to keep them coherent throughout an environment with many different authorization databases and resource managers, software vendors created "provisioning systems." I consider provisioning part of a security administration infrastructure and will discuss it in Section 1.4.4.

Another shift toward authorization service centralization occurred when extranet access management systems (EAMS) came to the market. EAMS centralize authorization decision making. In some products they also centralize authorization enforcement. I will discuss EAMS in more detail later.

The different shifts from decentralized to more centralized authorization services are illustrated in Figure 1.4.

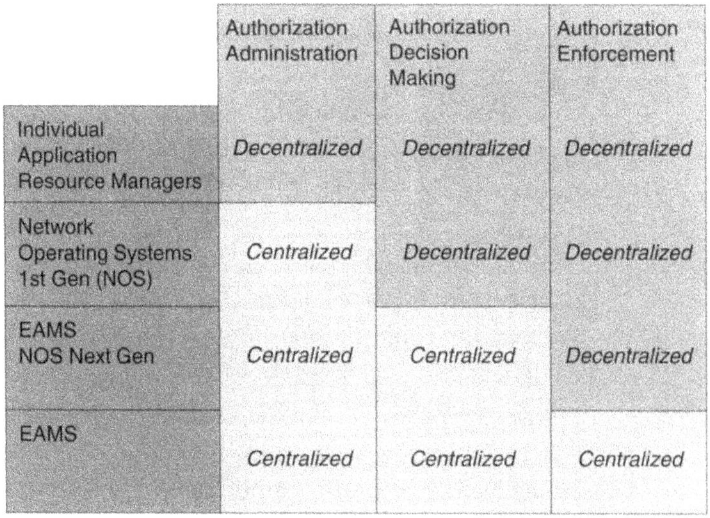

Figure 1.4 *Shift from authorization service decentralization to centralization.*

	Authorization Administration	Authorization Decision Making	Authorization Enforcement
Individual Application Resource Managers	*Decentralized*	*Decentralized*	*Decentralized*
Network Operating Systems 1st Gen (NOS)	*Centralized*	*Decentralized*	*Decentralized*
EAMS NOS Next Gen	*Centralized*	*Centralized*	*Decentralized*
EAMS	*Centralized*	*Centralized*	*Centralized*

An authorization infrastructure is made up of one or several authorization policy authorities. Authorization security policies can be managed by the authorization TSI itself or, depending on the degree of centralization, using tools that come with the security management infrastructure. The authorization infrastructure interacts with a repository (database or directory) to store and retrieve authorization data. Authorization infrastructure servers are obviously linked to an auditing system and may have management agents from the corporate IT infrastructure management software installed. Finally, the authorization services provided by the infrastructure will be used by a set of applications.

1.4.4 Security administration infrastructures

In a TSI environment the security administration infrastructure typically deals with security identity, authentication credential and authorization intermediaries, and policy management. To store this identity, credential, and authorization information, the security administration infrastructure uses a repository, typically a database or a directory. To provide more granular management capabilities, a security administration infrastructure may also provide self-service and delegated administration facilities for these data. Security administration infrastructures also guarantee that these critical data remain synchronized among the different repositories and applications of an IT infrastructure.

Security administration infrastructures often come integrated with other TSI solutions, such as authentication or authorization infrastructures. Examples are NOS such as Windows NT or 2000, or Netware, or EAMS such as Netegrity Siteminder and Oblix NetPoint.

For the moment there is one category of products that focuses on security administration infrastructure TSI functions. They are called provisioning systems and are discussed in a later section. Next we will explore the role of directories in identity management TSI solutions.

The important role of directories

Directories are commonly used as the central repository for security-related information. This information includes identities, authorization intermediaries (groups, roles), entitlements (what an identity is allowed to do), and identity or attribute certificates (produced by a PKI).

Lately, directories have been promoted as the cornerstone for enterprise identity management services. The main goal of identity management systems is to provide users with a single identity that can be used throughout the enterprise.

There are different technological approaches possible when using directories in the context of TSIs: using an enterprise directory, a directory synchronization utility, a metadirectory, or a virtual directory.

The concept of an enterprise directory is definitely the most straightforward approach to provide these functions to security infrastructures. The enterprise directory is the single authoritative source for identity information throughout an enterprise. All users and directory-enabled applications rely on the identities that are stored in the enterprise directory. Unfortunately, many enterprises cannot use this approach because of the presence of legacy directories. They can choose the directory synchronization utility, the metadirectory, or the virtual directory approach.

- Directory synchronization utilities are intelligent Lightweight Directory Access Protocol (LDAP)-based engines capable of synchronizing directory data between almost any type of directory.
- A metadirectory (also referred to as a centralized directory) provides a consolidated view on data that are stored in different directories. It pulls the data together in a central repository and keeps them synchronized in the different directories.
- A different approach to deal with multiple directories is the concept of a virtual directory. Unlike a metadirectory, a virtual directory does not build a central repository. It relies on directory server or client functions to access the data stored in different directory sources.

Table 1.3 gives an overview of directory solutions, one for every solution category: enterprise directory, metadirectory, directory synchronization, and virtual directory software.

Provisioning systems

Provisioning systems primarily deal with identity and resource provisioning. They allow companies to centralize and automate the process of supplying, or "provisioning," internal and external entities with access to the company's resources. In the mainframe era, identity and resource provisioning was relatively easy. The rise of the PC and the growing importance of distributed client-server applications have made provisioning an administrative nightmare. Provisioning systems extend the simplicity of mainframe provisioning to today's distributed PC networks. Remember that a provisioning system does not authenticate users or enforce authorization—those are the tasks of other TSI components.

Table 1.3 *Directory Solutions*

Vendor	Product	URL
Enterprise directory		
Novell	eDirectory	http://www.novell.com/products/edirectory/
Sun	Sun Java System Directory Server	http://www.sun.com/software/products/directory_srvr/home_directory.html
Metadirectory		
Microsoft	Microsoft Indentity Integration Server (MIIS)—formerly known as MMS	http://www.microsoft.com/windowsserver2003/technologies/directory/miis/default.mspx
CriticalPath	Metadirectory Server	http://www.cp.net/solutions/wirelessSP/dataDirectoryIntegration/metaDirectoryServer.jsp
Siemens	DirX	http://www.siemens.com/directory
Directory synchronization		
HP	LDAP Directory Synchronizer (Compaq LDSU)	http://www.hp.com/hps/messaging/mc_ldap_download.html
Virtual directory		
Radiant Logic	Radiant One Virtual Directory Server	http://main.radiantlogic.com/RLISite/

Provisioning systems extend the ease of administration available in NOS environments such as NT and Netware to cover other applications and platforms. They provide a centralized administration layer on top of the NOS' decentralized authorization enforcement. This makes them very different from EAMS (discussed later). In EAMS both authorization management and enforcement are centralized. Like NOS, provisioning systems are directory-focused to store identity, authentication, and authorization information.

The ultimate goal of a provisioning system is to provide a "one-click" administration system. For example, the deletion of an identity in the HR database will make the provisioning system automatically delete all other occurrences of this identity in all credential databases in your organization and all authorization settings of the resources of your organization. This can—if managed properly—significantly enhance the overall security quality of your IT systems. Used the other way around—to speed up the creation of new identities and authorization settings—it can make new employees become productive much faster. Obviously, centralized provisioning and one-click administration will also make identity and authorization management more consistent and easier to audit.

A provisioning system can do more than just identity and resource provisioning. These are major differentiators when comparing the functionalities of provisioning systems and identity management systems and metadirectory services. Most provisioning system software available on the market today is made up of the following services and components:

- A self-service administration facility to let users maintain their proper credential and profile information
- A delegated administration facility to delegate part of the administration of a subset of the accounts and/or resources maintained in the provisioning system to other administrators. This may be a much-needed option in organizations with decentralized administration models or in the context of Internet or application service providers (ISPs or ASPs).
- A password synchronization service to synchronize passwords between the different credential databases of an organization. This functionality may overlap with features offered by an authentication infrastructure providing SSO capabilities.
- A workflow engine to automate the processes behind account and resource provisioning. For example, in many organizations the creation of a corporate account requires approval by multiple instances before the account is allowed access to the company's knowledge base.
- A set of agents or connectors to link up the provisioning system with applications and other TSI components

The most important partners of provisioning systems are directories and metadirectories. A provisioning system considers one particular directory, (e.g., the one that is managed by the HR department) as the master of identity information. This master directory will drive all the actions initiated by the provisioning system. In that sense provisioning systems can add great value to corporate directory or metadirectory deployments. They link up different applications with the directory—something that many directory vendors have not succeeded in doing when they tried to directory-enable various applications. When analyzing the provisioning market and the metadirectory market, it will become clear that much overlap exists between both product categories. Some metadirectories such as Siemens DirX are

Table 1.4 *Provisioning Solutions*

Vendor	Product	URL
Business Layers	eProvision Day One	http://www.businesslayers.com
IBM Access360	enRole	http://www.tivoli.com/news/features/access360.html
Waveset Technologies*	Lighthouse	http://www.waveset.com

* The Waveset provisioning solution was acquired by Sun at the end 2003.

offering provisioning functions. In contrast, every provisioning system is LDAP-enabled to communicate with directories.

It becomes clear that there are some obvious benefits to the creation of an identity and resource provisioning system as part of a larger TSI deployment. In the future their scope may even be extended. The provisioning systems available today focus mainly on application and database access. Vendors are currently looking at extending their products to cover other provisioning areas such as physical building access and application deployment. Table 1.4 gives an overview of provisioning solutions available on the market today (a nonexhaustive list).

Major players such as Access360 (now a part of IBM) and Business Layers are also involved in the provisioning standardization efforts. The main goal is to standardize and thus to simplify the exchange of provisioning information between different systems, resources, and applications.

Access360 leads the independent Extensible Resource Provisioning Management (XRPM) working group (more info at http://www.xrpm.org). The goal of XRPM is to standardize the exchange of access right provisioning information between different systems and resources in an extensible markup language (XML) format. The Active Digital Profile (ADPr) working group—which is led by Business Layers—has a broader scope. Its goal is to create an XML-based specification that will allow companies to share provisioning information across multivendor systems.

1.5 The long road toward unified TSI solutions

By now it should be clear that trusted security infrastructures may change the face of IT security in the years to come. Obviously, the road ahead will be long and challenging.

One of the key TSI problems remains mature and interoperable security standards. Although lately a lot of new standardization efforts have been bootstrapped (efforts like XKMS, SAML, and so forth), all of them still have to gain widespread acceptance in the TSI marketplace. Another challenging question is how Web services will impact TSIs.

1.5.1 Overview

Figure 1.5 summarizes the current TSI product offerings. From this figure it becomes apparent that currently no universal TSI solution is available that spans all dimensions. This includes authentication, authorization, and security administration services, and also the different TSI client access methods: office/enterprise, Web-based, wireless-based, or remote access–based. Figure 1.5 also shows the important step forward made by EAMS products. The latter will be explained in more detail in Section 1.5.2.

From the architecture diagrams in this section, you should remember the commonalities between the different TSI services. For example, all of them deal with repositories and interact with an enterprise management system in one way or another. This underlines the importance of a global TSI approach: Too many large enterprises use an island approach when dealing with TSI. They may have a provisioning, PKI, and EAMS project, but they miss the glue that makes these projects come together. Communication, coordination, and standardization are key, certainly in this critical IT space.

1.5.2 Unified TSI example: EAMS

Extranet access management systems (EAMS) are a good example of TSI solutions where different security services are bundled in one commercial software offering. EAMS can be defined as a unified solution for Web authentication, SSO, authorization, and security administration. Because EAMS were born in the Web portal world, they are focusing on HTTP-based access to Web resources.

In the first place, EAMS are TSIs providing centralized authorization decision making and enforcement. EAMS decouple authorization decision making and/or enforcement from applications and services and centralize these services at TTPs. EAMS also include centralized security management (covering identities, credentials, and roles), can provide authentication services, and provide a set of accounting services.

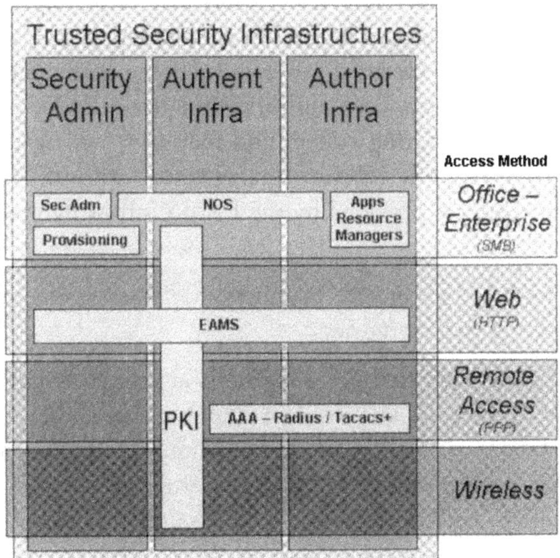

Figure 1.5 *TSI overview.*

In the future EAMS may be extended to cover other access methods as well. For example, a couple of EAMS vendors already provide RADIUS support for remote access. Ideally, EAMS should also be extensible to cover more than just Web-based applications. Some EAMS vendors have included this functionality in their product. However, in the latter case, the role of the EAMS is limited to centralized authorization decision making.

Over the last two years, EAMS have been a major success story in the security world that has been supported by many software vendors. With the creation of EAMS, vendors were responding to customer demands for more powerful extranet security features. Customers were asking for group-based and role-based authorization support, self-registration for users, SSO across multiple Web sites, and a centralized administration model that also allows managers to delegate administrative tasks.

EAMS are made up of a central policy engine containing the EAMS logic for authorization, authentication, auditing, and security administration services. Note that for authentication and security administration services, EAMS may call on some external authentication or security management TSI. The EAMS policy engine may also provide the intelligence for EAMS functions such as self-service administration, delegation administration, password synchronization, and so forth. Authorization security policies can be managed by the EAMS itself or, depending on the degree of centralization, using tools that come with the security management infrastructure. The EAMS infrastructure interacts with a repository (database or directory) to store and retrieve credentials, user identity information, attributes, and authorization data. EAMS servers are obviously linked to an auditing system and may have management agents from the corporate IT infrastructure management software installed. Finally, the security services provided by the EAMS infrastructure will be used by a set of applications.

The EAMS software products available on the market today can be grouped in two categories:

- In an agent-based EAMS, clients always communicate directly with the application servers. The latter have an EAMS agent installed that validates every client request with an EAMS policy server. The EAMS policy server makes the access control decision and sends the response back to the application server. The application server's EAMS agent then allows or denies client access accordingly.
- In a proxy-based EAMS, clients never communicate directly with the application servers. Situated between the two, an EAMS proxy intercepts every client request and enforces access control. The EAMS proxy communicates with an EAMS policy server. The latter is the access control decision maker—the proxy functions as an access control traffic filter.

Table 1.5 *Extranet Access Management System Vendors*

Vendor	Product	URL
Agent-based EAMS		
Netegrity	Siteminder	http://www.netegrity.com
Oblix	NetPoint	http://www.oblix.com
RSA (Securant)	ClearTrust	http:/www.rsa.com
Entrust	GetAccess	http://www.entrust.com
Hewlett Packard	SelectAccess	http://www.hp.com
Proxy-based EAMS		
Aventail	OnDemand and Connect	http://www.aventail.com
IBM (Tivoli)	Access Manager	http://www.ibm.com

Table 1.5 gives an overview of EAMS products out of the two categories available on the market today.

1.6 Microsoft and the challenge of TSIs

This book focuses on how Microsoft has provided built-in support for TSIs in the latest versions of its enterprise server operating system Windows Server 2003. These built-in TSI features are introduced in Section 1.6.1. We will also look at other Microsoft products that are not bundled with Windows Server 2003 and that can provide TSI services. These other Microsoft products will not be covered in detail in this book.

1.6.1 Windows server 2003 as a TSI security building block

Table 1.6 shows the TSI building blocks that come bundled with the Windows Server 2003 server operating system. The table shows only the software that Microsoft sells as a product. It doesn't show the free Microsoft tools—a good example is Microsoft Software Update Services (SUS).

Table 1.6 *Microsoft TSI Services Built into Windows Server 2003*

Windows Feature	TSI Service	Discussed In
Kerberos authentication infrastructure	Authentication infrastructure	Chapter 5
Web server authentication infrastructure	Authentication infrastructure	Chapter 6
Passport authentication infrastructure	Authentication infrastructure	Chapter 7
Authorization manager and framework	Authorization infrastructure	Chapter 12
Malicious mobile code protection	Authorization and security administration infrastructure	Chapter 11
Public key infrastructure	Key management infrastructure	Chapters 13–16
Built-in auditing system	Auditing infrastructure	Chapter 18
Built-in Security Policy enforcement (using group policy objects)	Security administration infrastructure	Chapter 18
Security patch management	Security administration infrastructure	Chapter 18

1.6.2 Other microsoft TSI building blocks

Table 1.7 provides an overview of other Microsoft software products that can be used to provide TSI services. The Microsoft Identity Integration Server 2003 (MIIS), the Microsoft Operations Manager (MOM), the Microsoft Systems Management Server (SMS), and the Microsoft Provisioning System (MPS), Microsoft Services for UNIX, are available now. TrustBridge is the name of a TSI product that will be released sometime near the end of 2003. Trustbridge will not be discussed in this chapter, but we will return to it in Chapter 9. The same is true for the Rights Management Service (RMS), which is discussed in Chapter 12, and Services for UNIX 3.0 (SFU 3.0), which are discussed in Chapter 8.

Microsoft Indentity Integration Server

Microsoft Indentity Integration Server 2003 (MIIS) is Microsoft's metadirectory solution. MIIS was formerly called Microsoft Metadirectory Services (MMS) In the context of trusted security infrastructures, MIIS can be used as the central repository for security-related information such as iden-

Table 1.7 *Other Microsoft Software Providing TSI Services*

Microsoft Software	TSI Service	More Information At
Microsoft Identity Integration Server (MIIS)—formerly known as MMS	Identity, authentication and authorization data management—security management infrastructure	http://www.microsoft.com/windowsserver2003/technologies/directory/miis/default.mspx
Microsoft Provisioning System (MPS)	Security management infrastructure—provisioning	http://www.microsoft.com/serviceproviders/mps
Microsoft Operations Manager (MOM)	Security management and auditing infrastructure	http://www.microsoft.com/mom
Microsoft Systems Management Server (SMS)	Security management and auditing infrastructure and	http://www.microsoft.com/sms
Microsoft Services for UNIX 3.0 (SFU 3.0)	Security management and authentication infrastructure	http://www.microsoft.com/windows/sfu
TrustBridge (code name for product to be released in 2004)	Authentication and authorization infrastructure	http://www.microsoft.com/presspass/press/2002/jun02/06-06trustbridgepr.asp
Rights Management Services	Authorization infrastructure	http://www.microsoft.com/windowsserver2003/technologies/rightsmgmt/default.mspx

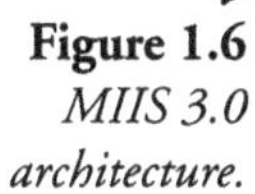

Figure 1.6 *MIIS 3.0 architecture.*

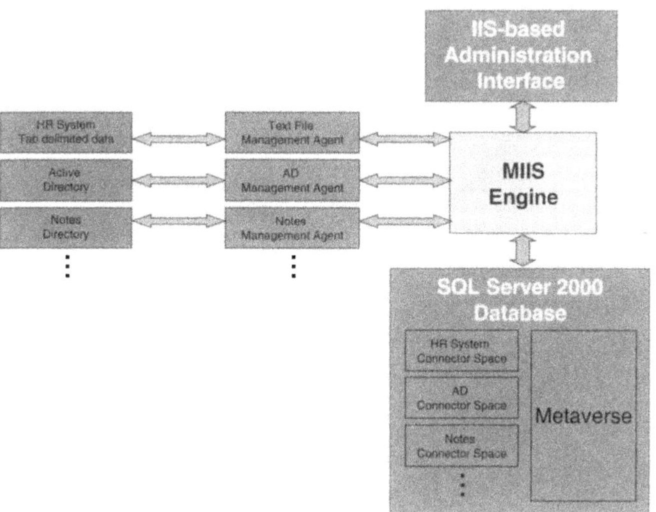

tities and authorization data. Microsoft bought the core MIIS engine from a company called Zoomit back in 1999. MIIS stores and integrates information stored in different directories or data sources into a unified view called the *metaverse*. Figure 1.6 shows the MIIS architecture.

Besides the metaverse, you will notice two other typical MIIS terms in Figure 1.6: management agents and connector spaces. A connector space (CS) is a representation of the objects and their associated attributes from a connected system (an HR system, another directory, and so forth) in the MIIS data repository. A management agent (MA) is the mechanism that processes and replicates data between a connected system and its MIIS connector space. MIIS ships with the following MAs: Active Directory (AD), Active Directory Application Mode (ADAM), Attribute value pair text files, Delimited text files, Directory Services Markup Language (DSML), Fixed width text files, LDAP Directory Interchange Format (LDIF), Lotus Notes/Domino 4.6 and 5.0, Microsoft NT 4 Domains, Microsoft Exchange 5.5, 2000 and 2003, Microsoft SQL 7 and 2000, Novell eDirectory v8.6.2 and v8.7.

Microsoft also provides a free reduced functionality version of MIIS: the Identity Integration Feature Pack. This add-on package for Windows Server 2003 can synchronize identity information between AD, AD Application Mode (ADAM), Exchange 2000 Server and Exchange Server 2003. It can also automate the provisioning of identity data between these different data sources. You can download it from http://www.microsoft.com/downloads/details.aspx?FamilyID=d9143610-c04d-41c4-b7ea-6f56819769d5&DisplayLang=en.

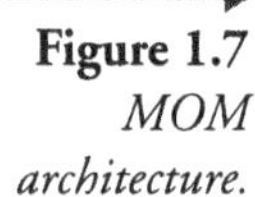

Figure 1.7 *MOM architecture.*

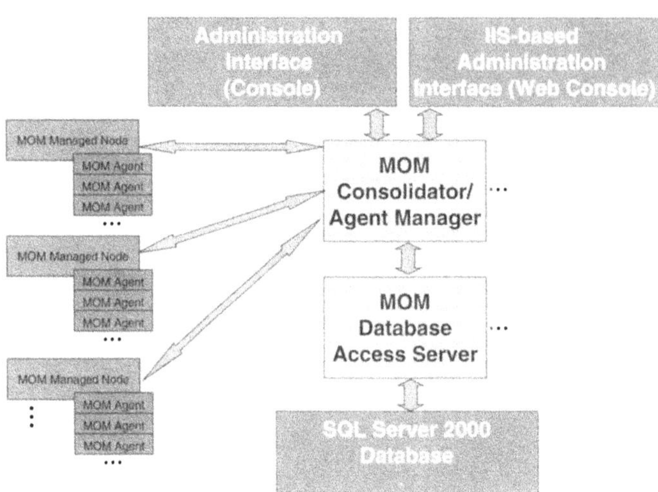

Microsoft Operations Manager

Microsoft Operations Manager (MOM) is Microsoft's solution for enterprise-wide event and performance management. In the context of trusted security infrastructures, MOM can be used to build a centralized auditing infrastructure. Microsoft licensed MOM's core engine from NetIQ and rebranded it. MOM's highly flexible and distributed architecture is illustrated in Figure 1.7.

Out-of-the-box MOM includes agents for the following platforms, applications, and services (as part of the base management pack): Windows 2000, Active Directory, Internet Information Server, Windows 2000 Terminal Server, Distributed Transaction Coordinator, WINS, DHCP, RRAS, Transaction Server, Message Queue Server, DNS, MOM, and SMS. MS also provides optional agents (as part of application management packs) for the following MS applications: Exchange, SNA Server, ISA Server, Proxy Sever, SQL Server, Commerce Server, Site Server, and Biztalk Server. Other agents covering many more applications and platforms (including non-Microsoft platforms and applications) are available from third-party software vendors.

Microsoft Systems Management Server

The functionality of Microsoft's Systems Management Server (SMS) is often confused with the functionality of Microsoft's MOM. Although there are some small overlaps, both products have different focus areas. Whereas MOM is focusing on performance monitoring and log consolidation, the

Figure 1.8
SMS architecture.

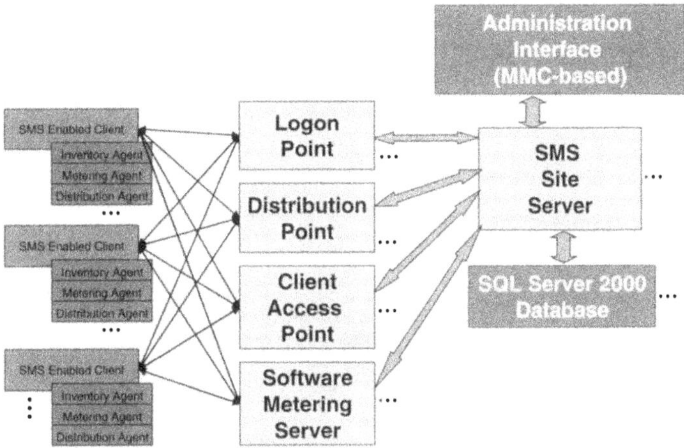

SMS's key strengths are in the areas of software distribution, hardware and software inventories, and help desk functions.

The latest SMS release is SMS 2003, which Microsoft released late 2003. Many enterprises are still using SMS 2.0. In 2003 Microsoft released an interesting add-on called the Software Update Services (SUS) Feature Pack that specifically extends SMS 2.0's capabilities in the security patch management space for the Windows OSs and the MS Office applications. The SUS Feature Pack functionality is included out-of-the-box in SMS 2003.

Figure 1.8 gives an overview of the SMS architecture. As for MOM, this architecture is highly flexible and distributed. Figure 1.8 does not show SMS's hierarchical site capabilities consisting of primary and secondary sites.

Provisioning system

The Microsoft Provisioning System (MPS) is Microsoft's provisioning solution. It is built on Microsoft-centric XML technology and provides a provisioning solution for some of the core Microsoft applications such as Active Directory, Exchange, FrontPage, SharePoint Team Services, and IIS. MPS can be extended to cover other applications as well (by building custom MPS providers). Figure 1.9 gives an overview of the MPS architecture. MPS is not a true Microsoft product offering, but rather a collection of different Microsoft technologies. It is currently available only through specific Microsoft partners such as eQuest Technologies (more information is available at http://www.eqinc.com/Servs/Microsoft%20Provisioning%20System%20Development.htm).

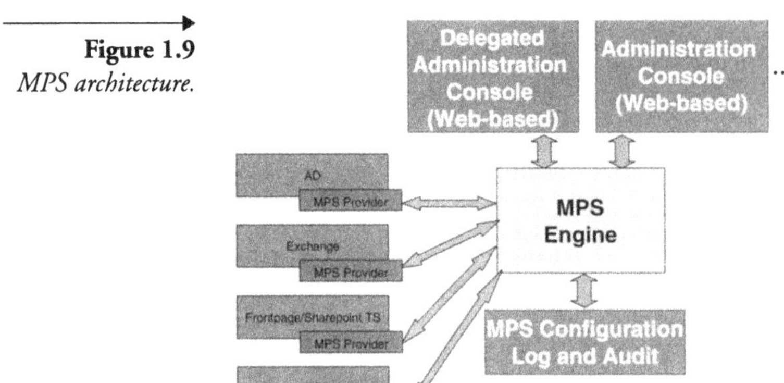

Figure 1.9
MPS architecture.

1.7 Conclusion

This chapter introduced the typical TSI services and showed how Microsoft can help in this space. It introduced the Microsoft TSI product offerings and shed some light on the TSI features that come bundled with the Windows Server 2003 Operating System, which is explored in greater detail in the rest of this book.

Selected bibliography

Authorization Infrastructures

- AMR Research, C. Quirk and C. Niven: "Achieving Access Management Efficiencies Through Single Sign-On."
- Burton Group Technical Position on "Access Management."
- Oppliger, R., "Using Attribute Certificates to Implement Role-Based Authorization and Access Controls."

Authentication Infrastructures

- Burton Group, Single Sign-On, Network Strategy Report.
- Burton Group Technical Position on "User Authentication."
- Network Applications Consortium (NAC) Position Paper: "Enterprise-Wide Security: Authentication and Single Sign-On."
- Smith, R. E., *Authentication: From Passwords to Public Keys*, Reading, MA: Addison-Wesley, 2002.

Provisioning Systems

- Active Digital Profile: http://www.adpr-spec.com/.
- Burton Group Network Strategy, Directory-Based Resource Provisioning Systems, Report.
- Burton Group Technical Position on "Identity Management."
- XRPM working group: http://www.xrpm.org.

Trust

- Essinger, J., *Internet Trust and Security*, Reading, MA: Addison-Wesley, 2001.

2

Windows Security Authorities and Principals

This chapter focuses on two building blocks of Windows Server 2003 operating system security: security authorities and security principals. Among the concepts discussed are security principal, domain, security identifier, domain controller, logon name, LSA, and LSA policy.

2.1 Security authorities

To illustrate the fundamental role of trust in the Windows Server 2003 operating system and to make the link with Chapter 1 on trusted security infrastructures (TSIs), we will first discuss the concept of Windows OS security authorities. In Windows OSs we have to deal with two types of security authorities: the local security authority (LSA) and the domain security authority. A security authority reigns over a kingdom of resources (represented by the ellipse in Figure 2.1) and has its proper database to store security-related information. We will reuse these representations as other Windows security concepts are introduced throughout this chapter.

2.1.1 The local security authority

The LSA is a Windows machine's local security authority. The LSA is available on all kinds of Windows machines: both stand-alone machines and machines that are a member of a Windows domain.

Physically the LSA is a protected OS subsystem (visible in the task manager as the lsass.exe process) that is running in OS user mode. The lsass process hosts a set of other important security processes [implemented as dynamic link libraries (dlls)] that are illustrated in Figure 2.2: the LSA authority process (lsasrv.dll), the SAM process (samsrv.dll), the AD process (ntdsa.dll), the Netlogon process (netlogon.dll), and a set of authentication packages [the NTLM authentication package (msv1_0.dll) and/or the

Figure 2.1
Security authority.

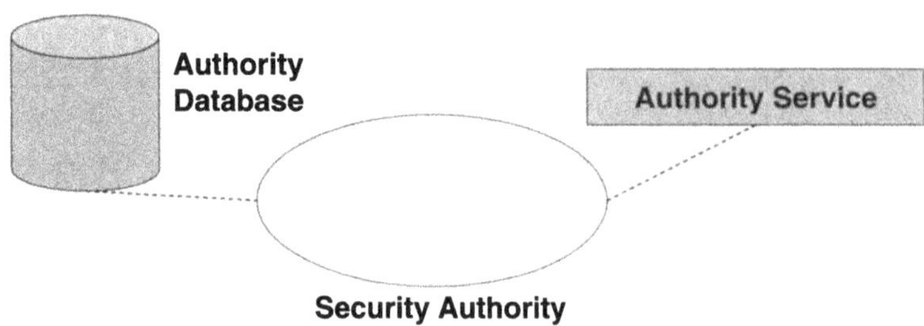

Kerberos authentication package (Kerberos.dll)]. The Netlogon process is only available on Windows domain controllers. The AD process is only available on Windows 2000 and later domain controllers. I will come back to the Netlogon process and the authentication packages in Chapter 4 on Windows authentication.

The LSA and its subprocesses play a crucial role in the authentication and authorization security processes. Among their tasks are security principal credential validation and access token generation. The LSA also enforces the local security policy, including the auditing policy, memory quotas, user logon rights, and privileges.

The LSA has its proper database, which is referred to as the LSA database. It holds system-specific security policy information. The information stored in the LSA database is known as the LSA policy. The objects stored in the LSA policy are known as policy objects. Physically the LSA security policy database is a secured part of the system registry.

The Security Accounts Manager (SAM) and Active Directory (AD) LSA subprocesses govern access to the local and domain credential databases. These databases contain security information about local or domain security principals. The SAM is used in all Windows versions to store local or

Figure 2.2
LSA process and subprocesses available on Windows domain controllers.

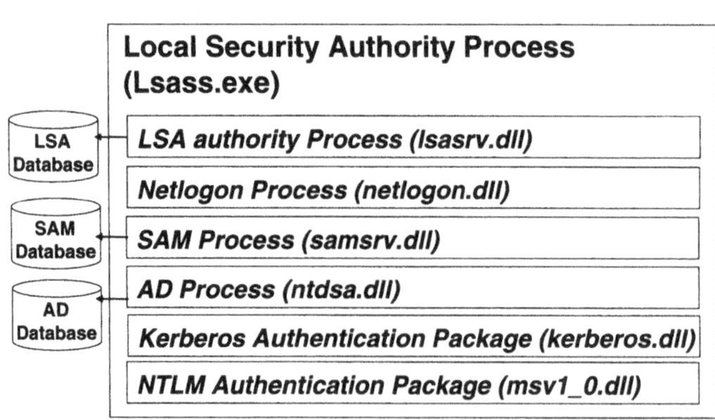

domain security principal information. The Active Directory is used from Windows 2000 on to store domain security principal-related security information on domain controllers. The concepts of domain and security principal will be explained in greater detail later in this chapter.

The LSA database

The LSA security policy database holds different types of policy objects: policy, account, and private data objects.

- A policy object determines who can access the LSA database. It also contains global system information such as system memory quota and auditing settings. Every system has a single policy object.
- An account object contains information that is specific to a user or group (e.g., special user logon rights, privileges, and quotas).
- A private data object is used to store confidential information such as system or service account passwords. LSA private data objects are also known as LSA secrets.

There is a limit on the number of LSA secrets that can be stored in the LSA database. In Windows Server 2003 this limit is 4,096. LSA secrets are encrypted using a system-specific key and stored in the HKEY_LOCAL_MACHINE\security container of the system registry.

LSA secrets can be one of the following types: local, global, or machine LSA secrets. Local LSA secrets can only be read locally from the machine that stores them; global LSA secrets are replicated between domain controllers; and machine LSA secrets can only be accessed by the operating system. Microsoft uses special naming conventions to store these special LSA secret types in the security key of the registry: "L$" for local, "G$" for global, and "M$" or "NL$" for machine LSA secrets.

To look at the LSA secrets stored on a Windows machine, you can use regedt32.exe or the lsadump2.exe command-line tool. Either method will reveal the LSA secrets' names and content in an encrypted format. Remember that LSA secrets are critical NT system data. After you obtain a listing, handle the listing with care and do not distribute it freely.

To use the registry editor to look at the LSA secrets, you must first change the permissions on the registry Security subkey and all its subkeys so that your account has full control access. The Security key is in the HKEY_LOCAL_MACHINE registry hive. Note that you should never change these permissions on a production system—always use a test system. Changing the permissions will reveal a new list of registry subkeys, including the Policy key. Underneath the Policy key you can find a list of LSA secrets.

Lsadump2 is a freeware tool that you can download from BindView's Razor security team download page (http://razor.bindview.com/tools/desc/lsadump2_readme.html). Lsadump2 lets you look at a machine's LSA secrets from the command prompt. To run Lsadump2, your account must have debug privileges on the machine. By default, this privilege is given only to administrator accounts. Again, do not run this tool on your production systems—use a test system.

2.1.2 The domain security authority

As was explained in Chapter 1, bringing multiple resources together in a kingdom that is ruled by a trusted third party facilitates security policy enforcement and provides ease of use to both users and administrators. In Windows Server 2003 a kingdom is called a domain and a trusted third party is called a domain controller (DC).

The domain concept

As in NT4 and Windows 2000, a Windows Server 2003 domain in the first place defines a management boundary. It is an administrative grouping of users, machines, and resources.

From Windows 2000 on a domain is also an Active Directory namespace partition. Because the namespace within the Active Directory is hierarchical, the domain structure in Windows 2000 and Windows Server 2003 is made up of a series of parent-child relationships between the different domains. Windows 2000 and Windows Server 2003 allow you to build AD domain trees and forests. Figure 2.3 shows an AD forest made up of several AD trees (hp.com, compaq.com, and tandem.com). In every AD tree there are multiple hierarchical parent-child domain relationships. Domains are linked using trust relationships (explained later in this chapter) and DNS domain names. Within the different domain trees in Figure 2.3, the DNS namespace is contiguous. Between domain trees there is a noncontiguous DNS namespace.

To a certain extent, a domain is also a security boundary: it can be linked to a specific security policy that is only valid within the domain. The introduction of the forest concept in Windows 2000, however, fundamentally changed the Windows security boundaries as they existed in earlier Windows versions. From Windows 2000 on, the notion of referring to a

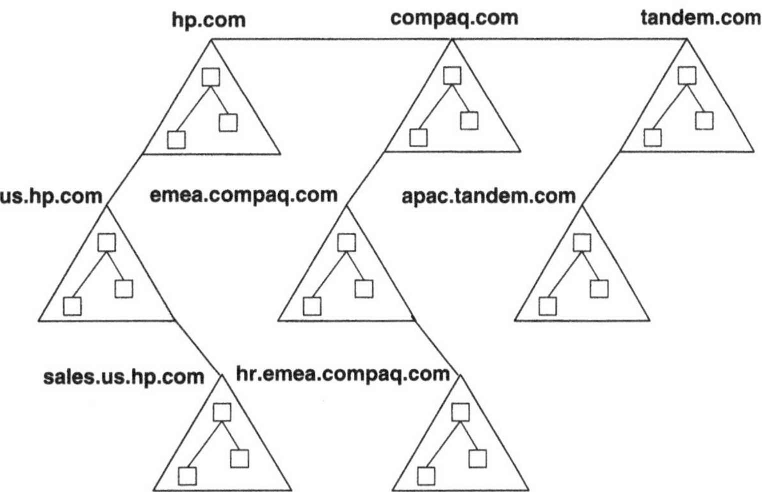

Figure 2.3 *Windows Server 2003 AD domains, trees, and an AD forest.*

domain as a security boundary is not completely valid anymore: The true security boundary is the forest. Domain administrators must always have a certain level of trust in the forest enterprise administrators. The latter have power in all domains in a forest.

Even though the concept of Windows Server 2003 domains, trees, and forests is completely different from the concept of a DNS domain,[1] both concepts are closely intertwined in the context of an AD infrastructure. AD uses DNS to name and locate AD domains and objects, and every Windows Server 2003 domain is identified by its DNS domain name. In fact, the AD namespace is contained within the DNS namespace. Every AD domain tree can be mapped to a DNS domain hierarchy, and every AD domain corresponds to a DNS domain.

Domain functionality levels

The most important property of a Windows 2000 domain was its mode. The most important property of a Windows Server 2003 domain is its functionality level.

A Windows 2000 domain can be in one of the following states: mixed or native mode. A mixed-mode Windows 2000 domain provides backward compatibility with Windows NT4 or earlier DCs. A native-mode Windows 2000 domain provides additional AD functionality. In a native-mode Windows 2000 domain, all DCs are Windows 2000 DCs.

1. An AD domain stores objects; a DNS domain stores resource records.

In Windows Server 2003, Microsoft provides a new set of AD functions that are only available if all the DCs are Windows Server 2003 DCs. This forced Microsoft to introduce more domain modes in order to link the correct AD functionality to a domain and its homogeneous or heterogeneous DC population. The Windows Server 2003 domain modes must be capable of differentiating between domains that are holding only Windows Server 2003 DCs and domains that contain a mixture of Windows Server 2003, Windows 2000, and NT DCs.

To deal with the domain-mode problem in Windows Server 2003 once and for all, Microsoft introduced the concept of functionality levels. It is just another name for a portable version management system that can be used in current and future versions of the Windows OS. Windows Server 2003 functionality levels not only apply to DCs and domains, but they are also applicable to forests. They allow the domain and forest functionality levels to be increased when all DCs in the domain or forest have reached the appropriate level.

Table 2.1 *Domain Functionality Levels*

Reference Name	Domain Functionality Level	Possible Domain Controllers	Available Features
Windows 2000 mixed-mode domain	Mixed + Level 0	Windows NT Windows 2000 Windows Server 2003	■ Ability to replicate to Windows NT Backup Domain Controllers (BDCs). ■ Windows 2000 feature set.
Windows 2000 native-mode domain	Native + Level 0	Windows 2000 Windows Server 2003	■ No ability to replicate to Windows NT BDCs. ■ Windows 2000 feature set.
Windows Server 2003 interim mixed-mode domain	Mixed + Level 1	Windows NT Windows Server 2003	■ Ability to replicate to Windows NT BDCs. ■ Windows 2000 DCs cannot join domain. ■ Windows 2000 feature set.
Windows Server 2003 mode domain	Level 2	Windows Server 2003	■ No ability to replicate to Windows NT BDCs. ■ Windows 2000 DCs cannot join domain. ■ Application Directory Partitions. ■ DC rename. ■ DNS stub zones in Application NC. ■ Kerberos KDC key version numbers. ■ Windows 2000 feature set.

Tables 2.1 and 2.2 give an overview of the Windows Server 2003 domain and forest functionality levels and their features. The tables also show what kind of DCs can be contained in a domain or forest with a certain functionality level. Table 2.3 lists some of the new Windows Server 2003 AD features and their functionality level requirements.

Domain controllers

A domain controller (DC) is a domain's trusted authority. It hosts the domain security database and authenticates security principals for domain

Table 2.2 *Forest Functionality Levels*

Reference Name	Forest Functionality Level	Possible Domain Controllers	Available Features
Windows 2000 forest	Level 0	Windows NT Windows 2000 Windows Server 2003	■ Level 0 mixed-mode domains can exist with Windows NT, Windows 2000, and Windows Server 2003 DCs. ■ Level 0 Windows 2000 native-mode domains can exist with Windows 2000 and Windows Server 2003 DCs. ■ Level 1 Windows Server 2003 interim mixed-mode domains can exist with only Windows NT and Windows Server 2003 DCs. ■ Level 2 Windows Server 2003 mode domains can exist with only Windows Server 2003 DCs. ■ Windows 2000 feature set.
Windows Server 2003 interim forest	Level 1	Windows NT Windows Server 2003	■ Level 1 Windows Server 2003 interim mixed-mode domains can exist with only Windows NT and Windows Server 2003 DCs. ■ Level 2 Windows Server 2003 mode domains can exist with only Windows Server 2003 DCs. ■ Windows 2000 feature set. ■ Link value replication among Windows Server 2003 DCs. ■ Prevent Windows 2000 domain controller from joining the forest. ■ New ISTG (KCC) algorithm among Windows Server 2003 DCs.

Table 2.2 *Forest Functionality Levels (continued)*

Reference Name	Forest Functionality Level	Possible Domain Controllers	Available Features
Windows Server 2003 forest	Level 2	Windows Server 2003	■ Level 2 Windows Server 2003 mode domains can exist with only Windows Server 2003 DCs. ■ Domain Rename. ■ Dynamic auxiliary classes. ■ New attribute replication only to global catalogs (no GC rebuild for Schema extensions and inclusion into the GC). ■ Schema deletions. ■ Transitive forest trusts.

Table 2.3 *Functionality Level Requirements for Windows Server 2003 Features*

Feature	Functionality Level Requirement
Application Directory Partitions	Domain Functionality Level = 2
Domain Controller Rename	Domain Functionality Level = 2
DNS Stub Zones in Application NC	Domain Functionality Level = 2
Kerberos KDC Key Version Numbers	Domain Functionality Level = 2
Link value replication	Forest Functionality Level = 1
Prevent Windows 2000 domain controller from joining the forest	Forest Functionality Level = 1
New ISTG (KCC) algorithm	Forest Functionality Level = 1
Domain Rename	Forest Functionality Level = 2
Dynamic auxiliary classes	Forest Functionality Level = 2
New attribute replication only to global catalogs (no GC rebuild for Schema extensions and inclusion into the GC)	Forest Functionality Level = 2
Schema deletions	Forest Functionality Level = 2
Forest trusts	Forest Functionality Level = 2

resource access. A domain can contain multiple DCs. All DCs hold a copy of the same domain security database. The security database contains the identifiers and authentication credentials of the different domain security principals. The use of a centralized security database simplifies centralized security administration.

The domain security database of Windows 2000 and Windows Server 2003 is the Active Directory. It replaces the SAM that was used in Windows NT 4.0. In Windows 2000 and Windows Server 2003, every domain controller contains a read-write copy of the domain directory database. This is different from Windows NT4 where the Primary Domain Controller (PDC) was the only one to host a read-write copy. All other Windows NT4 domain controllers held a read-only copy of the domain database and served as Backup Domain Controllers (BDCs). The NT4 domain security database replication model is referred to as a single-master replication model. The Windows 2000 and Windows Server 2003 models are referred to as a multi-master replication model.

Domain controller FSMO roles

Windows Server 2003 DCs can have (just like Windows 2000 DCs) special roles in a Windows Server 2003 domain or forest. These roles are called Flexible Single Master of Operations (FSMO) roles. FSMO roles exist because some of the AD services must operate in a single-master mode—even though the bulk of the AD services are built on a multimaster model. Table 2.4 gives an overview of the different FSMO roles. The PDC emulator, RID master, and infrastructure master FSMO roles are security-related.

2.2 Security principals

In a Windows environment any entity that can be uniquely identified is called a security principal. Unique identification allows security principals to be distinguished from one another. Users and machines are examples of security principals. Security principals are used in the context of both a local and a domain security authority (as illustrated in Figure 2.4). A security principal's entry in a local or domain security authority's security database (the SAM or AD) is usually referred to as an account. A user security principal has a user account in the SAM or AD, a machine—a machine account, and a service—a service account.

From Windows 2000 onward, machine security principals are true security principals: They can identify themselves to any other principal. This

Table 2.4 *Overview of Domain Controller FSMO Roles*

DC FSMO Role (Uniqueness)	Comments
Schema Master (1 for every AD forest)	The Schema Master is unique in the entire AD forest. AD schema extensions (new object classes or attributes) can only be created on the Schema Master DC.
Domain Naming Master (1 for every AD forest)	The Domain Naming Master manages the names of every domain in the forest. Only the Domain Naming Master can add and remove domains in the tree or forest. This avoids naming conflicts.
PDC Emulator (1 for every domain)	The PDC Emulator provides backward compatibility for downlevel clients and servers in the following ways: ■ It provides downlevel client support for password updates. ■ It performs replication to downlevel BDCs (NT 4.0). ■ It acts as the Master Domain Browser, if the Windows NT 4.0 Browser service is enabled. It also plays an important role regarding its peer Windows Server 2003 DCs. Windows Server 2003 DCs attempt to replicate password changes to the PDC emulator first. Each time a DC fails to authenticate a password it contacts the PDC emulator to see whether the password can be authenticated there, perhaps as a result of a change that has not yet been replicated down to the particular DC.
RID Master (1 for every domain)	When a security principal is created, it receives a domainwide *Security ID* (SID). A part of the SID is a domainwide unique *Relative ID* (RID). The RID master allocates a pool of RIDs for each of the DCs and keeps track of the sets of allocated RIDs.
Infrastructure Master (1 for every domain)	When an AD object from another domain is referenced, the reference contains the GUID, the SID, and the DN of the object. If the referenced object moves the following will happen: ■ The object GUID does not change. ■ The object SID changes if the move is cross-domain. ■ The object DN always changes. A DC holding the infrastructure master role is responsible for updating the SIDs and DNs in cross-domain object references for objects in the domain.

was not the case in NT4 and earlier Windows versions. A machine's account name always ends in a dollar sign ($).

The unique identifiers that Windows uses to refer to security principals are logon names and security identities (SIDs). These will be explained next.

To verify a security principal's claimed identity, Windows can use different authentication credentials. These credentials can be based on different

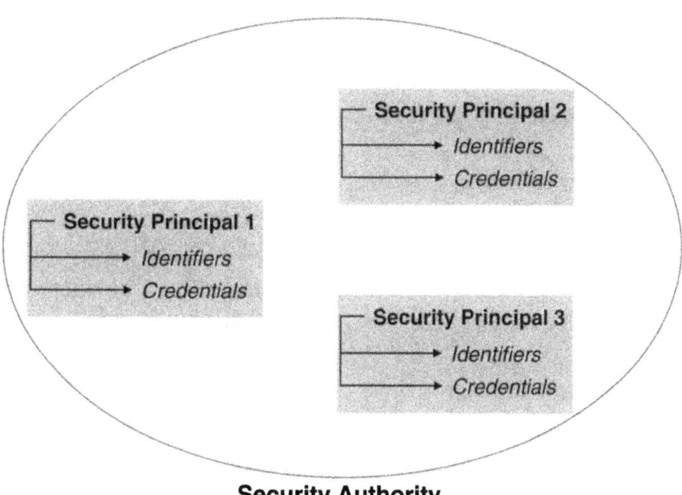

Figure 2.4 *Security authority and security principals.*

authentication methods: passwords, smart cards, biometric data, and so forth. The main difference between these methods is the use of different credentials or things that uniquely identify an entity. Out-of-the-box Windows Server 2003 supports password-based and smart card–based authentication. Other authentication methods can be supported by using third-party software. Next we will provide more details on the Windows security principal identifiers and the default Windows credentials—passwords. Authentication methods are discussed extensively in Chapter 4.

So what's the use, besides identification and authentication, of being a security principal? Every "security principal" can be used in other Windows security-related processes such as authorization, delegation, and auditing. A security principal can be granted access to resources (this process is known as authorization). It can also be granted administrative permissions (this process is known as delegation) and can be uniquely referred to in security logs (creating and maintaining security logs is the task of the auditing process). Authorization, delegation, and auditing will again be covered in later chapters.

Windows Server 2003 supports a new type of security principal: the iNetOrgPerson security principal. The enabler of this new principal type is the iNetOrgPerson AD object class. Contrary to the AD user object class (which is used to define plain user accounts) the iNetOrgPerson object class complies with an Internet standard: RFC 2798. The support for an RFC-compliant security principal type is important for companies planning to set up some kind of directory synchronization between AD and other non-Microsoft directories. iNetOrgPerson AD objects are true Windows security principals. Like any other user object, they can be used to define authorization settings or administrative delegation.

2.2.1 Security principal identifiers

Next we will discuss Windows Server 2003 security principal identifiers. We will look at logon names and security identifiers. Logon names are used by security principals when they authenticate themselves to a local or domain security authority. Security identifiers are of no use to normal users: They are used to refer to security principals by the Windows security processes.

Logon names

In a Windows Server 2003 environment, security principals can use different logon names. They can use their downlevel name or their user or service principal name (UPN or SPN).

A downlevel name has the format "domainname\username." It was a security principal's unique identifier in Windows versions before Windows 2000. Downlevel names can be used to refer to security principals in the kingdoms of both local and domain security authorities.

As mentioned earlier, Windows 2000 introduced the concept of a forest as an administrative and security boundary. The forest concept required the creation of a new type of unique security principal identifier. The latter is exactly the reason why Windows 2000 introduced the concepts of UPNs and SPNs.

User principal names

A UPN is of the format "username@company.com." It consists of a security principal's name, an @ symbol, and a DNS domain name. Their format is defined in RFC 822. The UPN is stored in the userprincipalname attribute of a Windows Server 2003 AD account object. UPNs can only be used to refer to security principals in the context of a domain security authority.

The uniqueness of a security principal's UPN is validated every time a new AD account object and UPN are created: first by searching the local Active Directory Domain naming context, then by searching the global catalog.

In Windows Server 2003 (like in Windows 2000), there is no need for the DNS domain name portion of a UPN to correspond to the DNS domain name of the domain that contains the security principal definition. It needs to correspond to a domain that has a trust relationship with

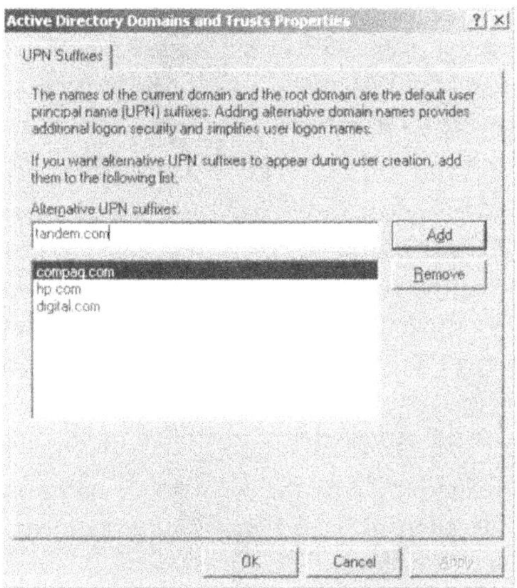

Figure 2.5 *Defining UPN suffixes.*

the principal's domain or to an alternate domain name listed in the UPN suffixes attribute of the AD Partitions container (which is a part of the Configuration container). How to define UPN suffixes from the Windows graphical user interface (GUI) is explained in the following side note. UPN suffixes can enable security principals to log on with their e-mail address. The latter may be risky from a security point of view: A hacker sniffing SMTP traffic can immediately catch half of the user's credentials.

Defining UPN Suffixes UPN suffixes can be set from the Windows Server 2003 GUI by using the properties of the Active Directory domains and trusts container in the Active Directory domains and trusts MMC snap-in—as illustrated in Figure 2.5. To add a UPN suffix, type the name of the suffix in the Alternative UPN suffix entry box, then click the Add button.

A nice thing about using a UPN for authenticating to a Windows Server 2003 domain security authority is that it takes away the requirement for a security principal to enter a domain name in the logon dialog box. When he or she types his or her UPN, the domain entry box will be automatically disabled. A UPN also stays the same independently of what happens with a security principal's account object after its creation. The following administrative actions do not affect the UPN:

- Moving a security principal to another domain in the forest
- Renaming a security principal's downlevel name

Service principal names

A service principal name (SPN) is a unique identifier for the security identity that is used by a Windows 2000 (or later) service. Like any other piece of code executing on a Windows machine, a Windows service must always run in the security context of a particular security identity.

SPNs were introduced in Windows 2000 to uniquely identify a service during the Kerberos authentication sequence. When a user sends a Kerberos ticket request for a particular service to the Windows Server 2003 Kerberos Key Distribution Center (KDC), it specifies the service he or she wants to connect to using its SPN. The SPN will also be specified in the ticket that is generated by the KDC. The user can use the ticket only to authenticate to the service that is identified by that particular SPN.

An SPN is very similar to the concept of a user principal name (UPN)—the unique identifier for a user in a Windows forest. Just like a UPN, an SPN must be unique in the Windows forest.

An SPN is stored in a security principal's AD object: in the ServicePrincipalName attribute. Because many Windows services run in the security context of a machine account, you often find them in the ServicePrincipalName attribute of a machine's AD object.

To look at the SPNs that are associated with a particular machine account, you can use the adsiedit or the setspn tools. Both are coming with the Windows Server 2003 Support tools. Adsiedit is a generic MMC-based tool that allows you to retrieve all kinds of AD information. Setspn is a command-line tool that specifically deals with SPN information.

Typing "setspn –L test1" at the command prompt will list all the SPNs that are linked to the machine called test1 (as illustrated in Figure 2.6). To add an SPN, use setspn with the -A switch. To delete one, use the -D switch.

To enable the user of a Windows service to construct the service's SPN without completely knowing it, SPNs have a fixed format. In most cases the Kerberos software just gets an LDAP or HTPP URL from the user. To deal with the conversion from, for example, a URL to an SPN Windows includes a special OS function called "DsCrackNames." The SPN format is specified here:

```
<ServiceClass>/<Host>:<Port>/<ServiceName>
```

The different SPN parts have the following meaning:

- <ServiceClass> is a string identifying the service. Examples are "www" for a Web service and "ldap" for a directory service.

Figure 2.6 *Using setspn to display the SPNs linked to a machine.*

```
K:\WINDOWS\system32\cmd.exe

K:\Program Files\Resource Kit>setspn -l test1
Registered ServicePrincipalNames for CN=TEST1,OU=Domain Controllers,DC=hr,DC=hew
    ldap/test1.hr.hewlettpackardtest.net/ForestDnsZones.hr.hewlettpackardtest.ne
    ldap/test1.hr.hewlettpackardtest.net/DomainDnsZones.hr.hewlettpackardtest.ne
    NtFrs-88f5d2bd-b646-11d2-a6d3-00c04fc9b232/test1.hr.hewlettpackardtest.net
    DNS/test1.hr.hewlettpackardtest.net
    GC/test1.hr.hewlettpackardtest.net/hr.hewlettpackardtest.net
    HOST/test1.hr.hewlettpackardtest.net/HR
    HOST/TEST1
    HOST/test1.hr.hewlettpackardtest.net
    HOST/test1.hr.hewlettpackardtest.net/hr.hewlettpackardtest.net
    E3514235-4B06-11D1-AB04-00C04FC2DCD2/eea70c07-6fec-4ff7-89cc-13de60f10642/hr
    ldap/eea70c07-6fec-4ff7-89cc-13de60f10642._msdcs.hr.hewlettpackardtest.net
    ldap/test1.hr.hewlettpackardtest.net/HR
    ldap/TEST1
    ldap/test1.hr.hewlettpackardtest.net
    ldap/test1.hr.hewlettpackardtest.net/hr.hewlettpackardtest.net

K:\Program Files\Resource Kit>_
```

- <Host> is the name of the computer on which the service is running. This can be a NetBIOS or a DNS name.
- <Port> is an optional parameter for the service port number. It enables differentiating between multiple instances of the same service that are running on the same machine and that are using a different TCP/IP port number.
- <ServiceName> is an optional parameter used to identify the data or services provided by a service or to identify the domain served by a service.

Next is a sample SPN identifying the AD LDAP service of domain controller called DC1 in the sales.hewlettpackard.net domain:

```
Ldap/DC1.sales.hewlettpackard.net/SALES
```

Security identifiers

Every Windows security principal has a security identifier (SID). SIDs are used by Windows security-related processes such as authorization, delegation, and auditing to uniquely identify security principals.

The SID for a domain account is created by a domain's security authority; the SID for a local account is created by a local security authority. The SID of a domain account is stored in the objectSid attribute of the account's AD object. The SID of a local account is stored in a secured registry portion.

An important property of a SID is its uniqueness in time and space: A SID is unique within the scope of the environment where it was created (domain or local computer). It is also unique in time: If you create an object "Paul," delete it, and recreate it with the same name, the new object will never have the same SID as the original object. The format of SIDs for local and domain authorities will be outlined next.

A set of interesting utilities to translate user account names to SIDs and the other way around are available on the Internet: look at the Web site of sysinternals for the getsid utility (http://www.sysinternals.com). On the Web site of ntbugtraq, you can find a copy of user2sid and sid2user (http://www.ntbugtraq.com). You can also use the Support Tools getsid tool. Even though this is a SID comparison tool, you can use it to translate user names to SIDs. To see the SID linked to the account you used to log on to a Windows machine or domain, together with the SIDs of the groups you're a member of, use the whoami tool with the /all switch.

Sysinternals provides a utility called newsid to generate new machine SIDs. This utility can be very useful when dealing with a machine cloning technology that doesn't automatically generate a new SID for every cloned machine. A good example is the copying of VMWare images to create new virtual machines. When you bring these identical VMWare images together in the same domain you will experience machine SID problems. You can run newsid from the command line or from the Windows GUI. To run newSID from the command line and to automatically reset a computer's SID, type

```
"newsid /a"
```

at the command prompt. In addition to generating new computer SIDs, newSID replaces all occurrences of the old SIDs with the new SIDs in the registry, in the registry objects' ACLs, and in the file-system objects' ACLs. newsid is available for free from http://www.sysinternals.com/ntw2k/source/newsid.shtml.

An SID is not the same as a global unique identifier (GUID). The SID is an object's unique identifier within a Windows domain. It can be used for security-related processes. The GUID is an object's unique identifier within the Active Directory database. It cannot be used in security-related processes. The GUID of an object never changes, whereas the SID can change. For example, when a user object is moved between two domains, it will receive a new SID—but the GUID will remain identical. To translate an object's GUID to its AD Distinguished Name, have a look at the guid2obj utility. This utility can be downloaded from the following URL: http://www.microsoft.com/windows2000/techinfo/reskit/tools/existing/guid2obj-o.asp.

Table 2.5 *SID Structure*

Field	Example: S-1-5-32-544
Character "S" identifying the object as a SID	S
The revision level of the SID structure (currently always 1)	1
An identifier for the top-level authority that issued the SID. Possible values are given in Table 2.6.	5 (= SECURITY_NT_AUTHORITY)
A variable number of identifiers for subauthorities, also known as relative identifiers (RIDs): they uniquely identify the security object "relative" to the authority issuing the SID.	32 (= SECURITY_BUILTIN_DOMAIN_RID)
	544 (= DOMAIN_ALIAS_RID_ADMINS)

SID layout

Let's have a look at what an SID looks like. The string representation of an SID and its different components together with an example are shown in Table 2.5.

Table 2.6 shows the predefined Windows SID layouts. In this table the following conventions are used:

- "TA" represents the identifier for the top-level authority (as shown in Table 2.7).

Table 2.6 *Predefined SID Layouts*

SID Type	Comments	SID Layout							
Special groups	—	S	1	TA	WID	—	—	—	—
Built-in groups	Refer to the built-in domain	S	1	5	32	WID	—	—	—
Logon sessions	—	S	1	5	5	X	Y	—	—
Local well-known SIDs	On workstations and member servers	S	1	5	21	WM1	WM2	WM3	WID
Local incremental SIDs	On workstations and member servers	S	1	5	21	WM1	WM2	WM3	RID
Shared well-known SIDs	On the domain level	S	1	5	21	D1	D2	D3	WID
Shared incremental SIDs	On the domain level	S	1	5	21	D1	D2	D3	RID

Table 2.7 *SID Top-Level Authorities*

Top-Level Authority Value	Meaning
0	SID_IDENTIFIER_AUTHORITY
1	SECURITY_WORLD_SID_AUTHORITY
2	SECURITY_LOCAL_SID_AUTHORITY
3	SECURITY_CREATOR_SID_AUTHORITY
4	SECURITY_NON_UNIQUE_AUTHORITY
5	SECURITY_NT_AUTHORITY
9	SECURITY_RESOURCE_MANAGER_AUTHORITY

- "X" and "Y" represent two 32-bit fields that are used to uniquely identify a logon session.
- "WM1," "WM2," and "WM3" represent three 32-bit fields used to uniquely identify a workstation or member server.
- "D1," "D2," and "D3" represent three 32-bit fields used to uniquely identify a Windows domain.
- "RID" represents a relative identifier. This is a value above 1,000 that is maintained in an incremental way by the OS.
- "WID" represents a well-known identifier or an RID with a predefined meaning.

Well-known SIDs and RIDs

Because an SID is unique in space and time, this does not mean that different Windows kingdoms cannot contain identical SIDs. Examples are the well-known SIDs such as the SIDs for the everyone or administrator groups. The administrator groups occur in the context of every Windows domain authority. A list of well-known SIDs and RIDs and their function is shown in Tables 2.8 and 2.9. In Table 2.9, the XXX represents domain SIDs.

2.2.2 Password credentials

Credentials are used by security authorities to verify a security principal's claimed identity. In this chapter we will explore the Windows default credentials: passwords. Chapter 4 contains more information on other

Table 2.8 *Well-Known SIDs*

SID	Meaning
S-1-0-0	Null session SID. Represents accounts with no known SID.
S-1-1-0	The everyone group SID.
S-1-2-0	The local group SID. Represents users who physically log on to the console of a computer.
S-1-3-0	The creator/owner group SID. This is a placeholder SID that's replaced with the SID of the actual creator/owner of an object.
S-1-3-1	The primary group SID. This is a placeholder SID that is replaced with a user's primary group. Primary groups are used in Posix and Macintosh.
S-1-5	The NT authority SID.
S-1-5-1	Dial-up SID.
S-1-5-2	Network logon SID.
S-1-5-3	Batch logon SID.
S-1-5-4	Interactive logon SID.
S-1-5-5-#-#	Session logon ID.
S-1-5-6	Service logon SID.
S-1-5-7	Anonymous logon SID.
S-1-5-8	Proxy SID.
S-1-5-9	Enterprise controllers SID. Includes all domain controllers (DCs) in an AD forest.
S-1-5-10	Self SID. This is a placeholder SID for a user.
S-1-5-11	Authenticated user SID. Used to differentiate users that were authenticated from members of the everyone group.
S-1-5-13	Terminal server users SID.
S-1-5-14	Remote interactive logon.
S-1-5-15	This organization.
S-1-5-18	Local system SID.
S-1-5-19	Local service SID.
S-1-5-20	Network service SID.

Table 2.8 *Well-Known SIDs (continued)*

SID	Meaning
S-1-5-21	Nonunique RIDs SID.
S-1-5-32	Built-in local groups SID.
S-1-5-1000	Other Organization.
S-1-5-64-10	NTLM authentication.
S-1-5-64-14	SChannel authentication.
S-1-5-64-21	Digest authentication.

Table 2.9 *Well-Known RIDs*

RID	Meaning
S-1-5-XXX-500	Administrator account[*]
S-1-5-XXX-501	Guest account[†]
S-1-5-XXX-502	Krbtgt account
S-1-5-XXX-512	Domain administration
S-1-5-XXX-513	Domain users
S-1-5-XXX-514	Domain guests
S-1-5-XXX-515	Domain computers
S-1-5-XXX-516	Domain controllers
S-1-5-XXX-517	Certificate publishers
S-1-5-XXX-518	Schema administrators
S-1-5-XXX-519	Enterprise administrators
S-1-5-XXX-520	Group Policy Creator Owners
S-1-5-XXX-533	RAS and IAS servers
S-1-5-XXX-1000	HelpServicesGroup
S-1-5-XXX-1002	TelnetClients
S-1-5-XXX-1106	DNSUpdateProxy
S-1-5-XXX-1109	IIS_WPG

Table 2.9 *Well-Known RIDs (continued)*

RID	Meaning
S-1-5-32-544	Administrators
S-1-5-32-545	Users
S-1-5-32-546	Guests
S-1-5-32-547	Power users
S-1-5-32-548	Account operators
S-1-5-32-549	Server operators
S-1-5-32-550	Print operators
S-1-5-32-551	Backup operators
S-1-5-32-552	Replicators
S-1-5-32-553	RAS servers
S-1-5-32-554	Pre-Windows 2000 compatible access
S-1-5-32-555	Remote desktop users
S-1-5-32-556	Network configuration operators
S-1-5-32-557	Incoming forest trust builders
S-1-5-32-558	Performance monitor users
S-1-5-32-559	Performance log users
S-1-5-32-560	Windows Authorization Access group
S-1-5-32-561	Terminal Server License Servers

* Contrary to Windows 2000, in Windows Server 2003 the Administrator account can be disabled. System or domain administrators may want to do this to better protect against misuse of this powerful account.

† Like the administrator account, the guest account can be disabled in Windows Server 2003 (which is the default). You can also delete it from a Windows system using the delguest utility that's available from http://ntsecurity.nu/toolbox/.

credential types that can be used in the context of a Windows Server 2003 setup.

Although password credentials are not the best way to identify security principals, they are certainly the most widely used credentials. They are the default Windows credentials, and any security principal can use them. Without them you have to install extra hardware or software. In the following

The Local Service and Network Service Accounts In Windows 2000 and earlier versions, Windows services and third-party applications typically ran in the security context of the local system account (also referred to as the LSA account: S-1-5-18). Running a service in the context of the local system account gives it almost unlimited privileges on the Windows system. The local system account's powers are comparable to those of the root account on UNIX systems.

To deal with this problem, Microsoft provides new accounts: the local service (S-1-5-19) and the network service (S-1-5-20). Both accounts have significantly fewer privileges than the local system account. The local service account can be used for services or applications that only access local system resources. The network service account can be used for services or applications that access network resources.

Examples of Windows Server 2003 services that are using the local service account by default are the smart card, remote registry, and telnet service. Examples of services using the network service account by default are the DNS client, the DHCP client, and the license logging service.

When you want to configure a service to use one of these new accounts, you must enter the service accounts manually—you cannot simply select them from a list. To configure the local service account, type NT Authority\LocalService; and to configure the network service account, type NT Authority\NetworkService (as illustrated in Figure 2.7).

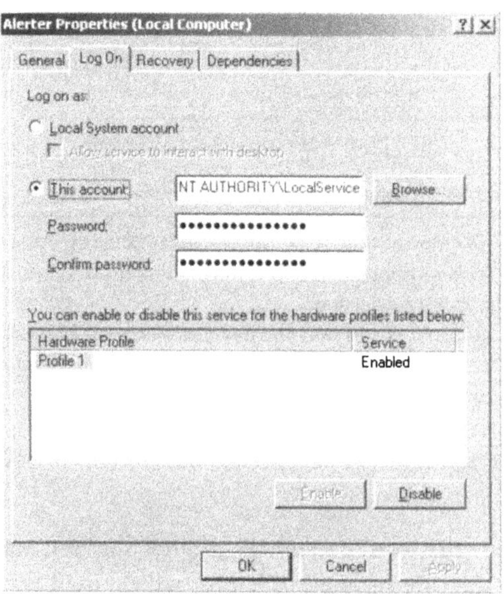

Figure 2.7 *Configuring a service to use the local service account.*

sections we will look at how password quality can be enhanced and how you can audit password quality. We will also pay special attention to machine passwords.

Enhancing password quality

Three important recommendations to enhance password quality in a Windows environment are to use the built-in Windows password policies, to provide your users with guidelines for choosing high-quality passwords, and to regularly audit the password quality. I strongly advise you to implement these guidelines—they are your first line of defense against hackers and malicious users trying to exploit the inherent weaknesses of passwords. These three guidelines will be explored in more detail in the following sections.

Microsoft is also aware of the importance of good password quality: law five of their 10 immutable laws of security[2] states: "Weak passwords trump strong security."

Password policy settings

Table 2.10 gives an overview of all password-related Group Policy Object (GPO) settings—of which the password policy settings are certainly the most important ones. GPOs are an important Windows administration tool that can be used by administrators to centrally control the system configuration settings of Windows workstations and servers in a domain environment. The table does not include the machine account password-related settings; these are discussed later.

Password policy settings can be just like any other account policy setting, only defined on the domain level. You cannot enforce a specific password policy for the users in a particular AD organizational unit (OU), for example.

User password guidelines

The most important guideline you can give your users is to choose truly random passwords. There are some tools available that you point your users to in order to help them choosing random passwords. The easiest solution is to let users use the net user command with the /random switch (as Figure 2.8 shows for user joe). The command automatically generates a strong random password and assigns it to the user account.

2. http://www.microsoft.com/technet/treeview/default.asp?url=/technet/columns/security/essays/10imlaws.asp.

Another solution is to use an online password generation service (like the one at http://www.winguides.com/security/password.php) or a stand-alone password generation program (like the one available from http://www.mark.vcn.com/password/). A Google search for "password generator" will reveal more similar tools. These password generation tools typically generate a random password of a length and complexity specified by the user—they also let you generate multiple random passwords in a single run. The online password generation services are accessible for free. Some of the stand-alone programs have to be purchased.

Table 2.10 *Windows Server 2003 Password Quality-Related GPO Settings*

Setting	Comments
Password policy (in Computer Configuration\Windows Settings\Security Settings\Account Policies GPO Container)	
Enforce password history	Value: 0–24 Sets the number of passwords Windows will remember and forces users to choose a password different from the one in the history.
Maximum password age	Value: 0–999 Specifies number of days a password remains valid. "0" means that the password never expires. This setting can be overridden by setting "Password never expires" in the account properties.
Minimum password age	Value: 0–999 Specifies number of days before a user is allowed to change his or her password. "0" means that the user can always change his or her password.
Minimum password length	Value: 0–14 Specifies the minimum password length. "0" means that the user is allowed to have no password at all. Like in Windows 2000, Windows Server 2003 supports a maximum password length of 127 characters. In NT4 the password length was limited to 14 characters.
Password must meet complexity requirements	Value: enabled-disabled Enabling this setting requires that passwords: ■ Are at least six characters long. ■ Contain a mix of uppercase letters, lowercase letters, numbers, and symbols. ■ Do not contain the user name or any part of the user's full name.
Store passwords using reversible encryption for all users in the domain	Value: enabled-disabled When this setting is enabled passwords will not be stored in a hashed format in the SAM or AD. This setting is used to support the HTTP-based Digest authentication protocol.

Table 2.10 *Windows Server 2003 Password Quality-Related GPO Settings (continued)*

Setting	Comments
Security options (in Computer Configuration\Windows Settings\Security Settings\Local Policies GPO Container)	
Accounts: Limit local account use of blank passwords to console logon feature only	Value: enabled-disabled Enabling this setting will make it impossible for users with blank passwords to perform a network or a remote desktop logon feature. Only local logon features will be allowed. The difference between local and network logon features is explained in Chapter 4.
Network Security: Do not store LAN Manager hash value on next password change	Value: enabled-disabled When this setting is enabled, no LAN Manager password hashes will be stored in the SAM or AD. The LAN manager password hash is insecure because it stores an identical hash for every password that's longer than 14 characters.*

* More details on the differences between the LAN Manager hash of a password and the more secure NT hash of a password will be provided in Chapter 4.

You may also recommend your users to choose passwords that include special characters that cannot be detected by password cracking tools (these tools are covered next). The 187 special characters that cannot be detected are listed on the Web site http://sysopt.earthweb.com/articles/win2kpass.

Checking password quality

To perform basic password quality tests, you can use the Microsoft Baseline Security Analyzer (MBSA). The MBSA tool (illustrated in Figure 2.9)

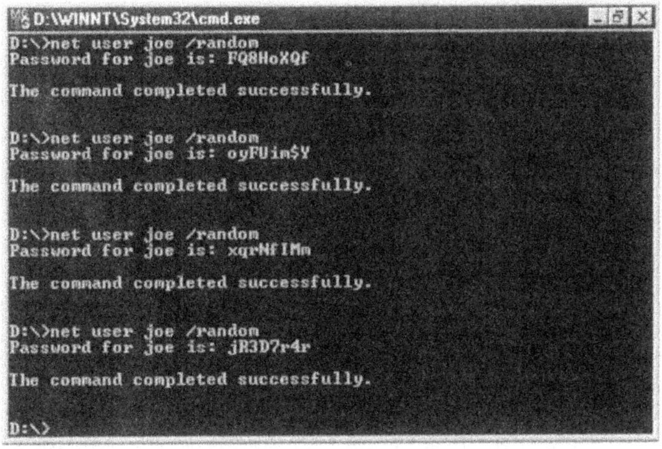

```
D:\WINNT\System32\cmd.exe
D:\>net user joe /random
Password for joe is: FQ8HoXQf

The command completed successfully.

D:\>net user joe /random
Password for joe is: oyFUim$Y

The command completed successfully.

D:\>net user joe /random
Password for joe is: xqrNfIMm

The command completed successfully.

D:\>net user joe /random
Password for joe is: jR3D7r4r

The command completed successfully.

D:\>
```

Figure 2.8 *Using net user with the /random switch.*

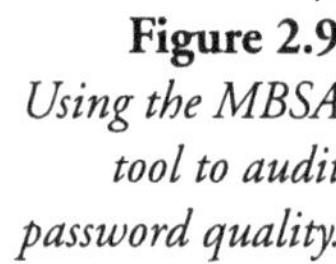

Figure 2.9 *Using the MBSA tool to audit password quality.*

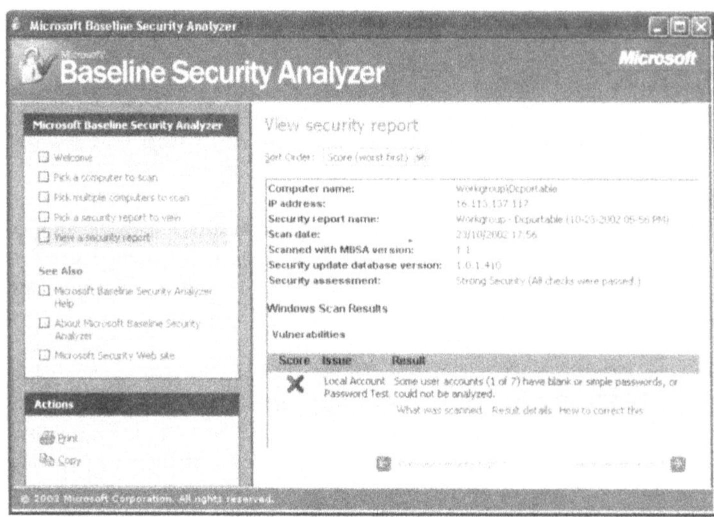

(version 1.1.1 at the time of this writing) can check for the following password conditions:

- Password is blank.
- Password is the same as the user account name.
- Password is the same as the machine name.
- Password uses the word "password."
- Password uses the word "admin" or "administrator."

MBSA version 1.1.1 also includes a command-line version (mbsacli.exe) that can perform the same checks.

For advanced password quality tests, I recommend that you look at a set of third-party tools that can crack the password hashes Windows stores in the security database (the SAM or Active Directory) and sends across the network during authentication exchanges. These tools are not just hacking tools; they are also excellent tools to run regular password quality audits on your Windows domains. To run the tools, you need administrator privileges on the local system. Next we will discuss two such tools: L0phtcrack and John the Ripper. Another tool with similar capabilities is the Elcomsoft Advanced NT Security Explorer (More information is available at http://www.elcomsoft.com/antexp.html.)

L0phtcrack L0phtcrack was originally developed by the hacker group, the Cult of the Dead Cow. You can get a trial copy of the latest version of the

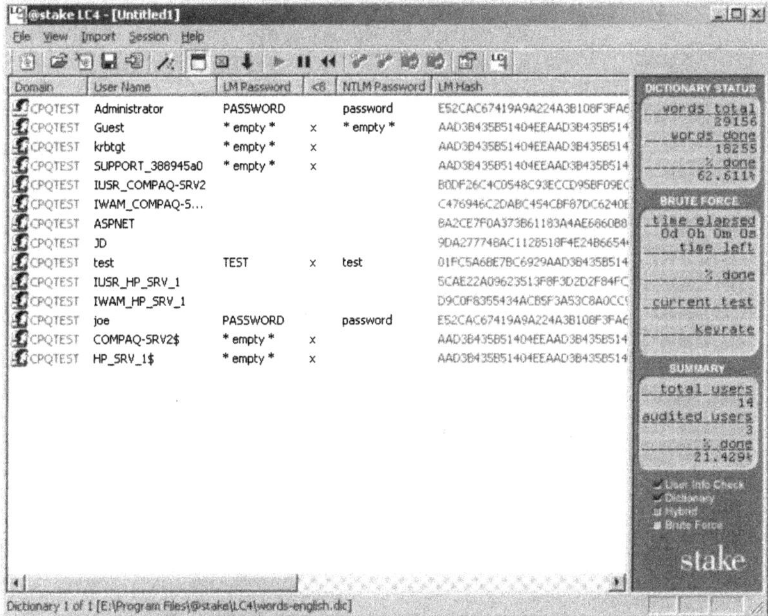

Figure 2.10
L0phtcrack GUI.

tool (currently version 4.0) from the @Stake Web site at http://www.atstake.com/research/lc/download.html. The tool is also referred to as LC4. Figure 2.10 shows the LC4 GUI.

In a Windows Server 2003 environment, LC4 can retrieve the password hashes from different sources:

- From the local SAM or AD database. This method requires administrator privileges.
- From a remote SAM or AD database. This method requires administrator privileges.
- By sniffing the network for an NTLM version 1 authentication-related challenge-response exchanges. If NTLM version 2 is used, LC4 cannot retrieve password hashes using this method. There is more information on the difference between NTLM versions 1 and 2 and how to configure Windows to use either or both of these versions in Chapter 4.
- By importing the output file of a pwdump3.exe-run. Pwdump3 is a command-line tool that can be used to retrieve password hashes from a Windows security database (AD or SAM). You can download the tool from the Polivec Web site at http://www.polivec.com/pwdump3.html. Pwdump3 uses a technique that is known as DLL

injection to run code in the security context of the LSASS process. It must be run in the security context of an administrator account. To use pwdump3.exe, extract the pwdump3 zip file, then run the Pwdump3 command from the directory that contains pwdump3.exe.

Another method that was available on pre-Windows 2000 systems was to retrieve the hashes directly from a SAM file. This method did not necessarily require that the user accessing the SAM was logged on with administrator privileges (he or she could easily retrieve the SAM from an Emergency Repair Disk (ERD) or by booting a Windows box in DOS). The reason why this does not work on Windows 2000 and later OS versions is because they have the syskey protection feature enabled by default. Syskey provides an additional layer of encryption for SAM password hashes. It can only be circumvented if the SAM is accessed in the security context of an administrator account. Syskey is explained in more detail in the following side note.

LC4 supports different methods for cracking Windows 2000 password hashes: dictionary, hybrid, and brute force cracks. When starting a cracking session, L0phtcrack runs the three methods in the following order: first dictionary, then hybrid, and finally brute force. You can disable or enable the crack methods using the LC4 Auditing options, which are available from the Session\Session Options menu option.

During a dictionary crack, LC4 encrypts (hashes) all of the passwords listed in a predefined password file and compares every result to the password hash. If they match, LC4 knows the actual password is the dictionary word. LC4 comes with a default password file, named the words-english file. Many other dictionary files can be downloaded from the Internet. You can also create your own custom password file and load it into L0phtcrack.

During a hybrid crack, LC4 extends the dictionary crack by adding simple number and symbol patterns to the word list in the password file. For example, as well as trying out the word "Galileo," L0phtcrack will also try "Galileo24," "13Galileo," "?Galileo," and so on. The number of characters in the pattern can be specified in the characters field of the Auditing Options dialog box. The default number of characters is 2.

When performing a brute-force crack, LC4 tries every possible combination of characters. The characters LC4 uses can be defined in a character set. This set can be specified in a password file or using the Character Set drop-down box in the Auditing Options dialog box. The default character set is the alphanumeric set, A–Z, 0–9. An important detail is that in LC4 the brute-force crack option is only available if you pay a license fee for the tool. The prices are about $350 for a normal license and $1,750 for a consultant license.

Syskey Protection of SAM and AD Security Data The Syskey adds an extra level of encryption for the password hashes stored in the SAM database and AD. By default, syskey is enabled on any Windows Server 2003 system.

Out of the box, the syskey encryption key is stored on the local system—definitely a bad idea for systems that require a very high level of security. That is why you might want to consider prompting for the syskey password at system startup. To set this up, type "syskey" at the command prompt, choose update, and select the "password startup" option. Syskey also offers the possibility to store the startup key on a floppy disk.

The easiest way to find out whether an NT machine has Syskey enabled is to type "syskey" at the command prompt. This command brings up the Securing the Windows Account Database dialog box (shown in Figure 2.11), which indicates whether Syskey encryption is enabled.

Alternately, you can check for the registry value HKEY_LOCAL_MACHINE\SYSTEM\CurrentControlSet\Control\Lsa\Secureboot. If the Secureboot value (of type REG_DWORD) exists and is set to a value of 0x1, 0x2, or 0x3, Syskey is enabled on the system.

More information on syskey can be found in the MS Knowledge Base article Q143475.

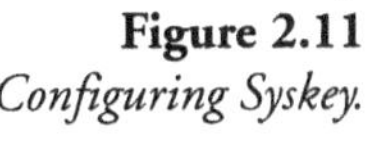

Figure 2.11
Configuring Syskey.

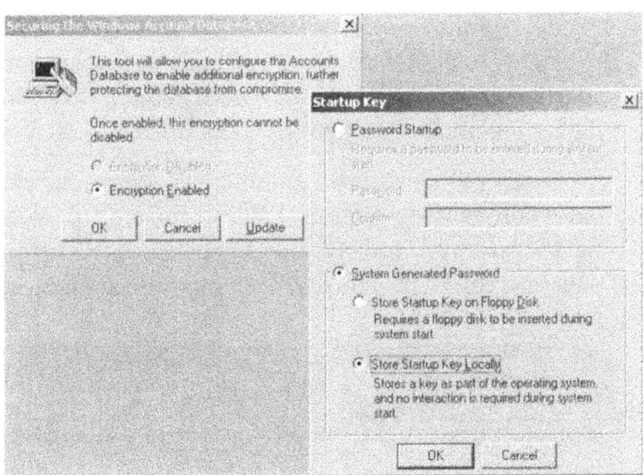

John the Ripper Unlike LC4, John the Ripper (JtR) is a command-line password cracking tool that is free (including its brute-force cracking function). You can download the tool from http://www.openwall.com/john. Be sure that you download the Win32 binaries. A distributed version of JtR (called Distributed John) is available from http://ktulu.com.ar/en/djohn.php. It can distribute the cracking load across different machines.

Also unlike LC4, JtR does not include tools to retrieve the password hashes from the NT SAM or Active Directory or to sniff the network for password hashes. To retrieve the hashes, you need a tool like pwdump3.exe (explained earlier). The following command dumps all password hashes to a file called passwd.lanman and stores the file in the D:\john\run directory:

```
Pwdump3 >D:\john\run\passwd.lanman
```

If you use Notepad to open the passwd.lanman file, you will see output similar to that in Figure 2.12. Note that the file contains one line for every user account in the SAM. A set of colon-separated alphanumeric values that represent the password hash follows each user account name.

Next, switch from the directory that contains pwdump3.exe to the directory that contains the JtR executable called john.exe, which by default is in the \john-16\run directory. Before starting the password cracking process, test whether JtR is operating properly on your system. To do so, type the following at the command line:

```
john -test
```

This command starts a JtR benchmarking test that checks the JtR cracking speed for different password hashing formats. You will notice that in addition to cracking NT password hashes, JtR can crack the password hashes on FreeBSD, OpenBSD, and other UNIX systems.

When the benchmark terminates without an error, you can start the password cracking process. JtR can do both dictionary-based and brute-force–based password cracking. By default, JtR performs a dictionary-based password crack. To start that cracking process on the password hashes in the

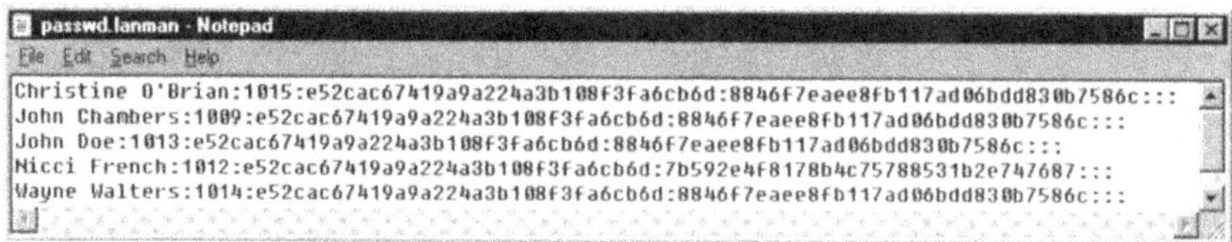

Figure 2.12 *Pwdump3 output.*

Figure 2.13 *Running John the Ripper.*

```
D:\WINNT\System32\cmd.exe

D:\john\john-16\run>john passwd.lanman
Loaded 10 passwords with no different salts (NT LM DES [24/32 4K])
PASSWOR          (Christine:1)
PASSWOR          (John:1)
PASSWOR          (John:1)
PASSWOR          (Nicci:1)
PASSWOR          (Wayne:1)
D                (Christine:2)
D                (John:2)
D                (John:2)
D                (Nicci:2)
D                (Wayne:2)
guesses: 10  time: 0:00:00:00 100% (2)  c/s: 422980  trying: D - A

D:\john\john-16\run>john -show passwd.lanman
Christine O'Brian:PASSWORD:1015:8846f7eaee8fb117ad06bdd830b7586c:::
John Chambers:PASSWORD:1009:8846f7eaee8fb117ad06bdd830b7586c:::
John Doe:PASSWORD:1013:8846f7eaee8fb117ad06bdd830b7586c:::
Nicci French:PASSWORD:1012:7b592e4f8178b4c75788531b2e747687:::
Wayne Walters:PASSWORD:1014:8846f7eaee8fb117ad06bdd830b7586c:::

10 passwords cracked, 0 left

D:\john\john-16\run>
```

passwd.lanman file, you would type the following at the command prompt (illustrated in Figure 2.13):

```
john passwd.lanman
```

To start a brute-force–based password cracking process, use the -incremental switch:

```
john -incremental:all passwd.lanman
```

When you use the -incremental switch, you must include an incremental option (e.g., all in this example), which specifies the brute-force cracking scheme used. For details about all the incremental options and how to configure them, see the documentation that accompanies the JtR tool.

JtR saves its results in the john.pot file. To see an overview of the cracked passwords for the passwd.lanman file, type the following at the command prompt, as Figure 2.13 shows:

```
john -show passwd.lanman
```

To speed up the password cracking process, JtR lets you use different dictionary files, test only specific password combinations, or spread the password cracking load across different computers. By default, JtR uses the password.lst dictionary file, which contains commonly used passwords and comes with the JtR software. To discover other dictionary files, simply do a Google or Yahoo! search for the term "dictionary file." You can use the -wordfile switch to specify other dictionary files. For example, the following command uses the mydict.lst dictionary file.

```
john -wordfile:mydict.lst passwd.lanman
```

To test only specific password combinations, you can specify a set of password rules in a file called conf.ini, add conf.ini to the JtR configuration file, then run the tool with the -rules switch:

```
john -rules passwd.lanman
```

Spreading the cracking process across multiple machines significantly speeds up the process but is rather complex to set up. Spreading the load uses a different JtR restore file for every computer that participates in the cracking process.

Machine passwords

Many people forget that in a Windows domain environment, machine security principals have—just like user security principals—a password. The reason why many people forget this is mainly because a machine's password cannot be dealt with directly from the Windows GUI—most of the machine password-related maintenance tasks occur automatically without any administrator intervention.

The OS changes machine passwords automatically every 30 days. Unlike user passwords, a machine's password cannot be reset from the Windows Server 2003 GUI. An administrator can reset a user password from the Users and Computers MMC snap-in: by right-clicking the account object and selecting "reset password..." You can, however, use the command prompt tool "netdom" with the "/resetpwd" switch (this tool comes with the Windows Server 2003 support tools) to force a machine password change. Doing so will write a copy of the new password to the local LSA database and to the Active Directory (the domain credential database).

Windows Server 2003 includes a set of GPO settings to change the machine password update behavior. The GPO settings together with their corresponding registry hacks are listed in Table 2.11. All registry keys are located in the HKEY_LOCAL_MACHINE\system\currentcontrolset\services\netlogon\parameters registry container.

One of the hacks allows you to disable password changes. From a security point of view, it is obviously a bad idea to disable password changes because it makes machines more vulnerable to hacker attacks.

2.2.3 Account lockouts

From its early versions Windows has come with a security feature known as account lockout. Account lockout assures that user accounts automatically become unusable when a user has entered a certain amount of bad pass-

Table 2.11 *Machine Password Update Registry Hacks*

Can Be Applied To...	Parameter (Type) *(Corresponding GPO Security Options Setting)*	Values	Meaning
Workstations	DisablePasswordChange (REG_DWORD) *("Domain member: Disable machine account password changes")*	0	Workstation automatically changes machine account password
		1	Workstation never changes machine account password (this value does not prevent manual change)
	MaximumPasswordAge (REG_DWORD) *("Domain member: maximum machine account password age")*	1–1000000 days	Interval for automatic machine password change (only used if DisablePasswordChange is disabled)
Domain controllers	RefusePasswordChange (REG_DWORD) *("Domain controller: refuse machine account password changes")*	0	Domain controller accepts machine password changes
		1	Domain controller rejects machine password changes

words. The bad password threshold is defined by an administrator in the account lockout security policy. Administrator accounts are not subjected to the account lockout policy. Account lockout protects your Windows systems against acount spoofing and hijacking. On the other hand, it can also be looked at as a great denial-of-service (DOS) attack tool: hackers could lock out all your Windows accounts, making it impossible for anyone except your administrators to log on the Windows infrastructure.

When an account is locked out, only an administrator can unlock it. To do so, the administrator must uncheck the "account is locked out" checkbox in the account tab of the account properties (using the AD Users and Computers MMC snap-in).

Account lockout should not be confused with disabling an account, which is the consequence of an explicit action performed by the administrator—it does not occur automatically following, for example, a set of security policy settings.

Account lockout process

Figure 2.14 illustrates the Windows 2000 and Windows Server 2003 account lockout process. In this process a domain's PDC emulator plays the key role.

- Step 1: A user attempts to log on to a Windows domain using a wrong password.
- Step 2: The authenticating DC detects the password is wrong. To make sure that the user really entered a wrong password—and that the problem is not caused by AD replication latency—the authenticating DC double-checks with the domain's PDC emulator.
- Step 3: The PDC emulator checks the password and detects it is really wrong. The PDC emulator increments the BadPwdCount attribute in the user account object's properties with 1.
- Step 4: The PDC emulator informs the authenticating DC about the fact that the user's password was really wrong.
- Step 5: The authenticating DC updates the BadPwdCount attribute in his local AD copy of the user account object.
- Step 6: The user is informed about the fact that he provided a wrong password.

If the user's BadPwdCount property exceeds the value defined in the Account Lockout Threshold of the domain's lockout policy (explained later), the user's account will be marked as locked out. The BadPwdCount property is automatically reset to 0 when the user enters a correct password following a set of bad password entries.

In Windows Server 2003 the DCs perform a password history check before a user's BadPwdCount attribute is incremented. The password provided by the user is checked against the two last passwords in the user object's password history (stored in the NtPwdHistory user object attribute).

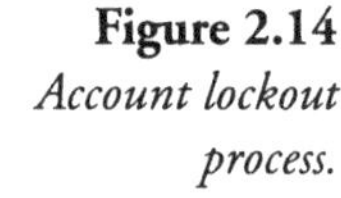

Figure 2.14 *Account lockout process.*

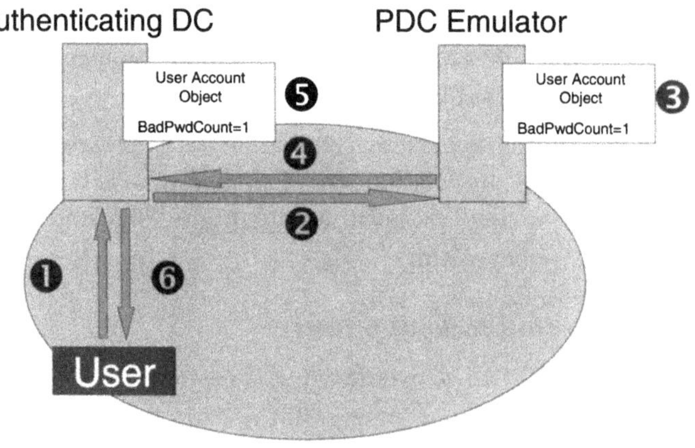

Besides the BadPwdCount property, every Windows Server 2003 account object also has the following account lockout–related property: the BadPasswordTime property. The BadPasswordTime property contains the last time the user, machine, or service submitted a bad password to the authenticating DC. Both the BadPwdCount and the BadPasswordTime property are not replicated between DCs. The authenticating DC only replicates it to the PDC emulator of the domain.

Account lockout policy

A Windows 2000 and later domain's account lockout policy settings are set from the account lockout portion of a domain group policy object. They are located in the Computer Configuration\Windows Settings\Security Settings\Account Policies GPO container. Like all other account policies (password and Kerberos policies), they can only be applied on the Windows domain level.

Table 2.12 shows a set of recommended values for the account lockout policy settings. To make sure that account policies (including account lock-

Table 2.12 *Account Lockout Policy Settings*

Account Lockout Policy Setting	Value/Meaning
Account lockout duration (ObservationWindow)	0–9999 minutes (Defaults to 30) Recommend value: 30 Specifies the amount of time after which an account's badPwdCount attribute is reset. Or in other words: specifies the amount of time a locked-out account remains locked out before the system automatically unlocks it. If the lockout duration is set to value 0 the account will remain locked out until an administrator explicitly unlocks it.
Account lockout threshold (LockoutTreshold)	0–999 invalid logon attempts (Defaults to 0) Recommend value: 10 Specifies the number of times a user can send a bad password to the authentication service before the account is locked out. An "account lockout threshold" with value 0 means that account lockouts are disabled in the domain.
Reset account lockout after (LockoutDuration)	1–99999 minutes (Defaults to 30) Recommend value: 1 (for environments with normal security requirements) and 30 (for environments for with high security requirements). Specifies the amount of time that lockout is enforced on an account that has exceeded the Account lockout threshold value.

out policies) are always evaluated (in other words, to make sure that logging on using cached credentials will not work), it is also advisable to use the "Interactive logon: require domain controller authentication to unlock workstation" GPO setting (also known as the forceunlocklogon registry hack). The latter is explained in the side note.

> **Making Sure That Account Security Policies Are Enforced When a User Unlocks the Windows Console** When a user unlocks the Windows console, he or she will be logged on using cached credentials (explained in Chapter 3). This means that the account security policies (including the account policies) are not enforced—which is a potential security hole.
>
> To make sure that the account security policies are enforced when a user unlocks the Windows console, change the following GPO setting: "Interactive logon: require domain controller authentication to unlock workstation." It is located in the Machine Configuration\Windows Settings\Security Settings\Local Policies\Security Options GPO container.
>
> Under the hood this GPO setting changes the ForceUnlockLogon registry key located in HKEY_LOCAL_MACHINE\Software\Microsoft\Windows NT\CurrentVersion\Winlogon\. Setting it to value 1 means the account policies will be checked on a DC when the console is unlocked. This also means you won't be able to unlock the console when no DC is available.

If you are setting the account lockout policies for the very first time (e.g., if you have defined an account lockout threshold), Windows Server 2003 will automatically suggest a set recommended settings for the "account lockout duration" and "reset account lockout counter after" account lockout policy settings. This is illustrated in Figure 2.15.

Account lockout–related management tools

Early Windows 2003 Microsoft added some interesting new account lockout–related tools to their management tool portfolio. Microsoft provides

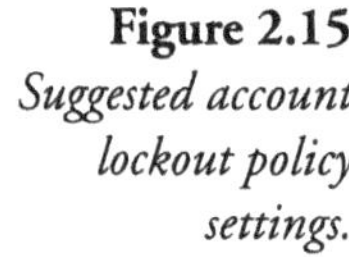

Figure 2.15 *Suggested account lockout policy settings.*

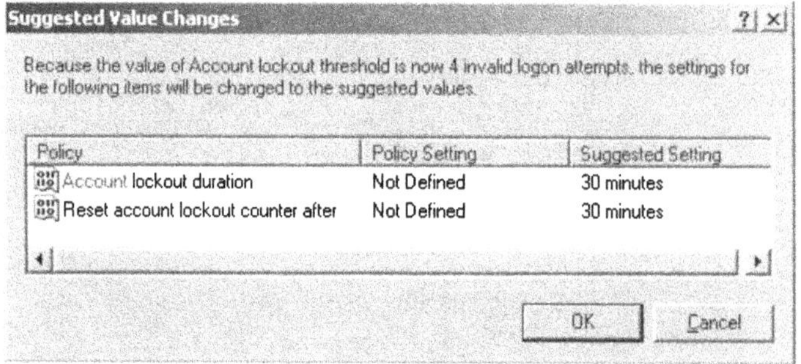

some of these tools as part of the Windows Server 2003 Resource Kit. All of them are also available in a software package that is downloadable for free from the Microsoft Web site (look for the altools.exe file). Table 2.13 gives an overview of these tools.

The acctinfo.dll adds a new property tab to an AD user account's properties (as illustrated in Figure 2.16). The new tab holds different types of account logon feature–related information. A very interesting feature of the tool is its capability to reset a user's password on a specific DC in the domain. This can be done by clicking the "Set PW on Site DC" push button at the bottom of the "Additional Account Info" tab. To add the tab to your AD account properties, register the acctinfo.dll on every machine from which you're using the AD Users and Computers MMC snap-in. To register a dll, use the regsvr32.exe command-line tool.

The alockout.dll helps with identifying the program or service that is causing an account lockout or—in other words—the entity that is sending the wrong credentials. In the altools.exe file it comes in two versions: one for Windows 2000 and Windows Server 2003 and another one for Windows XP. To install the tool, use the appinit.reg registry file that comes together with the tool. When the dll is installed and an account lockout occurs, alockout.dll generates an entry in the alockout.txt file—which is stored in the %windir%\debug folder. Microsoft does not recommend using this tool on servers running important network services or applications (such as Microsoft Exchange).

Aloinfo.exe is a command-line tool that can be used to display a list of the user accounts stored in AD and the amount of days that are left before

Table 2.13 *Account Lockout–Related Management Tools*

Tool Name (Available From)	Usage
AcctInfo.dll (Resource Kit and altools.exe)	Adds a new property page to the AD account properties that can help isolate and troubleshoot account lockouts. The tool can also be used to change a user's password on a domain controller in a particular site.
ALockout.dll (altools.exe)	Client-side tool that helps with identifying the process or application that is sending wrong credentials.
ALoInfo.exe (altools.exe)	Command line tool displaying all user account names and the age of their passwords.
LockoutStatus.exe (Resource Kit and altools.exe)	GUI tool (illustrated in Figure 2.17) that can query all domain controllers for user account lockout-related information.

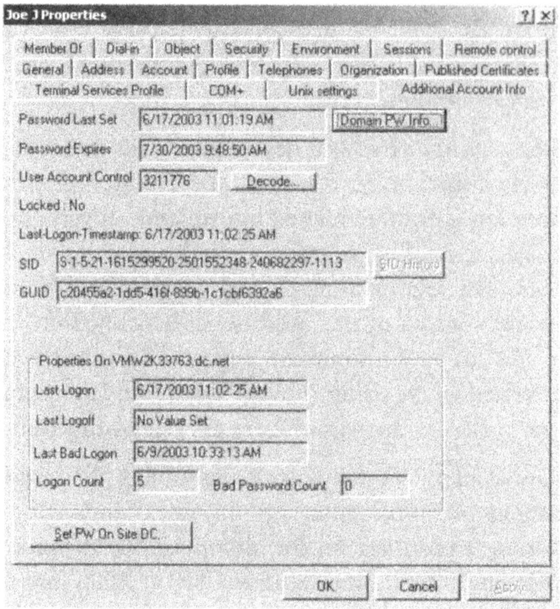

Figure 2.16
Additional account info tab.

their passwords expire. To retrieve this information, type the following aloinfo command at the command line:

```
Aloinfo /expires /server:<servername>
```

Another interesting tool is lockoutstatus.exe. It is a GUI tool (illustrated in Figure 2.17) that can be used to query for the account lockout–related information of a particular user account on the different domain controllers of a domain. It displays the following information:

- Status of the BadPwdCount attribute on different domain controllers
- Last time a bad password was entered
- Time the password was set for the last time
- Time when the account was locked out
- Name of the domain controller that locked the account (in the "originating lock" field): This is the domain controller that wrote to the Lockouttime attribute of the user account.

Under the hood, LockoutStatus.exe uses the NLParse.exe tool to parse the Netlogon logs for specific Netlogon return status codes. The tool's output can be saved to a comma-separated value text file.

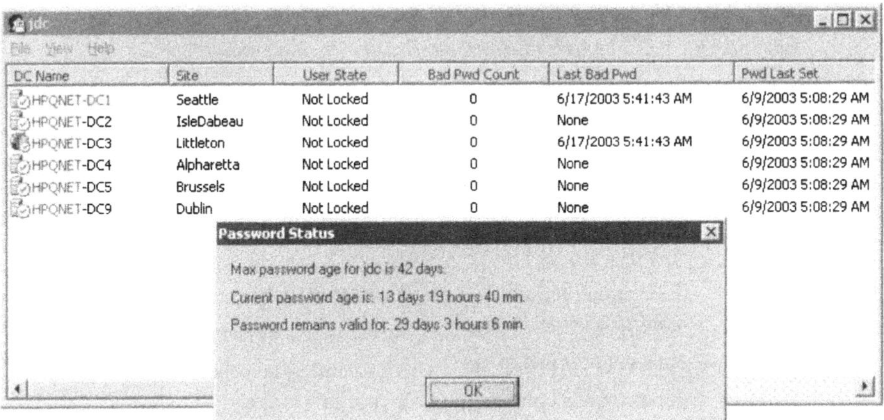

Figure 2.17 *LockoutStatus.exe tool.*

2.2.4 Security-specific AD replication mechanisms

Active Directory provides some specific replication mechanisms to efficiently distribute critical security information such as account lockouts, password updates, global LSA secret changes, and security policy changes in a Windows domain. By default, AD replication takes place at predefined intervals. AD has three security-specific replication mechanisms: immediate, urgent, and single-user-object "on-demand" replication. The differences between the three mechanisms are outlined in Table 2.14.

From an account lockout point of view, there is an important link between urgent and immediate replication: When an account is locked out or unlocked, urgent replication starts, which then triggers immediate replication.

Immediate replication works by default within an AD site. Between AD sites it only works if intersite change notifications are enabled. To enable intersite change notifications, you must enable it in the options attribute of the AD site link object. Site link objects are located at the following AD path: CN=IP,CN=Inter-Site Transports,CN=Sites,CN=Configuration,DC=<ForestRootDomainName>. To enable change notifications, set the rightmost bit in the site link object's options attribute to 1. To change the delay for intersite change notification messages, modify the value of the following registry key: HKEY_LOCAL_MACHINE\SYSTEM\CurrentControlSet\Services\NTDS\Parameters\ Replicator notify pause after modify. The default value is 300 seconds.

Table 2.14 *AD Security-Related Replication Mechanisms*

	Urgent Replication	Immediate Replication	Single-User-Object "On-Demand" Replication
Occurs between:	All DCs of the domain.	DCs and the PDC emulator of the domain.	A user's authenticating DC and the PDC emulator of the domain.
Occurs when:	The account lockout or password policies are changed. An account is locked out. An account is unlocked. A DC's password is changed. A global LSA secret is changed. The RID Manager state changes.	A password is changed. An account is locked out. An account is unlocked. A global LSA secret is changed on one of the DCs in a domain.	A DC contacts the PDC emulator to request for an update to a user object's attributes. This can occur when an authenticating DC wants to get an update on the status of the bad password count attribute of a user object.
Replication model:	Follows the AD replication topology.	Follows the AD replication topology.	Does not follow the AD replication topology. Uses a point-to-point replication mechanism.

Immediate replication can also be disabled within a site for specific DCs (e.g., if there is a slow WAN link between the DC and the PDC emulator). To do so, use the following GPO setting: "Contact PDC on logon failure" located in Computer Configuration\Administrative Templates\System\Net Logon.

Under the hood, this GPO setting changes the following registry key: HKLM\SYSTEM\CurrentControlSet\Services\Netlogon\Parameters\AvoidPdcOnWan (Value 1 means immediate replication is disabled).

Single-user-object on-demand replication can be enabled or disabled by changing the following registry key: HKEY_LOCAL_MACHINE\SYSTEM\CurrentControlSet\Control\Lsa SamDisableSingleObjectRepl. If this key holds value 1, single-user-object on-demand replication is disabled. More information on single-user-object on-demand replication can be found in the following Microsoft KB article: http://support.microsoft.com/?id=812499.

3

Windows Trust Relationships

Chapter 2 introduced Windows security authorities and security principals. In this chapter we will look at how we can establish security relationships between Windows domain security authorities using trust relationships.

3.1 Defining trust relationships

Trust relationships define an administrative and security link between two Windows domains or forests. They enable a user to access resources that are located in a domain or forest that is different from the user's definition domain or forest. The creation of a trust between domains or forests does not automatically grant users access to resources in the trusting domains or forests: The domain or forest administrator still has to assign access rights to the users for the appropriate resources.

In the context of a Windows domain or forest, a trust basically means that one domain trusts the authentication authorities of another domain, or, in other words, it creates cross-domain visibility and usability of security principals. When security authority A has authenticated a user, Joe, and security authority B trusts security authority A (as illustrated in Figure 3.1), B will not start another authentication process in order to verify user Joe's identity. In Windows domain speak, the fact that a domain controller (DC) in domain A has authenticated user Joe and the existence of a trust between domains A and B are enough for the DCs in domain B to trust user Joe's identity.

When a trust relationship is set up between two domains, there is always a trusted and a trusting domain. The trusting domain is the one that initiates the setup of a trust relationship. The trusted domain is the subject of the trust definition. If the domain compaq.com sets up a trust with the digital.com domain (as illustrated in Figure 3.2)—in which case digital.com is

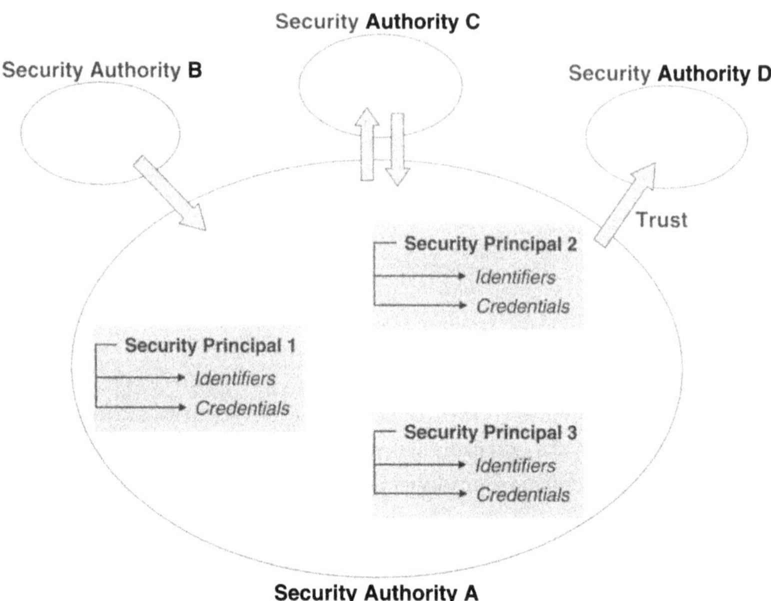

Figure 3.1 *Security authorities and trust relationships.*

the trusted domain and compaq.com is the trusting domain—all accounts defined in digital.com will be trusted. This means that all digital.com accounts can be used to set access control settings on resources in the compaq.com domain. The opposite is not true, unless another trust is defined going from digital.com to compaq.com—in that case compaq.com is the trusted domain and digital.com the trusting domain. The latter case is referred to as a two-way trust relationship. The former case is referred to as a one-way trust relationship.

In Windows Server 2003, trust relationships can be created automatically or manually:

- Windows Server 2003 trust relationships are created automatically as part of the "dcpromo" process. The dcpromo process builds an AD instance on a Windows server, or, in other words, it makes a server a domain controller.
- To create a trust manually, use the Active Directory Domains and Trusts MMC snap-in. During manual trust setup you will be prompted to enter a "trust password." When trusts are created automatically, this "trust password" is generated and exchanged without administrator intervention.

You cannot create a trust relationship if the NETBIOS domain name of the two domains are identical. In the example of Figure 3.2, the NETBIOS

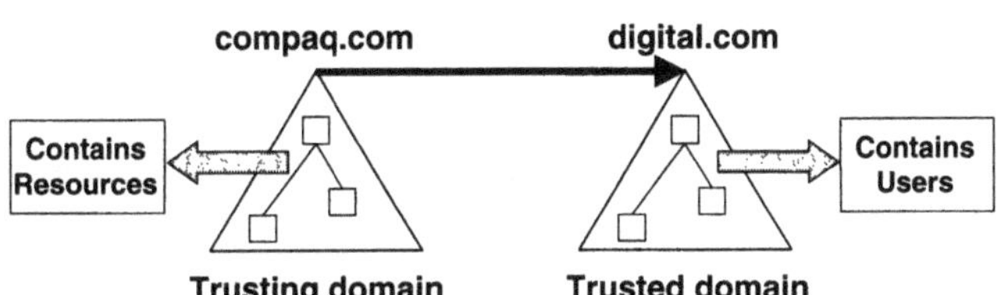

Figure 3.2 *Trust relationships: trusting versus trusted domain.*

name of the trusting domain is compaq, the NETBIOS name of the trusted domain is digital. If both the trusted and trusting domain had a NETBIOS name "root" creating a trust between the two would fail.

In the following sections we will discuss the Windows Server 2003 trust properties and types and how trust relationships work behind the scenes. We will pay special attention to a brand-new Windows Server 2003 trust type: cross-forest trust.

3.2 Trust properties and types

Trust relationships in a Windows environment can be classified based on the following properties: the way they are created (implicitly or explicitly), whether they are one- or two-way trust relationships, and whether they are transitive or not. The different trust types and their properties are listed in Table 3.1. They are illustrated in Figure 3.3.

A Windows Server 2003 administrator can view trust relationships and their properties through each domain object's properties in the AD Domains and Trusts MMC snap-in, or by using the netdom.exe or nltest.exe command prompt utilities (these utilities will be explained later on in this chapter). Figure 3.4 shows the trusts tab in the properties of a

Table 3.1 *Trust Types and Default Properties*

Trust Type	Default Properties
Tree-Root Trust	Implicitly created, transitive, two-way
Parent-Child Trust	Implicitly created, transitive, two-way
Shortcut Trust	Explicitly created, transitive, one- or two-way
Forest Trust	Explicitly created, transitive, one- or two-way
External Trust	Explicitly created, nontransitive, one- or two-way
Non-Windows Trust	Explicitly created, nontransitive, one- or two-way

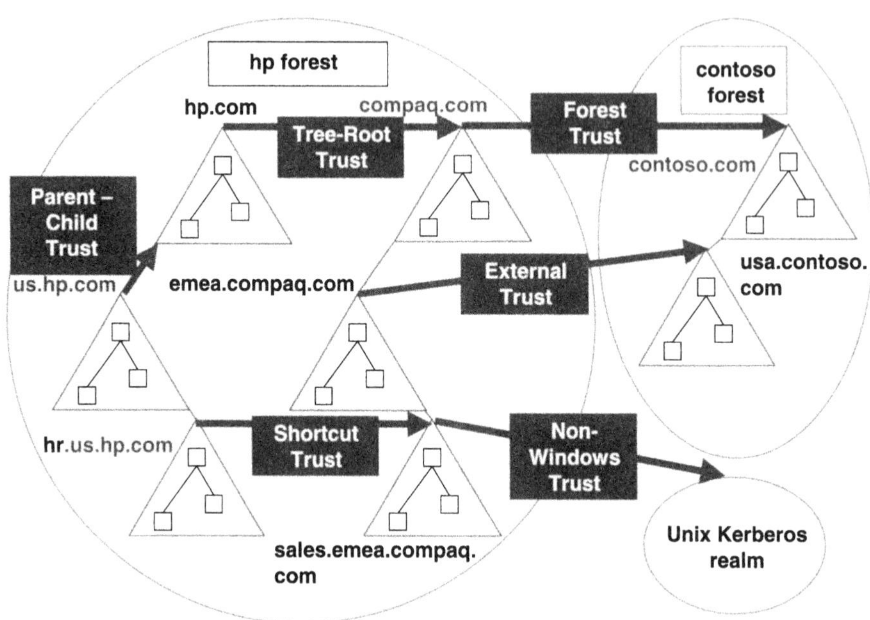

Figure 3.3 *Windows trust types.*

domain as you can see it from the AD Domains and Trusts MMC snap-in. If you open the properties of a particular trust relationship, you get more detailed information on the specific properties of that particular trust relationship (as shown in Figure 3.5).

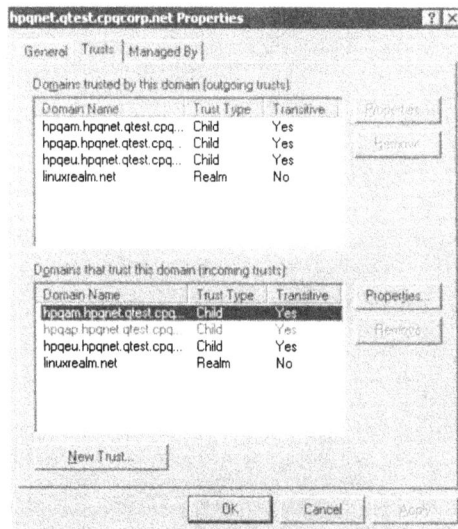

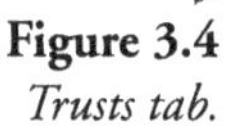

Figure 3.4 *Trusts tab.*

hpqnet.qtest.cpqcorp.net Properties

General | Trusts | Managed By

Domains trusted by this domain (outgoing trusts):

Domain Name	Trust Type	Transitive
hpqam.hpqnet.qtest.cpq...	Child	Yes
hpqap.hpqnet.qtest.cpq...	Child	Yes
hpqeu.hpqnet.qtest.cpq...	Child	Yes
linuxrealm.net	Realm	No

Properties... Remove

Domains that trust this domain (incoming trusts):

Domain Name	Trust Type	Transitive
hpqam.hpqnet.qtest.cpq...	Child	Yes
hpqap.hpqnet.qtest.cpq...	Child	Yes
hpqeu.hpqnet.qtest.cpq...	Child	Yes
linuxrealm.net	Realm	No

Properties... Remove

New Trust...

OK Cancel Apply

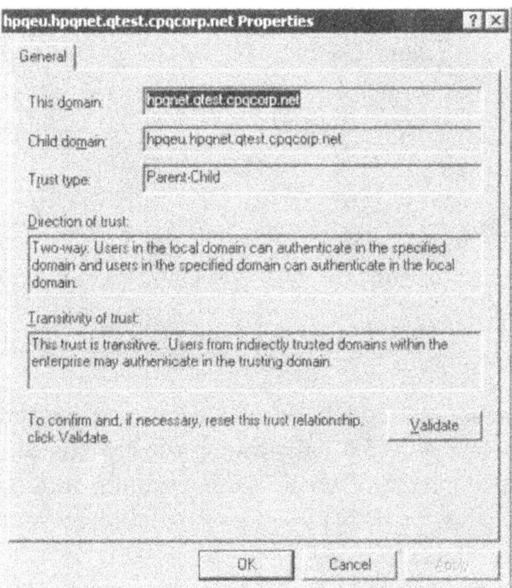

Figure 3.5
Trust properties.

Implicitly created trust relationships are created as part of the dcpromo process. Dcpromo—the process that installs an AD instance and domain controller—can automatically create trust relationships between AD parent and child domains and between the top-level domains of an AD tree and the root domain of the forest. All the other trust relationship types are created explicitly by domain administrators.

All implicitly created AD trust relationships are two-way transitive trust relationships. In other words, running dcpromo automatically defines two trust relationships. Also, in this case each domain is both a trusting and a trusted domain. All explicitly created AD trust relationships can be either one- or two-way trust relationships—depending on the administrators' decisions.

In Windows Server 2003 (and beginning with Windows 2000), Microsoft simplified trust creation and management by letting you create trusts automatically as part of the domain hierarchy building process and by allowing transitive trust relationships. Before, in NT4 and earlier Windows versions, all trust relationships had to be created manually and were nontransitive.

Transitive means that the trust extends beyond the trusted and the trusting domain. For example, if both the europe.hp.com and the us.hp.com domains trust the hp.com domain, then the europe.hp.com domain implicitly trusts the us.hp.com domain. Transitive trust reduces the number of

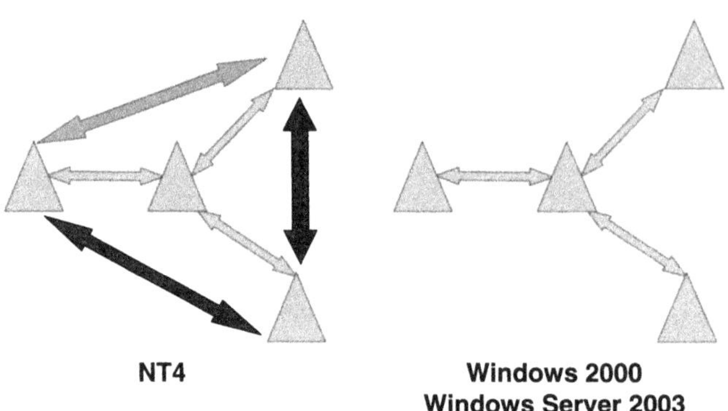

Figure 3.6 *Number of trust relationships required in Windows Server 2003 and NT4.*

trusts that are needed for authentication interoperability between different domains. In Figure 3.6, only four trusts are needed (between each parent and child domain) to obtain authentication interoperability between all three domains. In an NT4 setup we would have needed six trust relationships to do the same thing.

Users working from Windows 2000 or later workstations can see the effect of transitive trusts when they log on. They can choose every domain with which their domain has a direct trust or an indirect trust. An NT 4.0 end user sees only the direct trusts of his or her domain.

Transitive trust is only a logical concept—there is no shared secret between the domain controllers of the domains that share a transitive trust. This means that for authentication to occur between entities on opposite ends of a transitive trust, the authentication process will not flow across the transitive trust but along a path that is known as the *trust path*. This concept will be explained in more detail in Chapter 5 of this book.

3.3 Trust relationships: Under the hood

Let's look at what is behind a "trust relationship" and what happens when you manually set up a one-way trust relationship in Windows Server 2003.

In the example in Figure 3.7, the domain administrator of domain South decides to trust another domain, North. In this case South is the trusting domain and North is the trusted domain. When the administrator sets up the trust, Windows will create a Trusted Domain Object (TDO) for the North domain in the AD domain naming context of domain South (this is on the outgoing side of the trust). This account will be called South. Just as for any other AD account, there will be a security principal password linked to this object. This password is sometimes also referred to as the

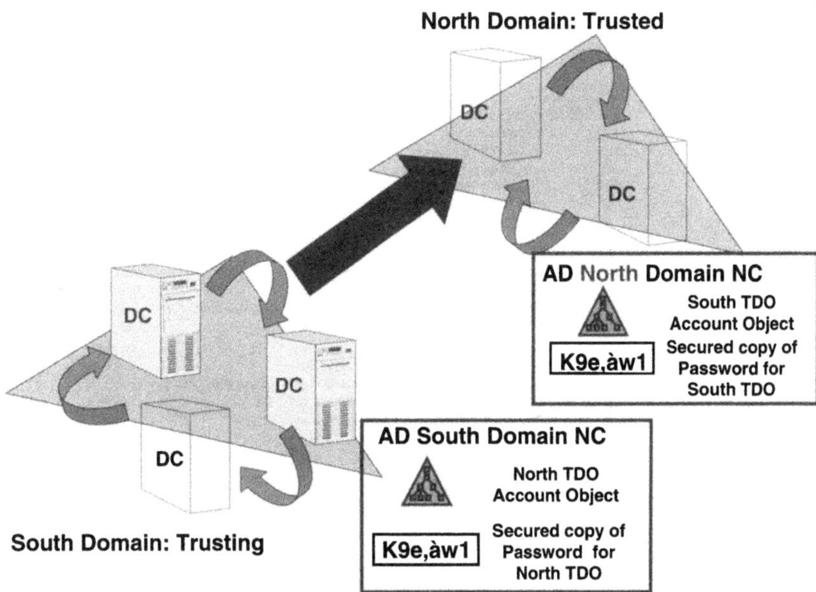

Figure 3.7 *Trust relationships: behind the scenes.*

interdomain secret. When you set up a trust relationship manually, the OS will actually prompt you for this password. When the administrator in the South domain or the administrator in the North domain creates the other side of the trust in the North domain (the incoming side), another TDO called South will be created in the AD domain naming context of domain North.

You can look at the TDO account objects using the AD Users and Computers MMC snap-in or using AdsiEdit. The TDOs are located in the domain naming context underneath the system container (as illustrated in Figure 3.8). Table 3.2 shows the most important trust-related attributes of an AD TDO object.

The South TDO account is replicated among the DCs in the North domain using plain AD domain naming context replication. The same is true for the North TDO in the South domain. The TDOs and some of their attributes are also replicated to the global catalog (GC). This makes them available to all entities in a Windows forest. The latter enables the routing of cross-domain and cross-forest authentication requests and object browsing (explained in the following sections).

What are these TDOs and their passwords (the interdomain secrets) used for? One of the things they are used for is the setup of a secure channel between the domains North and South. A secure channel is set up when the first domain controller of domain South boots up and on condition that a

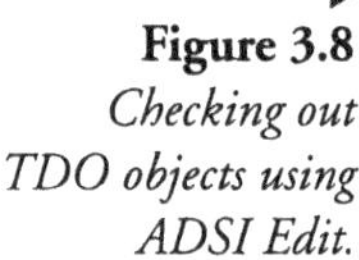

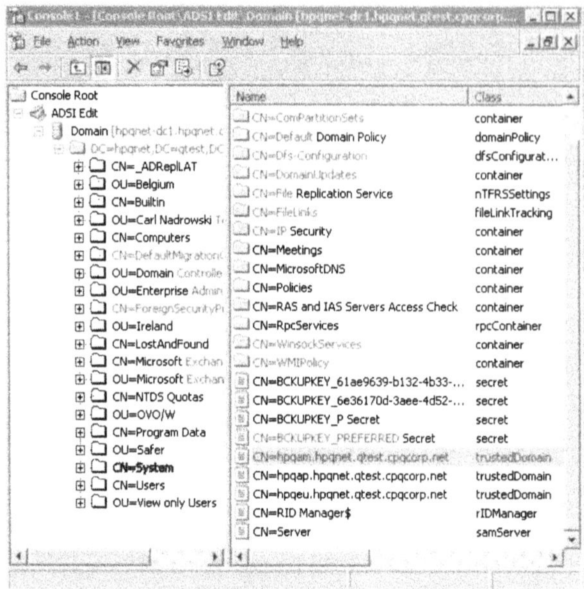

Figure 3.8 *Checking out TDO objects using ADSI Edit.*

Table 3.2 *Key AD TDO Object Trust-Related Attributes*

TDO Attribute	Meaning/Values
TrustAttributes	Trust properties. Values: ■ 1: trust is nontransitive ■ 2: trust valid only for Windows and later computers ■ 40 0000: trust to a parent domain ■ 80 0000: trust to root domain of another domain tree
TrustDirection	The direction of a trust. Values: ■ 1: incoming trust ■ 2: outgoing trust ■ 3: two-way trust
TrustPartner	The name of the domain with which a trust exists. For Windows 2000 and later this is a DNS name. For Windows NT this is a NetBIOS name.
TrustType	The type of trust. Values: ■ 1: downlevel trust (to a Windows NT domain) ■ 2: Windows 2003 trust (with an AD domain) ■ 3: MIT trust (with MIT Kerberos v5 realm) ■ 4: DCE trust (with DCE realm)
TrustAuthIncoming	Authentication information for the incoming portion of a trust.
TrustAuthOutgoing	Authentication information for the outgoing portion of a trust.

domain controller of domain North is available. It is used to secure the authentication traffic between the trusting and the trusted domain. As other domain controllers become available they will set up their proper secure channels.

3.4 Forest trust

Windows 2000 introduced the concept of a forest as a logical and administrative grouping of several Windows domains that are linked together using trust relationships. A forest provides ease of use and administration for resources that must be available to the users of different domains. It also facilitates the deployment, administration, and use of enterprise applications such an Exchange-based mail infrastructure.

As the knowledge of the forest concept matured, it became clear that it takes away some of the domain boundaries that are available in earlier Windows versions. In Windows 2000 the domain cannot be considered a true security boundary anymore: The final border is the forest. As a consequence, a certain amount of trust is required between the different domains in a forest and their administrators.

A lot of organizations cannot live with these trust requirements for political, legal, or purely administrative reasons and have deployed multiple Windows forests. Many organizations built multiple forests for reasons of a company merger or a set of company acquisitions. Another example is the requirement to build two forests for perimeter security reasons: one forest for the intranet and another one for the demilitarized zone (DMZ).

A major problem in Windows 2000 is the definition of cross-forest trust. From a security administration point of view, the creation of cross-forest trust is an administrative nightmare that basically puts your Windows 2000 environment back in the NT4 era (remember the spaghetti model of trust). A general shortcoming of Windows 2000 trust relationships is that, just like their predecessors, they can only define trust in a very coarse-grain way, a characteristic that is not particularly useful in a cross-forest environment where you may want to restrict what is exchanged and accessed between forests.

It is clear that Windows 2000 is not made to easily support multiple forests. In Windows Server 2003, Microsoft resolved most of the Windows 2000 multiple forest and cross-forest trust problems and shortcomings through the introduction of a new trust type called "forest" trust.

Windows Server 2003 forest trust relationships allow administrators to securely federate two AD forests using a single trust relationship. The forest trust features can provide a seamless AD object browsing, user authentication, and access control experience between different forests. Windows Server 2003 also offers new powerful tools to define fine-grain cross-forest trust security policies. In the following sections we will explore more in detail how these new cross-forest trust features work.

The cross-forest trust features are a fundamental building block for Microsoft's federation strategy. Windows Server 2003 cross-forest trust primarily focuses on federation between different Microsoft AD environments (e.g., to link together company forests or company partner or subsidiary forests). In the 2003–2004 time frame, the MS product range will be extended with a product that is specifically focusing on external federation between Windows forests and other organization's Trusted Third Parties (TTPs) (that are not necessarily rooted on MS AD technology): This product was, at the time of the writing of this book, codenamed "Trustbridge."

3.4.1 Features

Windows Server 2003 includes a set of important enhancements that facilitate the setup and administration of cross-forest trust relationships:

- *Forest trust relationships are transitive between two forests.* In Windows Server 2003 it is enough to have a single trust between the two root domains of two different forests to enable interforest authentication between all domains in the two forests. This is illustrated in Figure 3.9 for Domain C in the compaq.com forest: Because of the transitive forest trust between compaq.com and hp.com, domain C will automatically have a transitive trust relationship with domains D, E, and F in the hp.com forest (the same is true for the other domains). Transitive trusts greatly simplify forest trust administration and provide transparent SSO between all domains in the two forests. In Win-

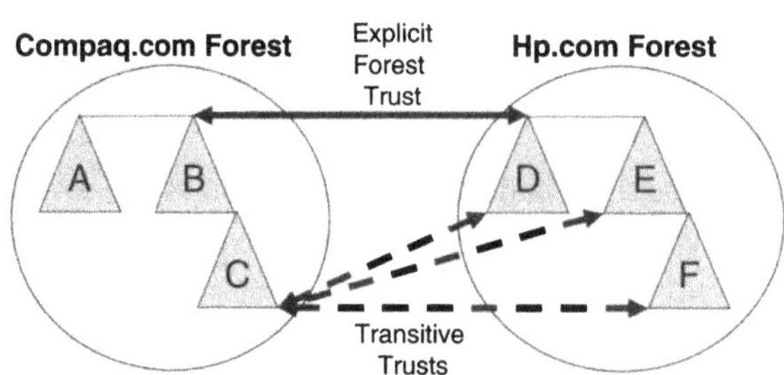

Figure 3.9 *Cross-forest trust transitivity between two forests.*

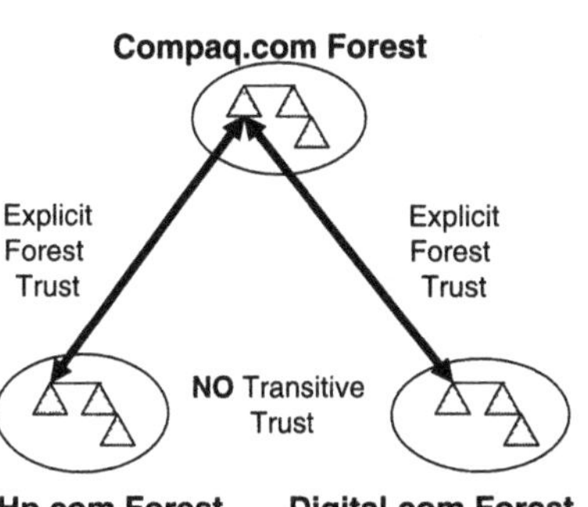

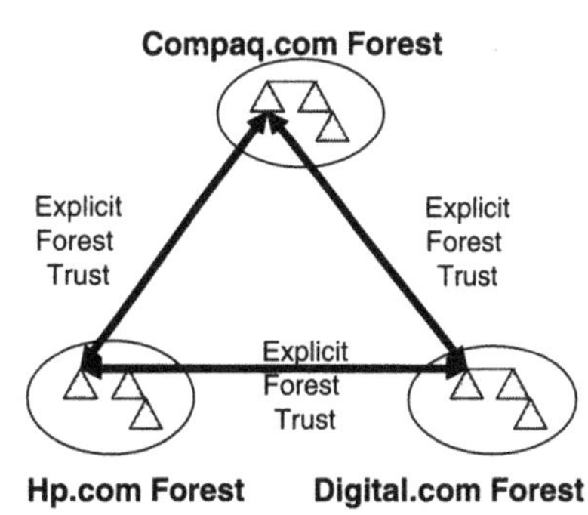

Figure 3.10 *Cross-forest trust between multiple forests.*

dows 2000 the same level of functionality required the definition of a trust relationship between every other domain in the two forests. Transitive forest trusts do not allow for transparent object browsing (e.g., when setting access control settings) between all domains in the two forests; this is only possible between the root domains of the two forests.

- *Forest trusts are not transitive between multiple forests* (as illustrated in Figure 3.10 for the digital.com, compaq.com, and hp.com forests). If forest trusts exist between the digital.com and the compaq.com forests and between the compaq.com and the hp.com forests, then there will not automatically be a transitive trust between digital.com and hp.com (as illustrated in the left picture of Figure 3.10). If a transparent SSO experience is required between the hp.com and the digital.com forests, an explicit forest trust relationship would be required between those two forests (as illustrated in the right picture of Figure 3.10).
- *Forest trust relationships can be defined in a very granular way.* Windows Server 2003 supports three ways to restrict forest trust: SID filtering, top-level name restrictions, and selective authentication (the latter feature is also known as the authentication firewall). These three concepts will be explained in greater detail later. Remember that in Windows 2000 trust definition is very coarse-grain:[1] When you set up a trust between forests in a Windows 2000 environment, you either trust everyone or don't trust anyone.
- *Forest trust relationships enable the use of different authentication protocols and methods for cross-forest resource access.* When performing a

1. Note that Windows 2000 supports SID filtering between domains from Service Pack 2 (SP2) onward.

cross-forest network logon, both Kerberos and NTLM are supported. For interactive cross-forest logon, users can use either a Kerberos PKINIT-based smart card logon feature or a User Principal Name (UPN)–based logon feature (the latter supports both the Kerberos and the NTLM authentication protocols).

- *Forest trust relationships create cross-forest visibility of universal and global groups and user accounts.* For example, when you create a forest trust relationship between the root domain of resource forest hp.com (the trusting forest) and the root domain of account forest compaq.com (the trusted forest) you can
  - put universal and global groups defined in the compaq.com forest into domain local groups in the hp.com forest.
  - put user accounts defined in the in the compaq.com forest into domain local groups in the hp.com forest.
- *Windows Server 2003 includes a new trust wizard* (accessible from the Active Directory Domains and Trusts MMC snap-in) that guides you through the different trust configuration options (illustrated in Figure 3.11). This wizard can be used to set up a forest trust and all other trust types (shortcut, external, and realm trusts). When the wizard detects that the trusted domain is a forest root domain, you can choose to set up either a forest trust or an external trust (the difference between the two is explained next). When setting up a forest trust, the wizard guides you through the following steps:
  - Specification of the DNS or NetBIOS name of the target domain
  - Specification of whether the trust will be bidirectional, one-way incoming, or one-way outgoing
  - Specification of whether you want to create the trust in both domains or just in your proper domain
  - Specification of whether the authentication firewall must be enabled
  - Specification of which DNS name suffixes should be enabled for cross-forest name suffix routing
  - Confirmation of the creation of the trust

An important requirement to use the Windows Server 2003 forest trust features outlined earlier (with the exception of the new trust wizard) is that both forests are in Windows Server 2003 functionality level 2. This forest functionality level is only available if all domains are at functionality level 2. The latter is only possible if all the domain controllers in a domain are running the Windows Server 2003 operating system.

Figure 3.11 *The new Windows Server 2003 Trust Wizard.*

Processing of GPOs, Logon Scripts, and Profiles in an Interactive Cross-Forest Logon Feature In Windows Server 2003 you can influence whether the logon scripts, the roaming profiles, and the user portions of the GPOs in the user's logon domain are made available to a user when logging on interactively over a forest trust link.

This can be done by modifying the "Allow Cross-Forest User Policy and Roaming User Profiles" GPO setting in the following GPO container: Computer Configuration\Administrative Templates\System\Group Policy\. By default this setting is disabled. In other words: by default user logon scripts and profiles are not applied in cross-forest logon scenarios.

This GPO setting is also available in Windows 2000 from Windows 2000 Service Pack 4 (SP4) onwards. Like in Windows Server 2003 the setting is also disabled by default. In pre-SP4 Windows 2000 setups the application of logon scripts and user profiles is enabled by default in cross-forest logon scenarios. All this is documented in the Microsoft Knowledge Base article Q823862.

3.4.2 Behind the scenes

The basic enabler behind forest trust is a new trustedDomain Active Directory object (TDO) type called "forest". TDOs of type forest contain a new attribute called msDS-TrustForestTrustInfo that is used to store information about the domains in the trusted forest. This is basically security and NetBIOS and DNS naming information of the root domain of the trusted forest and any top-level name (TLN) restrictions (explained next) related to the other domains in the trusted forest. The information stored in the

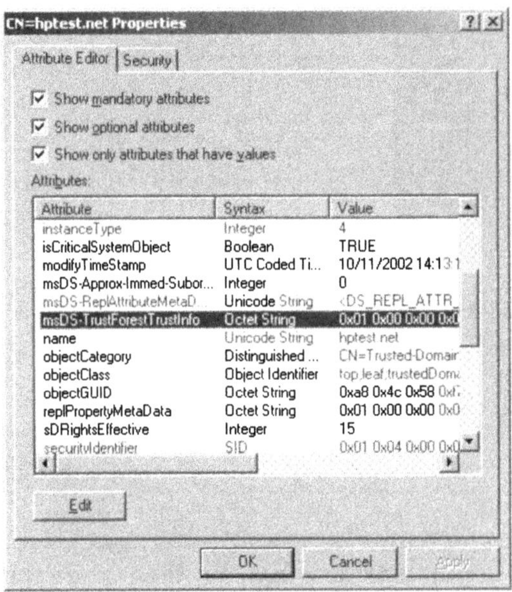

Figure 3.12 *Windows Server 2003 forest trust attributes (as viewed from AdsiEdit).*

msDS-TrustForestTrustInfo object is basically used to route authentication requests and object lookups between forests. The msDS-TrustForest-TrustInfo attribute is a binary blob which can be deciphered using the LsaQueryForestTrustInformation API (this API is documented in the Windows platform SDK).

Remember that the TDOs and their attributes are replicated to the global catalog (GC). As a consequence, any machine in the forest can look up forest trust TDO objects and use their content. To take a look at a TDO's attributes, you can use the AdsiEdit tool coming with the Windows Server 2003 support tools (as illustrated in Figure 3.12 for the hptest.net TDO).

Windows Server 2003 supports two ways to link forests together: using a forest or an external trust. The latter was the only way to link forests together in Windows 2000. The key difference between a forest trust and an external trust is that a forest trust contains information about all domains in the remote forest. As a consequence, it can support Kerberos-based authentication, UPN-based logon feature, and object lookups between any of the domains in the two forests. Figure 3.13 shows how two other forests "cpqtest.net" and "digitaltest.net" are displayed in the Windows object picker (used for setting access control settings) after two forest trust relationships have been defined: one between hewlettpackardtest.net and cpqtest.net and another one between hewlettpackardtest.net and digitaltest.net.

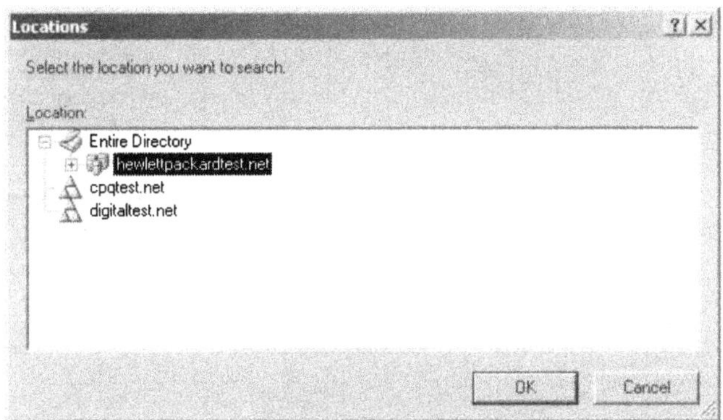

Figure 3.13 *Display of other forest "hptest.net" in Object Picker.*

The easiest way to find out a trust relationship's type is to use the AD Domains and Trusts MMC snap-in and open the properties of a domain container. In the Trusts tab you can find the domain name of the trust relationship, the trust type, and whether the trust is transitive (as illustrated in Figure 3.4).

3.4.3 Restricting forest trust

Windows Server 2003 includes several ways to restrict forest trust: top-level name restrictions, selective authentication, and SID filtering. These will be explained in the following sections.

Name suffix routing and top-level name restrictions

Windows Server 2003 uses a mechanism called name suffix routing to provide name resolution between forests linked together using a forest trust. As explained earlier, name resolution is needed to route cross-forest authentication and object query requests. The Windows Server 2003 cross-forest routing mechanism is rooted on a list of DNS domain suffixes that is stored in the TDO of the root domain of a forest. The suffixes can be disabled, enabled, or excluded to modify the cross-forest routing behavior. How to do this will be explained next. Name suffix routing modifications in the first place only affect Kerberos authentication behaviour. NTLM authentication messages passed between domains that are not requiring routing logic bypass the name suffix routing restrictions.

In the example in Figure 3.14, a one-way forest trust has been defined between the cpqtest.net and the hewlettpackardtest.net Windows forests. The hewlettpackardtest.net domain is the root domain of the forest with the same name. The hewlettpackardtest.net forest is made up of a second

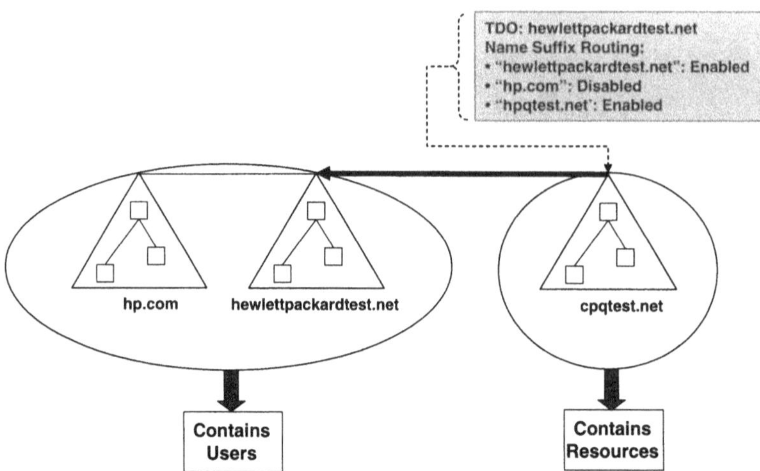

Figure 3.14 *TLN restrictions example: disabling DNS namespaces.*

domain tree called hp.com. In this scenario, cpqtest.net is the trusting domain containing the resources and hewlettpackardtest.net is the trusted domain containing the users. The administrator in the cpqtest.net domain decides that he or she does not want to trust the authentication requests or object query requests that are coming in from accounts in the hp.com domain. To do so, he or she can disable the "hp.com" namespace in the msDS-TrustForestTrustInfo attribute of the TDO for the hewlettpackardtest.net domain in the cpqtest.net AD naming context, which is on the outgoing side of the trust.

DNS namespaces can be disabled when running the new Windows Server 2003 Trust Wizard. The page where this is done is illustrated in Figure 3.15. The wizard displays all the DNS suffixes of the top-level domains in a forest (with the exception of the DNS suffix of the root domain itself) and all UPN suffixes that have been defined on the forest level. In the example of Figure 3.15, there is one additional top-level DNS suffix "hp.com" and one UPN suffix has been defined "hptest.net." To disable the routing of all incoming requests with a *.hp.com suffix in the cpqtest.net forest, simply uncheck the box—as illustrated in Figure 3.15. To enable routing (in the example, routing is enabled for *.hptest.net), simply leave the checkbox checked.

Remember that forest UPN suffixes are defined from the AD Domains and Trusts MMC snap-in. To add or delete additional UPN suffixes, right-click the Active Directory Domains and Trusts container and select properties.

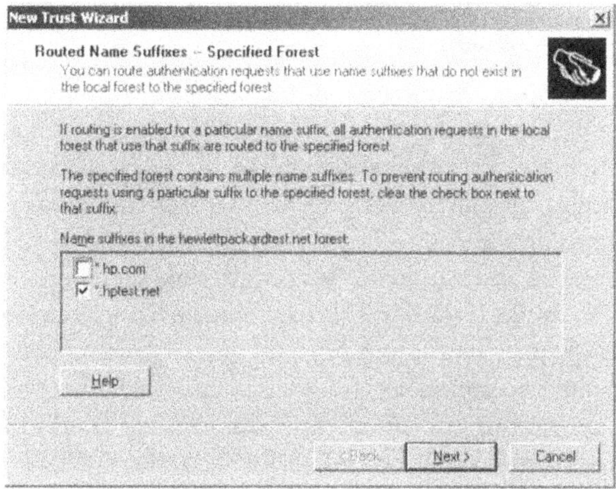

Figure 3.15 *TLN restrictions example: enabling DNS namespaces when running the Trust Wizard.*

DNS namespaces can also be disabled from the "Name Suffix Routing" tab in the properties of a trust object (available from the AD Domains and Trusts MMC snap-in). This is illustrated in Figure 3.16 for the hp.com suffix in the properties of the hewlettpackardtest.net trust object. To disable or enable a suffix, select them and click the "Enable" or "Disable" pushbuttons as needed. Note that the dialog box also shows another DNS suffix called "hewlettpackard.net" that is set to disable and marked as "New." This is a UPN suffix that was added to the "hewlettpackardtest.net" forest after the

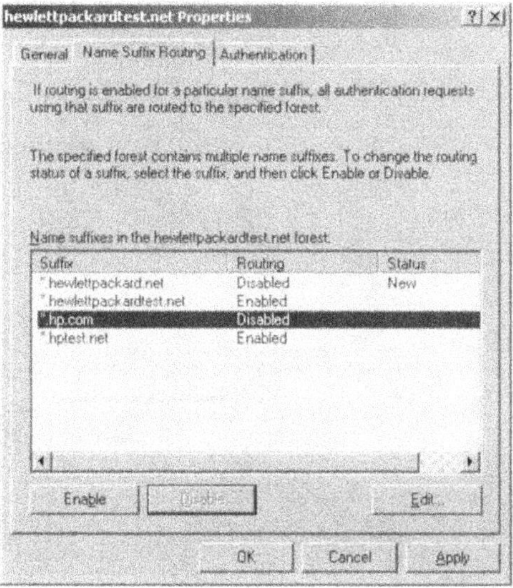

Figure 3.16 *TLN restrictions example: disabling DNS namespaces from the Trust Properties.*

Trust Wizard was run. By default, Windows Server 2003 disables these newly added suffixes.

Disabling a namespace in the properties of forest trust relationship fully disables the routing of requests from that namespace and all its subordinate namespace. For example, disabling the hp.com namespace will disable the routing from all subordinate namespaces, including emea.hp.com, americas.hp.com, and asiapac.hp.com. Top-level name (TLN) restrictions also allow you to exclude the routing of only certain subordinate namespaces. For example, if routing from the hp.com namespace was enabled, you could exclude just the routing from the emea.hp.com subordinate namespace. A key thing to remember is that TLN restrictions always modify the authentication routing behaviour for traffic coming from a particular namespace. They are always configured on the incoming side of a trust relationship.

TLN restrictions can also be used to avoid DNS namespace collisions during the routing of cross-forest authentication requests. A DNS namespace collision occurs when the Windows security software can follow two or more different DNS paths to get to a target domain or forest.

In the example in Figure 3.17, a bidirectional forest trust relationship has been set up between the hewlettpackardtest.net and hr.hewlettpackardtest.net forests. A one-way forest trust relationship exists both between the hewlettpackardtest.net and the cpqtest.net forests and between the hr.hewlettpackardtest.net and the cpqtest.net forests. Both the hewlettpackardtest.net and the hr.hewlettpackardtest.net forests contain resources; the cpqtest.net forest contains users.

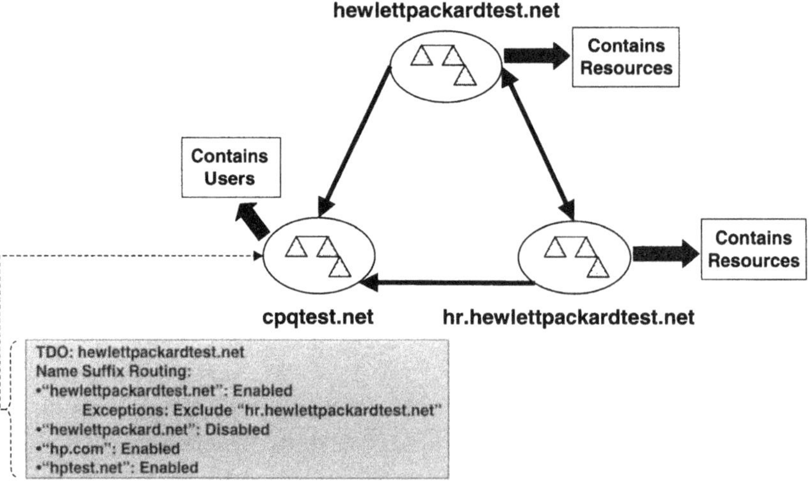

Figure 3.17 *TLN restrictions example.*

By default, the forest trust between hewlettpackardtest.net and cpqtest.net routes all authentication traffic for the *.hewlettpackardtest.net DNS suffix to the hewlettpackardtest.net forest. *.hewlettpackardtest.net includes both the hewlettpackardtest.net and hr.hewlettpackardtest.net DNS domains. Because of the lack of trust transitivity between multiple forests, this may lead to problems. An authentication request coming from the cpqtest.net forest for a service in hr.hewlettpackardtest.net—that is routed to hewlettpackardtest.net—cannot be forwarded by the DCs in the hewlettpackardtest.net forest to the hr.hewlettpackardtest.net forest.

In order to avoid these DNS namespace collisions, a TLN restriction should be set in the cpqtest.net forest on the hewlettpackardtest.net TDO to exclude the hr.hewlettpackardtest.net namespace from the forest trust with hewlettpackardtest.net.

TLN restrictions that exclude DNS namespaces are also defined on the "Name Suffix Routing" tab of the properties of a trust object (available from the AD Domains and Trusts MMC snap-in). This is illustrated in Figures 3.17 and 3.18 for the TLN restriction for the hr.hewlettpackardtest.net domain on the hewlettpackardtest.net trust. Note that the Status of the *.hr.hewlettpackardtest.net suffix in the name suffix routing tab says "Exceptions" (Figure 3.18). Switching to the Edit view (after selecting the *.hr.hewlettpackardtest.net entry in Figure 3.18) allows you to define the TLN restrictions (Figure 3.19). Contrary to the disabling and enabling of

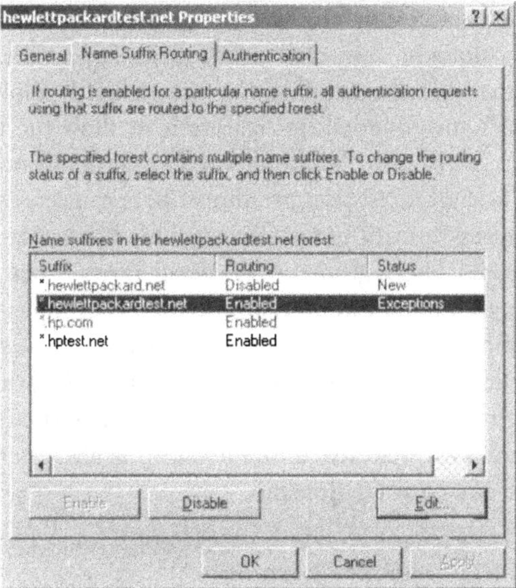

Figure 3.18
*TLN restriction for *.hr.hewlett-packardtest.net: main view.*

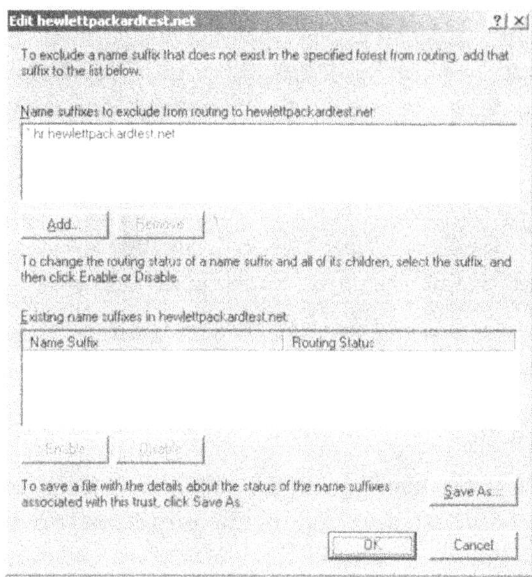

Figure 3.19 *TLN restriction for *.hr.hewlett-packardtest.net: edit view.*

DNS namespaces, TLN restrictions cannot be set from the new Windows Server 2003 Trust Wizard.

Selective authentication

When the selective authentication feature (this feature was previously known as the authentication firewall) of a forest trust[2] relationship is enabled, users accessing cross-forest resources will not be allowed to authenticate to a domain controller or resource server (file, print server, and so forth) in the other forest unless they are explicitly allowed to do so. The reason why Microsoft added this feature is to allow for a more granular cross-forest trust definition. Without selective authentication enabled, all users from the foreign forest become almost perfect peers of the local forest users from an access control point of view. This is because they are added to the Authenticated Users group of the local forest when they cross the trust. Even though foreign forest users will still be members of the Authenticated Users group when the selective authentication option is enabled, they will only be allowed to authenticate to the forest after they pass an additional access control check (that will be explained next). Note that contrary to TLN restrictions, selective authentication is always configured on the outgoing side of a trust relationship.

2. Selective authentication can also be set on external trust relationships.

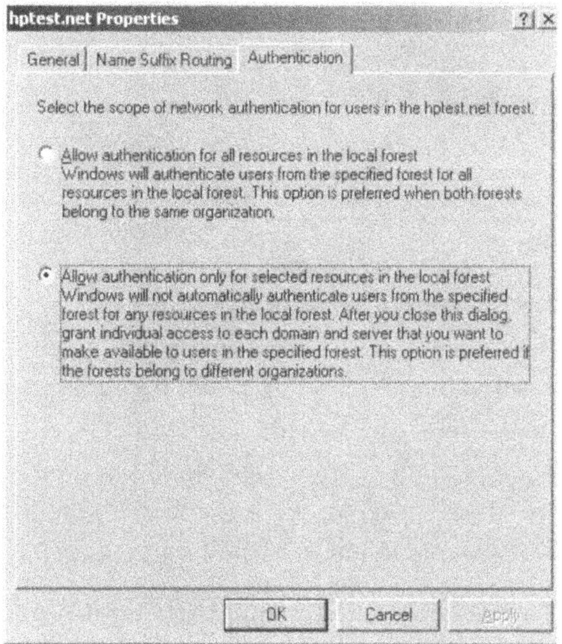

Figure 3.20 *Enabling the selective authentication feature of a forest trust relationship.*

A forest trust relationship's selective authentication function can be enabled from the Trust Wizard or from the properties of the trust relationship. To enable it from the trust properties, select the authentication tab and select the "allow authentication only for selected resources in the local forest..." (as illustrated in Figure 3.20). When you try to access a resource in a forest for which the selective authentication has been enabled from a machine in the other forest, the following error will be displayed: "Logon Failure: The machine you are logging onto is protected by an authentication firewall. The specified account is not allowed to authenticate to the machine."

For example, to enable users to authenticate to domain controllers in forests that have the selective authentication option enabled, the forest administrator must change the access control settings of the AD domain controller objects. To do so, use the Advanced Features view of the Active Directory Users and Computers MMC snap-in, open the properties of the appropriate domain controllers, and give the user the "Allowed to Authenticate" permission (as illustrated in Figure 3.21). Another example is if users wanted to access resources on a file server in a forest with the selective authentication option enabled, you would change the access control settings of the file server's machine account.

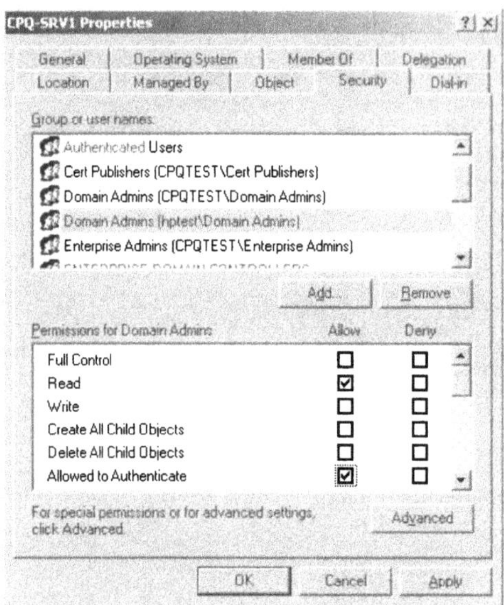

Figure 3.21 *Setting the "Allowed to Authenticate" permission for a foreign security principal.*

The additional access control check for the "Allowed to Authenticate" permission is triggered by a special security identity that is added to a user's access token when he tries to access a resource using a forest trust that has the selective authentication option enabled. This SID is called the "Other Organization" (SID Value S-1-5-1000). You can easily check for its presence in a user's access token using the whoami command-line tool and the / groups switch.

SID filtering

The idea behind SID filtering is that security identifiers for which the domain controllers in a forest are not authoritative should not be included in the access control information that is sent to other forests in cross-forest scenarios. When a user tries to authenticate to a DC of another forest, its authorization data (e.g., group memberships) are sent along with the authentication request. To make sure that only authorization data from the user's home forest are stored in the user's security token, the DC of the remote forest validating the authentication request will filter out all SIDs that are not local to the user's home forest.

SID filtering protects against attempts to add foreign SIDs to authorization data in order to elevate a user's privileges (these threats are also known as elevation of privilege attacks). For example, if a user would succeed in adding the SID of the Enterprise Administrators group of the other forest

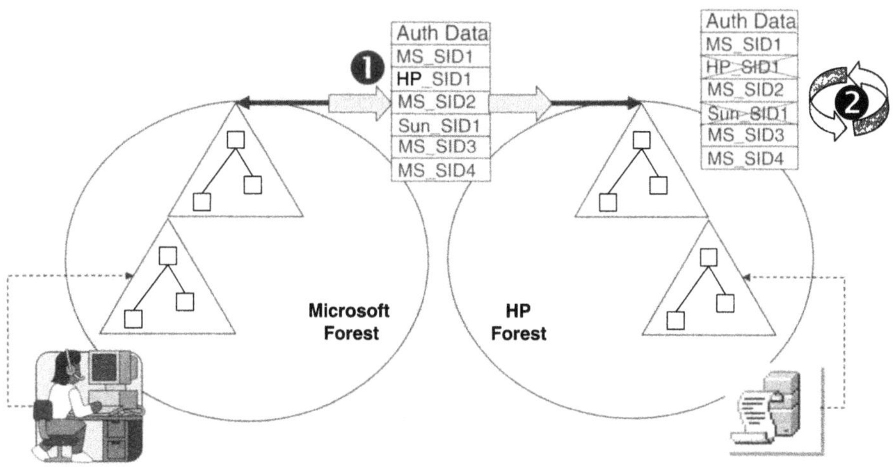

Figure 3.22 *SID filtering between two forests.*

to its access control data, he or she could gain enterprise administrator–level access to the other forest.

Figure 3.22 shows the effect of using SID filtering between two forests [the Microsoft (MS) forest and the HP forest]. In this example a user that is defined in and logged into the Microsoft forest wants to access a resource in the HP forest. In the first step his authorization data are sent along with his authentication request to a DC in the HP forest. In the second step the DC in HP forest filters out all SIDs that are not linked to the user's home forest (which is the Microsoft forest). In the example the DC automatically removes all SIDs referring to the HP forest and another forest called the Sun forest.

SID filtering is enabled automatically when you set up a Windows Server 2003 forest trust relationship. You can turn SID filtering on or off using the netdom command line utility. To turn SID filtering on, use "netdom /filtersids yes <FQDN>". To turn SID filtering off replace the yes in the previous command by a no. It is not recommended to use it for trust relationships between domains in the same forest—enabling SID filtering may break certain AD features. A good example is the use of SIDHistory in migration scenarios (see also Chapter 10). SID filtering was first introduced in Windows 2000 Service Pack 2. How to set up in Windows 2000 is explained in the Microsoft Knowledge Base article Q289243 available from http://support.microsoft.com/default.aspx?scid=kb;en-us;289243. Note that SID filtering is the only trust property that is not dependent on the availability of Windows Server 2003 functionality level 2.

Setting Forest Trust Properties from the Command Line Most forest trust restrictions explained in this chapter can be set from the command line. To do so you must use the netdom.exe utility: The most important forest trust–related switches are explained next.

General Netdom command:

```
Netdom trust <trusting_domain_name> /domain:<trusted_domain_name>
```

Specific Netdom command switches:

`/NameSuffixes`	Lists the routed name suffixes for trust_name on the domain named by trusting_domain_name.
`/ToggleSuffix`	Use with /NameSuffixes to change the status of a name suffix.
`/SelectiveAUTH`	Specifying "yes" enables selective authentication across this trust. Specifying "no" disables selective authentication across this trust. Specifying /SelectiveAUTH without yes or no will display the current state of this trust attribute.
`/AddTLN`	Adds the specified top-level name to the forest trust information for the specified trust.
`/AddTLNEX`	Adds the specified top-level name exclusion to the forest trust information for the specified trust.
`/RemoveTLN`	Removes the specified top-level name from the forest trust information from the specified trust.
`/RemoveTLNEX`	Removes the specified top-level name exclusion from the forest trust information from the specified trust.

3.4.4 Synchronizing forest data

Setting up a forest trust relationship between two Windows forests creates Windows authentication and authorization interoperability between the two environments. From a user and administrator perspective, it is also very useful to provide directory object visibility across the two forests. A user may, for example, want to connect to a printer (an AD printQueue object) or a file share (an AD volume object) in the other forest.

This basically means that resources like printers and file shares that are published in the Active Directory of one forest should be published in the Active Directory of the other forest. This can be done using an LDAP synchronization tool. Examples of tools providing this kind of functionality are

HP's LDAP Directory Synchronization Utility (LDSU) and metadirectory tools such as Microsoft Identity Integration Server 2003 (MIIS 2003—formerly known as MMS).

3.5 Trusts and secure channels

When a trust relationship is set up between two Windows domains, a secure channel will be created between these domains every time the domain controllers on both sides of the trust are started. In the context of a secure channel, "secure" means providing authentication of the requestor and also confidentiality, integrity, and data authentication services for the data sent across the channel. A secure channel always involves a domain controller.

In a Windows environment, secure channels are not only set up between domains and their domain controllers. They also provide a secure communication path between the security principals listed here:

- Between a workstation or member server and a domain controller located in the same domain
- Between domain controllers located in the same domain
- As mentioned earlier, between domain controllers located in different domains

A secure channel enables the secure replication of Active Directory data between domain controllers in the same and different domains. Also, the exchange of Kerberos authentication messages and the exchange of the challenge-response messages and pass-through authentication in an NTLM authentication sequence take place across a secure channel.

You can look at a secure channel as the enabler of secure communication between machines and their trusted authority in the same domain and between the trusted authorities of different domains. The security services offered by a secure channel are based on machine account passwords (within a domain) and on trustedDomain account passwords (between domains).

Secure channels are set up at system startup time. To authenticate the requestor of the secure channel, different accounts are used depending on where the secure channel is set up:

- Between a workstation or member server and a domain controller located in the same domain, the workstation or member server's machine account is used.

- Between domain controllers located in the same domain, the domain controller's machine account is used.
- Between domain controllers located in different domains, the trustedDomain account is used.

The service responsible for setting up the secure channel is the Net-Logon service. An important difference in the way a secure channel is set up between Windows 2000, Windows Server 2003, and NT4 is the way the requestor locates a domain controller: In NT4 the localization method was dependent on the way the machine's NetBIOS name resolution was configured; in Windows 2000 and Windows Server 2003 a domain controller is located using DNS.

3.5.1 Controlling secure channels setup

In Windows Server 2003 there are two ways to control secure channel setup: using an entry in the LMHosts file and using the nltest.exe utility (in NT 4.0, there was a third way: using the setprfdc.exe utility). The "control secure channel setup" means making sure that the secure channel is set up to a particular domain controller (DC). This may be an interesting option for cross-domain authentication traffic when domains are spanning different physical AD sites.

- Using the LMHosts file

  You can use the LMHosts file to preload DC entries for a particular domain in the NetBIOS name resolution cache. The following LMHosts entry will preload DC1 for domain HP in the client's Net-BIOS cache:

  ```
  10.0.0.1   DC1   #PRE  #DOM:HP
  ```

- Using the nltest.exe utility

  To set the secure channel to a domain "HP" to a DC called "DC1," use the following nltest command:

  ```
  Nltest /sc_reset:HP\DC1
  ```

3.5.2 Validating secure channels between domains

In Windows Server 2003 there are different methods to validate secure channels between domains. You can do so from the GUI or from the command line.

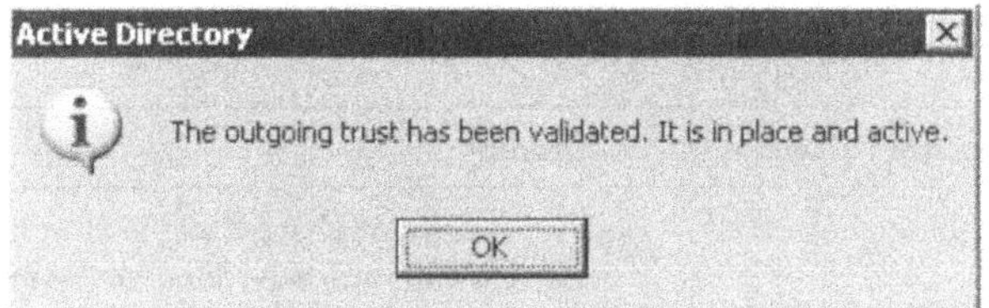

Figure 3.23 *Validating a secure channel from the GUI.*

To validate a secure channel between domains from the GUI, open the Domains and Trusts MMC snap-in, open the properties of the domain whose secure channel you want to verify, go to the trusts tab, then open the properties of the trust relationship whose secure channel you want to verify: Clicking the Verify button will verify the secure channel associated to that particular trust relationship. If the secure channel and the trust are OK, the system will pop up a dialog box similar to the one illustrated in Figure 3.23. If the secure channel is not okay, the system will automatically try to reset the secure channel.

To validate a secure channel from the command line, you can use the nltest.exe, netdom.exe, or dcdiag.exe command-line tool. The exact syntax needed to do this is explained in Section 3.5.4.

3.5.3 Fine-tuning secure channel security services

Besides authentication of the requestor, a secure channel also provides "confidentiality," "integrity," and "data authentication" services for the data sent across the channel. These security services can be fine-tuned using the registry hacks shown in Table 3.3 (located in the HKLM\System\CurrentControlSet\Services\Netlogon\Parameters registry folder). Obviously, these hacks can also be controlled using Windows 2000 and Windows Server 2003 Group Policy Object settings. By default, every Windows 2000, Windows XP, and Windows Server 2003 workstation and server has the "Sealsecurechannel" and"Signsecurechannel" parameters set.

These parameters (explained in Knowledge Base article Q183859) should not be confused with "SMB signing and sealing" (explained in Knowledge Base article Q161372).

3.5.4 Secure channel–related and trust-related management tools

Table 3.4 lists some tools you can use to monitor, test, and troubleshoot your Windows Server 2003 secure channels and where you can find them.

Table 3.3 *Secure Channel Security Registry Hacks*

Registry Parameter	Meaning
Requiresignorseal	If set to1, secure channel traffic must be either signed or sealed; if this cannot be done, the system refuses to set up a secure channel. If set to 0, the use of signing and sealing will depend on the outcome of the negotiation between the two entities.
Sealsecurechannel	Encrypt secure channel traffic (if set to 1).
Signsecurechannel	Sign secure channel traffic (if set to 1). If "Sealsecurechannel" is set, the channel will be sealed and not signed.
RequireStrongKey	If set to 1, enforces the use of a strong 128-bit key for securing the channel. The 128-bit key encryption will only be used if both sides of the channel support 128-bit encryption (in Windows 2000, this setting requires the high-encryption pack, which is available by default in Windows Server 2003).

Table 3.4 *Trust and Secure Channel Troubleshooting Tools*

Tool (Available From)	Function
Netdom.exe (Support Tools)	Command prompt tool enabling an administrator to manage trusts and secure channels, check their status, and reset them.
	Sample netdom commands: ■ To query the trusts defined: netdom query trust ■ To verify the status of a trust (secure channel) to a particular domain: netdom trust <trusting_domainname> / domain:<trusted_domainname /verify ■ To reset a trust (secure channel) to a particular domain: netdom trust <trusting_domainname> / domain:<trusted_domainname /reset ■ To create a trust from one domain to another: netdom trust <trusting_domainname> / domain:<trusted_domainname> /add

Table 3.4 *Trust and Secure Channel Troubleshooting Tools (continued)*

Tool (Available From)	Function
Nltest.exe (Support Tools)	Command prompt tool enabling an administrator to check the status of a trust and to reset it.
	Sample nltest commands: ■ To list the trust relationships existing from a particular domain controller: nltest /trusted_domains /server:<dcname> ■ To verify the status of a trust: nltest /sc_query:<domainname> ■ To reset a trust (secure channel) from a particular domain controller to a particular domain: nltest /server:<dcname> / sc_reset:<domainname> ■ To force a secure channel password change for a particular machine and a particular domain: nltest /server:<machinename> / sc_change_pwd:<domainname> ■ To reset a trust (secure channel) for a particular domain to a particular domain controller: nltest /sc_reset:<domainname>\<dcname> ■ To identify all domain controllers in a domain nltest /dclist:<domainname>
Dcdiag (Support Tools)	Command prompt tool to test domain controllers.
	Sample dcdiag command: ■ To test the secure channels originating from a particular domain controller to a particular domain: Dcdiag /s:<dcname> / test:outboundsecurechannels / testdomain:<domainname>
Netdiag (Resource Kit)	Command prompt tool that can be used to validate and test secure channels.
	Sample netdiag command: ■ To test and validate secure channels: Netdiag /test:Trust
Setprfdc.exe (NT4 SP4)	Enables the specification of a preferred list of domain controllers for secure channel setup.

The last tool in the list—the setprfdc.exe tool—can be used to influence the Windows secure channel setup behavior.

Monitoring Trust Relationships Using Windows Management Instrumentation (WMI) To monitor trust relationships using WMI, you can use one of the following three WMI classes. All three are part of the Root\MicrosoftActiveDirectory namespace:

- Microsoft_LocalDomainInfo: This class provides information about the domain on which the instance of the trust monitor is running.
- Microsoft_DomainTrustStatus: Instances of this class provide information about the domains that have a trust relationship with the local domain.
- Microsoft_TrustProvider: The properties of this class define the parameters of the operation of the trust monitor.

Here is a sample WMI Query Language (WQL) event query you can use to monitor a trust:

```
Select * From __InstanceModificationEvent Within 10 Where
TargetInstance ISA 'Microsoft_DomainTrustStatus' And
TargetInstance.TrustIsOk = "False"
```

3.6 Trusts and firewalls

Many enterprise environments require Windows trust relationships to be set up between domains or forests that are crossing firewalls. Because in Windows 2000 and later the true security boundary is the forest, this has become a common practice between different Windows forests: Some organizations, for example, maintain separate internal and external Windows forests that are separated by a firewall. Table 3.5 gives an overview of common multiforest enterprise scenarios and their trust-related firewall requirements, both for inbound and outbound traffic.

Windows trust setup and maintenance heavily rely upon RPCs. One of the key problems with RPCs in a firewall environment is its use of dynamic port allocations (see the previous side note). In order to limit the amount of firewall ports that must be opened to enable trust-related RPC traffic to pass through the firewall, Windows Server 2003 includes the following registry keys:

- The LSA RPC port, which is used for trust creation and access to the LSA Policy database, can be defined using the "TCP/IP Port" entry in HKEY_LOCAL_MACHINE\System\CurrentControlSet\Services\NTDS\Parameters.

Table 3.5 *Firewall Port Configuration for Multiforest Scenarios*

Scenario	Inbound Ports		Outbound Ports	
Trust setup on both sides from an internal forest (two-way trust)	LDAP	389 UDP and TCP		
	MS DS	445 TCP		
	Kerberos	88 UDP		
Trust validation from an internal forest domain controller to an external forest domain controller (outgoing trust only)	LDAP	389 UDP and TCP		
	MS DS	445 TCP		
	DCE endpoint resolution—portmapper	135 TCP		
	Netlogon	fixed port		
Using object picker on an external forest to add objects in an internal forest to groups and ACLs			LDAP	389 UDP and TCP
			LSA	fixed port
			Netlogon	fixed port
			Kerberos	88 UDP
			DCE endpoint resolution—portmapper	135 TCP
Set up a trust on the external forest from the external forest			LDAP	389 UDP and TCP
			MS DS	445 TCP
			Kerberos	88 UDP
Network logon feature from an internal forest domain controller to an external forest domain controller with Kerberos authentication	MS DS	445 TCP		
	Kerberos	88 UDP		
Network logon feature from an internal forest domain controller to an external forest domain controller with NTLM authentication			DCE Endpoint resolution—portmapper	135 TCP
			Netlogon	fixed port

- The Netlogon RPC port, which is used for NTLM and secure channel setup, can be defined using the "DCTcpipPort" entry in HKEY_LOCAL_MACHINE\System\CurrentControlSet\Services\Netlogon\Parameters.

Remote Procedure Calls (RPCs) and Dynamic Service-Port Mappings

An important goal behind the development of the remote procedure call (RPC) protocol was to build a solution for the limited number of service ports available in the TCP and UDP protocols. In both TCP and UDP, ports are defined in a 2-byte field, which limits the number of ports to 65,536.

Instead of using static service-port mappings, RPC provides a dynamic service-port mapping function. In RPC, incoming RPC calls are mapped to a variable port in the 1,024 to 65,535 range. Although RPC uses variable service ports, it needs a unique way to identify services. The RPC protocol resolves this need by using a special service identifier and a dedicated Portmapper service. The unique RPC identifier is called the RPC service number. Service numbers are defined in a 4-byte field, which provides up to 4,294,967,296 possible service numbers. The Portmapper service listens on a static port (TCP or UDP port 135). The service exists primarily to map the unique RPC service number on a variable TCP/UDP port. Thus, RPC can provide both a unique way to identify RPC services and a way to dynamically allocate the scarce number of TCP/UDP service ports.

Figure 3.24 illustrates how this dynamic port allocation works. In Step 1, the RPC server starts and registers with the RPC Portmapper service. The RPC portmapper maps the RPC service number to a port in the range 1,024 to 65,535. In Step 2, the Portmapper returns the port to the RPC server. The first two steps are known as the RPC registration steps. The RPC client then wants to connect to the RPC server. To find out the exact port on which the server is listening, the RPC client contacts the Portmapper (Step 3). The Portmapper then maps the RPC service number it received from the client to the server's port and returns the number to the client (Step 4). Finally, the RPC client connects to the server (Step 5), and the server replies to the client (Step 6).

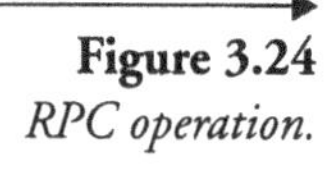

Figure 3.24
RPC operation.

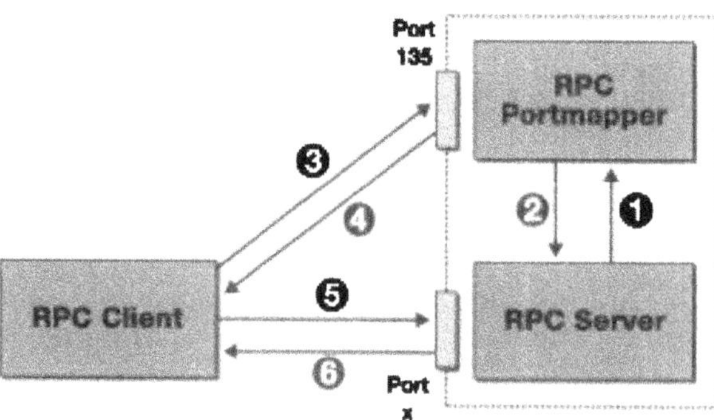

4

Introducing Windows Authentication

This chapter focuses on the most fundamental security service of any operating system: authentication. Before an entity is given access to a resource on a Windows system, the operating system must validate the entity's identity and check whether it can access that particular resource. The latter process is known as authorization, and it is discussed in greater detail later in this book. The first process is known as authentication and is the topic of discussion in this and the following chapters. The primary purpose of authentication is to prove and validate an entity's identity; it answers the question: to whom or what is the system talking?

The chapter starts off with a general explanation of authentication infrastructure terminology. Then it looks at the Windows authentication architecture and more detailed Windows authentication topics such as the NTLM authentication protocol, the secondary logon feature, credential caching, and strong authentication options for Windows.

4.1 Authentication infrastructure terminology

In an authentication infrastructure, users trust a set of authentication authorities to provide trustworthy authentication services. Authentication authorities are represented by one or more authentication servers. Authentication authorities are also referred to as authentication trusted third parties (TTPs). Every authentication authority reigns over a set of resources located on machines that are part of the authentication authority's kingdom. I will call this "kingdom" from now on a "domain" (in NT terminology)—but you may as well call it a "realm" (in Kerberos terminology) or a "cell" (in DCE terminology)—it does not really matter. Anyhow, when a user logs on successfully to the authentication authority's domain, he or she can transparently access all resources in the domain, without reauthenticating to every individual resource server.

Note the different authentication infrastructure–related terms:

- An *authentication infrastructure* refers to a set of authentication servers and authentication authorities, providing outsourced authentication services.
- *Authentication servers* are the physical machines performing the authentication functions.
- *Authentication authorities* are a logical trust-related concept: They are the entities that are trusted by users to perform reliable authentication functions.

In order to authenticate, a user shares a set of "credentials" with the authentication authority. The authentication authority stores its copy of the credentials in a secured database. For the moment, very popular types of credential databases are LDAP-accessible directories. Depending on the type of credentials, the user can simply remember them or "safeguard" them in some other way (e.g., store them on a smart card).

During a typical authentication process (like the one illustrated in Figure 4.1), a user submits his or her credentials (in the earlier example, a user ID and a password) or the result of a cryptographic operation involving his or her credentials to the authentication authority (which is represented by an authentication server). The authentication authority then validates the credentials using the data stored in its credential database. If the credentials supplied by the user and the ones stored in the database match or if the result of a cryptographic operation on the credentials stored in the database

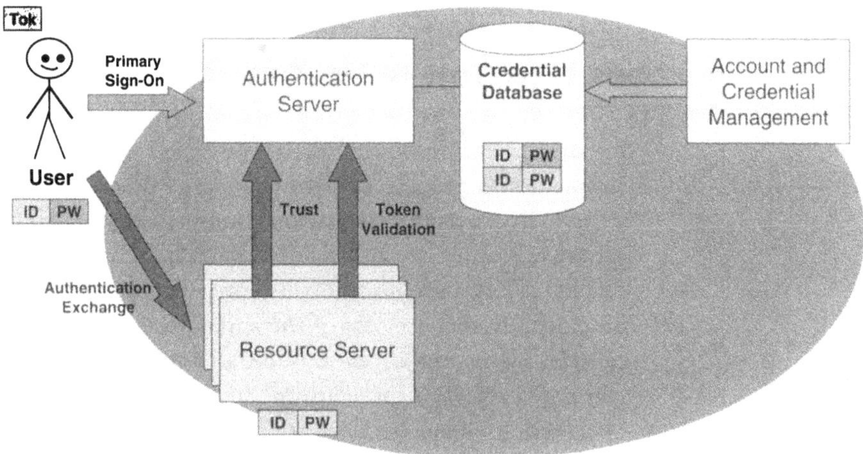

Figure 4.1 *Authentication Infrastructure terminology.*

equals the information supplied by the user, the user's identity is considered authentic. Consequently, the user is given or denied access to the authentication authority's kingdom. To prove that the user has been authenticated, the authentication authority will issue a cryptographic token to the user. This token is used as proof of authentication in subsequent accesses to other resources in the authentication authority's kingdom.

4.2 Qualifying authentication

The security quality of an authentication infrastructure largely depends on the following two factors: the security protocol and the authentication method.

From a protocol point of view, it always better to use a proven open security standard than a proprietary authentication protocol. This is because open standards tend to be better tested; this means tested by a larger community of vendor-neutral people. Open standards also tend to be supported on multiple platforms; proprietary protocols tend to be bound to a single platform. A well-known example of a proven open authentication protocol is the Kerberos protocol [defined in Request for Comments (RFC) 1510]. An example of a proprietary protocol is Microsoft's NTLM (NT–LAN Manager) authentication protocol.

Table 4.1 gives an overview of common authentication protocols used in IT today. Note that this list is not exhaustive.

The quality of the authentication method mainly depends on the number of factors (or credentials) it considers when authenticating a user. One of the most used authentication methods—user ID and password—is a one-factor authentication method. It uses a single "factor"—knowledge—to authenticate a user.

Multifactor authentication methods authenticate a user based on multiple factors. That is why they will also offer higher security quality than single-factor authentication methods. A good example of a multifactor authentication system is a smart card: It combines possession (of the card) and knowledge (of the card's PIN code). Table 4.2 gives an overview of different authentication methods and the number of authentication factors they support.

So far we have only discussed password-based credentials (see Chapter 2) as a means to authenticate users against a Windows authentication authority. You can obviously also provide stronger authentication methods to your

Windows users. Table 4.3 shows some of the stronger and/or multifactor authentication solutions that are available for Windows (note that this list is not exhaustive).

The number of authentication factors is not the only quality-related element of an authentication method. Much also depends on how the authentication method is implemented and how applications are using the authentication method. For example, a fingerprint-based authentication solution will not bring much extra security if the fingerprint image is sent in the clear to an authentication server after it has been recorded by a biometric device.

Many IT environments require the authentication infrastructure to support multiple authentication methods and protocols. This may be necessary because the environment supports internal and external users who are using a variety of methods and protocols to access resources. Another reason why different authentication methods and protocols may be needed is because

Table 4.1 *Common IT Authentication Protocols*

Authentication Protocol	Comment/References
Basic Authentication	Basic authentication is the authentication protocol defined in the HTTP standard. It uses a base64 user ID-password authentication exchange.
Digest Authentication	Digest authentication is another HTTP-based authentication protocol. Digest uses a challenge-response–based protocol. Like basic authentication, the credentials are user ID-password–based. Unlike basic authentication, the credentials are not sent across the network.
SSL/TLS	SSL stands for Secure Sockets Layer; TLS stands for Transport Layer Security and is the follow-up protocol to SSL that has been standardized by the IETF. SSL/TLS operates on the OSI transport layer and uses certificates to authenticate both the client side and the server side. It can be used to add strong authentication to SMTP, HTTP, NNTP, and other application-level protocols.
Kerberos	Defined in RFC 1510, Kerberos is the default authentication protocol in a Windows 2000 and Windows Server 2003 domain.
NTLM	Proprietary authentication protocol developed by Microsoft, NTLM is the default authentication protocol of Microsoft Windows NT4.

Table 4.2 *Overview of Authentication Methods*

	Authentication Method				
Authentication Factor	Password/ PIN	Smart card/ token	Biometric device	Biometric and smart card	Dial-back
Knowledge	X	X	—	X	—
Possession	—	X	—	X	—
Biometric Data	—	—	X	X	—
Location	—	—	—	—	X

resources have different value or contain more sensitive information. Access to confidential information, for example, may require a stronger authentication method than access to information published on the corporate Internet Web site. In some authentication infrastructures, this feature is known as "graded authentication." This simply means that the resources and information a user is allowed to access will vary depending on the strength of the authentication protocol and method the user used to authenticate. An example of a product providing this kind of functionality is Novell's Modular Authentication Service (NMAS).

When implementing a security solution, you should not just look at the quality of the authentication solution. Perhaps the most important factor to take into account is risk: The strength of the authentication solution that is

Table 4.3 *Strong and Multifactor Authentication Options for Windows*

Strong Authentication Option (Authentication Factors)	**Sample venDors (More Info At...)**
Smart card (knowledge and possession)	Built-in support with Windows 2000 and later OSs (more details are provided in Chapters 5 and 17)
Security token (knowledge and possession)	RSA Security SecurID (http://www.rsasecurity.com/products/securid/index.html)
Fingerprint (biometric data)	Identix Biologon (http://www.identix.com/products/pro_info_biologon.html)
Iris scan (biometric data)	Iridian Technologies Iris Recognition (http://www.iridiantechnologies.com)
Facial scan (biometric data)	Biovisec Nemesis (http://www.biovisec.com)

required for a particular IT environment depends on the security risks that are associated with that environment. The higher the risk, the stronger security solutions are required. Security risks are a function of the probability that a security incident will occur and the cost of a security incident for your organization.

4.3 Authentication authentication architecture

This section explains the Windows authentication architecture. As you will notice, the architecture used in Windows Server 2003 is not much different from the one used in earlier Windows versions.

4.3.1 Terminology

In a Windows environment, a user bootstraps the authentication process by pressing CTRL+ALT+DEL [this is known as the Secure Attention Sequence (SAS)] to log on to a machine or a domain. Microsoft calls this method of authenticating a user to the Windows system an interactive logon feature or local logon feature. A valid interactive logon feature results in a "logon session." If a user wants to access a resource that is located on another machine during its logon session, another authentication process will be started: This authentication process is referred to as a noninteractive logon method or network logon method. A valid noninteractive logon method results in a "network logon session."

Besides interactive and noninteractive logon methods, Windows also supports two other logon methods: the batch logon method and the service logon method. The batch logon method is used by task schedulers (e.g., the "at" or "WINat" service); the service logon method is used by services. All of them have slightly different architectures.

Every entity that authenticates to a Windows system is called a "principal." A principal is identified by its Security Identifier (SID); to prove its identity during an authentication process, a principal uses credentials. Credentials allow principals to be distinguished from one another and to identify them. Examples of credentials are a principal's account name and its password. If the operating system accepts this type of credentials for authentication, the fact that the principal knows its account name and password is regarded by the operating system as a proof of its identity. Do not confuse principal and account: An account is a record in an authentication authority's database; a principal is an entity that can be identified by a Windows system. These concepts were explained in great detail in Chapter 2.

The authentication authority differs depending on what you are logging on to. If you log on locally to a machine, it is the Local Security Authority (LSA) on the machine itself, but if you log on to a domain, authentication is performed against the LSA of a domain controller. To be able to validate a principal's identity, the authentication authority needs a copy of a principal's credentials, which are stored in the authentication database.

A Windows Server 2003 authentication process can use different authentication protocols: NTLM (NT LAN Manager), Kerberos, and SSL (TLS). The way support for these protocols is embedded in the Windows Server 2003 authentication architecture is explained in Section 4.3.2.

4.3.2 Architecture

Since its early days, one of the most important design principles of NT has been modularity. NT's authentication architecture is an excellent example of a modular architecture built on different abstraction layers. In Windows Server 2003, this architecture is basically the same as the one used in Windows 2000 and NT4. Ninety percent of the changes that Microsoft incorporated can be described as plugging in supplementary security modules. In the following sections we discuss the authentication architectures for interactive (local) and non-interactive (network) logon.

Architecture for interactive authentication

The architecture for interactive authentication is illustrated in Figure 4.2. An interactive authentication sequence starts whenever a user initiates an SAS sequence. This makes the Winlogon service call the GINA module. GINA stands for Graphical Identification and Authentication. Winlogon is the OS component that provides interactive authentication. GINA is the component responsible for displaying the logon interface, extracting the user's credentials, and passing them to the LSA.

The LSA is an OS kernel component that can act as a local authentication authority: It interacts with local and remote authenticaton databases, and authentication packages. When logging on locally to a machine it will interact with the local authentication database. When logging on to a domain it will interact with the domain authentication database (which can be on the local or a remote machine).

Authentication packages are software packages that implement different authentication protocols. In NT4 the only available authentication package was MSV1_0. MSV1_0 was the package that performed a pass-through authentication if there was no credential store (a SAM database) available

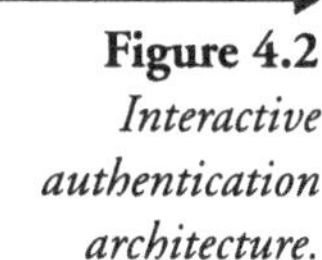

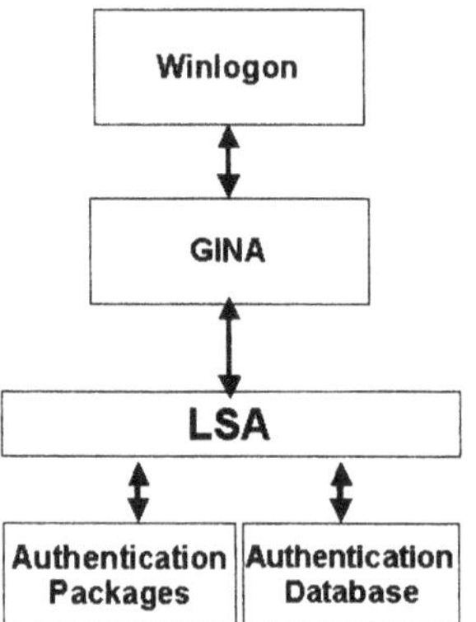

Figure 4.2 *Interactive authentication architecture.*

locally to validate the user's credentials. Software vendors can implement their own authentication package to support other authentication protocols. The MSV1_0 authentication package is still supported in Windows 2000, Windows XP and Windows Server 2003.

You can find out which authentication package dlls are available at your machine by looking into the following registry location: HKEY_LOCAL_MACHINE\System\CurrentControlSet\Control\Lsa\Authentication Packages.

The authentication database stores secured copies of the credentials needed during the authentication process. NT4 machines, Windows XP, Windows 2000 Professional workstations, and Windows 2000 and Windows Server 2003 member servers store credentials in the SAM database. In this case the SAM database contains local user accounts that can be used to log on locally to a machine. A Windows 2000 and Windows Server 2003 domain controller stores credentials in the Active Directory. The Active Directory database contains domain user accounts that can be used to log on to a Windows domain.

Architecture for noninteractive authentication

Figure 4.3 provides a simplified overview of the noninteractive authentication architecture used in a distributed application consisting of a client and a server component. A good example of a distributed application is an Outlook client accessing an Exchange mailbox. This architecture introduces two new important concepts: the Security Support Provider Interface (SSPI) and Security Support Providers (SSPs).

The communication between the client and the server component happens via communication protocols. These protocols can be typical LAN

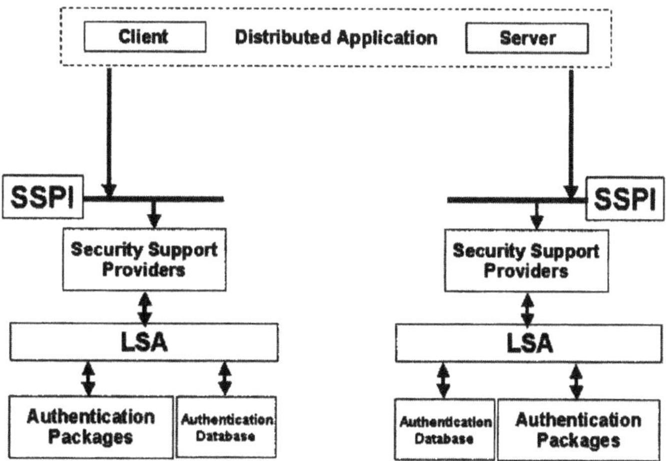

Figure 4.3 *Noninteractive authentication architecture.*

communication protocols such as SMB and RPC, or typical Internet-oriented communication protocols such as HTTP, POP3, NNTP, and LDAP.

The SSPI is an Application Programming Interface (API), sitting between the communication protocols and the security protocols. It has two important functions:

1. Its primary function is to abstract the commonalities of different authentication protocols and to hide their implementation details. For example, Kerberos and NTLM both use the concept of a master key; NTLM, however, uses a challenge-response mechanism, while Kerberos relies on a ticketing system.
2. Abstract communication protocols from security protocols. A security protocol should be available to any communication protocol, or, in other words, the implementation of a security protocol should not contain any communication-protocol–specific code.

An SSP is a software module that implements a security protocol. SSPs can be plugged into the SSPI. Out-of-the-box Windows Server 2003 supports the following SSPs: MSV1_0 (supporting both NTLM versions 1 and 2), Kerberos, SChannel (secure channel support using the SSL and TLS protocols), and Digest Authentication. NTLM is the default authentication protocol of NT4—it is explained in more detail later in this chapter. Digest Authentication is a challenge-response-based protocol that can be used in Web environments (for more information, see Chapter 6). Software vendors can also implement their own SSPs to provide other security models.

To get an overview of the SSPs supported on your machine, have a look at the following registry key: HKEY_LOCAL_MACHINE\System\CurrentControlSet\Control\Lsa\Security Packages.

Notice in Figure 4.3 that SSPs access authentication packages via the LSA. This figure also shows that the LSA communicates with the authentication database; remember from an earlier section that the LSA validates credentials by comparing them with the entries in its authentication database. One thing that Figure 4.3 does not show is that most SSPs rely on Cryptographic Service Providers (CSPs), modules that provide basic cryptographic functions, for example, encryption using the Data Encryption Standard (DES), signing using RSA, or hashing using Message Digest 4 (MD4). SSPs can call on different CSPs thanks to another abstraction layer that was introduced in NT4: the CryptoAPI (or CAPI). We will come back to CAPI in Chapter 13.

Because the model shown in Figure 4.3 contains multiple authentication protocols (SSPs), there has to be some kind of negotiation between the client and the server before the actual authentication can take place. To enable the negotiation, Microsoft included a special SSP called "Negotiate." Its operation is illustrated in Figure 4.4. This package is based on the SPNEGO (Simple and Protected GSS-API Negotiation Mechanism) Internet draft (RFC 2478: The Simple and Protected GSS-API Negotiation Mechanism). In order to negotiate an authentication protocol, the Negotiate package has to know how to communicate with the corresponding authentication package. So far, the Negotiate SSP can only deal with the Kerberos and NTLM package.

Figure 4.4 *Role of the Negotiate SSPI.*

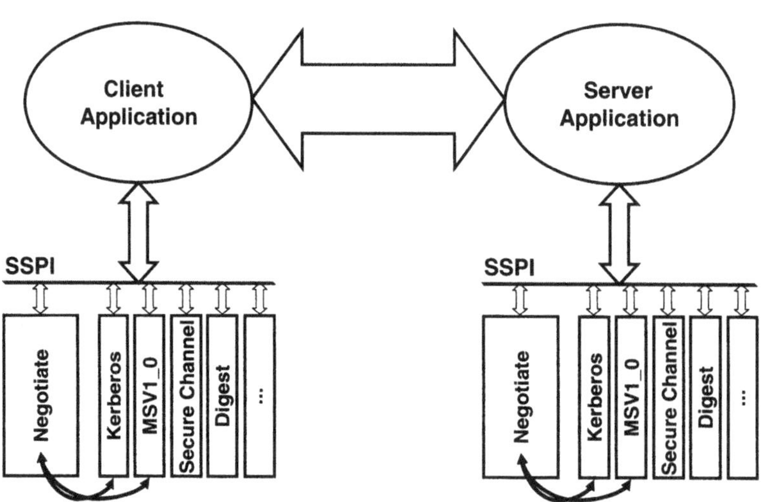

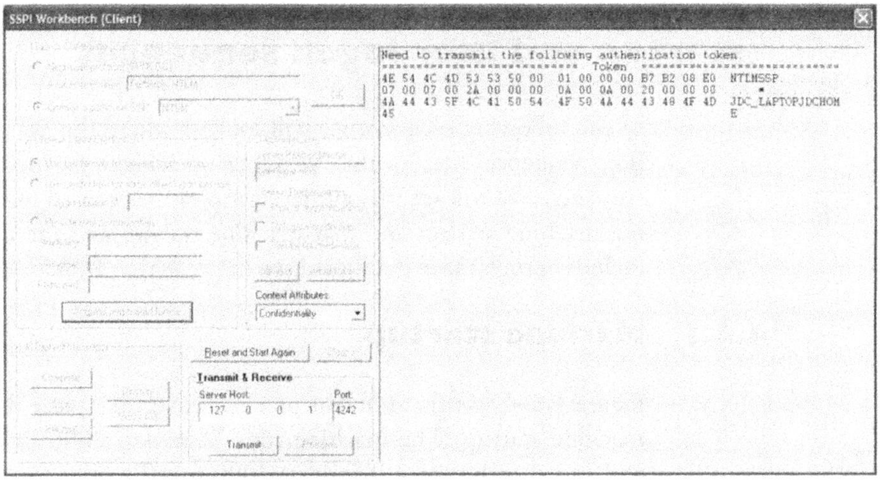

Figure 4.5 *Using SSPI Workbench.*

So how does this negotiation work? The first SSP called by the SSPI when a call for authentication comes in is the Negotiate SSP. The client Negotiate package then sends a list of available SSPs to the server. Finally, the server Negotiate package picks an SSP based on its locally available SSPs and communicates it to the client. Although this negotiation clearly adds some communication overhead, it offers much more flexibility.

In Windows 2000, Windows XP, and Windows Server 2003, the Negotiate SSP's first choice for authentication is Kerberos. It will fall back to NTLM if:

- The Kerberos KDC service in their domain is unavailable.[1]
- A service's Service Principal Name (SPN) is not registered (SPNs were explained in Chapter 2). For example, when a user tries to access a file share on a server whose "Host" SPN is not registered, the user will be authenticated using NTLM.

An excellent tool to get a deeper understanding of how the SSPI really works is the "SSPI workbench" tool (see Figure 4.5). It is written by Keith Brown from DevelopMentor and can be downloaded for free from http://www.develop.com/kbrown/security/samples.htm. More information on the tool is available at http://www.develop.com/kbrown/security/sample_sspibench.htm.

1. Kerberos only works in a domain environment—it cannot be used to logon locally to a workstation or member server. This is because the Kerberos KDC service is only available on a domain controller.

4.4 Authentication in the Windows machine startup and user logon sequences

In the following sections, we will look at where the Windows authentication sequence fits in the Windows machine startup and user logon sequence. We will see that authentication is performed more than once during machine startup and that machine startup and the user logon feature includes much more than just user and machine authentication.

4.4.1 Machine startup

Figure 4.6 shows the different processes that take place during a Windows machine startup. The machine runs Windows 2000 Professional or later and is a member of a Windows 2000 or Windows Server 2003 domain. The different processes are listed next:

- The client starts up. The network interface is initialized. If the machine is not configured with static IP configuration information, it will run through the Dynamic Host Configuration Protocol (DHCP) configuration process to obtain its IP configuration.
- Once the client's network interface has been configured and the network protocol stack has been initialized, the machine will launch a

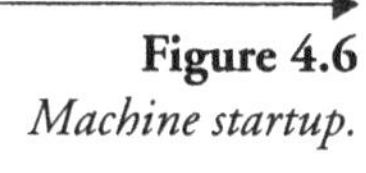

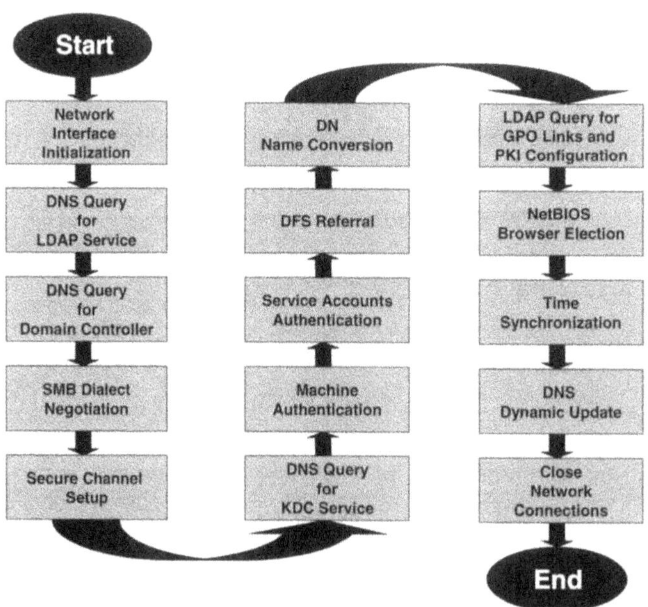

Figure 4.6 *Machine startup.*

DNS query for an LDAP service (read domain controller) to one of its configured DNS servers. The DNS query will look for an _ldap._tcp.default-first-site-name._sites.dc._msdcs.main.local service (SRV) record. The site name used in this SRV record depends on the one registered on the machine; by default, it is "default-first-site-name."

- When an LDAP service (read domain controller) has been located, the client will launch an LDAP query for a domain controller belonging to the machine's definition domain to the LDAP server.
- The client will then negotiate an SMB dialect with the domain controller.[2] The Server Message Block protocol (SMB) is an important file sharing protocol used in all Windows versions. It is used to provide remote file services in a distributed client-server environment. Later on in the startup, it will be used by the client to download configuration information (including GPO settings) from the domain controller.
- Next, the client will set up a secure channel with the domain controller. To do this it will connect to the domain controller's Netlogon service. The secure channel is needed to send confidential information, such as authentication data, from the client to the domain controller. Secure channels were explained in Chapter 3.
- Once the secure channel has been set up, the client will launch another DNS query to its DNS server to find an authentication server (in Windows 2000 and later, a domain controller running a KDC service). The DNS query will look for a _kerberos._tcp.default-first.site-name._sites.dc._msdcs.main.local SRV record. The site name used in this SRV record depends on the one registered on the machine; by default, it is "default-first-site-name."
- The machine Kerberos authentication phase takes place.
- The Kerberos authentication takes place for every service that is not running using the local system account.
- The client will then connect to the IPC$ share on the domain controller and start the Distributed File System (DFS) referral process. The DFS referral process downloads DFS configuration information

2. An important detail is that Windows Server 2003 has SMB signing enabled by default. This won't cause problems when using a Windows 98 or Windows 2000 Professional or later client, but may prohibit NT4 and Windows 95 clients to log on to your Windows Server 2003 infrastructure. Installing NT4 Service Pack 4 (SP4) or the Directory Services Client (dsclient.exe) on top of Windows 95 resolves this problem.

from the domain controller to the client (downloading happens using the SMB protocol).

- The client launches an RPC call to the domain controller to convert its name into a Distinguished Name (DN).
- Using the DN the client can then perform an LDAP query against its DC to find out the group policies applied to it. The group policy information is downloaded using the SMB protocol.
- The client then launches another LDAP query to the domain controller to find out PKI configuration information (e.g., what are the Enterprise CAs available in the forest?).
- If NetBIOS is enabled on the client, it will start a browser election.
- The client performs time synchronization with its domain controller using the Simple Network Time Protocol (SNTP).
- Finally, the client launches a DNS query for the start of authority of its DNS domain. The client then performs a dynamic update of its DNS records on the DNS server returned from the previous query.
- The client startup will be completed by closing down the connections with the domain controller.

4.4.2 User logon process

Once a machine has been started up, a user can log on to it interactively. Figure 4.7 shows the different processes that take place during a regular Windows 2000 or Windows Server 2003 domain user logon process from a Windows 2000 Professional or later workstation. As we will see, the user logon process is much shorter than the machine startup process. The different processes are listed next:

- After the machine has started up successfully, a CTRL-ALL-DEL screen will be displayed on the screen, permitting the user to start an interactive logon session by pushing CTRL-ALT-DEL.
- The user presses CTRL-ALT-DEL, fills in a set of credentials, and presses OK or Enter.
- The user Kerberos authentication sequence takes place.
- The machine launches an RPC call to the domain controller to convert the user name to a DN.

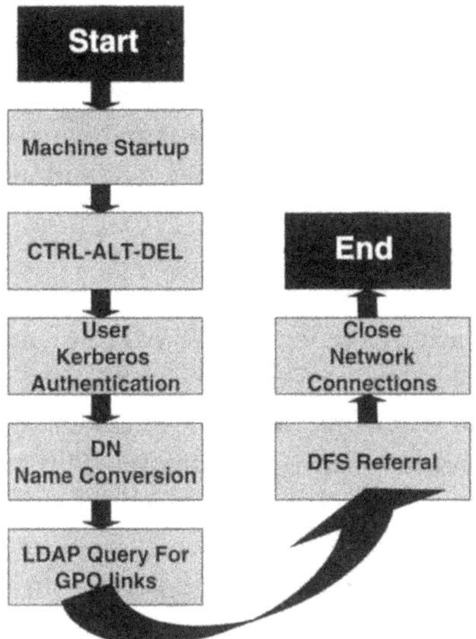

Figure 4.7
User logon process.

- Using the DN the client can then perform an LDAP query against its DC to find out the group policies applied to the user. The user group policy information is downloaded using the SMB protocol. At the same time DFS referral information linked to the user will be downloaded.
- The user logon will be completed by closing down the connections with the domain controller.

An Easy Way to Find Out a User's Authenticating Domain Controller The easiest way to find out the authenticating DC is to check the content of the environment variables that are available in the user's logon session. To do so, open a command prompt window, then type "set l"; this will bring up all environment variables starting with an l (see Figure 4.8). The user's authenticating DC is listed on the LOGONSERVER= line.

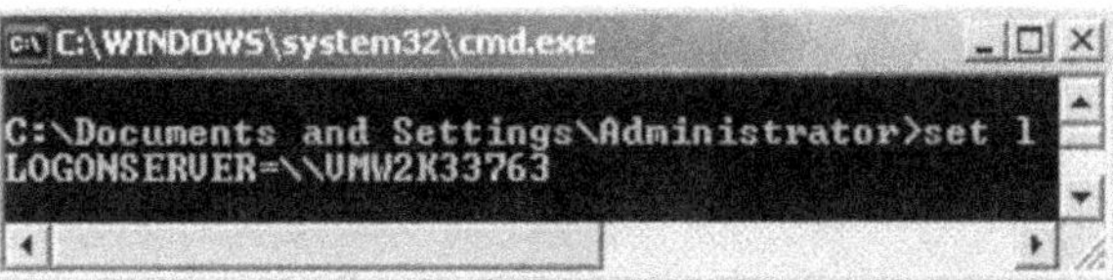

Figure 4.8
Finding out the authenticating DC using "set l."

4.5 NTLM-based authentication

NTLM is a challenge-response-based authentication protocol. It is the default authentication protocol of NT 4.0 and is—for backward compatibility—still supported in Windows 2000 and Windows Server 2003.

4.5.1 The protocol

Let's look at the basic operation of the NTLM authentication protocol using the example of a user running Outlook XP who wants to access his or her mailbox on an Exchange server. The Exchange server is running Exchange 2000 and is installed on a Windows 2000 member server—it is a member of a Windows Server 2003 domain. The reason why we take an Outlook XP–Exchange 2000 scenario is because in Outlook 2003, Exchange 2003 Microsoft embedded support for the Kerberos authentication protocol.

In this example, the client, the Exchange server, and the domain controller will run through the following six authentication steps (as illustrated in Figure 4.9):

- Step 1: The client tells the Exchange server the user wants to access his mailbox.
- Step 2: The Exchange server sends an NTLM challenge (i.e., a random string) to the client.

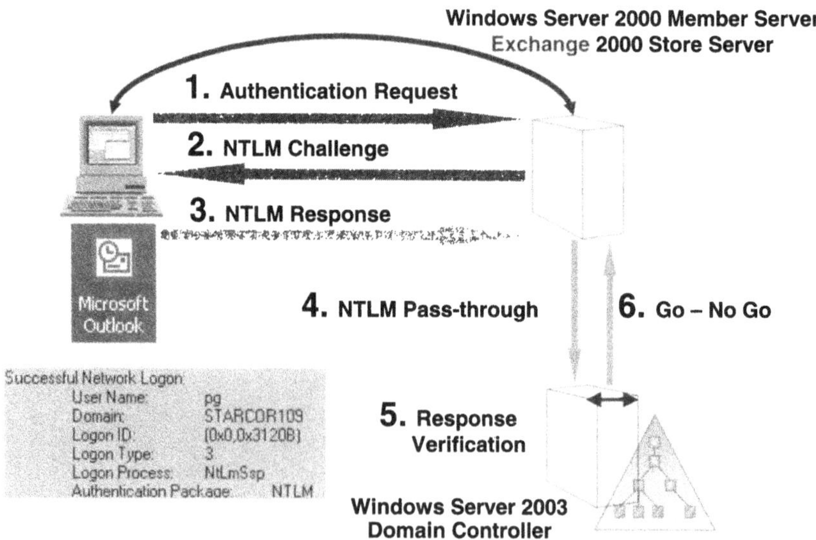

Figure 4.9 *Basic NTLM authentication flow.*

- Step 3: The NTLM response that the client sends back to the Exchange server consists of the server's challenge, encrypted using the hashed version of the user password.
- Step 4: Because the Exchange server is not a domain controller and does not have access to a secured copy of the user's credentials (the hashed password), it will forward the NTLM response (together with the NTLM challenge) to a domain controller. The latter process is known as NTLM pass-through authentication.
- Step 5: The domain controller validates the response it received from the domain controller by encrypting the original NTLM challenge with its local copy of the hashed user password. It then compares the result to the NTLM response that the Exchange receiver received from the client.
- Step 6: If the two values are identical, the domain controller will inform the Exchange server that the user is authenticated. If they are not, the domain controller informs the Exchange server that the credentials the user provided are not valid to authenticate the user.

The NTLM authentication protocol consists of two subprotocols: the NT and LM protocols. This basically means that in response to the server's NTLM challenge, the client replies with two messages: an NTLM and an LM response.

Windows 9x, Windows 3.x, DOS, and OS/2 only support LM authentication. For backward compatibility, NT 4.0, Windows 2000, Windows XP, and Windows Server 2003 support both authentication flavors. This means they can authenticate requests coming from Win9x, Windows 3.x, DOS, and OS/2 clients. By default, every NT and Windows client responds to an NTLM challenge by sending back both an NT and an LM response. In doing so, they can also authenticate against Win9x, Windows 3.x, DOS, and OS/2 machines.

In addition to the two NTLM authentication protocols (the NT and LM protocols), Microsoft also offers an enhanced version of NTLM—called NTLMv2—from NT4 SP4 on. One of the advanced security features that NTLMv2 provides is sealing a user's authorization data in an NTLM pass-through message. It also better protects against man-in-the-middle attacks.

NTLMv2 is available on any NT machine running SP4 or later. Microsoft provides NTLMv2 support for Win9x with the Directory Services Client (dsclient.exe) that is available from the Windows 2000 CD (at the moment of the writing of this book, dsclient was not included on the

Windows Server 2003 CD). How to enforce the use of the more secure NTLMv2 authentication protocol is explained in Section 4.5.2.

4.5.2 Controlling the NTLM subprotocols

Before NT4 SP4, no easy way existed to disable the LM portion of the NTLM authentication protocol. In all later Windows versions, administrators can control the NTLM subprotocols that Windows clients use, and Windows server administrators can set the NTLM subprotocols that they will accept.

To control the NTLM subprotocols, you can use a GPO setting or the LMCompatibilityLevel (REG_DWORD) registry entry. The registry entry is located in the HKEY_LOCAL_MACHINE\SYSTEM\CurrentControlSet\Control\Lsa registry subkey. The GPO setting is called "Network Security: LAN Manager Authentication Level" and is located in Computer Configuration\Windows Settings\Security Settings\Local Policies\Security Options. Table 4.4 shows the LMCompatibilityLevel and the GPO settings

Table 4.4 *LM Compatibility Level Settings*

LM Compatibility Level Setting	GPO Setting	Meaning
0	Send LM and NTLM responses.	Clients use LM and NTLM authentication, and never use NTLMv2 session security.
1	Send LM and NTLM responses—use NTLMv2 session security if negotiated.	Clients use LM and NTLM authentication, and use NTLMv2 session security if the server supports it.
2	Send NTLM response only.	Clients use only NTLM authentication, and use NTLMv2 session security if the server supports it.
3	Send NTLMv2 response only.	Clients use NTLMv2 authentication, and use NTLMv2 session security if the server supports it.
4	Send NTLMv2 response only/refuse LM.	Clients use NTLM authentication, and use NTLMv2 session security if the server supports it. DCs refuse LM authentication.
5	Send NTLMv2 response only/refuse LM and NTLM.	Clients use NTLMv2 authentication, use NTLMv2 session security if the server supports it. DCs refuse LM and NTLM authentication, and accept only NTLMv2.

and their meanings. The default LMCompatibilityLevel value for Windows Server 2003 is "Send NTLM Response Only."

4.5.3 Removing the LM hashes from the credential database

The two NTLM authentication protocols NT and LM also use different hashing methods to securely store the user's password in the Windows security database (SAM or AD). As a consequence, the Windows security database contains an LM hash and an NT hash (also known as the Unicode hash) for every user account's password.

The LM hash is weak compared to the NT hash (see the following side note) and can easily be cracked using brute-force attacks (using, for example, LC4—as explained in Chapter 2). Because of the way LM hashing works, the effective password length is limited to seven characters (even if the user uses a longer password), and all characters are stored in uppercase (even if the user uses a combination of uppercase and lowercase characters). The LM hash weaknesses do not mean that the NT portion is unbreakable; it simply takes much more time to break it. For more details about the weaknesses of the LM hash, visit http://www.atstake.com/research/lc.

The only protocol using the LM hash is the LM authentication protocol (in both NTLM and NTLMv2). The NT authentication protocol (in both NTLM and NTLMv2) and the Kerberos authentication protocol both use the NT hash during their authentication sequence.

From Windows 2000 Service Pack 2 (SP2) on, Microsoft offers the capability to remove the LM hashes from the credential database. To do this you can use the NoLMHash registry hack or the "Network security: Do not store LAN Manager hash value on next password change" GPO setting. The NoLMHash (REG_DWORD) registry hack is located in the HKEY_LOCAL_MACHINE\SYSTEM\CurrentControlSet\Control\Lsa registry key and should be set to 1 to disable LM hash storage. The GPO setting is located in Computer Configuration\Windows Settings\Security Settings\Local Policies\Security Options. Two other lesser known methods to disable LM hash storage are the following:

- Using a password that is longer than 15 characters
- Using ALT characters in your password

When you use one of these options, no more LM hashes will be stored in the credential database at the next user password change. In Windows 2000 the LM hash history entries in the security database will not be cleared when enabling the NoLMHash setting. They will be cleared in Windows XP and Windows Server 2003. If you enable the NoLMHash setting in a domain environment, you must enable it on all domain controllers of the domain.

Because the LM protocol is still used for authenticating Windows 9x (or older) Windows clients, you cannot use these settings when you have these client platforms in your Windows 2000 or Windows Server 2003 environment.

The LM Hash Versus the NT Hash Windows computes the LM hash as follows:

- Convert all lowercase characters in the password to uppercase.
- Pad the password with NULL characters until it is exactly 14 characters long.
- Split the password into two 7-character chunks.
- Use each chunk separately as a DES key to encrypt a specific string.
- Concatenate the two cipher texts into a 128-bit string and store the result.

As a result of the way the LM hash is generated, it is very easy to crack. Most password cracking tools (such as LC4) will start by cracking the LM hashes.

In AD the LM hash is stored in the DbcsPwd account property; the LM hash history is stored in the LmPwdHistory account property.

The NT Hash is calculated by taking the plaintext password and generating an MD4 hash of it. The NT hash is much more resistant to brute-force attacks than the LM hash.

In AD the NT hash is stored in the UnicodePwd account property; the LM hash history is stored in the NtPwdHistory account property.

4.6 Secondary logon service

The Windows Server 2003 Secondary Logon Service (SLS) allows users to start logon sessions with other credentials within their current logon session. Before Windows 2000, Microsoft provided a special utility to provide this functionality. This utility came with the Windows Resource Kit and was called su.exe (yes, the name is borrowed from UNIX's switch-user utility). Now this functionality is provided by the SLS that is installed by default and starts automatically when the system boots.

Using a secondary logon session is a security best practice. Too many security incidents happen because administrators stay logged on with their high-privilege account all the time. They use it to do both administrative

Figure 4.10 *Running runas.exe from the command line.*

```
C:\WINDOWS\system32\cmd.exe
C:\Documents and Settings\Administrator>runas /U:Joe explorer.exe
Enter the password for Joe:
Attempting to start explorer.exe as user "DC\Joe" ...

C:\Documents and Settings\Administrator>_
```

tasks and nonadministrative tasks, such as reading their e-mail or, even worse, surfing the Internet.

The easiest way to start a secondary logon session with other credentials is by using the runas.exe command-line utility. To start explorer.exe in the context of, say, the user Joe, you would type the following runas command at the command line:

```
Runas /u:Joe explorer.exe
```

After typing this command, runas will prompt you to enter Joe's password; if the password is correct, it will start a new instance of explorer.exe (as illustrated in Figure 4.10).

Running the NT Shell in an Alternate Security Context A little-known detail is that you can also use runas to start the complete Windows shell in an alternate security context. To do so, kill the explorer.exe process from the Task Manager. Then, using the Task Manager's File\Run menu option, start the secondary logon by typing, for example, "runas /u:Joe explorer.exe." This can be interesting when you want to use drive mappings in your secondary logon session. A drive mapped from the command line in a secondary logon session will not be accessible from your Windows Explorer. It will be accessible if you start the complete Windows shell in the alternate security context.

The Windows XP and Windows Server 2003 version of runas by default open the user profile of the user who is specified in the /u: switch. This is different from Windows 2000, where runas by default loaded the default user profile. In Windows XP and Windows Server 2003, you can still load the default user profile by specifying the /noprofile switch. Another key difference from Windows 2000 is that runas now supports the smart card logon process: This is done using the /smartcard switch (as illustrated in Figure 4.11). Table 4.5 gives an overview of the most important runas switches.

The secondary logon process can also be started from the Windows Explorer. To do so, right-click the icon for an executable or its shortcut and select Run as... (as illustrated in Figure 4.12). This will bring up the Run As dialog box that will allow you to enter the alternate credentials.

```
D:\WINNT\System32\cmd.exe - runas /smartcard /user:administrator explorer
D:\efstest>runas /smartcard /user:administrator explorer
Reading smart cards...
Reading smart cards...
Reading smart cards...
Reading smart cards...
Reading smart cards...
PIN:

Attempting to start "explorer" as user "Administrator - WhistlerRootCA
"...
```

Figure 4.11 *Running runas.exe from the command line with smart card credentials.*

Table 4.5 *Runas Switches*

Runas Switch	Meaning
/env	Instructs runas to use the environment variables of the currently logged on user rather than the ones of the alternate user specified in the runas command.
/noprofile	Instructs runas to use the default user profile instead of the profile of the alternate user specified in the runas command.
/savecred	Instructs runas to use logon credentials previously saved by the user (in the credential manager). This switch will not prompt for the password of the alternate user specified in the runas command.
/smartcard	Instructs runas to use the smart card logon process for the secondary logon process.

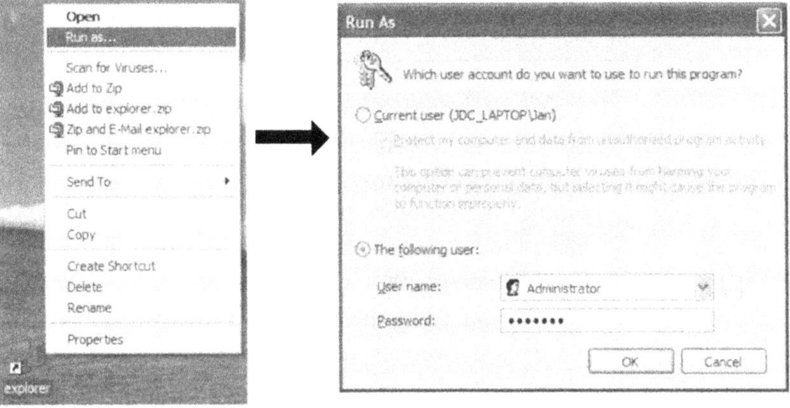

Figure 4.12 *Secondary logon process from Windows Explorer.*

4.7 Anonymous access

In Windows Server 2003, Microsoft included several new features to restrict what can be done to a Windows Server 2003 system and its resources using anonymous access. Anonymous access was introduced in the Windows OS to allow users who are lacking Windows credentials to access Windows-hosted resources. Microsoft, however, opened too many gates for anonymous users—giving way to many (in)famous security exploits.

A key security enhancement is that the Anonymous group is no longer a member of the Everyone group. In Windows, anyone who tries to access a resource without providing credentials is by default part of the Anonymous group. This behavior can easily be reversed by setting the following GPO setting: "Network access: Let Everyone permissions apply to anonymous users." It is located in the Computer Configuration\Windows Settings\

Table 4.6 *Anonymous Access–Related Security Options in the GPO Settings*

GPO Setting	Meaning
Network Access: Allow anonymous SID/ Name translation	Determines if an anonymous user can request SID attributes for another user, for example, retrieve the administrator account name given the administrator SID (which always ends in 500).
Network Access: Do not allow anonymous enumeration of SAM accounts	Determines whether anonymous users are allowed to perform certain activities, such as enumerating the names of domain accounts.
Network Access: Do not allow anonymous enumeration of SAM accounts and shares	Determines whether anonymous users are allowed to perform certain activities, such as enumerating the names of domain accounts and network shares.
Network Access: Restrict anonymous access to Named Pipes and Shares	Determines whether anonymous access will be allowed to named pipes and shares.
Network Access: Shares that can be accessed anonymously	Determines which network shares can be accessed by anonymous users.
Network Access: Named Pipes that can be accessed anonymously	Determines which named pipes can be accessed by anonymous users.

Security Settings\Local Policies\Security Options GPO container. This brand new GPO setting corresponds to the following registry key:

```
HKEY_LOCAL_MACHINE\System\CurrentControlSet\Control\LSA\
everyoneincludesanonymous
```

Microsoft also included other new anonymous access–related security options in the GPO settings. They are listed in Table 4.6 and are also located in the Computer Configuration\Windows Settings\Security Settings\Local Policies\Security Options GPO container. The sidenote below explains how to set up auditing for anonymous access-based AD data enumeration.

Enabling auditing for anonymous access AD data enumeration To enable auditing for anonymous access AD data enumeration, do the following:

- Log on to a domain controller of the forest root domain using an account with Domain Admins credentials.
- Open the ADSI Edit MMC snap-in.
- Connect to Domain naming context of the forest root domain.
- Open the properties of the CN=Server,CN=System,Dc=<FQDN> AD object.
- In the Security tab, click Advanced.
- On the Auditing tab, set the following auditing settings:

  "Success" "Anonymous Logon" "Read All Properties" "This object only"

  "Success" "Anonymous Logon" "Enumerate Entire SAM Domain" "This object only"

4.8 Credential caching

Each time you log on interactively to a Windows domain, your Windows system securely caches your domain credentials. Thanks to this feature, you can log on to the domain when no DCs are available or when your machine is disconnected from the network. Secure caching means that the system's LSA will store a hash of the password hash in the system registry. In other words: the cached credentials cannot be used to derive either the password hash or the original password. The cached credentials are stored in the following registry key: HKEY_LOCAL_MACHINE\Security\Cache. In order to see the content of the Security registry container you must change its default permissions. Logging on with cached domain credentials gives you access only to the local resources on your machine, not to resources that are hosted on other domain-member machines.

From a security standpoint, this feature clearly has risks. Users can intentionally disconnect a local machine from the network, for example, to get around the fact that the administrator disabled the machine's domain account, then still log on to the domain. This type of logon method, however, gives the user access only to local resources.

You can disable cached-account logon sessions and force a user's machine to contact a DC before the user can log on to the domain. You can do so using a registry hack or a GPO setting. To disable cached-account logon sessions using a registry hack, create the CachedLogonsCount registry entry of type REG_SZ and set the value to 0 in the HKEY_LOCAL_MACHINE\SOFTWARE\Microsoft\Windows NT\CurrentVersion\Winlogon registry subkey. To do the same thing using a GPO setting, enable the "Interactive logon: number of previous logons to cache (in case domain controller is not available)" setting. This setting is located in the Computer Configuration\Windows Settings\Security Settings\Local Policies\Security Options GPO container. Do not set the number of logons to cache to 0 on mobile users' laptops. These users would be unable to log on with their domain credentials when away from the office.

You must restart your computer for this change to apply. When credential caching is disabled and no DC is available, a user can still logon to a machine using a local account. Although this key doesn't appear in the registry by default, NT caches a set of 10 domain credentials by default. The maximum value for CachedLogonsCount is 50.

The credential caching discussed in this section should not be confused with Windows XP and Windows Server 2003's capability to store user credentials in the user's profile, a feature that is known as the credential manager and that is discussed in more detail in Chapter 9. Also, this credential caching is different from the caching mechanisms offered by certain authentication protocols. Kerberos, for example, offers client-side ticket caching. Kerberos is discussed in greater detail in Chapter 5.

4.9 General authentication troubleshooting

This section contains an overview of general authentication troubleshooting tools—"general" meaning not related to specific authentication protocols. We will discuss authentication-related event logging and netlogon logging.

4.9.1 Authentication-related event logging

Windows auditing includes the following authentication-related event categories:

- Audit account logon events (Success, Failure): when this auditing category is enabled events will be logged for logon attempts against a Windows security database (SAM or AD).
- Audit logon events (Success, Failure): when this auditing category is enabled events will be logged at the machine where the actual authentication takes place. During an interactive logon this is at the local computer. During a network login this is at the machine where the resource is located.

Enabling auditing for the above event categories can be of great use when troubleshooting Windows authentication problems. This section covers only an introduction to authentication-related event logging: We will come back to Windows auditing in more detail in Chapter 18.

When auditing is enabled for logon events, your event logs will contain entries similar to the ones shown in Figures 4.13 and 4.14. Figure 4.13 shows the event details for a successful logon event. Figure 4.14 shows the event details for a logon failure event. Table 4.7 shows all the event detail fields for Windows user authentication events.

Table 4.8 shows the most important authentication-related event IDs. Table 4.9 shows the values of the Logon Type field and their meaning. The

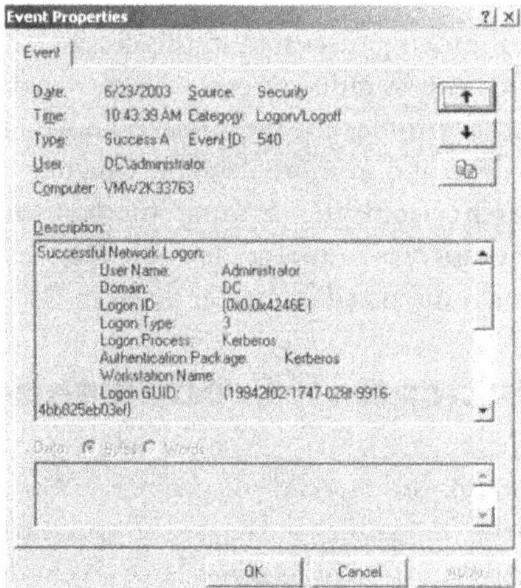

Figure 4.13 *Successful logon event.*

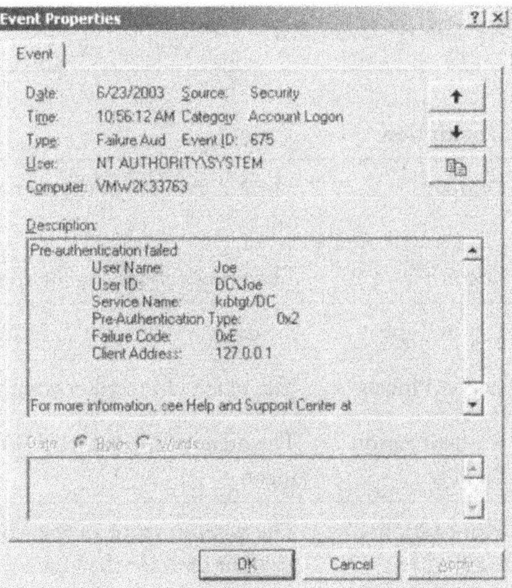

Figure 4.14 *Failed logon event.*

Table 4.7 *Logon Process Field Values*

Event Detail Field Name	Description	
Date	The date on which the event occurred.	
Time	The time at which the event occurred.	
User	The user account performing the logon event.	
Computer	The account name of the computer on which the event occurred.	
Event ID	The identifier for the event. For an overview of Windows 2000 event IDs (still applicable to Windows Server 2003), see the Microsoft articles on "Security Event Descriptions" Parts 1 and 2 (Knowledge Base articles Q299475 and Q301677).	
Source	The source of the event.	
Type	The type of event: successful (Success Audit) or failure (Failure Audit).	
Category	The category of the event.	
Description	A short description of the event. This field holds the following user authentication-related information:	
	Reason	An explanation of why the authentication failed (applies only to authentication failures).
	User Name	The name of the user account that tried to log on.

Table 4.7 *Logon Process Field Values (continued)*

Event Detail Field Name	Description	
	Domain	The NT domain of the user account that tried to log on.
	Logon ID	The unique identifier for a logon session.
	Logon Type	A numeric value that indicates the NT logon type.
	Logon Process	The name of the process that performed the logon.
	Authentication Package	The name of the authentication package used for the logon.
	Workstation Name	The account name of the workstation that the user account used for the logon event.

Table 4.8 *Authentication-Related Event IDs*

Event ID	Meaning
514	An authentication package has been loaded by the LSA.
515	A trusted logon process has registered with the LSA.
518	A notification package has been loaded by the Security Account Manager.
528	Successful Logon.
529	Logon Failure: Unknown user name or bad password.
530	Logon Failure: Account logon time restriction violation.
531	Logon Failure: Account currently disabled.
532	Logon Failure: The specified user account has expired.
533	Logon Failure: User not allowed to log on at this computer.
534	Logon Failure: The user has not been granted the requested logon type at this machine.
535	Logon Failure: The specified account's password has expired.
536	Logon Failure: The NetLogon component is not active.
537	Logon Failure: An unexpected error occurred during the logon process.

Table 4.8 *Authentication-Related Event IDs (continued)*

Event ID	Meaning
538	User Logoff.
539	Logon Failure: Account locked out.
540	A user successfully logged on to a network.
548	Logon Failure: The security ID (SID) from a trusted domain does not match the account domain SID of the client.
549	Logon Failure: All SIDs corresponding to untrusted namespaces were filtered out during an authentication across forests.
551	A user initiated the logoff process.
552	A user successfully logged on to a computer using explicit credentials while already logged on as a different user.
644	User Account Locked Out.

Table 4.9 *Logon Type Field Values*

Logon Type	Meaning
2	Interactive logon process
3	Network logon process
4	Batch logon process
5	Service logon process
6	Proxy logon process
7	Unlock workstation
8	Network cleartext logon process
9*	Newcredentials logon
10	Remote desktop (RDP) or terminal services logon process
11	Logon process using cached credentials

* This logon type means that a a security principal cloned its current token and specified new credentials for outbound connections. The new logon session has the same local identity, but uses different credentials for other network connections.

Table 4.10 *Logon Process Field Values*

Logon Process Field Entry	Description
User32 or WinLogon\MSGina	A typical NT logon process occurred. Winlogon.exe and msgina.dll are the files that the NT authentication UI uses.
SCMgr	The NT Service Control Manager (SCM) logged on and started a service.
Advapi	An application called the LogonUser functions to initiate a logon process.
MS.RADIU	The Remote Authentication Dial-In User Service (RADIUS) initiated a logon process.
Ntlmssp	The NT LAN Manager (NTLM) authentication protocol Security Support Provider (SSP) initiated the logon process.
IIS	Microsoft IIS initiated the logon process (this situation occurs when you use anonymous access or basic authentication on the IIS level).
Kerberos	KerberosThe Kerberos authentication protocol SSP initiated the logon process.

most frequently occurring Logon Type values are 2 and 3. When you see a Logon Type 2 in the Event Viewer logs, you know that somebody has logged on interactively to your machine. When you see a Logon Type 3, you know that somebody has tried to access a resource on your computer from the network. When you see a Logon Type 4, you know that the Windows Scheduler service has run a script or program in batch. When you see a Logon Type 5, you know that a Windows service has started using a specific user account.

The Logon ID field uniquely identifies a logon session on a particular machine. Because both a logon session's logon and logoff events refer to the same Logon ID, you can use the Logon ID to find the logoff event that corresponds to a particular logon event. A logoff event has event ID 538.

The Logon Process field shows the name of the process that initiated the logon session. Table 4.10 shows some of the possible values for this field and their meaning.

4.9.2 Netlogon logging

The Netlogon service is one of the key LSA processes that is running on every Windows domain controller (see Chapter 2 for more information on the LSA). It plays a critical role during interactive and noninteractive logon sequences. When troubleshooting authentication problems, it can be very useful to turn on Netlogon service logging.

To turn on Netlogon logging, type the following nltest command at the command line:

```
nltest /dbflag:2080ffff
```

Enabling Netlogon logging, also requires a Netlogon service restart. You can do this using the net stop netlogon and net start netlogon commands. To disable netlogon logging type:

```
nltest /dbflag:0
```

Then again restart the Netlogon service. The Netlogon service stores its log data in a special log file called netlogon.log, which is stored in the %Windir%/debug folder.

Great tools to query the Netlogon log files are the nlparse.exe and the findstr.exe tools.

The nlparse.exe is a GUI tool that comes with the MS account lockout tools, which can be downloaded for free from the Microsoft Web site (look for altools.exe). Figure 4.15 shows the nlparse GUI: It contains the most common Netlogon error codes and their meaning. Nlparse stores the output of its queries in two files (that are both stored in the %Windir%\debug folder)—the netlogon.log-out.scv and the netlogon.log-summaryout.txt.

Findstr.exe is a command-line tool that is included with the default installation of Windows 2000, Windows XP, and Windows Server 2003.

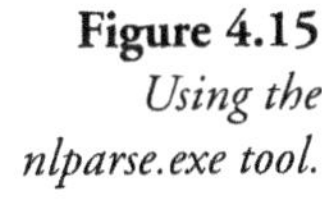

Figure 4.15 *Using the nlparse.exe tool.*

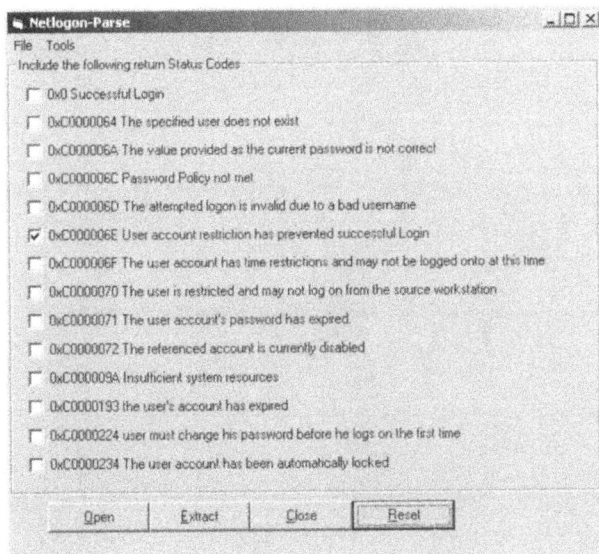

You can use it to query a single or multiple Netlogon files for occurrences of a particular user account or error codes. The following command queries the netlogon.log file for occurrences of user JoeJ and stores the results of the query in the output.txt file.

```
Findstr "JoeJ" netlogon.log >c:\output.txt
```

4.10 What's coming up in the next chapters?

The following five chapters will cover different aspects of Windows Server 2003 authentication technology and infrastructures:

- Chapter 5 focuses on the Kerberos authentication protocol.
- Chapter 6 explains the authentication features of Internet Information Server 6.0, the new Web server shipping with Windows Server 2003.
- Chapter 7 explains Microsoft's Passport single sign-on solution for the Internet.
- Chapter 8 focuses on Windows and UNIX authentication integration.
- Chapter 9 gives an overview of different single sign-on architectures available for a Windows environment.

5

Kerberos

This chapter focuses on the Kerberos authentication protocol, the default authentication protocol of Windows Server 2003. We will look at how the protocol is works, how it has been implemented in Windows Server 2003, and some advanced Kerberos topics.

5.1 Introducing Kerberos

In Greek mythology Kerberos is a three-headed dog guarding the entrance to the underworld. In the context of this book Kerberos refers to the authentication protocol developed as part of the MIT Athena project.[1]

Microsoft introduced Kerberos as the new default authentication protocol for enterprise environments in Windows 2000. Every Windows 2000, Windows XP, and Windows Server 2003 OS platform includes a client Kerberos authentication provider. Neither Windows 2000 nor Windows Server 2003 includes Kerberos support for other legacy Microsoft platforms. Your NT4, Windows 95 or 98 clients will not be able to authenticate using Kerberos—you'll need to upgrade these workstations to either Windows 2000 Professional or Windows XP. In the early days of Windows 2000, Microsoft promised to include Kerberos support for Windows 95 and 98 in the "Directory Services Client" (dsclient.exe), an add-on for Windows 95 and 98 that can be found on the Windows 2000 Server CD.

A little more about the dog's three heads: They stand for authentication, authorization, and auditing. The basic Kerberos protocol (Version 5, as defined in RFC 1510) only deals with authentication. Microsoft's implementation of the protocol also includes extensions for authorization. So far,

1. More historical information on the MIT Athena project is available from the following URL: http://www-tech.mit.edu/V119/N19/history_of_athe.19f.html.

no Kerberos implementation covers auditing. Kerberos can also offer more than the three A's: Later in this chapter we will explain how one of the secret keys exchanged during the Kerberos authentication sequence can be used for packet authentication, integrity, and confidentiality services.

Another analogy to the dog's three heads is the number of basic entities the Kerberos protocol is dealing with. There are always three: two entities that want to authenticate to one another (e.g., a user and a resource server) and an entity that mediates between the two, a trusted third party, or, in Kerberos terminology, the key distribution center (KDC).

5.1.1 Kerberos advantages

In this section, we will explain the key differences between the NTLM and the Kerberos authentication protocols and the advantages that Kerberos brings to the Windows 2000, Windows XP, and Windows Server 2003 operating systems and their users. Many of the terms used in this section will be explained in greater detail later on in this chapter.

Faster authentication

The Kerberos protocol uses a unique ticketing system that provides faster authentication:

- Every authenticated domain entity can request tickets from its local Kerberos KDC to access other domain resources.
- The tickets are considered as access permits by the resource servers.
- The ticket can be used more then once and can be cached on the client side.

When a resource server or the KDC gets a Kerberos ticket and a Kerberos authenticator from the client, the server has enough information to authenticate the client. The NTLM authentication protocol requires resource servers that are not domain controllers, to contact a domain contoller in order to validate a user's authentication request (this process is known as pass-through authentication). Thanks to its ticketing system, Kerberos does not need pass-through authentication. This is why Kerberos accelerates the authentication process. A downside to the ticketing system is that it puts a greater workload on the client. On the other hand, it offloads the resource servers; they must not bother about pass-through authentication anymore.

Mutual authentication

Kerberos supports mutual authentication. This means that the client authenticates to the service that is responsible for the resource and that the service also authenticates to the client. This is a big difference from NTLM. The NTLM challenge-response provides only client authentication: The server challenges the client, the client calculates a response, and the server validates that response. Using NTLM, users might provide their credentials to a bogus server.

Kerberos is an open standard

Microsoft based its Kerberos implementation on the standard defined in RFC 1510 (this is Kerberos Version 5). This is why Kerberos can provide single sign-on (SSO) between Windows Server 2003 and other OSs supporting an RFC 1510-based Kerberos implementation. RFC 1510 can be dowloaded from the Internet Engineering Task Force (IETF) at http://www.ietf.org.

Over the past years, Microsoft has been actively involved in the Kerberos standardization process. Microsoft software engineers participated in the creation of several Kerberos-related Internet drafts (see also http://www.ietf.org).

Support for authentication delegation

Authentication delegation can be looked at as the next step after impersonation: Thanks to impersonation, a service can access local resources on behalf of a user; thanks to delegation, a service can access remote resources on behalf of a user. What delegation really means is that user A can give rights to an intermediary machine B to authenticate to an application server C as if machine B was user A. This means that application server C will base its authorization decisions on user A's identity rather than on machine B's account. Delegation is also known as authentication forwarding. In Kerberos terminology this basically means that user A forwards a ticket to intermediary machine B, and that machine B then uses user A's ticket to authenticate to application server C.

You can use delegation for authentication in multitier applications; an example of such an application is database access using a Web front end. In such a setup the browser, the Web server, and the database server are all running on different machines. In a multitier application, authentication happens on different tiers. In such application if you want to set authorization on the database using the user's identity, you should be capable of using the user's identity for authentication both on the web server and the database server. This is impossible if you use NTLM for authentication on every link, simply because NTLM does not support delegation. We will come back to delegation in greater detail later on in this chapter.

Support for the smart card logon feature

Through the Kerberos PKINIT extension, both Windows 2000 and Windows Server 2003 include support for the smart card logon feature. The smart card logon feature provides much stronger authentication than the password logon feature does because it relies on a two-factor authentication: To log on, a user needs to possess a smart card and know its PIN code. The smart card logon feature also offers other security advantages; for example, it can block Trojan horse attacks that try to grab a user's password from the system memory.

Table 5.1 *Kerberos–NTLM Comparison*

	NTLM	Kerberos
Cryptographic technology	Symmetric cryptography	Basic Kerberos: symmetric cryptography Kerberos PKINIT: symmetric and asymmetric cryptography
Trusted third party	Domain controller	Basic Kerberos: domain controller with KDC service Kerberos PKINIT: domain controller with KDC service and Enterprise CA
Microsoft-supported platforms	Windows 95, Windows 98, Windows ME, Windows NT4, Windows 2000, Windows XP, and Windows Server 2003	Windows 2000, Windows XP, and Windows Server 2003*
Features	Slower authentication because of pass-through authentication	Faster authentication because of unique ticketing system
	No mutual authentication	Mutual authentication
	No support for delegation of authentication	Support for delegation of authentication
	No support for smart card logon feature	Support for smart card logon feature
	Proprietary Microsoft authentication protocol	Open standard
	No protection for authorization data carried in NTLM messages†	Cryptographic protection for authorization data carried in Kerberos tickets

* Remember from the previous chapter that Kerberos can only be used for domain logon to a Windows 2000 or Windows Server 2003 domain.

† This was the case for NTLM version 1; this problem has been resolved in NTLM version 2.

5.1.2 Comparing Kerberos to NTLM

Table 5.1 compares Kerberos, the default authentication protocol of Windows 2000 and Windows Server 2003, to NTLM, the default authentication protocol of NT4. It also lists the main features of both protocols introduced in the previous sections.

5.2 Kerberos: The basic protocol

The following sections explain the basic Kerberos protocol as it is defined in RFC 1510. Those not familiar with Kerberos may be bewildered by the need for numerous diverse keys to be transmitted around the network. In order to break down the complexity of the protocol, we will approach it in five steps:

- Step 1: Kerberos authentication is based on symmetric key cryptography.
- Step 2: The Kerberos KDC provides scalability.
- Step 3: A Kerberos ticket provides secure transport of a session key.
- Step 4: The Kerberos KDC distributes the session key by sending it to the client.
- Step 5: The Kerberos Ticket Granting Ticket limits the use of the entities' master keys.

Before starting to explore how Kerberos works, we must explain the notations that will be used in the illustrations:

- The u stands for user, s stands for resource server, and k stands for KDC.
- S stands for session key; Sus means the session key shared between the user and the resource server.
- M stands for master key; Mu is the master key of the user.
- Drawing (1) in Figure 5.1 represents the session key shared between the user and resource server.

Figure 5.1 *Session keys and encrypted session keys.*

- Drawing (2) represents the same session key, but this time encrypted.
- Drawing (3) represents the same session key, encrypted using the master key of the user.

To ease reading we will talk about a "client," Alice, and a "resource server" that authenticates using Kerberos. The identities used in this Kerberos authentication exchange are Alice's SID and the SID of the service account that is used by the application or the service responsible for the resource. To be fully correct we should talk about the "service account of the service," but this would not promote ease of reading. Also, when we talk about Alice, we really mean the LSA on Alice's machine impersonating Alice and acting on her behalf. From now on, the following words are synonyms: principal and security principal and entity, and domain and realm.

5.2.1 Kerberos design assumptions

Before diving into the nuts and bolts of the protocol, let's have a quick look at some of the design assumptions the Kerberos designers at MIT took. It is very important to keep these assumptions in mind as we run through the Kerberos internals.

- Kerberos always deals with three entities: users, servers, and a set of security servers that mediate between the users and the servers for authentication.
- Time is trusted. This is because Kerberos uses timestamps to protect against replay attacks.
- The user trusts its workstation completely. This is because Kerberos caches authentication tokens on the client side.
- The security server must be online all the time. Kerberos requires the availability of the security server in order to generate new Kerberos security tokens.
- The servers are stateless. Kerberos wants to limit the amount of security principal–related information that is kept on the server side.
- Users' password time on user machine must be minimized. Kerberos looks at a user password as a weak secret—it should be protected the best possible. One of the ways to do this is to limit its time on the user workstation. Another way is to create a key hierarchy.

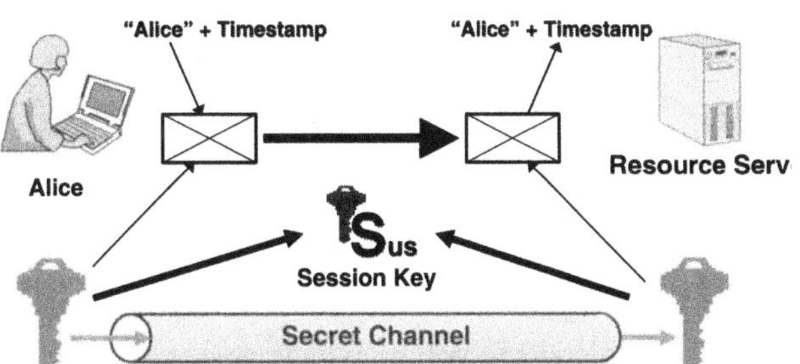

Figure 5.2 *Kerberos authentication is based on symmetric key cryptography.*

5.2.2 Step 1: Kerberos authentication is based on symmetric key cryptography

To authenticate entities Kerberos uses symmetric key cryptography.[2] In symmetric key cryptography the communicating entities use the same key for both encryption and decryption. The basic mathematical formula behind this process is the following:

$$D_K(E_K(M)) = M$$

If the encryption (E) and decryption (D) processes are both using the same key K, the decryption of the encrypted text (M) results in the readable text (M).

This is what happens when Alice wants to authenticate to a resource server using a symmetric key cipher (illustrated in Figure 5.2):

- Alice encrypts her name and the current timestamp using a symmetric key.
- The encrypted message and Alice's name are sent to the resource server.
- The resource server decrypts the message.
- The resource server checks Alice's name and the timestamp (this is the result of the decryption process). If they are okay, Alice is authenticated to the server.

Why does this process authenticate Alice to the resource server? If the resource server can successfully decrypt the message, this means if the decryption process results in Alice's name and an acceptable timestamp, the resource server knows that only Alice could have encrypted this information,

2. When the Kerberos design was started, public key cryptography was still patented (by RSA). This explains why the default Kerberos protocol (as defined in RFC 1510) relies on symmetric key cryptography.

because she is the only one, besides the resource server, who also knows the symmetric key. In this context acceptable means the following: Upon receipt of Alice's encrypted packet, the resource server will compare the timestamp in Alice's packet against the local time. If the time skew between these two timestamps is too big, the resource server will reject the authentication attempt, because a hacker could have replayed Alice's original authentication packet.

In this explanation you may have noticed the differences and similarities with the NTLM authentication protocol. Both Kerberos and NTLM use symmetric cryptography for authentication: "If you can prove you know your secret key, I believe you are who you say you are." In NTLM the knowledge of the secret key is proven using a challenge-response mechanism. Kerberos uses symmetric encryption of the timestamp and the user's name to do the same thing.

The encrypted packet containing Alice's name and the timestamp is known in Kerberos as the authenticator, and the symmetric key is called a session key. A session key exists between all Kerberos principals that want to authenticate to each other.

A critical element in this exchange is the timestamp: It provides "authenticator uniqueness" and protects against replay attacks. Without the authenticator, a hacker could grab a ticket off the network and use it to impersonate Alice to a resource server. The timestamp explains the time sensitivity of the Kerberos protocol and of Windows 2000 and Windows Server 2003.

Remember from the introduction that Kerberos can provide "mutual" authentication: To provide this the Kerberos protocol includes an additional exchange that authenticates the server to the client. In this example, it means that, in turn, the server will encrypt its name and the current timestamp and send it to Alice.

A big problem when using a symmetric protocol is the secure distribution of the secret key. The secret key is generated at one side of the communication channel and should be sent to the other side of the communication channel in a secure way. Secure means that the confidentiality and integrity of the key should be protected. If anybody could read the secret key when it is sent across the network, the whole authentication system becomes worthless: The secrecy of the secret key is a vital part of a symmetric cipher.

Steps 2, 3, and 4 explain how the Kerberos developers have resolved the problem of secure session key distribution.

5.2.3 Step 2: The Kerberos KDC provides scalability

The Kerberos protocol always deals with three entities: two entities that want to authenticate to one another and one entity that mediates between these two entities for authentication: the key distribution center (KDC). Why do we need a KDC?

Suppose that Alice is part of a workgroup consisting of five entities that all want to authenticate to one another using symmetric key cryptography. Because every entity needs to share a secret key with every other entity, we will need 10 keys. The mathematical formula behind this is n (n – 1)/2. In a 50,000-employee company we would need about 1.5 billion keys. Not only would we have to deal with an enormous amount of keys, but there would also be an enormous amount of small authentication databases: On every client there would be one, containing all the secret keys of the entities with which the client wants to authenticate. This solution is clearly not scalable to the level of a big environment. Imagine having to use such a solution on the Internet.

To make Kerberos more scalable, the Kerberos developers included the concept of a KDC. KDC is a trusted third party with which every entity shares a secret key: This key is called the entity's master key. All entities trust the KDC to mediate in their mutual authentication. The KDC also maintains a centralized authentication database containing a copy of every user's master key.

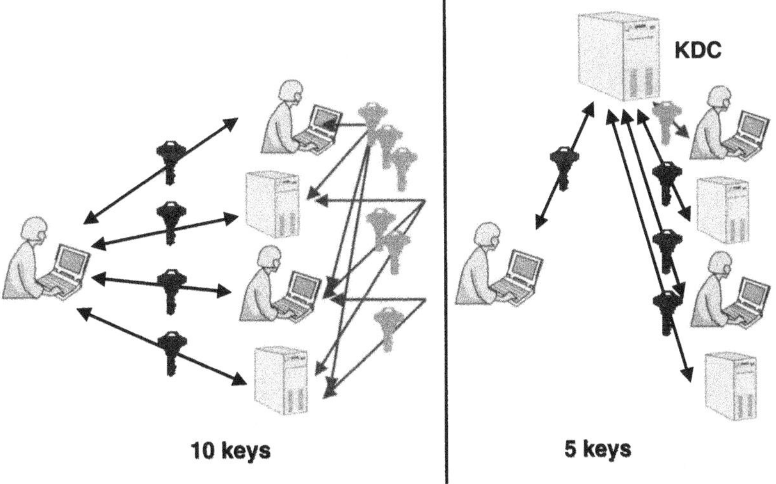

Figure 5.3 *A KDC provides scalability.*

In Windows Server 2003 the KDC is a service that is installed on every domain controller as part of the dcpromo Active Directory installation process. Every Windows Server 2003 domain controller runs a KDC service[3] and hosts an Active Directory (AD) instance, the central authentication database.[4] As a consequence, a domain with multiple domain controllers provides fault tolerance for the authentication process and the authentication database. If one DC is down, another one can automatically take over. Also, the AD authentication database is replicated between domain controllers.

The concept of a master key is not new to Windows 2000, Windows Server 2003, and Kerberos: It already existed in NT4 and earlier Windows versions. In Windows the master key is derived from a security principal's password.

The password is a secret key that is shared between each individual security principal and the central authentication authority (in the Kerberos case the KDC). Both the entity and the KDC must know the master key before the actual Kerberos authentication process can take place. For obvious security reasons, the AD never stores the plain password but a hashed version (the hash algorithm used is MD4).

An entity's master key is generated as part of the domain enrollment process (e.g, when the administrator enrolls the user and enters a password). A machine's master key is derived from the machine password that is automatically created when an administrator joins the machine into a domain.

5.2.4 Step 3: The ticket provides secure transport of the session key

Figure 5.4 shows the three basic entities with which the Kerberos protocol deals: a client (Alice), a resource server, and a KDC. Figure 5.4 also shows the master keys that are shared between the entities participating in the authentication process and the KDC.

Remember that in the first step we talked about the problem of distributing the secret key (the session key) when dealing with symmetric key ciphers. This section explains how Kerberos resolves this problem. It makes

3. The KDC itself is made of two subservices: the Authentication Service (AS) and the Ticket Granting Service (TGS); in other Kerberos implementations these two subservices can run on different machines, but this is not possible in Windows 2000 and Windows Server 2003.
4. On an interesting note, a standard Kerberos domain is made up of a master KDC and one or more slave KDCs. The master KDC is collocated with a read-write copy of the authentication database (single-master model). In Windows 2000 and Windows Server 2003 every KDC server hosts a read-write copy of the domain portion of the Active Directory (multimaster model).

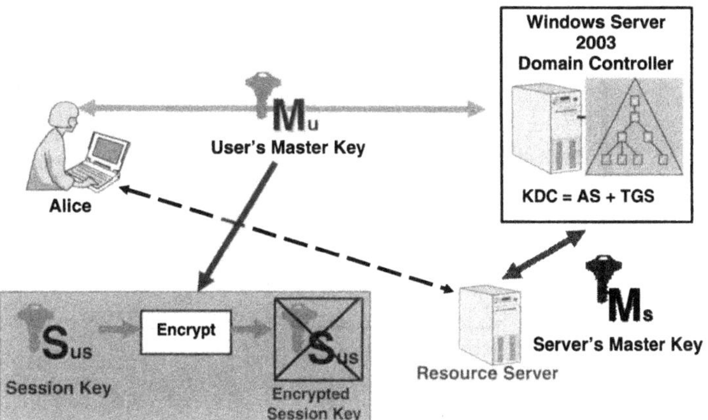

Figure 5.4 *Kerberos entities and master key concept.*

the link between the session key and the master key (introduced in step 2) and explains why we really need a master key in the Kerberos protocol.

In Section 5.2.3, we explained that every entity shares a master key with the KDC. We also said that all entities trust the KDC to mediate in their mutual authentication. Trust in this context also means that every entity trusts the KDC to generate session keys. In the scenario shown in Figure 5.4, the resource server would never trust Alice to generate session keys, because Alice has not authenticated yet to the resource server (the other way around would not work either).

So far, so good. Alice needs to authenticate to the resource server and requests a session key from the KDC. The KDC will generate the session key[5] and distribute it to both entities. After the KDC has generated the session key, it must communicate it to both Alice and the resource server. To secure the transport of the session key to a particular entity, Kerberos encrypts it with the master key of that entity.

Because there are two entities, Alice and the resource server, two encrypted versions of the session key must be generated:

- One encrypted with Alice's master key
- One encrypted with the master key of the resource server

In Kerberos terminology, the session key encrypted with the resource server's master key is known as a "ticket." A Kerberos ticket provides a way to transport a Kerberos session key securely across the network. Only the

5. The security quality of the session key depends on the quality of the random number generator used to generate the session key.

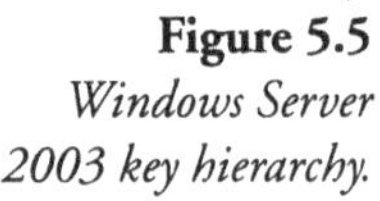

Figure 5.5 *Windows Server 2003 key hierarchy.*

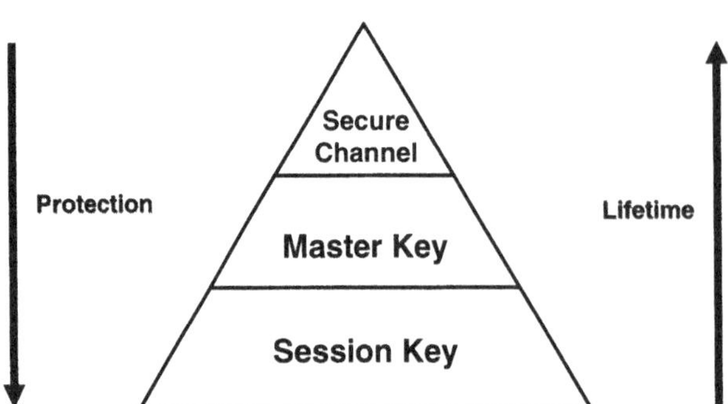

destination resource server and a Windows Server 2003 domain controller can decrypt it.

By securing the transport of the session key using the master key, Kerberos creates what is known as a key hierarchy. Figure 5.5 shows the Windows Server 2003 key hierarchy, which consists of:

- *The session key (or short-term key):* A session key is a secret key that is shared between two entities for authentication purposes. The session key is generated by the KDC. Because it is a critical part of the Kerberos authentication protocol, it is never sent in the clear over a communication channel: It is encrypted using the master key.
- *The master key (or long-term key):* The master key is a secret key that is shared between each entity and the KDC. It must be known to both the entity and the KDC before the actual Kerberos protocol communication can take place. The master key is generated as part of the domain enrollment process and is derived from a user, a machine, or a service's password. The transport of the master key over a communication channel is secured using a secure channel.
- *The secure channel:* When Windows is using a secure channel, it is using a master key to secure the transport of another master key. The following example illustrates the secure channel concept. When you create a new user, the user's password will be sent to the domain controller using a secure channel. The secure channel is in this case made up of the master key shared between the workstation you're working on and the domain controller. In other words, the master key is derived from the workstation's machine account password. The concept of a secure channel was also explained in Chapter 2.

In this key hierarchy the following are also true:

- Higher-level keys protect lower-level keys.

- Higher-level keying material has a longer lifetime than lower-level keying material.
- Lower-level keying material is used more frequently for sending encrypted packets across the network. As a consequence, there is a higher risk for brute-force attacks on these packets. In other words, the associated keys should be changed more often.

5.2.5 Step 4: The KDC distributes the session key by sending it to the client

The KDC can distribute the encrypted session keys to Alice and the resource server in two ways:

- Method 1: The KDC could send it directly to both Alice and the resource server (as shown in Figure 5.6).
- Method 2: The KDC could send the two encrypted session keys to Alice. Alice could then send out the resource server's encrypted copy of the session key later on in the Kerberos authentication sequence (as shown in Figure 5.7).

  The first method has the following disadvantages:

- The resource server has to cache all the session keys: one session key for each client that wants to access a resource on the server. This would impose a huge security risk on the server side.
- Synchronization problems could occur: The client could already be using the session key, while the resource server has not even received its copy yet.

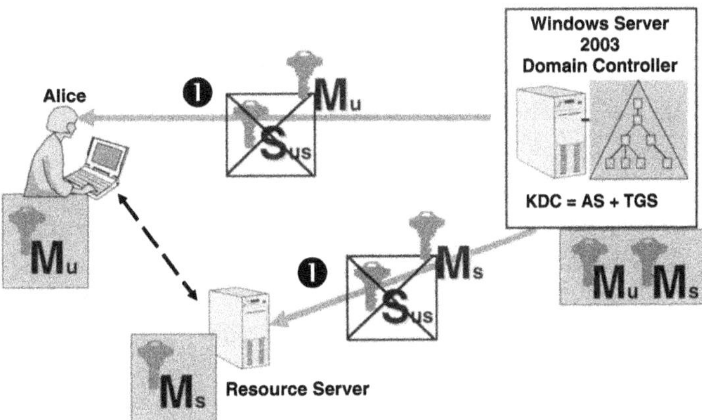

Figure 5.6 *Kerberos ticket distribution Method 1.*

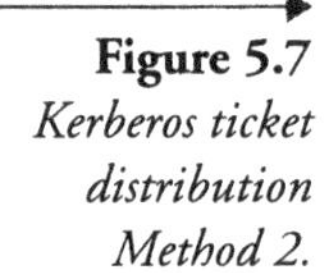

Figure 5.7 *Kerberos ticket distribution Method 2.*

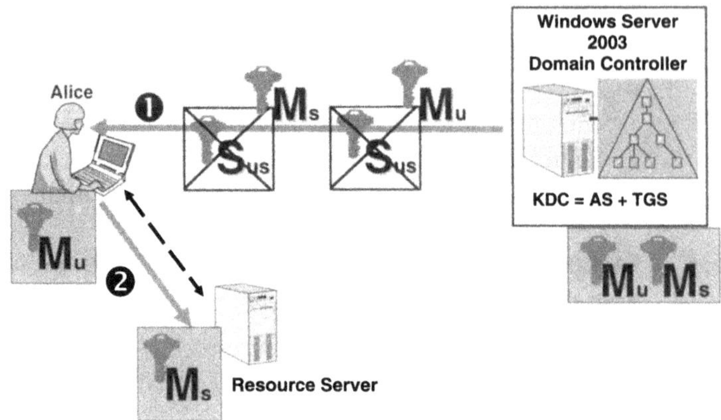

Because of the disadvantages associated with Method 1, Kerberos uses the alternative explained next as Method 2 (see Figure 5.7):

- Both the encrypted session keys (the one for Alice, encrypted with Alice's master key, and the one for the resource server, encrypted with the resource server's master key) are sent to Alice.
- Alice can decrypt the packet encrypted with her master key and get out the session key. Alice's system can now cache both Alice's copy of the session key and the server's copy of the session key (contained in the ticket).
- When Alice needs to authenticate to the resource server, the client will send out the server's copy of the session key.

The key advantage of Method 2 lies in its unique caching architecture: Alice's machine can cache tickets and reuse them. Also, it takes away the need for the server to cache the tickets: It receives them from the clients as needed. This architecture makes the Kerberos protocol stateless on the server side. This has obvious advantages if you want to implement a load balancing or redundancy solution on the server side: There is no need to bother about keeping the session keys synchronized between the different domain controllers.

On the client side, tickets are kept in a special system memory area, which is never paged to disk. The reuse of the cached tickets is limited because of a ticket's limited lifetime and renewal time. Windows 2000, XP, and Windows Server 2003 maintain a ticket cache for every security principal logon session. The ticket cache is purged when the logon session ends. The cache is preserved and written to disk when a system goes into hibernation mode.

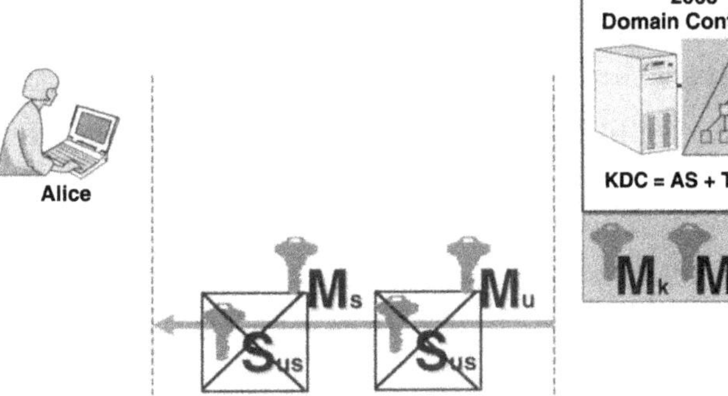

Figure 5.8
The use of the master key.

5.2.6 Step 5: The Ticket Granting Ticket limits the use of the master keys

There is yet another important weakness in the protocol that we have not addressed so far: The session key that is sent back from the KDC to Alice is encrypted using Alice's master key (as shown in Figure 5.8). This encrypted packet is sent over the network every time Alice needs a session key to authenticate to a resource server. This means that every time there is an opportunity for hackers to intercept the encrypted packet and to perform—possibly offline—a brute-force attack on the encrypted packet and derive the user's master key.

In a brute-force attack, a hacker tries to guess the key that was used to encrypt a packet by trying out all the possible keys and looking at the result. Such attacks are not unrealistic: Remember some of the tools that were mentioned in Chapter 2 (L0phtcrack, John the Ripper…) to do brute-force attacks on the SAM or AD database or on the authentication packets sent across the network?

There is clearly a need here for a strong[6] secret to replace Alice's master key: This will be the role of the session key that is shared between each entity and the KDC. This session key will replace Alice's password, and it will be used to authenticate Alice to the KDC after the initial authentication.[7]

6. Strong means less susceptible to brute-force attacks. To resist these attacks there are two possibilities: (1) Use longer keys—longer keys create bigger key spaces and make it more difficult to guess the right key; (2) change the keys more often—this limits the chance for brute-force attacks. In other words, limit the lifetime of the keys; this principle is often referred to as perfect forward secrecy (PFS). The Kerberos developers have chosen the latter solution.
7. There are also other reasons why the concept of a session key shared between every Kerberos entity and the KDC is important: it allows for the KDC's AS and TGS services to be hosted on different machines (this cannot be done in Windows, but is often done in UNIX Kerberos implementations), and it enables cross-domain authentication referrals (explained later).

Although it has an identical function (authentication), the session key introduced in this step is *not* the same as the one used in the previous sections. This session key is shared between Alice and the KDC, and the other session key is shared between Alice and the resource server.

Just like Alice's master key, both Alice and the KDC must know this session key. To securely transport this session key, we will use the same mechanism as the one described in steps 3 and 4:

- Step 3: Kerberos uses a ticket to provide secure transport of the session key. The special ticket used here is known as the Ticket Granting Ticket (TGT).
- Step 4: Kerberos distributes the tickets by sending them out via Alice. The KDC sends the TGT to Alice; Alice caches the TGT and can send it to the KDC when needed. Again, there is no need for the KDC to cache the TGTs of every client, and once more this makes the Kerberos protocol stateless on the server side. If you do not consider these arguments, it may sound silly that the KDC generates the session key and sends it out to the client to get it back from the client at a moment later in time.

Figure 5.9 shows how this new session key (S_{ku}) and the associated TGT are used in the basic Kerberos protocol exchange:

- Alice sends a logon message to the domain controller. This message is secured using Alice's master key, derived from Alice's password.[8]
- The KDC will then send out a secured copy of the session key to be used for authentication between Alice and the KDC for the rest of the logon session (this session key will replace the user's master key). The copy of the session key encrypted with the KDC's master key is called the TGT.
- The session key and the TGT will be cached in Alice's local Kerberos ticket cache.
- Later on, when Alice wants to access a resource on the resource server, the security process acting on Alice's behalf will send out a request for a ticket to the KDC using the locally cached TGT. The request for the resource will be secured using the session key S_{ku}.
- Finally, the KDC will send back a ticket and a new session key to Alice, which she can use later on to authenticate to the resource

8. The encryption of this request is not a part of the basic Kerberos protocol as defined in RFC 1510; it is based on a Kerberos extension known as Kerberos preauthentication. It will be explained later on in this chapter.

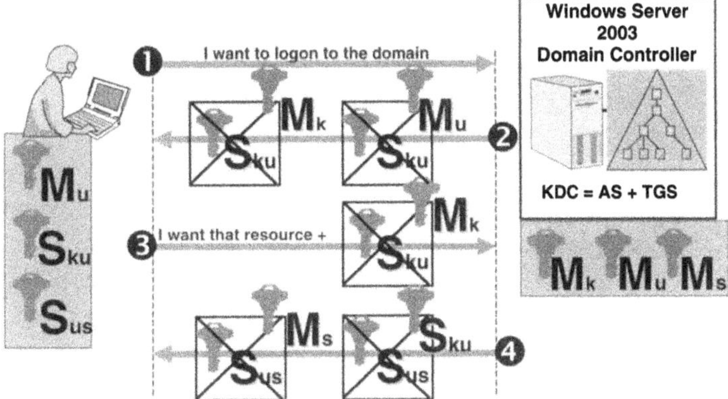

Figure 5.9 *The role of the Kerberos TGT.*

server. Notice that in Figure 5.9 the new session key is not encrypted using Alice's master key, but using the newly created session key S_{ku}.

This sequence shows how in the basic Kerberos exchange:

- The TGT is reused to request tickets for other application or resource servers. The reuse of the TGT is limited by its lifetime. The lifetime of the TGT not only limits the usage of the TGT itself but of all the tickets that were obtained using a particular TGT. For example, if I have a TGT that is about to expire in a half-hour, every new ticket I get will also expire at the same point in time (even though the default lifetime of a ticket may be one hour).
- Ticket requests do not require further use of the client's master key.[9] During the logon session, a weak secret (the master key derived from a client's password) is exchanged for a strong secret (the session key contained within the TGT). In other words, at logon time and at each TGT renewal the user will authenticate to the KDC with his master key; in subsequent ticket requests he will authenticate using the session key, which is contained in the TGT.
- The newly created session key (S_{ku}) doesn't need to be cached on the KDC: The KDC gets it from the client each time the client requests a new service ticket. S_{ku} is encrypted using the KDC's master key (remember: this is what they call the TGT). This feature makes Kerberos stateless on the KDC side, which has, as for resource serv-

9. This also means that once you have a session key, in a standard Kerberos implementation there's no more need to cache the master key on the client, which is very good from a security point of view. Microsoft Windows 2000, XP, and Windows Server 2003 still cache the master key because they need it to perform NTLM authentication to downlevel clients.

ers, obvious advantages if some load balancing or redundancy technology has to be implemented on the KDC side.

5.2.7 Bringing it all together

In this section we will bring together all the elements that were brought up in the previous five steps. Figure 5.10 shows the complete Kerberos protocol: It consists of three subprotocols (or phases), each one made up of two steps. In the following list, the cryptic names between parentheses are the names of the Kerberos protocol messages as they are called in the Kerberos standard documents.

- Phase 1: Authentication Service Exchange (occurs once for every logon session)
  - Step 1: Authentication Server Request (KRB_AS_REQ). Alice logs on the domain from her local machine. A TGT request is sent to a Windows KDC. Ntsecurity.nu makes available two tools (kerbsniff and kerbcrack) to retrieve a user's password from the KRB_AS_REQ network exchange. To capture the KRB_AS_REQ packets, use kerbsniff. Then use kerbcrack to perform a brute-force or dictionary attack on the captured packets. The tools can be downloaded from http://www.ntsecurity.nu/toolbox/kerbcrack/.
  - Step 2: Authentication Server Reply (KRB_AS_REP). The Windows KDC returns a TGT and a session key to Alice.
- Phase 2: Ticket-Granting Service Exchange (occurs once for every resource server)
  - Step 3: TGS Request (KRB_TGS_REQ). Alice wants to access an application on a server. A ticket request for the application server is sent to the Windows KDC. This request consists of Alice's TGT and an authenticator.
  - Step 4: TGS Reply (KRB_TGS_REP). The Windows KDC returns a ticket and a session key to Alice.
- Phase 3: Client-Server Authentication Exchange (occurs once for every server session)
  - Step 5: Application Server Request (KRB_AP_REQ). The ticket is sent to the application server. Upon receiving the ticket and the authenticator, the server can authenticate Alice.

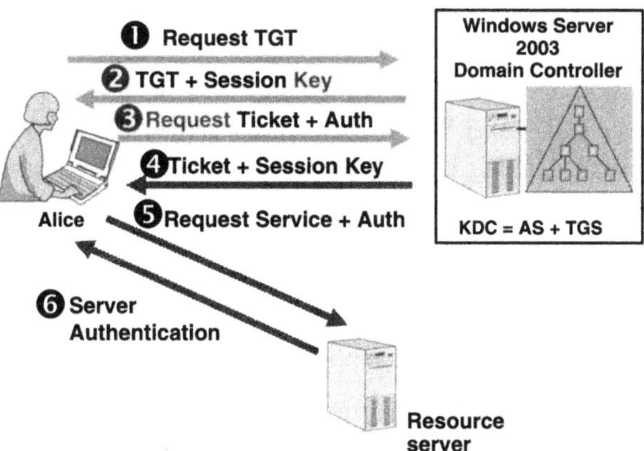

Figure 5.10 *The complete Kerberos protocol.*

- Step 6: Application Server Reply (KRB_AP_REP). The server replies to Alice with another authenticator. On receiving this authenticator, Alice can authenticate the server.

During these exchanges the following keys and tickets are cached on Alice's computer: the TGT, the ticket used to authenticate to the resource server, and two session keys—one to authenticate to the KDC and one to authenticate to the resource server.

5.2.8 Kerberos data confidentiality, authentication, and integrity services

Windows 2000, XP, and Windows Server 2003 all include the Kerberos extensions that can be used to provide data confidentiality, authentication, and integrity for messages that are sent after the initial Kerberos exchange outlined in the previous sections. These extensions are known as the KRB_PRIV (providing data confidentiality) and the KRB_SAFE (providing data authentication and integrity) Kerberos extensions. They are based on the existence of a session key between two entities at the end of a Kerberos authentication protocol exchange:

- The session key can be used to sign a message. A hash, which is the result of applying a hash function to a message, can be encrypted using the session key. A hash encrypted with a session key is also referred to as a message authentication code (MAC).
- The session key can be used to seal a message by encrypting the message using the session key.

5.3 Logging on to windows using Kerberos

Now that we have explained the basic Kerberos protocol, we can discuss some real-world Windows Kerberos logon examples. In this section we will look in detail at both local and network logon features in single and multiple domain environments and in a multiple forest scenario.

5.3.1 Logging on in a single domain environment

Typical examples of logon method in a single domain environment are:

- Alice is logging on from a machine that is a member of the domain where Alice's user account has been defined (this is a local logon method).
- Alice accesses a resource located on a machine that is a member of Alice's logon domain (this is a network logon method).

Local logon process

Figure 5.11 shows what happens during a local logon process in a single domain environment.

Everything starts when Alice presses <CTRL><ALT><DEL> and chooses to log on to the domain.

1. The client Kerberos package acting on behalf of Alice tries to locate a KDC service for the domain; it does so by querying the DNS service.[10] The Kerberos package will retry up to three times to contact a KDC. At first it waits 10 seconds for a reply; on each retry it waits an additional 10 seconds. In most cases a KDC service for the domain is already known. The discovery of a domain controller is also a part of the secure channel setup that occurs before any local logging on.
2. Once the DC is found, Alice sends a Kerberos authentication request to the DC. This request authenticates Alice to the DC and contains a TGT request (KRB_AS_REQ).
3. The Authentication Service authenticates Alice, generates a TGT, and sends it back to the client (KRB_AS_REP).

10. Windows 2000 and Windows Server 2003 publish two Kerberos-specific SRV records to DNS: _kerberos and _kpasswd. The list of all published SRV records can be found on a domain controller in the "%windir%\system32\config\netlogon.dns" file. The SRV DNS records are created automatically during the domain controller setup (as part of the dcpromo process).

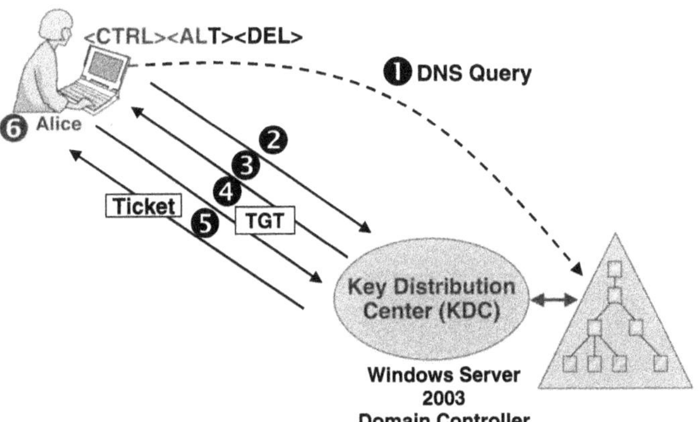

Figure 5.11 *Local logon process in a single domain environment.*

4. The local machine where Alice logged on is—just like any other resource—a resource for which Alice needs a ticket. Alice sends a ticket request to the DC using her TGT (together with an authenticator) (KRB_TGS_REQ).
5. The TGS of the DC checks the TGT and the authenticator, generates a ticket for the local machine, and sends it back to Alice (KRB_TGS_REP).
6. On Alice's machine, the ticket is presented to the Local Security Authority, which will create an access token for Alice. From then on, any process acting on behalf of Alice can access the local machine's resources.

Network logon process

When Alice is already logged onto a domain and wants to access a resource located on a server within the same domain, a network logon process will take place. In this case, the logon sequence is as follows (see Figure 5.12):

1. Alice sends a server ticket request to the DC using her TGT (together with an authenticator) (KRB_TGS_REQ).
2. The TGS of the DC checks the authenticator, generates a server ticket, and sends it back to Alice (KRB_TGS_REP).
3. Alice sends the ticket (together with an authenticator) to the application server (KRB_AP_REQ).
4. The application verifies the ticket with the authenticator and sends back his or her authenticator to Alice for server authentication (KRB_AP_REP).

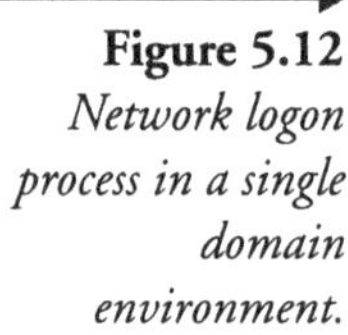

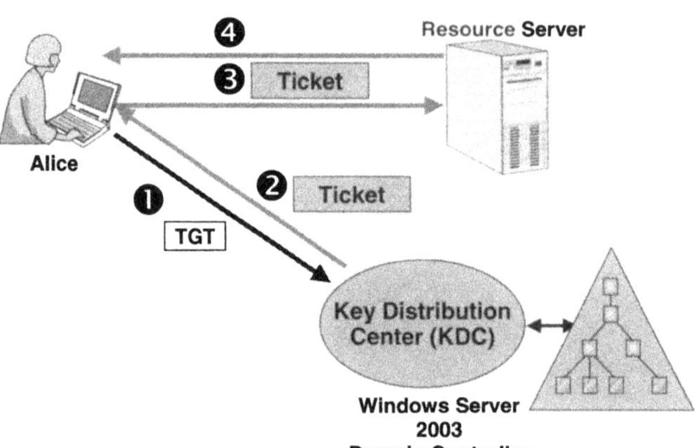

Figure 5.12 *Network logon process in a single domain environment.*

Disabling Kerberos in migration scenarios

In certain migration scenarios it may be necessary to disable the Kerberos authentication protocol on your Windows Server 2003 domain controllers. Remember from Chapter 4 that for Windows 2000 Professional and later clients, the first authentication protocol of choice is always Kerberos—at least if the client is talking to a Windows 2000 or later DC.

Imagine the following migration scenario: You have migrated all your client platforms to Windows XP and you upgraded one of your Windows NT4.0 DCs to Windows Server 2003—all the remaining DCs are still on NT4.0. In this scenario the one and only Windows Server 2003 DC may become overloaded by Kerberos authentication traffic because all Windows XP clients try to authenticate against it. Also, if this DC becomes unavailable, the clients cannot be authenticated anymore. Once a client has been authenticated by a Kerberos KDC it will not fall back to NTLM and NT4 DCs. This is a typical scenario where you may want to temporarily disable the Kerberos authentication protocol on the Windows Server 2003 DC.

To disable Kerberos, Microsoft provides a registry hack (the hack is available from Windows 2000 Service Pack 2 onward). The hack is called NT4Emulator (REG_DWORD) and should be added to the HKEY_LOCAL_MACHINE/System/CurrentControlSet/Services/Netlogon/Parameters registry key of the Windows 2000 SP2 or later DC and set to value 1.

The creation of this key on the Windows 2000 SP2 or later DC creates another problem because it will make it impossible to manage the AD using any of the MMC-based AD management tools. To get around this problem, you must make a registry change on the clients from which you want to use the AD management tools. Add the NeutralizeNT4Emulator registry value (REG_DWORD) in the HKEY_LOCAL_MACHINE/System/CurrentControlSet/Services/Netlogon/Parameters registry key and set it to value 1.

The role of SPNs

One of the great features of Kerberos is its support for mutual authentication. The enabling technologies for mutual authentication are the Kerberos protocol itself, User Principal Names (UPNs), and Service Principal Names (SPNs). The UPN and SPN concepts were introduced in Chapter 2. In the following we will look at how SPNs are used during the Kerberos authentication exchanges.

Let's take the example of a network logon process: A user decides to access a file on another server during his or her logon session. In this example the following SPN-related events will occur during the authentication exchanges:

- The Kerberos software on the client side constructs a Kerberos "KRB_TGS_REQ" message, containing the user's TGT and the SPN of the service that is responsible for the file the user wants to access. This message is sent to the user's domain controller. A Kerberos client can always construct a service's SPN—how this works was explained in Chapter 2.
- The KDC queries the AD[11] to find an account that has a matching SPN (this process is also known as "resolving" the SPN). The service's SPN must be unique in the AD. If more than one account is found with a corresponding SPN, the authentication will fail.
- Given the service account corresponding to the SPN and the associated master key, the KDC can construct a service ticket and send it back to the client. (This is the "KRB_TGS_REP" message.)
- In the next step the client sends a "KRB_AP_REQ" message to the file server (including the service ticket and a Kerberos authenticator).
- Finally, the service will authenticate back to the client (this is the "KRB_AP_REP" message). This is where the real mutual authentication happens.

11. In the first place it will query the local domain Naming Context of the user's authentication DC; after that, it will query the global catalog.

5.3.2 Logging on in a multiple domain environment

Typical examples of scenarios where a multiple domain logon process occurs are the following:

- Alice is logging on from a machine member of a different domain than the one where Alice's account has been defined (this is a local logon process).
- Alice is accessing a resource located on a machine that is a member of a different domain than the one where Alice initially logged on (this is a network logon process).

In the following examples, we will frequently use the concepts "referral ticket" and "inter-realm key." These concepts will be explained in more detail in the section on "multiple domain logon: under the hood."

Local logon process

Figure 5.13 shows a typical multidomain environment, consisting of a parent domain hp.com and two child domains, North America (NA) and Europe. In the local logon example, Alice's account is defined in the Europe domain. Alice logs on from a workstation whose account is defined in the NA domain.

The local logon process can be broken down into the four following steps:

- Step 1: AS exchange (KRB_AS_REQ and KRB_AS_REP):
  - To log on Alice, a TGT request is sent to a KDC in Europe.hp.com.
  - The AS Request is sent to a KDC in Europe.hp.com. The selected KDC will sent back the AS Reply. Only a KDC of Alice's account domain can authenticate Alice (Windows credentials are never replicated between the domain controllers of different domains).
- Steps 2, 3, and 4: TGS exchanges (KRB_TGS_REQ and KRB_TGS_REP):
  - To request a ticket for Alice to work on the NA workstation, a TGS request is sent to the KDC of Europe.hp.com.
  - The KDC of Europe.hp.com cannot issue a ticket that allows Alice to work on a workstation in NA. Only a KDC of NA can return such a ticket.[12] Therefore, the TGS reply contains a referral

12. This is because only a KDC of NA knows the workstation's master key.

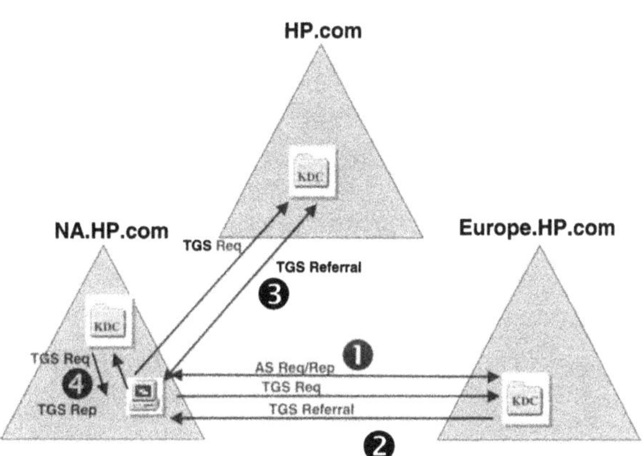

Figure 5.13 *Local logon in a multiple domain environment.*

ticket to the domain closest to NA.hp.com (from a DNS point of view) and with which NA.hp.com has a real (nontransitive) Kerberos trust. In this example, this is hp.com.

- On receiving the referral ticket, Alice locates a KDC of the intermediary domain hp.com and sends a TGS request including the referral ticket to that KDC.
- The KDC in hp.com decrypts the referral ticket using an interdomain key shared between Europe.hp.com and hp.com. The KDC detects that the referral ticket contains a ticket request for a ticket for a workstation in NA. The KDC checks on the domain closest to NA.hp.com from hp.com's point of view and sends Alice a referral ticket to this domain.
- Alice asks a KDC of NA.hp.com for a ticket for the local workstation. Finally, the KDC of NA.hp.com will send Alice a TGS reply with a valid ticket for the workstation.

The amount of interdomain authentication traffic occurring in this scenario should not be overestimated for several reasons:

- The size of Kerberos tickets is relatively small.
- Tickets have a lifetime and are cached.
- The referral traffic does not occur for every resource access.

An interesting side note is to look at what happens if at some point in this exchange, the administrator of the Europe domain decides to disable Alice's account. The answer to this question is pretty straightforward: The KDC of Europe will continue to issue tickets as long as the original TGT is valid. The disabled account will only be detected when Alice tries to get a new TGT.

Network logon process

Let's look at what happens with a local logon process in a multidomain environment. Again, we are using the example of a parent domain and two child domains. In the following network logon example, Alice is logged on to the NA domain (Alice and computer account are defined in the NA domain). Alice wants to access a resource hosted on a server in the Europe domain.

The network logon process can be split into the following four steps (as illustrated in Figure 5.14):

- Steps 1, 2, and 3: TGS exchanges:
  - Before Alice can contact the KDC in realm Europe.hp.com, she must have a valid ticket to talk to the KDC of that domain. Because there is no direct trust between Europe.hp.com and NA.hp.com, Alice must request the ticket via an intermediary domain.
  - Alice first tries to request a ticket for the KDC of the domain closest to the Europe.hp.com domain; this is hp.com. Because there is a direct trust between NA.hp.com and hp.com, Alice can request this ticket to her own KDC. The KDC will return a referral ticket that is encrypted with the interdomain key shared between NA.hp.com and hp.com.
  - Armed with this referral ticket, Alice can send a TGS request to the KDC of the hp.com domain, requesting a ticket for the KDC of the Europe.hp.com domain. Because there is a direct trust between hp.com and Europe.hp.com, the KDC of hp.com can answer this request. The returned referral ticket will be encrypted with the interdomain key shared between hp.com and Europe.hp.com.

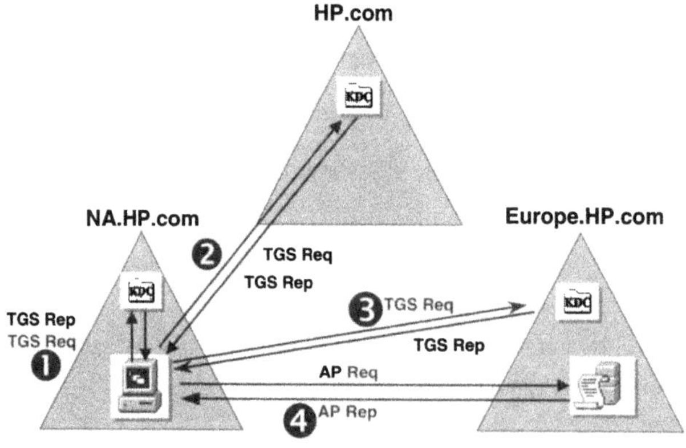

Figure 5.14 *Network logon in a multiple domain environment.*

- With this referral ticket, Alice finally can send a TGS request to a KDC of the Europe.hp.com domain to request a ticket for the target file server.

- Step 4: Application Server Exchange:
  - With the ticket she received from the target server's KDC, Alice can send an authentication request (consisting of the ticket and an authenticator) to the target server.
  - During the last step, the target server will also authenticate back to Alice.

The effect of shortcut trusts on multiple domain logon traffic

A typical scenario where you would create a shortcut trust is a Windows Server 2003 domain tree where a massive amount of authentication traffic occurs between two domains that are logically linked together using a transitive trust (such as the example shown in Figure 5.15). The shortcut trust example illustrated in Figure 5.15 shows how the number of referrals is reduced and how the trust path used during authentication is shortened. Note that the KDC in the user domain can detect the existence of shortcut trust when querying the AD. It has enough intelligence to refer Alice directly to the KDC in the resource domain.

In the example illustrated in Figure 5.14, Alice would go through the following steps to access the resource located in the Europe domain when a shortcut trust is defined between the Europe and the NA domains:

- Step 1: Alice uses her TGT to obtain a ticket from the KDC in the NA domain for the resource server in the Europe domain. The KDC in the NA domain is not the authoritative KDC for the resource server's Europe domain, so the KDC in the NA domain refers Alice

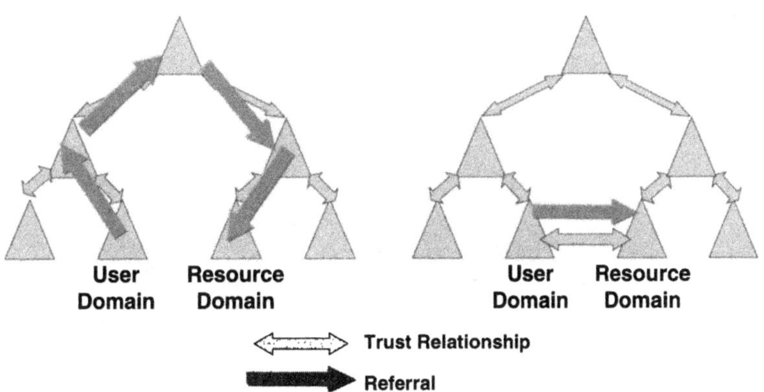

Figure 5.15 *Effect of a shortcut trust on multiple domain logon traffic.*

to the domain closest to the target domain with which the NA domain has a Kerberos trust relationship. This domain is Europe.

- Step 2: The KDC in the Europe domain is the authority for the resource server's Europe domain, so The KDC in the Europe domain can generate a ticket for Alice.
- Step 3: Alice uses the ticket from the KDC in the Europe domain to access the resource server.

Transitive Trusts in Domains Containing Windows 2000, Windows Server 2003, and NT 4.0 DCs Be careful when relying on transitive trust in domains containing both Windows 2000 or Windows Server 2003 and NT 4 DCs. Because NT4 domain controllers do not support Kerberos, transitive trust will only work if a user is authenticated by a Windows 2000 or later DC.

Consider the network logon example illustrated in Figure 5.16. A user defined in NA logged on from a Windows 2000 workstation in NA is accessing a resource in the "Belgium" domain (be.emea.compaq.com). There is a transitive trust between the NA and Europe and between the NA and Be domains. In this scenario, authentication will fail if the DC authenticating the user in the Be domain is an NT4 DC. Because of the NT4 DC, authentication will fall back to NTLM. NTLM does not understand transitive trust and requires a "real" trust.

What does this mean? When the NT4 domain controller receives the authentication request from the user in NA, it cannot create a trust path back to the Be domain because NT4 and NTLM can only deal with "single hop" trusts. NTLM would work in this scenario if an "explicit" trust relationship was defined between the NA and Be domains.

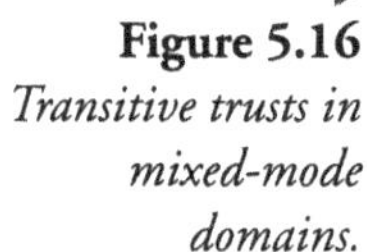

Figure 5.16
Transitive trusts in mixed-mode domains.

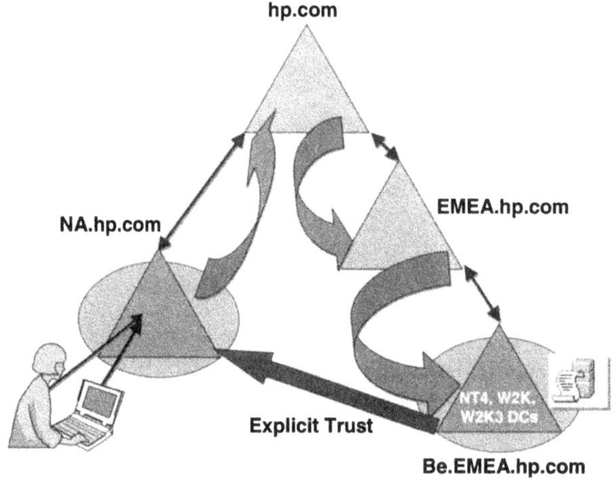

Multiple domain logon process: Under the hood

In this section we will explain some of the concepts behind the multiple domain logon process: referral tickets and the KDC's Authentication Service (AS) and Ticket Granting Service (TGS). To fully understand the multiple domain logon process, we will also introduce a special Kerberos principal—the krbtgt principal.

We will not come back to the concepts of trusteddomain account object (TDO) and interdomain secret. To enable interdomain authentication, every domain that is trusted by another domain is registered in the domain's AD domain naming context as a security principal. These principals are also known as TDOs. The TDO's master key is often referred to as an interdomain secret. TDOs were also explained in Chapter 3.

Interdomain authentication traffic (the referral tickets mentioned before) are secured using the master key and the session key of the TDO principals. Like for any other account, the domain trust account's master key is derived from the account's password. The creation of the TDOs and their master keys can happen automatically during the dcpromo process or manually when an administrator explicitly defines a trust relationship.

To explain the use of the krbtgt account, we must first explain why the Kerberos KDC is made up of two subservices: the Authentication Service (AS) and the Ticket Granting Service (TGS). The services offered by a Kerberos KDC can be split into two service categories; each subservice has a set of different tasks:

- The Authentication Service authenticates accounts defined in the domain where the AS is running and issues TGTs for these accounts.
- The Ticket Granting Service issues service tickets for resources defined in the domain where the TGS is running.

The AS and TGS share a secret that is derived from the password of the krbtgt principal, which is the security principal used by the KDC. Its master key will be used to encrypt the TGTs that are issued by the KDC. The krbtgt account is created automatically when a Windows 2000 or Windows Server 2003 domain is created. It cannot be deleted and renamed. Like for any other account, its password is changed regularly. In the Windows 2000 and Windows Server 2003 Users and Computers snap-in, this account is always shown as disabled.

Now that we have explained the TDO, interdomain secret, and krbtgt concepts, let's look once more at how the multiple domain logon process works. A basic rule in Kerberos is that to access a resource a user needs a

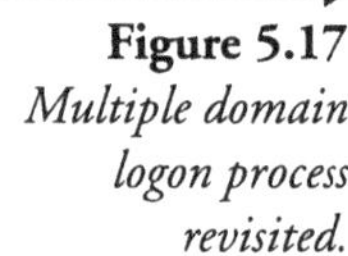

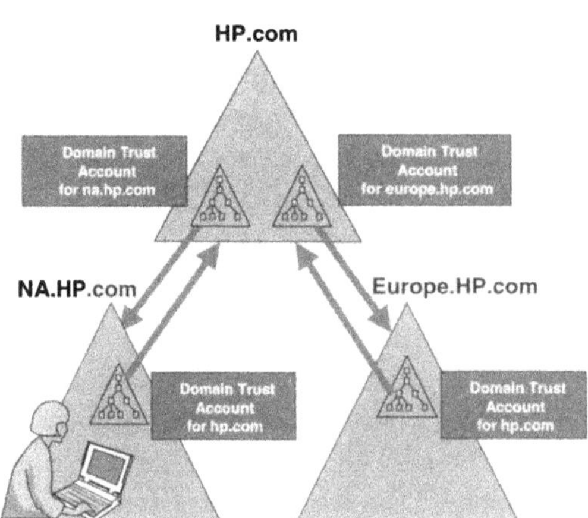

Figure 5.17 *Multiple domain logon process revisited.*

ticket. How can Alice get a ticket for a resource contained in a domain different from Alice's definition domain? Let's once more take the example of Alice defined and logged on in domain na.hp.com, who decides to access a resource in europe.hp.com (as illustrated in Figure 5.17).

In this scenario, the KDC of na.hp.com would issue a referral ticket to Alice to access hp.com. What exactly is a referral ticket? A referral ticket is a TGT that Alice can use in domain hp.com to get a ticket for the resource in that domain. The KDC of na.hp.com can issue such a TGT because hp.com is a security principal [it has a TDO, Trusted Domain Object, account (see Chapter 3)] in his or her domain. How can the KDC of hp.com trust a TGT that was issued not by itself, but by the KDC of na.hp.com? The KDC of hp.com will decrypt the TGT with the interdomain secret of its TDO account in na.hp.com to retrieve the session key—it will then use this session key to validate the associated Kerberos authenticator. If the authenticator is valid, the KDC will consider the TGT trustworthy. The same things will happen when hp.com issues a referral ticket for Alice to authenticate to a domain controller in europe.hp.com.

The referral process we just explained relies heavily on the AD and more particularly on the global catalog (GC). First, it uses the GC to find out, given the SPN, in which domain the resource is located, and thus which domain controller can issue a ticket to access the resource. Then it uses the AD to find out the domain closest to the target domain to which Alice should be referred.

Figure 5.18 explains the process outlined in the previous sections a bit more in detail and using UNIX Kerberos terminology: It illustrates an inter-realm (interdomain) Kerberos authentication exchange between the

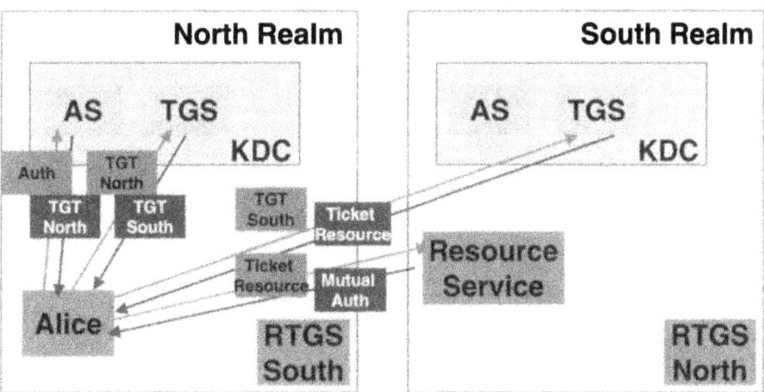

Figure 5.18 *Multiple domain logon process: under the hood.*

North and the South realms. In the example of Figure 5.18, Alice wants to access a resource service in the North realm. In the UNIX Kerberos terminology, they call the Windows TDO accounts from the previous example Remote Ticket Granting Service (RTGS) accounts: Figure 5.18 shows that there is an RTGS account for North in the South realm and vice versa.

5.3.3 Multiple forest logon process

In Windows Server 2003, Microsoft has added additional information in the TDO account objects to enable interforest authentication traffic. Let's look at an example that shows how Windows Server 2003 uses the extra information stored in the TDO to route Kerberos authentication requests during a cross-forest resource access.

In the example (illustrated in Figure 5.19), a user that is logged on to the emea.compaq.com domain (the user and machine accounts are defined in emea.compaq.com) wants to access a resource located on a server in the us.hp.com domain. Both forests are at functionality level 2, and a bidirectional forest trust relationship has been set up between them. From a Kerberos point of view, the user is already logged on to the emea.compaq.com domain and has a valid TGT. The remote resource is identified using an SPN of the following format: <servicename>/us.hp.com.

In this example the authentication requests will be routed as follows:

1. The user's machine contacts the local DC to request a Kerberos service ticket for the resource in the us.hp.com domain. The DC in emea.compaq.com cannot find an entry for the remote service in its local domain database and asks a GC server in the emea.compaq.com for help. The GC suspects (based on the DNS suffix) that the service is located in the hp.com forest, and it sends

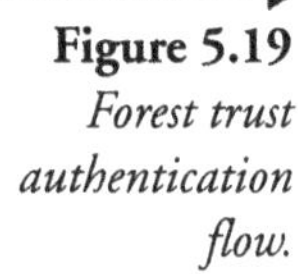

Figure 5.19 *Forest trust authentication flow.*

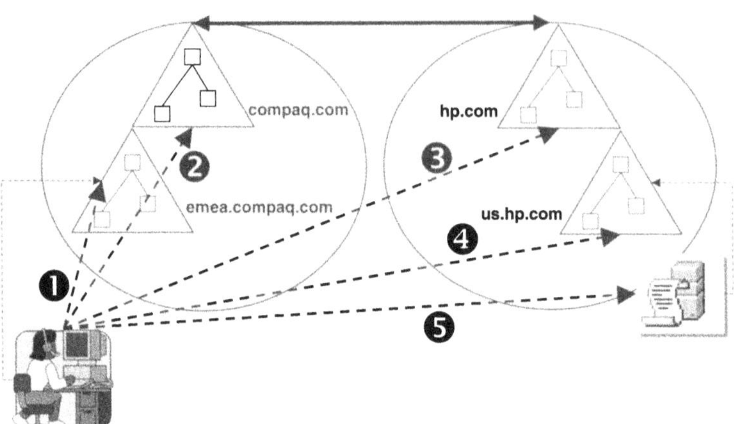

this routing hint to the DC and tells the DC to refer the user to a DC in the compaq.com root domain.

2. The user's machine contacts a DC in the root domain of the compaq.com forest. This DC refers the user to a DC in the root domain of the hp.com forest.
3. The user's machine contacts a DC in the root domain of the hp.com forest. The DC of the hp.com forest double-checks with the local GC whether the service is in his or her forest. After validation it refers the user to a DC in the us.hp.com domain.
4. The user's machine contacts a DC in the us.hp.com domain. This DC can issue a service ticket to the user for the resource in the us.hp.com domain.
5. The user uses the service ticket to authenticate to the resource server in the us.hp.com domain.

5.4 Advanced Kerberos topics

In this section we will focus on some advanced Kerberos topics: delegation of authentication, the link between authentication and authorization, the content of Kerberos tickets and authenticators, the details behind the smart card logon process, Kerberos transport protocol, and port usage.

5.4.1 Delegation of authentication

Delegation refers to the facility for a service to impersonate an authenticated client in order to relieve the user of the additional burden of authenticating to multiple services. To the latter services it will look as if they are communicating directly with the user, whereas in reality another service will sit between them and the user.

A classical example of where delegation is a very useful feature is when a user asks a print server to print a file that is located on another server. In today's Internet world there are many more examples. Basically, any Web-based multitier application can take advantage of delegation. Examples are Web sites launching user queries against a database located on some back-end server, or a user accessing his or her mailbox from a Web interface [a good example is Microsoft's Outlook Web Access (OWA)]. In the future, when Web services become widespread, the need for authentication delegation support will only become bigger. Web services are rooted on highly distributed architectures that can make data and other resources available to a wide range of users. Web services are typically accessed using open Internet protocols (such as HTTP and SMTP). In such environments it would not be a very smart idea to host the data on the Web servers. Web services require multitier application designs and the ability to reuse the user identity end-to-end.

The ability to refer to a user's identity end-to-end in a multitier application scenario is one of the key advantages of the Kerberos delegation support. It means that administrators can enforce authorization settings at the different tiers using a single user identity. This not only simplifies management but also facilitates user tracking and auditing on the different levels of a multitier application. Finally, because of its ability to transparently authenticate a user on multiple tiers, delegation provides SSO support.

Kerberos' ability to support delegation is a consequence of its unique ticketing mechanism. When sending a ticket to a server, the Kerberos client can add additional information to it so the server can reuse it to request other tickets on the user's behalf to the Kerberos KDC.

Delegation: Behind the scenes

The Kerberos delegation uses specific flags that can be set in a Kerberos ticket. The Kerberos standard (RFC 1510) defines four types of flags, shown in Table 5.2. Windows 2000 and Windows Server 2003 currently only support the "forwardable" and "forwarded" flags. Notice in Table 5.2 that "forwardable" is a much more powerful concept than "proxiable": A forwardable ticket is a TGT, a proxiable ticket is a plain ticket; a ticket can be used for one single application, and a TGT can be used for multiple applications.

Table 5.2 *Kerberos Ticket Delegation Flags*

Flag	Meaning
Proxiable	Tells the TGS that a new service ticket with a different network address may be issued based on this ticket
Proxy	Indicates that the ticket is a proxy ticket
Forwardable	Tells the TGS that a new TGT with a different network address may be issued based on this TGT
Forwarded	Indicates that this ticket has been forwarded or was issued based on an authentication using a forwarded TGT

What's missing in Windows 2000 Kerberos delegation?

One of the reasons why Kerberos delegation in Windows 2000 is only used rarely is because few people really know and understand it. Another reason is that the Windows 2000 implementation lacks some important security-related configuration options.

In Windows 2000, when a computer is "trusted for delegation," it can impersonate a user to any other service on any other computer in the Windows 2000 domain. In other words, when a Windows 2000 administrator trusts a computer for delegation, the delegation is "complete"; there are no configuration options to make the delegation more granular.

Another obstacle is that Kerberos delegation in a Windows 2000 Web scenario only works if the user has authenticated to the Web server using Kerberos or Basic authentication. There is no way to use delegation when you prefer to use the more secure digest authentication protocol to authenticate your users to the Web server. We also have to keep in mind that the use of Kerberos between a browser and a Web server is only possible when the browser supports Kerberos and the Kerberos KDC is accessible from the browser. The latter is clearly a problem in Internet scenarios: Very few companies are willing to expose their KDC to Internet users. Also, on the Internet, not every user has a Kerberos-enabled Web browser. So far, only Microsoft's Internet Explorer (from version 5.0 on) is Kerberos-enabled.

In Windows Server 2003, Microsoft embedded a set of Kerberos protocol extensions to remedy these problems. These extensions are referred to as the "Service-for-User" (S4U) Kerberos extensions. There are two new extensions: the Service-for-User-to-Proxy extension (S4U2Proxy) and the Service-for-User-to-Self extension (S4U2Self). Microsoft is planning to submit the specifications of both Kerberos extensions to the IETF some time in the near future.

The new Kerberos extensions are only available if your Windows Server 2003 domain is in Functionality Level 2 (which is the native Windows Server 2003 functionality level).

The S4U2Proxy Kerberos extension

The way that delegation works in Windows 2000 is by letting a Kerberos client forward a user's TGT to a service. In Kerberos-speak, a TGT is a very powerful security token: It is a digital piece of evidence that proves that a user's identity has been validated by the Kerberos KDC. A service can use a TGT to get many other service tickets on the user's behalf. This is why in Windows 2000 delegation is considered "complete." What makes the possessor of a TGT even more powerful is the fact that in Windows 2000 Microsoft uses the TGT to transport user-related authorization data [embedded in the Privilege Attribute Certificate (PAC) field].

The S4U2Proxy Kerberos Extension allows a service to reuse a user's "service ticket" to request a new service ticket to the KDC. In other words, there is no more need to forward a user's TGT to the service. The simple fact that the service can present a user's ticket to a KDC is enough to prove a user's identity. The Kerberos exchanges occurring in a typical S4U2Proxy scenario are illustrated in Figure 5.20.

In Figure 5.20 steps 1 through 3 illustrate the Kerberos exchanges related to a user authenticating to server 1.

- Step 1: The user requests a service ticket for server 1 to the KDC (Kerberos TGS_REQ message).
- Step 2: The KDC returns a service ticket for server 1 to the user (Kerberos TGS_REP message).
- Step 3: The user presents the service ticket for server 1 to server 1 (Kerberos AP_REQ message).
- Server 1 then needs to access a resource on server 2 on the user's behalf. Server 1 is running Windows Server 2003 and thus supports the S4U2Proxy extension.
- Step 4: The S4U2Proxy extension on server 1 requests a service ticket for server 2 to the KDC on the user's behalf. To prove the user's identity to the KDC, server 1 presents the user's service ticket for server 1 (Kerberos TGS_REQ message).

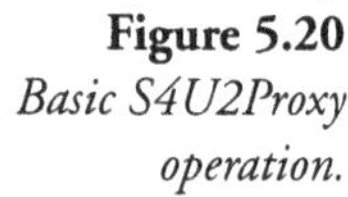

Figure 5.20
Basic S4U2Proxy operation.

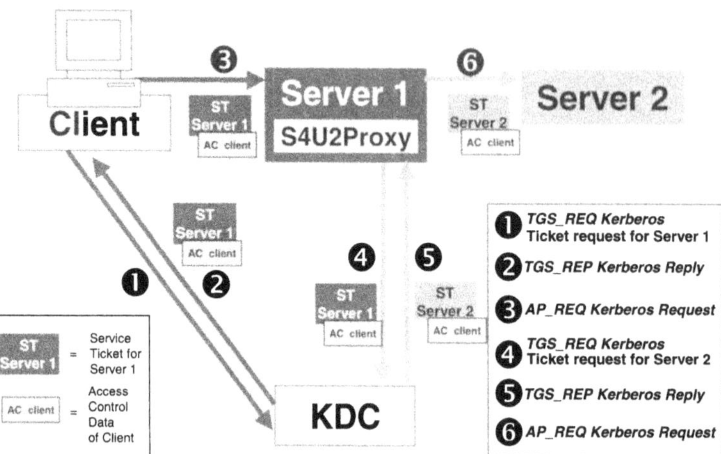

- Step 5: The KDC returns a service ticket for server 2 to server 1. Even though this new ticket is passed to server 1, it contains the user's authorization data (Kerberos TGS_REP message).
- Step 6: Server 1 presents the service ticket for server 2 to server 2 (Kerberos AP_REQ message).

If a service could do this with any user ticket it receives, the S4U2Proxy feature would create a security hole: The service would be allowed to access any other service on the user's behalf. That is why Microsoft has added support for fine-grain delegation configuration. In Windows Server 2003 an administrator can configure which services a machine or service is allowed to access on a user's behalf. How to set this constrained delegation up is explained in the next section.

Configuring constrained delegation

When you open the properties of a machine or a service account in Windows Server 2003 (from the Users and Computers MMC snap-in), you will notice the new "Delegation" tab. This tab is not available in the properties of a plain user account. It only shows up if the account has an associated SPN.

From the Delegation tab you can configure delegation in three different ways (as illustrated in Figure 5.21):

- *Disallowed:* This is done by checking the "Do not trust this computer for delegation" option.
- *Allowed for all services:* This can be done by checking the "Trust this computer for delegation to any service (Kerberos only)" option. This

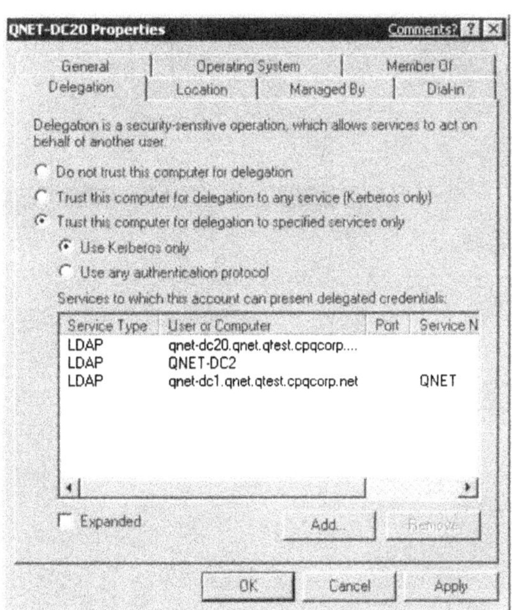

Figure 5.21 *Configuring delegation in Windows Server 2003.*

is the default option and refers to delegation the way it was available in Windows 2000.

- *Only allowed for a limited set of services:* This can be done by checking the "Trust this computer for delegation to specified services only" option. This is the new "constrained" delegation option coming with Windows Server 2003.

When selecting the latter option (constrained delegation), you can select the SPNs of the services for which the delegation is allowed. You can do so using the "Add..." push button. Pushing this button will bring up the "Add Services" dialog box. Initially, the available services list in this dialog box appears empty. To fill the list, press the "User or Computers..." push button. The latter will bring up the Active Directory object picker dialog box, which will allow you to select the appropriate SPNs. You can only select the SPNs of machines that are a member of the machine's domain.

The SPNs for which delegation is allowed are stored in a new AD account object attribute called "msDS-AllowedToDelegateTo." You can examine the content of this multivalued attribute using the Support Tools "AdsiEdit" tool (as illustrated in Figure 5.22). When the Kerberos authentication service receives a delegation request for a ticket for a particular service, it compares the SPNs listed in the Kerberos ticket request with the ones listed in the computer or service account's "msDS-AllowedToDele-

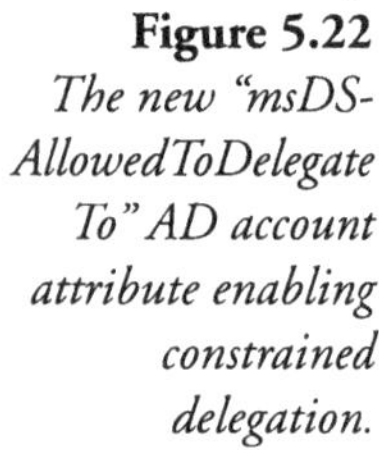

Figure 5.22
The new "msDS-AllowedToDelegateTo" AD account attribute enabling constrained delegation.

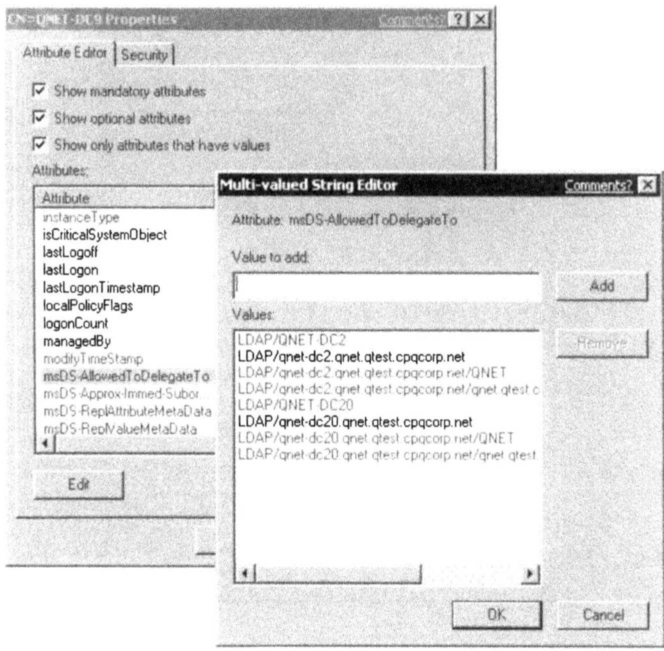

gateTo" attribute. If there are no matches, the delegation request is denied. Remember that an account's SPNs are stored in the "servicePrincipalName" attribute.

In the scenario illustrated in Figure 5.20, you would set up constrained delegation in the account properties of server 1. You would trust server 1 for delegation to the SPN of server 2.

The S4U2Self Kerberos extension

An important problem when using Kerberos delegation in a Web-based Windows 2000 environment is that it can only be used when the client uses Kerberos or Basic authentication to authenticate to the Web server. The Web server (IIS 6.0) that ships with Windows Server 2003 comes with many other interesting authentication options, such as MS Passport–based, Digest-based, or certificate-based authentication. In Windows Server 2003 you can use the latter authentication options together with Kerberos delegation thanks to the combination of the S4U2Proxy (explained earlier) and another new Windows Server 2003 Kerberos extension called Service-for-User-to-Self (S4U2Self).

The service provided by the S4U2Self extension provides a service known as "protocol transition." It allows for the combination of any of the

IIS authentication protocols listed earlier on the IIS front end with the Kerberos authentication protocol on the IIS back end. In other words, the Web server can use Kerberos authentication and delegation with a user's identity to a back-end server independently of how the user authenticated to the Web server. Behind this new extension there is nothing else than the ability for an application or service to request to the Kerberos KDC a new service ticket on behalf of a user account defined in the domain or the forest. If this appears to you as a dangerous password-less logon process, keep in mind that before an application or service is allowed to request a service ticket on a user's behalf, it must already have authenticated the user. Also, the application or service itself must hold a valid Kerberos TGT. The basic operation of the S4U2Self Kerberos extension is illustrated in Figure 5.23.

In Figure 5.23, step 1 illustrates the user authenticating to server 1. When server 1 is an IIS6.0 Web server, he or she can do so using Digest-based, Basic-based, MS Passport–based, or client certificate–based authentication. In steps 2 through 3 server 1 requests a Kerberos ticket for server 1 on the user's behalf.

- Step 2: The S4U2Proxy extension on server 1 requests a service ticket for server 1 to the KDC on the user's behalf (Kerberos TGS_REQ message).
- Step 3: The KDC returns a service ticket for server 1 to server 1. Even though this new ticket is passed to server 1, it contains the user's authorization data (Kerberos TGS_REP message).

This clearly illustrates the authentication "transition": A user who was initially authenticated to server 1 using another authentication protocol is

Figure 5.23
Basic S4U2Self operation.

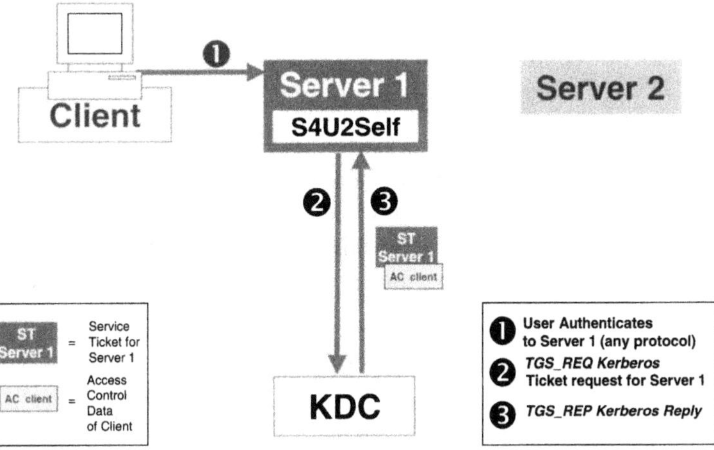

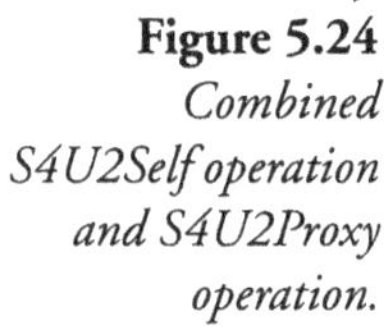

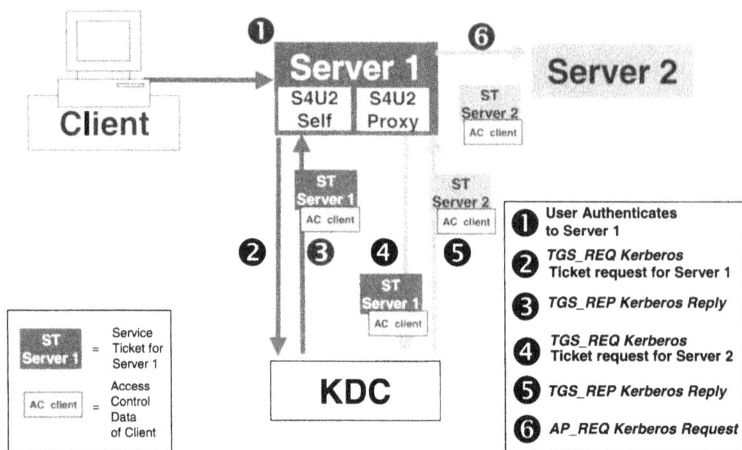

Figure 5.24 *Combined S4U2Self operation and S4U2Proxy operation.*

transparently authenticated to server 1 using the Kerberos protocol. Once the user has authenticated using Kerberos to server 1 and the KDC has issued a service ticket for server 1, server 1 (in fact, the S4U2Proxy extension) can reuse this ticket to request a ticket for server 2 on the user's behalf. This combined S4U2Self and S4U2Proxy operation is shown in Figure 5.24.

Configuring protocol transition

Configuring protocol transition is relatively easy. So far I did not explain the "Use Kerberos only" and "Use any authentication protocol" configuration options (as illustrated in Figure 5.21). These are exactly the options that enable or disable the S4U2Self Kerberos extension. If you select "Use any authentication protocol," protocol transition will be possible; if you select the other one, it will not.

In order for protocol transition to function correctly, the following two conditions should also be met. They are both related to the service account of the service or application that is requesting a new ticket on the user's behalf.

1. In order for the service to obtain an impersonation token, its service account should have the "act as part of the operating system" privilege. If this is not the case, the service will only get an identification token.

2. In order to get the user's authorization data into the newly constructed user ticket, the service account also needs permission to enumerate the user's group memberships. This can be done by

adding the service account to the ACL of the "TokenGroupsGlobalAndUniversal" user object attribute or by adding the service account to the "Pre-Windows 2000 Compatible Access" group.

In the scenario illustrated in Figures 5.23 and 5.24, you would set up protocol transition in the account properties of server 1. If in this scenario the service impersonating the user is the IIS Web service, you would give the extra permissions and privileges mentioned earlier to the IIS Web service account.

A sample scenario

You can test the new Kerberos services in a small lab environment. Figure 5.25 shows the test scenario that I used. This scenario consists of a simple Web application that queries an SQL Server database on the back end. The database query is defined in a COM+ application that is running on the Web server. The query is called from an ASP page. The Web server and SQL server are members of the same domain. The client machine need not necessarily be a domain member.

The goal of this test scenario from an authentication point of view is to let the user use any authentication protocol (with the exception of Kerberos) to authenticate to the Web server. On the back end, to authenticate to the COM+ application and the SQL Server database, we would like to use Kerberos and Kerberos delegation. This can only be set up if the new Kerberos services (S4U2Proxy and S4U2Self) are available on the Web server. Table 5.3 summarizes the software requirements and configuration options you need to keep in mind when setting this up.

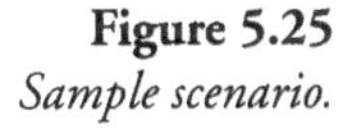

Figure 5.25
Sample scenario.

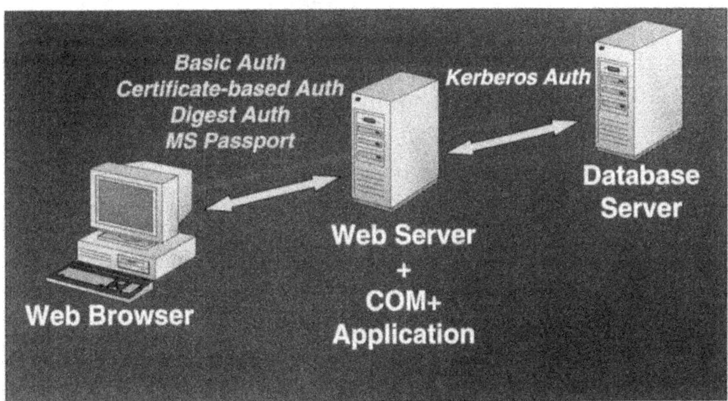

Table 5.3 *Configuration of Different Components*

Component	Software Requirements and/or Configuration Settings
Web Browser	Support for Basic authentication, Digest authentication, certificate-based authentication (SSL), or MS Passport–based authentication. The user account is a member of the domain.
Web Server	Delegation settings for computer account: ■ Trust this computer for delegation to specified services only. ■ Use any authentication protocol. ■ Add the SQL service of the database server's Service Principal Name (SPN) (A). ■ Web application is set to support Basic authentication, Digest authentication, certificate-based authentication (SSL), or MS Passport–based authentication. ■ The user has the appropriate access permissions to the Web site. ■ The Web server is a member of the domain. ■ Web server is running Windows Server 2003.
COM+ Application	The impersonation level of COM+ application must be set to "delegate." The user has the appropriate access permission to the COM+ dll.
Database Server	The SQL Server is configured to support Windows Integrated authentication. The SQL Server service has a registered SPN that is the one referred to in the Web server's computer account delegation settings [see (A) above]. The user has the appropriate access permissions to the database. The database server is a member of the domain. The database server is running Windows 2000 or Windows Server 2003 and SQL Server 2000.

5.4.2 From authentication to authorization

In this section we will explain the link between Windows Server 2003 authentication and authorization in the context of a Kerberos authentication exchange. Figure 5.26 illustrates the link between these two core operating system security services.

Next we will explain how we get from the Kerberos ticket (the basic entity used for authentication) to the access token (the basic entity used for authorization). An important component in this process is the Kerberos Privilege Attribute Certificate (PAC). Microsoft extended the base Kerberos protocol to include authorization data (e.g., global group memberships). A Windows Server 2003 ticket and TGT both contain a PAC.

Let us start off with a normal Kerberos authentication sequence. We are once more dealing with three entities: a user (Alice), a resource server, and a

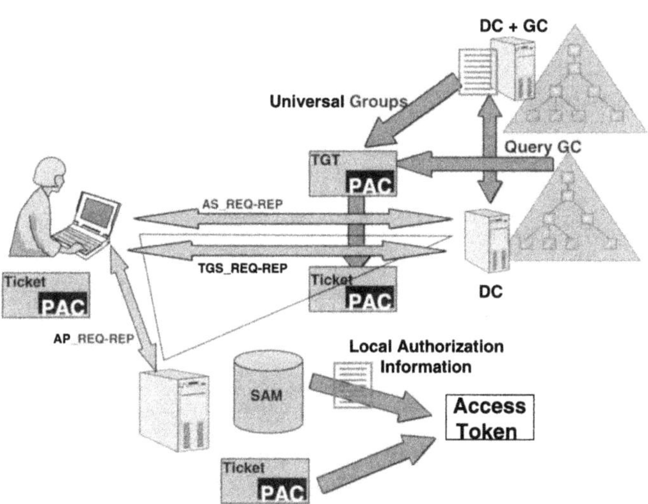

Figure 5.26 *From Windows Server 2003 authentication to authorization.*

Kerberos KDC. Once Alice's workstation has located a domain controller, it will request a TGT. The KDC will generate the PAC, embed the authorization data listed next, put the PAC into a TGT, and send the TGT to Alice.

- Alice's global group memberships and domain local group memberships: These are available from the KDC's local Active Directory (Domain NC).
- Alice's universal group memberships: These are available:
  - In the global catalog. If the KDC server himself or herself does not host a global catalog, the KDC service will need to query a global catalog on another domain controller.
  - In the domain naming context of Alice's logon domain. This is only true if the site of Alice's authenticating DC has universal group caching enabled (see following side note). The GC-less logon process or universal group caching is a new Windows Server 2003 feature that caches a user's universal group membership in the msDs-Cached-Membership attribute of a user account. Universal group memberships are cached in this attribute at the first user logon instance and are by default refreshed every 8 hours.
- The user rights assigned to Alice or any of her groups (universal, global, and domain local). These are available from the domain controller's LSA database.

Table 5.4 gives an overview of which group memberships are available where.

Table 5.4 *Windows Server 2003 Groups: Group Membership and Definition Storage Locations*

Group Type	Group: Available Where?	Group Membership: Available Where?
Universal group	AD: Global catalog	AD: Global catalog AD: Domain NC: only if Universal Group Caching (GC-less logon) is enabled.
Global group	AD: Global catalog	AD: Domain NC
Domain local group	AD: Domain NC	AD: Domain NC
Local group	Local machine: SAM	Local machine: SAM

Alice then decides she wants to access a resource hosted on a member server. Alice sends a request for a ticket to the KDC. This ticket will contain the same PAC as the one contained in the TGT. The ticket is sent back to Alice.

Alice authenticates to the resource server using the ticket. The LSA on the resource server will generate Alice's access token (for use in subsequent authorization decisions). In the access token the LSA will embed:

- Alice's authorization data found in the ticket's PAC (her universal, global, and domain local group memberships and user rights, assigned to her or any of the groups of which she is a member)
- Alice's authorization data found in the local security database (SAM): These are the local group memberships of Alice, the local group memberships of the groups (universal, global, or domain local) of which Alice is a member, and the user rights of Alice and Alice's groups.

To look at the contents of your access token, use the whoami tool (with the /all switch) that comes with the Windows Server 2003 code.

Key things to remember from this section are the following:

- The PAC data are added to a ticket on the KDC level and are inherited between subsequent TGT and ticket requests and renewals. The PAC data are not refreshed at ticket-request time. This means that if a user's group memberships change during its logon session, he or she will have to log off-log on (just as in NT4), wait for an automatic TGT renewal to occur, or purge the Kerberos ticket cache (using the klist or kerbtray utilities explained next). Note that even though

Enabling a GC-Less Logon Process A GC-less logon or universal group caching is a new Windows Server 2003 feature that enables Windows Server 2003 domain controllers to cache a user's universal group memberships in the msDS-Cached-Membership attribute of a user account. It is enabled in the NTDS settings properties of a site object—as illustrated in Figure 5.27.

Windows 2000 requires the availability of a GC server to retrieve a user's universal group membership when logging on to a domain. In Windows 2000 Microsoft provides a workaround for this requirement by enabling DCs to ignore GC failures, when a GC could not be contacted to find out about a user's universal group memberships. This workaround was based on a registry key called IgnoreGCFailures, which had to be added to the HKEY_LOCAL_MACHINE\System\CurrentControlSet\Control\Lsa registry folder of every DC. This hack also took away the possibility to use universal groups in a Window 2000 forest. (This is documented in Microsoft Knowledge Base article Q241789.)

The new Windows Server 2003 feature does not fully take away the need to put a GC in every site—or at least to have one reachable GC for every site. Although GCs are not needed anymore to find out about a user's universal group memberships, you still need them to resolve UPN names when users are logging on using a UPN.*

* This UPN resolution process will only occur when using alternate UPN suffixes. These are suffixes that are different from the standard suffixes as they occur in the Windows DNS domain names.

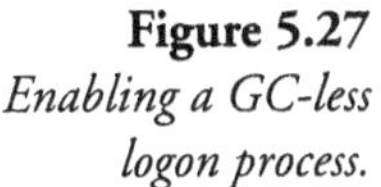

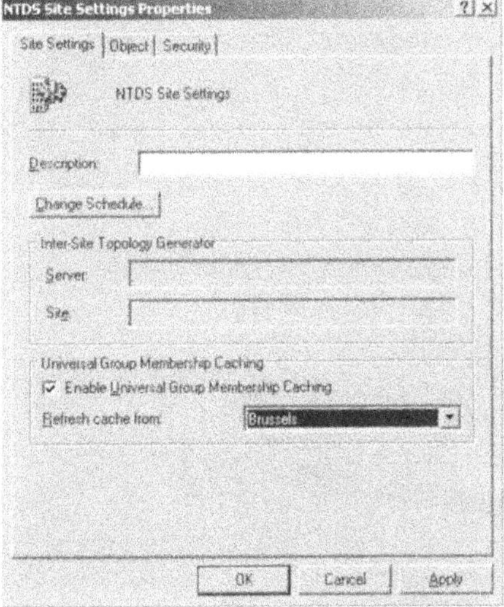

Figure 5.27 *Enabling a GC-less logon process.*

Windows does not refresh the authorization data it will check whether the account hasn't been disabled (see also the sidenote on "Kerberos and disabled accounts").

Kerberos and Disabled Accounts The following example illustrates how the fact that Kerberos TGTs are reusable as long as they are valid, together with the action of disabling a Windows account can lead to security holes in a Windows multi-domain environment. The AD environment illustrated in Figure 5.28 consists of a single forest with a single domain tree. A user's Windows account and machine account are defined in domain emea, a file server is part of the asiapac domain. When the user logs on to emea, he or she will receive a TGT for the emea domain. When the user accesses the file server in asiapac he or she will in addition get a TGT for the asiapac domain (see also Section 5.3.2). When the administrator disables the user account in emea, he or she won't be able to get any more tickets for resources in emea. The user will however still be able to get new tickets for resources in the asiapac domain—this will be possible as long as the user's TGT for asiapac remains valid. The reason for this is that the DCs in the asiapac domain don't check the user's account status when they issue tickets.

- Unless you have enabled the GC-less logon process (see the previous side note), the presence of at least one domain controller hosting a global catalog per domain tree is mandatory to log on a normal user. An exception to this rule is accounts that are member of the Administrators or Domain Administrators groups: They can log on even when a global catalog server is not available.

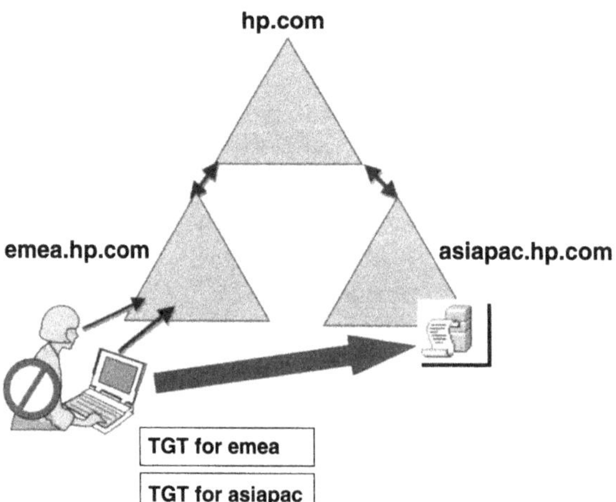

Figure 5.28 *Kerberos and disabled accounts: Example*

5.4.3 Analyzing the Kerberos ticket and authenticator

This section provides some inside information on the Kerberos ticket and authenticator. The concepts of a ticket and an authenticator and the relationship between the two are illustrated in Figure 5.29.

Remember that the primary purpose of a ticket is to securely transport the session key to be used for authentication between two entities. A ticket can only be decrypted by a KDC and the destination resource server. This way the client cannot decrypt and change its own authorization data (the information contained in the PAC). An authenticator is the Kerberos object that is providing the actual authentication. An authenticator can be checked by anyone possessing the corresponding session key. A detailed overview of the content of both the ticket and the authenticator is given in the following sections.

Ticket content

Table 5.5 shows the ticket fields, their meaning, and whether they are sent in encrypted format across the network.

Kerberos encryption types

Windows Server 2003 Kerberos supports the following cryptographic algorithms: RC4-HMAC, DES-CBC-CRC, and DES-CBC-MD5. The default encryption algorithm is "RC4-HMAC"—it was defined in an Internet draft called draft-brezak-win2k-krb-rc4-hmac-05.txt.

The default Kerberos encryption type can be changed using the "Use DES encryption types for this account" AD account property. The property can be set in the account options, which are available from the account tab in the account properties. Enabling this property is required when you're looking after UNIX and Windows Kerberos interoperability. DES encryption is the default in most UNIX Kerberos implementations.

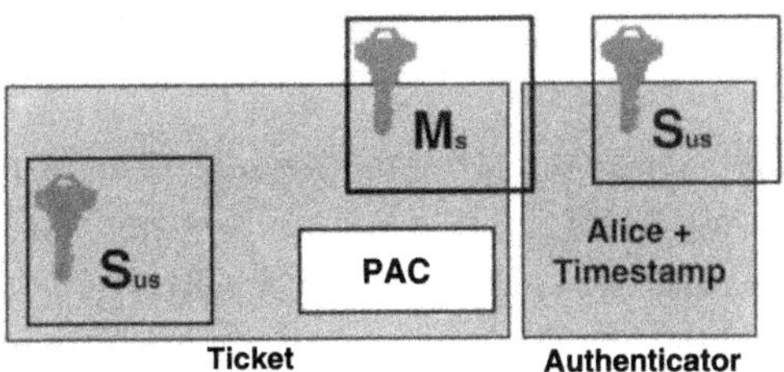

Figure 5.29 *Relationship between Kerberos ticket and authenticator.*

Table 5.5 *Kerberos Ticket Content*

Encrypted?	Name	Meaning
	Tkt-vno	Version number of the ticket format.
	Realm	Name of the realm (domain) that issued the ticket.
	Sname	Name of the server (Principal name).
✓	Flags	Ticket options. These are explained in more detail later in the chapter.
✓	Key	Session key.
✓	Crealm	Name of the client's realm (domain).
✓	Cname	Client's name (Principal name).
✓	Transited	Lists the Kerberos realms that took part in authenticating the client to whom the ticket was issued.
✓	Authtime	Time of initial authentication by the client. The KDC places a timestamp in this field when it issues a TGT. When it issues tickets based on a TGT, the KDC copies the authtime of the TGT to the authtime of the ticket.
✓	Starttime	(Optional) Time after which the ticket is valid.
✓	Endtime	Ticket's expiration time.
✓	Renew-till	(Optional) Time period during which the ticket is automatically renewed without the client having to provide his or her master key.
✓	Caddr	(Optional) One or more addresses from which the ticket can be used. If omitted, the ticket can be used from any address.
✓	Authorization data	(Optional) Privilege attributes for the client. Microsoft calls this part the Privilege Attribute Certificate (PAC).

There are two reasons why Microsoft did not use DES as the default algorithm:

- *Ease of upgrading from NT4 to Windows 2000 or Windows Server 2003.* The key used for RC4-HMAC can also be used with the Windows NT 4 Password Hash.
- *Export law restrictions.* In the early stages of the Windows 2000 development, 56-bit DES could not be exported outside of the United States. Because MS wanted to use the same Kerberos encryption technology in both the domestic and export versions of the product, they chose the 128-bit RC4-HMAC alternative. RC4-HMAC was already exportable at that point in time.

Table 5.6 *Kerberos Encryption Types: Key Lengths in Bits*

Algorithm	Authentication	Signing	Confidentiality Protection
RC4-HMAC	128	128	128 (56)
DES-CBC-CRC	56	56	56
DES-CBC-MD5	56	56	56

The algorithm used for a Kerberos ticket can be checked using the "klist" or "kerbtray" resource kit utilities. These utilities are explained later in this chapter.

Table 5.6 shows the algorithms and their supported key lengths. When the Windows 2000 "Strong encryption fix" has been installed, RC4-HMAC can use 128-bit keys for bulk encryption. This is the default in Windows Server 2003. A Windows domain can contain a mix of clients with and without the fix installed. Windows Kerberos will automatically choose the strongest available encryption algorithm.

The Privilege Attribute Certificate

The Privilege Attribute Certificate (PAC) enables the Kerberos protocol to transport authorization data—in the Windows case these data are user group memberships and user rights. We already explained part of the reason for existence of the PAC in the section on "From authentication to authorization."

Shortly after the release of Windows 2000, Microsoft received some negative press attention because of the proprietary way they used the PAC field in a Kerberos ticket. This forced Microsoft to release the PAC specifications. They can be downloaded from http://www.microsoft.com/downloads/details.aspx?displaylang=en&familyid=BF61D972-5086-49FB-A79C-53A5FD27A092. This document can be used only for informational purposes; it explicitly forbids the creation of software that implements the PAC as described in the specifications. A summary of the specifications can be found at http://msdn.microsoft.com/library/default.asp?url=/library/en-us/dnkerb/html/MSDN_PAC.asp. Microsoft also submitted their PAC definition as an Internet Draft to the IETF—it's called draft-brezak-win2K-krb-authz-01.txt.

Most non-Microsoft Kerberos implementations ignore the PAC field and its content. Interoperability issues may arise though if a user is a member of a large amount of groups. In that case, the PAC size may become so big that it cannot be transported in a single UDP packet anymore. If this happens, a Windows KDC will request the client to switch to TCP, which cannot be done by some of the early Kerberos implementations (see also Section 5.5.3).

An important PAC security detail is that its content is digitally signed. By signing the authorization data, a hacker cannot make modifications to the data without being detected. This was possible in NTLM version 1: Authorization data for part of NTLM version 1 messages were not protected. Microsoft corrected this error in NTLM version 2, which is included in Windows 2000, XP, Windows Server 2003, and all the NT4 Service Packs from SP4 onward (see also Chapter 4 for more information).

The Kerberos PAC content is signed twice:

- Once with the master key of the KDC (this is the master key linked to the krbtgt account). This signature prevents malicious server-side services from changing authorization data. The LSA on the server side will require a validation of the signature for every ticket coming from a service that is not running using the local system account. To validate the signature, the server will need to set up a secure channel with the KDC that signed the authorization data. This extra validation step might remind you of NTLM and its pass-through authentication. This time, however, the pass-through is not used for validation of a response but for validation of a digital signature.
- Once with the master key of the destination service's service account (the destination service is the one responsible for the resource the user wants to access). This is the same key as the one used to encrypt the ticket content. This signature prevents a user from modifying the PAC content and adding its own authorization data.

The Kerberos ticket has a fixed size, which indirectly also limits the PAC size. If a user is a member of a large amount of groups, this size may be exceeded and, as a consequence, authentication and group policy processing may fail. Microsoft allows you to adjust the maximum size of a Kerberos ticket using the MaxTokenSize registry parameter. This parameter is a REG_DWORD value and is contained in the HKEY_LOCAL_MACHINE\System\CurrentControlSet\Control\Lsa\Kerberos registry container. The value should be adjusted on all Windows machines users are logging from to a domain to using Kerberos.

In Windows 2000, the default MaxTokenSize value is 8,000 bytes. In Windows 2000 Service Pack 2 (SP2) and Microsoft Windows Server 2003, the default value is 12,000 bytes.

The MaxTokenSize parameter is documented in Microsoft Knowledge Base article Q327825.

In order to reduce the PAC size, Microsoft implemented a new method to store authorization data in the PAC in Windows 2000 Service Pack 4 (SP4) and later, and in Windows Server 2003. This solution is also available as a hotfix for pre-Windows 2000 SP4 machines (see also Q327825). This new PAC authorization data storage method can be summarized as follows:

- If the global and universal groups a user belongs to are local to the domain the user is in, then only the RID (relative identifier) is stored.
- If the groups are local groups or are from other domains, the entire SID is stored.

This means for example that instead of storing an "S-1-5-21-1275210071-789336058-1957994488-3140" value (the SID), you would only store the "3140" value (the RID) in the PAC. Microsoft provides a special process on the client and server side to explode the RIDs back to the SID format during the Windows authorization process.

Even on platforms where this new PAC authorization data storage method is available, it may be required that the maxtokensize registry value be adjusted.

Kerberos preauthentication data

"Preauthentication" is a feature introduced in Kerberos version 5. With preauthentication data, a client can prove the knowledge of its password to the KDC before the TGT is issued. In Kerberos version 4, anyone, including a hacker, can send an authentication request to the KDC; the KDC does not care. It does not even care about authenticating the client: Authentication is completely based on the client's ability to decrypt the packet returned from the KDC using its master key.

Preauthentication also lowers the probability of an offline password-guessing attack. Without preauthentication data, it is easy for a hacker to do an offline password-guessing attack[13] on the encrypted packets returned from the KDC. A hacker can send out dummy requests for authentication; each time he or she will get back another encrypted packet, which means he or she gets another chance to make a brute-force attack on the encrypted packet and to guess the user's master key.

13. During an offline password-guessing attack, a hacker intercepts an encrypted packet, takes it offline, and tries to break it using different passwords This kind of offline attack is also known as a brute-force attack: The hacker tries out different keys (in this case "passwords") to decrypt a packet until he or she finds the right key that decrypts the packet in cleartext.

Table 5.7 *Kerberos Authenticator Content*

Encrypted?	Name	Meaning
✓	Authenticator-vno	Version number of the authenticator format. In Kerberos v.5 it is 5.
✓	Crealm	Name of the realm (domain) that issued the corresponding ticket.
✓	Cname	Name of the server that issued the corresponding ticket (Principal name).
✓	Cksum	(Optional) Checksum of the application data in the KRB_AP_REQ.
✓	Cusec	Microsecond part of the client's timestamp.
✓	Ctime	Current time on client.
✓	Subkey	(Optional) Client's choice for an encryption key to be used to protect an application session. If left out, the session key from the ticket is used.
✓	Seq-number	(Optional) Initial sequence number to be used by the KRB_PRIV or KRB_SAFE messages (protection against replay attacks).

In a standard Kerberos authentication sequence, the preauthentication data consist of an encrypted timestamp. When logging on using a smart card, the preauthentication data consist of a signed timestamp and the user's public key certificate. In Windows 2000 and Windows Server 2003, preauthentication is the default. An administrator can turn it off using the "Do not require Kerberos preauthentication" checkbox in the account properties ("account" tab). This might be required for compatibility with other implementations of the Kerberos protocol. Preauthentication affects the content of a ticket: Every ticket contains a special flag that is reserved for preauthentication.

Authenticator content

Table 5.7 shows the authenticator fields, their meaning, and whether they are sent in encrypted format across the network.

TGT and ticket flags

In this section, we will analyze the content of a Kerberos TGT and a service ticket; we will focus on the TGT and ticket "flags." The ticket flags and their meaning are explained in Table 5.8.

Next are some important notes on usage of the ticket flags in Windows 2000 and Windows Server 2003 Kerberos.

- By default, every ticket has the "forwardable" flag set. This default behavior can be reversed by setting the "account is sensitive and cannot be delegated" property on an account object. Windows 2000 and Windows Server 2003 Kerberos do not support "proxy" tickets.

- By default, every ticket has the "renewable" flag set. When a ticket expires and a new ticket is needed, the system will not automatically request a new ticket (a TGT or a service ticket) (automatic ticket requests will work as long as a user's cached credentials are available).
- By default, every ticket has the "preauthenticated" flag set.
- Every Windows 2000 TGT has the "initial" flag set.

Table 5.8 *Kerberos Ticket Flags*

Flags	Meaning
Forwardable	Indicates to the ticket-granting server that it can issue a new Ticket Granting Ticket with a different network address based on the presented ticket.
Forwarded	The ticket has either been forwarded or was issued based on authentication involving a forwarded Ticket Granting Ticket.
Proxiable	Indicates to the ticket-granting server that only nonticket-granting tickets may be issued with different network addresses.
Proxy	The ticket is a proxy ticket.
May be postdated	Indicates to the ticket-granting server that a postdated ticket may be issued based on this Ticket Granting Ticket.
Postdated	Indicates that a ticket has been postdated. The end service can check the ticket's auth-time field to see when the original authentication occurred.
Invalid	The ticket is invalid.
Renewable	The ticket is renewable. If this flag is set, the time limit for renewing the ticket is set in RenewTime. A renewable ticket can be used to obtain a replacement ticket that expires later.
Initial	The ticket was issued using the AS protocol instead of being based on a Ticket Granting Ticket.
Preauthenticated	Indicates that, during initial authentication, the client was authenticated by the KDC before a ticket was issued. The strength of the preauthentication method is not indicated, but is acceptable to the KDC.
Hardware preauthentication	Indicates that the protocol employed for initial authentication required the use of hardware expected to be possessed solely by the named client. The hardware authentication method is selected by the KDC and the strength of the method is not indicated.
Target trusted for delegation (OK as delegate)	This flag means that the target of the ticket is trusted by the directory service for delegation.

- A ticket has the "Target trusted for delegation" (OK as delegate) flag set if the service or user account for which the ticket was issued has the "account is trusted for delegation" property set, or, in the case of a computer account, if the computer object has "trust computer for delegation" set.

A single ticket can contain multiple flags. The flags are added to a ticket's properties as a hexadecimal 8-bit number, of which only the first 4 bits are significant. One bit can refer to different flags. If flags refer to the same bit position, they are added hexadecimally. This hexadecimal number is displayed when looking at the TGTs in the Kerberos ticket cache using the resource kit tool "klist"; the other resource kit tool "kerbtray" automatically converts the number to its appropriate meaning.

5.4.4 Kerberized applications

Kerberized applications are applications that use the Kerberos authentication protocol to provide authentication (and maybe in a later phase to provide encryption and signing for subsequent messages). Windows 2000 and Windows Server 2003 include the following Kerberized applications:

- LDAP to AD
- CIFS/SMB remote file access. Common Internet File System (CIFS) is the new name of Microsoft's SMB protocol that is mainly used for file and print sharing.
- Secure dynamic DNS update
- Distributed File System Management
- Host to Host IPsec using ISAKMP
- Secure intranet Web services using IIS
- Authenticate certificate request to certification authority (CA)
- DCOM RPC security provider

Smart card logon process

Windows 2000 and Windows Server 2003 include extensions to Kerberos Version 5 to support public-key–based authentication. These extensions are known as PKINIT—which stands for use of Public Key cryptography for INITial authentication—and are defined in an IETF Internet draft available from http://www.ietf.org. PKINIT enables the smart card logon process to a Windows 2000 or later domain. PKINIT allows a client's master key to be replaced with its public key credentials in the Kerberos Authentication

Using Klist and Kerbtray The Windows Server 2003 Resource Kit contains two utilities you can use to look at the content of the Kerberos ticket cache: kerbtray.exe (illustrated in Figure 5.30) and klist.exe (illustrated in Figure 5.31). Kerbtray.exe is a GUI tool, and klist.exe is a command-line tool. Both tools can be used to display and/or purge the content of the Kerberos ticket cache.

To bring up the kerbtray dialog box and look at your logon session's Kerberos ticket cache, double-click the kerbtray icon in the status area of your Windows desktop. The kerbtray icon is only displayed if you started the kerbtray program—it looks like a green ticket. The upper pane of the kerbtray dialog box shows all Kerberos tickets (both service tickets and TGTs) that are cached in your logon session's Kerberos ticket cache. The lower part of the dialog box has four tabs: Names, Times, Flags, and Encryption Types. The content of these tabs differs depending on the ticket that is selected in the upper pane.

- The Names tab shows the name of the security principal the Kerberos ticket was issued to [this is the user's User Principal Name (UPN)], together with the name of the service for which the ticket was issued [this is the service's Service Principal Name (SPN)].
- The Times tab shows the validity period of the ticket: its start and end time. For both TGTs and tickets, the default validity period is 10 hours.
- The Flags tab shows the Kerberos ticket flags that have been set in the ticket. Examples of ticket flags are the forwarded and proxy flags used during the Kerberos delegation process. For a more detailed explanation of all the Kerberos ticket flags, I refer to the Kerberos Version 5 (V5) standard document [Request For Comments (RFC) 1510], which can be downloaded from the IETF Web site at http://www.ietf.org.
- Finally, the Encryption Types tab shows the names of the symmetric encryption algorithms that were used by the Kerberos software to encrypt the tickets' content.

```
C:\WINDOWS\system32\cmd.exe

C:\Documents and Settings\Joe>klist tickets

Cached Tickets: (3)

   Server: krbtgt/DC.NET@DC.NET
      KerbTicket Encryption Type: RSADSI RC4-HMAC(NT)
      End Time: 6/9/2003 20:36:57
      Renew Time: 6/16/2003 10:36:57


   Server: ldap/VMW2K33763.dc.net/dc.net@DC.NET
      KerbTicket Encryption Type: RSADSI RC4-HMAC(NT)
      End Time: 6/9/2003 20:36:57
      Renew Time: 6/16/2003 10:36:57


   Server: host/vmw2k33763.dc.net@DC.NET
      KerbTicket Encryption Type: RSADSI RC4-HMAC(NT)
      End Time: 6/9/2003 20:36:57
      Renew Time: 6/16/2003 10:36:57


C:\Documents and Settings\Joe>
```

Figure 5.30 *Looking at the Kerberos ticket cache using the Klist utility.*

To purge the tickets in the Kerberos ticket cache, right-click the kerbtray icon in your desktop's status area and select Purge Tickets. This option deletes *all* tickets in your ticket cache. Use this option with extreme caution: Deleting tickets may stop you from authenticating to other Windows services during your logon session. If you have purged your tickets, you can only obtain new ones by logging off and then logging on again.

To display the content of the Kerberos ticket cache using the klist command-line utility, type the following at the command prompt:

```
Klist tickets
```

or

```
Klist tgt
```

The first command will bring up the service tickets in the cache, and the second command will bring up the TGTs in the cache. To purge the cache from the command line, type:

```
Klist purge
```

Again, use the latter command with extreme caution.

The kerbtray utility displays more ticket information than the klist utility does—it also displays the information in a much more readable format. For example, the klist utility displays the TGT tickets flags altogether in a single hexadecimal string: It is up to the user to decipher this string and retrieve the associated ticket flags.

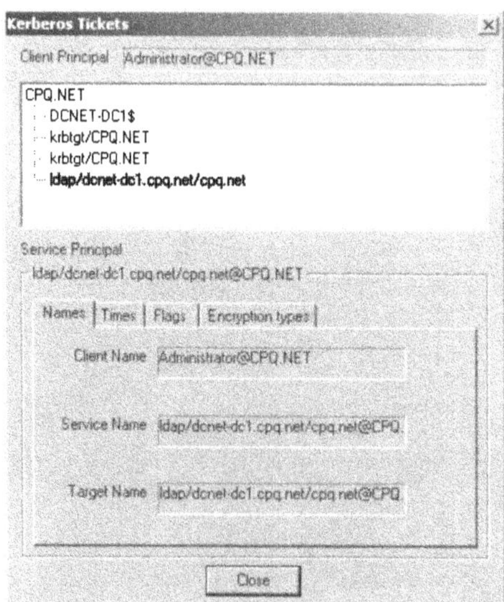

Figure 5.31 *Looking at the Kerberos ticket cache using the Kerbtray utility.*

Table 5.9 *Mapping the Standard Kerberos "Master Key" to the PKINIT "Public-Private Key"*

Standard Kerberos Usage of Master Key	PKINIT Replacement
Client-side encryption of the preauthentication data	Private key
KDC-side decryption of the preauthentication data	Public key
KDC-side encryption of session key	Public key
Client-side decryption of session key	Private key

Request (KRB_AS_REQ) and Reply (KRB_AS_REP) messages. This is illustrated in Table 5.9.

PKINIT introduces a new trust model (illustrated on the right side of Figure 5.32) in which the KDC is not the first entity to identify the users (as is the case for classical Kerberos). Before KDC authentication, users are identified by the certification authority in order to obtain a certificate. In this new model the users and the KDC obviously both need to trust the same CA.

Figure 5.33 shows the way the Kerberos smart card logon process works (notice that the cryptic names of the Kerberos messages have changed):

- Alice starts the logon process by introducing her smart card and by authenticating to the card using her PIN code. The smart card contains Alice's public key credentials: her private key and certificate.
- A TGT request is sent to the KDC (AS); this request contains the following (PA-PK-AS-REQ):
  - Alice's principal name and a timestamp
  - The above signed with Alice's private key
  - A copy of Alice's certificate

Figure 5.32 *Smart card logon trust model.*

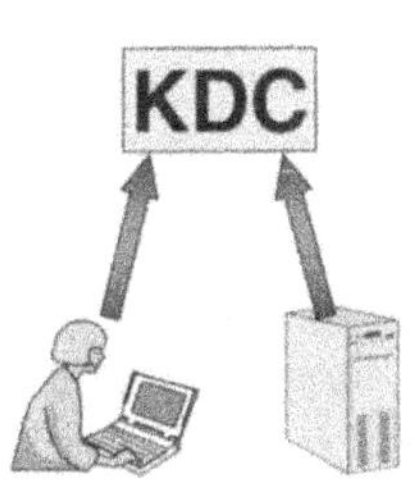

Standard Kerberos V5

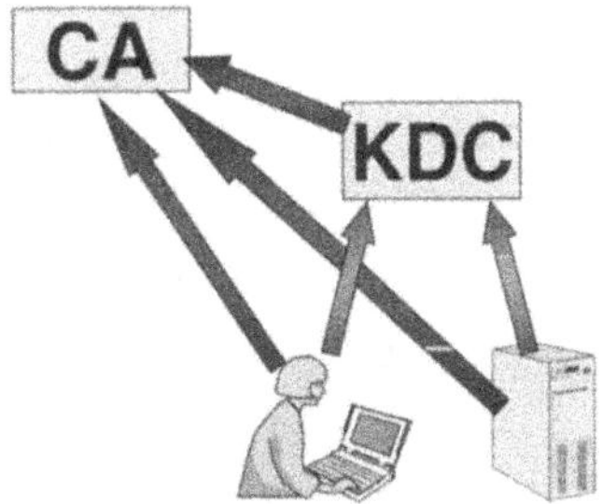

Kerberos PKINIT

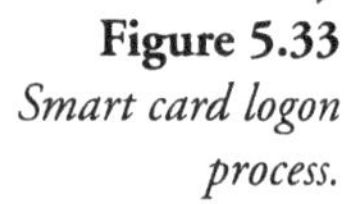

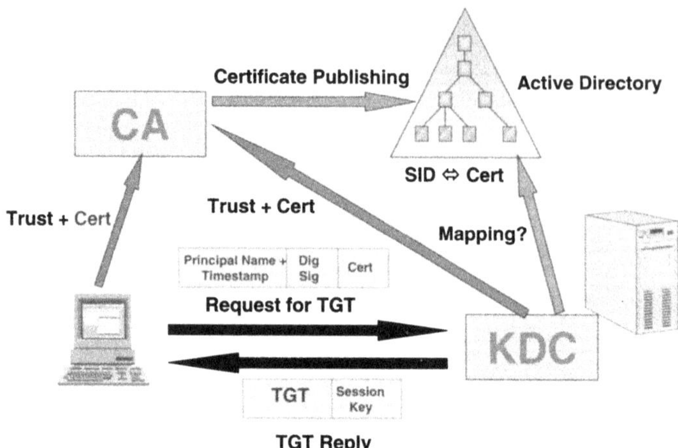

Figure 5.33 *Smart card logon process.*

- To validate the request and the digital signature on it, the KDC will first validate Alice's certificate. The KDC will then query the Active Directory for a mapping between the certificate and a Windows account. If it finds a mapping, it will issue a TGT to the corresponding account.
- The KDC sends back the TGT to Alice. Alice's copy of the session is encrypted with her public key (PA-PK-AS-REP).
- To retrieve her copy of the session key, Alice uses her private key.

We will come back to smart card support in Windows Server 2003 in Chapter 17.

5.5 Kerberos configuration

5.5.1 Kerberos GPO settings

The Windows Server 2003 Account Policies [Part of the Group Policy Object (GPO) computer configuration] include a special subfolder for Kerberos-related policy settings (illustrated in Figure 5.34). It contains the following GPO entries:

- Enforce user logon restrictions: This setting enforces the KDC to check the validity of a user account every time a ticket request is submitted. If a user does not have the right to log on locally or if his or her account has been disabled, he or she will not get a ticket. By default, the setting is on.

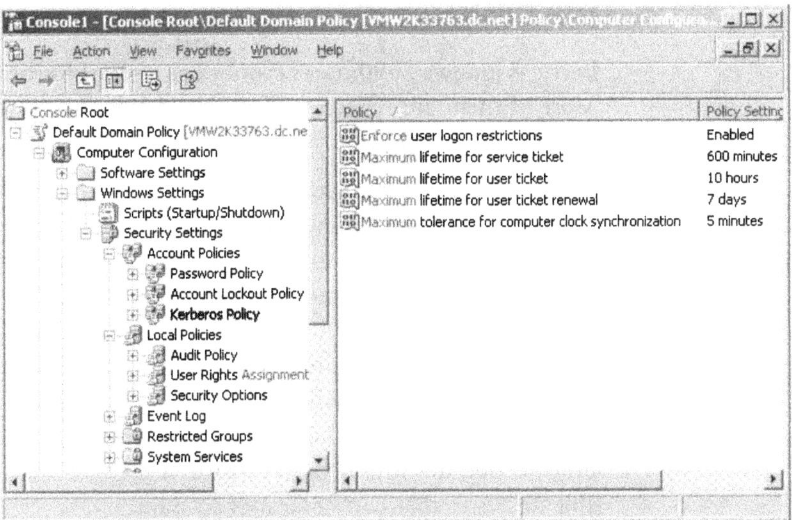

Figure 5.34 *Kerberos-related GPO settings.*

- "Maximum lifetime for service ticket": In Microsoft terminology, a service ticket is a plain Kerberos ticket. Its default lifetime is 10 hours.
- "Maximum lifetime for user ticket": In Microsoft terminology, a user ticket is a Kerberos TGT. Its default lifetime is 10 hours.
- "Maximum lifetime for user ticket renewal": By default, the same ticket [service or user ticket (TGT)] can be renewed up until 7 days after its issuance. After 7 days, a brand-new ticket has to be issued.
- Maximum tolerance for computer clock synchronization: This is the maximum time skew that can be tolerated between a ticket's time-stamp and the current time at the KDC. Kerberos is using a time-stamp to protect against replay attacks. Setting this setting too high creates a bigger risk for replay attacks. The default setting is 5 minutes.

These Kerberos policies can only be set on a per-domain basis (the same is true for account lockout policies and password policies). You cannot define, for example, different Kerberos account policy settings per individual organizational unit (OU).

Another Kerberos-related GPO entry is located in Local policies\user rights assignment: "enable computer and user accounts to be trusted for delegation" sets the "trusted for delegation" property of user and computer objects in a domain, site, or organizational unit. Kerberos delegation was explained earlier in this chapter.

5.5.2 Kerberos-related account properties

Every Windows 2000 user account has a set of Kerberos-related properties. Most of them are related to Kerberos delegation, and one is related to the use of preauthentication.

Every user account has the property "Account is sensitive and cannot be delegated." Every machine account has a special delegation tab in its properties that can be used to define machine-related Kerberos delegation settings. This is a brand-new tab in the machine properties that was not available in Windows 2000. The details behind the machine-related delegation settings were explained in Section 5.4.1. One more point worthy of mentioning is that domain controllers are by default trusted for delegation. If a user account has the "account is sensitive and cannot be delegated" property set, the administrator instructs the KDC not to issue any forwardable tickets to that particular user account.

The "Use DES encryption types for this account" account property changes the default Kerberos encryption type from RC4 to DES (as explained in Section 5.4.3).

Every user account also has a "Do not require Kerberos preauthentication" property. This setting must be enabled when the account is used in a Kerberos implementation or application that supports preauthentication. This is usually the case in UNIX Kerberos implementations. Windows Kerberos preauthentication was discussed earlier in this chapter.

5.5.3 Kerberos transport protocols and ports

RFC 1510 defines that a Kerberos client should connect to a KDC (port 88) using the connectionless UDP protocol. Microsoft Kerberos by default uses UDP. Microsoft Kerberos can also use TCP to take advantage of TCP's bigger Maximum Transmission Unit (MTU) capacity. Microsoft uses TCP if the ticket size is bigger than 2 kB. Any ticket fitting in a packet of 2 kB is sent using UDP, which has a 1,500-octet MTU limit. The Windows 2000 Kerberos ticket can easily grow beyond this limit if it is carrying a large PAC field—this can, for example, occur when a user is a member of a large number of groups.

The default 2-kB limit can be changed using the following registry hack. Setting this value to 1 will force Kerberos to use TCP all the time.

```
HKEY_LOCAL_MACHINE\SYSTEM\CurrentControlSet\Control\Lsa\
Kerberos\Parameters
Value Name: MaxPacketSize
```

```
Data Type: REG_DWORD
Value: 1–2000 (in bytes)
```

Kerberos uses port 88 on the KDC side and a variable port on the client side. If your Kerberos clients communicate only with KerberosV5 KDCs (the Kerberos version used in Windows 2000 and Windows Server 2003), it is enough to keep port 88 open on your firewall. If they communicate with KerberosV4 KDCs, you must also open port 750. Table 5.10 gives an overview of all Kerberos-related ports.

5.5.4 Kerberos time sensitivity

Time is a critical service in Windows 2000 and Windows Server 2003. Timestamps are needed for directory replication conflict resolution, but also for Kerberos authentication. Kerberos uses timestamps to protect against replay attacks. Computer clocks that are out of sync between clients and servers can cause authentication to fail or extra authentication traffic to be added during the Kerberos authentication exchange.

To illustrate the importance of time for Kerberos authentication, let's look at what really happens during a KRB_AP_REQ and KRB_AP_REP Kerberos exchange:

1. A client uses the session key it received from the KDC to encrypt its authenticator. The authenticator is sent out to a resource server together with the ticket.

Table 5.10 *Kerberos-Related Ports*

Port	Protocol	Function Description
88	UDP TCP	Kerberos V5
750	UDP TCP	Kerberos V4 Authentication
751	UDP TCP	Kerberos V4 Authentication
752	UDP	Kerberos password server
753	UDP	Kerberos user registration server
754	TCP	Kerberos slave propagation
1109	TCP	POP with Kerberos
2053	TCP	Kerberos demultiplexer
2105	TCP	Kerberos encrypted rlogin

2. The resource server compares the timestamp in the authenticator with its local time. If the time difference is within the allowed time skew, it goes to step (4). By default, the maximum allowed time skew is 5 minutes—this setting can be configured through domain-level GPOs.

3. If step (2) failed, the resource server sends its local current time to the client. The client then sends a new authenticator using the new timestamp it received from the resource server.

4. The resource server compares the timestamp it received from the client with the entries in its "replay cache" (this is a list of recently received timestamps). If it finds a match, the client's authentication request will fail. If no match is found, client authentication has succeeded, and the resource server will add the timestamp to its replay cache.

The service responsible for time synchronization between Windows 2000, Windows XP, and Windows Server 2003 computers is the Windows Time Synchronization Service (W32time.exe). The Windows time service is compliant with the Simple Network Time Protocol (SNTP) as defined in RFC 1769 (available from http://www.ietf.org/rfcs/rfc1769.txt). SNTP makes sure that the computer clocks are within 20 seconds of each other. A protocol that can provide more accurate time synchronization than SNTP is the Network Time Protocol (NTP). NTP is defined in RFC 1305 (available from http://www.ietf.org/rfcs/rfc1305.txt). Because the Windows 2000 AD replication and Kerberos do not require the level of time accuracy offered by NTP, the Windows developers decided to implement the SNTP protocol as the time protocol for Windows 2000 and later OSs.

Basic SNTP operation

All Windows 2000, XP, and Windows Server 2003 machines have the W32Time service installed by default. In the service list the service is referred to as the Windows Time service—in Windows Server 2003 and XP it is started automatically. The time service will automatically perform time synchronization at machine startup and at regular intervals (initially every 8 hours).

At machine startup, the client contacts an authenticating domain controller and exchanges packets to determine the latency of communication between the two computers. W32time will determine what time the local machine time should be converged to—this time is referred to as the target time. If the target time is ahead of local time, local time is immediately set to the target time. If the target time is behind local time, the local clock is slowed over the next 20 minutes to align the two times, unless local time is more than 2 minutes out of synchronization, in which case the time is immediately set.

At regular intervals, the client machine will perform periodic time checks. To do this the client connects to the "inbound time partner" (the Windows authenticating domain controller) once each "period." The initial period is 8 hours. If the local time is off from the target time by more than 2 seconds, the interval check period is divided in half. This process is repeated at the next interval check until either:

- The local time and target time remain within 2 seconds of each other.
- The interval frequency is reduced to the minimum setting of 45 minutes.

If accuracy is maintained within 2 seconds, the interval check period is doubled, up to a maximum period of 8 hours.

The default time convergence hierarchy constructed in a Windows 2000 and Windows Server 2003 forest follows the following rules:

- All client desktops and member servers nominate as their inbound time partner the authenticating domain controller. If this domain controller becomes unavailable, the client reissues its request for a domain controller.
- All domain controllers in a domain nominate the primary domain controller (PDC) emulator Flexible Single Master Operation (FSMO) to be the inbound time partner.
- All PDC emulator FSMOs in the enterprise follow the hierarchy of domains in their selection of an inbound time partner.
- The PDC emulator FSMO at the root of the forest is authoritative and can be manually set to synchronize with an outside time source.

Many organizations also rely on an external time source for time synchronization. This usually means that the PDC emulator of their root domain synchronizes with an external time server. In organizations that have a Windows forest that is geographically spread out, an external time source for a DC in every geography may be preferred over one time source for the root domain only.

The external time source can be a time server on the Internet such as the server of the Swiss Federal Institute of Technology in Zurich. It can also be a time server appliance hosted in the enterprise—one of the companies sell-

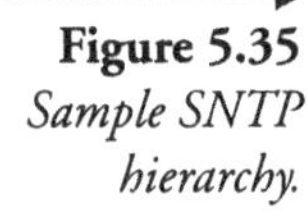

Figure 5.35
Sample SNTP hierarchy.

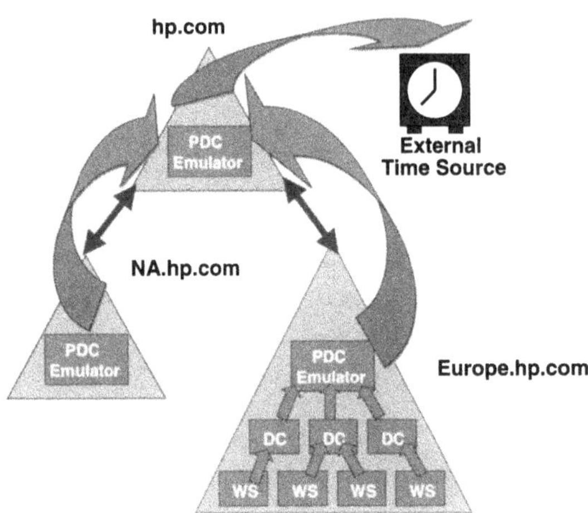

ing time server appliances is Symmetricom (previously known as Datum—more info at http://www.datum.com).

A sample SNTP hierarchy is shown in Figure 5.35. This default SNTP hierarchy can be modified by using the utilities that will be explained in the next section.

Configuring the windows time service

Microsoft provides two tools to configure and diagnose the Windows Time service:

- Net time—which is used to configure the time service and the synchronization hierarchy. The following net time command will change the time server on the local machine to mytimeserver.hp.com:

  ```
  Net time /setsntp:mytimeserver.hp.com
  ```

- w32tm—which is used to diagnose and configure the time service. For example, to monitor and analyze the time synchronization in the hp.com domain, I would type:

  ```
  w32tm /monitor /domain:hp.com
  ```

Both tools allow you to configure the time hierarchy to use the Windows defaults (as explained earlier in this section) or to use special designated time servers.

In Windows Server 2003, Microsoft added a new section in the GPO settings to configure the Windows Time Service. You can find it under Computer Configuration\Administrative Templates\System\Windows

Time Service. The time service's configuration data are kept in the following registry key: HKEY_LOCAL_MACHINE\System\CurrentControlSet\Services\w32Time.

For many more Windows time service configuration details, read the Microsoft white paper available from http://www.microsoft.com/windows2000/docs/wintimeserv.doc.

5.6 Kerberos and authentication troubleshooting

In the next two sections, we will explore some basic Kerberos and Windows Server 2003 authentication troubleshooting tools. An indispensable tool for every administrator is the Event Viewer. The next section will list some common Kerberos error messages as they appear in the Event Viewer. The following side note explains how to enable advanced Kerberos event logging.

Enabling Advanced Kerberos Event Logging Advanced Kerberos event logging can be enabled using the following Windows registry hack. Set the Loglevel registry key (REG_DWORD) to value 1. Loglevel is located in the following registry key: HKEY_LOCAL_MACHINE\SYSTEM\CurrentControlSet\Control\Lsa\Kerberos\Parameters.

5.6.1 Kerberos error messages

In Windows Server 2003, Microsoft included some Kerberos-specific event IDs. They are listed in Table 5.11. If you want to go even more in detail, Table 5.12 shows the Kerberos-related error messages as they appear in the Windows Event Viewer. Both can give interesting hints when troubleshooting Kerberos authentication problems.

Table 5.11 *Kerberos-Specific Event IDs*

Event ID	Meaning
672	An authentication service (AS) ticket was successfully issued and validated.
673	A ticket granting service (TGS) ticket was granted.
674	A security principal renewed an AS ticket or TGS ticket.
675	Kerberos preauthentication failed. This event is generated on a key distribution center (KDC) when a user types in an incorrect password.

Table 5.12 *Kerberos Error Messages and Meaning*

Code	Short Meaning	Error Explanation
0x6	Client Principal unknown	The KDC could not translate the client principal name from the KDC request into an account in the Active Directory. To troubleshoot this error, check whether the client account exists in AD, whether it has not expired, and whether AD replication is functioning correctly.
0x7	Server Principal unknown	The KDC could not translate the server principal name from the KDC request into an account in the Active Directory. To troubleshoot this error, check whether the client account exists in AD, whether it has not expired, and whether AD replication is functioning correctly.
0x9	Null key error	Keys should never be null (blank). Even null passwords generate keys because the password is concatenated with other elements to form the key.
0xE	Encryption type not supported	The client tried to use an encryption type that the KDC does not support, for any of the following reasons: The client's account does not have a key of the appropriate encryption type; the KDC account does not have a key of the appropriate encryption type; the requested server account does not have a key of the appropriate encryption type. The type may not be recognized at all, for example, if a new type is introduced. This happens most frequently with MIT compatibility, where an account may not yet have an MIT-compatible key. Generally, a password change must occur for the MIT-compatible key to be available.
0x17	Password has expired	This error can be caused by conflicting credentials. Let the user log off and then log on again to resolve the issue.
0x18	Preauthentication failed	This indicates failure to obtain ticket, possibly due to the client providing the wrong password.
0x1A	Requested server and ticket do not match	This error will occur when a server receives a ticket destined for another server. This problem can be caused by DNS problems.
0x1F	Integrity check on decrypted field failed	This error indicates that there is a problem with the hash included in a Kerberos message. This could be caused by a hacker attack
0x20	Ticket has expired	This is not a real error; it just indicates that a ticket's lifetime has ended and that the Kerberos client should obtain a new ticket.
0x22	Session request is a replay	This error indicates that the same authenticator is used twice. This can be caused by a hacker attack.
0x19	Preauthentication error	The client did not send preauthentication, or did not send the appropriate type of preauthentication, to receive a ticket. The client will retry with the appropriate kind of preauthorization (the KDC returns the preauthentication type in the error).
0x25	Clock skew too great	There is time discrepancy between client and server or client and KDC. To resolve this issue, synchronize time between the client and the server.

Table 5.12 *Kerberos Error Messages and Meaning (continued)*

Code	Short Meaning	Error Explanation
0x26	Bad address in Kerberos session tickets	Session tickets include the addresses from which they are valid. This error can occur if the address sending the ticket is different from the valid address in the ticket. A possible cause of this could be an Internet Protocol (IP) address change. In Windows 2000, this change is dynamic and existing cached tickets could be invalidated. Another possible cause is when a ticket is passed through a proxy server. The client is unaware of the address scheme used by the proxy server, so unless the program caused the client to request a proxy server ticket with the proxy server's source address, the ticket could be invalid.
0x3C	Generic error	A generic error that may be a memory allocation failure. The event logs may be useful if this error occurs.
0x29	Kerberos AP exchange error	This indicates that the server was unable to decrypt the ticket sent by a client, meaning that the server does not know its own secret key, or the client received the ticket from a KDC that did not know the server's key. This can be tested by determining if the server can obtain a ticket to itself, or if anybody else can locate the server. The secure channel used by NTLM is also an indicator of the validity of the password on local machine accounts.

5.6.2 Troubleshooting tools

Microsoft delivers several tools to troubleshoot Kerberos (see Table 5.13). They are spread across the resource kit, the support tools, and the platform SDK. Most of them are command prompt tools.

Table 5.13 *Kerberos Troubleshooting Tools*

Tool	Comments
mytoken.exe (Platform SDK)	Command prompt tool to display the content of a user's access token: This includes the user's rights and group memberships.
whoami.exe (Default Windows installation)	Command line tool to look at the content of the user's access token (use the /all switch).
klist (Resource Kit)	Command prompt tool to look at the local Kerberos ticket cache. Klist can also be used to purge tickets. Klist is a very simple but very important tool that you can use to find out how far the authentication got.
Kerbtray (Resource Kit)	GUI tool that displays the content of the local Kerberos ticket cache.

Table 5.13 *Kerberos Troubleshooting Tools (continued)*

Tool	Comments
Netdiag (Support tools)	Netdiag helps isolate networking and connectivity problems by providing a series of tests to determine the state of your network client. One of the "NETDIAG" tests is the Kerberos test. To run the Kerberos test, type "netdiag /test:Kerberos" at the command prompt.
Replication monitor (replmon) (Support tools)	Using Replication monitor, an administrator can not only check the replication traffic but also the number of AS and TGS requests and the FSMO roles.
Network monitor (Server CD)	Network monitor does not come out of the box with a parser for the Kerberos protocol. However, a special Kerberos parser dll is available from Microsoft.
Setspn (Support Tools)	Tool allowing you to manage (view, reset, delete, add) service principal names (SPNs).

5.7 Kerberos interoperability

As mentioned earlier in this chapter, Kerberos is an open standard that is implemented on different platforms. Because of this Kerberos can be used as an SSO solution between Windows and other platforms.

5.7.1 Non-Windows Kerberos implementations

Table 5.14 lists other Kerberos implementations and the platforms on which they are available.

5.7.2 Comparing Windows Kerberos to other implementations

Before going into the details of the interoperability scenarios, it is interesting to look at what makes Windows 2000 and Windows Server 2003 Kerberos different from the other implementations. The Microsoft implementation of Kerberos is different in the following ways:

- It is tightly integrated with the Windows 2000 and Windows Server 2003 OS kernel: Every Windows 2000 and Windows Server 2003 system runs the Kerberos Security Support Provider (SSP) and every DC has a KDC service.

Table 5.14 *Non-Windows Kerberos Implementations*

Kerberos Implementation	Platform
MIT Kerberos v1.1	NetBSD
CyberSafe TrustBroker	UNIX, MVS, Windows 95, NT4
Sun SEAM	Solaris
DCE Kerberos (IBM)	AIX, OS/390
Computer Associates Kerberos [Platinum (OpenVision)]	Windows 95, 3.1, 3.11
Kerberos PAM	Linux, HP-UX
Heimdal	UNIX

- Kerberos principals locate the KDC using DNS. Windows 2000 and Windows Server 2003 DNS includes special SRV records that provide the location of a Kerberos KDC.
- MS implemented the RC4-HMAC encryption algorithm (56/128 bit keys) as the preferred Kerberos encryption type. MS still supports DES-CBC-CRC and DES-CBC-MD5 (56-bit keys) for interoperability reasons. See Section 5.4.3 for more information about this.
- The MS implementation does not support the MD4 checksum type.
- Windows Kerberos KDCs require Kerberos clients to perform preauthentication by default. More information about this is available in Section 5.5.2.
- The MS implementation does not include support for DCE-style cross-realm trust relationships.
- Microsoft uses their proprietary SSPI API (see Chapter 4) to access Kerberos services. They do not support the raw krb5 API.
- Microsoft uses the authdata field in the ticket to embed authorization data. Microsoft refers to this field as the Privilege Attribute Certificate (PAC). See also Section 5.4.3 for more information about this.

5.7.3 Interoperability scenarios

In this section we will focus on setting up Kerberos interoperability between Windows 2000 or Windows Server 2003 Kerberos and a Kerberos implementation that runs on top of UNIX platforms. Kerberos authentication interoperability can be set up in three different ways:

- The Windows Kerberos KDC is the KDC for both Windows and UNIX security principals (the principals are administered from the Windows KDC) (Scenario 1).
- The UNIX KDC is the KDC for both Windows and UNIX security principals (the principals are administered from the UNIX KDC). This scenario includes no Windows domain controllers (Scenario 2).
- A cross-realm trust relationship is defined between a Windows domain and a UNIX Kerberos realm. A part of the principals is administered from the Windows KDC, another part is administered from the UNIX KDC. In this case, there are two KDCs—one KDC on each side of the trust relationship (Scenario 3).

Next we will explain these three scenarios using examples of Windows-UNIX Kerberos authentication interoperability.

Lots of valuable information on how to set up interoperability can be found in the following white papers:

- "Windows 2000 Kerberos interoperability" available from http://www.microsoft.com/windows2000/techinfo/howitworks/security/kerbint.asp
- "Windows 2000 Kerberos Interoperability" by Christopher Nebergall available from http://www.sans.org/rr/paper.php?id=973

Principals defined on a Windows KDC

This scenario allows for Kerberos principals on both Windows and non-Windows platforms to log on using Windows credentials and a Windows KDC. To enable a user to log on to Windows from a UNIX workstation, the UNIX krb5.conf Kerberos configuration file must be edited to point to the Windows KDC. Afterward, the user can log on using his or her Windows account and the "kinit" command (kinit is the equivalent of logon in UNIX Kerberos implementations).

The setup gets a little bit more complicated when enabling a service, running on a UNIX platform, to log on using Windows credentials and a Windows KDC. In this scenario the Windows administrator has to run through the following configuration steps:

- Edit the krb5.conf file on the UNIX machine to point to the Windows KDC.

- Create a service account for the UNIX service in the Active Directory.
- Use ktpass.exe to export the newly created service account's credentials from AD and create a keytab file. The keytab file contains the password that will be used by the UNIX service to logon to the Windows domain.
- Copy the keytab file to the UNIX host and merge it with the existing keytab file.

Ktpass comes with the Windows support tools. It allows an administrator to configure a UNIX computer or UNIX-based service as a security principal in the Active Directory.

The following example illustrates this last scenario. A company has a UNIX database server whose content should be accessible through a Web interface for every Windows user. To set this up, configure the database service as a principal in the Windows domain, and install an IIS server as a Web front end for the database server. To allow for credential forwarding between a Windows user and the IIS server, the IIS server must be "trusted for delegation."

Principals defined on a non-Windows KDC

This scenario allows for Kerberos principals on both Windows and non-Windows platforms to log on using UNIX credentials and a UNIX KDC. For a stand-alone Windows workstation or member server to use a UNIX KDC, the following has to be done:

- Create a host for the workstation in the UNIX realm.
- Configure the Windows workstation or member server using ksetup.exe to let it point to the UNIX KDC and realm and to set the machine password (this will automatically switch the workstation or member server to workgroup mode). Ksetup.exe also comes with the Windows support tools.
- Restart the workstation or member server and run ksetup.exe again to map local machine accounts to UNIX principals.

Cross-realm trust

This is probably the most flexible interoperability scenario available. This scenario will enable non-Windows Kerberos principals to log on to their UNIX KDC and to access resources in a Windows domain and also the other way around: For Windows principals to log on to their Windows KDC and to access resources in a UNIX realm.

The setup of a cross-realm trust between Windows and a UNIX realm is relatively straightforward. On the Windows side two things must be done: A trust relationship must be created using the AD Domains and Trusts snap-in, and a realm mapping for the UNIX realm should be added to the system registry. To add a realm mapping, use the ksetup tool. A realm mapping should not only be added on the Windows Domain controller, but also on every machine from which resources will be accessed in the UNIX realm. On the UNIX side, a trust relationship can be created using the kadmin tool.

If all user accounts are defined in the UNIX realm, a domain layout that is very similar to the NT4 master domain model of account domains and resource domains is created. In that case, the UNIX realm acts as a master account domain containing all the accounts. The Windows domain acts as a resource domain, containing resources and mappings from the UNIX accounts to Windows SIDs.

If you are planning to use this domain-realm layout, some extra configuration, besides the creation of a cross-realm trust, is needed on the Windows side. The reason for this is the difference in the accounting and aauthorization systems used in Windows and UNIX. Whereas UNIX relies on principal names for both accounting and authorization, Windows relies entirely on security identities (SIDs). Even though there is a trust relationship between the UNIX realm and the Windows domain, users authenticated through the KDC in the UNIX account domain can by default not access any resource in the Windows, because they do not have an SID.

To resolve this problem, shadow or proxy accounts must be created on the Windows side. A proxy account is an attribute (the "altSecurityIdentities" attribute) of a Windows account that contains a UNIX principal name. In other words, proxy accounts provide a way to map a UNIX account to a Windows account or SID.

Setting Up Kerberos Proxy Accounts Kerberos proxy or shadow accounts can be defined from the AD Users and Computers MMC snap-in.

- In the MMC snap-in's View menu option, select Advanced Features…
- Right-click the user account for which you want to define the proxy account and select Name Mappings… This will bring up the Security Identity Mapping dialog box (illustrated in Figure 5.36).
- Select the Kerberos Names tab, and then Add… to add the UNIX Kerberos Principal Name.

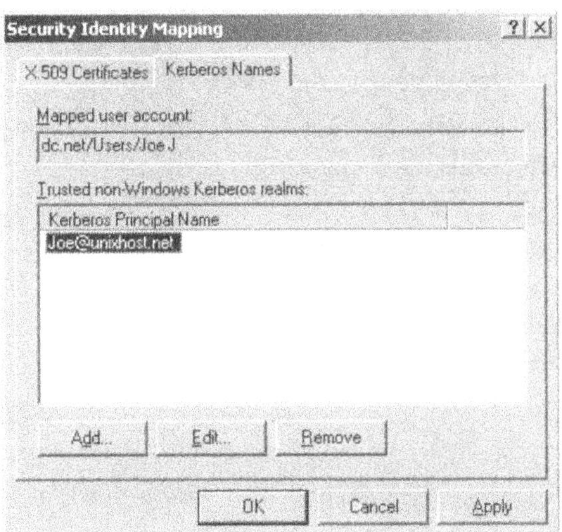

Figure 5.36 *Defining Kerberos account mappings.*

Let's look at what will happen now when a UNIX principal wants to access a resource that is hosted on a machine that is a member of a Windows domain (illustrated in Figure 5.37):

- The UNIX principal is logged on to the UNIX domain; his or her credential cache contains a TGT for the UNIX domain.
- The UNIX principal wants to access resource A in the Windows domain. His or her local KDC refers him to the Windows KDC.
- The Windows KDC creates a new service ticket for the UNIX principal to access resource A. Because the TGT used by the UNIX principal contains an empty PAC, the Windows KDC will query the Active

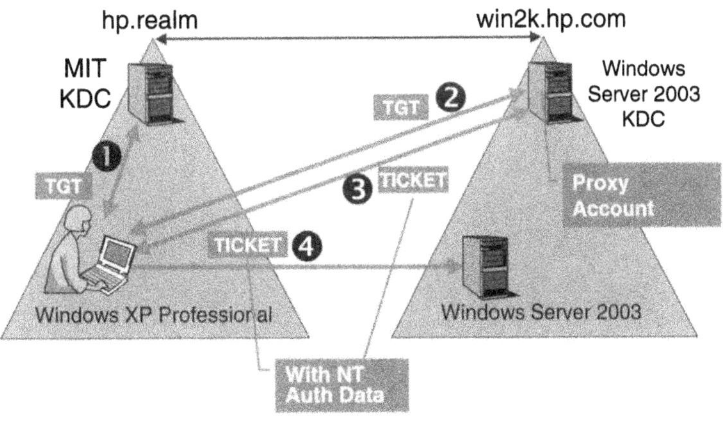

Figure 5.37 *UNIX-Windows Server 2003 Kerberos interoperability using a cross-realm trust.*

Directory for an account mapping between the UNIX principal and a Windows SID. The newly issued service ticket will contain the PAC data corresponding to the Windows SID.

- Using the service ticket, the UNIX principal authenticates to the machine hosting resource A.

In case the Windows domain also contains NT4 servers that can only authenticate using NTLM, this scenario also requires some password synchronization tool between the UNIX Realm (where the accounts and their passwords are defined) and the Windows domain. Such a tool is available in CyberSafe's Trustbroker product.

6

IIS Authentication

This chapter focuses on the Internet Information Services (IIS) 6.0 authentication methods. Microsoft has made radical changes to its Web server in Windows Server 2003. Some of these changes and their impact on the overall security quality of the Web server are explored in Section 6.1. The rest of the chapter focuses on the authentication methods supported in IIS 6.0.

6.1 Secure by default in IIS 6.0

Windows Server 2003 is Microsoft's first enterprise operating system that ships with the label "secure by default." One of the most visible effects of this is that IIS is now an optional service and is not installed by a default Windows Server 2003 installation.[1] This really makes sense if you keep in mind the numerous IIS security exploits that have occurred over the past years. Domain administrators can even prevent other administrators from installing IIS 6.0 on a server in a Windows Server 2003 domain using the following GPO setting: "Prevent IIS installation," which is located in the Computer Configuration\Administrative Templates\Windows Components\Internet Information Server GPO container. Note that this setting will not prevent an administrator from installing an IIS 5.0 or earlier Web server on a Windows Server 2003 machine.

Like Windows Server 2003, when IIS 6.0 is installed, it will be in a locked-down state. By default, IIS 6.0 is only capable of providing static Web page support ("static" meaning: plain html files). The dynamic content (for example, active server pages) that can be served by IIS is controlled using a new administration feature called Web Service Extensions in the IIS Manager MMC snap-in (also known as the Internet Services Manager [ISM]).

1. This is not true for Windows Server 2003 Web Edition, the OS's edition that is specifically targeting Web servers.

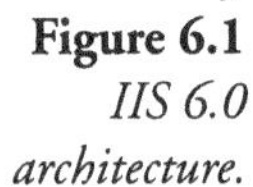

Figure 6.1 *IIS 6.0 architecture.*

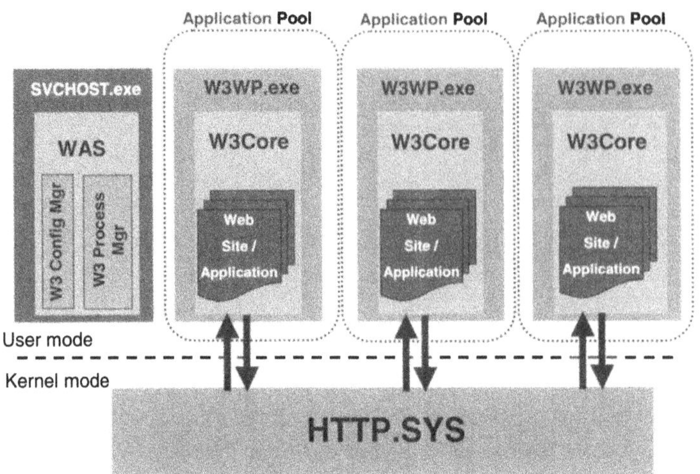

Other features illustrating IIS 6.0's secure by default are the fact that URLscan-like functionality has been implemented as an integral part of the Web server and that stronger access control settings are set on the IIS log files and cache directories. URLscan is a tool that scans all incoming HTTP requests to IIS. If it spots suspicious URLs, it blocks the HTTP request. Many Web server hacks consist of sending a URL to the Web server that contains a string that can be interpreted by the Web server as an instruction to execute a particular command. For IIS 4.0 and 5.0, URLscan is available as an add-on tool.

Perhaps the most fundamental change that makes IIS 6.0 more secure by default is its brand-new architecture: Microsoft completely reengineered the HTTP portion[2] of the Web server. The key characteristic of this architecture is isolation. IIS 6.0 supports an operation mode that is known as Worker Process Isolation Mode (WPIM), which enables different Web sites (and their worker processes) that are running on the same physical server to operate completely independent of one another—much like a logical firewall has been set up between them. This enables a per Web site configuration of security parameters (e.g., the security identity used by a Web site) and performance parameters (e.g., the amount of system resources that can be consumed by a Web site). This architecture also provides better protection against denial-of-service (DOS) attacks: An attack on one Web site can never bring down the complete Web server and all the other Web sites running on it.

2. This new architecture does not apply to the SMTP, NNTP and FTP portions of the web server.

Figure 6.1 illustrates the new IIS architecture. The entities providing application and Web site isolation are the application pools. As Figure 6.1 shows, an application pool can host several Web applications and sites. Each application pool can be assigned different security and performance parameters—application pools are logically separated from one another. Each application pool shows up in the Windows task manager as a separate instance of the w3wp.exe process. In IIS 6.0 Microsoft also provides separate processes for the administration and housekeeping of the Web server (the Web Administration Service [WAS] or the svchost.exe process) and the treatment of incoming and outgoing HTTP messages (the kernel-mode HTTP.sys driver).

6.2 Introducing IIS authentication

Microsoft's Web server supports the classical HTTP authentication methods—basic and digest authentication—and certificate-based authentication based on the Secure Sockets Layer (SSL) and Transport Layer Security (TLS) protocols. These three authentication methods are discussed extensively in this chapter. Besides these three, IIS also includes support for the typical Windows authentication methods—NTLM and Kerberos authentication—and Microsoft's Internet Single Sign-On authentication protocol—MS Passport. NTLM and Kerberos authentication were explained in great detail in the previous chapters. In this chapter we will look at how the Kerberos and NTLM protocols fit into the IIS authentication exchange and configuration. The built-in support for MS Passport authentication is new to IIS 6.0. It will be explained in greater detail in Chapter 7.

The IIS authentication options can be set from the properties of an IIS Web site, directory, or file (as illustrated in Figure 6.2) in the ISM: Go to the Directory Security tab, then click the Edit... pushbutton in the "Authentication and access control" section. To set SSL authentication options for a Web site, directory, or file, click one of the buttons in the secure communications section of the Directory Security tab. You can also set the authentication options globally for the complete Web server using the master Web site properties. The latter are accessible from the properties of the Web sites container in the ISM.

By default, every Web resource has both anonymous access and integrated Windows authentication enabled. This means that IIS will always first attempt to give a user access using anonymous (or unauthenticated) access. If this does not succeed, IIS will try to give the user access using integrated Windows authentication and the user's Windows credentials. If you

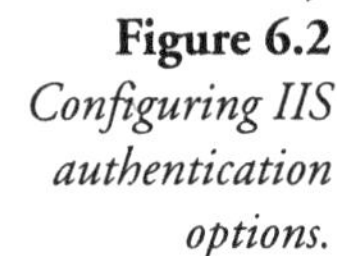

Figure 6.2 *Configuring IIS authentication options.*

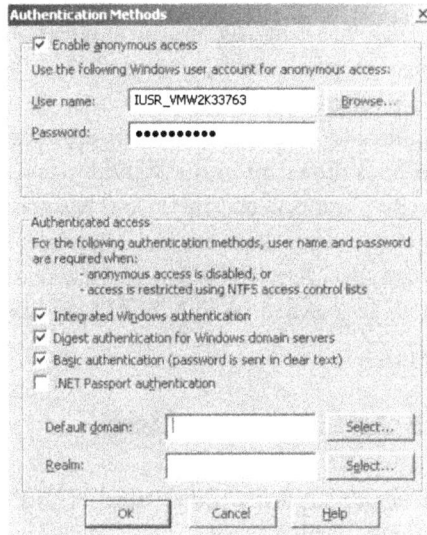

have enabled the integrated Windows, digest, and basic authentication options, IIS will first try to give users access using the integrated Windows and digest authentication protocols—only after trying these two methods and failing will it try with the basic authentication protocol.

These authentication options are not the only authentication options that can be made available to an IIS user. Web site administrators and application developers can also build their custom authentication methods or rely on authentication solutions provided by other software vendors. A good example of an IIS authentication solution from another vendor is the SecurID authentication plug-in from RSA Security[3] (illustrated in Figure 6.3; more information can be found at http://www.rsasecurity.com/products/securid/techspecs/windows.html). A good example of a custom authentication method is forms-based authentication.

In a forms-based authentication scenario, a user enters his or her authentication credentials on a Web page and then the Web page's code logic validates the credentials against a credential database. The credential database can be any kind of repository (an LDAP-accessible directory, an SQL database, and so forth). Some of these custom authentication methods do not rely on the built-in Windows security mechanisms and services such as security principals, accounts, and credential databases (like the AD

3. At the time of writing, no SecurID agent was available for IIS 6.0. More info is available at the following URL: http://www.rsasecurity.com/products/securid/techspecs/windows.html..

Figure 6.3 *SecurID-based IIS authentication.*

and the SAM). Custom IIS authentication methods are not explained in this book. A good example of a custom authentication method is explained in the IIS 6.0 Resource Kit; the example is named CustomAuth Version 1.0. Another example is Exchange Outlook Web Access (OWA) forms-based authentication.

6.3 HTTP authentication

The HTTP protocol specification includes a set of specific HTTP headers to deal with authentication in a Web environment. The HTTP specification also defines Web authentication methods: basic authentication—which is a part of the HTTP version 1.0 specification—and digest authentication—which is a part of the HTTP version 1.1 specification. Both authentication protocols are explained next.

Figure 6.4 shows the different messages that are exchanged between a Web browser[4] and server during an HTTP-based authentication exchange:

1. The browser requests data from the Web server using an HTTP GET verb.

4. Or any other HTTP client: for example an HTTP proxy server.

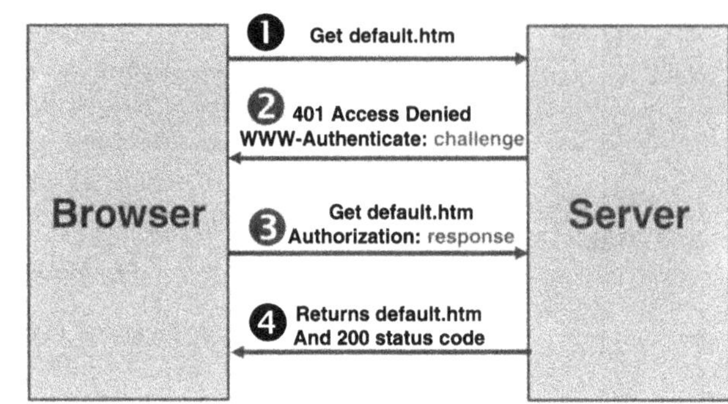

Figure 6.4 *Typical HTTP authentication exchange.*

2. If the Web server requires the client to authenticate himself or herself, it sends an HTTP 401 error back to the browser, along with:
   - A list of the authentication schemes it supports
   - A challenge. Not all web authentication protocols use this challenge. When using digest authenticaton for example the browser uses it to calculate the authentication reply that is sent back to the server. The challenge is sent as one or more WWW-Authenticate headers in the server's response.
3. The browser chooses one of the Web authentication protocols that it supports and constructs an authentication response. The response is based on the user's credentials and—depending on the authentication protocol used—also on the challenge that was sent by the server. To obtain the user's credentials the browser will prompt the user. The response is sent back to the server as part of an authorization header.
4. The server authenticates the data it got from the browser and, assuming everything is okay, sends the response, and the requested resource, back to the user. The latter message includes an HTTP 200 status code—which is a "no errors" message.

Step 2 of this authentication exchange begins with "if the Web server requires the client to authenticate himself of herself." Authentication is indeed an option. Many Web sites do not care about the identity of a user—good examples are Web sites containing public information that should be available to everyone. For such sites authentication is just overhead, slowing down the information exchange. That is why most Web servers (including IIS) also provide an anonymous access method. If a Web site is configured to use this access method, anyone is allowed to access the site,

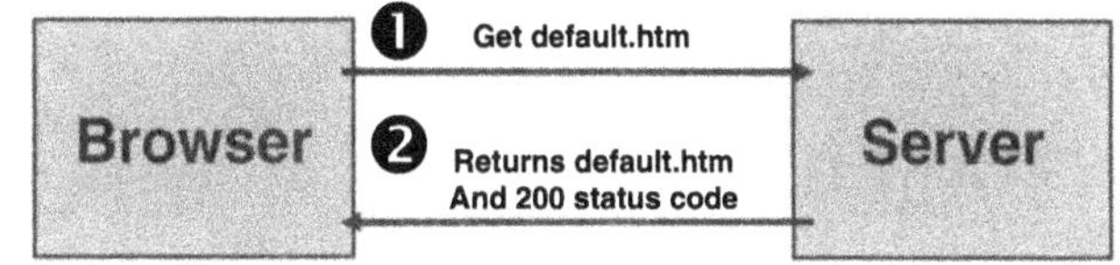

Figure 6.5 *Anonymous access exchange.*

even those users who do not provide credentials. Anonymous access is explained in more detail in the next section.

6.3.1 Anonymous access

Even though—from an end-user point of view—"anonymous access" appears as "no identification at all," there will be an authentication process at the Web server level. IIS always authenticates every anonymous session against the Windows security infrastructure using a preconfigured anonymous account. By default, this account is the IUSR_<computername> account (which is also known as the Internet guest account). This account is created automatically in the Windows Security database (SAM or AD) when an IIS Web server is installed. Figure 6.5 shows an anonymous access message exchange between a Web browser and server. In this instance the web server has been enabled for anonymous access and thus any request that does not contain credentials is a valid request.

The advantage of the back-end anonymous authentication process is that regular Windows authorization settings can be applied to Web resources that are accessed by anonymous users. This also means that if a Web resource has specific authorization settings that do not give access to the Internet guest account, the user will be asked to provide credentials.

Examining Web Authentication Exchanges A great tool for testing and troubleshooting Web servers is the IIS 6.0 Resource Kit tool WebFetch (wfetch) (illustrated in Figure 6.6). WebFetch does not render the HTTP content that it receives from the Web server—which makes it an interesting tool for analyzing HTTP messages. Note the WWW-Authenticate headers that are sent back by the Web server in the example of Figure 6.6.

The IIS 6.0 Resource Kit tools can be downloaded from the following URL:

http://www.microsoft.com/downloads/details.aspx?FamilyID=56fc92ee-a71a-4c73-b628-ade629c89499&DisplayLang=en.

The Internet guest account can be changed for every individual Web server, virtual directory, directory, and file. This can be done by clicking the

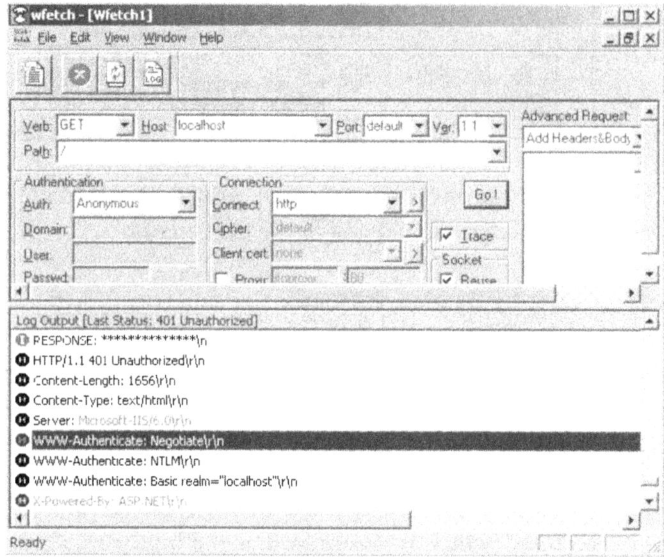

Figure 6.6 *Using the IIS Resource Kit WebFetch (WFetch) tool.*

Browse button in the anonymous access section in the Authentication Methods dialog box (see also Figure 6.2). Changing the Internet guest account on a particular virtual directory allows you to set different authorization settings on that directory. For example you may not want everyone to have access to every directory on every server using the same anonymous access account.

By default, IIS performs a network logon when an authentication occurs using the Internet guest account (by default, the Internet guest account is assigned the network logon user right). In IIS 5.0 and earlier versions the default logon type was interactive. Interactive logon requires the interactive logon user right. The latter imposes a security risk, because of the high amount of system privileges that are associated with it. The use of network logon as the default logon type in IIS 6.0 is another proof of how much more IIS 6.0 is secure by default.

6.3.2 Basic authentication

The basic authentication protocol is part of the HTTP 1.0 protocol specification. Because of this it can work with any browser type. Basic authentication provides a simple mechanism to transmit user credentials (a user ID and password) to a Web server.

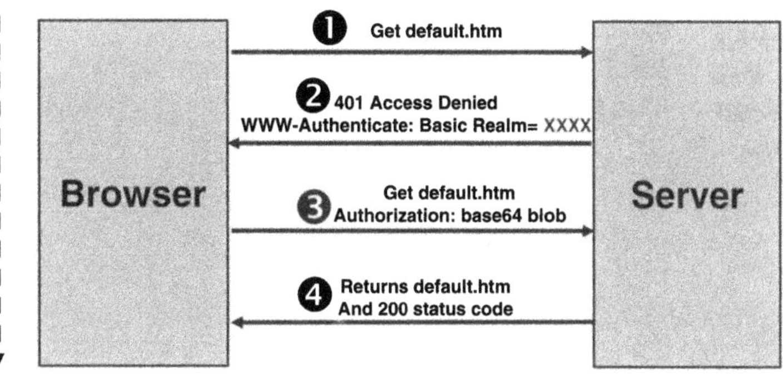

Figure 6.7 *Basic authentication exchange.*

Figure 6.7 shows the different messages that are exchanged between a Web browser and server during a basic authentication exchange.[5]

1. The browser requests data from the server by using an HTTP GET verb.
2. If the Web server requires the client to authenticate himself or herself, it sends an HTTP 401 error back to the browser, along with:
   - A list of the authentication schemes it supports, this time including the "basic" verb
   - The name of the basic authentication realm. The concept of a realm will be explained below.
3. Before replying to the challenge, the browser prompts the user for its username and password (as illustrated in Figure 6.8). This credential prompt will not occur if the user has previously cached his or her credentials in the user profile (using the "Remember my password" option) or if the URL that was used to access the website contains the username and password. The browser then responds to the authentication request by base64 encoding its username, password, and the authentication realm and sending the encoded blob back to the Web server as an authorization host header.
4. The server authenticates the browser's response and, if everything is okay,[6] sends the response, and the requested resource, back to the user. The latter message includes an HTTP 200 status code.

5. You can shortcut the basic authentication exchange by including the user credentials in the URL that is passed to the Web server. To do so use the following URL format: http://username:password@yourwebsite.com.
6. By default, IIS gives a user three basic authentication attempts.

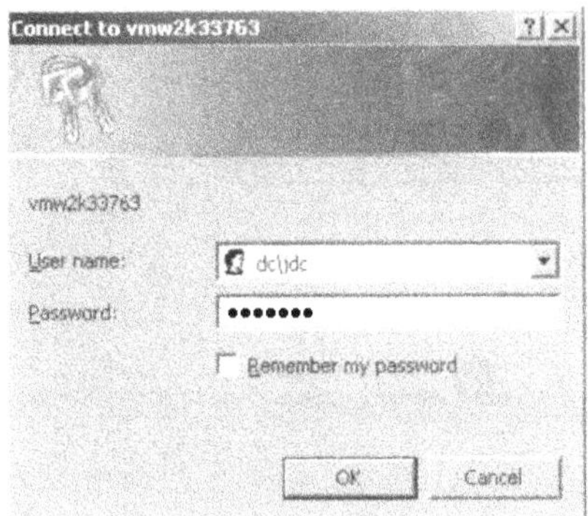

Figure 6.8 *Basic authentication credential prompt.*

The credential information, which is sent between a Web browser and server when using basic authentication is not secured, it is just base64 encoded. Because it is relatively easy to decode a base64 encoding (see also the following sidebar on decoding base64 encoding), it is advisable to secure the HTTP traffic using the SSL-TLS (Secure Sockets Layer—Transport Layer Security) protocols. We will come back to these protocols later in this chapter. When enabling basic authentication on a Web resource, IIS warns you about this potential security hole (as shown in Figure 6.9).

Decoding Base64 Encoding Decoding Base64-encoded messages is relatively easy. Base64 encodes messages by storing every three 8-bit characters in four 6-bit characters.

The easiest way to decode base64 is to use one of the online base64-decoder tools such as the tool at http://www.robertgraham.com/tools/base64coder.html.

Try to decode the following basic authentication string at the above URL:

ZG9tYWluXHVzZXJuYW1lOnBhc3N3b3Jk

What is the result of the decoding?

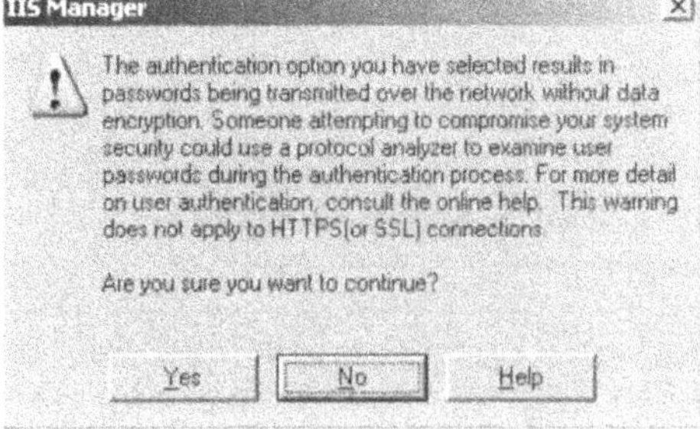

Figure 6.9 *Basic authentication warning.*

When setting basic authentication for a Web resource, you can also configure the default domain and realm at the bottom of the ISM authentication methods dialog box (see also Figure 6.2).

- The default domain allows you to set the domain to which a user should be authenticated when no domain is provided during the authentication process. In the example of Figure 6.8, the user provided an authentication domain called "dc" by preceding his or her username with dc\ In the example of Figure 6.8, the default domain specified in the authentication properties will be ignored. To enable User Principal Name (UPN) -based logon in a Windows 2000 or later domain environment you must specify "\" in the default domain field.

- The realm is a level within the IIS metabase hierarchy that a user is allowed to access when using basic authentication. By default, it is the IIS computer name—which provides access to all levels in the IIS metabase hierarchy (as illustrated in Figure 6.8 for machine vmw2k33763). The realm always appears in the left top corner of the basic authentication dialog box. Figure 6.10 shows how the custom realm /LM/W3SVC/1/Root/MyVirtualDir is displayed in the basic authentication dialog box. A Web resource's realm property can be set from the bottom of the Authentication Methods dialog box or in the IIS metabase. How to specify custom realms is explained in the IIS documentation. Both digest and advanced digest authentication (explained below) also use the realm concept.

Other interesting basic authentication options that cannot be set from the ISM GUI but only by editing the IIS metabase directly are the following:

- The logon type (LogonMethod metabase property) specifies the logon type that IIS performs when a basic authentication Web logon

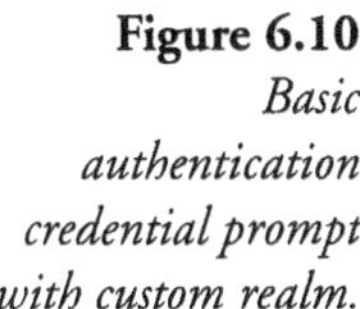

Figure 6.10 *Basic authentication credential prompt with custom realm.*

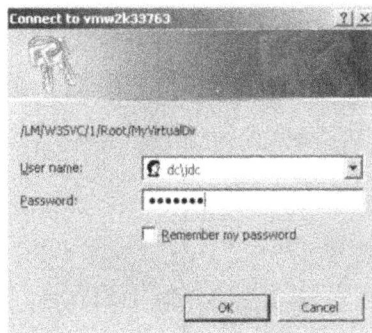

session occurs. As for anonymous access, by default, IIS performs a network logon (LogonMethod value 2). Other possible LogonMethod values are 1 (for batch logon) and 3 (for network clear-text logon).

- The token cache time (UserTokenTTL metabase property) specifies the amount of time a user's access token is cached and remains valid on the Web server. The default is 15 minutes. If you do not want to cache tokens on the Web server, set the UserTokenTTL to 0.

6.3.3 Digest authentication

Digest authentication was originally specified as part of the HTTP 1.0 protocol specification—an enhanced version is defined in the HTTP 1.1 protocol specification. Both versions are defined in RFC 2617. Like the NTLM authentication protocol, it uses a challenge-response–based authentication method. One of the key advantages of digest authentication is that it does not transmit the user credentials in the clear over the network (like basic authentication does) and thus does not require the use of the SSL or TLS protocols.

HTTP 1.1 and digest authentication are not yet supported by all browser and Web server types and versions. On the Microsoft side it is supported by IE5.0 and IIS 5.0 and later versions.

A major disadvantage of digest authentication is that it requires Active Directory user accounts (IIS warns you for this when enabling digest authentication—see Figure 6.11) and the clear-text storage of the password in the AD. In AD clear-text password storage can be set using a property of the user object: "Store Password using Reversible Encryption." You can also enforce clear-text password storage using the "Store Passwords using Reversible Encryption" Group Policy Object setting (located in the Security Settings\Account Policies\Password Policy container). After making this setting, the user or administrator must set a new password to activate the clear-text password storage.

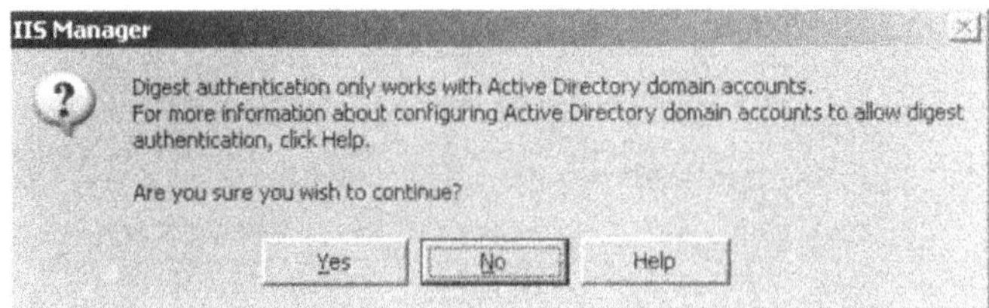

Figure 6.11 *Digest authentication warning.*

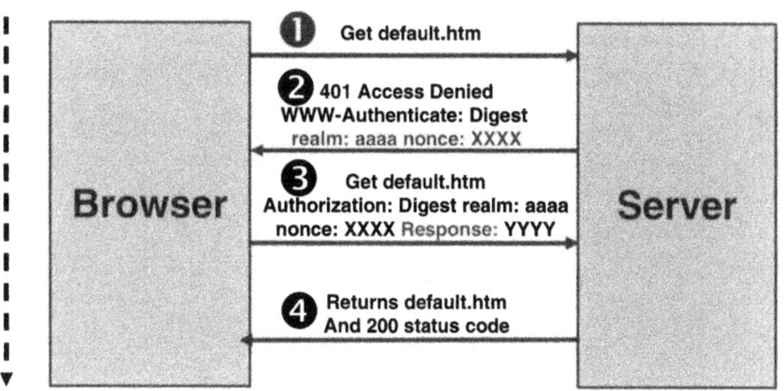

Figure 6.12 *Digest authentication exchange.*

Figure 6.12 shows how digest authentication works:

1. The user's browser requests access to the default.htm Web page.
2. The Web site replies with a 401 access denied message. The server's reply also tells the browser that the Web page requires digest authentication (the WWW-authenticate contains the word "digest") and lists the digest authentication realm to which the Web page belongs (in the example, realm "aaaa"). Most important, the reply also contains a digest challenge—which is usually referred to as the nonce (in the example, "XXXX").
3. Before replying to the challenge, the browser prompts the user for its username and password. The browser hashes[7] the challenge using the user's password. The outcome of this hash (in the example, response "YYYY") together with the nonce (in the example, "xxxx") and the realm (in the example, "aaaa") are then sent back to the Web server.
4. The Web server validates the response it gets from the browser by calculating the same hash and comparing it with what it got back from the browser. The Web server can calculate the hash because it also has access to the user's password (which is stored in AD). If everything is okay, the Web server sends the requested resource back to the user. The latter message includes an HTTP 200 status code.

The use of digest authentication will generate a typical authentication dialog box on the browser side. This dialog box is illustrated in Figure 6.13. The dialog box explicitly refers to the name of the resource the user tries to access and the use of the digest authentication protocol.

7. Digest authentication uses the MD5 hashing algorithm.

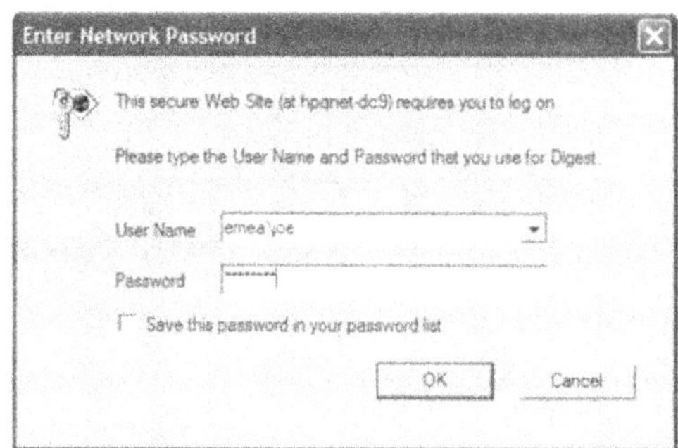

Figure 6.13 *Digest authentication dialog box.*

Two big architectural changes related to digest authentication in Windows Server 2003 are the inclusion of a digest security support provider (SSP) and the support for advanced digest authentication.

- In Windows Server 2003, Microsoft has implemented digest authentication (and advanced digest authentication—explained next) in the operating system using an SSP—SSPs were explained in Chapter 4. This does not mean that you cannot use digest authentication on an IIS server that is running on top of Windows 2000. In the latter case you must enable a special digest subauthentication dll called iissuba.dll and set the UseDigestSSP IIS metabase property to 0 (false). For more information on how to do this, I refer to the IIS 6.0 documentation.
- Advanced digest authentication is an enhanced version of the digest authentication protocol. The key advantage of advanced digest authentication is that it does not require clear-text storage of users' passwords (even though it requires the use of an AD account). Advanced digest authentication is only available for Web authentication if IIS 6.0 is running on a Windows Server 2003 box, if the browser used on the client side is at least IE 5.0 or later, if the user account used for authentication is defined in a Windows Server 2003 domain that is at functionality level 2 (meaning that it only contains Windows Server 2003 domain controllers), and if the UseDigestSSP metabase property is set to 1 (true). If one of these conditions is not met, simple digest authentication will be used.

As with basic authentication, you can configure the default domain and realm properties in the ISM when setting digest authentication for a Web resource. For digest authentication only, the metabase realm property is useful (even though the default domain box is also enabled when setting digest authentication).

```
HTTP/1.1 401 Unauthorized\r\n
Content-Length: 1656\r\n
Content-Type: text/html\r\n
Server: Microsoft-IIS/6.0\r\n
WWW-Authenticate: Digest qop="auth",algorithm=MD5-sess,nonce="50b32f19f058c301bb7f5f3483819789afb
"fc53c01756531dfbe02d9cabf7f2a55c",charset=utf-8,realm="Digest"\r\n
X-Powered-By: ASP.NET\r\n
Date: Sat, 02 Aug 2003 12:17:53 GMT\r\n
\r\n
```

Figure 6.14 *WFetch advanced digest authentication exchange.*

Recognizing Advanced Digest Authentication Support The key element allowing you to recognize whether advanced digest authentication is available on the Web server is the quality of protection (qop) parameter (see Figure 6.14) in the WWW-authenticate header. In IIS 6.0 the qop parameter typically has the "auth" value

In IIS 6.0 Microsoft did not implement the authentication message replay protection and mutual authentication features of improved digest authentication. They did implement the "frequent HTTP client" feature. This feature can be recognized by the presence of the algorithm=MD5-sess parameter in the WWW-authenticate header (see Figure 6.14). It protects against attacks that are based on an offline analysis of the HTTP messages. It forces the client to change the MD5 hash key that is used by the digest protocol periodically.

6.4 Integrated Windows authentication

The IIS Integrated Windows authentication option really consists of two authentication protocols: the NTLM and the Kerberos authentication protocol. It calls on three different Security Support Providers (SSPs): the Kerberos, NTLM, and Negotiate SSP. These SSPs and authentication protocols are normally available and used on Windows networks. However, instead of using the RPC communication protocol, in a Web environment the authentication protocol messages are transported using the HTTP protocol. Both the NTLM and Kerberos authentication protocols were explained in detail in Chapters 4 and 5.

Because Integrated Windows authentication includes several authentication protocols (NTLM and Kerberos), it needs a negotiation phase before the actual authentication between Web browser and server can take place. During this negotiation phase the Negotiate SSP will determine which authentication protocol to use (NTLM or Kerberos) between the Web browser and server.

As with digest authentication, Integrated Windows authentication never transmits the password in the clear—and thus does not require the use of SSL or TLS. From all Web authentication protocols listed so far in this chapter, Integrated Windows authentication also requires the least configuration and user intervention. Integrated authentication will automatically retrieve the user's credentials from its logon session's credential cache—unless integrated windows authentication has been disabled in the Internet Explorer (IE) configuration settings. In IE integrated authentication support can be enabled or disabled using the "Enable Integrated Windows Authentication" setting in the advanced configuration options. Changing this setting requires an IE restart. Unfortunately, both NTLM and authentication support are specific to Microsoft browsers.

Both the Negotiate SSP and NTLM authentication do not work across HTTP proxies because both require a point-to-point connection between the Web browser and server in order to function correctly. When using an HTTP proxy together with the Negotiate SSP or NTLM authentication the proxy can never respond to requests from the web server for user credentials. The reason for this is that on no occasion the credentials are transmitted to the proxy itself. That is why Integrated Windows authentication is best suited for intranet Web authentication and is not a good option for authentication in an extranet or Internet environment.

Kerberos authentication is only available on IE 5.0 browsers and IIS 5.0 Web servers or later. In order for Kerberos authentication to work, both the browser and the server also must be in the same or trusted Windows 2000 or later domain, and the Web server must have a valid Service Principal Name (SPN) that is registered in the Active Directory. Remember from Chapter 5 some of the key advantages of using Kerberos over NTLM:

- Kerberos is faster than NTLM.
- Kerberos is more secure than NTLM.
- Kerberos supports mutual authentication: it authenticates both the server and the client.
- Kerberos supports multihop delegation (also known as credential forwarding). Kerberos delegation was explained in chapter 5.
- Kerberos is an open standard.

Unless the user's current logon credentials can be used to authenticate to the Web server the use of integrated Windows authentication will generate a typical authentication dialog box on the browser side. This dialog box is

Figure 6.15 *Integrated Windows authentication dialog box.*

illustrated in Figure 6.15. In the left top side of the dialog box it always shows "Connecting to" followed by the name of the resource the user tries to connect to.

6.5 Passport-based authentication

Passport-based authentication in an IIS environment is explained in greater detail in Chapter 7.

6.6 Certificate-based authentication

Certificate-based authentication is based on the SSL and TLS protocols. SSL stands for the Secure Sockets Layer protocol. It is a security protocol operating at the transport layer of the OSI networking stack. SSL was initially developed by Netscape. The latest SSL specification (3.0) can be downloaded from http://wp.netscape.com/eng/ssl3. In 1999 SSL was standardized by the IETF in RFC2246 under the name Transport Layer Security (TLS) protocol (more information is available at http://www.ietf.org/rfc/rfc2246.txt). TLS is also referred to as SSL version 3.1. A great book revealing all the nuts and bolts of both protocols is Eric Rescorla's book, *SSL and TLS: Designing and Building Secure Systems* (Addison-Wesley, 2001).

SSL/TLS can provide the following security services:

- *Server authentication:* SSL/TLS uses X.509 server certificates to authenticate the Web server.
- *Data confidentiality and integrity services:* SSL/TLS always provides channel encryption services.

- *Optional client authentication:* SSL/TLS uses X.509 client certificates to authenticate the clients.

The last one is the most interesting one in the context of this chapter on IIS authentication methods. Contrary to the methods discussed earlier, certificate-based client authentication does not use the HTTP AUTH headers. Note that SSL can provide these authentication, confidentiality, and integrity services to a wide range of application-level protocols: not only HTTP but also including SMTP, NNTP, and so forth.

The SSL/TLS protocols are built on symmetric and asymmetric cryptographic protocols (also known as public key crypto) and X.509 certificates. For more information on X.509 certificates, see Chapter 13 on public key infrastructures (PKI).

When users connect to Web pages that are secured using SSL/TLS, they must use a secure URL that begins with https://. The use of https tells the browser it should try to establish a secure SSL connection with the Web server. By default these secure connections are made over port 443. In Internet Explorer a small lock symbol shows up at the bottom of the screen to show the user that they are connected over a secure SSL/TLS connection (illustrated in Figure 6.16). If you move over the lock symbol with your mouse pointer, you can see the SSL encryption strength that has been used. If you double-click the lock symbol, you will see the properties of the Web server's SSL/TLS certificate. If something is wrong with the Web server's certificate, the lock symbol will be covered with an exclamation mark.

In short, this is how an SSL/TLS connection is set up between a browser and a Web server:

- The browser connects to the Web server using a secure URL (https://).
- The Web server sends the browser the server certificate (containing its public key).
- The browser and Web server negotiate the encryption level to be used.
- The browser encrypts a session key (to be used for SSL channel encryption) with the Web server's public key and sends the encrypted blob to the Web server.

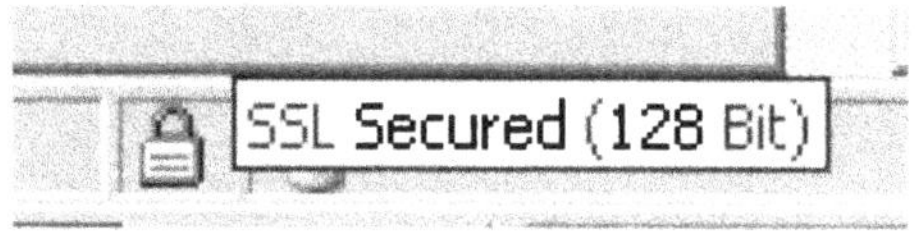

Figure 6.16 *Internet Explorer SSL/TLS lock symbol.*

- The Web server decrypts the encrypted blob using its private key.
- The browser and Web server exchange data—the data are secured using the session key.

6.6.1 SSL setup

The use of SSL/TLS requires X.509 certificates. You always need a server certificate, and if you also want client certificate-based authentication, you will also need client certificates. Setting up SSL in IIS 6.0 typically includes the following steps:

- Generate a server certificate request file.
- Submit the request file.
- Generate the server certificate.
- Install the server certificate on the Web site.
- Configure SSL on the Web site.
- Optionally, generate, acquire, and install client certificates.
- Install the issuing CA's certificate in the browser's trusted root certificate store.

In this chapter, only SSL-specific topics are discussed; for general information about certificates, public key infrastructures (PKIs), and the Windows Server 2003 PKI software, see Chapters 13, 14, and 15.

The easiest way to generate a server certificate request file is to use the IIS Web server certificate wizard (illustrated in Figure 6.17)—that guides you through the request file generation process. You can start the wizard from the ISM: right-click the Web site on which you want to set up SSL, select properties, then in the directory security tab—in the secure communications section—select Server Certificate (as illustrated in Figure 6.18).

In the wizard you have the option to send the request immediately to an online CA or generate the request offline. The first option will not only generate and send the certificate request file; it will also automatically install the certificate. This option will only work if you have an operational Windows enterprise CA. When you choose to generate the request offline, you will have to submit the request to the CA and install the certificate on the Web server all by yourself.

A very important step in the certificate request file generation wizard is the specification of the Web site's common name. You must make sure that the common name you enter in the wizard matches the name that the

Figure 6.17
SSL Web server certificate wizard.

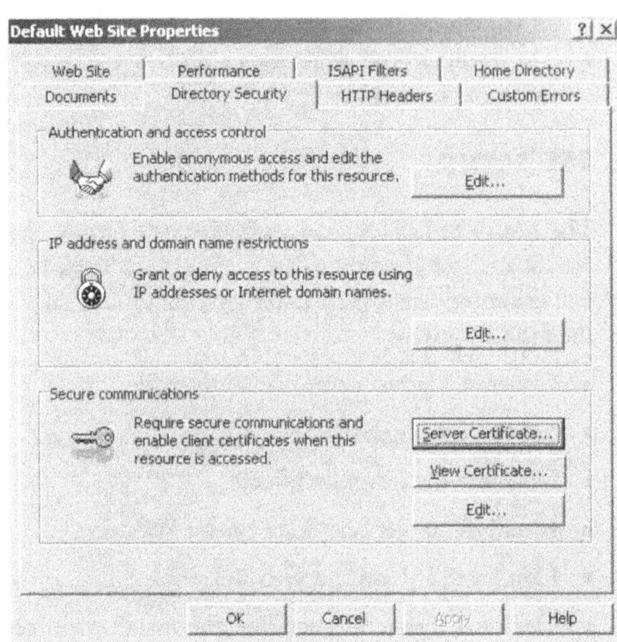

browser uses in the URL to securely connect to your Web site. This is because the common name appears in the server certificate, and if the name in the certificate does not match with the name in the URL, the browser will generate an SSL error. Microsoft supports the use of wildcards in the certificate's common name.

Figure 6.18
Starting the Web server certificate wizard.

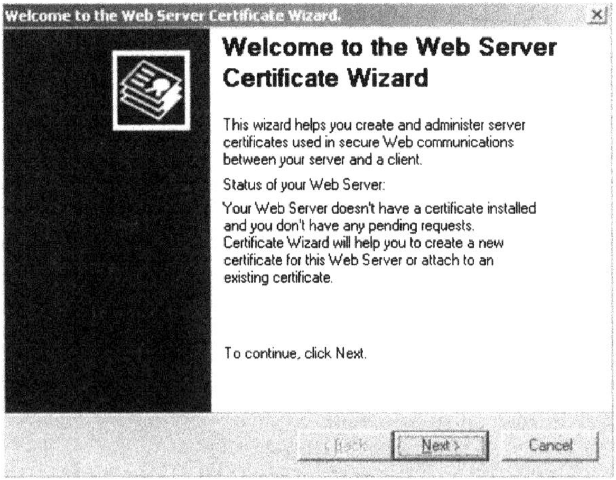

Welcome to the Web Server Certificate Wizard
Welcome to the Web Server Certificate Wizard
This wizard helps you create and administer server certificates used in secure Web communications between your server and a client.
Status of your Web Server:
Your Web Server doesn't have a certificate installed and you don't have any pending requests. Certificate Wizard will help you to create a new certificate for this Web Server or attach to an existing certificate.
To continue, click Next.
< Back
Next >
Cancel

Using Wildcards in the Common Name of SSL Server Certificates

Microsoft supports the use of wildcards in the common name of SSL server certificates. Using wildcards you can reuse the same certificate for different physical Web sites. This may be an interesting option for Web farms where only the machine is different between the different Web farm members.

The IIS SSL/TLS provider supports the following wildcards (the examples are all matching www.hp.com):

- *.hp.com
- w*.hp.com
- *w.hp.com
- www.h*.com
- www.hp.*

Microsoft's support for wildcards is in line with RFC 2595 and is documented in the Microsoft Knowledge Base article at http://support.microsoft.com/default.aspx?scid=kb;en-us;258858.

Once you have generated the certificate request file, you must use it to generate the actual certificate. SSL/TLS server certificates can be generated in different ways:

- They can be generated by an internal Certification Authority (CA), which is for example using the Windows Server 2003 PKI software.
- They can be generated by an external commercial CA (e.g., Verisign).
- You can generate self-signed certificates using the IIS 6.0 Resource Kit utility SelfSSL.

SelfSSL is a command-line tool allowing you to generate self-signed SSL/TLS certificates—in other words, you do not need a CA or PKI infrastructure. When you run SelfSSL, it will not only generate a self-signed certificate, but it will also install it on the Web server. If you use it with the /T switch, it will also add the self-signed certificate to the list of trusted certificates in the local machine's certificate store.

If you did not submit the request file to an online Windows enterprise CA or if you did not use the SelfSSL tool, you will have to manually submit the request to the CA that will issue the server certificate. If the CA you are using is an internal Windows CA, the easiest way to do this is to use the CA's Web interface. To do so, connect to the CA's Web site using the http://<servername>/certsrv URL. On the welcome page, select "request a certificate," then "submit an advanced certificate request," and finally, select "submit a certificate request by using a base64-encoded CMC or PKCS#10 file, or submit a renewal request by using a base64-encoded PKCS#7 file." The next Web page will then allow you to paste the base64-encoded content of the certificate request file in the page (the part that starts with --BEGIN NEW CERTIFICATE REQUEST-- and ends with --END NEW CERTIFICATE REQUEST--). If you are using an external commercial CA, consult the CA's operational procedures.

Once you get the server certificate back from the CA (again, this step is not needed if you used an operational Windows enterprise CA or SelfSSL), you can install it on your Web server. To do so, you can use once more the Web Server Certificate Wizard or the IIScertdeploy.vbs script that comes with the IIS 6.0 Resource Kit. If you use the wizard, this time select the "Process the pending request and install the certificate" option.

SSL/TLS can be configured from the Directory Security tab, using the Edit... button in the Secure Communications section (see also Figure 6.11). This button is only enabled if you successfully installed a server certificate. The configuration screen is shown in Figure 6.19. In the configuration screen you can:

- Enable/disable SSL for a Web site.
- Require 128-bit encryption, which provides extra protection for Web sites that deal with sensitive personal and financial information.
- Set client certificate-based authentication options. Both the "Accept client certificates" and "Require client certificates" options require the deployment of certificates to your browser clients. As with server certificates, SSL/TLS client certificates can be acquired from an internal CA or from an external commercial CA.
- Enable certificate mapping (explained in the next section).
- Enable certificate trust lists (CTLs) (explained later in this chapter).

If you want to configure the port that is used for SSL communications, this can be done from the Web site tab in a Web site's properties (the default port is 443). The Advanced button also allows you to add multiple SSL identities for the site using different ports.

Client SSL/TLS certificates can also be requested from an internal or external CA. If you are using a Windows Server 2003–rooted PKI, users can request certificates using their Certificates MMC snap-in or the CA's Web interface (accessible using http://<servername>/certsrv). Administrators can

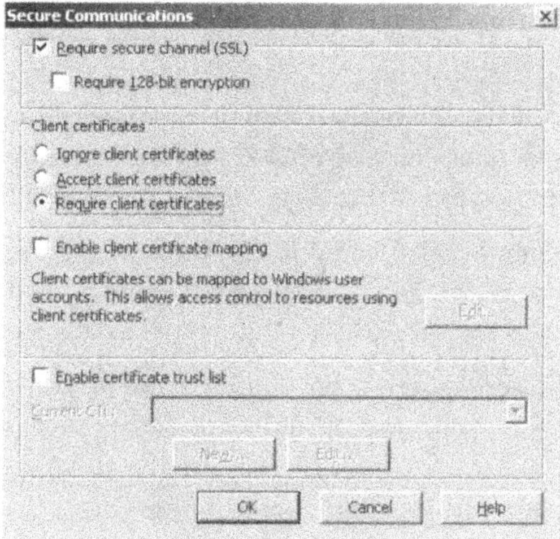

Figure 6.19 *Configuring SSL/TLS.*

also automatically enroll users for SSL/TLS certificates using a GPO setting. More details on user certificate enrollment can be found in Chapter 15. To add the server and client certificate's issuing CA's certificate to the user browser's trusted root certificate store, you can use different methods (these are explained in greater detail in Chapter 14):

- Use the IE Deployment Kit to create an install kit with CA's certificate added to the trusted root domains.
- Put the CA's certificate on a publicly accessible Web site where users can download and choose to trust it.
- Distribute the CA's certificate using a GPO setting.

An interesting property of the SSL implementation in Internet Explorer (IE) 6.0 and later is that users can manually clear the SSL cache from the IE GUI. This means that the client-side SSL authentication certificates can be removed from the browser cache. Normally certificates remain in the cache until the computer is restarted. To clear the SSL cache use the Clear SSL State pushbutton in the Internet Options\Content tab.

6.6.2 Certificate mapping

In order to facilitate Web server access control enforcement, SSL client authentication certificates can be mapped to Windows security identities. This feature is called certificate mapping. It allows you to apply authorization settings that are defined for Windows security identities to users who have authenticated to IIS using a certificate.

Certificate mapping can be defined in the IIS metabase or in the Active Directory (AD). In the latter case we're using a service that is known as the "Windows directory service mapper." AD-based mapping is an interesting option if you have multiple Web servers that all need to have certificate mappings defined. Instead of defining the mappings on every individual Web server, you can define them once in the central AD repository.

IIS metabase-based mapping can be defined from the ISM secure communications dialog box (illustrated in Figure 6.19) and is only available if you have checked the "enable client certificate mapping" checkbox.

Certificate mapping defined in the metabase can be set up in one of two modes: one-to-one mapping and many-to-one mapping.

- When using one-to-one mapping, IIS looks at the complete content of the client certificate to map it to a Windows security identity.
- Many-to-one certificate mapping is based on rules (as illustrated in Figure 6.20). In this case IIS looks at particular attributes of the client certificate (as defined in the rules) to map it to a Windows security identity.

AD-based mapping can be defined from the Users and Computers MMC snap-in: Use the Name mappings... option in an account object's context menu—this option is only available if the snap-in is in Advanced

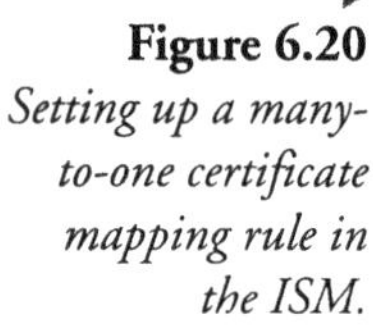

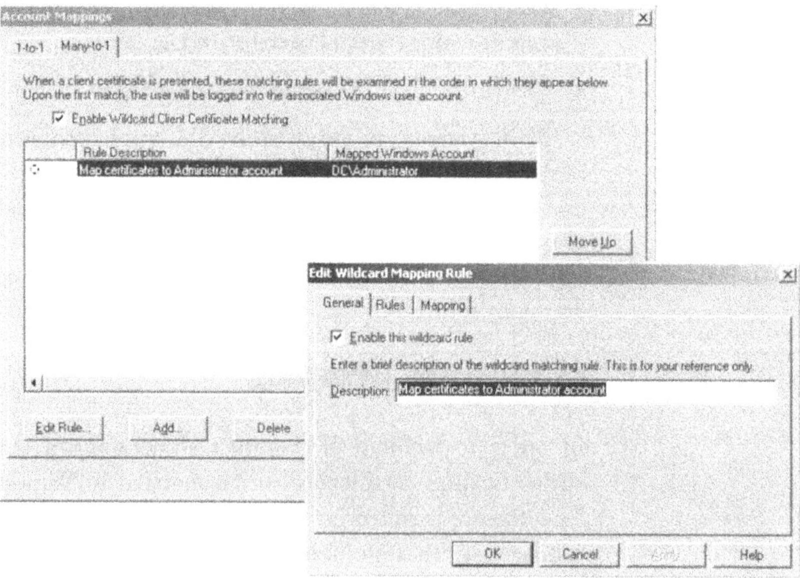

Figure 6.20 *Setting up a many-to-one certificate mapping rule in the ISM.*

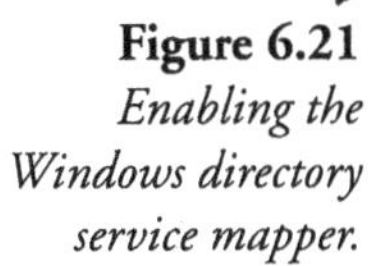

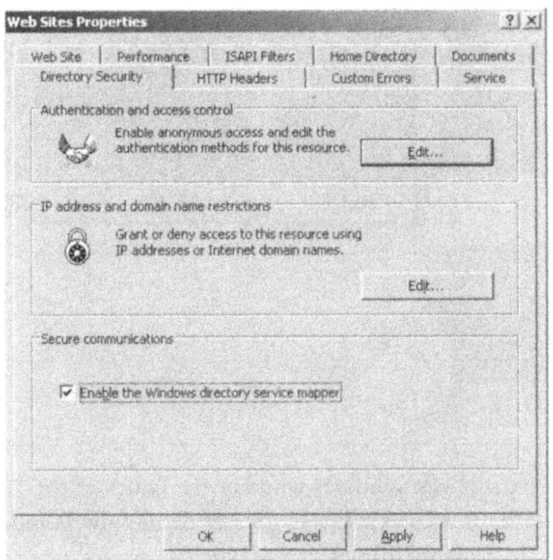

Figure 6.21 *Enabling the Windows directory service mapper.*

Features viewing mode. AD-based mapping only allows for one-to-one mapping. AD-based mapping or the Windows directory service mapper is enabled from the properties of the Web Sites container in the ISM (as illustrated in Figure 6.21).

6.6.3 Certificate validation

During the SSL/TLS protocol exchanges, both the browser and the Web server must validate each other's certificates (for the server side this is only true if also client-side certificate authentication has been enabled). SSL/TLS certificate validation includes the following checks (illustrated in Figure 6.22): an X.509 digital signature check, a trust check, a time check, a revocation check, and a formatting check. The certificate validation process is explained in greater detail in Chapter 15.

Every X.509 certificate includes a digital signature that is validated when the certificate is used. The digital signature check includes:

- *An integrity check:* A check that the certificate has not been tampered with
- *An authentication check:* A cryptographic check to determine that the Web site owns the private key that is associated with the public key stored in the certificate

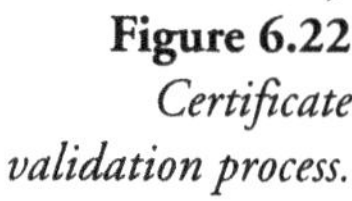

Figure 6.22 *Certificate validation process.*

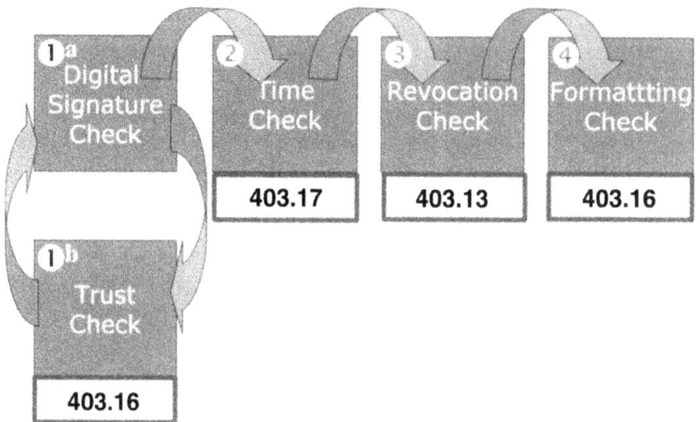

The trust check validates whether the issuer of the Web site's certificate is trusted. Chapter 14 explains in greater detail how Windows and its users and services (including IIS) determine whether or not a certificate is trustworthy. One feature that is worth pointing out here is the IIS support for Certificate Trust Lists (CTLs). A CTL is a signed list of trustworthy CA certificates that can be generated by the Web server administrator. A CTL can be configured using the CTL wizard that can be started from the secure communications dialog box (see also Figure 6.15). If the certificate's issuer is not trustworthy, IIS will generate a 403.16 HTTP error. On the browser side a security alert will be generated stating that "The security certificate was issued by a company you have not chosen to trust. View the certificate to determine whether you want to trust the certifying authority" (see Figure 6.23(a)).

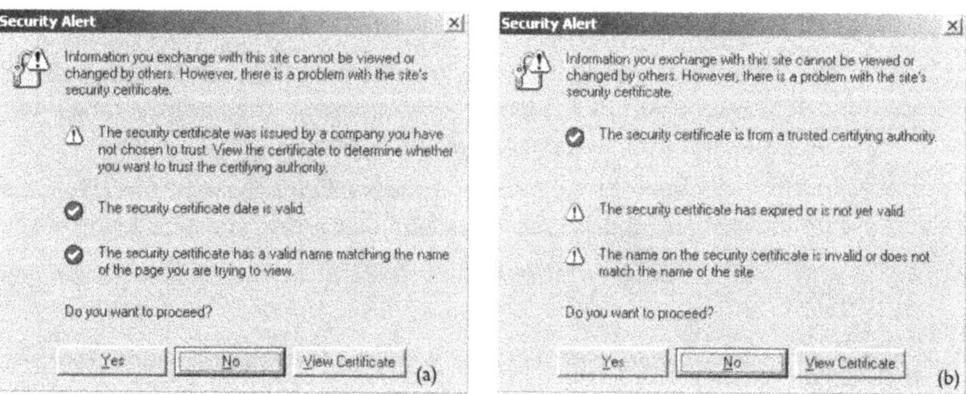

Figure 6.23 *(a) Browser-side certificate trust error, and (b) browser-side certificate time and name error.*

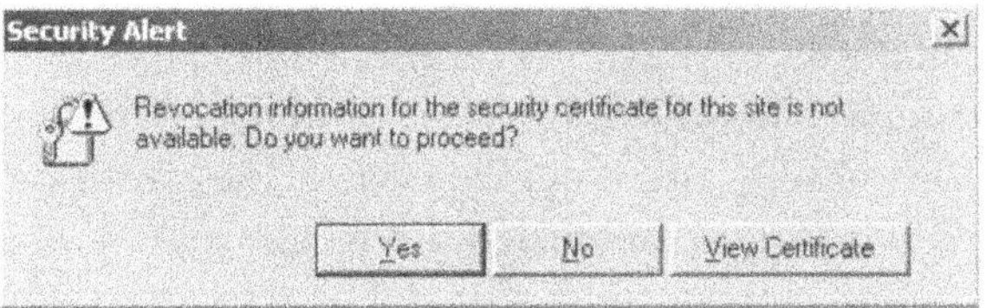

Figure 6.24 *Browser-side SSL/TLS revocation check error.*

The time check validates whether the certificate has expired. Every X.509 certificate has a limited lifetime. If the certificate has expired, IIS will generate a 403.17 HTTP error. On the browser side a security alert will be generated stating that "The security certificate has expired or is not yet valid" (see Figure 6.23(b)).

The revocation check validates whether the certificate has been revoked. By default, this check is not performed by Internet Explorer, but rather it is performed by IIS. In IIS revocation checking can be controlled using the certcheckmode metabase parameter (value 1 means revocation checking is disabled/value 0 means revocation checking is enabled). If the certificate has been revoked or if the CRL is not available, IIS generates a 403.13 HTTP error. On the browser side a security alert like the one shown in Figure 6.24 will be generated if the CRL is not available. Also, on the browser side revocation checking is controlled using the "check for server certificate revocation" entry in the browser's Internet options (illustrated in Figure 6.25).

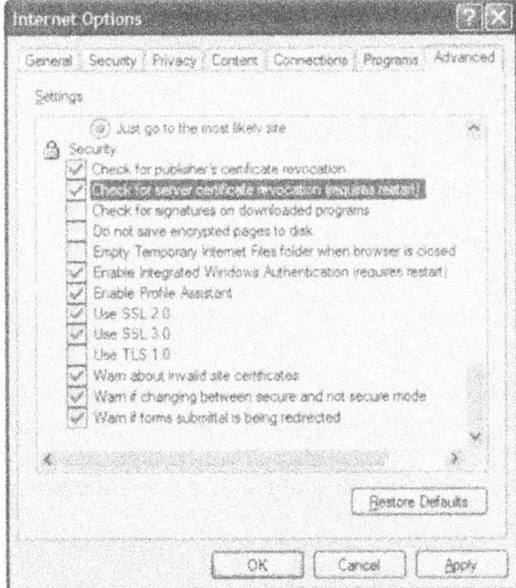

Figure 6.25 *Browser-side SSL/TLS certificate revocation checking option.*

The formatting check validates whether the content of an X.509 certificate conforms to the X.509 certificate format specification. The check also validates whether the common name in the certificate matches the name of the Web site—as entered in the URL. If the certificate is ill-formed or if the common names do not match, IIS will generate a 403.16 HTTP error. On the browser side a security alert will be generated stating that "The name of the security certificate is invalid or does not match the name of the site" (illustrated in Figure 6.23(b)).

6.6.4 Deployment considerations

In most enterprise environments you must consider the following deployment issues when setting up SSL/TLS for securing Web resources:

- SSL/TLS cannot be used in combination with HTTP host headers.
- SSL/TLS can have a performance impact on the Web server side.
- The combination of SSL/TLS and HTTP load balancing.
- SSL/TLS and HTTP proxy and/or firewall combined operation. This issue is discussed in greater detail in the next section.

When using https, you cannot use HTTP host headers to differentiate between different Web sites on the same Web server. This is because the SSL connection is set up before the HTTP connection and the HTTP information is sent in an encrypted format over the wire.

Table 6.1 *SSL/TLS Crypto Accelerator Devices*

Vendor	Device	More Information At:
Broadcom	■ CryptoNetX SSL800 ■ CryptoNetX SSL1600 ■ CryptoNetX SSL4000	http://www.broadcom.com
F5	■ Big IP SSL 400 ■ Big IP SSL 800	http://www.f5.com/f5products/bigip/SSL400800
HP (Compaq)	■ Atalla AXL 300	http://h18000.www1.hp.com/products/servers/security/axl300
Intel	■ Netstructure	http://www.intel.com/support/netstructure/index.htm
nCipher	■ nFast 800 ■ nFast 300	http://www.ncipher.com/nfast/index.html
Rainbow	■ Cryptoswift PCI	http://www.rainbow.com/products/cryptoswift/PCI.asp

Table 6.2 *SChannel Caching Registry Parameters*

Registry Parameter	Data Type	Default Value	Meaning
MaximumCacheSize	REG_DWORD	10,000	Maximum number of SSL sessions to maintain the cache
ClientCacheTime	REG_DWORD	10 hours	Time in milliseconds to expire a client-side cache element
ServerCacheTime	REG_DWORD	10 hours	Time in milliseconds to expire a server-side cache element

The asymmetric cryptographic operations behind the certificate-based authentication in SSL/TLS can impact the Web server performance. To deal with this performance issue, you can do three things:

1. Use hardware crypto accelerators devices. These devices offload the main system processor by using a dedicated processor for the cryptographic operations. Table 6.1 gives some example devices (this is a nonexhaustive list).

2. Limit the Web page size. Limiting the Web page size reduces the amount of data that need to be cryptographically processed.

3. Reuse cached SSL sessions to limit the number of SSL negotiations. You can fine-tune the SSL caching behavior by using the registry parameters in Table 6.2. They are located in the HKEY_LOCAL_MACHINE\system\currentcontrolset\control\securityproviders\schannel registry key.[8]

When using SSL in a Web load balancing environment (e.g., in a Web farm setup), you must make sure that your load balancing solution supports sticky sessions (also known as server affinity). Sticky sessions assure that the HTTP connection always returns to the same Web server in a server farm during a user Web connection sequence. This is key when the Web server maintains user session data.

6.6.5 SSL in proxy and firewall environments

SSL can be configured in different ways when dealing with HTTP proxies: The different approaches can be categorized as either SSL tunneling or SSL

8. These registry settings were available for IIS 4.0 and 5.0 and documented in the following KB article: http://support.microsoft.com/default.aspx?scid=kb;en-us;247658. At the time of writing, no update to the KB article was available for IIS 6.0.

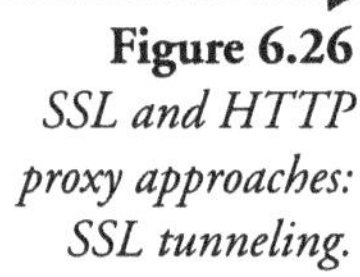

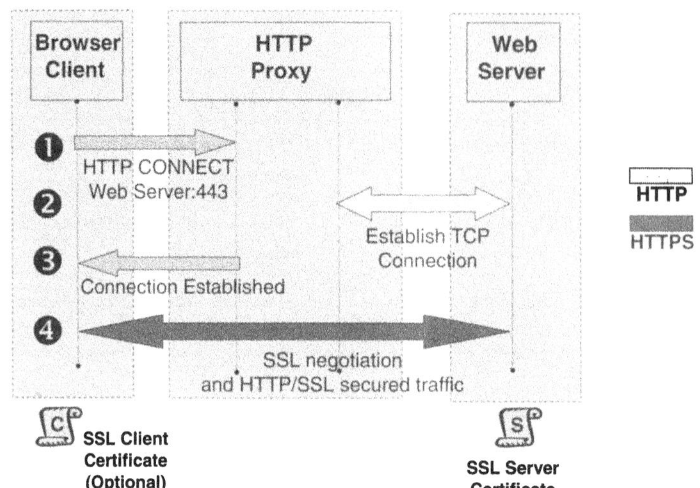

Figure 6.26 *SSL and HTTP proxy approaches: SSL tunneling.*

bridging. HTTP proxies are used in almost every perimeter security solution that includes application proxy-based firewalls and/or HTTP proxies.

An SSL tunneling setup provides true end-to-end SSL: The SSL tunnel starts on the browser and ends on the Web server. It is illustrated in Figure 6.26. It requires an SSL authentication certificate on the Web server and optionally an SSL client certificate on the client side. The problem with SSL bridging is that it breaks the role of an HTTP proxy. An HTTP proxy typically inspects the content of an HTTP request before it lets the request through. When using SSL the HTTP request cannot be inspected because the HTTP content is encrypted by the SSL tunnel. This is because an SSL tunnel is always set up before the HTTP application-level traffic reaches the destination host. SSL operates on the session level of the TCP/IP networking stack, while HTTP operates on the application level.

Does this mean that it is impossible to let an SSL tunnel flow through a firewall or HTTP proxy? No. To enable SSL tunnels to flow through HTTP proxies, SSL-enabled applications can use the HTTP CONNECT method. This method tells the proxy to ignore the content of an SSL session and to simply forward the SSL packets to the destination host (in this case a Web server). The HTTP CONNECT method is defined in RFC 2817 (available from the IETF Web site at http://www.ietf.org). It is important to stress that from a pure security point of view, SSL tunneling is not the best approach; it basically punches holes into your firewalls.

The alternative to SSL tunneling is SSL bridging. Using SSL bridging takes away the security concern expressed earlier for SSL tunneling. SSL

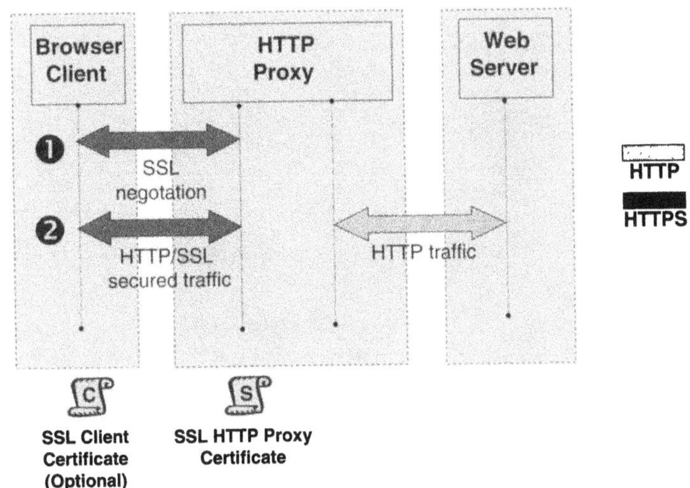

Figure 6.27 *SSL and HTTP proxy approaches: SSL bridging (single tunnel terminated on proxy).*

bridging basically means that the SSL tunnel is started or terminated on the HTTP proxy. As a consequence, there is no more end-to-end SSL tunnel setup. SSL bridging can be set up in different ways:

- Using a single SSL tunnel that starts on the client side and terminates on the HTTP proxy. This approach is illustrated in Figure 6.27. It requires an SSL certificate for the HTTP proxy and optionally an SSL certificate for the client side (if strong client-side authentication is required).
- Using a single SSL tunnel that starts on the HTTP proxy and terminates on the Web server. This approach is illustrated in Figure 6.28. It

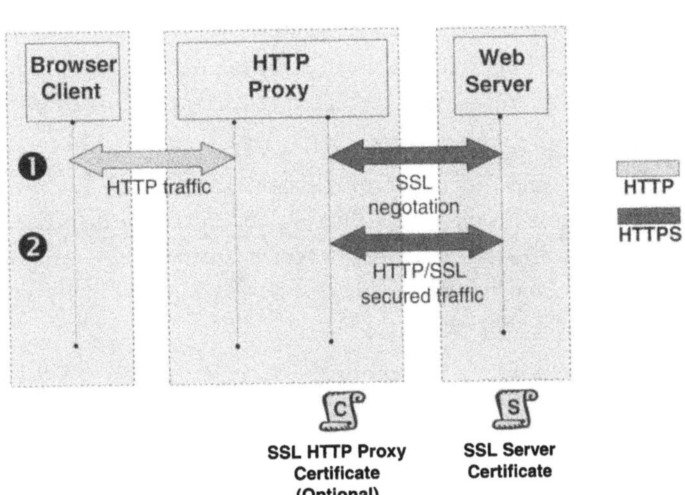

Figure 6.28 *SSL and HTTP proxy approaches: SSL bridging (single tunnel terminated on Web server).*

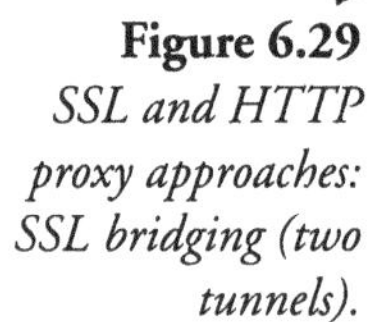

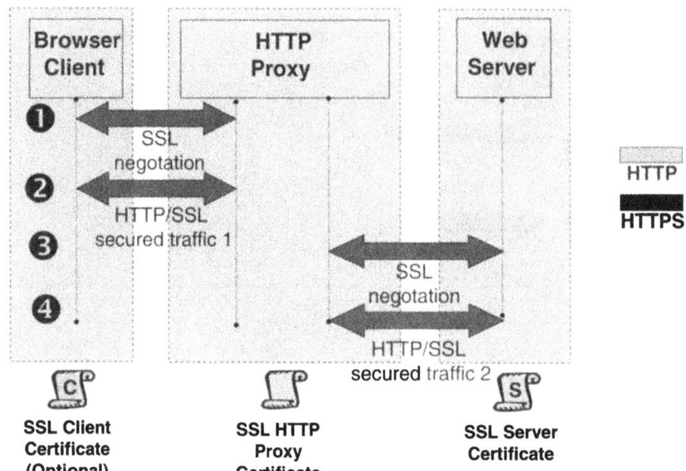

Figure 6.29 *SSL and HTTP proxy approaches: SSL bridging (two tunnels).*

requires an SSL certificate for the Web server and optionally an SSL certificate for the HTTP proxy (if strong client-side authentication is required).

- Using two SSL tunnels: one starting on the client and terminating on the HTTP proxy and another one starting on the HTTP proxy and terminating on the Web server. This approach is illustrated in Figure 6.29. It requires an SSL certificate on the HTTP proxy and Web server and optionally an SSL certificate on the client side (if strong client-side authentication is required).

Setting up SSL Bridging and Tunneling in an MS ISA Server Environment

ISA Server is Microsoft's follow-up product to Proxy Server 2.0. Unlike its predecessor, which was primarily a Web caching solution, ISA Server can serve as a full-blown firewall. In addition, ISA Server provides advanced packet filtering and application proxy firewall functions.

To set up SSL bridging on ISA Server, you must create an ISA Server destination set and Web publishing rule. To facilitate the configuration of SSL bridging in an OWA environment, Microsoft provides an OWA Publishing Wizard in Feature Pack 1 for ISA Server (illustrated in Figure 6.30). ISA Server Feature Pack 1 can be downloaded from http://www.microsoft.com/downloads/details.aspx?FamilyID=2f92b02c-ac49-44df-af6c-5be084b345f9&DisplayLang=en.

To configure ISA Server for SSL tunneling you need to use ISA Server's Server Publishing feature. Compared to setting up SSL bridging, setting up SSL tunneling is relatively easy, mainly because no SSL certificate must be set up for the ISA Server.

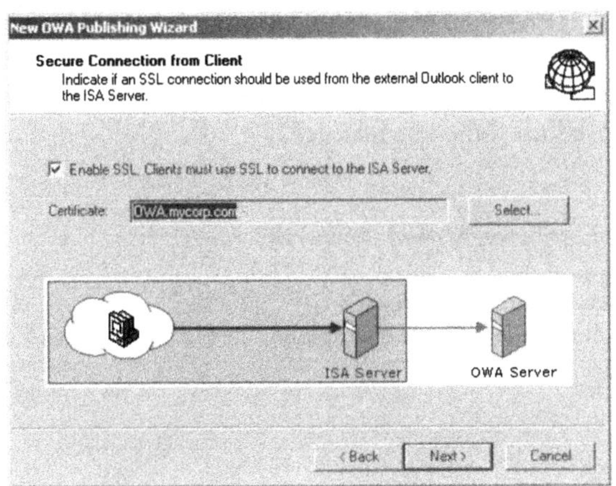

Figure 6.30 *Setting up SSL bridging using the OWA Publishing Wizard.*

Table 6.3 shows the different SSL approaches and their advantages and disadvantages.

Table 6.3 *SSL and HTTP Proxy Approaches*

SSL Approach	Pros	Cons
SSL Tunneling	■ End-to-end SSL	■ Security hole on HTTP proxy and firewall level: the proxy cannot screen for exploit infected content anymore
SSL Bridging—Option 1: Single SSL tunnel, started on client and terminated on proxy	■ HTTP content inspection on HTTP proxy and firewall level (no security hole) ■ Offloads SSL processing from Web server	■ No end-to-end SSL ■ HTTP traffic goes in the clear between proxy and Web server
SSL Bridging—Option 2: Single SSL tunnel, started on proxy and terminated on Web server	■ HTTP content inspection on HTTP proxy and firewall level (no security hole) ■ HTTP traffic is encrypted between proxy and Web server	■ No end-to-end SSL ■ HTTP traffic goes in the clear between browser and HTTP proxy
SSL Bridging—Option 3: Two SSL tunnels	■ HTTP content inspection on HTTP proxy and firewall level (no security hole) ■ HTTP traffic is encrypted both between browser and proxy and between proxy and Web server	■ No end-to-end SSL

6.7 IIS Authentication method comparison

Table 6.4 contains a comparison of the different IIS authentication protocols based on some key features.

Table 6.4 *IIS Authentication Method Comparison*

	Basic Authentication	Digest Authentication	NTLM	Kerberos	Certificate-Based	Passport
Protocol based on Open Standard	Yes	Yes	No	Yes	Yes	No
Relies on Windows accounts	Yes	Yes	Yes	Yes	No*	No†
Delegation support (credential forwarding)	Yes	No	No	Yes	No	No
Supports non-IE browsers	Yes	No	No	No	Yes	Yes
Requires SSL	Yes	No	No	No	Yes	No
Requires Windows 2000 or later clients and servers	No	Yes	No	Yes	No	No
Supports authentication through firewalls and proxies	Yes	Yes	No	No	Yes	Yes

* Can be mapped to Windows accounts
† Same as previous footnote.

7

Microsoft Passport

Passport, Microsoft's single identity and sign-on solution for the Web, has since its initial release back in 1999 been a controversial technology. Most Passport-related discussions concerned the product's security and privacy features. The primary goal of this chapter is to explore the security and privacy features of Passport. To do so, we will need to dive into the nuts and bolts of the Passport message exchanges. This chapter focuses particularly on how Microsoft has integrated Passport with its latest operating system platforms: Windows XP and Windows Server 2003.

7.1 Passport-enabling Web technologies

Passport uses common Web technologies that are supported by all browsers. These technologies are the Hypertext Transport Protocol (HTTP), Dynamic Web Pages with embedded JavaScript code, Cookies, and the Secure Sockets Layer (SSL) protocol. It is worth pointing out that so far (through Passport version 2.5)[1] Passport uses no (or very little) XML-based technology. In a future version of Passport the service will adopt a new SOAP- and XML-based authentication protocol derived from the WS-Security specification.[2]

Passport uses HTTP to retrieve Passport Web pages from Passport-enabled Web servers, in order to transport Passport-related user information, to create client-side cookies, to retrieve information from client-side cookies, and to redirect browsers from one Web site to another. Passport makes extensive use of HTTP redirect messages. HTTP redirect messages allow Web sites to communicate with one another without setting up a

1. At the time of writing (end 2003) version 2.5 was the most recent Passport version.
2. More info on WS-Security can be found at msdn.microsoft.com/ws-security.

direct communication between the Web sites' Web servers: all communications go via the user browser.

JavaScript code embedded in Web server pages enables Passport to deliver dynamic Web content like personalized Web pages to the user's browser. The reason why Microsoft has selected JavaScript over typical MS scripting technologies like VBScript is because JavaScript is supported on all browsers, not just in Microsoft browsers.

Cookies allow for both the temporary and persistent storage of Passport-related information on the user desktop. They are created by code on the Passport infrastructure servers. To store confidential user information, Passport uses encrypted cookies.

Passport uses SSL to create secure tunnels for the transport of confidential user data between browsers and Web servers. The SSL tunnel provides data authentication, confidentiality and integrity protection, and server-side authentication. The SSL protocol was explained in Chapter 6.

7.2 Passport infrastructure

Before diving into the nuts and bolts of how Passport works, we need a clear view of the Passport infrastructure. The Passport infrastructure components can be classified into three categories: the Microsoft Passport Nexus servers, the Passport domain authority servers, and the Web servers of the participating Web sites (as illustrated in Figure 7.1). The infrastructure servers a Passport user deals with are the domain authorities and participating Web sites.

- Participating Web site is a site that provides its users with the possibility to log on using Passport SSO. The owners of the site have installed some Passport-specific code on the Web server (including the Passport Manager COM object) and have signed an agreement with Microsoft or one of the Passport domain authorities to join the Passport SSO network. Examples of participating Passport sites are MoneyCentral, Starbucks, eBay, and ActiveState. An up-to-date list of participating Passport Web sites can be found at http://www.passport.com/directory. This directory only lists those participating sites which have chosen to be listed.
- A domain authority server is a trusted third party that owns a Passport domain and acts as a Passport authentication authority for that domain. Examples are the domain authority servers for the msn.com,

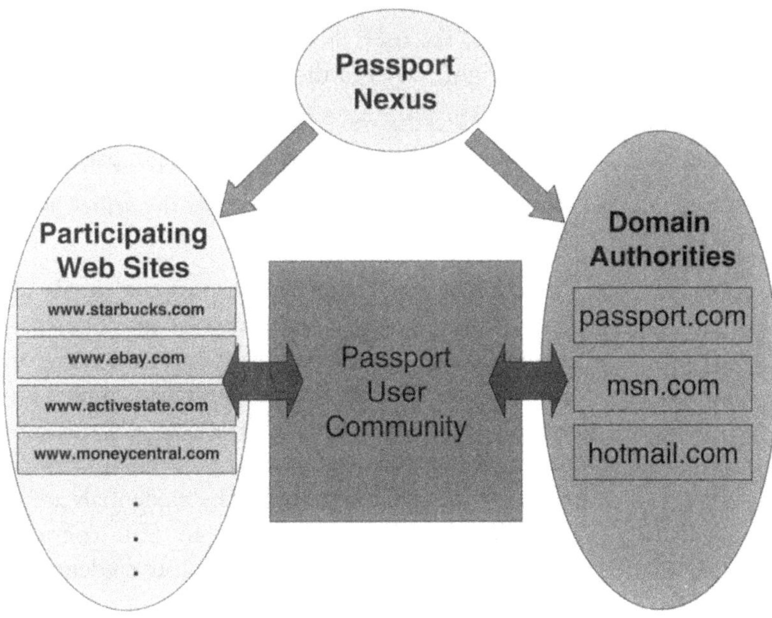

Figure 7.1 *Passport infrastructure.*

hotmail.com, and passport.com domains. Until now, all domain authorities were run by Microsoft or by business entities that are very closely related to Microsoft. Every domain authority manages a domain authority database that contains a secured copy of the users' Passport credentials and profile information.

- The Microsoft Passport Nexus servers make up the core of the Passport system. They provide configuration information to all other servers in the Passport Infrastructure, which includes things like the Passport user profile schema and the cryptographic keys used to secure certain Passport cookies.

7.3 Basic passport authentication exchange

In the following sections we will first explain how a basic Passport authentication exchange works in a non-Windows XP or Windows Server 2003 environment. In the following scenario, the user is working from a Windows 2000 machine. The user already has a set of Passport credentials and is not logged on to Passport. The scenario starts when the user enters the http://www.moneycentral.com URL in his browser. Let's look at what happens next from a Passport message exchange point of view (the exchanges are illustrated in Figure 7.2):

- Step 1: In order to authenticate to Passport and the MoneyCentral Web site, the user clicks the Passport "Sign In" icon located in the upper right corner of the MoneyCentral homepage.
- Step 2: Clicking the "Sign In" icon causes an HTTP redirect to the Passport domain authority server's login page.
- Step 3: The Passport domain authority server presents the user with a Passport login page.
- Step 4: The user enters his Passport credentials in the Passport login page. Javascript code embedded in the login page parses the username, extracts the domain portion of the name and uses it to determine which Passport domain authority to post the credentials to. As mentioned above there are three Passport domain authorities: MSN (for all msn.com users), Hotmail (for all hotmail.com users) and Passport (for all other domains). The credentials are sent to the Passport domain authority server over an SSL connection. The domain authority server then validates the user credentials.
- Step 5: If the user's Passport authentication is okay, the Passport domain authority server generates an HTTP redirect back to the MoneyCentral server.
- Step 6: The Passport domain authority server writes a set of domain- and user-specific Passport data to the user's machine.
- Step 7: The MoneyCentral Web server sends a new copy of the MoneyCentral homepage to the user's browser. On this new copy the Passport "Sign In" icon has changed to a "Sign Out" icon. The

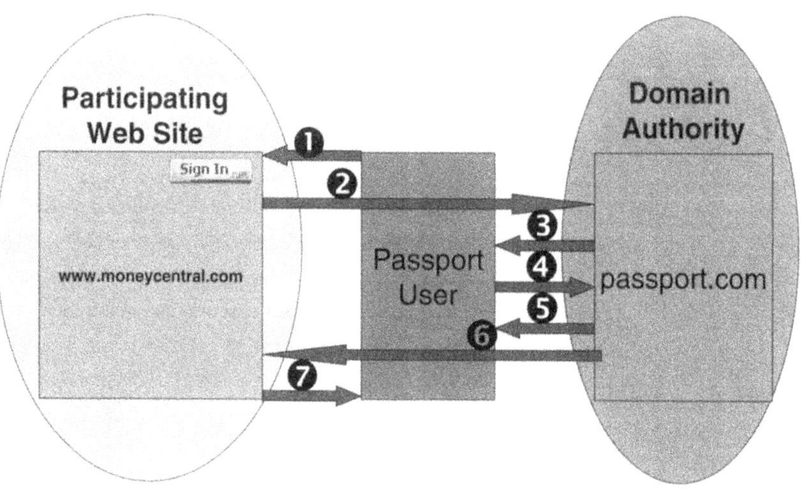

Figure 7.2 *Passport authentication sequence.*

MoneyCentral Web server also writes a set of site- and user-specific Passport data to the user's machine.

If the user hadn't already obtained a set of Passport credentials before clicking the "Sign In" icon in step 1 of the exchange, the scenario would look slightly different: In this case Passport would first redirect the user to a registration Web page in order to create a set of Passport credentials.

The actual URL for the redirect in Step 5 is specified by the participating site in the original authentication redirect of Step 2. This URL is validated against the site's Passport Site ID before the user is redirected back. The redirect URL must be within the primary domain of the site as registered in the Passport Nexus. This also means that authenticated users can be sent to locations other than the participating site's homepage: for example sending authenticated MSN users to the "My MSN" page rather than the MSN homepage after authentication.

An important feature of the basic Passport authentication sequence explained above is that the user's Passport credentials are never sent to the participating Web site. The participating Web site relies on a Passport-specific mechanism to actually authenticate the user. This mechanism is explained in Section 7.5.

The credentials that the user uses to authenticate to Passport in Step 4 are the user's e-mail address and a password or PIN code of at least six characters. Beginning with version 2.0, Passport supports a feature that is known as "strong-credential sign-in." It requires the user to enter, besides this e-mail address and password, a four-digit security key in order to authenticate to Passport. Passport will automatically block the user's Passport account key after ten attempts to log on with the wrong security key. Strong-credential sign-in is a Passport infrastructure feature: Its availability is independent of the platform that is used on the Passport user side. Strong-credential sign-in combined with Passport's use of the SSL protocol for the exchange of authentication-related data greatly enhances the security of the Passport protocol.

Another initiative that will certainly enhance the Passport security quality is to make Passport users aware of a Passport spoofing problem and its associated risks. A simple trick you can teach your users is how to check the authenticity of the name attributes of an SSL Passport server certificate (e.g., making sure that the certificate was issued to the "passport.com" Web site and not "pasport.com") or a Passport Web site's URL (e.g., making sure the URL shows http://login.passport.com and not http://login.pasport.com). These spoofing attacks on earlier Passport versions were also known as "Bogus Merchant" attacks. For an overview of these attacks, take a look at David Kormann and Aviel Rubin's paper available at http://avirubin.com/passport.html.

7.4 XP and Windows Server 2003 changes

When the user is using a Windows XP or Windows Server 2003 operating system platform, the Passport authentication exchange can be slightly different. In XP and Windows Server 2003, part of the Passport authentication can be managed by the operating system instead of the browser. In XP and Windows Server 2003, Microsoft implemented a security feature called the credential manager. It is a single sign-on solution based on a secure client-side credential cache. Credential manager is explained in greater detail in Chapter 9.

In XP and Windows Server 2003 Passport can use a login dialog box that is generated by the operating system (illustrated in Figure 7.3) rather than the web-based dialog that is retrieved from the Passport domain authority server. You may have noticed in Figure 7.3 that the Passport login dialog box has a different layout depending on the participating Web site from which the Passport authentication process was started—this feature is known as "cobranding."

This aspect of Windows integration is optional. The participating site controls whether they want the OS-based or Web-based login dialog box based on the specific calls that are made to the Passport Manager COM object. Due to limitations in cobranding on the OS-based dialog, most participating sites opt for the web-based approach. Both approaches use the credential manager.

When using the OS-based Passport login dialog box, only Steps 3 and 4 of the Passport authentication exchange are different (Steps 1 and 2 and 5 through 7 remain identical; see Figure 7.2):

- Step 3: The Passport domain authority server requests the user's operating system platform (Windows XP or Windows Server 2003) to display the Passport login dialog box rather than presenting the user with a Passport login page. (This is the case on pre-XP and Windows Server 2003 Passport platforms.)
- Step 4: The user enters his Passport credentials in the Passport login dialog box. The credentials are sent to the Passport domain authority server over an SSL connection. The domain authority server then val-

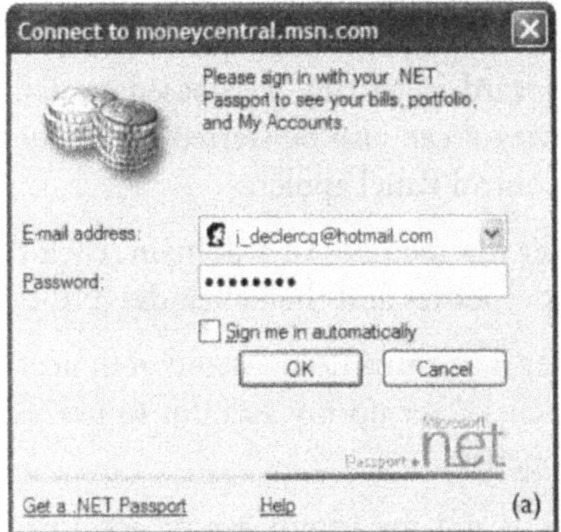

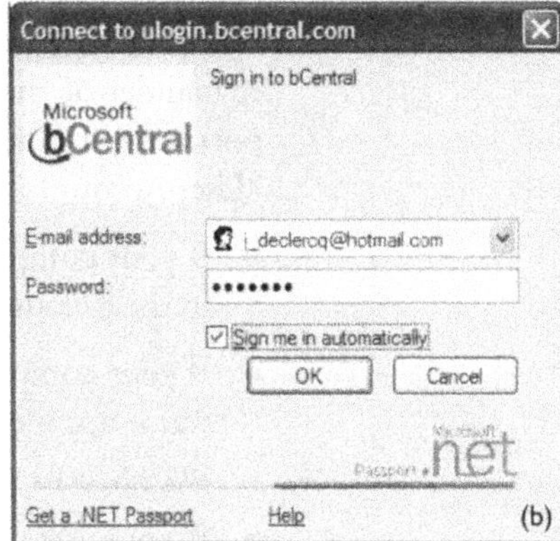

Figure 7.3 *Windows XP and Windows Server 2003 built-in MS Passport login dialog box: (a) MoneyCentral login and (b) bCentral login.*

idates the user credentials. With the exception of the use of the Passport "login dialog box," this step is identical to the way it worked on pre-XP and Windows Server 2003 Passport platforms.

Passport credentials can be saved in the credential manager. Because the credential manager's data are stored in the user profile, the credentials can be cached locally on the user's machine or remotely on a server (in the case of a roaming profile). To store your Passport credentials in the credential manager cache, check the "Sign me in automatically" checkbox (as illustrated in Figure 7.3).

In Windows XP and Windows Server 2003, Passport registration also works differently: Instead of redirecting the user to a Passport registration page, XP and Windows Server 2003 start the .NET Passport wizard (illustrated in Figure 7.4). The wizard, which comes bundled with the Windows

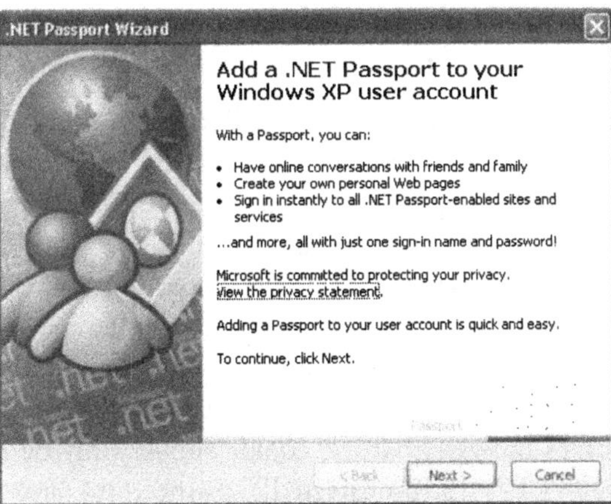

Figure 7.4 *.NET Passport Wizard.*

Server 2003 and XP OSs, will guide the user through the Passport registration process. Only the first page of the wizard is hard-coded in the OS, the remainder of the wizard is actually web-based content hosted by the Passport servers. The wizard can also be started manually at any time from the "User Accounts" Control Panel applet.

- If your computer is a member of a domain, click the "Advanced" tab in the account properties and then click the .NET Passport Wizard.
- If your computer is not in a domain and your account is an administrator account, click "Set up my account to use a .NET Passport" in the account properties.
- If your account is not an administrator account, click "Set up my account to use a .NET Passport" in the "Pick a task" bar.

7.5 Passport cookies

To understand the way Passport works, it is especially interesting to look at the different Passport cookies that are exchanged between the user browser, the participating Web sites, and the domain authorities.

The easiest way to see the cookies that are sent to the user browser during a Passport authentication sequence is to disable automatic cookie handling and set the cookie "prompt" option in the properties of your Internet Explorer browser. When you do this, your browser will prompt you each time a cookie is sent to your browser. To set this up in Internet Explorer 6.0 (this is the IE version that comes bundled with Windows XP and Windows Server 2003), select Internet Options from the Tools menu option, and go to the privacy tab. Click the "Advanced" button (as illustrated in Figure 7.5) and check the "Override automatic cookie handling" box—then select "Prompt" for both first-party and third-party cookies.

The next time you perform a Passport authentication sequence, your browser will generate several "Privacy Alert" warning dialog boxes (like the one illustrated in Figure 7.6) each time the Web site you are accessing tries to save a cookie to your machine. If you click "More Info," the dialog box is expanded and shows all the cookie properties. Interesting cookie properties to observe are the cookie name, the cookie domain (which is the domain that is attempting to write a cookie to your machine), the "expires" property (which informs you when the cookie expires), the secure property (indicates to the user's browser that the cookie should only be returned to the server over an HTTPs [SSL-protected]) connection) and the session property

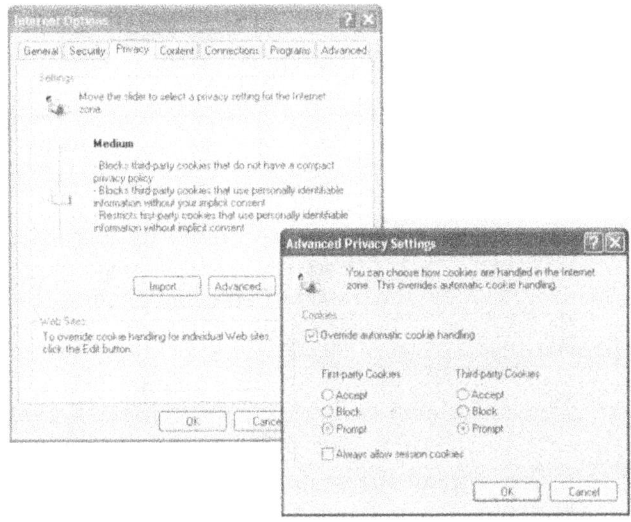

Figure 7.5 *Disabling automatic cookie handling in Internet Explorer 6.0.*

(which informs you whether the cookie is persistent or deleted at the end of the browser session).

Table 7.1 lists the most important cookies the Passport authentication system deals with. By default all Passport cookies are session cookies (also known as nonpersistent cookies) that are deleted from the cookie cache at the end of the browser session. Passport cookies can also "expire" at the end of the time period that is specified in the cookie by the Passport domain authority or participating Web site. If a user selects the "Sign me in automatically" option on the Passport login dialog the Passport cookies become persistent cookies.

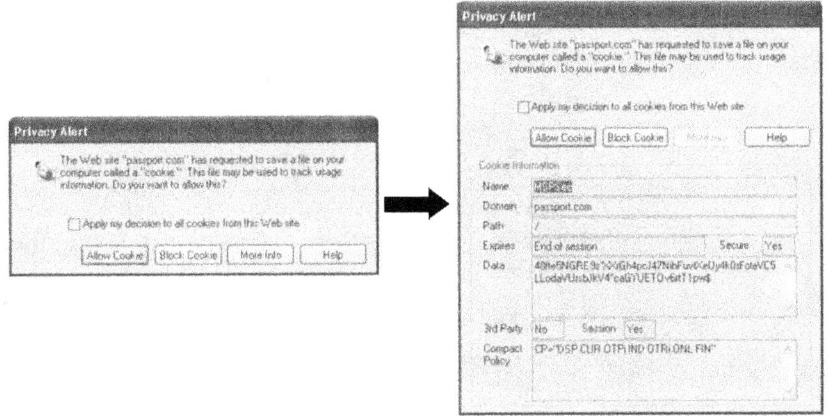

Figure 7.6 *Internet Explorer cookie "privacy alert."*

Table 7.1 *Passport Cookie Types*

Cookie Name	Cookie Short Name	Encryption?
Ticket-Granting Cookie	MSPSec	Encrypted using domain authority's encryption key
Ticket Cookie	MSPAuth	Encrypted using domain authority's or participating Web site's encryption key
Profile Cookie	MSPProf	Encrypted using domain authority's or participating Web site's encryption key
Visited Sites Cookie	MSPVis	Encrypted using domain authority's encryption key

The last column of Table 7.1 shows how the content of the cookies is secured. Passport uses a set of symmetric encryption keys in order to provide data confidentiality protection of cookie content. Every domain authority has an encryption key and also every participating Web site has an encryption key. The latter key is known to both the domain authority and the participating Web site. The encryption key is a 168-bit key that is regularly updated. The encryption algorithm used from Passport version 2 onward is Triple DES (3DES).

Passport uses two types of ticket cookies: ticket-granting cookies and "plain" ticket cookies. This system is very much inspired by the Kerberos authentication protocol.

The Passport ticket-granting cookie is the cookie that is generated at the beginning of a Passport logon session, which begins when the user signs in to Passport using the Sign In icon. It ends when the user closes his browser or when he signs out from Passport by clicking the Sign Out icon on a Participating Web site. The ticket-granting cookie is used to silently request a renewal of the ticket cookie for the domain authority or to request a new ticket cookie for a participating Web site to the Passport domain authority. Thanks to the ticket-granting cookie a user must not enter his Passport credentials repeatedly every time a ticket cookie must be renewed or a new ticket cookie must be requested. The ticket-granting cookie contains a user's Passport Unique IDentifier (PUID) and a hash of the user's credential information. The content is encrypted using the domain authority's encryption key.

A ticket cookie is used to authenticate a user to the domain authority or to a participating Web site during a Passport logon session. It contains the user's PUID and a set of encrypted timestamps. The latter protect against replay attacks. A ticket cookie's content is encrypted using the domain authority's encryption key (in the case of the ticket cookie for the domain authority) or using the participating Web site's encryption key (in the case of a ticket for a participating Web site).

The visited sites cookie contains a list of the participating Web sites that a user has visited from his or her computers since last Sign Out. This site list is used to clear all Passport-related cookies when a Passport user clicks the Sign Out icon to sign out of his Passport account.

A Profile cookie contains a Passport user's profile data. Like ticket cookies, profile cookies provide ease of use to a Passport user, who does not have to keep retyping his personal data every time he accesses another Web site. Passport deals with two different profile cookie types:

- One profile cookie contains the user's general profile information (also known as the user Passport "core" profile). Its content is encrypted using the domain authority's encryption key.
- The other profile cookie contains a user's general profile information and optionally additional profile information that is specific to a participating Web site. Its content is encrypted using the participating Web site's encryption key. At the time of writing, the content of the Passport profile cookies in the domain authority's domain and in the participating site's domain were identical. Passport did not store or pass site specific profile information within its cookies.

The user's general or core profile always contains the user's e-mail address and may optionally contain the user's first and last name, country/region, postal code, state, time zone, preferred language, gender, accessibility, occupation, and full birth date. By default, the option to include or not include the latter data in the user's profile is entirely up to the user. Some domain authorities, such as Hotmail, require these profile fields to be specified during registration. Passport stores the user data into the Passport core profile at registration time. From Passport 2.0 on a user can at any time after the initial registration change the content of the profile and decide which profile data to share with Passport participating Web sites.

Table 7.2 gives an overview of the Passport user data discussed so far. It shows the required and optional data for Passport registration and whether the data are by default shared with participating Passport sites during a Passport logon session.

Table 7.2 *Passport User Data*

Passport User Data Type	Content		Required During Registration?	Shared During Passport Logon Session?
PUID	Passport Unique Identifier		Yes	Yes
User General or Core Profile	E-mail address		Yes	User-defined default=No
	First and last name Country/region, postal code, state Time zone, preferred language, gender, accessibility, occupation Full birth date		No	User-defined default=No
Passport Credentials	Standard	E-mail address	Yes	User-defined default=No
		Password or PIN	Yes	No
	Strong credential sign-in	Four-digit key	No	No

7.6 Passport authentication revisited

Let us now revisit the Passport authentication exchange of Figure 7.4 and look at which cookies are sent back and forth between the different Passport components. This exchange is illustrated in Figure 7.7.

An important component in the Passport authentication cookie exchanges is the Passport Manager COM object. It is a server-side automation object that is installed on all participating Web sites. The Passport Manager object provides encryption services to protect Passport user data and handles the Passport cookie setting, parsing, and expiration logic. It also silently communicates with the Passport Nexus servers to determine the current configuration of the Passport network. Besides cookies, it also uses the HTTP query string as an intermediary for querying the central user store at the Passport domain authority. The advantage of using cookies over the HTTP query string as a data storage intermediary is that the URL display in the user's browser (the Internet Explorer "Address Bar") does not become cluttered with cryptic information:

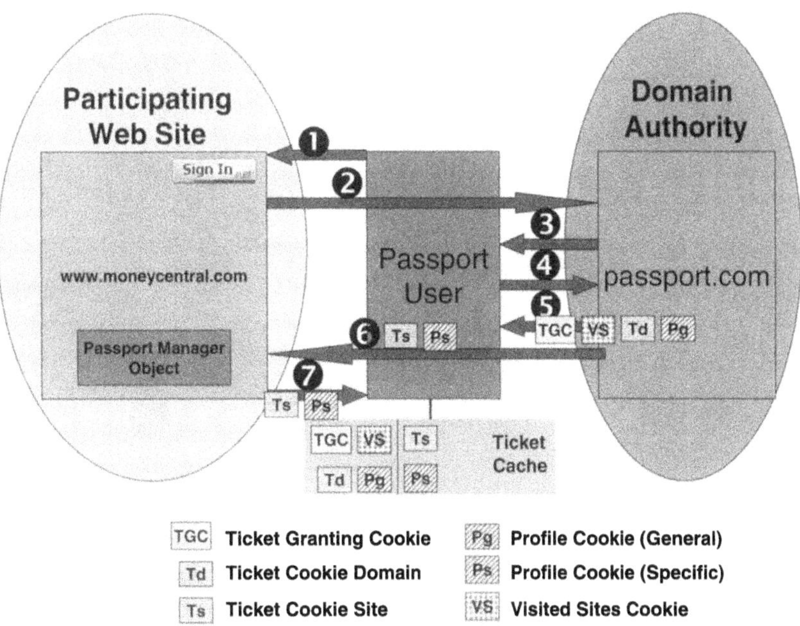

Figure 7.7 *Passport authentication sequence including cookies: initial login (Windows XP and Windows Server 2003).*

- During Step 5 the Passport domain authority redirects the user to the participating Web site. In the query string of the HTTP redirect message, the domain authority appends the ticket cookie and the specific profile cookie for the participating Web site.
- During Step 6 the Passport domain authority writes the ticket-granting cookie, the ticket cookie for the domain, the general profile cookie for the domain, and the visited sites cookie to the user's machine.
- During Step 7 the Passport Manager COM object on the participating Web site decrypts the cookies it received from the domain authority, validates them, and then writes them to the user's machine.

Note the different cookies that are stored in the user's cookie store on the user's machine. In Windows XP and Windows Server 2003, user-specific cookies are stored in the "cookies" folder of the user profile.

Figure 7.8 shows the Passport cookies that are exchanged when the user accesses another Web site (in the example "Starbucks.com" during the user's Passport logon session0. In this case the Passport Authentication Sequence will be slightly shorter:

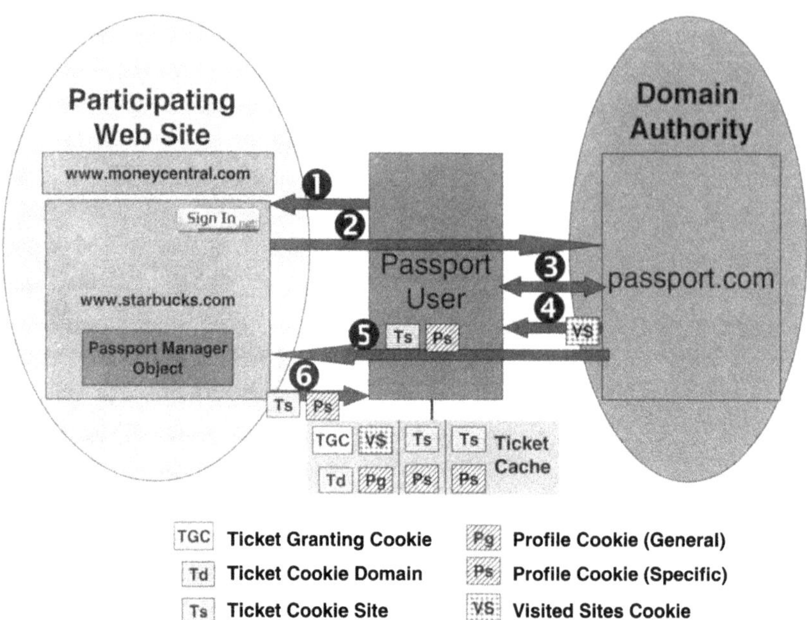

Figure 7.8 *Passport authentication sequence including cookies: log in to second site (Windows XP and Windows Server 2003).*

- Step 1: The authentication sequence starts when the user clicks the "Sign In" icon on the Starbucks homepage.
- Step 2: Clicking the "Sign In" icon causes an HTTP redirect to the Passport domain authority server's login page.
- Step 3: The Passport domain authority server queries the user's cookie cache and detects that the user has a valid ticket-granting cookie. As a consequence, the domain authority will not request the user's operating system platform to display the Passport login dialog box.
- Step 4: The Passport domain authority redirects the user to the participating Web site. In the query string of the HTTP redirect message, the domain authority appends the ticket cookie and the specific profile cookie for the Starbucks Web site.
- Step 5: Because the user has a set of valid domain cookies, the Passport domain authority only updates the visited sites cookie to include a reference to Starbucks.com and writes it to the user's machine.
- Step 6: The Passport Manager COM object on the Starbucks Web site decrypts the cookies it received from the domain authority, validates them, and then writes them to the user's machine.

7.7 Passport and the privacy of user information

Tightly intertangled with the ubiquity of the World Wide Web is the problem of universal distribution of personal information. The latter is better known as the privacy problem. Microsoft understands the importance of addressing privacy issues effectively in order to win universal acceptance for its Passport Single Sign-On technology. Among the Microsoft privacy-related initiatives are its support for the TRUSTe initiative (http://www.truste.org), the W3C's P3P initiative, and the inclusion of privacy-related features in its latest software products (including the latest Passport versions). To read Microsoft's general privacy statement, go to http://www.microsoft.com/info/privacy.htm. To read the Passport-specific privacy statement, go to http://www.passport.com/consumer/privacypolicy.asp.

From Passport version 2.0 forward, a Passport user can easily modify the content of his or her Passport user profile and decide which data he or she wants to share with other participating Web sites during a Passport logon

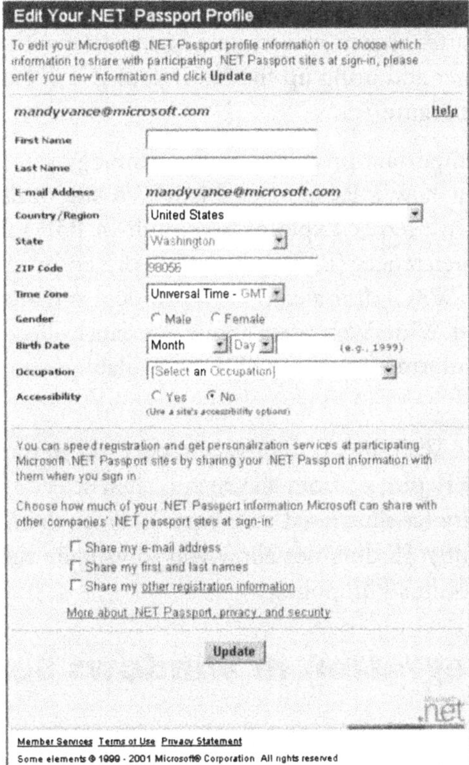

Figure 7.9 *The "Edit your .NET Passport profile" dialog box.*

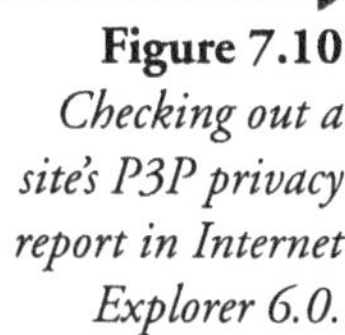

Figure 7.10 *Checking out a site's P3P privacy report in Internet Explorer 6.0.*

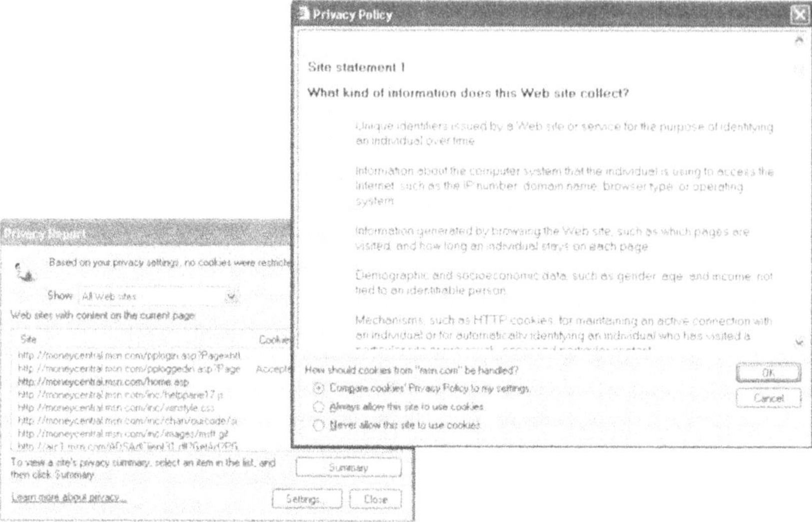

session. To do so in Windows XP, select "Change my .NET Passport" and then "Change Passport Attributes" from the Control Panel "User Account" applet. The latter actions will set up a connection with the Passport domain authority server and bring up the "Edit your .NET Passport Profile" dialog box shown in Figure 7.9.

Another important privacy-related technology you can use when you are worried about how a Passport-enabled Web site deals with your personal information is Internet Explorer 6.0's built-in P3P support. The Platform for Privacy Preferences (P3P) is a project driven by the World Wide Web Consortium (W3C). It is a combined protocol and architecture designed to inform World Wide Web users about the data-collection practices of Web sites. More information about P3P is available from http://www.w3.org/P3P.

To check a Web site's P3P privacy report in Internet Explorer 6.0, select View\Privacy Report... from the menu, then select a Web site's URL and click Summary (as illustrated in Figure 7.10 for the MoneyCentral homepage). Currently, IE does not allow you to validate the local IE P3P policy against a Web site's P3P policy.

7.8 Passport integration in Windows Server 2003

In Windows Server 2003, Microsoft included the following Passport integration features:

- *The ability to authenticate to a Windows Server 2003 IIS Web server using a set of Passport credentials.* "Passport Authentication" is now listed as one of the authentication method options in the properties of an IIS Web site. To use this feature, your IIS Web site must be joined to the Passport infrastructure as a participating Web site. Windows Server 2003 does not support the creation of enterprise Passport infrastructures, where an organization would be its own domain authority and not linked in any way to the Microsoft Web Passport infrastructure. If you want to use Passport to authenticate users of your Web site, you must join the MS Web-based Passport infrastructure.
- *The ability to define a mapping between a Passport PUID and a Windows Security Identifier (SID).* Thanks to this, an administrator can apply Windows SID-based access control settings to users who have authenticated using Passport credentials. The PUID-SID mapping is defined in the altSecurityIdentities property of an Active Directory account object. Unlike alternate Kerberos identities and certificate mappings, PUID-SID mappings can currently not be added using the "Name Mappings..." option in the advanced view of the Users and Computers MMC snap-in. To set them up, you can use an LDAP-based editing tool (like LDIFDE or AdsiEdit) or you could also script the creation of the mappings using ADSI.
- *The ability to let IIS construct an SID for a Passport PUID on the fly.* This feature allows for Windows SID-based access control enforcement for users who have authenticated to IIS-using Passport credentials but who do not have an AD PUID-SID mapping defined. In this case the Passport Manager object will derive the newly generated SID from the Passport PUID. The problem with this feature is that the newly generated SID will not pop up in the resources' access control editors. In other words,access control enforcement using this SID requires some custom access control logic coding.

Recognizing IIS Passport Authentication Messages To recognize and troubleshoot IIS Passport authentication exchanges, you can use the WebFetch (WFetch) tool coming with the IIS 6.0 Resource Kit. An IIS 6.0 Web site that has Passport authentication enabled will send out a WWW-authenticate message containing the Passport verb (see example in Figure 7.11).

Even though Windows Server 2003 includes advanced Passport support, it does not include a Passport-specific Security Support Provider

```
HTTP/1.1 302 Object moved\r\n
Date: Tue, 05 Aug 2003 19:48:32 GMT\r\n
Server: Microsoft-IIS/6.0\r\n
X-Powered-By: ASP.NET\r\n
Content-Type: text/html\r\n
Location: https://current-login.passporttest.com/ppsecure/secure.srf?lc=1033&id=1&ru=https://localhost/&tw=1800&fs=1&kv=1&ct=1060112912&cb=
er=2.1.6000.1&tpf=cc452f8f5e2b24da57210747a281216a\r\n
Content-Length: 0\r\n
WWW-Authenticate: Passport1.4 lc=1033,id=1,tw=1800,fs=1,ru=https://localhost/,ct=1060112912,kv=1,ver=2.1.6000.1,seclog=10,tpf=57859df77e
b2b4429\r\n
\r\n
```

Figure 7.11 *WFetch HTTP Passport authentication trace.*

(SSP). The Passport support in IIS is enabled using a dynamic link library (DLL) called "passport.dll." As a consequence, Passport authentication cannot be negotiated between a Passport user and a Passport-enabled Windows Server 2003 server; it must be explicitly set in a Web site's authentication methods property.

7.9 Passport futures

The continuing stream of product enhancements and developments and—as a result—the many Passport versions released over the last three years illustrate the important role Microsoft has reserved for the product. In 2001 Microsoft positioned Passport as the basic building block for its consumer-oriented Web services initiative—also known as "Hailstorm." In late 2001 Microsoft commissioned Ready Run Software to port the Passport SSO solution to Sun Solaris and Redhat Linux (more information is available at http://www.rtr.com/Ready-to-Run_Software/passport_press_release.htm).[3] In 2002, Microsoft revealed plans for an MS Passport version 3.0 that will be rooted on the WS-security standards (explained below).

Microsoft has to face many competitors in this space. The growing industry focus on identity management gave way to many players in the Web SSO space. At the time of writing, we can easily say that all major software vendors are involved in this game.

The standardization efforts in the federation and Web identity management space are also progressing in a very competitive way. Whereas Microsoft, IBM, and Verisign are pushing the Web services security stan-

3. The Passport SDK for Solaris and Linux can be downloaded from http://msdn.microsoft.com/library/default.asp?url=/downloads/list/websrvpass.asp.

dardization initiative (WS-Security),[4] most other major software vendors stick to the Liberty Alliance[5] and the Security Assertion Markup Language (SAML)[6] as the building blocks for a Web-based SSO infrastructure and federated Web services. Federation will be covered in Chapter 9.

4. See http://msdn.microsoft.com/library/default.asp?url=/library/en-us/dnwssecur/html/securitywhitepaper.asp.
5. See http://www.projectliberty.org.
6. See http://www.oasis-open.org.

8

UNIX and Windows Authentication Interoperability

Many of today's organizations have an IT infrastructure that is made up of a mix of Windows, UNIX, and mainframe computers. Although we surely should not neglect the importance of the mainframe and its applications, we must also admit that more and more organizations are moving critical applications to the UNIX platform and, lately, to even the Windows platform. CIOs usually also do not want to bet on a single horse; they prefer not to stick to a single platform and vendor.

All of these arguments have put a growing focus on the integration of Windows and UNIX platforms and their applications. Platform and application integration inevitably includes integration of core security services such as account management and authentication. Account management deals with the management of security principal identities and their attributes (and possibly also user privileges). An authentication service deals with the verification of a security principal's identity.

The goal of this chapter is to give an overview of the different Windows and UNIX account management and authentication integration solutions currently available on the IT market.

- Regarding Windows, this chapter focuses on the Windows 2000, Windows XP, and Windows Server 2003 platforms—all of them are running in an AD-centric environment.
- Regarding UNIX, I will try to cover the most common UNIX flavors in use today: HP-UX, Sun Solaris, IBM AIX, and Linux.

8.1 Comparing Windows and UNIX authentication

Table 8.1 provides an overview of different authentication characteristics and how they are typically implemented on the Windows and the UNIX platform.

Table 8.1 *Windows and UNIX Authentication Characteristics*

Authentication Characteristic	Windows	UNIX
Authentication Mechanisms	■ Native support for UserID-Password and Smart Card (only Windows 2000 and later) ■ Other mechanisms available through third-party extensions	■ Native support for UserID-Password ■ On some UNIX platforms: Smart Card (through special PAM modules) ■ Other mechanisms available through third-party extensions
Authentication Authorities	■ Local authority ■ Domain authority	■ Local authority ■ Domain authority (NIS, NIS+ domain, Samba domain)
Authentication Protocol	■ Plain UserID-password ■ NTLM ■ Kerberos V5 (Windows 2000 and later)	■ Plain UserID-password ■ Protocol based on crypt(3) hash function ■ Other protocols using special PAM or other modules (Kerberos and others)
Credential Database	■ Local (SAM) or Centralized (SAM or AD) ■ SAM (Security Database): Any NT4 machine (local or domain authority) and Windows 2000 and later standalone machines and member servers. ■ AD (Active Directory): Windows 2000 domain authorities (domain controllers (DCs))	■ Local or Centralized (NIS, NIS+, LDAP, or Samba (smbpasswd))
Security Principal Identifiers	■ SIDs (Security Identifiers): for users, groups, machines	■ UIDs (User Identifiers): for users ■ GIDs (Group Identifiers): for groups
User Principal Names	■ Maximum of 20 characters ■ Case insensitive ■ Cannot be identical to group names	■ Typically a maximum of eight characters ■ Case sensitive ■ Can be identical to group names

8.2 Interoperability enabling technologies

The key Windows enablers for account management and authentication interoperability in a mixed UNIX and AD-centric Windows environment are AD's support for the LDAP directory access protocol and for the Kerberos distributed authentication protocol. Both protocols were shipped for the first time with Windows 2000. Microsoft's adoption of both protocols for Windows 2000 and later operating systems is largely driven by the fact that they are both based on open standards.

8.2.1 LDAP

The Lightweight Directory Integration Protocol (LDAP) defines a set of protocols to access X.500-based directories. LDAP version 3 is the latest version. LDAP v3 has been standardized by the IETF in RFCs 2251 through 2256 and 2829 through 2831. In Windows 2000 Microsoft adopted LDAP as the default protocol to access the information stored in their Active Directory.

Next is a short list of some of the particularities of the MS LDAP implementation—these may be important when discussing Kerberos interoperability with other platforms.

- AD uses MS-specific schema extensions: They use MS-specific OIDs for certain schema elements, added MS-specific attributes to the top object class, and by default AD does not support the inetOrgPerson object class. Microsoft has, however, provided an add-on software kit to support the inetOrgPerson class in Windows 2000. The class is also supported out of the box in the Windows Server 2003 AD release.
- AD cannot be deployed as a stand-alone LDAP directory. Using AD as an LDAP repository requires the deployment of a complete Windows 2000 or later infrastructure. This will change with the release of ADAM (AD Application Mode) in 2003.

8.2.2 Kerberos

Over the years the Kerberos authentication protocol has proven itself to be a secure and efficient authentication protocol in a distributed client-server environment. Kerberos version 5 (the version used in Windows 2000 and later) has been standardized in RFC 1510.

The following is a short list of some of the particularities of the MS Kerberos implementation—again these may be important when discussing Kerberos interoperability with other platforms:

- MS Kerberos supports the 128-bit RC4-HMAC encryption algorithm as its default encryption type. It also supports 56-bit DES-CBC-CRC and DES-CDB-MD5 for interoperability with MIT Kerberos.

- MS Kerberos does not support postdated and forwarded Kerberos tickets.
- MS Kerberos uses case-insensitive Kerberos principal names.
- MS includes user authorization data (user group memberships and so forth) in Kerberos tickets in the Privilege Attribute Certificate (PAC) field.

8.3 UNIX security-related concepts

The next sections introduce some typical UNIX security-related concepts that will be referred to throughout this chapter. We will discuss PAM, UNIX naming services (NIS, NIS+ and the NSS), and Samba.

8.3.1 PAM

The Pluggable Authentication Module (PAM) architecture provides a pluggable authentication model for UNIX platforms. For a great introduction to PAM, read the Sun white paper on "Making Login Services Independent of Authentication Services" available from http://wwws.sun.com/software/solaris/pam/pam.external.pdf.

Thanks to PAM, UNIX system administrators can plug different authentication methods and protocols into the UNIX OS. This makes the different authentication methods and protocols available to the different UNIX system entry applications such as login, ftp, telnet, su, passwd, and rlogin. The following is a nonexhaustive list of authentication methods and protocols that PAM can make available to applications:

- UNIX file-based authentication (using the /etc/passwd or /etc/shadow files)
- LDAP-based authentication
- NIS or NIS+-based authentication
- Kerberos-based authentication
- S/Key-based authentication
- SecurID-based authentication
- NTLM-based authentication

PAM can also enable single sign-on (SSO) on the UNIX platform; if the passwords used for different services are identical, PAM can be used to share

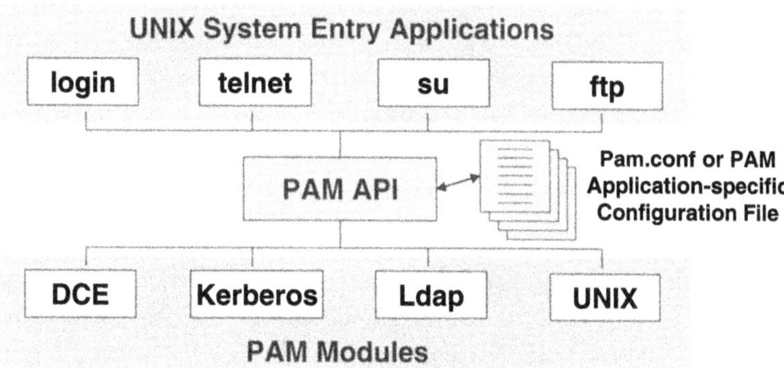

Figure 8.1 *The PAM architecture.*

the password transparently between the application's possibly different authentication mechanisms.

Figure 8.1 shows the basic PAM architecture. A key element in the PAM architecture is the PAM configuration file. PAM authentication behavior can be configured differently for each individual PAM-enabled service. This can be done for all services together in the /etc/pam.conf file or for an individual service in its proper PAM configuration file—the latter is located in the /etc/pam.d directory.

Among the configuration parameters specified in a PAM configuration file are the authentication modules that must be loaded for a particular system entry application's authentication process to complete. PAM modules are stackable—this means that during the authentication process a service may be configured to call on different PAM modules. All this is illustrated in the following example showing the content of a PAM configuration file that holds the PAM authentication configuration for the login, ftp, and telnet services:

```
login auth required /lib/security/pam_unix_auth.so
login session required /lib/security/pam_unix_session.so
login account required /lib/security/pam_unix_account.so
login password required /lib/security/pam_unix_passwd.so
ftp auth required /lib/security/pam_skey_auth.so
ftp session required /lib/security/pam_unix_session.so
telnet session required /lib/security/
pam_unix_session.so
```

As you may have noticed in this sample configuration file, PAM provides more than just authentication services. It also provides the following services that are closely related to authentication: account, password, and session management services. PAM account management modules allow system entry applications to retrieve account-related information (such as logon hours, account expiry date, and so forth) from a local or central repository. Password management modules allow system entry applications to change users' passwords. Session management modules allows for the setup and closing of a user's session. It also allows for the logging of session information in a local or central repository.

The PAM architecture is supported on most Linux platforms (e.g., Redhat 7.2 and later) and on the HP-UX (from version 11.0 on), Solaris, and AIX platforms. In the context of this discussion on UNIX and Windows authentication integration, the following PAM modules are of particular interest:

- pam_unix: A PAM module supporting authentication, account, and password and session management. The pam_unix supports UNIX crypt(3) password hashing.
- pam_ldap: A PAM module used in conjunction with the pam_unix module for authentication and password management with an LDAP server.
- pam_kerberos: A PAM module that adds support for the Kerberos authentication protocol (as defined in RFC 1510).

Another PAM module that could be used in the context of a Windows-UNIX security integration project is pam_smb. The pam_smb supports the NT Lan Manager (NTLM) authentication protocols and can be used to authenticate UNIX hosts and users against a Windows server or domain controller (DC). I will not discuss the pam_smb in this chapter. It does not use any of the key protocols for Windows-UNIX security integration in an AD-centric world: LDAP and Kerberos. Also, the NTLM authentication protocols are based on proprietary standards and are considered less secure than the Kerberos authentication protocol. More information on pam_smb can be found at http://www.csn.ul.ie/~airlied/pam_smb. Note that I will discuss Samba; the latest Samba version (2.2.8) is still using NTLM authentication as well. Samba, however, will provide Kerberos authentication support in a future release.

The Windows equivalent of PAM is the Security Support Provider Interface (SSPI) and its Security Support Provider (SSP) modules. Here is an interesting side note: Back in the 1990s a team at the University of Michigan succeeded in developing a PAM-like architecture for NT (more information on this can be found at http://www.citi.umich.edu/u/itoi/ni_pam_usenix.pdf).

8.3.2 UNIX naming services

A general definition of a naming service is a repository that stores all kinds of information and that allows this information to be queried by clients (users and applications) in an easy way. This information typically includes host to IP address mappings, user account names, credential information (secured passwords), access permissions, access intermediaries (groups) and their membership, and printer definitions. Naming services not only allow users and applications to retrieve information, but they also allow them to update information and to perform name resolution (or to query for name mappings). In the context of this chapter, naming services are primarily used to enable different computers to share authentication- and authorization-related information by storing them in a central repository governed by a naming service.

Examples of typical Windows naming services are flat files (the hosts and lmhosts files), the Windows Internet Name Service (WINS), the Domain Name System (DNS), and the LDAP-based naming services. Also, the Windows security database (SAM or AD) that is governed by the local or domain security authority can be designated as a naming service: one that is specifically focusing on security-related information.

Over the years the UNIX OS has supported a wide range of naming services. As with Windows, these include flat files (stored in the /etc directory), DNS, and LDAP-based naming services. UNIX also supports two other UNIX-specific naming services: the Network Information System (NIS) and the Network Information System Plus (NIS+). The UNIX-specific naming services are discussed in more detail next.

Table 8.2 *Common UNIX Naming Services*

UNIX Naming Service	DNS	LDAP	NIS	NIS+
Namespace	Hierarchical	Hierarchical	Flat	Hierarchical
Data Storage	Files/Resource records	Directories	Two column binary maps	Multicolumned tables
Server Types	Primary/Secondary	Master/Replica	Master/Slave	Root domain master/subdomain master/replica
Security	Public Key Extensions	SSL (LDAPs)	None	DES/public-private key-based authentication

Table 8.2 summarizes the characteristics of most common UNIX naming services. (This list is not exhaustive: less common naming services such as the Federated Naming Service [FNS] are not discussed.)

8.3.3 NIS

In 1985 SUN Microsystems produced NIS: the Network Information Service, which is also referred to as the Yellow Pages (yp). NIS was one of the first UNIX-based distributed naming services. The primary focus of NIS was to make network management easier by providing a centralized naming service and repository.

An NIS repository centralizes information such as machine names and addresses, user names, network services, and so forth. This collection of information is referred to as the NIS namespace. The NIS namespace is stored in binary files that are known as NIS maps. A typical NIS service has maps such as passwd, group, automount, services, and rpc. Often there are two or more key fields in a map; the passwd map, for example, services lookups both by username and by UID.

The way that a UNIX client interacts with an NIS service is relatively simple. It is all based on the fact that the information stored in the NIS maps is augmenting or replacing information stored in local UNIX configuration files such as /etc/passwd, /etc/hosts. Let us illustrate this using the example of the /etc/passwd file, which stores account-password mappings and is used for local user authentication on a UNIX host. Thanks to NIS, a UNIX host can be redirected to a central NIS server when validating a user's credentials. This happens if the user's entry in the host's local /etc/passwd file is marked with a + sign. For example, the following entry in the /etc/passwd file will redirect the UNIX host to the passwd map on the NIS server to find out the credentials of user johndoe (in this entry the number 2003 is the UNIX UID of johndoe, 103 is the GID of johndoe).

```
+johndoe::2003:103:::
```

Like NT, NIS uses the notion of a domain to provide an administrative grouping of machines. A UNIX host's NIS domain basically determines which NIS server the host will query. Within an NIS domain, NIS uses a single-master information replication model that is made up of a master and multiple slave NIS servers. Figure 8.2 shows the NIS architecture. Figure 8.2 also shows some of the typical NIS commands: "ypbind" to connect to a NIS server, "yppush" to push changes from NIS master to slave servers (also note that the yp in these commands stands for "yellow pages").

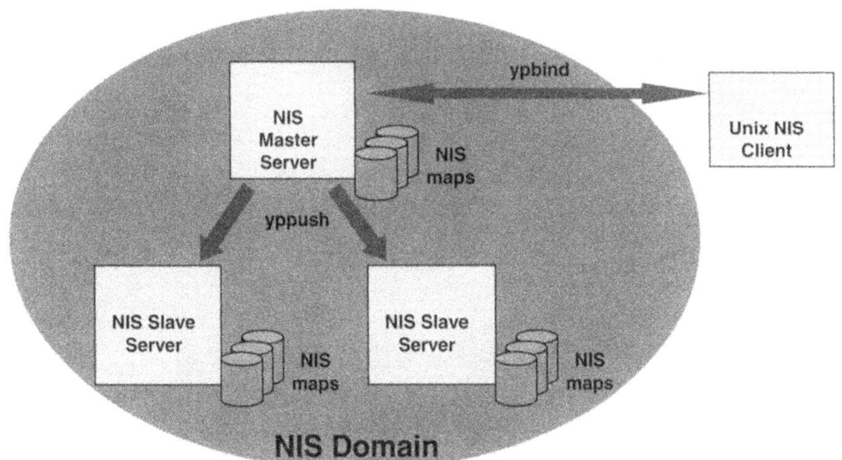

Figure 8.2 *The NIS Architecture.*

One of the biggest deficiencies of NIS is its complete lack of security: NIS does not authenticate its users, NIS data are transmitted in the clear, NIS updates can be spoofed, and so forth. NIS also lacks an easy extensible data structure and an efficient information replication model.

8.3.4 NIS+

NIS+ was introduced by Sun as part of the Solaris 2 OS as an enhanced naming service for NIS. Like for NIS, the primary focus of NIS+ was to make network management easier by providing a centralized naming service and repository. The most important enhancements coming with NIS+ compared to NIS are support for a hierarchical namespace, client authentication (both users and hosts), secured data transmission, NIS+ object access control lists (ACLs), incremental updates between master and slave servers, and a better data storage model. Instead of using binary files, NIS+ stores its information in database-like tables.

NIS+ architecture can be made up of several hierarchical layers of master and replica NIS+ servers: At the top of the hierarchy sits a root master server, and underneath it can be one or more subdomain master servers. Each of the master servers can have one or more replica servers. Figure 8.3 shows the NIS+ architecture.

Many NIS+ concepts are very similar to the concepts used by LDAP-rooted naming services. Because of these similarities and because of the adoption of LDAP as the default naming service in Solaris version 9, Sun considers NIS+ an end-of-feature (EOF) naming service.

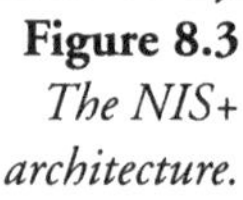

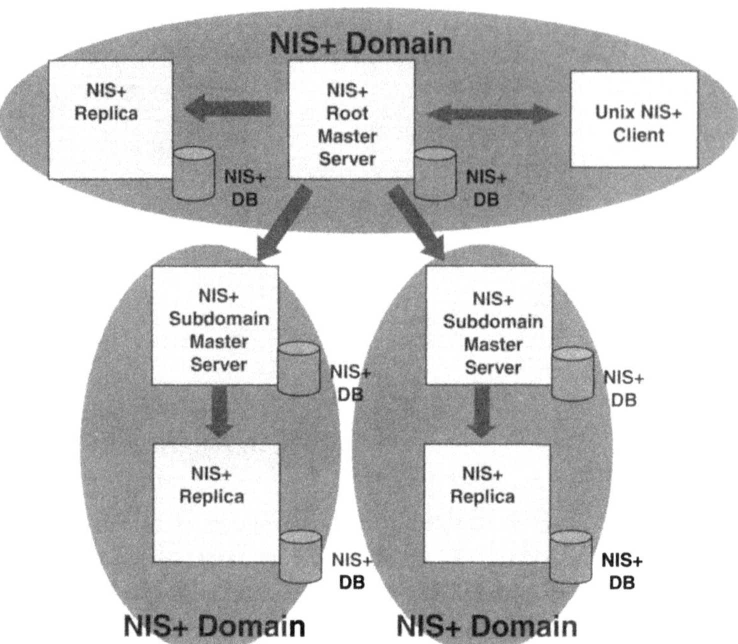

Figure 8.3 *The NIS+ architecture.*

8.3.5 NSS

Because many different naming services (DNS, NIS, NIS+, LDAP, and so forth) can be made available to UNIX clients and applications, Sun developed the concept of a universal naming service: the Naming Service Switch (NSS). Just like PAM, NSS is implemented using shared code libraries. The latter facilitates reconfiguration and makes it relatively easy to plug in a new naming service.

NSS is a client-side technology. Thanks to it, UNIX clients and applications do not have to be aware about which naming service stores which information. When the client or application wants to resolve a name, it simply calls on the NSS API. NSS then determines which naming services should be searched and in which order they should be searched. The NSS configuration is nailed down in the nsswitch.conf file. Figure 8.4 shows the NSS architecture. Notice that PAM modules can also call on NSS for naming services.

Next is an example of the configuration data that can be found in the nsswitch.conf file. Note that unlike PAM, NSS does not allow configuration on a per service basis. As shown in the example NSS can, however, be configured on a per data type basis. For the different data types that may

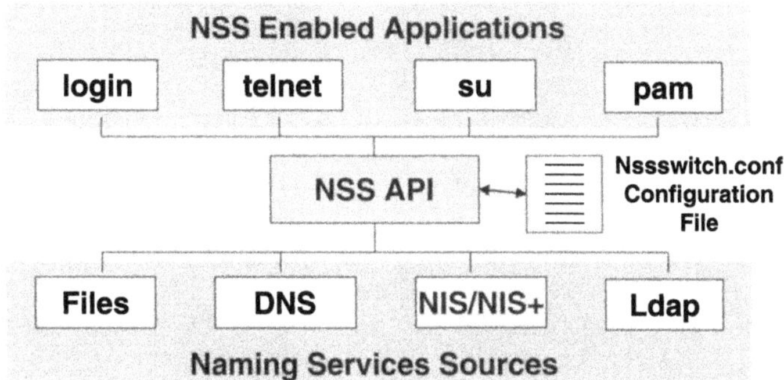

Figure 8.4 *The NSS architecture.*

need to be resolved on a host, the nssswitch.conf file can specify different name resolution sources and the order in which these sources should be tried.

```
passwd: files nisplus nis
shadow:  files nisplus nis
group:  files nisplus nis
hosts:  files nisplus nis dns
services: nisplus files
```

In order to speed up name resolution, most UNIX NSS clients also support a caching mechanism known as the name service caching daemon (nscd).

NSS is currently supported on Solaris, Linux, and HP-UX (from version 11.0 onward). AIX has a similar concept called Information Retrieval System (IRS), which is rooted on Bind 8 code.

8.3.6 NIS futures and LDAP integration

Unlike NIS+, NIS is not considered an end-of-feature solution and until now Sun has not announced any plans to migrate it to LDAP. Because Windows AD is an LDAP-centric repository, some kind of NIS/LDAP integration will be needed in IT environments where integrated Windows and UNIX account management is needed and where NIS naming services are still required. Two common approaches are to store NIS data in an LDAP directory or to provide an NIS-to-LDAP gateway service. In the latter approach NIS queries must be translated into LDAP queries.

The first approach is described in RFC 2307 "An Approach for Using LDAP as a Network Information Service" (an IETF Internet draft) and RFC 2307bis (a revised version of RFC2307). Both RFCs describe an LDAP directory schema for storing NIS data in an LDAP directory. The

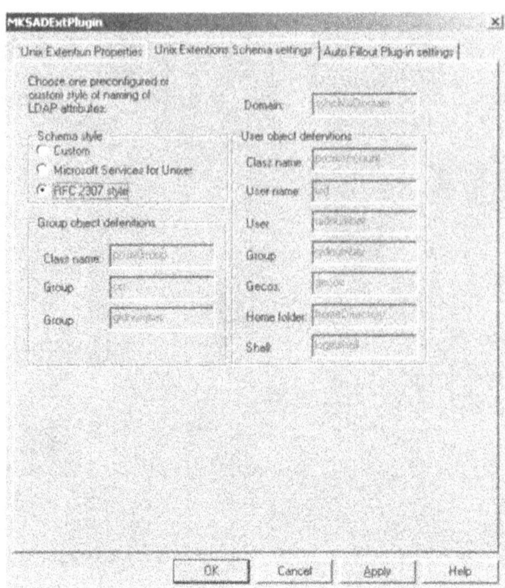

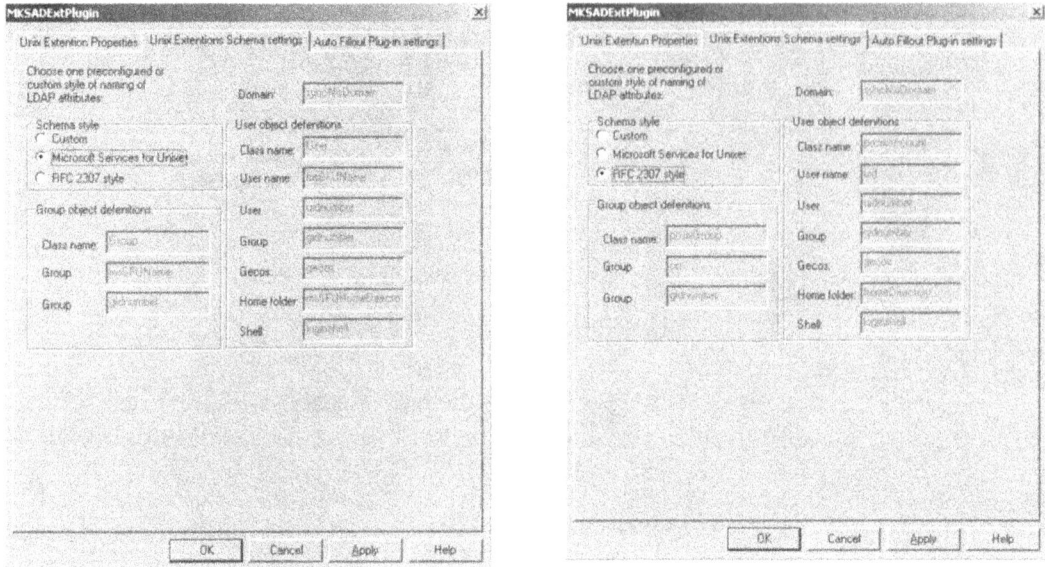

Figure 8.5 *AD4Unix AD schema style configuration.*

RFCs provide mappings for all the common NIS maps: passwd, group, hosts, shadow, services, netgroup, protocol, ethers, and so forth. Both RFCs describe directory objectclasses and attributes, but none of them mandates the use of a particular LDAP tree structure.

The default Microsoft AD schema is not RFC 2307-compliant. The same remains true when adding the MS SFU 3.0 NIS schema extensions.

The AD schema can be made RFC 2307-compliant by adding the AD4Unix schema extensions—a set of freeware extensions that can be downloaded from http://www.css-solutions.ca/ad4unix. AD4Unix supports both RFC 2307- and SFU-compliant schema extensions. Figure 8.5 shows the AD4Unix configuration dialog box that is used to set the "schema style." Note the naming differences between the SFU- and the RFC 2307-naming conventions.

Both NIS-LDAP integration solutions are discussed in greater detail later in this chapter.

8.3.7 Samba

Samba is a collection of software that provides the following two important services to the UNIX platform:

- Samba allows UNIX clients to access file and print services using the Server Message Block (SMB) and Common Internet File System (CIFS) network protocols.
- Samba allows the UNIX server to provide file and print services using the SMB and CIFS network protocols.

SMB is the default Microsoft file and print sharing protocol. CIFS is the name Microsoft uses to designate the SMB flavor that can run without requiring NetBIOS over TCP (NBT).

These two services make Samba the ideal gateway for sharing file and print services and integrated authentication between a Windows and a UNIX environment "the Microsoft way" (using the SMB protocol). Later this chapter also covers some solutions that can be used for file service sharing and integration authentication between Windows and UNIX "the UNIX way" (using the Network File System [NFS] protocol).

Samba runs on a variety of server platforms, many of which are UNIX flavors (AIX, Linux, and so forth) but also on VMS, Netware, and OS/2. Samba is freeware software that is available under the GNU public license (more information on this license is available at http://ftp.easynet.be/samba/docs/GPL.html). Plenty of Samba-related information can be found on the Samba Web site at http://www.samba.org.

From a security point of view, Samba comes with the following features and functionality:

- Can act as the only Windows Primary Domain Controller (PDC) (only from Samba version 2 onward) in an NT 4.0-like (non AD-based) domain.
- Can be configured as a Backup Domain Controller (BDC) in a pure Samba environment. This can be done by replicating the smbpasswd file whenever changes are made to the SAM database.
- Can be a member server in a Windows NT 4.0, Windows 2000, or Windows Server 2003 domain.
- Can support NTLM authentication and Windows pass-through authentication.
- Can provide NetBIOS name resolution services. A Samba server can even act as a WINS server.

At the time of writing it was impossible for Samba (version 2.2.8) to operate as a domain controller in a Windows 2000 or later environment.

Also, Samba currently does not support Windows interdomain trust relationships. As pointed out in this list, Samba can be a member server in an NT4.0, Windows 2000, or Windows Server 2003 domain. For Windows 2000 this is independent of the domain mode (mixed or native). For Windows Server 2003 this is independent of the functionality level.

In a future release (the Samba TNG or Samba version 3.0 project), Samba may include LDAP and Kerberos support, enabling it to interact with AD as a true Windows 2000 or later server.

Later this chapter discusses two Samba-based solutions:

- One that is based on coexistence between a UNIX and a Windows infrastructure and that uses Samba for SMB-based file and print sharing between the two platforms.
- Another one that can provide true integrated Windows and UNIX account management and authentication integration for UNIX users of SMB resources. This solution is based on the Samba Winbind service.

8.4 Windows and UNIX account management and authentication integration approaches

The account management and authentication integration approaches for the Windows and UNIX platforms that are discussed in this chapter can be categorized as follows:

- *Coexistence Solutions:* In these solutions the NIS and AD/LDAP infrastructures coexist. Usually these solutions do not provide a single point of administration. Also they do not provide single sign-on (SSO), but they do provide integrated authentication. In this context "integrated authentication" means using the same authentication credentials and/or protocols in the UNIX and the Windows environment. A well-known set of solutions in this category is credential synchronization services. Such services simply synchronize the credentials between the UNIX and Windows security authentication authorities and their repositories.
- *Centralized User Management:* Solutions that are using this approach provide a single point of administration for both UNIX and Windows accounts and credentials. This approach is also referred to as single-source sign-on. In an AD-centric Windows environment, it is

Table 8.3 *Solution Overview*

Coexistence Solutions (Mixed NIS and AD Infrastructure)	Centralized User Management using AD/LDAP Repository
■ Server for NIS (AD-integrated NIS) (SFU 3.0)	■ PADL NIS/LDAP gateway
	■ pam_unix-centric
■ User Mapping Service (SFU 3.0)	■ pam_ldap-centric
■ Samba	■ pam_kerberos-centric
■ Password Synchronization	■ Vintela Authentication Services (VAS)
Password Synchronization using SFU 3.0	■ Samba WinBind

quite obvious to use AD as the central repository. Some solutions in this category provide a special front end to AD, so users can keep using their legacy communication protocol (e.g., NIS) and do not need to change to LDAP to communicate with AD.

- *Single Sign-On (SSO):* Whereas the two previous approaches still require users to enter a set of credentials each time they access another environment, true SSO only requires users to enter their credentials once: to the primary authentication authority (e.g., a Windows DC). Afterward, authentication to secondary authentication authorities (e.g., a UNIX resource server) happens transparently. There are quite a few different SSO architectures available. For a high-level outline of the different SSO architectures and examples of commercial software supporting them, see Chapter 9.

The solutions for integrated account management and authentication discussed in this chapter are listed in Table 8.3. Note that there is a strong focus on the integration solutions that MS offers as part of their Services for UNIX 3.0 (SFU 3.0) suite.

8.4.1 Coexistence solutions between an NIS and an AD infrastructure

This section focuses on the coexistence solutions coming with the MS Services for UNIX 3.0 suite: Server for NIS, the User mapping service, and the Password Synchronization Service. In late 2002, Microsoft released version 3 of its Services for UNIX (SFU) software suite: a collection of software facilitating the integration of the Windows and the UNIX platform. We will also look at how Samba can be used to provide security coexistence between UNIX and Windows for SMB-based file and print sharing.

SFU server for NIS

Server for NIS is an SFU 3.0 service that allows Windows 2000 and Windows Server 2003 domain controllers (DCs) to act as NIS master servers. During the installation of Server for NIS, SFU extends the AD schema to enable AD to store the NIS-specific data. Figure 8.6 shows how the AD user and group properties are extended to provide a single point of administration for both Windows and UNIX authentication and authorization data. The overall architecture of this solution is illustrated in Figure 8.7.

Server for NIS allows Windows administrators to define the UNIX user and group attributes in AD. This can be done manually or the attributes can also be pulled over all at once from an existing UNIX NIS server. To do the latter, the Server for NIS installation installs a set of migration utilities. Migration can be done from the command line using the nis2ad executable or using the GUI-based Migration Wizard.

A Server for NIS-enabled Windows DC can receive NIS query requests from UNIX NIS clients, translate them into AD queries, and return the data to the NIS clients in an NIS format. It can also replicate the NIS data to both Windows and UNIX NIS servers (as illustrated in Figure 8.7). The Windows servers with which it replicates are also Windows DCs. In this case the NIS data are replicated using the AD replication model. The

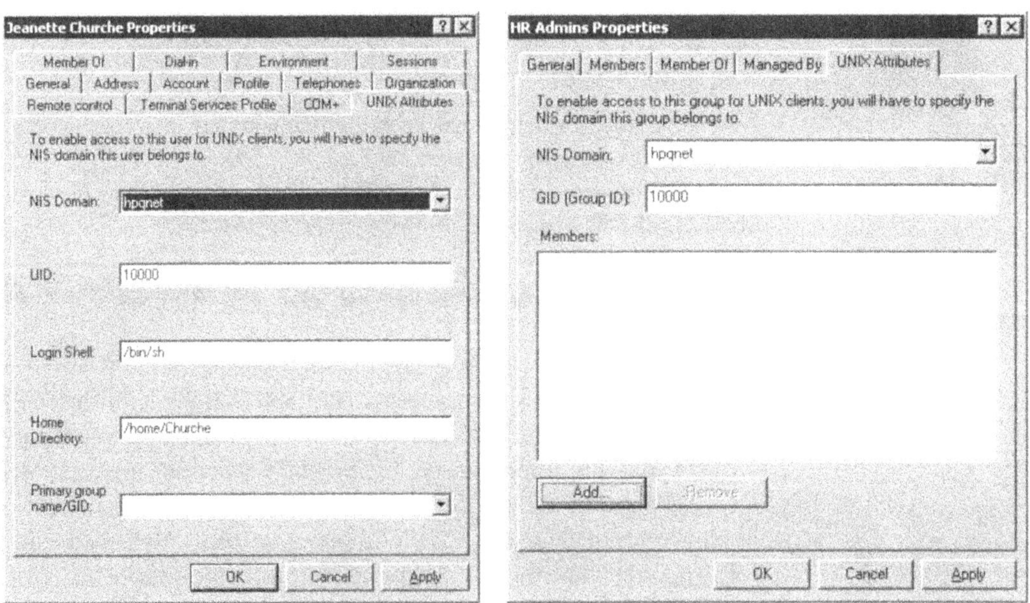

Figure 8.6 *AD user and group object properties with a UNIX-specific property tab.*

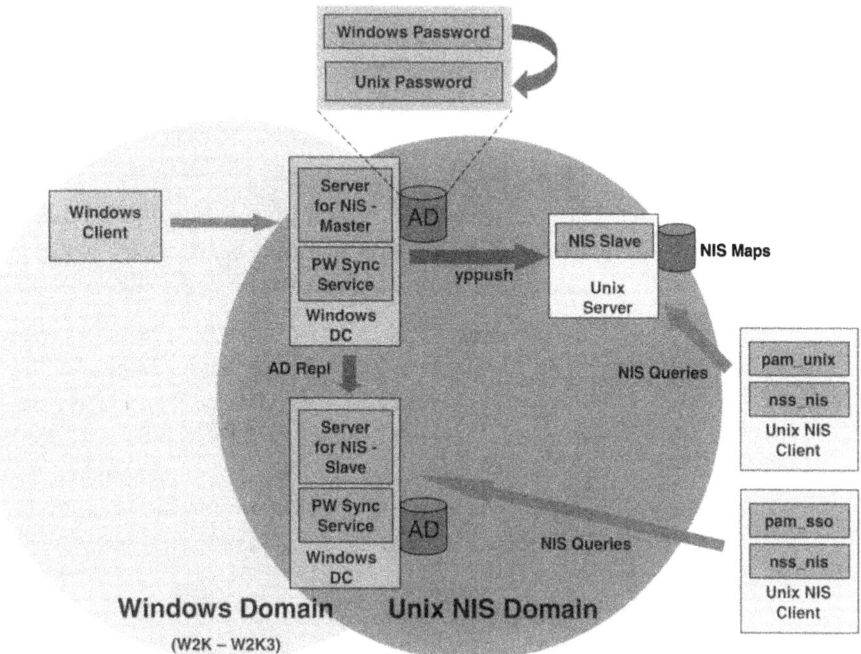

Figure 8.7 *SFU Server for NIS architecture.*

UNIX servers with which it replicates are NIS slave servers. In this case NIS data are replicated using the NIS yppush protocol.

Server for NIS also provides a one-directional password synchronization service: If a user's Windows password is changed in AD, it will be automatically changed in the corresponding UNIX password property of the AD user object. Server for NIS will automatically replicate the password change to the other Windows NIS servers and the UNIX NIS slave servers.

This automatic password synchronization facilitates user management in a mixed environment. It is made possible thanks to a password synchronization service shipping with SFU. This service is automatically installed when Server for NIS is installed. If you want bidirectional password synchronization in order to also replicate the password changes that are originating in the UNIX environment, read the text concerning SFU password synchronization service later in this section.

This password synchronization feature mandates that in a Windows domain that is made up of multiple DCs, Server for NIS (together with the password synchronization service) is installed on all DCs. In a multimaster directory replication model like the one AD uses, a user's original password change can occur on any of the DCs in the domain.

To enable UNIX users to authenticate against a UNIX host using the credentials stored in the AD-based NIS server, one of the following PAM modules should be installed on the UNIX host:

- The pam_unix module: This is the default UNIX PAM module, supporting crypt(3) hash-based authentication, password updates, and account management using a local or NIS-based repository.
- The Microsoft SFU pam_sso module: This is a special PAM module that MS provides as part of SFU 3.0. It can be used for crypt(3) hash-based authentication and also for password updates. The nice thing about pam_sso is that it uses 3DES to secure the exchanges between the UNIX host and the Windows AD server. Contrary to the pam_unix module, the pam_sso module cannot be used to let a UNIX host communicate with a non-AD-based NIS server.

Samba

Samba can be used to provide an integrated authentication solution between Windows and UNIX for the users of SMB-based file and print services. This capability (which is illustrated in Figure 8.8) is based on the following Samba features:

- Samba's capability to let a UNIX machine become a member server of a Windows 2000 or later domain
- Samba's support for Windows NTLM-based pass-through authentication

This solution cannot provide integrated account management because on the UNIX side a UID and GID are needed for every user. UNIX needs UIDs and GIDs in order to maintain file ownership and permissions on UNIX file system resources. A UID and GID on their turn require a UNIX account for every user. In other words, even though the password is kept in AD and the Windows 2000 or later DC can take care of integrated authentication, there's still a double bookkeeping problem: Every UNIX SMB user needs both a UNIX account (and UID and GID) and a Windows account.

Remember that Samba does not support the Kerberos authentication protocol. Samba can be configured to use the NTLM challenge/response-based authentication protocol. NTLM is not the default authentication protocol in Samba versions 2.2 and earlier: By default, they use an insecure plaintext password-based authentication mechanism. In these versions

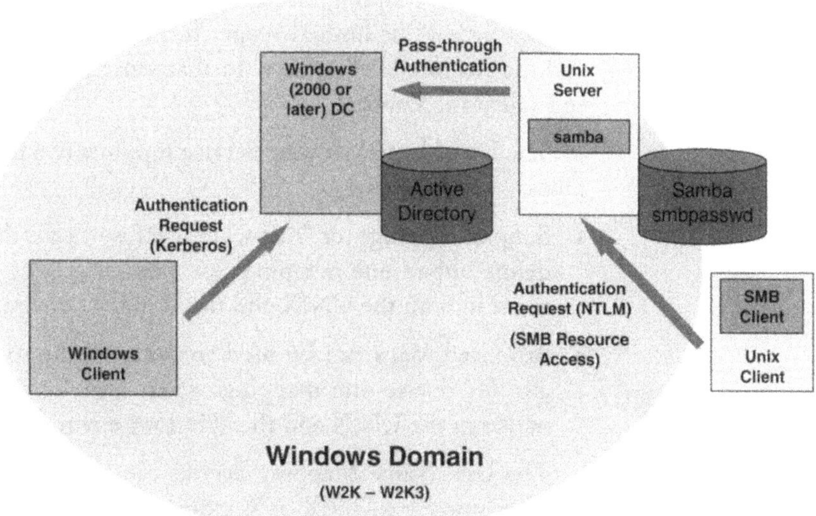

Figure 8.8 *Samba architecture.*

Samba will only use NTLM if the "encrypt passwords" directive is set to yes in the Samba configuration file. The encrypt passwords directive will be switched on by default in Samba 3.0.

On the UNIX client-side SMB resource access obviously requires an SMB client. One of the following SMB clients can be used:

- The smbclient program coming with the Samba software kit
- The smbfs filesystem: This feature is only available on the Linux platform.
- The smbsh program: This client is available on most UNIX clients with the exceptions of HP-UX and Linux.

SFU user name mapping service

The SFU 3.0 User Name Mapping Service enables other SFU applications to automatically retrieve the Windows credentials corresponding to a set of UNIX credentials (or the other way around) from a central location. The User Name Mapping Service provides this service to the following SFU applications: Microsoft Interix, the client for NFS, Gateway for NFS and Server for NFS, and the Remote Shell Service. The service can be installed on a Windows NT 4.0, Windows XP, Windows 2000, or Windows Server 2003 platform. Because it does not use Active Directory as the repository to store its mapping data, it can be installed on any Windows server.

The Name Mapping Service cannot be categorized as a true SSO solution because of its limited scope. It only works for NFS-based file access and the Remote Shell service. In that sense you can look at it as an NFS-equivalent for Samba.

The User Name Mapping Service supports two types of user name mappings:

- Simple mappings (or "maps," as Microsoft calls them) can be used to define one-to-one mappings for users or groups that have the same name in both the UNIX and the Windows environment.
- Advanced maps can be used to define many-to-one mappings and also for one-to-one mappings when users or groups have different names in the UNIX and the Windows environment.

The User Name Mapping Service can get its UNIX information from different sources: a UNIX or Windows NIS server, or a UNIX or Windows client that has the PCNFS daemon installed (as illustrated in Figure 8.9). PCNFS is a fairly simple service that allows users to obtain UNIX authorization information (UIDs and GIDs) given their username and password. Users simply have to send their username and password to the PCNFS service, the latter compares the password to the one stored in its local password file, and if the two match, the PCNFS service returns the UNIX authorization information to the user.

In order to authorize machines to query the User Name Mapping Service, the User Name Mapping Service maintains a text-based authorization file called .maphosts. The file lists all hostnames of the machines that are authorized to query the User Name Mapping Service. The file is stored in the %SFUDIR%/mapper directory.

The operation of the User Name Mapping Service in combination with an NFS resource access is illustrated in Figure 8.9. The figure shows two different scenarios:

- Access from a Windows host to a UNIX-based NFS Server (steps A and B). In this case we have the client for NFS software installed on the Windows host. When a user tries to access an NFS resource, the NFS client will query the User Name Mapping Service using the user's Windows credentials for the corresponding UNIX credentials. The mapping service will return the matching UID, password, and GID. These can then be used by the NFS client to access the resources on the NFS server.

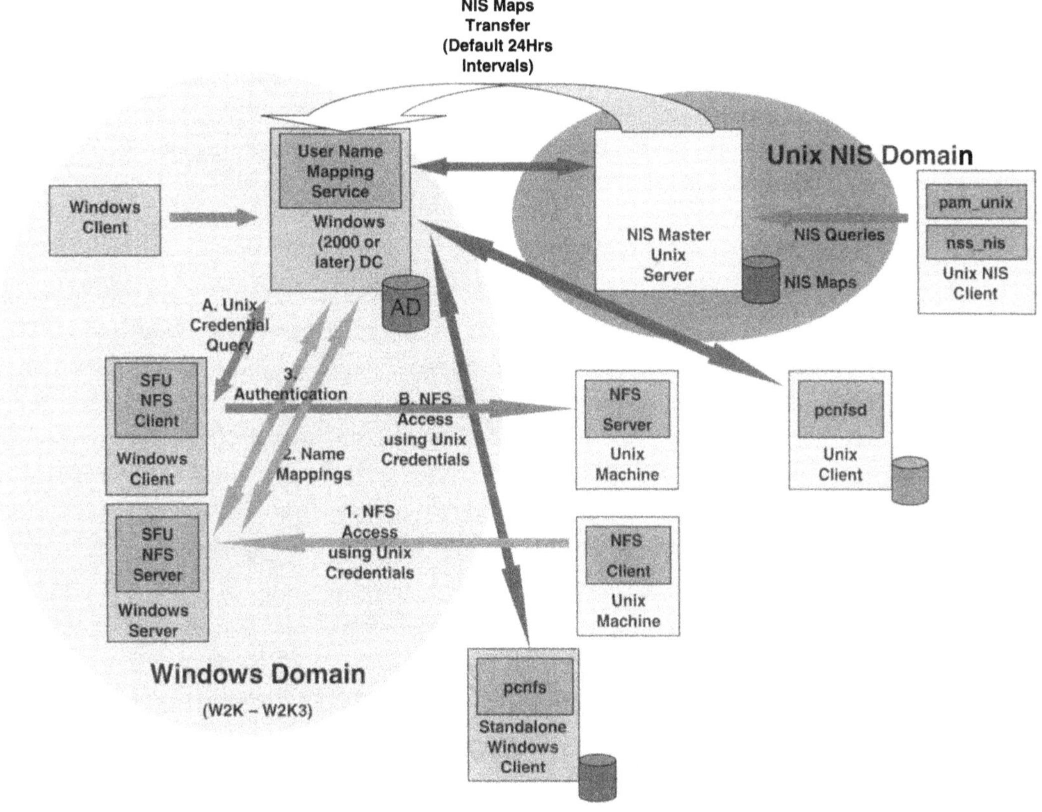

Figure 8.9 *SFU Name User Mapping Service architecture.*

- Access from a UNIX host to a Windows-based Server for NFS (steps 1, 2, and 3). In this case a UNIX NFS client tries to access an NFS resource on a Windows-based Server for NFS. The UNIX host offers his or her UNIX credentials to the Windows server. The Windows Server queries the User Name Mapping Service for the Windows credentials corresponding to the UNIX credentials. If matching credentials are found, the mapping service returns them to the NFS server. The NFS server can then use them to authenticate the user to a Windows DC. Finally, the NFS server performs an authorization check for the user.

Solutions providing password synchronization

Another alternative for providing security coexistence between a Windows and a UNIX environment is to keep the passwords synchronized between the two worlds. Because both Windows and UNIX use specific hashing algorithms to securely store user passwords, true password synchronization between the two credential databases is impossible. Password synchronization can only occur when the password is set or reset, before the hashing algorithm is applied. Hashing algorithms have the unique property that they are one-way functions.

SFU password synchronization

The Password Synchronization Service SFU version 3 allows for password synchronization between the Windows NT4 Server and Workstation, Windows 2000 Professional and Server, Windows XP, and Windows Server 2003 platforms on the Windows side, and the HP-UX 11, AIX 4.3.3, Redhat Linux 7.0, and Solaris 7 platforms on the UNIX side. For all the above-mentioned UNIX platforms—with the exception of AIX—password synchronization works in both directions: from Windows-to-UNIX and from UNIX-to-Windows. AIX password synchronization only works from Windows-to-UNIX.

SFU's password synchronization provides secure password synchronization. The passwords are encrypted using the 3DES algorithm and a secret key that is shared between the UNIX and Windows platforms.

Figure 8.10 shows how password synchronization works from Windows-to-UNIX. The figure shows two scenarios: Windows-to-UNIX password synchronization in a Windows domain environment and Windows-to-UNIX password synchronization from a Windows stand-alone machine.

- A Windows domain user initiates a password update to its Windows domain controller (DC).
    - If password synchronization is set up between the AD and a UNIX NIS domain, the SFU password synchronization service will synchronize the password with the UNIX NIS database. This setup always requires the SFU password synchronization service to be installed on all Windows DCs (remember that a password update can occur on any server in a multimaster model).

      If the NIS master server is running on a UNIX platform, the Single Sign-On daemon (ssod) must be installed on the NIS master server (this daemon is also referred to as the password synchronization daemon). The ssod daemon will update the NIS maps and initiate a push to the other UNIX NIS slave servers.

      If the NIS master server is a Windows AD machine running the SFU Server for NIS extensions (this scenario is not shown in

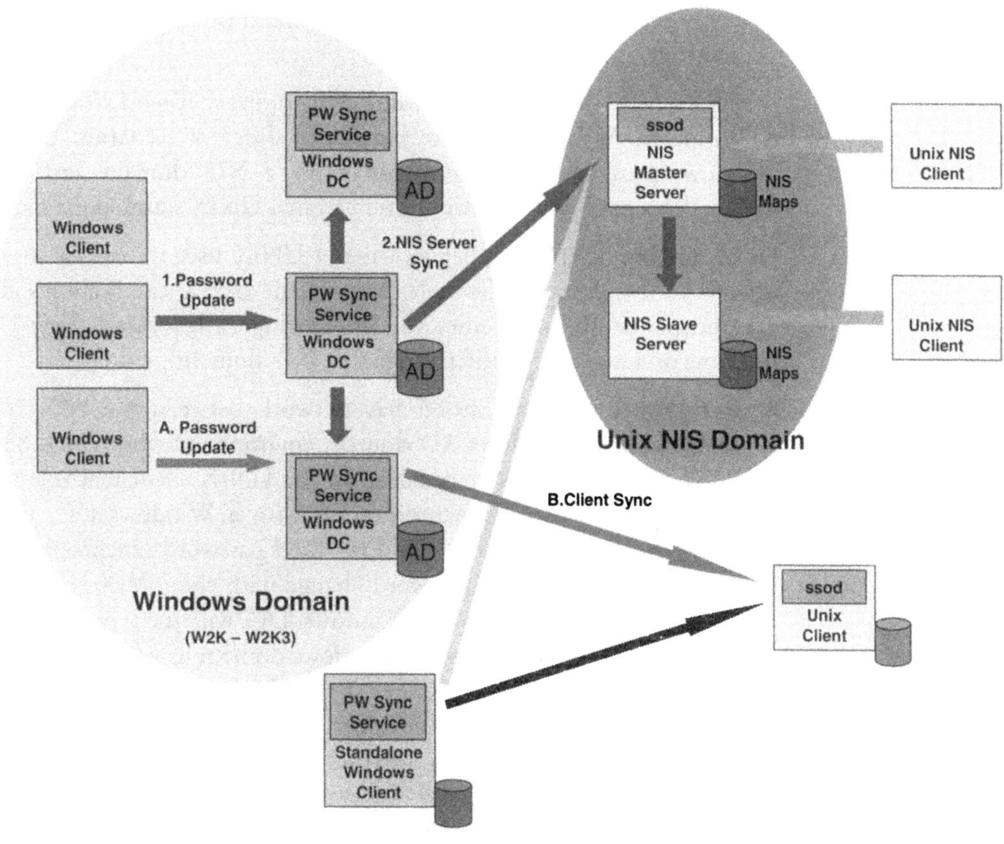

Figure 8.10 *SFU password synchronization architecture: Windows to UNIX.*

Figure 8.5), then the AD NIS master server will make sure that the changes are pushed to the other AD machines and the UNIX NIS slave servers.

- If password synchronization is set up between the AD and a UNIX stand-alone machine (a machine that is not participating in a UNIX NIS domain), the SFU password synchronization service will synchronize the change with the UNIX machine. The UNIX machine's local ssod daemon will make sure the change is made to the machine's local credential database.

- A Windows user (working from a Windows stand-alone machine) initiates a password update to its local authority. This scenario requires the SFU password synchronization service to be installed on the Windows stand-alone machine. On the UNIX side the password synchronization operation and requirements are the same as the ones mentioned in the Windows domain scenario (for both a UNIX NIS and stand-alone setup).

Figure 8.11 shows how password synchronization works from UNIX-to-Windows. Again this picture shows two different scenarios: UNIX-to-Windows password synchronization from a NIS domain and UNIX-to-Windows password synchronization from a UNIX stand-alone machine.

In this case everything begins when a UNIX user initiates a password update. In this scenario, the basic setup on the UNIX side is always identical (independently of whether you are dealing with a stand-alone UNIX machine or a machine participating in an NIS domain).

- If password synchronization has to work between a UNIX NIS domain and a Windows AD domain environment, the UNIX SSO PAM module (pam_sso) installed on the UNIX client machine will initiate the password synchronization with a Windows DC. Only when this is done will the Windows SFU password synchronization service synchronize the password change with the UNIX NIS database. At the same time the Windows DC will then replicate the change to all other DCs in the Windows domain using the AD replication model. This setup requires the SFU password synchronization service to be installed on all Windows DCs. Also, SFU password synchronization has to be configured for two-way synchronization with the NIS master server and one-way synchronization (UNIX-to-Windows) with the UNIX NIS clients.

  In this scenario, if the NIS master server is a Windows machine that has the SFU Server for NIS extensions installed (not shown in Figure 8.6), UNIX NIS clients can directly update their password to the Windows NIS master server (using the NIS yppasswd command and having the pam_sso module installed).

- If password synchronization has to work between a UNIX stand-alone machine and a Windows AD domain environment, the UNIX SSO PAM module (pam_sso) installed on the UNIX client machine will synchronize the password change with a Windows DC. The Windows DC will then replicate the change to all other DCs in the Windows domain using the AD replication model. In this scenario the Windows DC must have the SFU password synchronization service installed: It has to be configured for one-way synchronization (UNIX-to-Windows) with every stand-alone UNIX client.

  If password synchronization has to work between a UNIX stand-alone machine and a stand-alone Windows machine, the UNIX SSO

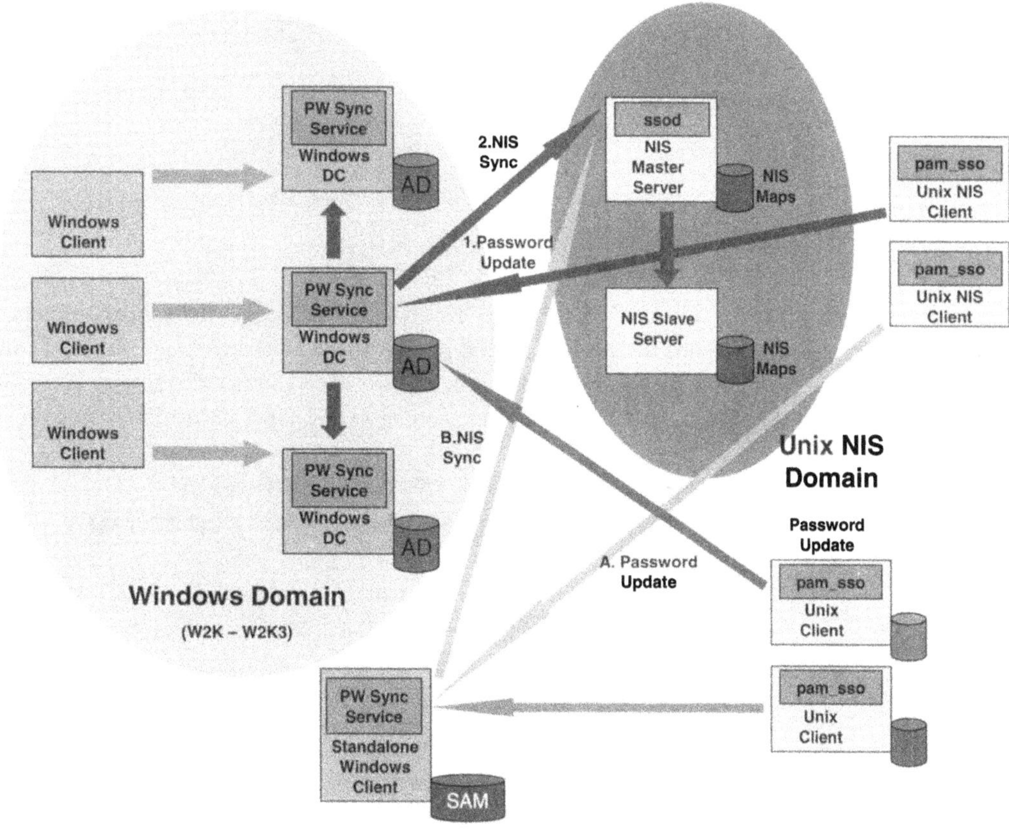

Figure 8.11 *SFU password synchronization architecture: UNIX to Windows.*

PAM module (pam_sso) installed on the UNIX client machine will simply synchronize the password change with the Windows stand-alone machine. In this scenario the Windows stand-alone machine must have the SFU password synchronization service installed: It has to be configured for one-way synchronization (UNIX-to-Windows) with the stand-alone UNIX client.

Other password synchronization solutions

Many IT software vendors provide password synchronization solutions for mixed Windows/UNIX environments. Table 8.4 provides a nonexhaustive list of some commercial solutions. A detailed discussion of these solutions is beyond the scope of this book.

A very interesting open source solution for password synchronization between Windows and UNIX is the solution proposed in the OpenLDAP-

Table 8.4 *Password Synchronization Solutions*

Vendor/Product	URL
Passgo InSync	http://www.passgo.com
Proginet SecurPass-Sync	http://www.proginet.com
M-Tech P-Synch	http://www.psynch.com

based "LDAP Account Synchronization Project." This solution is based on a password filtering DLL that intercepts password changes on the Windows DC and then synchronizes them with the OpenLDAP server. More information is available from http://acctsync.sourceforge.net.

8.4.2 Solutions providing centralized user management using an AD/LDAP repository

The following sections discuss solutions providing centralized user management for Windows 2000 (and later) and UNIX platforms using a central AD/LDAP repository. It is rather obvious that for this to work we will need to install extra software on the UNIX side.

Next we begin with a solution that is centered around an NIS-to-LDAP gateway. Then we explore several PAM-centric solutions: a solution using pam_unix, a solution using pam_ldap, and another solution using the Kerberos authentication protocol. Finally, we discuss a Samba-based solution that unfortunately only works for file and print sharing in a Linux environment.

NIS/LDAP gateway

NIS to LDAP gateway functionality is provided by ypldapd—a product from PADL software (http://www.padl.com). Ypldapd basically provides an NIS server interface. Contrary to a normal NIS server, however, the NIS server behind the ypldapd interface stores its data in an LDAP directory (and not in NIS maps). The intent of ypldapd is to allow an organization to leverage the scalability and distributed nature of LDAP directory services, while maintaining an existing NIS infrastructure. The ypldapd architecture is illustrated in Figure 8.12.

The ypldapd allows an organization to replace an NIS server with ypldapd without having to reconfigure any NIS client. The ypldapd acts as a broker between UNIX NIS clients and the LDAP server. Classical NIS utilities such as ypcat, ypmatch, and login will work unmodified. The only exception is the NIS password-changing utility (yppasswd): Because pass-

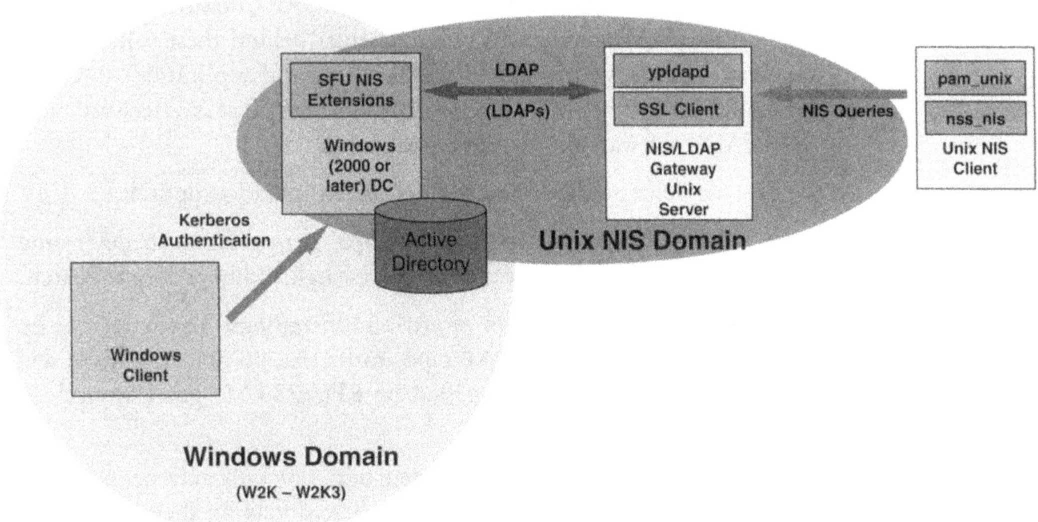

Figure 8.12 *NIS/LDAP gateway architecture.*

words are stored in LDAP, the classic NIS password-change utility will not work. To deal with this problem, ypldapd provides a special password-changing utility called ldappasswd.

When ypldapd starts, it binds to the LDAP server specified in its configuration file. This binding action is similar to logging into an operating system or application. An identifier is sent to the LDAP server along with an associated password. If the password matches, a connection to the LDAP server is established. This connection is maintained as long as ypldapd and the LDAP server are running.

Before ypldapd can access the data in the LDAP repository, special objects that can hold NIS data must be defined on the LDAP server. In Active Directory these special containers are created when the Services for UNIX (SFU) Server for NIS schema extensions are installed.

The binary distribution of ypldapd is available for Solaris 2.6, 7, and 8, Linux, and AIX 4.3.3 (on PowerPC). Source licensees may build ypldapd for other platforms, except for HP-UX. The ypldapd for HP-UX is available directly from HP.

Nss_ldap

Contrary to what was discussed earlier, in all the following solutions UNIX clients can access the AD/LDAP repository directly. In these solutions there is no more need for NIS servers or NIS-to-LDAP gateways translating NIS requests to LDAP queries. The basic enabler behind these solutions is the nss_ldap module, which allows UNIX clients and applications to communicate directly with an LDAP repository. The nss_ldap is a freeware module from PADL software (http://www.padl.com).

The nss_ldap module has a rich set of configuration options:

- It allows UNIX users to specify LDAP search filters to determine where in the directory tree to start the search and how deep to search.
- It allows for the definition of attribute mappings. The latter can be useful when searching LDAP repositories that do not store name service data in the format specified by RFC 2307 (a good example is SFU's Server for NIS).

Two of the four solutions outlined next not only rely on nss_ldap to retrieve user profile information (home directory, login shell, and so forth) but also to help with the user authentication process.

Pam_unix-centric approach

The pam_unix module supports the typical UNIX authentication protocol that is based on the crypt(3) hash function. Pam_unix has the capability to calculate a crypt(3) hash given a user password, to compare this hash to another hash stored in some repository, and—based on the outcome of the comparison—to decide whether the user's identity is authentic or not. The pam_unix module also provides password management and is supported on all UNIX flavors discussed in this chapter: Linux, HP-UX, Solaris, and AIX.

When UNIX clients rely on the pam_unix module, user authentication occurs as follows:

- Pam_unix first retrieves the user's password hash from the LDAP repository. To connect to the LDAP repository, pam_unix calls on nss_ldap.
- The hash nss_ldap retrieved is then validated on the UNIX host by pam_unix. This means that pam_unix will compare it to the local password hash. The latter is the outcome of the application of a hash function on the password that was entered by the user.
- If the validation process by the pam_unix module is okay, the user is given access to the UNIX client.

- After the initial authentication, the UNIX login program usually calls on nss_ldap for a second time—this time to retrieve additional user profile information from the LDAP repository.

In this scenario the LDAP repository is not the true authentication authority—this is the local pam_unix module's role. The LDAP repository provides only authentication data to the pam_unix module (via the nss_ldap module).

Security specialists can argue against this solution because it always uses the same account to access the LDAP repository. Access to the LDAP data does not occur using the identity of the user that must be authenticated, but using the identity of proxy account defined on the UNIX host. Some setups even dare to use anonymous access.

In order to support this in an AD environment (as illustrated in Figure 8.13), AD must have the SFU NIS extensions installed. Because the UNIX user password must be stored in the UNIX crypt(3) hash format.

In order to secure the LDAP network traffic between the UNIX client and AD, it is advisable to use LDAP over SSL or TLS (LDAPs). SSL/TLS support is available out of the box on the AD side. To support it on the UNIX side, you can use the stunnel software (http://www.stunnel.org).

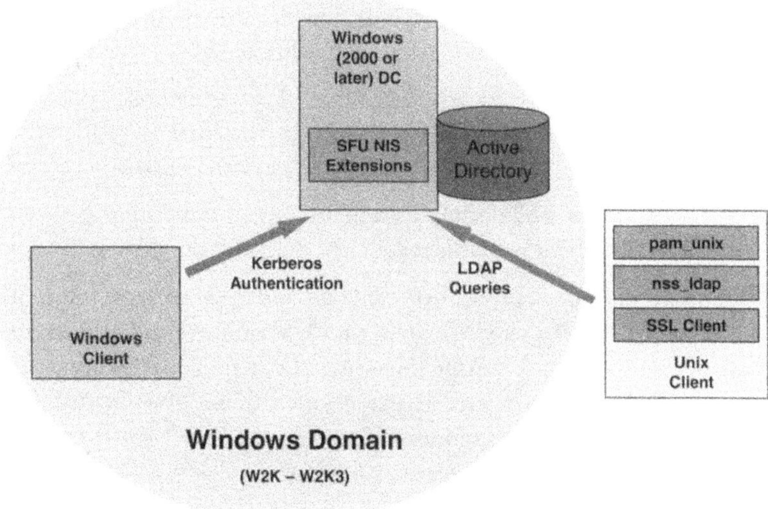

Figure 8.13 *The pam_unix-centric architecture.*

Pam_LDAP-centric approach

The pam_LDAP module supports one or more LDAP-based authentication mechanisms: simple authentication (also known as plaintext authentication or a simple LDAP bind), CRAM-MD5-based authentication, or digest authentication (the last two are used in conjunction with the SASL negotiation protocol).

Pam_LDAP also provides password management. It does not provide account and session management services. That is why once a user is authenticated using pam_ldap, applications will need to call on another PAM module to retrieve user profile information. Just like pam_unix, pam_ldap calls on nss_ldap to retrieve user profile information from the LDAP repository.

A pam_LDAP module for HP-UX 11, Linux, and Solaris 2.6 and above is available from PADL software (http://www.padl.com). AIX can support it but requires reconfiguration (more information on this topic can be found in the IBM Redbook "AIX and Linux Interoperability").

The pam_LDAP solution has several security advantages over the pam_unix solution:

- Contrary to the pam_unix-centrix approach, the LDAP repository acts as a true authentication authority. In this solution the LDAP server will decide whether the user authentication is successful or not and then return the result to the UNIX host.
- Access to the LDAP repository does not occur in the security context of a proxy account. In this case pam_LDAP authenticates to the LDAP server using the user credentials.
- All authentication attempts can be subjected to a central security policy that is stored in the LDAP repository.

Pam_LDAP can only work in conjunction with AD (as illustrated in Figure 8.14) when the AD4Unix AD schema extensions have been applied to AD. AD4Unix provides RFC2307-compliant AD schema extensions. The AD4Unix extensions can be downloaded from http://www.css-solutions.ca/ad4unix. To secure the LDAP traffic between the UNIX client and the LDAP server, it is once more advisable to use LDAP over SSL or TLS.

Pam_Kerberos-centric approach

Pam_Kerberos lets a UNIX host authenticate to a Kerberos Key Distribution Center (KDC). Most pam_kerberos modules also provide account, password, and session management capabilities. Most UNIX Kerberos

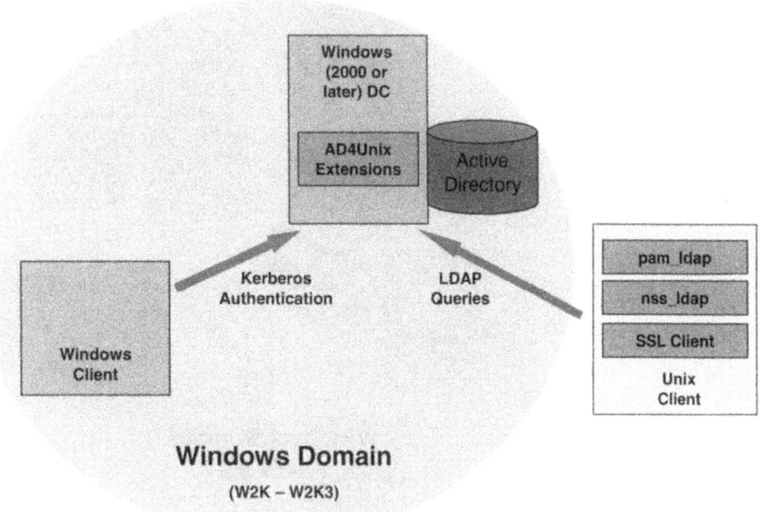

Figure 8.14 *Pam_LDAP-centric architecture.*

PAM modules are known as pam_krb5, where krb5 refers to version 5 of the Kerberos authentication protocol.

The nice thing about using the Kerberos authentication protocol for a UNIX and Windows integration project is that it can also be used as an SSO solution for Windows and UNIX applications that understand the protocol. These applications are also referred to as Kerberized applications. Unfortunately, in the UNIX world, there are very few Kerberized applications.

In an AD-centric environment two Kerberos-based Windows-UNIX interoperability approaches are possible:

- Using only Windows KDCs (as illustrated in Figure 8.15). In this scenario UNIX Kerberos users and services will receive Kerberos tickets that are issued by a Windows KDC. Even though Windows embeds profile data in the Kerberos tickets (authorization data), these cannot be used by the UNIX principals. UNIX principals can, however, fall back to nss_ldap to retrieve their profile data from the LDAP repository.
- Using both Windows and UNIX KDCs and by setting up cross-realm trust relationships between the UNIX and Windows KDCs (as illustrated in Figure 8.16). In this scenario UNIX Kerberos users and services will receive Kerberos tickets that are issued by a UNIX KDC.

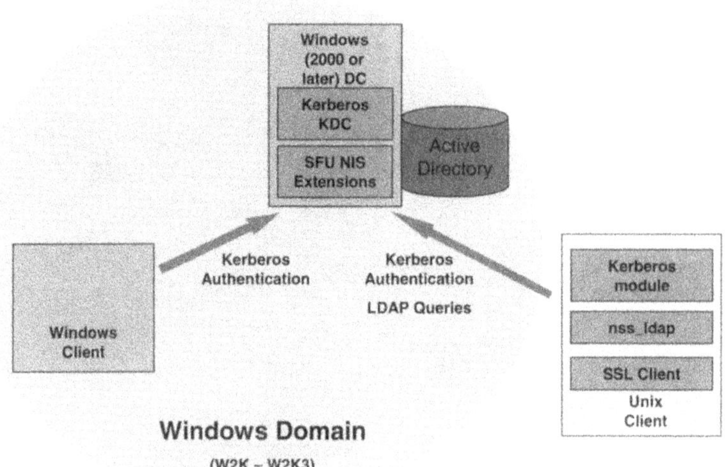

Figure 8.15 *Kerberos-centric architecture: Windows KDCs.*

As in the previous scenario, in this setup the UNIX hosts require nss_ldap in order to retrieve profile data from the LDAP repository.

For more information on Windows Kerberos interoperability, refer to Chapter 5 or the Microsoft Windows Kerberos Interoperability white paper available from http://www.microsoft.com/windows2000/docs/Kerbinterop.doc.

Vintela Authentication Services (VAS)

Vintela Authentication Services (VAS) is a commercial software offering from Vintela that provides centralized AD-based account management for Windows and certain UNIX clients. The most important feature of this solution is that it integrates UNIX machines into a Windows domain environment. By doing so, it can take advantage of the UNIX machine's Kerberos session key to secure users' authentication exchanges. That is also why—as opposed to the previous solutions—there is no more need to set up an SSL-secured connection between the UNIX client and the AD server. This also eliminates the need for dummy user accounts (or proxy accounts—see Chapter 5) and allows AD UNIX machine account attributes to be protected by the default AD authorization mechanisms. Just like all previous solutions, VAS enables users to use the same credentials on Windows and UNIX without needing special credentail sychronization software. VAS version 2.2 supports the following UNIX platforms: RedHat

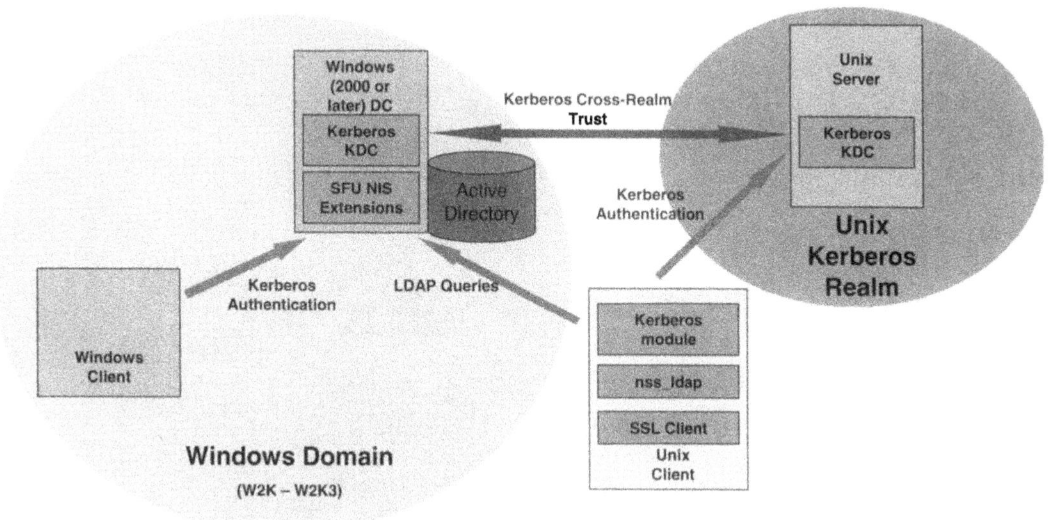

Figure 8.16 *Kerberos-centric architecture: UNIX and Windows KDCs.*

Linux 7.2 – 9.0, Suse Linux 8.x, Solaris 8,9, HP-UX 11.0, 11i, 11.11, 11.22, AIX 4.3 – 5.2

Besides LDAP and Kerberos, VAS also builds on the following open standards—SASL, GSSAPI and SPNEGO:

- The Simple Authentication and Security Layer (SASL) protocol provides a method for adding authentication support to connection-based protocols. SASL includes a negotiation phase before the actual authentication takes place. More information on SASL can be found at http://asg.web.cmu.edu/sasl.
- The Generic Security Services API (GSSAPI) is an API for authentication in a distributed client-server environment. It is basically an abstraction layer that enables applications to call on different authentication methods and protocols. GSSAPI can be compared to the Windows SSPI (explained in Chapter 4). Most UNIX Kerberos implementations have a Kerberos authentication GSSAPI plug-in. More information on GSSAPI can be found at http://www.faqs.org/faqs/kerberos-faq/general/section-84.html.
- The Simple and Protected GSSAPI Negotiation Mechanism (SPNEGO) is closely linked to the GSSAPI. It allows applications to negotiate which authentication mechanism to use. SPNEGO is documented in RFC 2478 (available from http://www.ietf.org).

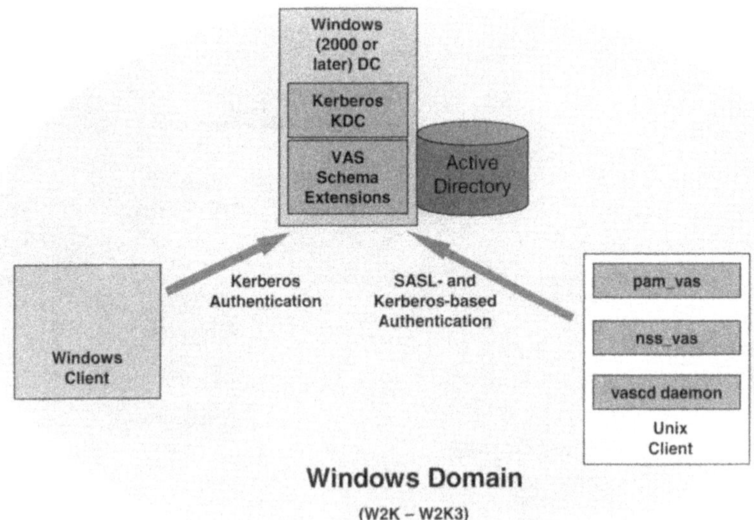

Figure 8.17 *Vintela Authentication Services (VAS)*

VAS includes several components for both the Windows and the UNIX side (as illustrated in Figure 8.17). On the Windows side it comes with a set of AD schema extensions (that are RFC 2307-compliant) and an extension for the AD Users and Computers MMC snap-in. On the UNIX side it comes with a special PAM (pam_vas) and NSS (nss_vas) module, and a special daemon called the vascd daemon. More information on VAS can be found at http://www.vintela.com/products/vas.

Other key VAS security features are the following:

- Automatic keytab maintenance. By joining UNIX workstations and servers to the domain, VAS eliminates the traditional Microsoft UNIX Kerberos interoperability steps of exporting and importing the keytab files. VAS automatically handles the creation of keytab files for both UNIX computer and UNIX service accounts.
- Full support for Microsoft Password Policies. VAS fully supports Microsoft password policies for password age, complexity, history and length.VAS users with expired passwords are prompted to change their password when logging on to UNIX workstations.
- Per workstation login access control based on users.allow/users.deny files. VAS introduces the concept of users.allow/users.deny files which can be configured to allow or deny login access based on Active Directory user name, group, or domain.

- Intelligent caching for better scalability. VAS uses patent pending caching technology that limits the amount and complexity of NSS/PAM driven LDAP traffic and LDAP server load while allowing the immediate realization of AD stored identity changes.
- Disconnected Operation. VAS can be configured to continue to allow Active Directory user authentication when the Active Directory server is unavaliable—such as in dial-up environments or on laptop computers.
- Script friendly command line utilities. VAS delivers script friendly command line utilities that can be used to build extremely rich authentication and identity management solutions based on popular Unix scripting languages (Perl, PHP, Python, shell, etc).
- Simplified time synchronization. VAS includes time synchronization functionality that allows UNIX hosts to synchronize time with Windows domain controllers.

Samba Winbind

Winbind can provide both a unified logon and account management experience between UNIX and Windows systems for SMB-based file and print access. Remember that the Samba solution discussed previously only provided a unified logon experience. The great thing about Winbind is that it takes away the need to define UNIX accounts (and UIDs and GIDs) in the Samba smbpasswd database (remember the double bookkeeping problem). The Winbind architecture is illustrated in Figure 8.18.

Unfortunately, so far the Samba Winbind daemon is only available for the Linux operating system. A stable version of Winbind is available from Samba release 2.2.2 onward (the latest Samba release is 2.2.8).

Samba's Winbind daemon is built on a UNIX implementation of Microsoft Remote Procedure Calls (RPCs), a special Pluggable Authentication Module (PAM) called pam_winbind, and the Name Service Switch (NSS).

- Winbind uses RPCs to enumerate Windows domain users and groups, to obtain Windows domain user and group details from a Windows domain controller, to authenticate users against an NT domain (using pass-through authentication), and to change passwords.
- Pam_winbind allows NT users to log in to the Samba Linux box and be authenticated by a Windows DC.

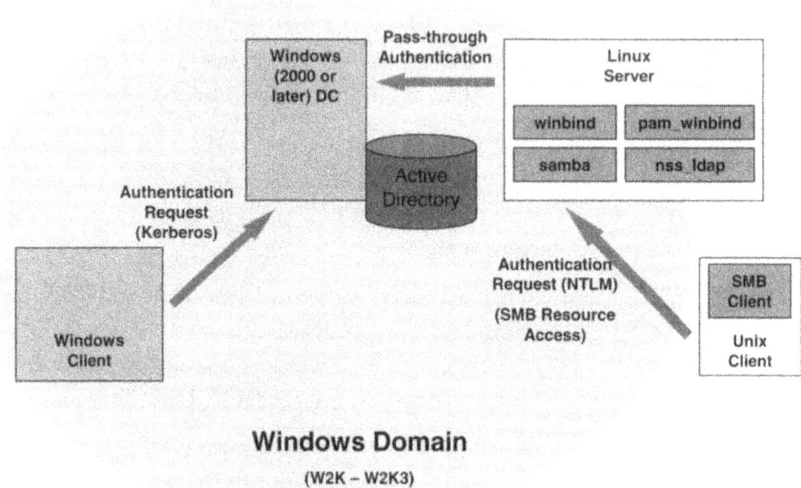

Figure 8.18 *Samba Winbind architecture.*

- The NSS module allows the Linux host and its services to resolve host-, group-, and user-names by calling on an LDAP repository (in this case AD).

The net result of all this together is that Windows domain users and groups will appear and work as UNIX users and groups on the UNIX box, and, most important, there is no more need for double bookkeeping.

A more detailed overview of the technologies behind Winbind can be found in Tim Potter and Andrew Tridgell's paper "Unified Logons between Windows NT and UNIX Using Winbind," available from http://us6.samba.org/samba/ftp/appliance/winbind.pdf. More information on how to set up Winbind and its different components can be found in the Samba documentation at http://de.samba.org/samba/ftp/docs/htmldocs/Samba-HOWTO-Collection.html#WINBIND.

8.5 Summary

This chapter provided an introduction to the different approaches one can take for UNIX and Windows account management and authentication integration. The list of solutions in this chapter is certainly not complete. The primary goal was to illustrate the different integration mechanisms that can be put in place and how MS supports them in SFU 3.0.

The combination of the Kerberos authentication protocol and an LDAP repository is definitely the most promising integration approach. Both LDAP and Kerberos are available on every Windows 2000 and later domain controller: Every DC hosts a Kerberos authentication authority (the KDC) and an LDAP-accessible repository (Active Directory). As long as UNIX Kerberized platforms and applications cannot take advantage of the authorization data Microsoft embeds in its Kerberos tickets (in the PAC field—see Chapter 5), the need for a special repository to centrally store the users' authorization data will remain.

9

Single Sign-On

A major driver behind the creation of authentication infrastructures is single sign-on (SSO). In short, SSO is the ability for a user to authenticate once to a single authentication authority and then access other protected resources without reauthenticating. The Open Group defines SSO as the mechanism whereby a single action of user authentication and authorization can permit a user to access all computers and systems where that user has access permission, without the need to enter multiple passwords.

This chapter focuses on the architectural approaches one can take when designing an SSO solution for a large IT infrastructure and on the security technology building blocks that can be used to construct such an SSO infrastructure. This chapter does not address the architecture of every SSO solution that is currently available on the software market. Many of them have a relatively small scope and only span a couple of applications, platforms, or authentication methods.

Remember that SSO is "authentication"-related, not "authorization"-related. Too many people confuse authentication and authorization. Authentication is a security process that assures that a user's identity is authentic, or in other words that another user, application, or service knows who it is talking to. Authorization is a security process that decides what a particular user is allowed or not allowed to do with a resource.

9.1 Single sign-on: Pros and cons

A study conducted by the Network Applications Consortium (http://www.netapps.org) in large enterprises showed that users spend an average of up to 44 hours per year to perform logon tasks to access a set of four applications. The same study measured the content of the calls to companies' helpdesk: 70% of the calls were password reset requests.

SSO is advantageous for both users and administrators. There is no need to point out that a user and an administrator's life becomes much easier if they have to deal only with a single set of credentials—one for every user. An average user will have to provide his or her logon credentials only once every day, and he or she will need to change only a single set of credentials at regular intervals. Indirectly this will increase a user's productivity. The authentication infrastructure, its administrators, and helpdesk operators will only need to keep track of the changes to a single entry for every user in the credential database. A key advantage is also that all authentication data are centralized and can be accessed and manipulated using the same tools and procedures. The latter may also be a weakness: If a malicious person gets to the database and can bypass its security system, he or she gets access to all of the data at once.

The advantages of SSO are not only related to the ease of administration and use, but SSO also brings important security advantages. Centralization eases the enforcement of a consistent authentication policy throughout the enterprise. Obviously, it is also much easier to secure a centralized than a distributed infrastructure. The lack of SSO services increases the risk for compromise of an authentication service's security. For example, because users need to keep track of different password credentials, they may start writing them down on Post-it notes and stick them to the back of their keyboards. Indirectly the absence of SSO can also affect the availability of an authentication service. The more passwords users have to remember or keep track of, the greater the chances that they forget or lose them.

A good SSO solution is also platform- and/or application-neutral: It can hide the authentication implementation details on different operating system platforms from the SSO user and can provide support to "outsource" the application-level authentication logic to a centralized SSO authentication authority.

An often-heard argument against SSO is that SSO credentials are the "key to the kingdom." If one can obtain the SSO credentials, one obtains access to all resources secured by them. This risk may be reduced when choosing SSO credentials that are not knowledge-based (a classic example of knowledge-based credentials are passwords) but rather biometric-based (e.g., using fingerprints) or possession-based (e.g., using cryptographic tokens or smart cards). The use of multifactor authentication solutions for SSO will further reduce this risk.

9.2 SSO architectures

9.2.1 Simple SSO architectures

SSO is relatively easy to implement in authentication infrastructures that are using a single authentication authority. Such an environment is illustrated in Figure 9.1. In this environment users have a single set of credentials. Remember that the concept of "users" must be interpreted in a large sense: It covers all security principals that are accessing the resources under the control of the authentication authority. Figure 9.1 shows a user and a resource server security principal trusting the same authentication authority. Linked to the authentication server is a credential database, which is the primary source for account and credential management.

Over the past years operating system vendors such as Novell and Microsoft have proven that SSO can easily be implemented in homogeneous LAN and intranet environments where all machines are running the same operating system and trusting the same authentication authority. Extranet Access Management System (EAMS) software vendors such as Netegrity, RSA (Securant), Baltimore, Entrust, and many others have proven the same thing for homogenous Web portal environments. Finally, remote-access authentication infrastructures using RADIUS, TACACS, or

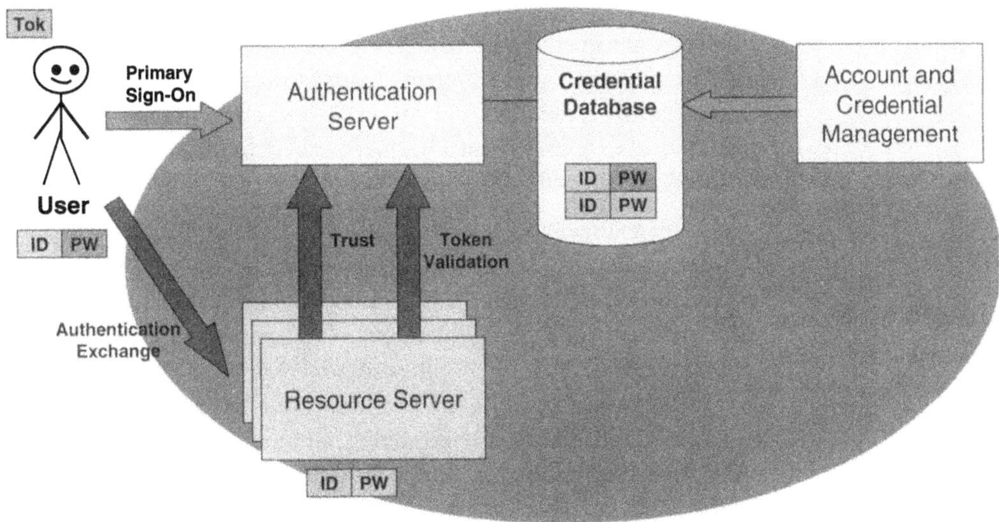

Figure 9.1 *SSO with a single authentication authority and a single authentication server.*

Table 9.1 *Simple SSO Solutions (Nonexhaustive List)*

SSO Solutions Bundled with Operating System Software	
Microsoft Windows NT, Windows 2000	http://www.microsoft.com
Novell Netware	http://www.novell.com
SSO Bundled with Extranet Access Management System (EAMS) Software	
Netegrity SiteMinder	http://www.netegrity.com
HP SelectAccess	http://www.openview.hp.com/products/select/index.html
Oblix Netpoint	http://www.oblix.com
SSO Using Centralized Remote Access Security Software	
Cisco (TACACS, TACACS+ solutions)	http://www.cisco.com
Microsoft (IAS RADIUS solution)	http://www.microsoft.com

TACACS+ showed that setting up SSO is relatively straightforward in environments using a centralized authority that communicates with a set of authentication proxies using a single well-defined authentication protocol. A nonexhaustive list of software products supporting simple SSO is given in Table 9.1.

Things get much more complex if the SSO scope is extended to cover different platforms and different organizations, which are using different authentication credentials and protocols and are governed by many different authorities. Usually this also means that the infrastructure has to deal with multiple credentials per user.

Having a single authentication authority does not necessarily mean that only one authentication server and a single credential database are available. For scalability and performance reasons, a single authentication authority may consist of multiple authentication servers and a set of replicated credentials databases. Figure 9.2 illustrates SSO in an environment with a single authentication authority and multiple authentication servers. Note that the credential database is replicated to all authentication servers. To avoid ambiguous user authentication, the replication of security credentials requires a single-master replication model. For the same reason, account and credential management can only be done on the data stored in the master credential database.

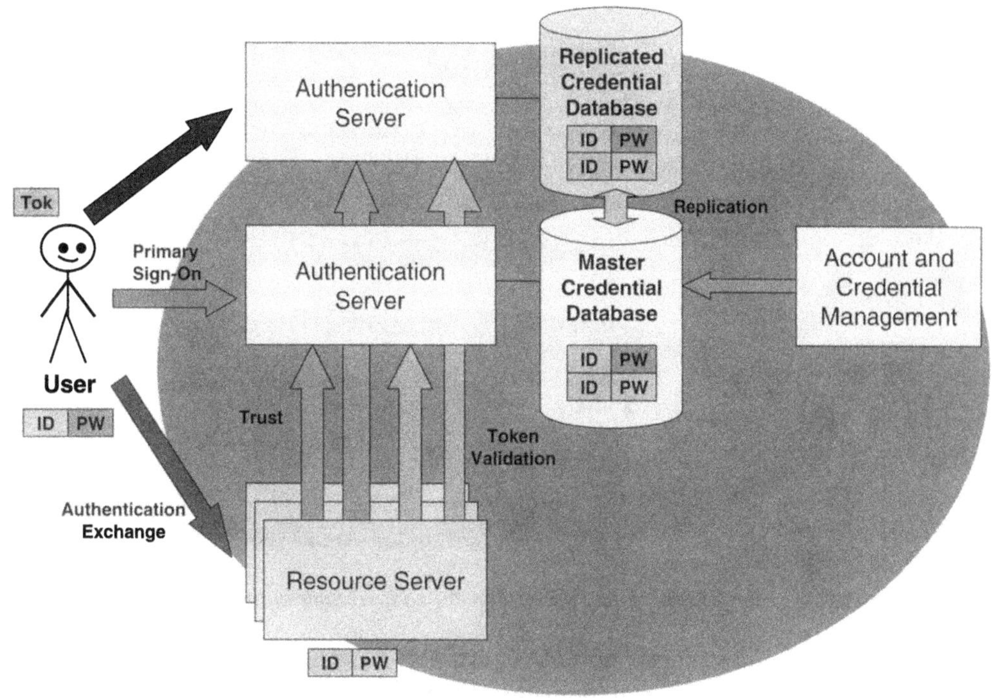

Figure 9.2 *SSO in an environment with a single authentication authority and multiple authentication servers.*

9.2.2 Complex SSO architectures

A big challenge in today's authentication infrastructures is to extend the SSO scope to cover many "different" authentication authorities. "Different" in this context means implemented on different platforms and governed by different organizations. In most scenarios these infrastructures also have to deal with multiple credentials per user and many different authentication protocols.

To ease the explanation of the different SSO architectures used in complex SSO setups, let us first look at how authentication works in an environment with multiple authentication authorities but without SSO support (as illustrated in Figure 9.3).

In the setup illustrated in Figure 9.3, the domain that the user uses most often is called the user's primary authentication domain. Domains that users use less often are called secondary authentication domains. Because in

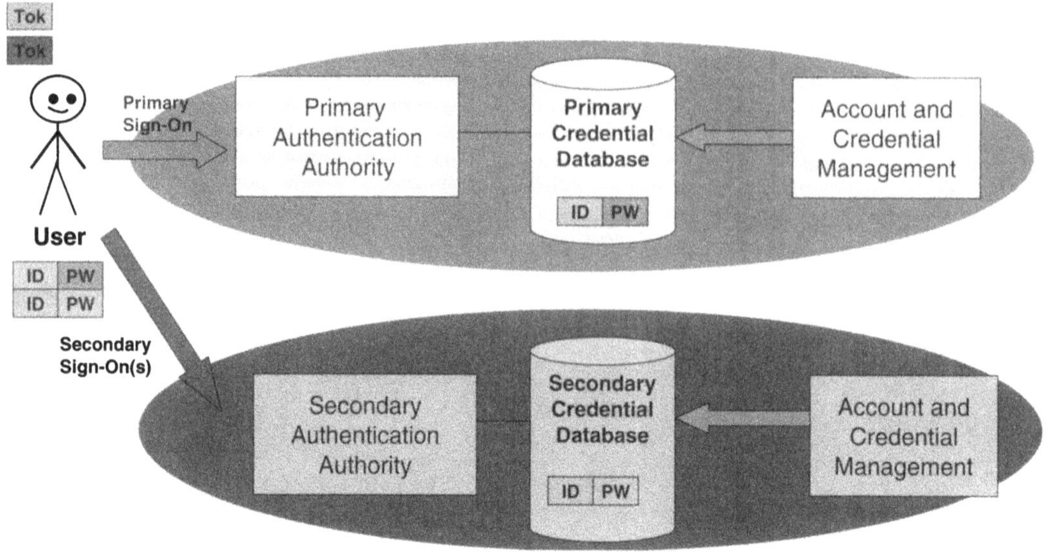

Figure 9.3 *Authentication in an environment with multiple authentication authorities.*

the example no SSO is available between the primary and the secondary authentication domains, when a user wishes to access resources in the secondary domains, he or she has to authenticate to the TTPs of those domains using credentials as defined in that particular secondary authentication domain. Every secondary authentication domain also has its proper credential database. There is no need to explain that this setup creates an enormous credential-safeguarding burden for the end users. Note that in this setup the user uses different authentication tokens, one per authentication authority.

SSO architectures dealing with a single set of credentials

The simplest complex SSO architectures are the ones using a single set of credentials, recognized by many different authentication authorities. There are two important flavors of complex SSO architectures dealing with a single set of credentials: token-based and public key infrastructure–based SSO systems.

Both SSO architectures provide SSO in a rather homogeneous environment. Homogeneous in this context means using a single account naming format and authentication protocol that are supported by every entity, application, and service participating in the SSO environment.

Token-based SSO systems

A classic example of an authentication protocol used for token-based SSO is the Kerberos authentication protocol. Kerberos is an open standard defined by the IETF that has been implemented on many different platforms.

In a token-based SSO architecture users get a temporary software token when they have been successfully authenticated to the TTP (as illustrated in Figure 9.4). This token can be cached on the user's machine and can be reused to prove the user's identity to other secondary authentication domain TTPs. To validate the user token, the TTPs use cryptographic methods that are based on secret keys that are set up between the secondary authentication domain TTPs and the primary authentication domain TTP. This cryptographic key material represents a trust relationship between primary and secondary authentication domains.

Contrary to the tokens we will discuss in other SSO architectures, the tokens used in token-based SSO systems are valid for more than a single authentication authority. Agreed that in some token-based setups users do have more than a single token, but in that case the authentication protocols support the automatic and transparent exchange of the token of one authentication authority for a token issued by another authentication authority.

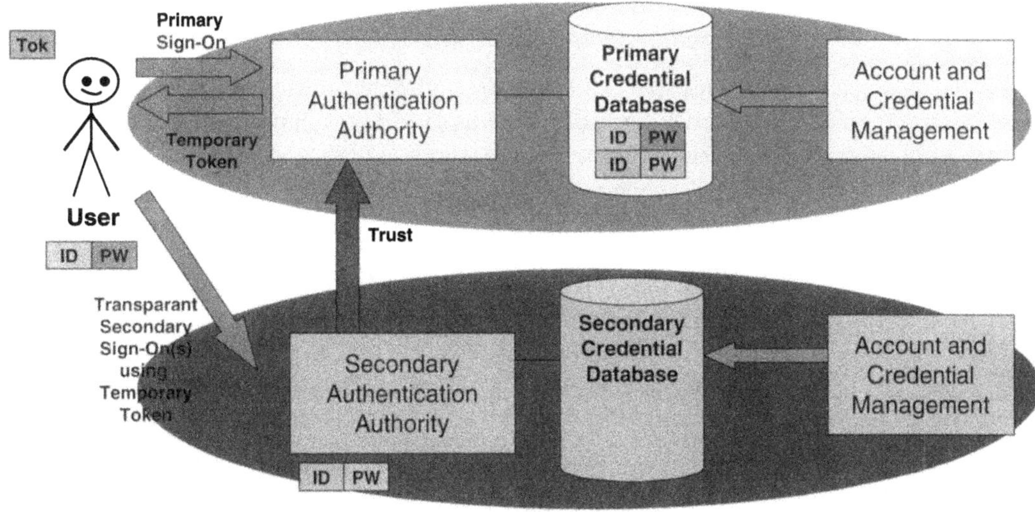

Figure 9.4 *Authentication in a token-based SSO environment.*

In the Kerberos case, users authenticate to a central authentication service, called the Kerberos key distribution center (KDC) (the authentication TTP). If their authentication credentials are valid, they receive a ticket (the software token), which enables the user to request other tickets from the KDC in order to access other resources in the primary and secondary authentication domains. The tickets prove to the resource servers that the user has been authenticated before by a trusted authentication service—the Kerberos KDC.

The Kerberos authentication protocol has inspired the developers of the authentication services for the Open Software Foundation's (OSF) Distributed Computing Environment (DCE). Microsoft has implemented Kerberos as the default authentication protocol of Windows 2000. CyberSafe sells plug-ins that can be used to enable an operating system platform to generate, understand, and validate Kerberos credentials (this process is also known as "Kerberizing").

The Kerberos token-based SSO typically uses remote procedure calls (RPCs) to transport authentication tickets. In HTTP-based environments, token-based SSO can be provided using HTTP cookies. The latter mechanism is used by many Extranet Access Management Systems (EAMS) such as Netegrity's SiteMinder or Oblix's Netpoint when dealing with multiple authentication authorities. Microsoft currently uses a similar cookie-based token system to extend the SSO functionality of its Passport Web authentication solution across different Web sites.

Token-based SSO software comes out of the box with many of today's most popular operating system platforms (Windows 2000, Netware, and so forth). Table 9.2 gives some examples of software products providing token-based SSO support.

Table 9.2 *Token-Based SSO Solutions (Nonexhaustive List)*

Kerberos-Based	
Microsoft Windows 2000	http://www.microsoft.com
Cybersafe ActiveTrust	http://www.cybersafe.ltd.uk
Cookie-Based	
Netegrity SiteMinder	http://www.netegrity.com
Oblix Netpoint	http://www.oblix.com
HP SelectAccess	http://www.openview.hp.com/products/select/index.html

Public key infrastructure–based SSO

In a public key infrastructure–based (PKI-based) SSO architecture (illustrated in Figure 9.5) users first register themselves at a trusted authentication authority [in this case called a certification authority (CA)] or at one of the authentication authority's registration agents [called registration authorities (RAs)]. During this registration process, different things occur: Users identify themselves using a set of credentials; a piece of client-side software generates an asymmetric key pair; and the public key of this key pair is offered to the CA (or RA) for certification. Upon receipt of the user's credentials and the public key, the CA (or RA) will verify the user's credentials. If the credentials are valid, it will generate a public key certificate and send it back to the user. The user's public key certificate and the user's private key are cached on the user's machine (or on a smart card or cryptographic token). They both are used to generate a kind of software token similar to the ones used in token-based SSO systems. These tokens are used to prove the user's identity to other secondary authentication authorities in subsequent authentication requests.

A major difference between a token-based and a PKI-based SSO architecture is that in the PKI case the cryptographic methods that are used to validate the user token are asymmetric cryptography-based (using public and private keys). The outcome of this validation process also largely depends on the trust relationship that is set up between the secondary authentication authorities and the primary authentication authority. In the

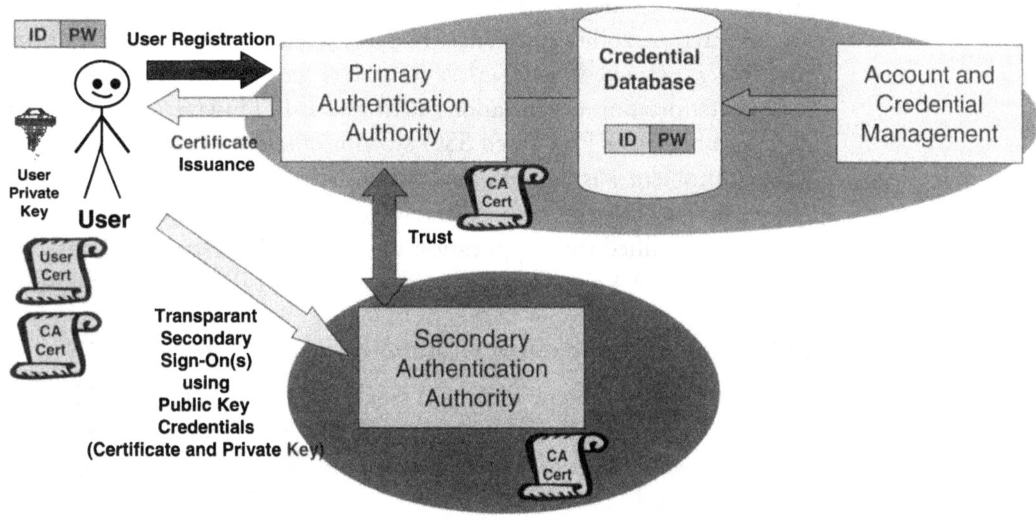

Figure 9.5 *Authentication in a PKI-based SSO environment.*

Table 9.3 *PKI-Based SSO Solutions (Nonexhaustive List)*

In-House PKI Products	
Baltimore Unicert PKI*	http://www.baltimore.com
Entrust Authority PKI	http://www.entrust.com
Smarttrust PKI	http://www.smarttrust.com
RSA Keon PKI	http://www.rsa.com
Microsoft PKI (Windows 2000, Windows Server 2003)	http://www.microsoft.com
External PKI Products	
Verisign	http://www.verisign.com
Globalsign	http://www.globalsign.com

* In september 2003 BeTRUSTed planned to acquire the Baltimore Unicert PKI software.

case of a PKI-based SSO architecture, the trust relationship between primary and secondary authentication authorities is represented by a secondary authentication authority's certificate (issued by the primary authentication authority). Similar to the tokens discussed in token-based SSO architectures, the tokens used in PKI-based SSO systems are valid for more than a single authentication authority.

Contrary to token-based SSO systems, PKI-based SSO systems are a relatively new technology. Early implementers of the technology experienced lots of interoperability problems. The latter were mainly related to immature PKI standards. Over the last two years the security software industry and standardization organizations such as the IETF have made important efforts to make the PKI-based SSO systems enterprise-ready. Another early adopter problem was that few applications were PKI-enabled. Although the latter problem has not been fully resolved, most application software vendors have modified their application to let them understand PKI-based credentials. Table 9.3 gives some popular examples of PKI software solutions.

SSO architectures dealing with many different credentials

There are three different flavors of SSO architectures that can deal with many different credentials: architectures that use credential synchronization, architectures using a secure client-side cache, and architectures using a secure server-side cache.

Contrary to token-based SSO, these three SSO architectures can provide SSO in a more heterogeneous environment. Besides different credential types, they can also support different account formats and multiple authentication protocols.

Credential synchronization

Figure 9.6 shows an SSO architecture that is using a credential synchronization system. A classic example is a system that synchronizes user passwords between the credential databases of different authentication authorities. Although this architecture supports multiple credentials for every user, they are kept identical using the credential synchronization mechanism. Credential synchronization systems typically use a single master credential database, which can be used by administrators to update the user credentials.

Because in this setup the user is still prompted to enter his or her credentials by every single authentication authority, these systems are not considered true SSO systems. Many security experts consider it a very dangerous practice to synchronize credentials between the databases of different authentication authorities. Their objections are based on the "key to the kingdom" argument mentioned earlier. Table 9.4 gives some examples of credential synchronization software products.

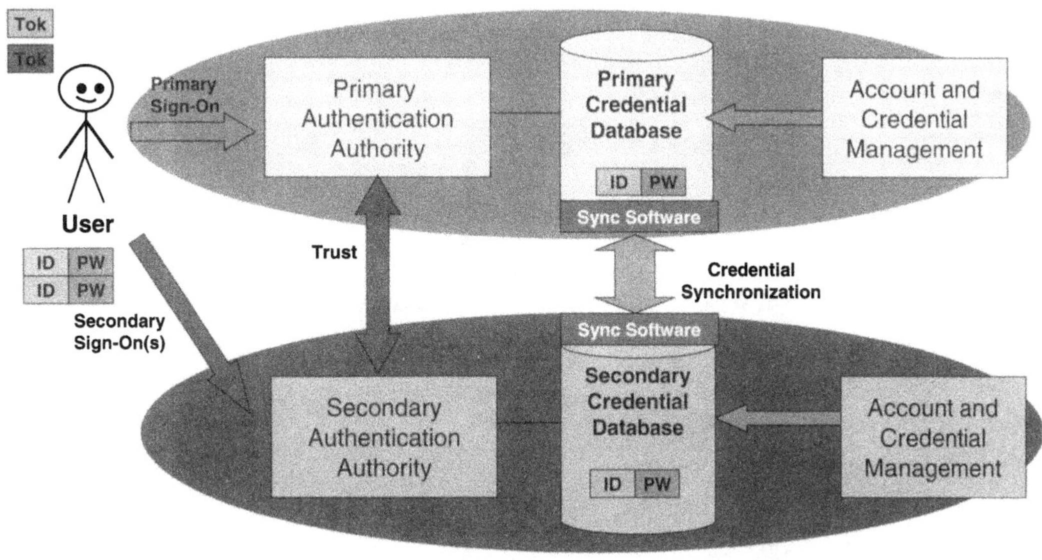

Figure 9.6 *Password synchronization-based SSO.*

Table 9.4 *Credential Synchronization-Based SSO Products (Nonexhaustive List)*

Passgo InSync	http://www.passgo.com
Proginet SecurPass-Sync	http://www.proginet.com
M-Tech P-Synch	http://www.mtechit.com
M-Tech ID-Synch	http://www.mtechit.com

The technology behind credential synchronization software is not as simple as Figure 9.6 may make you think. A key problem is the credential storage format in the credential databases of the different authentication providers. Very few authentication providers use the same storage format. Also, credentials are typically stored in a hashed format, which means that it is impossible to derive the original password from the hash. Because most providers use a different hash format, you cannot just synchronize the credentials between databases. That is why credential synchronization can only occur when the credentials are updated (e.g., when a user updates his or her password).

Secure client-side credential caching

Figure 9.7 illustrates an SSO architecture that is using a secure client-side credential caching mechanism. In this setup a set of "primary credentials" is

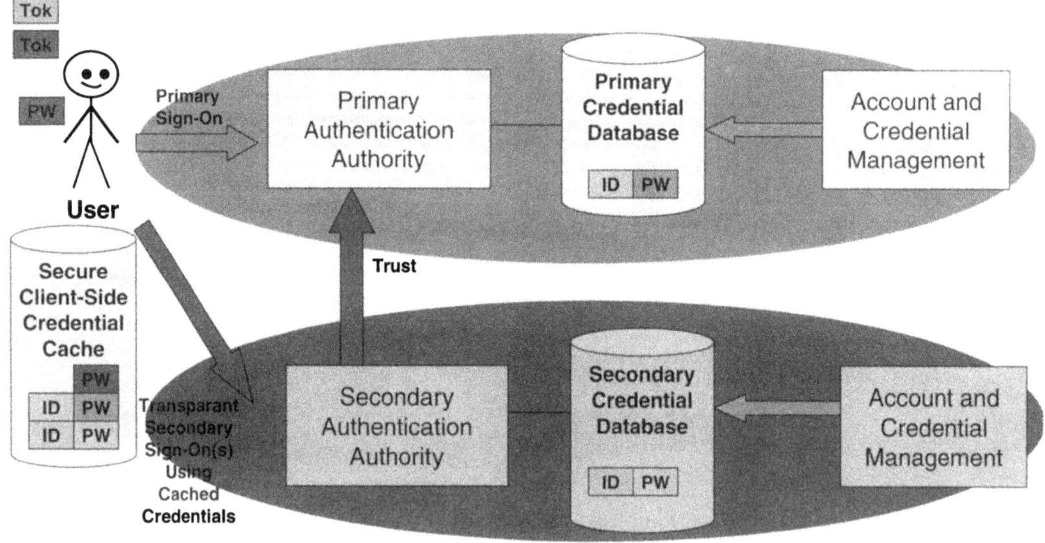

Figure 9.7 *Authentication in an SSO environment using a client-side secure cache.*

used to unlock a user's credential cache. Later on, when the user wants to access resources requiring different authentication credentials, the other credentials are automatically retrieved from the local credential cache and presented to the authentication authority. If the credentials are valid, the user will be logged on transparently to the other resource servers. Because in this setup authentication to the secondary authentication domains relies on the credentials for the primary domain to unlock access to the credentials of secondary domains, the secondary domains must trust the primary domain.

In the early days of secure client-side credential caching, it was combined with client-side scripting to automate the SSO process. This created a lot of administrative overhead. Nowadays credential caching is combined with more intelligent and adaptive client-side software that can automatically retrieve and provide the correct credentials to the destination server. Table 9.5 gives some examples of secure client-side cache-based SSO software products.

In the context of this SSO architecture, "secure storage" of the cached credentials is absolutely vital. This is certainly the case if the cached credentials are used to give access to business-critical applications or data. In the latter case it is not recommended to use this SSO architecture on portable client devices (such as laptops or PDAs) or on operating system platforms that have a bad security reputation.

SSO based on a secure client-side cache can be implemented without the use of an authentication "infrastructure." In this case the primary credentials unlocking the cache would be local credentials—"local" meaning defined in the local machine's security database and only valid for accessing local machine resources. In the context of an authentication infrastructure, the user's primary credentials are generally not local credentials but domain credentials.

Table 9.5 *Secure Client-Side Cache SSO Products (Nonexhaustive List)*

Bundled with OS Software	
Microsoft Windows XP, Windows Server 2003 (Credential Manager)	http://www.microsoft.com (also covered later on in this chapter)
Bundled with Other Software Products	
Entrust Entelligence (PKI client)	http://www.entrust.com
Identix BioLogon (Client-side biometrics software)	http://www.identix.com

Secure server-side credential caching

Figure 9.8 illustrates a secure server-side credential caching SSO architecture. Contrary to the use of a secure client-side cache, secure server-side credential caching SSO architectures store credentials in a central repository on the server side. Contrary to a credential synchronization-based SSO architecture, the credentials used in a secure server-side credential caching SSO architecture are not necessarily the same for every authentication authority.

In a secure server-side credential caching SSO architecture, the master credential database contains (besides the user's primary credentials) the mappings between a user's primary and secondary credentials. That is why the primary authentication authority in this architecture is sometimes referred to as the "authentication gateway." Another copy of the secondary credentials is kept in the secondary authentication domain databases.

In a secure server-side credential caching SSO setup, a user always first logs on to the primary authentication authority using his or her primary credentials and a predefined authentication protocol. If logon to the primary authentication authority is successful, the user-side SSO software usually provides the user with a list of available applications. When accessing an application that requires a logon to a secondary authentication authority,

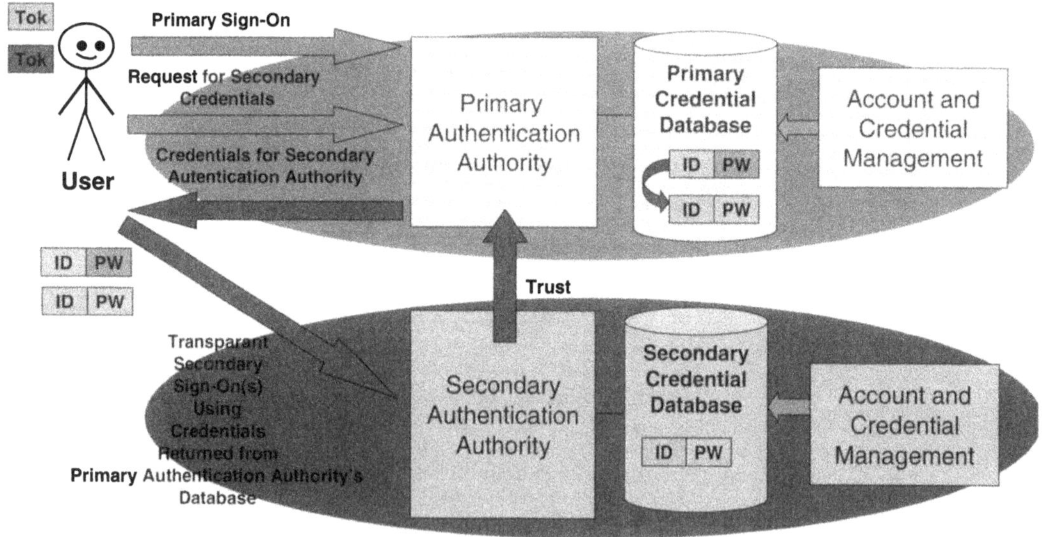

Figure 9.8 *Authentication in a secure server-side credential caching SSO environment.*

the user-side SSO software will first communicate with the primary authentication authority to retrieve the appropriate user credentials. These are then forwarded to the user in a secure way. Finally, the user-side SSO software will use the secondary domain credentials to transparently log the user on to the secondary domains.

Because in this architecture the secondary authentication authorities trust the primary authentication authority to store a copy of their credentials in the primary credential database, a trust relationship is required between every secondary and the primary authentication authority.

Server-side caching generally provides better security because the credentials are not stored on the client's hard disk (also remember the security concerns brought up for client-side caching). The credentials may be temporarily downloaded to the client but will disappear when the client shuts down. Also, access to the server-side credential cache is only allowed after a successful logon to the central authentication authority.

An important challenge in these architectures is how to keep the copies of the credentials in the primary credential database and the ones in the secondary credential databases synchronized. Different products use different approaches to resolve this problem:

- Some products contain password synchronization services.
- Some products rely on the password synchronization services of specific software products (Passgo, Proginet, and so forth) or the password synchronization services that are built into systems management software (BMC Patrol, CA Unicenter, Tivoli).
- Some products do not use any password synchronization and rely on administrators or users (self-administration) to perform the credential updates.

Examples of secure server-side credential caching SSO systems are IBM's Tivoli Secureway Global Sign-On, Computer Associates eTrust, and Vasco's SnareWorks Secure SSO (as listed in Table 9.6). SecureWay Global Sign-On's primary authentication method, for example, is a DCE token-based. After the initial authentication, the SecureWay Client-Side Global

Table 9.6 *Secure Server-Side Credential Caching SSO (Nonexhaustive List)*

IBM Tivoli Secureway Global Sign-On	http://www.ibm.com
Computer Associates eTrust	http://www.ca.com

Sign-On software retrieves the correct credentials from the primary credential database and provides them transparently to the correct secondary authentication authority.

9.2.3 SSO architectures: Summary

So far we discussed simple SSO solutions and SSO architectures that can span multiple authentication authorities. Table 9.7 gives an overview of the advantages and disadvantages of the SSO architectures discussed so far. A big challenge for today's SSO products is to extend their scope to cover authentication authorities that are governed by different institutions and companies and to integrate as an authentication provider with a wide range of applications. This topic is discussed in the following sections.

9.3 Extending SSO

9.3.1 Extending the SSO scope to cover different organizations

One of the driving factors behind extending SSO to cover different organizations are companies' e-business requirements to easily authenticate users defined in other organizations and transaction requests initiated by business partners. The demand for SSO scope extension is very high in the world of Internet portals. SSO clearly benefits the Internet experience of any portal user from an ease-of-use point of view.

There are two approaches when dealing with SSOs spanning different organizations. In the first approach an organization deals with the credential information and authentication of users in other organizations locally by using its proper credential database and authentication authority. In the second approach organizations agree to set up a federation[1] agreement between their authentication authorities. In the latter case users will always authenticate to their proper organization's authentication authority.

When dealing with authentication locally, an organization can define a set of local credentials or decide to synchronize credential databases. In the first case an organization simply provides every external entity with a set of new credentials that is kept in the organization's authentication database.

1. The Burton Group defines federation as follows: "The use of agreements, standards, and technologies to make identity and entitlements portable across autonomous identity domains."

Table 9.7 *Advantages and Disadvantages of Different SSO Architectures*

	Pros	Cons
Token-based	■ Single set of credentials simplifies life of user and administrator ■ Software usually comes bundled with OS software	■ Requires a homogeneous authentication infrastructure environment ■ Relies on symmetric cryptography
PKI-based	■ Single set of credentials simplifies life of user and administrator ■ Software usually comes bundled with state-of-the-art OS software ■ Relies on asymmetric cryptography	■ Can only deal with a single set of credentials ■ Complex certificate validation logic Requires a lot of processing on the client side ■ Requires a homogeneous authentication infrastructure environment (all services and applications must be PKI-enabled)
Credential Synchronization	■ Can deal with many different credentials ■ Does not require a homogeneous authentication infrastructure environment ■ Does not impact the client side (no extra software needed)	■ Credentials are kept identical on different platforms ■ Does not provide true SSO (unless it is combined with a secure client-side caching mechanism) ■ "Key to the kingdom" argument ■ Multiple sets of credentials complicate life of user and administrator ■ Requires extra software on server infrastructure side
Secure Client-Side Credential Caching	■ Can deal with many different credentials ■ Does not require a homogeneous authentication infrastructure environment ■ Has important impact on client side (requires extra software or state-of-the-art OS)	■ Requires a "secure" client-side credential cache—it is not recommended to use it from portable client devices or OSs with a bad security reputation ■ Multiple sets of credentials complicate life of user and administrator
Secure Server-Side Credential Caching	■ Can deal with many different credentials ■ Does not require a homogeneous authentication infrastructure environment ■ Has impact on client side (requires extra software)	■ Requires a credential synchronization mechanism (may be part of the SSO product) ■ Multiple sets of credentials complicate life of user and administrator ■ Requires extra software on server infrastructure side

Some organizations may even agree to delegate the administration of these credentials to an external administrator. A major disadvantage of this setup is that a user will end up with multiple credentials. In other words, there is no more SSO. In the second case an organization decides to synchronize account information between an external organization's directory and its proper directory. Even though in this scenario users may end up with a set of credentials that is identical between different organizations, users will still be prompted to enter their credentials by every other authentication authority.

A real SSO solution would accept the external entities' "foreign" credentials to authenticate to the organization's authentication authority and would not require a user to reenter his or her credentials. These goals are driving distributed authentication or "federation"-based authentication infrastructures.

In a federated authentication infrastructure, foreign credentials have been validated by a foreign TTP and are also accepted by an organization's proper authentication authority. The reason why they are accepted is because there is an agreement, trust, or federation between the foreign authentication authority and a company's proper authentication authority. This setup does not require a copy of the foreign organization's credential database. Also, in this case, the users only have to take care of a single set of credentials.

As long as the SSO solution behind federated authentication infrastructures supports a mechanism to set up federation or trust relationships between different authentication infrastructures, it can use any of the architectures discussed earlier in this chapter. They can use secure caching, credential synchronization, a token-based architecture, or a PKI-based architecture.

PKIs use the concept of CA hierarchies, cross-certification, bridge CAs, or any other CA-to-CA interoperability solution to set up federations. Kerberos-based infrastructures support federations through cross-realm trust relationships. The following are some examples of commercial authentication infrastructure products and how they support "trust" or "federation":

- Novell NDS eDirectory (version 8.5 and later) uses the concept of NDS tree federations.
- Microsoft Windows NT and 2000 domains use interdomain trust relationships. In Windows 2000 these trust relationships are built on Kerberos cross-realm authentication.

An interesting new language that will help with the creation of federations in the future is the Security Assertion Markup Language (SAML).[2] SAML is a new standard that uses XML to encode authentication and authorization information. Because its basis is XML, SAML is platform-independent. SAML is also authentication method–neutral: For example, it could be used to set up federations between PKI- and Kerberos-based authentication infrastructures. The development of SAML is driven by OASIS (the Organization for the Advancement of Structured Information Standards), a nonprofit, international consortium that creates interoperable industry specifications based on public standards such as XML and SGML.

At the time of writing, the standardization efforts in the federation space were progressing in a very competitive way. Whereas Microsoft, IBM, and Verisign are pushing the Web services security standardization initiative (WS-Security),[3] most other major software vendors stick to the Liberty Alliance[4] and SAML as the building blocks for a Web-based SSO infrastructure and federated Web services. Whether Microsoft will ever join the Liberty Alliance remains an open question. In July 2002 Microsoft announced they would support a limited version of the SAML 1.0 specification in their future security product line. At the time of writing Microsoft was building two new softwares that will be rooted on the WS-Security federation protocols: MS Passport version 3.0 (a Web federation solution) and a product codenamed Trustbridge (an inter-organization federation solution).

Table 9.8 compares Kerberos-, PKI-, and SAML-based authentication infrastructure federations.

9.3.2 Extending SSO to cover different applications

Another important authentication infrastructure feature that can help extend the SSO scope to cover different applications is the supported authentication application programming interfaces (APIs). Although this is not always an architect's primary concern, I found it useful to provide a list of popular authentication APIs. An architect should at least know about them.

Table 9.9 lists a set of well-known authentication APIs. APIs such as GSSAPI, JAAS, and CDSA provide vendor-neutral APIs—they also provide more than just authentication APIs. SSPI, PAM, NMAS, and XUDA are not vendor-neutral and only provide authentication services.

2. See http://www.oasis-open.org/committees/security/.
3. See http://msdn.microsoft.com/library/default.asp?url=/library/en-us/dnwssecur/html/securitywhitepaper.asp.
4. See http://www.projectliberty.org.

Table 9.8 *Comparing Federation Mechanisms*

	Kerberos-Based Federation	PKI-Based Federation	SAML-Based Federation
Authentication technology	Kerberos	PKI	Any
Platform support	Many	Many	Many
Support for entity authentication	Yes	Yes	Yes
Support for data authentication	No	Yes	Under development
Authorization federation support	Yes, but not standardized	Yes, but very few products support it	Yes
Granularity of trust relationship and security policy support	Very Monolithic, no policy support	Support for granular trust and security policies in some products	Under development
Status	Standardized	Standardized, though standardization is not complete	Under development

Table 9.9 *Authentication APIs*

Authentication API Name	Comments
Generic Security Service API (GSSAPI)	Security services API providing authentication, confidentiality, and integrity services. Defined in RFC 2078.
Security Support Provider Interface (SSPI)	Microsoft's Authentication API—has been inspired by the GSSAPI.
Pluggable Authentication Modules (PAMs)	Sun's pluggable authentication architecture.
Java Authentication and Authorization Service (JAAS)	The Java Authentication and Authorization API. Includes a Java implementation of Sun's PAM. Obviously, the JAAS development is driven by SUN.
Common Data Security Architecture (CDSA)	Security Services API for authentication, confidentiality, and integrity services driven by the Open Group.
Novell Modular Authentication Service (NMAS)	Novell's pluggable authentication architecture.
XCert Universal Database API (XUDA)	XCert's API to provide strong certificate-based authentication to applications (XCert is now a part of RSA).

9.4 SSO technologies in Windows Server 2003 and XP

Table 9.10 provides an overview of the specific SSO technologies that are currently provided or that will be provided in the near future by Microsoft. Some of them (as mentioned in Table 9.10) are covered in more detail in this book.

9.4.1 The Credential Manager

The requirement that users must reenter the same credentials whenever they access resources on the same Internet or intranet server .can be frustrating for users, especially when they have more than one set of credentials. Administrators often must cope with the same frustration when they have to switch to alternative credentials to perform administrative tasks.

Prior to Windows XP and Windows Server 2003, Microsoft provided similar application-specific solutions, such as the Microsoft Internet Explorer's (IE's) credential-caching mechanism. In Windows Server 2003 and XP, Microsoft integrates a universal solution: the Credential Manager. The Credential Manager is a client-based SSO solution that uses an intelligent credential-caching mechanism.

Table 9.10 *Windows Server 2003 and XP SSO Technologies*

SSO Technology	SSO Focus	Covered In:
Credential Manager	Enterprise and Web SSO	This chapter
MS Passport	Web SSO	Chapter 7
MS TrustBridge (to be released sometime in 2004)	Web SSO	Mentioned in this chapter.
MS Internet Authentication Service IAS	Network SSO	This chapter
MS Host Integration Server	Extending SSO to IBM RACF and Mainframe environments	Not covered in this book (HIS 2003 is a separate MS product)
MS Services for UNIX 3.0	Extending SSO to UNIX environments	Chapter 8

Credential Manager consists of three components: the credential store, the key ring, and the credential collection component. The Credential Manager keeps user credentials in a client-side credential store. Windows 2003 and XP use the Data Protection API (DPAPI) to secure access to the credential store content. Because the credential store is part of a user's profile, the store supports roaming. The store is unlocked using the user's "primary credentials" (they are also referred to as the default credentials). When users log on locally to a machine or domain, they use their primary credentials. The credential store contains credential-target maps.

- A set of credentials can take one of three forms: a user ID and password, a user ID and a certificate/private key, or a set of MS Passport credentials. Certificate/private key–based credentials can be stored on hard disk or on a smart card.
- A target is the resource the user accesses. To specify a target, you can use a DNS name or NetBIOS name. A target name can contain wildcards. For example, entering *.hp.com as the target name makes the associated credentials available to all targets whose DNS name ends in hp.com. A target name is independent of the communication protocol that is used to access it—in other words, credential manager can deal with HTTP-, HTTPs-, FTP- and SMB-based resource access.

Similar to a ring that holds the keys your house, office, or car, the Credential Manager key ring holds sets of credentials. The key ring component lets you manage the credential store's credential-target mappings and their properties. You view and modify the mappings and properties through the Stored User Names and Passwords dialog box, which Figure 9.9 shows. How you access the Stored User Names and Passwords dialog box depends on the OS and the OS's User Interface (UI):

- Windows Server 2003—Open the Control Panel Stored User Names and Passwords applet.
- XP's classic UI—Open the Control Panel User Accounts applet. Click the Advanced tab, then select the Manage Passwords option.
- XP's user-friendly UI—Open the Control Panel User Accounts applet and open the properties of the account with which you're currently logged on. In the Related Tasks list, select Manage my network passwords.

You can't modify all the credentials from the key ring UI. For example, you can't modify Passport credentials. You must modify Passport credentials from the Passport Web site.

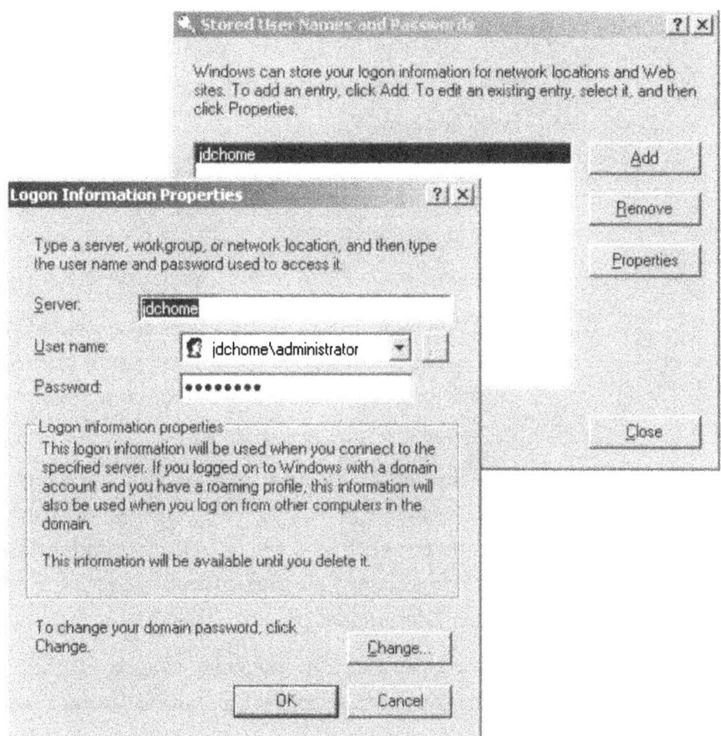

Figure 9.9 *Credential Manager key ring UI.*

When Credential Manager detects that it can't use the primary credentials (or the credentials with which the user is currently logged on) to access a target, its credential collection component displays the Connect to dialog box. This dialog box prompts the user for alternative credentials. When the user selects the Remember my password check box, Credential Manager adds the credentials to the credential store. Then, the next time the user accesses the same target, Credential Manager automatically uses these credentials without prompting the user.

When a user uses RAS to remotely log on to a Windows domain, Credential Manager automatically adds a wildcard target for the user's logon domain (e.g., *.hp.net) and corresponding credentials to the credential store. Credential Manager uses these credentials as the user's primary credentials during the RAS logon session. This entry represents a permanent credential cache addition—it remains in the cache after the RAS session has ended.

To see how Credential Manager operates, let's consider a user named Bob who is working from his workstation, which is called bobws. Bob wants to access a share resource that's on a server called devserv. As Figure 9.10 shows, the following events occur:

1. User Bob logs on at machine bobws as bobws\bob (which is a local account).
2. Bob uses a Credential Manager aware application (e.g., Windows Explorer) or API to access a file share on a server named devserv. Bob accesses the share using the following Universal Naming Convention (UNC) name: \\devserv\share.
3. The application calls on the Local Security Authority (LSA) and an authentication package (Kerberos or NTLM; authentication packages were explained in Chapter 4) to authenticate to \\devserv.
4. The authentication package queries Credential Manager for a set of credentials to use when accessing \\devserv. Credential Manager does not find a specific set of credentials and returns Bob's primary credentials bobws\bob (these are the credentials with which Bob logged on).
5. The authentication package tries to authenticate to \\devserv\share using the primary credentials (bobws\bob) but fails.
6. The failure is communicated to the application, which calls on the credui component. Credui brings up the Credential Collection dialog box.
7. Bob enters appropriate credentials in the Credential Collection dialog box and selects the Remember my password check box to save the credentials.
8. The credentials are passed to the Credential Manager, which stores them in the credential store.
9. The application and authentication package use the new credentials to authenticate to \\devserv\share. This time the authentication succeeds.

As Figure 9.10 shows, Credential Manager provides a great deal of automation. However, it doesn't automate all credential-relatedmanagement tasks. For example, suppose that the Credential Manager on your PC stores the credentials necessary to access a remote share on a file server. If the administrator for that file server changes the password to access the share, the password won't automatically be changed in your PC's Credential Manager, which might lead to an account lockout.

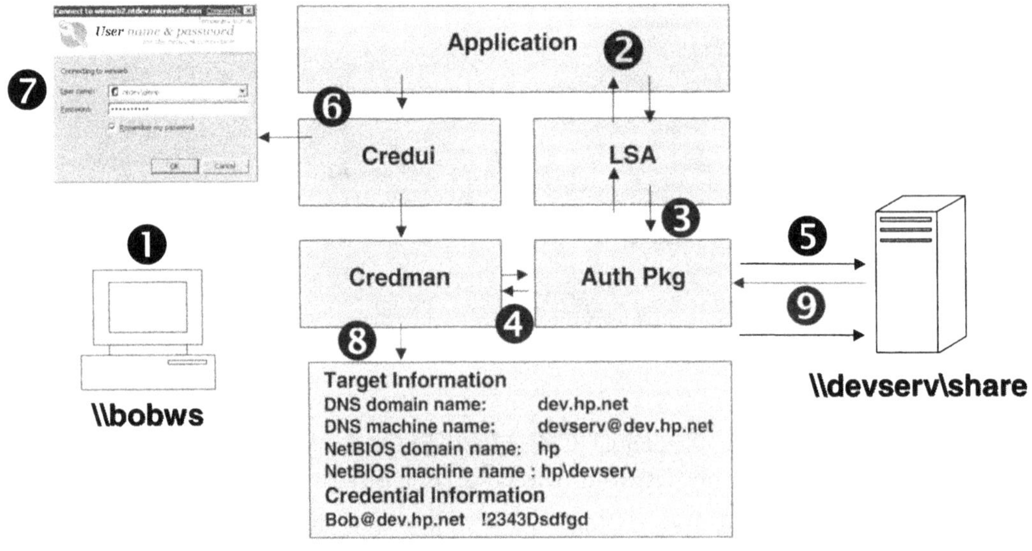

Figure 9.10 *Credential Manager operation.*

Administrators who don't want client-side credential storage can disable Credential Manager with the Network Access: Do not allow storage of credentials or .NET Passports for network authentication Group Policy Object (GPO) setting. You can find this setting in the Windows Settings\Security Settings\Local Policies\Security Options directory. When configuring this setting, the change will not take effect until you restart Windows. This setting can be used in both domain and standalone Windows Server 2003 and Windows XP setups. In a domain environment an administrator can use a GPO to enforce the setting. In a local setup you would use the Local Security Policy settings to configure it. When credential manager is disabled, the Stored User Names and Passwords dialog box will show up empty and with disabled push-

Figure 9.11 *Dialog boxes after disabling Credential Manager.*

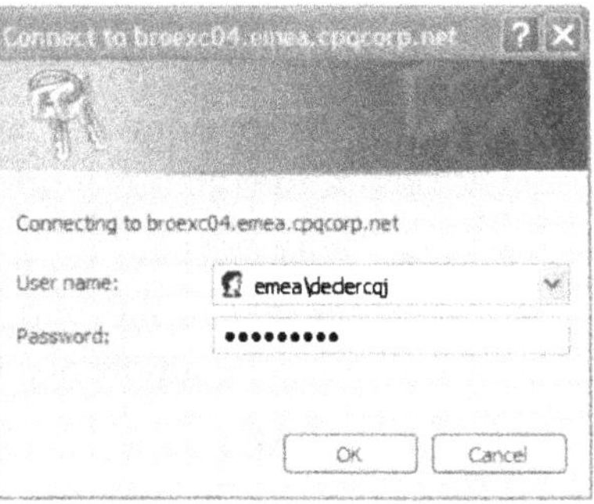

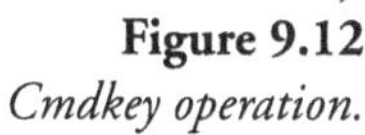

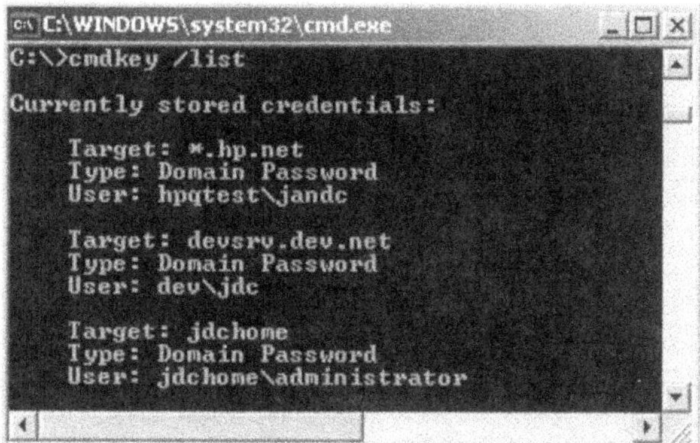

Figure 9.12
Cmdkey operation.

buttons; the Credential Collection Component dialog box will lack the "Remember my password" checkbox (as illustrated in Figure 9.11).

Windows 2003 includes the Cmdkey tool, which lets you manage the credential store from the command line. You can use Cmdkey to add, delete, and list credentials from the command line (as illustrated in Figure 9.12 for a list operation).

9.4.2 Internet authentication service

The Internet Authentication Service (IAS) is Microsoft's implementation of a Remote Authentication Dial-in User Service (RADIUS) server and proxy. RADIUS is an IETF standard defined in RFCs 2865 and 2866. The IAS software comes with all Windows Server 2003 versions with the exception of the Web server edition. The RADIUS proxy function is new to Windows Server 2003. It allows the forwarding of RADIUS requests to other IAS or RADIUS servers.

In a Windows environment, IAS is often used in conjunction with Microsoft's Routing and Remote Access Server (RRAS) to provide access control functions to dial-up users.

The meaning of the word RADIUS is confusing because it does not reveal the full capabilities of a RADIUS server:

- A RADIUS server not only deals with the authentication, but it also provides authorization and accounting services. As such, RADIUS is a good example of a triple A service.
- A RADIUS server not only serves dial-in (remote access) users, but it can also handle the access control requests of wireless users and users

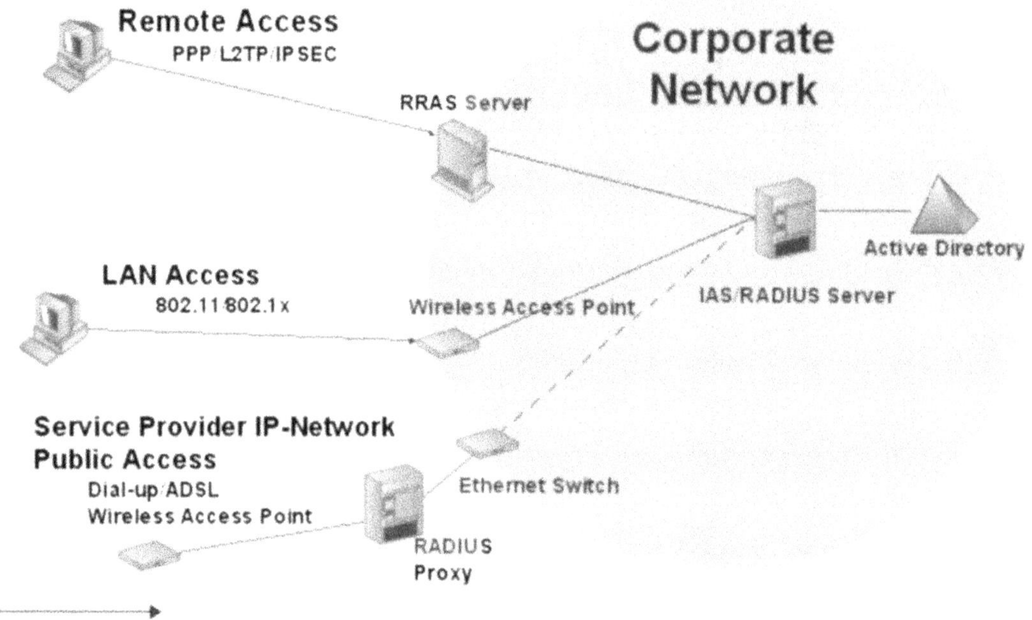

Figure 9.13 *IAS scenarios.*

connecting over a virtual private network (VPN) connection. This is illustrated in Figure 9.13.

The main reason why IAS is discussed in this chapter is because it can provide an integrated SSO solution for Windows domain and network access—independently of whether the user connects over a dial-up, wireless, or VPN connection. IAS can provide this functionality because it can be integrated with Active Directory. This integration basically means that IAS uses the AD credential database to authenticate users.

IAS SSO also works across multiple Windows domains that are in the same or in different forests:

- To make SSO work across different domains, add the IAS and RRAS (used for remote access) servers to the built-in RAS and IAS Servers group in every domain of the forest.
- To make SSO work across different forests, use an IAS RADIUS proxy in every forest that is pointing to a central RADIUS server.

IAS supports different authentication methods, which are listed in Table 9.11.

Table 9.11 *IAS Authentication Methods*

Authentication Method	Meaning
Password Authentication Protocol (PAP)	A very trivial authentication protocol for dial-up users. Transmits user password in the clear.
Shiva PAP (SPAP)	Special version of PAP developed by Shiva. Transmits user password in a reversibly encrypted format.
Challenge Handshake Authentication Protocol (CHAP)	Challenge-response based authentication protocol.
Microsoft CHAP (MS-CHAP)	Microsoft proprietary version of the CHAP protocol.
Microsoft CHAP v2 (MS-CHAP v2)	Enhanced version of MS CHAP. Supports mutual authentication and other security enhancements.
Extensible Authentication Protocol (EAP)	Not an authentication protocol but a negotiation protocol to determine the authentication method to be used between a client and a server. Allows for the use of smart cards, tokens, and certificates as authentication mechanisms. Windows Server 2003 supports the MD5-CHAP and certificate/smart card EAP authentication packages.
Protected Extensible Authentication Protocol (PEAP)	Negotiation protocol based on EAP that uses TLS to provide a secure communication channel. Only used for authentication of wireless 802.11 clients.

9.5 Summary

This chapter illustrated the complexity behind setting up an SSO architecture. This is the main reason why for many companies SSO will remain a holy grail for years to come.

As for any security solution, it is also recommended for an SSO solution to keep it simple and rely on open standards. For many organizations it may be much more realistic and feasible to plan for a reduced sign-on solution instead of a universal single sign-on solution. Also, open standards (like the Kerberos and PKI SSO mechanisms) provide better security quality and more flexible interoperability options. If you choose a vendor-specific SSO

solution (like the password synchronization and client-side and server-side credential caching mechanisms), you make your IT infrastructure very dependent on a single software vendor.

A critical new concept in the Web SSO world is "federation." Federation technologies and initiatives such as SAML, Liberty Alliance, and WS-Security may revolutionize the use of SSO in Web authentication infrastructures.

10

Windows Server 2003 Authorization

Once an entity has been authenticated, we need some way to restrict its access to the resources that are available on a computer or in a domain. In most environments, not just anyone can access every computer or domain resource. This is the goal of an authorization service: It protects against unauthorized use and provides an answer to the questions: What can an entity do with a resource and how can it interact with the resource?

10.1 Authorization basics

Authorization always deals with two entities (illustrated in Figure 10.1): a subject that wants to access an object. Authorization is typically executed and enforced by a third entity that is generally referred to as the reference monitor. In a Windows environment, this third entity is known as the Security Reference Monitor (SRM). The SRM is the only key security component of the Windows OS that is running in the highly privileged OS kernel mode. It checks all access to resources as requested by code that is running in user mode.

Authorization not only deals with access to visible Windows objects such as files, printers, registry keys, and AD objects. It also deals with access to less visible objects such as system processes and threads. Authorization also controls the ability to perform system-related tasks, such as changing the sys-

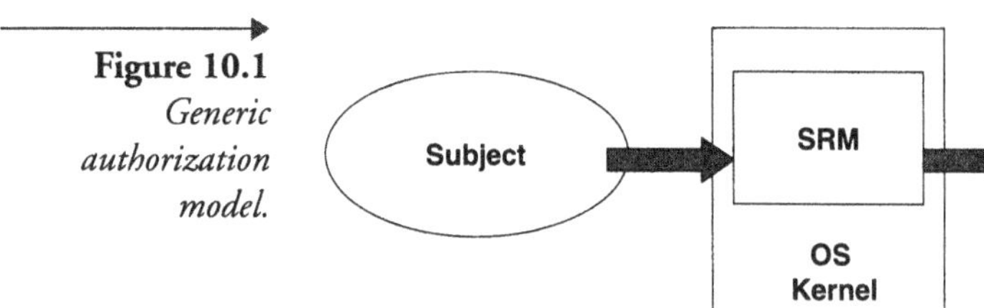

Figure 10.1 *Generic authorization model.*

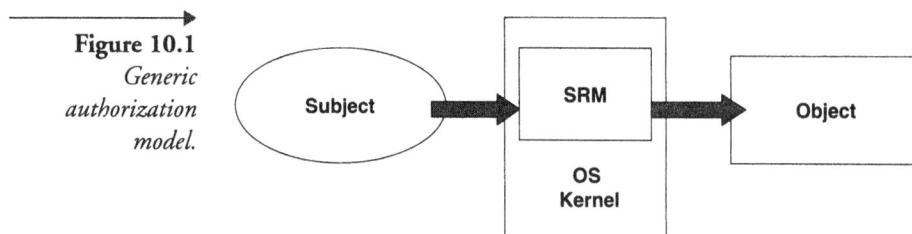

tem time or the ability to shut down the system. Microsoft calls these system-related tasks user rights.

10.2 The Windows authorization model

Although Windows Server 2003 includes quite a few new authorization features, the authorization model is basically the same as the one that was used in Windows 2000 and NT4. It is based on the following key concepts: access token, access mask, security descriptor, and impersonation.

Figure 10.2 brings the different Windows authorization concepts together. It shows how upon every object access, the security reference monitor (SRM) checks the access token and the access mask against an object's security descriptor. The access token and access mask are both linked to a process that impersonates a user. Let's have a closer look at the these key authorization concepts.

- Impersonation means that a process acts on behalf of a user.
- The access token contains a user's authorization data (such as group memberships and user rights).
- The access mask tells the SRM what the process wants to do with the resource (e.g., read a file? write to a file?).
- The security descriptor of an object tells the SRM who can do what with a particular object.

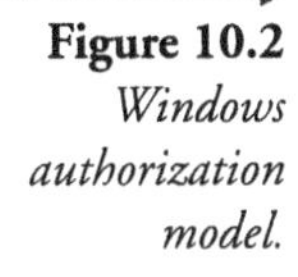

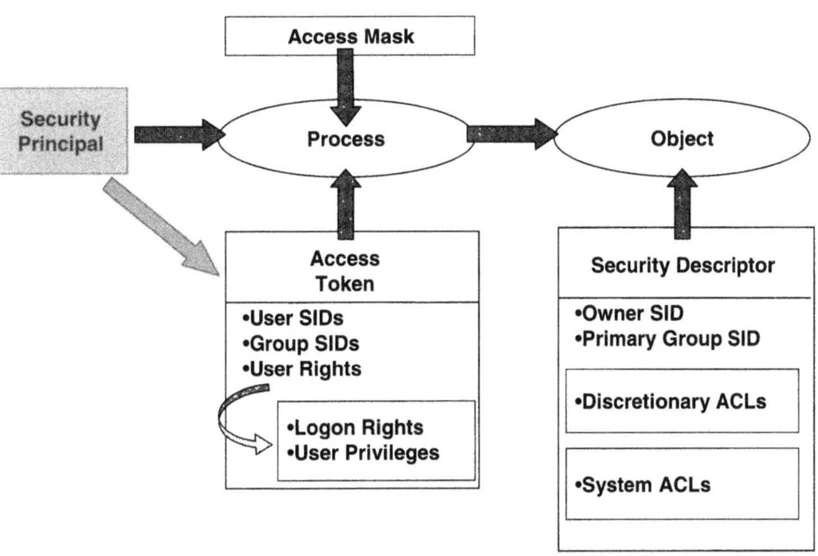

Figure 10.2 *Windows authorization model.*

Based on the outcome of the authorization comparison process, the SRM decides if the process can access the resource. To inform the process of what it can do with the resource, the SRM will return another access mask, the granted access mask. In the following section we will examine these key concepts more in detail and link them to the subject and object we introduced in Section 10.1.

To allow the operating system to associate a user's authorization data (the user's rights and group memberships, explained next) with every process that is started by the user, Windows uses an object called the access token. Access tokens are linked to a user's logon session. They are generated on every machine to which the user logs on, independent of the logon type (interactive, network, and so forth). An access token is always local and never travels across the network. The operating system component that generates access tokens is the Local Security Authority (LSA). Besides the user's domain authorization data, an access token also contains the user's local authorization data. The latter are the authorization data that are stored in a system's local security database (the SAM): It includes a user's local group memberships and local user rights. A complete overview of all the fields in the access token can be found in the Windows Server 2003 resource kit or the Microsoft Windows platform SDK. To look at the content of your Windows access token (including group memberships and user rights), use the whoami tool with the /all switch (as illustrated in Figure 10.3).

The main authorization attribute on the object side is called a security descriptor. A security descriptor tells the authorization system who can do

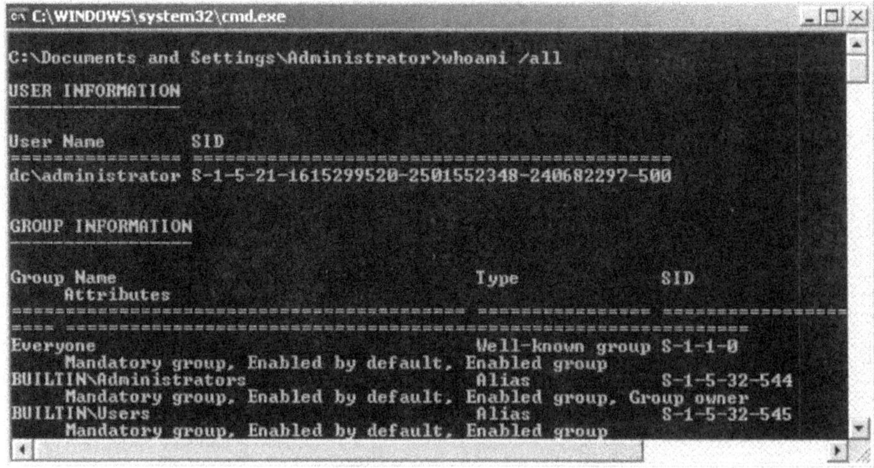

Figure 10.3 *Using whoami /all to look at the access token content.*

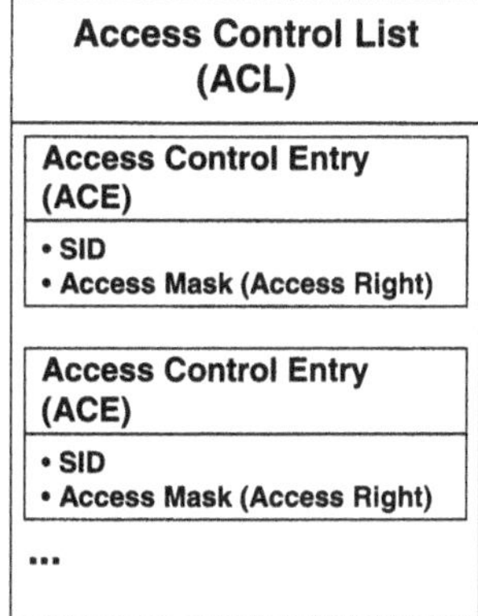

Figure 10.4 *Access control list (ACL) content.*

what with the object. Every object that has a security descriptor linked to it is called a securable object. Securable objects can be shared between different users—and every user can have different authorization settings. Examples of securable objects are a file, a folder, a file system share, a printer, a registry key, an AD object, and a service. The security descriptor of an AD object is stored in the object's nTSecurityDescriptor attribute (which is also replicated to the Global Catalog). The security descriptor of a file system object is stored in the NTFS file system.

Every object's security descriptor contains a set of Access Control Lists (ACLs), illustrated in Figure 10.4. An ACL is composed of multiple Access Control Entries (ACEs). An ACE is also referred to as a permission. An ACE links a security identity (SID) to an access right (e.g., read, write, delete, execute). Typical examples of permissions are "Joe can read the monthly expense claim report," or "Alice can print on the human resource department printer."

In a security descriptor, an access right is represented using a hexadecimal value called the access mask. Table 10.1 shows some access mask values and their meaning. If an access right is made up of multiple access rights,

Table 10.1 *Typical Windows Access Masks and Their Meaning*

Access Mask Values	Meaning (Associated Access Right)
0x10000	Delete
0x20000	Read
0x40000	Write

then the associated access mask value will be the sum of the individual access rights. For example, an access right holding the read and write access right will have an access mask of 0x60000.

Every security descriptor contains two types of ACLs: discretionary and system ACLs.

- Discretionary ACLs (DACLs) contain ACEs that are set by the owner of an object. They are called discretionary because their content is set at the object owner's discretion.

  Ownership is a key concept in the Windows security model. It is a very powerful concept because the owner of an object is always granted the right to manage the object's permissions. By default, the object owner is the Windows user account that created the object. In the case in which a domain administrator or a member of the local administrators group creates an object, by default the Domain Admins or Administrators groups become the object owner. This behavior can be changed in Windows Server 2003 thanks to the following GPO setting (part of the Security Options): "System objects: default owner for objects created by members of Administrators group." This GPO setting affects the nodefaultadminowner (REG_DWORD) registry value that's located in the HKEY_LOCAL_MACHINE\System\CurrentControlSet\Control\Lsa registry key.

  An account can take ownership of an object if it has the modify owner permission on the object or if it has the Take ownership of files or other user objects user right—by default, this right is given to members of the Administrators group. In an object's security descriptor, the owner is represented by its SID in the Owner SID field.

  To look at an object's discretionary ACLs from the Windows GUI, you will typically use the ACL editor (explained in detail as follows). To look at the DACLs of a file system object from the command prompt, you can use the cacls, xcacls, or showacls tools. For an AD object, you can use dsacls. We will come back to these tools at the end of this chapter.

- System ACLs (SACLs) contain an object's auditing settings and are set by an administrator. They are nondiscretionary: They are not related in any way to the owner of an object. SACLs are not the only thing that is needed in order to enable auditing on the object level. You also must enable "Audit object access" in a machine's audit policy. We will come back to Windows auditing in Chapter 18 of this book.

To look at an object's system ACL from the Windows GUI, you will also use the ACL editor. However, Windows does not include a native command-line utility to do this.

Besides the discretionary and system ACLs, an object's security descriptor also contains two other fields:

- The Owner SID field holding the SID of the owner of the object
- The Primary group SID field holding the SID of the object owner's primary group. The concept of a primary group is used for Posix and Macintosh compatibility reasons.

In the Windows authroziation model, a user never accesses a resource all by himself or herself: There is always a server process that acts on behalf of a user. This process is known in Windows terminology as impersonation. When a process impersonates a user, it means that it runs in the security context of the user and that it uses the user's authorization attributes.

The degree to which a process can act on behalf of a user can be controlled using impersonation levels, which are set in a user's access token. Windows Server 2003 uses the following impersonation levels: anonymous, identify, impersonate, and delegate. They are explained in Table 10.2. The anonymous and delegate impersonation levels were introduced in Windows 2000. The delegate level is the only impersonation level that can be controlled from the administration interface. Chapter 5 contains more information on the delegate impersonation level (or, in short, delegation) and they way it differs from the impersonate impersonation level.

Table 10.2 *Windows Impersonation Levels*

Impersonation Level	Meaning
Anonymous	The process impersonates an anonymous user (this means unidentified user). The access token will not contain any authorization information.
Identify	The process can use the identity of the user for its proper security processes. It cannot impersonate the user.
Impersonate	The process can act on behalf of a user to access resources on the local machine. The access token will contain the user's authorization information.
Delegate	A service can act on behalf of a user to access resources on the local machine and also on remote machines. The access token will contain the user's authorization information.

10.3 Windows 2000 authorization changes

Windows 2000 introduced quite a few fundamental authorization changes. Because these are so important, we will also discuss them in the context of this book on Windows Server 2003 security. Most of the authorization changes applicable to Windows 2000 are still valid for Windows Server 2003. If this is not the case it will be explicitly mentionned.

Microsoft included the following major authorization changes in Windows 2000:

- Inclusion of a new ACL editor
- Fine-grain control over inheritance
- Support for object-type ACEs
- Support for property-based and property set–based ACEs
- Support for extended rights
- New ACL evaluation rules

In the following, objects can refer to any securable object. These can be file system, share, printer, registry, Active Directory (AD), or service objects. As mentioned before, a securable object can also be a less tangible object, such as a process or a Windows station.

Some securable objects can contain other securable objects; they are called container objects. A container object can be a file system container (a folder), a registry container (a key), a printer container (a printer contains documents), or an Active Directory container (an Organizational Unit).

Table 10.3 shows a subset of the securable objects available in Windows 2000 and Windows Server 2003 and which new authorization feature is or can be applied to their ACLs. This table does not list all Windows objects on which authorization settings can be set. For example, service and windows station objects are not listed.

Some of the new features (the ones marked with (*) in Table 10.3) are part of a new ACL structure version (version 4). In Windows 2000 and Windows Server 2003, this new ACL structure has been implemented only for AD objects. The main change in version 4 ACLs is the support for object-type ACEs, which enable property-based ACEs, extended rights, and property sets. The principal reason why Microsoft incorporated this new ACL version change was to enable the definition of authorization data on AD objects in a more granular way. These ACL changes, for example, enable fine-grain administrative delegation on AD objects.

Table 10.3 *New Windows 2000 Authorization Features*

Securable Object/ Authorization Feature	AD Object Permissions	NTFS Object Permissions	Registry Object Permissions	Share Object Permissions	Printer Object Permissions
New ACL editor	Yes	Yes	Yes	Yes	Yes
Fine-grain inheritance control	Yes	Yes	Yes	No	No
Object-type ACEs (*)	Yes	No	No	No	No
Property-based ACEs (*)	Yes	No	No	No	No
Extended rights and property sets (*)	Yes	No	No	No	No
New ACL evaluation rules	Yes	Yes	Yes	Yes	Yes
ACL version	4	2	2	2	2

10.3.1 New ACL editor

To enable a proper display of the ACE changes mentioned earlier, Microsoft provided a new ACL editor, which was shipped for the first time with NT4 SP4. In NT4 you can install it as part of the Security Configuration Editor (SCE) installation.

The most important characteristic of this ACL editor is its object independency: The same editor is used to set authorization settings on different types of securable objects. The new ACL editor also supports deny ACEs and the new ACL evaluation rules.

Although NT4 supported deny ACEs, the ACL editor could not display them properly. In NT4 you set deny ACEs programmatically. An error message was displayed when opening an ACL that was holding a deny ACE using the NT4 ACL editor. NT4 can display deny ACEs properly in the ACL editor on systems that have the Security Configuration Tool Set (SCTS) installed.

The new ACL editor also has a brand-new Graphical User Interface (GUI), consisting of a basic view and an advanced view. Figure 10.5 shows the basic view of the new ACL editor. Pushing the Advanced... button brings you to the advanced view. The advanced view is used to set more granular access permissions, control inheritance, change ownership, see the

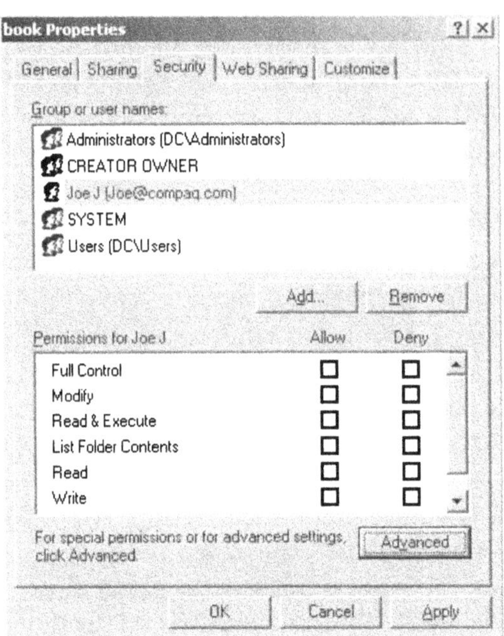

Figure 10.5 *Windows 2000 ACL editor GUI.*

effective permissions for a particular account (a new feature in Windows Server 2003), and set auditing settings.

The permissions displayed in the basic view of the ACL editor are, in fact, groups of permissions. To see what permissions are contained in a group of permissions, go to the advanced view of the ACL editor. The use of groups of permissions in the basic view can lead to situations such as the one illustrated in Figure 10.5. In this example the administrator denied access to user Joe to read the attributes of the book file system folder. Because read attributes are an individual permission rather than a group of permissions, they will not be displayed in the ACL editor's basic view.

10.3.2 Fine-grain control over inheritance

ACL inheritance is a mechanism that lets container objects pass access control information to their child objects. A container's child objects can be noncontainer objects but also other container objects. From an administrator point of view, ACL inheritance simplifies authorization management. An administrator can set the ACL on a parent object and, if inheritance is enabled, he or she should not bother about setting ACLs on each individual child object. From a software logic point of view, ACL inheritance makes

authorization evaluation much more complex. During the authorization process the SRM needs to consider multiple ACLs: not just an object's proper ACLs (also known as explicit ACLs), but also all the inherited ACLs. Inherited ACLs can come from an object's immediate parent, but also from parent objects that are higher up in the object hierarchy.

Comparing NT4 and Windows 2000 inheritance

Table 10.4 compares ACL inheritance in NT4 and Windows 2000. NT4 clearly offers no or very limited means to control ACL inheritance.

As in NT4 and Windows 2000, Windows Server 2003 uses static ACL inheritance. Static inheritance means that an object inherits permissions from its parent object when the object is created and when the permissions on the parent object are changed. In NT4 static inheritance happened following an explicit administrator action: he or she had to select "Replace Permissions" on Subdirectories and Replace Permissions on Existing Files" in the NT4 Folder Permissions dialog box to apply permissions to child objects when they were changed at the parent object. Windows 2000 and Windows Server 2003 will automatically update the child's ACLs when an administrator changes a parent object's ACL's change and clicks apply in the ACL editor.

Static inheritance obviously takes some processor power while the permissions are copied to all child objects, but the impact of this is almost negligible when compared to the impact of dynamic inheritance. With

Table 10.4 *Comparing NT4 and Windows 2000 Inheritance*

NT4	Windows 2000/Windows Server 2003
Static inheritance	Static inheritance
ACL inheritance can be configured on file system objects.	ACL inheritance can be configured on file system, registry and AD objects
ACL inheritance can be enforced	ACL inheritance can be blocked and enforced
Inherited ACLs overwrite existing ACLs	Inherited ACLs do not overwrite existing ACLs they are simply added to the existing ones
No way to remove inherited ACLs	Inherited ACLs are removed automatically from child objects when they are removed from the parent object
Inherited ACLs are not recognizable	Inherited ACLs are recognizable: they are displayed differently in the ACL editor

dynamic inheritance (which is, for example, used in NDS), each opening of an object requires checking not only the explicit permissions on the object itself but also the permissions of all its parent objects.

Another important difference is that Windows 2000 does not overwrite the child's proper explicit ACEs with the inherited parent ACEs. Windows 2000 simply adds inherited ACEs to the child's ACLs and tags them with a special inherited flag. You can observe the presence of this flag in the basic and advanced view of the ACL editor (as illustrated in Figures 10.6 and 10.7 for the advanced view).

To stress the fact that inherited ACLs cannot be edited in the ACL editor of a child object, Microsoft grays out the keys in the type column. Also, Microsoft added an explanatory text in the dialog box telling the user "this permission is inherited" and "you can edit the permission only at the parent object." The latter two features are only available in Windows 2000 (as shown in Figure 10.6). In Windows Server 2003, Microsoft got rid of the keys and the explanatory text and instead added a new "Inherited From" column showing from which parent object a child object inherits a particular permission. The new interface is illustrated in Figure 10.7. In the ACL editor's basic view inherited permissions are associated to a grey checkbox.

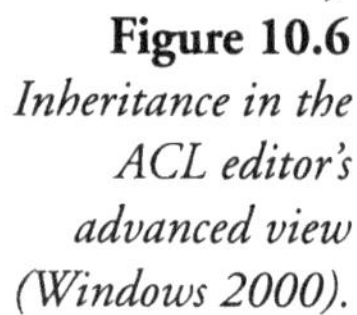

Figure 10.6 *Inheritance in the ACL editor's advanced view (Windows 2000).*

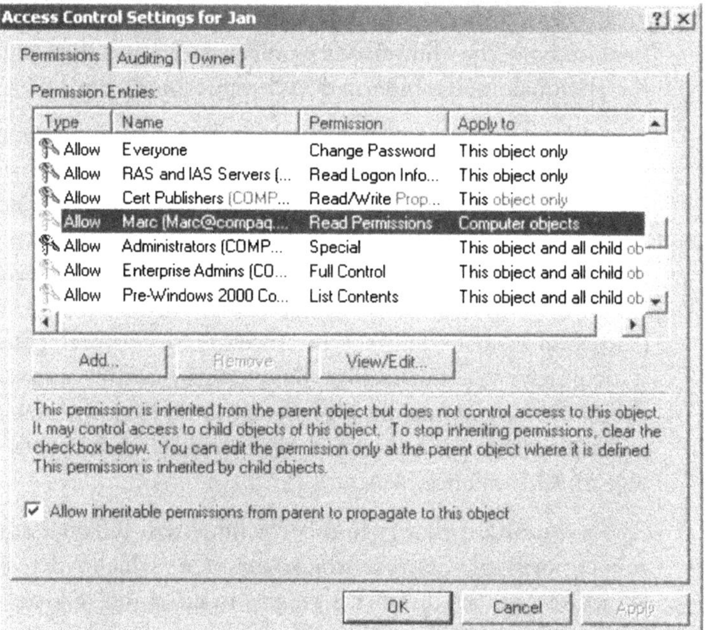

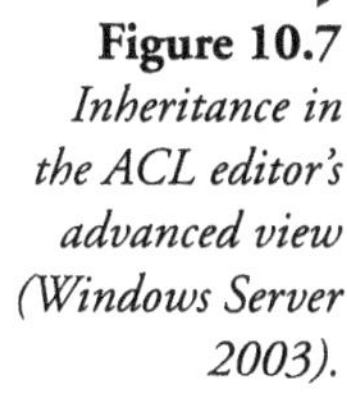

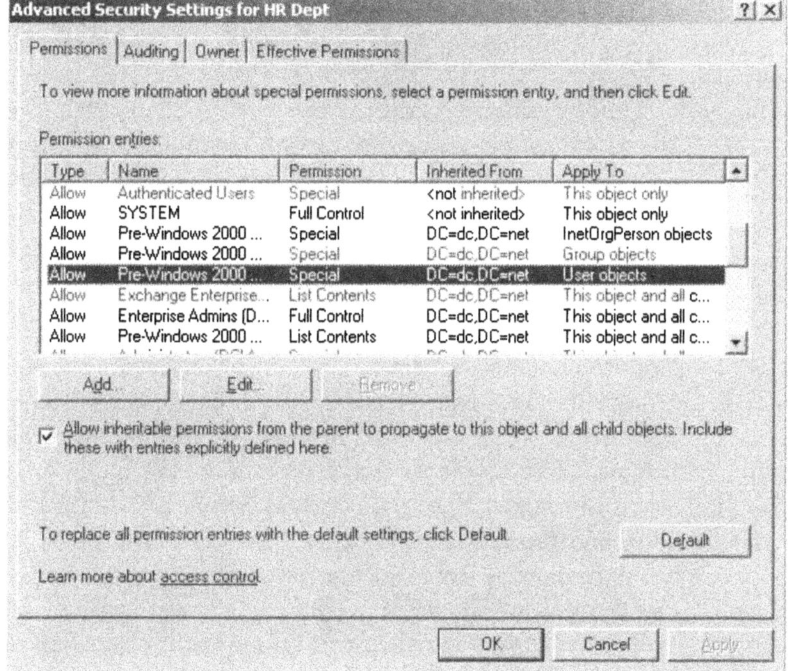

Figure 10.7 *Inheritance in the ACL editor's advanced view (Windows Server 2003).*

In NT4 inherited permissions could be edited on the child object, because both the child object's proper ACLs and the inherited ACLs were merged, making the inherited ACLs unrecognizable.

An interesting detail from both an ACL inheritance and an AD replication point of view is the way ACL changes on AD container objects are replicated in the Active Directory. Because AD is a multimaster database, ACL changes made on one instance of the AD also need to be replicated to every other instance of the AD database. To limit the bandwidth impact, Microsoft only replicates the explicit permissions—and not the inherited permissions—between AD instances. This feature, combined with the static inheritance, means that when the permissions are evaluated on an AD child object, it should always have the latest ACL information, unless some permission change on another AD instance has not replicated to the child object's AD instance.

An important change in the way inherited ACEs are stored in AD is the concept of single-instance storage for ACEs which Microsoft introduces in Windows Server 2003. This feature significantly reduces the space that is required in the AD database for ACE storage. The internal HP AD, for example, shrank from 12 GB down to 7 GB because of this feature. Single-

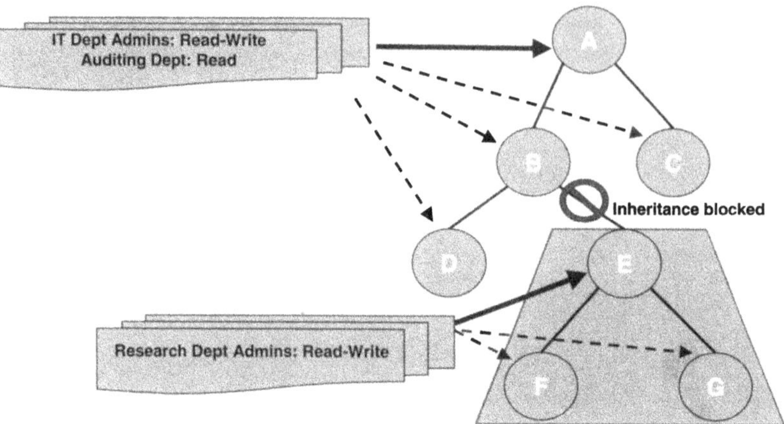

Figure 10.8 *Controlling inheritance using blocking.*

instance storage for ACEs basically means that child objects just contain a pointer to the inherited ACEs that are stored in the parent object's explicit ACEs—inherited ACEs are not copied to every single child object.

Controlling inheritance

By default, Windows 2000 ACL inheritance makes permissions automatically flow down from container objects to all child objects. This default behavior can be modified by blocking ACL inheritance on a child object or by enforcing inheritance[1] or limiting the inheritance scope on a container object. Thanks to these features, both entire subtrees and leaf objects can be excluded from ACL inheritance in an object hierarchy (as illustrated in Figure 10.8). What these features really mean is that ACEs that are marked as inheritable are or are not written to the ACLs of all or specific child containers or objects.

You may want to use inheritance control to apply special authorization rules to the file system folder or AD organizational unit of your organization's very special departments. In the example of Figure 10.8, the inheritance of the permissions that are explicitly set on the AD Organizational Unit A is blocked on the level of the E OU. As a consequence, inheritance is also blocked on all underlying OUs (F and G). On OU E an explicit permission is set that gives only read-write access to the research department admins.

To block inheritance on the child object level, uncheck the "Allow inheritable permissions from the parent to propagate to this object and all child

1. Enforcement of inherited permissions is not possible for AD permission inheritance.

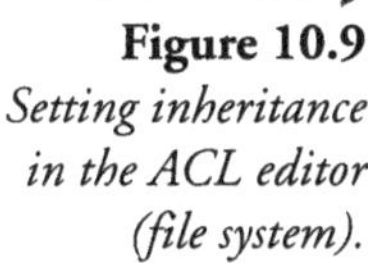

Figure 10.9
Setting inheritance in the ACL editor (file system).

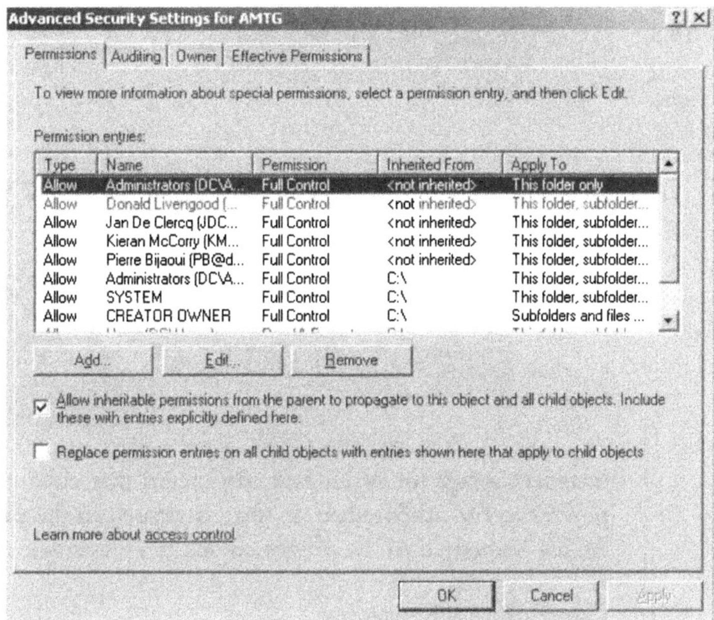

objects" (available only in the advanced view of the ACL editor[2]) (as illustrated in Figure 10.7 for AD and in Figure 10.9 for the file system). If you uncheck this box, Windows will bring up a dialog box (illustrated in Figure 10.10) that gives you the option to "Copy the previously inherited permissions to the object," to "Remove the inherited permissions and keep only the permissions explicitly specified on this object," or to cancel the action. The first choice removes the inherited flag from inherited ACEs and makes them explicit ACEs. The second choice effectively removes inherited ACEs.

When you recheck the "Allow inheritable permissions from the parent to propagate to this object and all child objects" checkbox (after you first unchecked it and removed the inherited permissions), you can reapply all inherited permissions. Before doing so in AD, the security system will warn you about the possible directory size and performance impact of reapplying all the inherited permissions (illustrated in Figure 10.11).

To reset the inheritance-blocking settings mentioned previously, the administrator of a child's parent container can enforce the writing of the inheritable ACEs to the child object's ACEs. This is done using the "Replace permission entries on all child objects with entries shown here that

2. This was not true in Windows 2000. In Windows 2000 this option was available in both the basic view and the advanced view of the ACL editor.

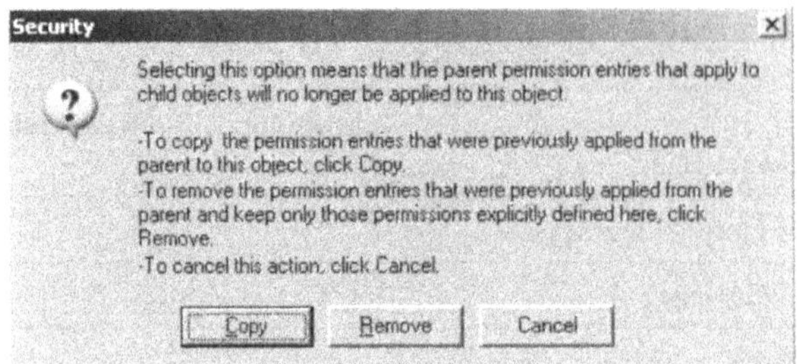

Figure 10.10 *ACL editor warning message.*

apply to child objects" checkbox (as illustrated in Figure 10.9). "This setting will only provoke the system to overwrite existing ACLs and re-enable inheritance for once, which is when the administrator presses OK. It will not ensure that inheritance blocking won't occur again later on when the administrator of the child object decides to do so. This option is available for file system and registry permission inheritance. It is not available for AD permission inheritance.

Another way to control inheritance on the parent container level is by using ACL inheritance scoping, which is based on special inheritance flags that are added to a parent object's ACEs. The flags are listed in the top row of Table 10.5. The ones listed in Table 10.5 apply to file system ACEs only.

The flags can be set from the advanced view of the ACL editor, using the View/Edit... push button (as illustrated in Figure 10.12). In the Apply onto listbox, different scopes can be selected: "This folder only," "files only," and so forth. Table 10.5 shows the inheritance flags corresponding to the setting chosen from the Apply onto... listbox. A noncontainer object obviously does not have these settings. In this case the Apply onto... box just shows "this object only."

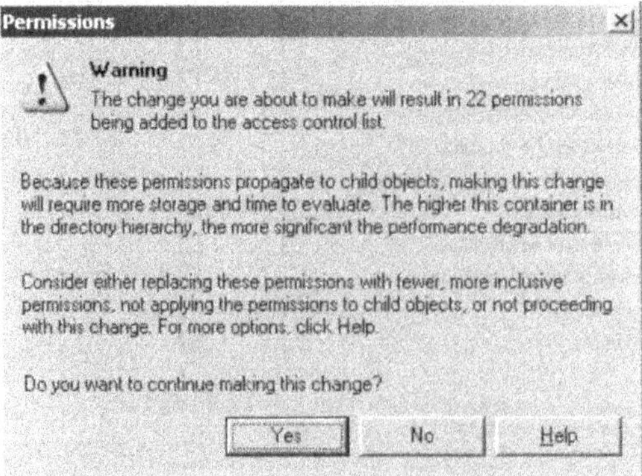

Figure 10.11 *ACL editor warning message (AD only).*

Table 10.5 *Inheritance Flags Corresponding to the File System ACL Apply Onto… Setting*

Inheritance Flag	Inherit Only (IO)	Container Inherit (CI)	Object Inherit (OI)
"Apply Onto…" setting	—	—	—
This folder only	—	—	—
This folder, subfolders, and files	—	X	X
This folder and subfolders	—	X	—
This folder and files	—	—	X
Subfolders and files only	X	X	X
Subfolders only	X	X	—
Files only	X	—	X

A flag that is not listed in Table 10.5 is the nonpropagate flag. This flag cannot be set using the Apply onto… drop-down box but by using the "Apply these permissions to objects and/or containers within this container only" checkbox (this checkbox is available from the advanced view only using the View/Edit… pushbutton)—as illustrated in Figure 10.12. The

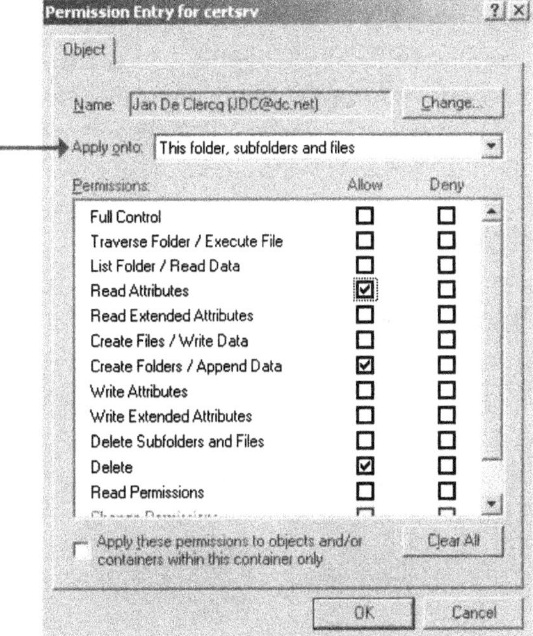

Figure 10.12 *Setting inheritance in the ACL editor (file system).*

nonpropagate flag and the corresponding checkbox control the recursion depth of permission inheritance. If you check the checkbox, the parent's permissions will only be propagated one level down the hierarchy (only to child objects, not to grandchild objects). If you uncheck it, permission inheritance will be applied recursively all the way down the object tree.

AD permissions have a much richer set of inheritance scoping flags. In short, the AD permission inheritance scopes can be classified as follows:

- *This object only:* Permissions will only be set explicitly on the selected object and will not be inherited by child objects.
- *This object and all child objects:* Permissions will be set explicitly on the selected object and will be inherited by child objects.
- *Child objects only*: Permissions will not be set on the selected object but will only be inherited by child objects.
- *Specific object type:* Permissions will only be inherited by child objects of the specified type. The object type can be any object available in the Active Directory, including object types created by extending the AD schema. Inheritance based on the object type will be covered in more detail in the section on object type–based ACEs.

10.3.3 Object type–based ACEs

Object type–based ACEs are a new feature of version 4 ACLs. Microsoft implemented them in Windows 2000 and Windows Server 2003 for AD objects. Object type–based ACEs include two new ACE fields: an object type field and an inherited object type field. Using these two fields, an administrator can create fine-grain authorization settings for AD objects:

- He or she can define to which object types an ACE applies. The object type field of an ACE refers to an object GUID. The GUID can be linked to an object type, an object property, a set of object properties, or an extended right.
- He or she can define which object types will inherit the authorization information defined in an ACE. The ACE field used for this feature is the inherited object-type field. Like the object-type field, it contains a GUID.

The following sections explain how you can set authorization based on the object type, a property, a property set, or an extended right. We will also come back to the effect of object type–based ACEs on AD object ACL inheritance.

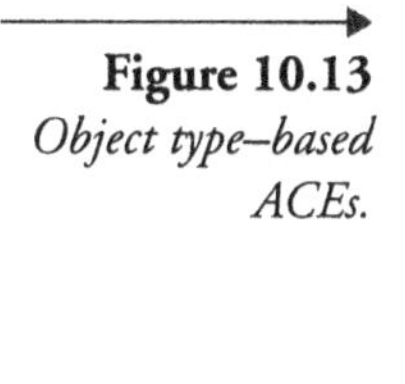

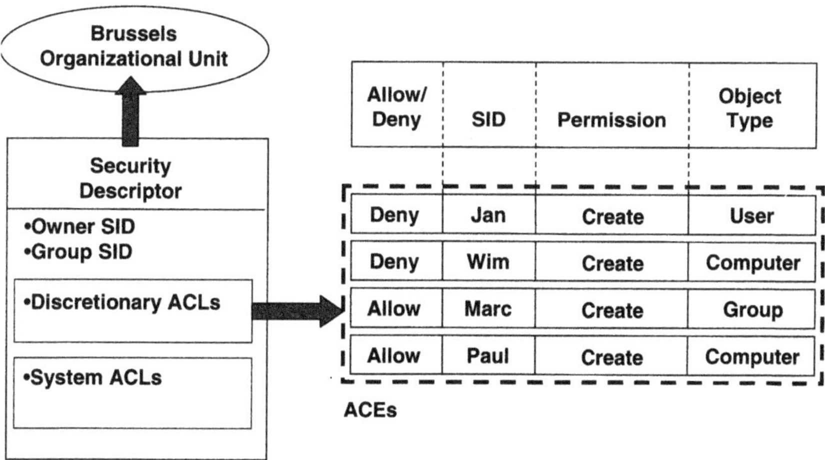

Figure 10.13 *Object type–based ACEs.*

Setting authorization based on the object type

Object type–based ACEs can be used to set permissions based on the AD object type. Let's illustrate this with an example. As mentioned earlier in this book, AD objects can be grouped in containers, called Organizational Units. Figure 10.13 shows how authorization could be set on the "Brussels" OU using object type–based ACEs:

- Jan cannot create user child objects in the Brussels OU.
- Wim cannot create computer child objects in the Brussels OU.
- Marc can create group child objects in the Brussels OU.
- Paul can create computer child objects in the Brussels OU.

Figure 10.14 shows how these object type–based ACEs are displayed in the ACL editor. You get this view from the Advanced View of the ACL editor. Notice that the ACEs are ordered in canonical order. The concept of canonical order will be explained below in Section 10.3.4. Figure 10.15 shows how one of the ACEs (the one that allows Marc to create group objects) is set in the advanced view.

Setting authorization based on a property or a property set

Object type–based ACEs can also be used to set authorization based on an AD object property or a set of object properties. Examples of user object properties are a user's first name, Home Directory, City, and Manager's name. An example of a property set is Personal Information: It includes a

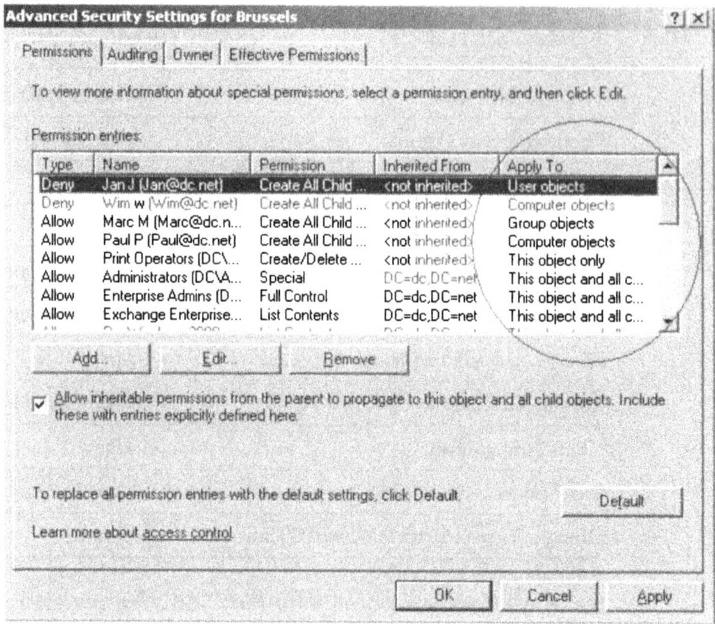

Figure 10.14 *Object type-based ACEs in the ACL editor—advanced view.*

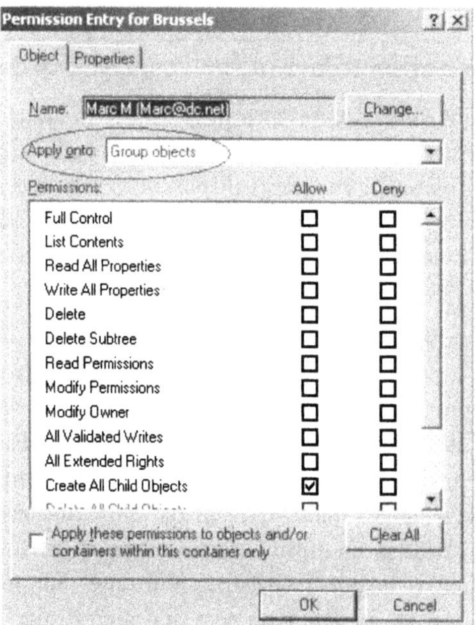

Figure 10.15 *Object type-based ACEs in the ACL editor—advanced view, permission entry details.*

Table 10.6 *Windows Server 2003 Property Sets and the Objects to Which They Can Be Applied*

Property Set Name	Can be applied to...
Phone and Mail Options	User, Group
General Information	User
Group Membership	User
Personal Information	User, Computer, Contact
Public Information	User, Computer
Remote Access Information	User
Account Restrictions	User, Computer
Logon Information	User
Web Information	User, Contact
Domain Password and Lockout Policies	Domain

user's Address, Telephone Number, and 39 other attributes. Table 10.6 provides an overview of the property sets available in Windows Server 2003 AD and the object classes to which they can be applied. Contrary to Windows 2000 in Windows Server 2003 the default property sets can be edited.

Modifying the AD Authorization Information Displayed in the ACL Editor

Because the number of different object classes and properties that are available in the AD is relatively big, by default, the Advanced View of the ACL editor only displays a subset of the object classes and properties. To change the items displayed in the ACL editor, you can edit the dssec.dat file (illustrated in Figure 10.16) that is located in the %systemroot%\System32 directory of every machine, where the Active Directory Users and Computers MMC snap-in is installed.

The dssec.dat file contains a bracketed entry for every object class. If an object class's @ value is set to 7, the type is not displayed in the ACL editor; if it is set to 0, it is displayed. The same is true for the different object properties. If a property's value is set to 7, it is not displayed, 6 means that only the read permission is included, 5 means that only the write permission is included, and 0 means that both the read and write permissions are included for the property. To reflect the changes made to dssec.dat close and restart the MMC AD User and Computers snap-in. Another solution is to simply edit the AD object permissions using the ADSIEdit tool which is installed with the Windows Support Tools. This tool bypasses the display restrictions set in the dssec.dat file and displays all object tyypes, attributes, and permissions.

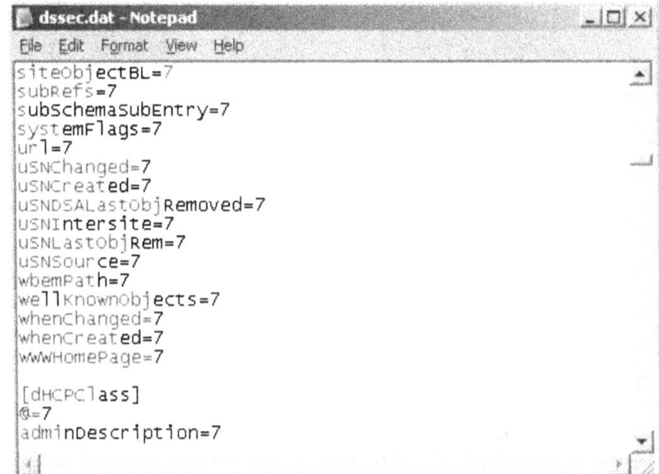

```
siteObjectBL=7
subRefs=7
subSchemaSubEntry=7
systemFlags=7
url=7
uSNChanged=7
uSNCreated=7
uSNDSALastObjRemoved=7
USNIntersite=7
uSNLastObjRem=7
uSNSource=7
wbemPath=7
wellKnownObjects=7
whenChanged=7
whenCreated=7
wWWHomePage=7

[dHCPClass]
@=7
adminDescription=7
```

Figure 10.16 *Dssec.dat content.*

How to create custom property sets for your organization is explained in the Windows platform SDK. For more information on how property sets are stored in AD, see the following sidebar on "How Property Sets are Defined."

Figure 10.17 shows how authorization can be set on an AD user object Jan, based on its properties and the available property sets.

- Jan cannot change the name of his manager. (Note that in the ACL user Jan is referred to using the Self security identity.)
- Wim can change all properties of Jan's user object.
- Jan can change his personal information.

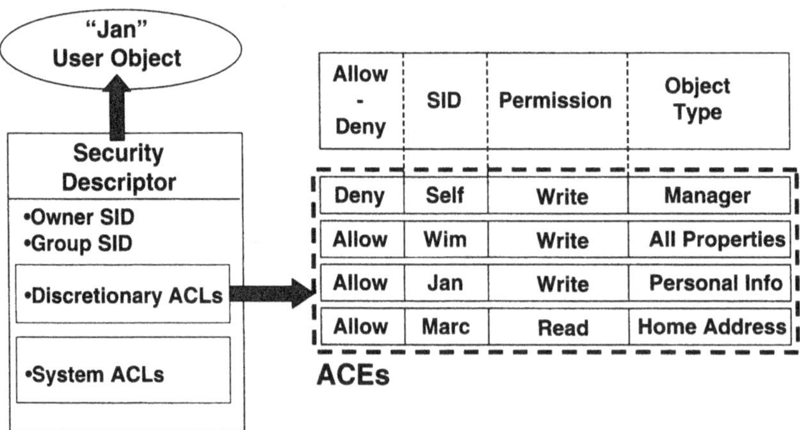

Figure 10.17 *Property-based ACEs.*

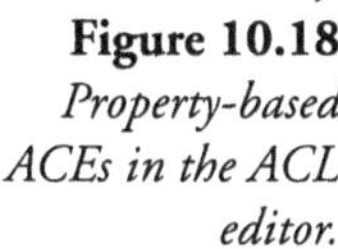

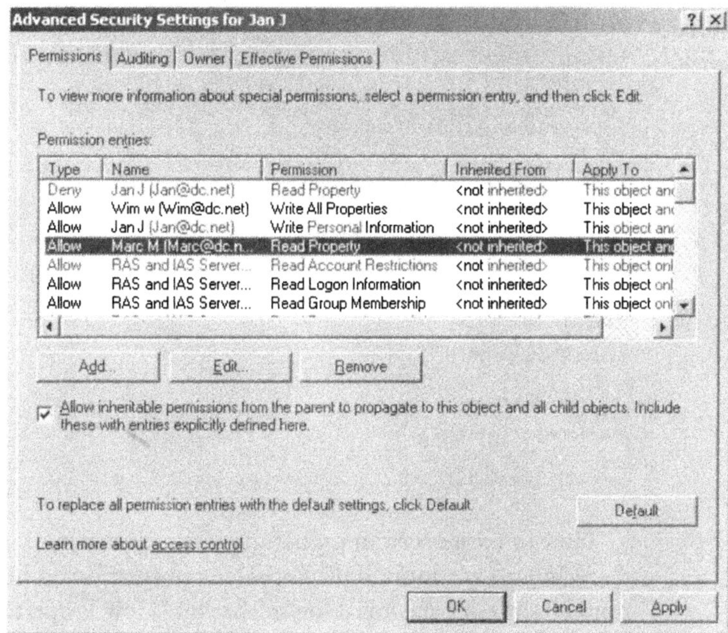

Figure 10.18 *Property-based ACEs in the ACL editor.*

- Marc can read all information contained in Jan's Home Address property set.

Figure 10.18 shows how these property-based ACEs are displayed in the ACL editor. Figure 10.19 shows how one of the ACEs (the one that allows Jan to change his personal information) is set in the advanced view of the ACL editor.

How AD Property Sets Are Defined Property sets allow attributes to be grouped for authorization purposes. They enable administrators, for example, to set read-write access on an AD object using a single ACE.

Each property set is identified by a GUID. The GUID is stored in the rightsGUID of the property set's ControlObjectAccess object in the Configuration naming context Extended-Rights container. All member attributes of the same property set have the same GUID stored in their attributeSecurityGUID property. This is illustrated in Figure 10.20 for the Telephone-Number attribute, which is part of the Personal Information property set.

Setting authorization using extended rights

Extended rights are special AD object–related actions or operations that are not covered by any of the standard Windows access rights (read, write, exe-

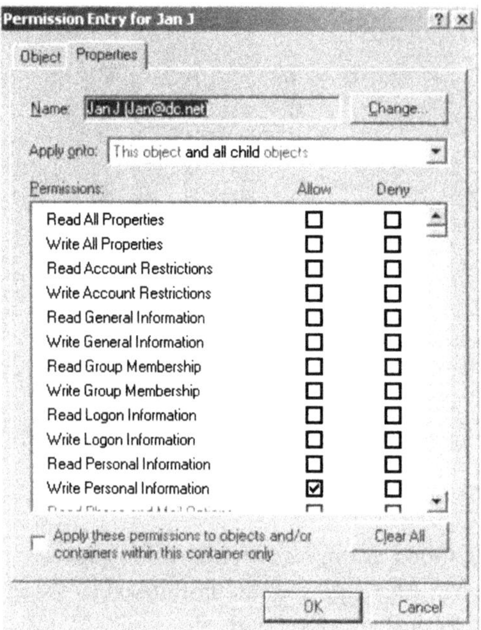

Figure 10.19 *Property-based ACEs in the ACL editor.*

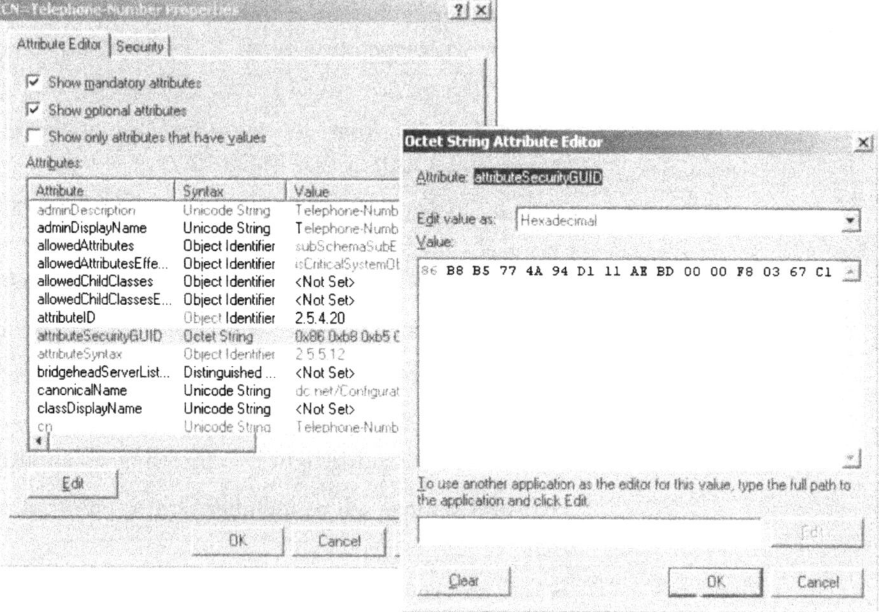

Figure 10.20 *Changing the attributeSecurityGUID property for the Telephone-Number attribute.*

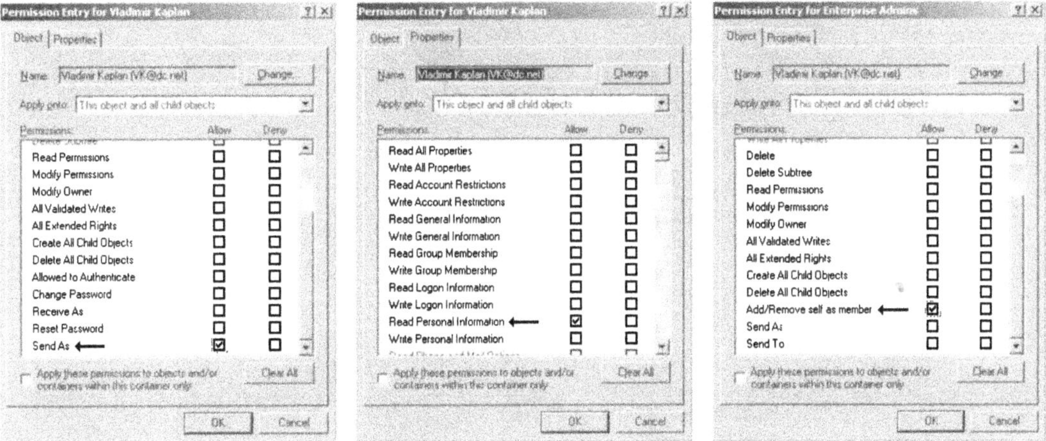

Figure 10.21 *Extended rights types.*

cute, delete). Good examples are the mailbox-specific send as and receive as extended rights. Although they are not linked to object properties, extended rights are displayed together with the standard object permissions in the ACL editor (as Figure 10.21 shows).

Extended rights can be classified in three types:

1. Extended rights that are enforced by the AD. They grant or deny a read or write operation to an Active Directory property set (see Table 10.7).

2. Extended rights that are enforced by applications such as Exchange or Outlook (see Table 10.7).

3. Extended rights that are enforced by the system. These are rights for specific operations that require validation before modification. They are also referred to as Validated Writes (see Table 10.8).

Figure 10.21 shows an example of each of the three extended right types:

1. The Read Personal Information extended right is enforced by the AD.

2. The Send As extended right is enforced by an application.

3. The Add/Remove self as member right is enforced by the system itself.

To get an overview of the extended rights, look at the Extended-rights container in the AD configuration naming context. As for property sets, an organization can create additional custom extended rights. Also as for prop-

Table 10.7 *New Windows Server 2003 Extended Rights*

Extended Right	Meaning
Allowed-To-Authenticate	Used for cross-forest selective authentication (feature of forest trust).
Create-Inbound-Forest-Trust	Allows the creation of inbound forest trust relationships.
DS-Execute-Intentions-Script	Should be granted to the partitions container. Allows the Rendom.exe or prepare operation to be used in a domain rename.
DS-Query-Self-Quota	Allows a user to query the user's own AD quotas (quotas are explained later in this chapter).
DS-Replication-Get-Changes-All	Allows the replication of secret domain data.
DS-Replication-Monitor-Topology	Allows the reading of replication monitoring data, such as replication status and object metadata.
Enable-Per-User-Reversibly-Encrypted-Password	Allows users to enable or disable the "reversible encrypted password" setting for user and computer objects.
Generate-RSoP-Logging	The user who has this right on an OU/Domain will be able to generate logging mode RSoP data for the users/computers within the OU.
Generate-RSoP-Planning	The user who has this right on an OU/Domain will be able to generate planning mode RSoP data for the users/computers within the OU.
Migrate-SID-History	Enables a user to migrate the SID-History without administrator privileges.
Reanimate-Tombstones	Allows for the restoration of deleted AD objects.
Refresh-Group-Cache	Used for GC-less logon. No GC logon relies on caching group memberships and this control access right is used to permission administrators and operators with rights to cause an immediate refresh of the cache, contacting an available GC.
SAM-Enumerate-Entire-Domain	Allows usage of NetAPI calls that read whole domain.
Unexpire-Password	Allows a user to restore an expired password for a user object.
Update-Password-Not-Required-Bit	Allows a user to enable or disable the "password not required" setting for user objects.

Table 10.8 *Windows Server 2003 Validated Writes*

Validated Write	Meaning
Add/Remove self as member (Self-Membership)	Enables updating membership of a group in terms of adding or removing one's own account.
Validated write to DNS host name (Validated-DNS-Host-Name)	Enables setting of a DNS host name attribute that is compliant with the computer name and domain name.
Validated write to service principal name (Validated-SPN)	Enables setting of the SPN attribute which is compliant to the DNS host name of the computer.

erty sets, the way to set these up is explained in the Windows platform SDK. Table 10.7 gives an overview of the new extended rights coming with Windows Server 2003. Table 10.8 gives an overview of the validated writes coming with Windows Server 2003 (which are also available in Windows 2000).

Object type–based ACEs and inheritance

An object type–based ACE also contains a special field that can be used to define which child objects will inherit the ACE. This feature can be controlled from the ACL editor GUI using the permission entry dialog box (see Figure 10.17). To set which object types will inherit the permission you set, select the object type from the Apply onto... drop-down box. Then check the "apply these permissions to objects and/or containers within this container only" property to limit permission inheritance to direct child objects only. Unchecking this property will apply the permissions to all container objects and all objects of that particular type all the way down the object tree.

10.3.4 ACL evaluation process

In Section 10.2 on the Windows authorization model, we introduced the entities that are involved in the authorization evaluation process: the subject (using an access token and an access mask), the object (having a security descriptor), and, of course, the Security Reference Monitor (SRM). In this section we look at how the SRM decides on letting a process access a resource or keeping a process from accessing a resource. We explain how the SRM generates the granted access mask, based on the access token, the access mask, the security descriptor, and the ACL Evaluation Rules.

The basic process

The basic ACL evaluation process can be summarized as follows:

- The SRM receives an access token and an access mask from some server process. Remember that the access mask tells the SRM what the process wants to do on behalf of a user.
- For every access right contained in the access mask, the SRM will then check the DACL of the object's security descriptor. It will check every ACE for an allow or deny permission matching that particular access right and the user SID or one of the user's group SIDs. Remember that user and group SIDs are contained in the access token.
- This ACL evaluation process will end when one of the following conditions occurs:

- The SRM finds a deny permission for one of the access rights that was requested in the access mask. The granted access mask will be empty and access will be denied.
- The SRM finds matching allow permissions for all the access rights that were requested in the access mask. The granted access mask will be complete and access will be granted.
- The SRM reaches the end of the object's security descriptor and did not find a match for every requested access right. The granted access mask will be cleared and access will be denied. This is very important: If no matching entry is found for every single requested access right, access is denied.

Evaluation rules and order

All of the authorization changes listed in the previous sections forced Microsoft to review the Discretionary ACL evaluation rules and order. The new DACL evaluation order is illustrated in Figure 10.22. Microsoft calls the new evaluation order the canonical order.

This canonical evaluation order contains three fundamental rules:

1. Explicitly defined authorization settings always have precedence over inherited authorization settings. This is a direct consequence of the Windows discretionary access control model.
2. Parent object authorization settings defined at a lower level in the object hierarchy have precedence over parent object authorization settings defined at a higher level of the object hierarchy.
3. Deny permissions have precedence over allow permissions at the same level. If this was not the case, a user with a deny access right could still be allowed to access a resource based on, for example,

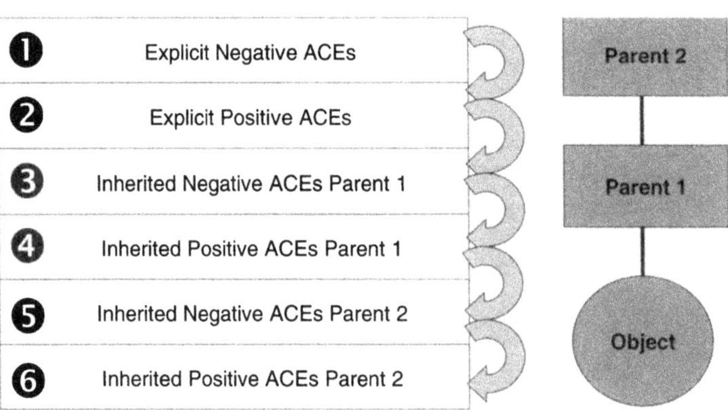

Figure 10.22 *Canonical evaluation order.*

an allow ACE for one of the user's groups. In this case the evaluation order would be: Allow for the group/Deny for the user. Because ACL processing stops when all access rights in the access mask are granted, the evaluation process would not even get to the deny ACE for the user object. Allow permissions may still have precedence over allow permissions based on the first rule: an explicit allow permission always has precedence over an inherited deny permission.

Figures 10.23 and 10.24 give some ACL evaluation examples. In both examples a process impersonating a user Jan is requesting read and delete access to a resource. The user Jan is a member of two groups: consultants and AMTG:

- In the first example (Figure 10.23), access is denied based on a deny delete permission for the consultants group (this is an inherited ACE). Note that even though Jan was granted read access, the granted access mask is empty. The impersonating process requests both read and delete access.
- In the second example (Figure 10.24), access is allowed based on an allow read permission for Jan (explicit permission) and an allow delete permission for AMTG (inherited permission). The granted access mask has both the read and delete access rights set.

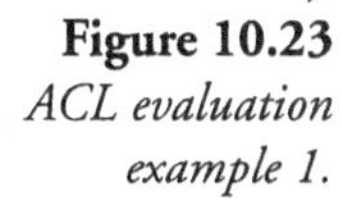

Figure 10.23
ACL evaluation example 1.

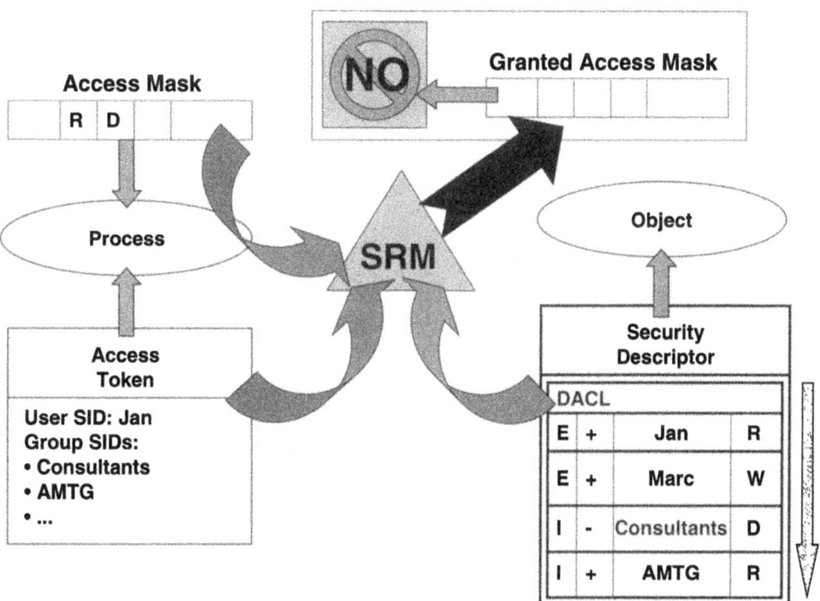

An interesting property of the Windows 2000 ACL editor is that it displays the ACLs in canonical order in the advanced view (as illustrated in Figures 10.7, 10.9, 10.14, and 10.18). But the Windows 2000 ACL editor's support for canonical order also has its limits: it can only display ACLs that are in canonical order and fails if ACLs are set in a different order. This could be an explicit allow permission preceding an explicit deny permission, which is called a non-canonical order. This does not mean that you cannot set ACLs in a noncanonical order—it simply means when you want to do this, you cannot use the ACL editor and you will have to do it programmatically. When you try to edit noncanonical ACLs in the AD Users and Computers MMC snap-in, the ACL Editor returns the following error: "Windows can not edit the permissions on <object_name> because they have been written in a non-standard format by another application. To enable editing, you must use the application to restore the permissions to a standard format."

Putting ACLs in noncanonical order can be interesting for certain applications. For example, in Exchange noncanonical order allows you to hide distribution list member objects from the global address list (GAL) for everyone (deny read members for everyone ACE), while still allowing Exchange servers to read and edit the objects (allow read-write members for Exchange Servers). In noncanonical order the allow ACE for Exchange

Figure 10.24 *ACL evaluation example 2.*

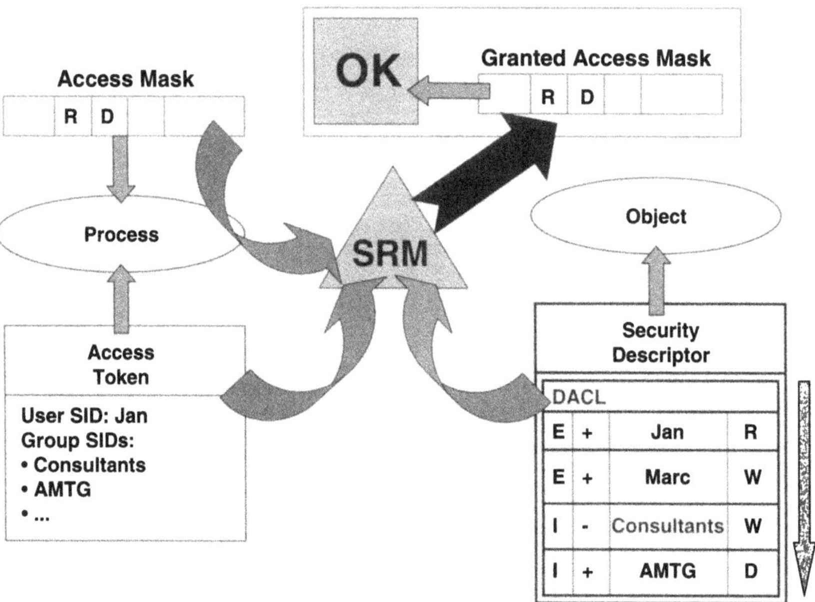

Servers precedes the Deny ACE for everyone on objects to be hidden in the GAL.

In the ACL evaluation process, special care must be taken of empty and missing DACLs. A missing DACL is also known as a null DACL. An empty DACL does not grant access to anyone. A null DACL gives access to everyone. In the case of a null DACL, the SRM simply copies the requested access mask to the granted access mask.

10.3.5 SID History

SID History is an AD user account attribute[3] that is used to facilitate the authorization process in Windows domain migration scenarios. It was introduced in Windows 2000 and is still used in Windows Server 2003. SID History helps in migration scenarios where a new domain infrastructure is created in parallel with the old domain infrastructure. In other words, there is a period of coexistence where the old and the new domains are both operational. In such scenarios it is typically required that newly created user accounts in the new infrastructure can still access resources in the old infrastructure. The key problem here is that the resources in the old infrastructure are secured using ACLs that refer to the old security identities (SIDs) of the user accounts defined in the old infrastructure.

To resolve this problem Microsoft's provides an API—called the cloneprincipal API—that when a new user or group object is created in AD (e.g., during a migration), can be leveraged to automatically add the old objects's SID to the SID history attribute of the new object. The content of the SID history attribute of the user's proper user account and of the groups which the user is a member of are also added to the user's access token. This means that when the user logs on to the new infrastructure using his or her new account, the security system will create an access token that not only refers to the new SID, but also to the old SID. That way the user will be able to access resources secured with the old SID that are hosted in the old infrastructure transparently.

The cloneprincipal API is used by Microsoft's Active Directory Migration Tool (ADMT-currently version 2), as well as other third party migration tools on the market. ADMT is a freeware migration tool downloadable from the Microsoft Web site.

SID History is not available in a Windows 2000 mixed-mode domain. It is available in Windows 2000 native mode and all higher Windows Server

3. The exact name of the attribute is SidHistory.

2003 domain functionality levels (Windows Server 2003 interim and Windows Server 2003).

Although SID History eases the migration process, it also represents some problems:

- The fact that a migrated user can use different security identifiers can be regarded as a security breach. Because there is no one-to-one mapping between a user's account and its security identifier, security auditing becomes a more difficult task.
- Another problem is token bloat. It is a direct result of augmenting the number of entries in access tokens. It may make you end up with decreasing network performance or access tokens that grow beyond the size of 8 Kb, which is the default access token limit. Token bloat can also occur if a user belongs to too many groups.

10.4 Windows Server 2003 authorization changes

In this section we discuss the Windows Server 2003 Authorization changes. We cover the effective permissions tab, the changes to the default AD object security descriptor, and the notion of quotas for AD objects.

10.4.1 More restrictive authorization settings

A direct consequence of the Microsoft security push is that Windows Server 2003 includes much more restrictive default authorization settings. Here are some examples:

- The NTFS root directory permissions have been tightened such that nonadministrators cannot write into the root directory nor can they modify files created by other users off of the root. In Windows 2000 Everyone had Full Control permission. The permissions in Windows Server 2003 are:
  - Administrator, System Account, Creator Owner: Full Control
  - Everyone: Read/Execute
  - Users:

    Read/Execute
    Create Folders/Append Data (this and subfolders)
    Create Files/Write Data (subfolders)
- More restrictive default share permissions: Everyone has now read-only permission. In Windows 2000 Everyone had Full Control per-

mission. This means that by default even administrators only have read access to newly created shares.

- More restrictive permissions on critical console applications, such as cmd.exe. Cmd.exe now has the following default ACL:
  - Administrators: Full Control
  - System: Full Control
  - Interactive: Read and Execute
  - Services: Read and Execute
- The Anonymous account is no longer a member of the Everyone group. As a result, Everyone now only contains Authenticated users and Guests.
- Tightened security on Windows event logs
  - For the application and custom logs:

    Interactive users can read and write to it locally.
    Administrators can access it remotely.
  - For the system log:

    Interactive users can read it locally.
    Localsystem, localservice, and networkservice can write to it locally.
    Only administrators can read it remotely.

Also, the default security settings on the event logs can be customized in Windows Server 2003 using the registry keys next. The permissions in these registry keys are defined in the SDDL format (explained shortly):

- HKEY_LOCAL_MACHINE\System\CurrentControlSet\Services\Eventlog\Application\CustomSD
- HKEY_LOCAL_MACHINE\System\CurrentControlSet\Services\Eventlog\System\CustomSD

10.4.2 Effective Permissions

The advanced view of the Windows Server 2003 ACL Editor contains a new tab called Effective Permissions (illustrated in Figure 10.25). This tab allows a member of the Domain Admins group to let the system calculate the effective permissions that will be applicable for a particular user account or group when accessing an object. The effective permissions logic takes both the explicit and inherited permissions into account. It also incorporates the

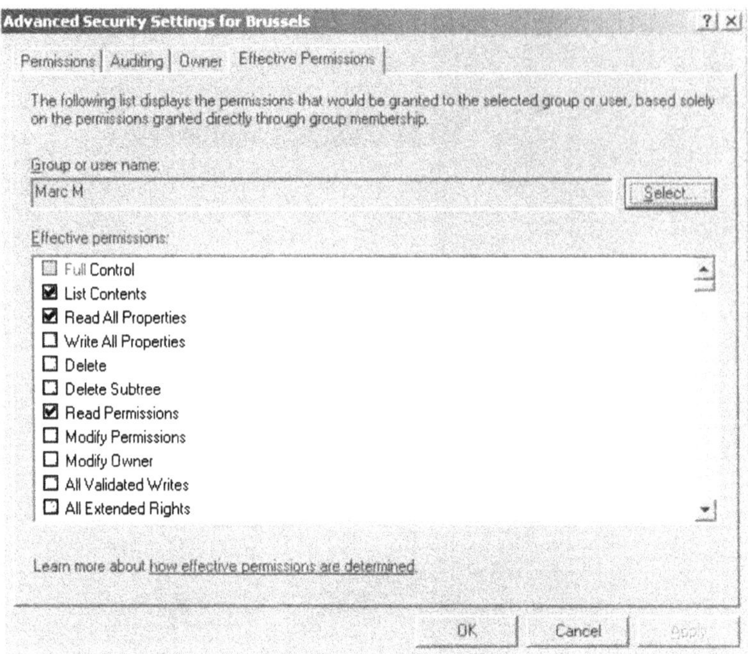

Figure 10.25 *Effective permissions tab.*

group memberships—with the exception of the well-known group memberships—of the account (or group) in its effective permission calculations.

10.4.3 Default AD security descriptor changes

Windows Server 2003 includes some interesting changes related to the management of the default security descriptor for AD objects. For every AD object class (user, group, and so forth) Microsoft has defined a default security descriptor that describes the default permissions that are set when an AD object instance of a particular object class is created. Windows Server 2003 includes changes to the way you define the content of this security descriptor and the way that you can apply and reapply a particular object instance.

The default security descriptor can be set from the properties of an AD object class. The easiest way to do this is by using the Active Directory Schema MMC snap-in. Before you can use this snap-in you must register the schmmgmt.dll. To do so, type the following at the command line:

```
Regsvr32 schmmgmt.dll
```

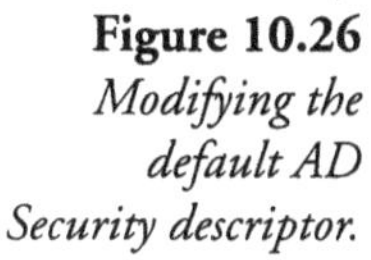

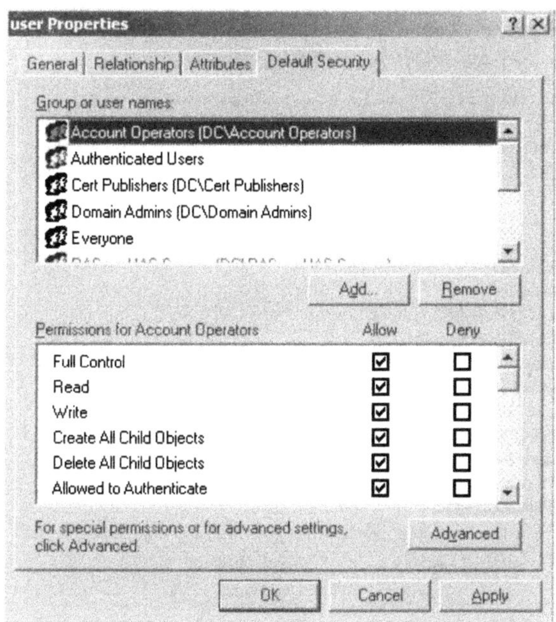

Figure 10.26 *Modifying the default AD Security descriptor.*

To set, for example, the default security descriptor for the user object class, open the Active Directory Schema MMC snap-in, locate the user object in the classes container, then open up the class properties: To change the default security descriptor, go to the default security tab (as illustrated in Figure 10.26). Before, in Windows 2000, this tab was simply named Security—which was a bit confusing.

You can also retrieve the content of the default security descriptor attribute of an AD object class using other tools: You can, for example, use ldp.exe or the AdsiEdit MMC snap-in. In that case look for the defaultSecurityDescriptor attribute of the AD object class. In both cases you will have to decipher the content of the attribute. Both tools display the content of the attribute in a Security Descriptor Definition Language (SDDL) format (see the sidebar on SDDL). SDDL is the native format used to store security descriptor information in the AD. Following is another sidebar on how to use ldp.exe to retrieve the defaultSecurity-Descriptor attribute.

To retrieve all default security descriptors stored in the AD schema, you can also use the following ldifde command:

```
Ldifde - f ADdefaults.txt -d
cn=schema,cn=configuration,dc=<domainname> -r
(objectCategory=classSchema) -l defaultsecuritydescriptor
```

To reset an object instance's security descriptor to the content of the default security descriptor of the object class, Microsoft added a new pushbutton in the advanced view of the ACL editor. This pushbutton is called Default and is illustrated in Figures 10.7, 10.14, and 10.18. Resetting the security settings of an object to the defaults will only replace the explicit permissions that are set directly on the object. The inherited permissions will stay as they are.

Introducing the Security Descriptor Definition Language (SDDL) The Security Descriptor Definition Language is a text format defined by Microsoft for storing and transporting information in a security descriptor. The SDDL syntax is explained in great detail at the following MSDN URL: http://msdn.microsoft.com/library/en-us/security/security/security_descriptor_string_format.asp.

An SDDL string can contain four tokens to indicate each of the four main components of a security descriptor: owner (O:), primary group (G:), DACL (D:), and SACL (S:). Next are an SDDL string example and its meaning.

```
O:BA G:SY D: (D;;0xf0007;;;BG) (A;;0x3;;;SU)
```

`O:BA`	Object owner is the built-in administrator (BA)
`G:SY`	Primary group is the system (SY)
`D:`	Start of the DACL portion
`(D;;0xf0007;;;BG)`	Deny built-in guests (BG) all access
`(A;;0x3;;;SU)`	Allow service accounts read and write permission

10.4.4 AD link value replication and group membership updates

An important deficiency of the way that groups are implemented in Windows 2000 AD is that a group's membership attribute is completely replicated between DCs every time a group membership change occurs. A change can be as small as adding or removing a single user to/from the group. This is because group membership is implemented as a multivalue AD attribute and multivalue attributes are replicated as a single data blob.

The key problem with this implementation is that when administrators are updating group membership simultaneously on different DCs, during replication of these updates one of the administrator's changes will be overwritten by the other administrator's changes. In Windows 2000 AD the last writer wins and the first writer's changes are lost.

Windows Server 2003 AD replication introduces a new feature known as Link Value Replication (LVR) that resolves the above problem. Thanks to LVR, individual values of a multivalue attribute can be replicated separately between AD instances. Besides reducing AD replication traffic, network bandwidth usage, processor, and memory usage, LVR also helps AD get rid of the group membership limit (approximately 5,000) that exists in Windows 2000.

LVR is only available if the Windows Server 2003 forest is in the Windows 2003 interim or native Windows 2003 functionality level (meaning that the forest does not include Windows 2000 DCs).

Using Ldp.exe to Retrieve the defaultSecurityDescriptor AD Attribute

You can start Ldp* by typing ldp at the command line or in the Run... menu option. Then complete the following steps:

- From the Connection menu option, select Connect... Enter the name of the AD server in the Connect dialog box.
- From the Connection menu option, select Bind... Enter a set of valid credentials in the bind dialog box.
- From the View menu option, select Tree. Enter the following base DN to retrieve, for example, the defaultSecurityDescriptor attribute of the user object class:

```
cn=user,cn=schema,cn=configuration,
DC=<domainname>,DC=<domainextension>
```

- Locate the content of the defaultSecurityDescriptor attribute in the right pane (as illustrated in Figure 10.27).

* Ldp is part of the Windows support tools.

10.4.5 Quotas for AD objects

AD object quotas determine the number of objects that can be owned in a given AD naming context or partition by a particular security principal. Quotas can help prevent denial of service (DOS) attacks on AD domain controllers. Without them (which is the case for Windows 2000), a security principal could, for example, create AD objects until a domain controller runs out of storage space.

AD object quotas are specified and administered for each individual AD naming context and partition. You cannot define them for the schema naming context. You can define a default quota for every AD naming con-

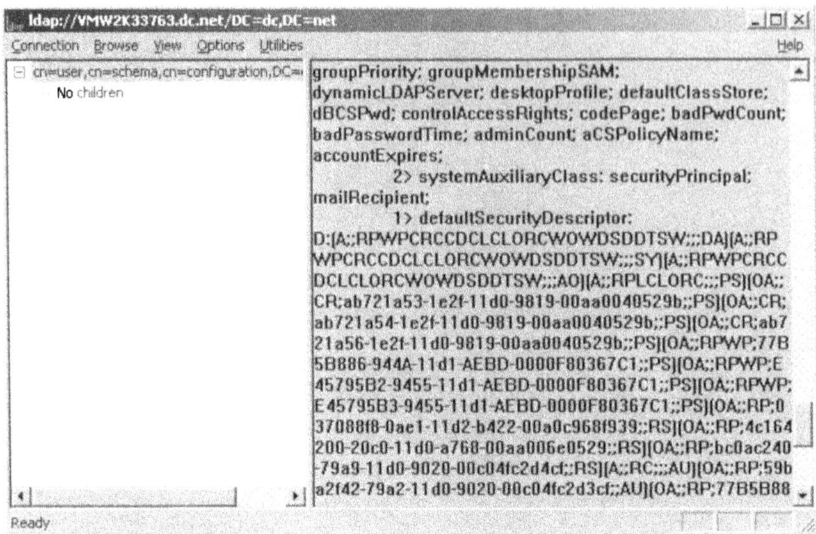

Figure 10.27 *Using ldp.exe.*

text and partition. If you do not explicitly set a default quota on a partition, the default quota of the partition is unlimited.

Tombstone objects owned by a security principal are also counted as part of the AD object quota consumption of the principal. For each naming context and partition, you can specify a tombstone quota factor that determines the weight that is given to a tombstone object in quota accounting. For example, if the tombstone quota factor for a given naming context or partition is set to 25, then a tombstone object in the partition is counted as 0.25 of a normal AD object. The default tombstone quota factor for each partition is set to 100. This means that, by default, normal and tombstone objects are weighted equally.

You can assign quotas to every security principal: This includes users, computers, groups, and iNetOrgPerson objects. When a security principal is covered by multiple quotas, the effective quota is the maximum of the quotas assigned to the security principal. A user could, for example, be assigned an individual quota and also belong to a security group that has quotas assigned to it. Members of the Domain and Enterprise Administrator groups are exempt from quotas.

AD object quotas are stored in the NTDS Quotas container of the AD naming context or partition as objects of the msDS-QuotaControl class.

Only domain controllers running Windows Server 2003 can enforce quotas. Quotas are enforced only on originating directory operations; they are not enforced on replicated operations. To effectively use AD object quo-

tas in an AD domain directory partition, all domain controllers in that domain must be running Windows Server 2003. To use AD object quotas in an AD configuration partition, all domain controllers in the forest must be running Windows Server 2003. In other words, all domains and the forest should be at Windows Server 2003 functionality level 2. The availability of the quota feature itself is not related to any specific functionality level—it is available right away on any Windows Server 2003 domain controller. However, if there are still Windows 2000 domain controllers in a domain where quotas are enforced, then users could still connect to one of these domain controllers and work around the quota restrictions.

Windows 2000 includes a very limited version of the AD quota system that is coming with Windows Server 2003: You can restrict how many computer accounts can be created by a particular user account. To do so, use the ms-DS-MachineAccountQuota attribute of the AD domain object. The restriction does not apply to members of the Domain Admins and Account Operators groups. The ms-DS-MachineAccountQuota attribute is still supported in Windows Server 2003 (default value is 10).

To disable the addition of computer accounts, you can set this attribute to 0. A similar effect can be obtained by taking away the "Add workstations to domain" user right from the Authenticated Users group. In both Windows 2000 and Windows Server 2003, this right is given by default to the Authenticated Users group.

Setting and Testing AD Object Quotas To set an AD object quota of 10 for user Joe in the Accounting domain naming context, type the following dsadd command:

```
Dsadd quota -part DC=Accounting,DC=COM -acct Accounting\Joe -qlimit
10 -desc "Quota for Joe"
```

If user Joe tries to create more than 10 AD objects in the Accounting domain, an error similar to the one shown in Figure 10.28 will be generated.

To modify the tombstone quota factor for the Accounting domain naming context, use the following dsmod command:

```
Dsmod partition DC=Accounting,DC=COM -qtmbstnwt 25
```

To modify the default object quota setting to 0 for the Accounting domain naming context, use the following dsmod command:

```
Dsmod partition DC=Accounting,DC=COM -qdefault 0
```

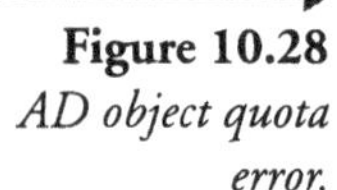

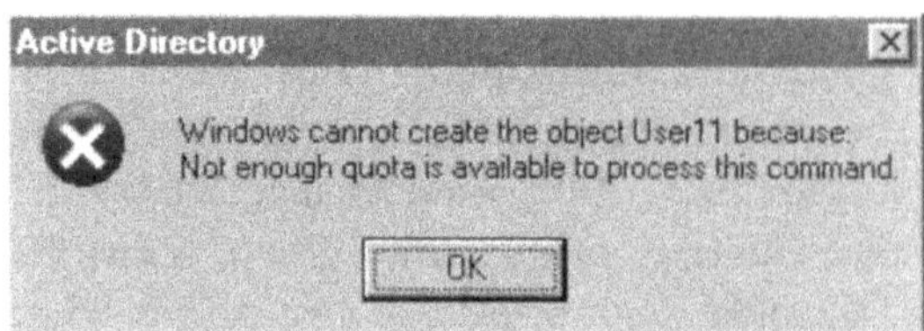

Figure 10.28 *AD object quota error.*

10.5 Authorization intermediaries

In large distributed computing environments such as a Windows domain, consisting of many subjects and even more objects, the management of authorization data may become a very tedious and time-consuming task. With the exception of the full control permission that is automatically given to the owner of the object, all other permissions must be set manually by an administrator or by the object's owner. To ease authorization management, Windows includes the following authorization intermediaries: groups and user rights.

- Groups provide a way to group entities with similar capabilities. They facilitate authorization management of object permissions. Administrators typically add all authenticated Windows entities (users and machines) that have similar resource permissions or user rights to the same group.
- User rights define the capabilities of subjects to manage system resources and to perform system-related tasks. For instance, who can log on locally to a domain controller? Who can change the system time? Who can load device drivers? They facilitate authorization management for system resources and system-related tasks. User rights should not be confused with access rights or permissions. User rights apply to a computer system; access rights apply to an object.

Group intermediaries can be used to ease the administration of user rights intermediaries. For example, you can give all the members of the IT support department the right to add computers to the domain.

10.5.1 Groups

The following list gives an overview of the four major differences between the way groups are implemented in NT4 and in Windows 2000/Windows Server 2003.

Windows 2000 and Windows Server 2003 support two types of groups: security groups and distribution groups. Distribution groups are mail-oriented. They demonstrate the tight integration of the Microsoft Exchange mail server (Exchange 2000 and Exchange 2003) and the Windows Operating System. Contrary to a security group, a distribution group does not have an SID and cannot be used in any security-related process (authorization or delegation).

Windows 2000 and Windows Server 2003 support four types of security groups. They are listed in Table 10.9 together with their usage scope (where can I use the group?), their content scope (what can be contained in the group?), and the database or file that holds the group definition and membership.

Table 10.9 *Windows 2000/Windows Server 2003 Security Groups*

	Usage Scope	Content Scope	Group Definition Storage*	Group Membership Storage
Universal groups	Global (anywhere in the forest or trusted domains or trusted forests)	Principals from any domain in the forest Universal groups Global groups from any domain in the forest	AD Domain NC Global Catalog	AD Domain NC Global Catalog
Global groups	Global (anywhere in the forest or trusted domains or trusted forests)	Principals from the same domain Global groups from the same domain	AD Domain NC Global Catalog	AD Domain NC
Domain local groups	Local domain	Principals from any domain in the forest Universal groups Global groups from any domain in the forest Domain Local groups from the same domain	AD Domain NC Global Catalog	AD Domain NC
Local groups	Local computer	Principals from any domain in the forest Universal groups Global groups from any domain in the forest	SAM	SAM

* This means: where the group's name, type and SID are stored.

The usage scope deserves some more explanation. A global usage scope means that the group can be used in the ACL of any object, anywhere in the forest (or trusted domains or trusted forests). A local usage scope means that the group can be used only in the ACL of an object in the local domain (for a domain local group) or in the ACL of an object on the local computer (for a local group).

Windows 2000 and Windows Server 2003 groups can be nested. An administrator can, for instance, create a global group Employees and embed two other global groups in it: Consultants and Managers. This feature is only available if your domain does not include any NT4 domain controllers. The group scope and group type of domain local, global, and universal security and distribution groups can be changed, as long as the domain does not include any NT4 domain controllers. Furthermore, the members of the group and the group itself need to meet the criteria for the usage scope and content scope that the group would require to have after the conversion takes place. For example, you cannot convert a domain local group to a universal group, if the domain local group contains another domain local group as a member. Similarily, you cannot convert a universal group to a global group, if the universal group is a member of another universal group in a different domain.

- A universal group can be converted to a domain local or a global group.
- A domain local group can be converted to a universal group.
- A global group can be converted to a universal group.
- A security group can be converted to a distribution group and the other way around. Before a security group is converted to a distribution group, Windows warns you about the possible authorization consequences of doing so (as illustrated in Figure 10.29).

A special note should be made on local groups. As Table 10.6 shows, local groups are very different from the three other group categories. They are only meaningful on the local computer, cannot be nested, and are stored

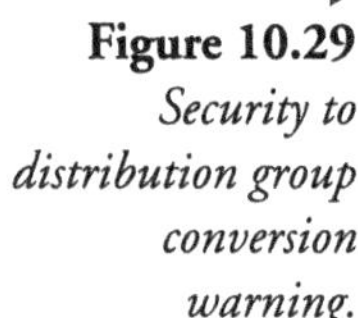

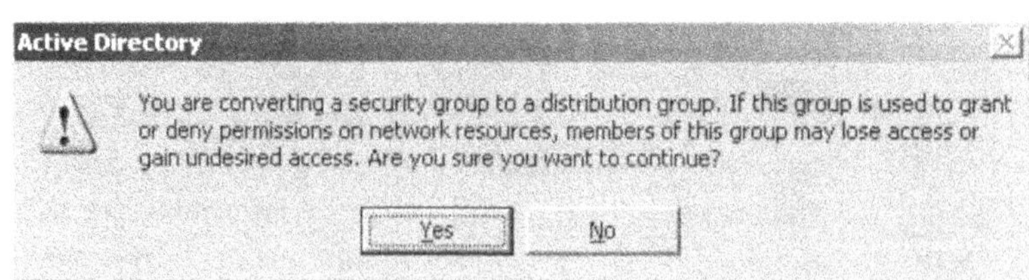

Figure 10.29 *Security to distribution group conversion warning.*

Table 10.10 *Effect of the Windows Domain Modes on Windows Group Features*

All Domains Supporting NT4 DCs	Domains Including Only Windows 2000 or Windows Server 2003 DCs
Three group scopes: global, local and universal*	Four group scopes: global, domain local, local, and universal
Two group types: security and distribution	Two group types: security and distribution
Domain controllers share local groups	Domain computers share domain local groups
Custom local groups can be defined on any machine	Custom local groups can be defined on any machine with the exception of domain controllers
Groups of the same type cannot be nested	Groups of the same type can be nested
Group scope and type cannot be changed	Group scope and type can be changed

* Universal groups can be created in mixed mode domains, but these can only be universal distribution groups.

in the SAM. Local groups are sometimes referred to as aliases. An alias identifies an object in a different way.

Groups in Windows 2000 mixed and native mode

The availability of some of the group features listed in the previous section depends on whether your Windows domain contains NT4 domain controllers or not. Translated in Windows Server 2003 speak: They are dependent on the functionality level of your Windows domain. For more information on the Windows Server 2003 functionality levels, see Chapter 2 of this book. Table 10.10 gives an overview of the Windows group features and their availability.

Built-in security groups

The goal of this section is not to provide a complete overview of the built-in Windows Server 2000 and Windows Server 2003 security groups. We will focus on the differences with NT4. Table 10.11 lists the new Windows 2000 built-in security groups. Table 10.12 lists the new Windows Server 2003 built-in security groups.

The Domain Controllers, Domain Computers as well as the Domain Users group are used as the primary group of the respective security principals. As such, AD objects are not an explicit member of these groups: the OS computes their membership dynamically. Every AD object can only have one of them as its primary group. Also the pre-Windows 2000

Table 10.11 *New Built-In Windows 2000 Groups*

Built-In Group Name	Group Scope	Meaning
Pre-Windows 2000 Compatible Access	Domain Local	Members of this group have read access to most attributes on user and group AD objects.
Enterprise Admins	Universal	The Enterprise Admins group exists only in the root domain of an AD forest. The members of this group can make forest-wide changes and change the AD configuration-naming context.
Schema Admins	Universal	The Schema Admins group exists only in the root domain of an AD forest. The members of this group can change the AD schema-naming context
Group Policy Creator Owners	Global	Members of this group are authorized to create new Group Policy Objects in the AD.
Domain Controllers	Global	Includes all domain controllers of the domain.
Domain Computers	Global	Includes alll computers that are joined to the domain with the exception of domain controllers.
DnsAdmins	Domain Local	Members of this group can administer the Windows 2000 DNS service.
Replicator	Domain Local	Supports file replication in a domain.
Cert Publishers	Domain Local	Members of this group are permitted to publish certificates to the Active Directory.
RAS and IAS Servers	Domain Local	Servers in this group can access remote access properties of users.
DNSUpdateProxy	Global	DNS clients who are permitted to perform dynamic updates on behalf of some other clients (such as DHCP servers).

Table 10.12 *New Built-In Windows Server 2003 Groups*

Built-In Group Name	Group Scope	Meaning
HelpServicesGroup	Domain Local	Group for the Help and Support Center.
IIS_WPG	Domain Local	IIS Worker Process Group.
TelnetClients	Domain Local	Members of this group have access to Telnet Server on this system.

Table 10.12 *New Built-In Windows Server 2003 Groups (continued)*

Built-In Group Name	Group Scope	Meaning
Windows Authorization Access Group	Domain Local	Members of this group have access to the computed token-GroupsGlobalAndUniversal attribute on User objects.
Terminal Server License Servers	Domain Local	Terminal Server License Servers.
Remote Desktop Users	Domain Local	Members in this group are granted the right to log on remotely.
Performance Monitor Users	Domain Local	Members of this group have remote access to monitor this computer.
Performance Log Users	Domain Local	Members of this group have remote access to schedule logging of performance counters on this computer.
Network Configuration Operators	Domain Local	Members in this group can have some administrative privileges to manage configuration of networking features.
Incoming forest trust builders	Domain Local	Members of this group can create incoming, one-way trusts to the forest.

compatible Access group deserves some more explanation. It enables applications that cannot run using the AD authorization settings as they are enforced by a Windows 2000 Domain Controller, to run in a Windows 2000 or Windows Server 2003 environment. If the application's security identity is a member of this group, the application will be capable of reading AD user and group objects.

Well-known security principal groups

A very powerful type of group is the security group, whose membership is controlled automatically by the operating system. A user becomes a member of a well-known security principal group if he or she meets a certain condition. Although their membership cannot be controlled, they can be used, like any other group, for delegation and authorization settings. An interesting characteristic of these groups is the way they are replicated between AD instances: Even though they may contain thousands of objects, their membership is not replicated. Like the three primary groups (Domain Users, Domain Controllers and Domain Computers) that were mentioned above, the OS computes their membership dynamically. The well-known security principal groups are stored in the AD configuration-naming context Well-known Security Principals container. All of the special security groups are listed in Table 10.13. The ones that are new to Windows Server 2003 are listed in Table 10.14.

Table 10.13 *Well-Known Security Principal Groups: Windows Server 2003*

Well-Known Security Principal Groups	Membership—Meaning
Digest Authentication	Digest is another authentication packet. This security principal allows specifying who can log on using digest and who cannot.
Network Service	For services not requiring local system, but network access.
NTLM Authentication	Allows setting special permissions for down-level clients authenticating using the less secure NTLM protocol. Whenever a user logs on to a DC using NTLM, this group/SID is added to his or her access token. Access to resources can thus be restricted by using this group in a deny ACE.
Other Organization	Used for forest trust selective authentication. Selective authentication allows distinguishing between users from your own forest and users that come in through a forest trust. See Chapter 3 for more information.
Remote Interactive Logon	Allows assigning permissions for users logged on via Terminal Services/ Remote Desktop.
SChannel Authentication	Allows setting special permissions for clients authenticating via a secure channel.
This Organization	See Other Organization.
Well-Known-Security-ID-System	Local System account.

Table 10.14 *Well-Known Security Principals: Windows 2000*

Well-Known Security Principal Groups	Membership—Meaning
Everyone	Includes all authenticated users and guests. In Windows Server 2003 the anonymous account is not longer a member of the Everyone group
Anonymous Logon	Includes all users that logged on anonymously.
Authenticated Users	Includes all uses that authenticated to the operating system
Network	Includes all users logged on through a network connection.
Dialup	Includes all users logged on through a dial-up connection.
Batch	Includes all users logged on through a batch scheduler connection.
Interactive	Includes all users logged on interactively.
Service	Includes all principals that logged on as a service.
Enterprise Domain Controllers	Includes all domain controllers in a Windows 2000 forest

Table 10.14 *Well-Known Security Principals: Windows 2000 (continued)*

Well-Known Security Principal Groups	Membership—Meaning
Terminal Server User	Includes all users that have logged on to a terminal services server.
System	Represents the local system.
Creator Owner	Placeholder used for inheritance: is replaced by the creator owner of the object that inherits the permission.
Creator Group	Placeholder used for inheritance: is replaced by the primary group of the creator owner of the object that inherits the permission.
Self	Placeholder—represents the object to whose ACLs Self is added.
Proxy	Reserved for future use
Restricted Code	Reserved for future use

Administrator groups

The pyramid shown in Figure 10.30 shows the level of administrative privileges Windows 2000 gives to its default security groups. Table 10.15 shows the default memberships of these groups on a Windows 2000 workstation, member server, and domain controller. Notice that some groups are not available on all Windows computer types (N/A) and that some groups, by default, do not have members (—).

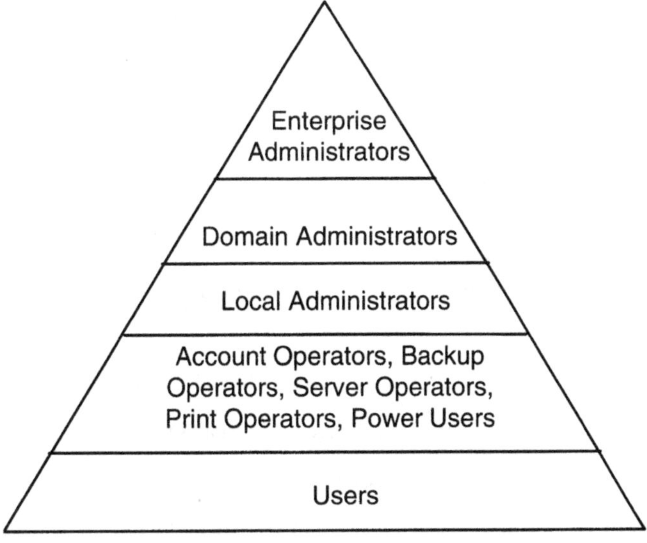

Figure 10.30 *Windows administrator pyramid.*

Table 10.15 *Windows Administrator Groups*

Group	Default Members on Workstations, Member Servers	Default Members on Domain Controllers
Enterprise Admins	N/A	Administrator of forest root domain
Domain Admins	N/A	Administrator of the domain*
Administrators	Administrator, Domain Admins†	Administrator, Domain Admins, Enterprise Admins
Users	Authenticated Users, Domain Users	Authenticated Users, Domain Users, Interactive
Power Users	Interactive Users	N/A
Account Operators	N/A	—
Server Operators	N/A	—
Backup Operators	N/A	—
Print Operators	N/A	—

* The enterprise admins group is only defined on the domain controllers of the root domain of a forest.

† The Domain Admins group is added to the local Administrators group when the machine joins a domain. The same is true for the Domain Users and the local Users group.

Let's look a bit more in detail at the power of the Windows Enterprise Admins, Domain Admins, and Administrators groups. It is also worth comparing these groups to the administrator groups that were available in NT4.

NT4 had two administrator groups: Domain Admins and Administrators:

- The Administrators group on domain controllers was one and the same group shared between all domain controllers of a domain. A member of this group had the right to manage all domain resources, including users, groups, rights, account policy, audit policy, trusts, shares, and the services on all domain controllers.
- The Administrators group on a member server or a workstation had the right to manage all resources on the local workstation or member server system.
- The Domain Admins group did not have proper rights. Members of the Domain Admins group receive administrative right over every system in a domain because, by default, when a system joined the

domain, the Domain Admins group was added to the local Administrators group.

A key problem of NT4 is its inflexible nature on the level of granular administration. If you wanted to give an administrator permission to manage a subset of domain accounts, you either added him to the Account Operators or Domain Admins group. This gave him or her administrative control not just over the subset but over every account in your domain. The Account Operators group merely denied its members to change administrative accounts in the domain.

Windows 2000 and Windows Server 2003 have three administrator groups: Enterprise Admins, Domain Admins, and Administrators:

- The Enterprise Admins group is created in the first domain that is created in the forest. The Enterprise Admins group is added automatically to every Administrators group of the domain controllers in every domain that joins the forest. This means that, by default, a member of the Enterprise Admins can manage the configuration of a forest and also every domain controller in the forest. Table 10.16 lists some Windows administrative tasks that require enterprise administrator rights and permissions.

  The Enterprise Admins group is not added to the Domain Admins group and the Administrators group on member servers and workstations. By default, it is also not possible for a member of the Enterprise Admins group to grant himself administrative rights on all servers and workstations in a forest simply by changing the group memberships of the Domain Admins groups. This is because:

- Domain Admins are global groups in their respective domain;
- Enterprise Admins is a universal group in the root domain;
- A universal group cannot be added to a global group;
- The group-type of the Domain Admins group cannot be changed;
- A user from one domain cannot be added to a global group of another domain.
- Members of the Enterprise admins group have however the power to create other accounts (in each domain of the forest) which they can then add to the respective domain admins group. They can also use the restricted groups GPO settings to enforce the addition of the Enterprise Admins group to all local Administrators groups.

Table 10.16 *Administrator Tasks That Require Enterprise Administrator Permissions*

Task	Reason
Create new domain in forest	Creates crossRef objects in CN=Partitions, CN=Configuration subtree.
Manage Sites and Subnets	Creates and modifies objects in CN=Sites, CN=Configuration subtree.
Install Enterprise Certification Authority	Creates CA object in CN=Public Key Services, CN=Services, CN=Configuration subtree.
Install Certification Authority for a child domain	Creates objects in CN=Public Key Services, CN=Services CN=Configuration subtree.
Create Admission Control Service (ACS) policies	Creates subnet objects in CN=Subnets, CN=Sites, CN=Configuration. Creates CN=ACS, CN=Subnets, CN=Sites, CN=Configuration and objects in this subtree.
Install first Exchange server in forest	Extends schema configuration naming context. Creates objects in CN=DisplaySpecifiers, CN=Configuration subtree. Creates CN=MS Exchange, CN=Services, CN=Configuration and objects in this subtree.
Authorize a DHCP server	Creates CN=DHCPRoot, CN=NetServices, CN=Services, CN=Configuration and objects in this subtree.
Set up printer location tracking	Sets location attribute on subnet or site objects in CN=Sites, CN=Configuration subtree. Sets location attribute on computer object in any domain.
Set up Simple Certificate Enrollment Protocol (SCEP)	Changes ACL on objects in CN=Public Key Services, CN=Services CN=Configuration subtree.

- The same rules as in NT4 apply to the Domain Admins and the Administrators group on member servers and workstations.

Both Windows 2000 and Windows Sever 2003 include major enhancements on the level of granular administration. In both OSs it is also possible to grant an administrator the permission to manage only a subset of the domain accounts. We will come back to this in Section 10.7.

AdminSDHolder and permissions on administrator accounts

To protect against unauthorized modification of the permissions set on accounts that are members of one of the built-in Windows administrator groups, Microsoft provides a mechanism that automatically resets the permissions on these accounts at regular intervals.

In Windows 2000 this feature applies to members of the Enterprise Admins, Schema Admins, Domain Admins, and Administrators groups. In Windows Server 2003[4] it also applies to members of the Account Operators, Server Operators, Print Operators, Backup Operators, and Cert Publishers groups.

This mechanism is based on a special AD container object called AdminSDHolder (Administrator Security Descriptor Holder object). Every hour the holder of the PDC Emulator master of operations (FSMO) role compares the permissions on the administrator accounts against the permissions on the CN=AdminSDHolder, CN=System, DC=*<DomainName>*,DC=*<DomainExtension>* container. If the permissions are different, the security descriptor on the administrator object is changed to reflect the permissions on the AdminSDHolder container. In order for this process to work, AdminSDHolder also automatically disables permission inheritance on the AD administrator objects.

To change the permissions the PDC emulator applies to the administrator accounts, you must change the permissions on the AdminSDHolder container. Because AdminSDHolder is a container object, not all permissions applicable to a user account object can be set from the Windows GUI. For example, you cannot set the change password permission from the GUI. To do so, you can use the dsacls command-line utility as shown in the following example:

```
dsacls cn=adminsdholder,cn=system,dc=<domainname> /G
"Everyone:CA;Change Password"
```

10.5.2 Group usage guidelines

Windows 2000 and Windows Server 2003 administrators are facing the same authorization administration problem as they did in NT4: They must give a universe of users access to a universe of resources. It is obvious that groups can make the life of administrators much easier. What are some of the basic rules an administrator should use when dealing with groups for authorization? Here is a starting point (illustrated in Figure 10.31):

- Use global groups to group users, use local groups (SAM local or domain local) to set the ACLs on resources, and put global groups into local groups to apply authorization settings.

4. The same is true on Windows 2000 if you have installed the hotfix that is mentioned .in Microsoft KB article Q327825 or you have installed Windows 2000 Service Pack 4 (SP4).

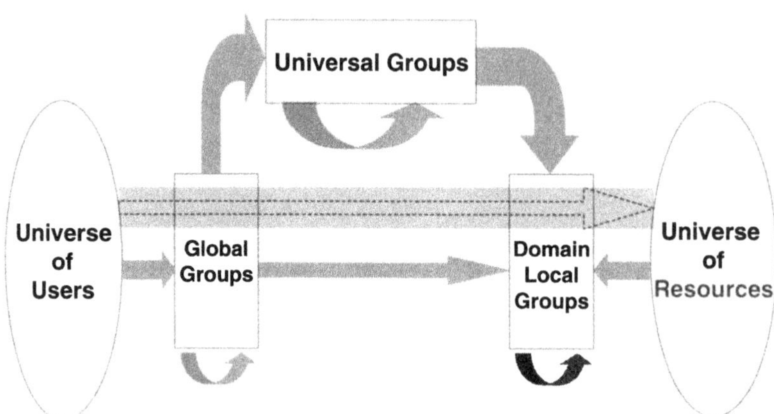

Figure 10.31 *Group usage guidelines.*

- Use universal groups to give users access to resources that are located in more than a single domain. This means that you should put global groups into universal groups, put the universal groups into local groups, and then use these local groups to set the resources' ACLs.
- Use universal groups when the group's membership is close to static. Universal groups cause more network traffic when their membership changes frequently, than this is the case with domain local or global groups. The reason for this was shown in Table 10.6: The membership of a universal group is stored in the Global Catalog (GC) that is replicated forest-wide. Specific applications may demand more usage of universal groups than would make sense from a pure AD replication perspective. For example, you should always use universal groups as distribution lists for Exchange 2000 and later. This is because of the way Exchange resolves distribution list (DL) memberships. An Exchange server talks to a GC server to resolve a DL's membership. If a DL contains a global group from another domain, then the global group will always be emtpy from an Exchange perspective. Remember that global group memberships are only available on the DCs of the global group's definition domain.

10.6 User rights

User rights can be split into two categories: logon rights and user privileges. Logon rights control who can log on to a computer system and how he or she can do the logon. User privileges are used to control access to system resources and system-related operations.

User rights are machine-specific and are enforced by the LSA. As in NT4, user rights in Windows 2000 and Windows Server 2003 can be set on the machine level. To set them, you can use the Local GPO editor (LGPO) or the command prompt utility "ntrights.exe" (part of the resource kit). From Windows 2000 onward, user rights can also be set and enforced globally using GPO settings.

10.6.1 New Windows 2000 user rights

Table 10.17 lists user rights that are new to Windows 2000.

10.6.2 New Windows Server 2003 user rights

Table 10.18 lists user rights that are new to Windows Server 2003.

10.6.3 User rights versus user permissions

User rights are very different from user permissions (defined in an object's ACL). User rights ease authorization management for system resources and system-related tasks. Permissions are not authorization intermediaries. They control the access to any securable object. Also, permissions affect only a particular object or a group of objects on a computer system. User rights

Table 10.17 *New Windows 2000 User Rights*

User Right	Meaning
Deny access to this computer from network Deny logon as a batch job Deny local logon Deny logon as a service	Prohibits an entity from connecting to the computer from the network, to log on as a batch job, to log on locally, or to log on as a service. These four rights all have a corresponding grant right. If both the grant and deny rights are set, the deny right will overrule the grant right.
Enable computer and user accounts to be trusted for delegation	Allows the user to change the Trusted for Delegation property on a user or computer object. Besides this right the user must also have write access to the object's account control flags.
Remove computer from docking station	Allows the user of a portable computer to undock the computer by clicking Eject PC on the Start menu. This feature protects against theft on docking stations that have special security options to anchor the portable.
Synchronize directory service data	Allows a process to synchronize AD data. Obviously, this right is relevant only on domain controllers.

Table 10.18 *New Windows Server 2003 User Rights*

User Right	Meaning
Impersonate a client after authentication	When you assign this right to a user, you permit programs that run on behalf of that user to impersonate a client.
Allow log on through Terminal Services	Allows a user to log on to a machine using terminal services. When you grant this user right, you no longer have to grant the user the Log on locally right (which was a requirement in Windows 2000).
Create global objects	This user right is required for a user account to create global objects in a Terminal Services session.
Deny log on through Terminal Services	Denies a user to log on to a machine using terminal services. When you deny this user right, you no longer have to deny the user the Log on locally right (which was a requirement in Windows 2000).
Adjust memory quotas for a process	Determines who can change the maximum memory that can be consumed by a process.
Perform volume maintenace tasks	Determines which users and groups can run maintenance tasks on a volume, such as remote defragmentation.

* Both the "Impersonate a client after authentication" and "create global objects" user rights were introduced in Service Pack 4 (SP4) for Windows 2000.

affect the entire computer. Finally, user rights are set by a GPO administrator. Permissions are set by the owner of an object or by the local administrator of a computer system.

If user rights conflict with permissions, user rights have precedence. For example, if an administrator has the right to back up files and directories on a system, and the owner of some files stored on the system has explicitly denied the administrator access to these files, the administrator will still be able to back up the files.

10.7 Administrative delegation

Administrative delegation is the ability to delegate Windows AD infrastructure-related administrative tasks to a particular administrator account or group. Delegation is possible thanks to the changes to the Windows authorization model coming with AD. Administrative delegation is a must in large AD environments to assign administrative control over different AD objects (OUs, sites, domains, GPOs, and so on).

10.7.1 Organizational units

An important enabler for the administrative delegation of AD objects is the inclusion of a container object in AD, called an organizational unit (OU). You can use an OU to delegate the administrative control over the objects contained in it.

When dealing with OUs, we must always keep the following in mind:

- An OU is an AD container object that is primarily used to organize AD objects in a hierarchical way and to delegate control over these objects to different administrators.
- OUs are not security principals. They do not have a security identity (SID). This is why they cannot be used in ACLs. Also, you cannot delegate administrative tasks to an OU. This makes an OU very different from a group. This does not mean that you cannot use ACLs to set authorization settings on OU objects.
- An object can only be contained in a single OU, although from a hierarchical point of view an object can have multiple parent OUs.
- An OU is bound to a single domain. It cannot span multiple domains.

The example in Figure 10.31 illustrates the use of organizational units: It shows the OU structure of an AD infrastructure spanning several geographical locations. The top-level OUs reflect the geographical locations (Continent and City) of the infrastructure: Europe is the top OU and underneath there is an OU for Brussels (BRO), Dublin (DBO), Amsterdam (AMS), and London (LON). Per location, the OUs are then split into subOUs that are based on the object types that must be administered:

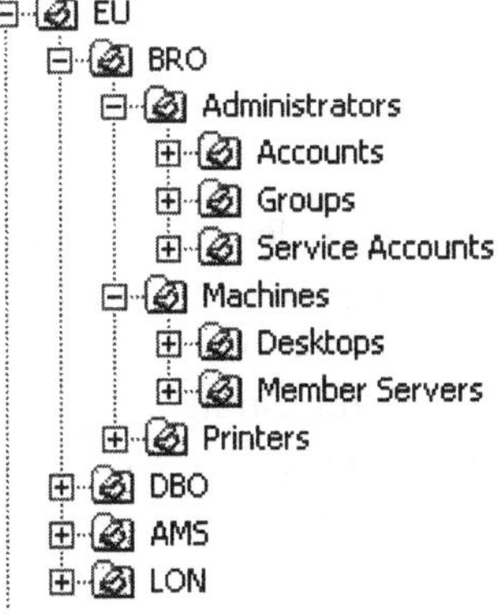

Figure 10.32 *Organizational unit hierarchy example.*

There is an OU for administrators, one for users, one for machines, and one for printers.

The nesting of OUs is reflected in an AD object's Distinguished name—this is illustrated in the following example of an object that is part of the OU structure in Figure 10.32:

```
CN=FileServer1, OU=Member Servers, OU=Machines, OU=BRO, OU=
EU, DC= hp, DC=com
```

10.7.2 Setting up administrative delegation

To set up administrative delegation, Microsoft provides a delegation wizard (illustrated in Figure 10.33). The wizard is accessible from the Windows GUI on the level of sites, domains, and OUs. The delegation wizard allows an administrator to choose among a set of predefined delegation tasks (listed in Table 10.19). An administrator can also create custom tasks to better reflect the organizational needs. Custom tasks can be defined from the delegation wizard or you can add them as predefined tasks to the wizard. How to add predefined tasks to the delegation wizard is explained in the following sidebar.

Administrators that are familiar with the new ACL editor and the changes on the level of the ACL model in Windows 2000 and Windows Server 2003 can do without the delegation wizard, and set delegation through the ACL editor of a site, an OU, or any other object's ACL editor.

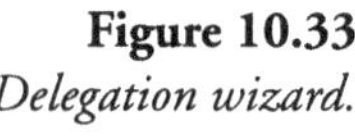

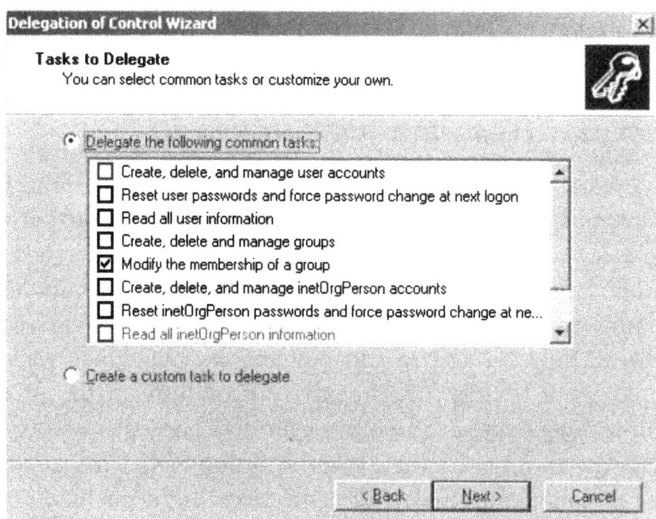

Figure 10.33
Delegation wizard.

Table 10.19 *Predefined Windows Server 2003 Delegation Tasks*

Domain	Join a computer to the domain
	Manage group policy links
Site	Manage group policy links
OU	Create, delete, and manage user accounts
	Reset user passwords and force password change at next logon
	Read all user information
	Create, delete, and manage groups
	Modify the membership of a group
	Manage group policy links
	Generate Resultant Set of Policy (Planning)
	Generate Resultant Set of Policy (Logging)
	Create, delete and manage inetOrgPerson accounts
	Reset inetOrgPerson passwords and change password change at next logon
	Read all inetOrgPerson information

A new management tool that is very convenient to delegate administrative control over group policy objects is the Group Policy Management Console (GPMC). The GPMC GUI contains a special delegation tab for every GPO (as illustrated in Figure 10.34). GPMC is a free add-on tool that can be downloaded from the Microsoft Web site at http://www.microsoft.com/downloads/details.aspx?FamilyId=F39E9D60-7E41-4947-82F5-3330F37ADFEB&displaylang=en.

Undelegating administrative permissions can be done from the ACL editor or by using one of the command-line tools listed at the end of this chapter. A big problem in this area is how to easily remove all the permissions that are set for an account on child objects (e.g., in the case in which administration was delegated on the level of an OU), as the delegation wizard can only be used to add permissions, but not to remove them. You could write a script that iteratively runs through the ACLs of all child objects and removes all occurrences of a particular account. Microsoft is planning to provide a new command-line tool called dsrevoke.exe to ease and automate the removal of permissions on hierarchical object structures. The tool was first presented to the public at TechED 2003.

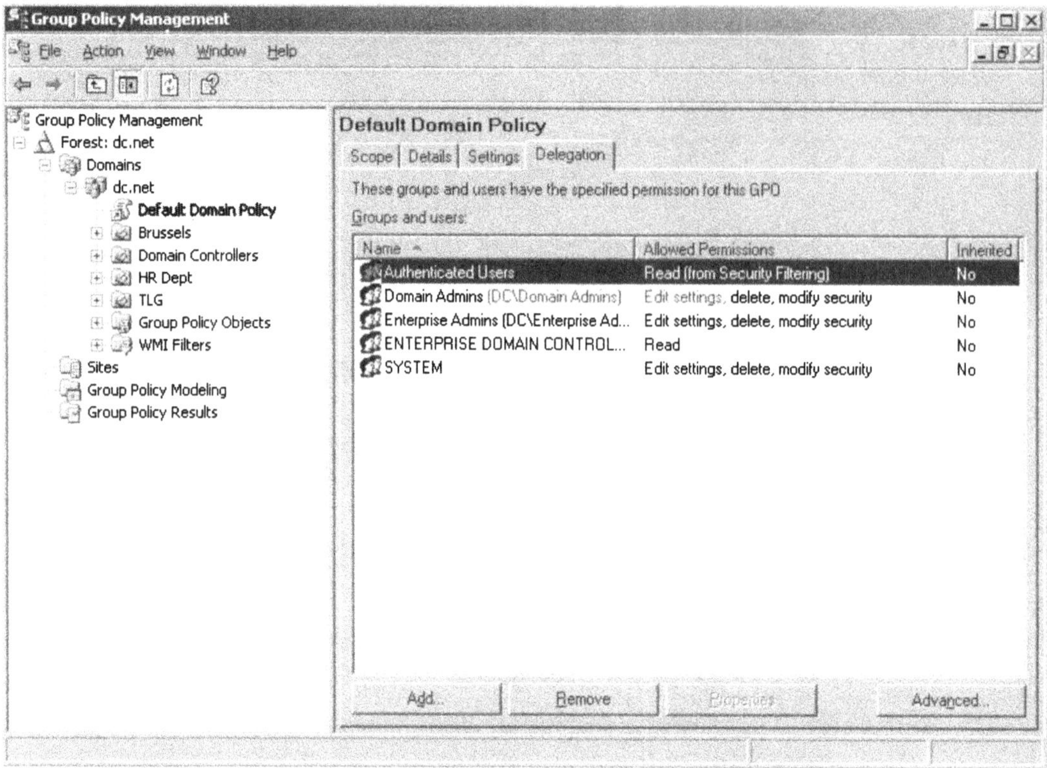

Figure 10.34 *Delegation tab in GPMC.*

To reflect the administrative delegation on the level of the administrator interface, Windows 2000 and Windows Server 2003 allow you to develop customized administration interfaces. Microsoft calls these interfaces taskpads. To create a taskpad, you use the Taskpad View Wizard. To get to the wizard, open a new MMC console and add a snap-in. Right-click the snap-in container and select New Taskpad View. Customized MMC consoles and taskpads can be saved as regular files. If you want, you can, for example, send them by mail to the administrators who need it.

Customizing the Predefined Tasks in the Delegation Wizard The predefined tasks appearing in the delegation wizard can be modified using the delegwiz.inf file configuration file (illustrated in Figure 10.35), located in the %Windir%/inf directory. How to customize the task list is explained in the Microsoft Knowledge Base article Q308404 available from http://support.microsoft.com/default.aspx?scid=kb;en-us;308404.

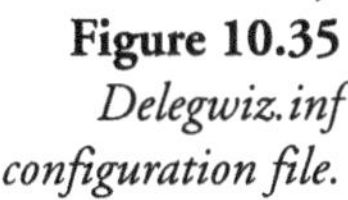

Figure 10.35 *Delegwiz.inf configuration file.*

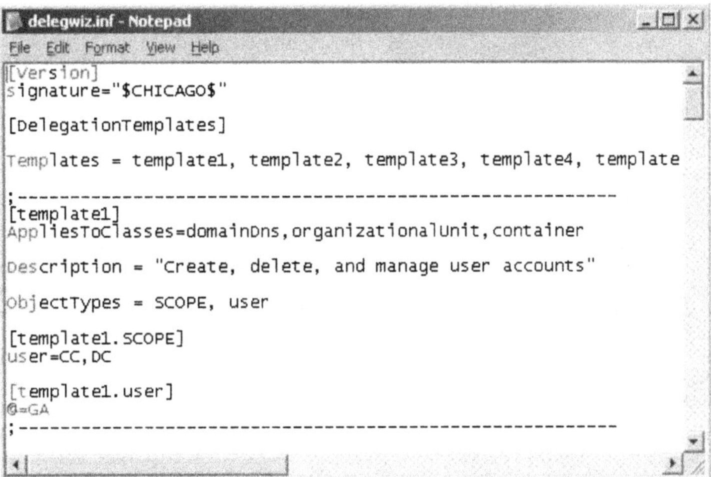

```
delegwiz.inf - Notepad
File Edit Format View Help
[Version]
signature="$CHICAGO$"

[DelegationTemplates]

Templates = template1, template2, template3, template4, template

;-------------------------------------------------------
[template1]
AppliesToClasses=domainDns,organizationalUnit,container

Description = "Create, delete, and manage user accounts"

ObjectTypes = SCOPE, user

[template1.SCOPE]
user=CC,DC

[template1.user]
@=GA
;-------------------------------------------------------
```

10.7.3 Delegation guidelines

It is not recommended to use delegation on the level of AD domains and sites. Microsoft even recommends to only delegate on the OU level.

Delegation on the domain level cannot fully isolate the administrative authority of a particular administrator. As mentioned in Chapter 2 of this book, a Windows domain is only a boundary for AD replication. From Windows 2000 onward, the true security boundary is the forest. If you want to provide complete isolation between administrative entities, set up multiple AD forests.

It is not recommended to delegate administration tasks on the site level because sites are bound to the physical layout of the network used for your AD infrastructure. Sites are based on IP addresses and subnets. The fact that a single site can span different forests, domains, and OUs may make the ACL evaluation process too complex.

It is also not recommended to delegate the following AD infrastructure-related administrative tasks:

- Management of AD security settings, including the management of the Default Domain and Domain Controller Group Policies
- Backup and Restore of AD
- Promotion and demotion of AD Domain Controllers

10.7.4 Administrative delegation examples

The following examples illustrate how you could use administrative delegation in a Windows Server 2003 domain.

Help-desk scenario

A typical scenario where AD administrative delegation is very helpful is a help-desk scenario. From a Windows account management point of view, organizations typically want to give the following abilities to their help-desk administrators:

- Reset an account's password.
- Set the "User must change password at next logon" account property.
- Unlock an account by unchecking the "Account is locked out" account property.

To delegate these administrative tasks to your help-desk administrators you must set the following permissions on the OU for which you want to delegate permissions:

- Allow—Reset Password for user objects (grants permission to reset an account's password).
- Allow—Write lockoutTime for user objects (grants permission to unlock an account)
- Allow—Write pwdLastSet for user objects (grants permission to set Üser must change password at next logon").
- Allow—Read AccountRestrictions for user objects (grants permission to read all account options, for example allowing to determine if an account is enabled or not).

In order to display the pwdLastSet and lockoutTime user account attributes in the advanced view of the ACL editor of Windows 2000 machines, you must edit the dssec.dat configuration file. You must set the lockoutTime and pwdLastSet attributes to value 0 (default is 7). This process is illustrated in Figure 10.36.

User self-management scenario

By default, Active Directory allows specific user account attributes to be edited by the user. Examples are the user's phone number, office location,

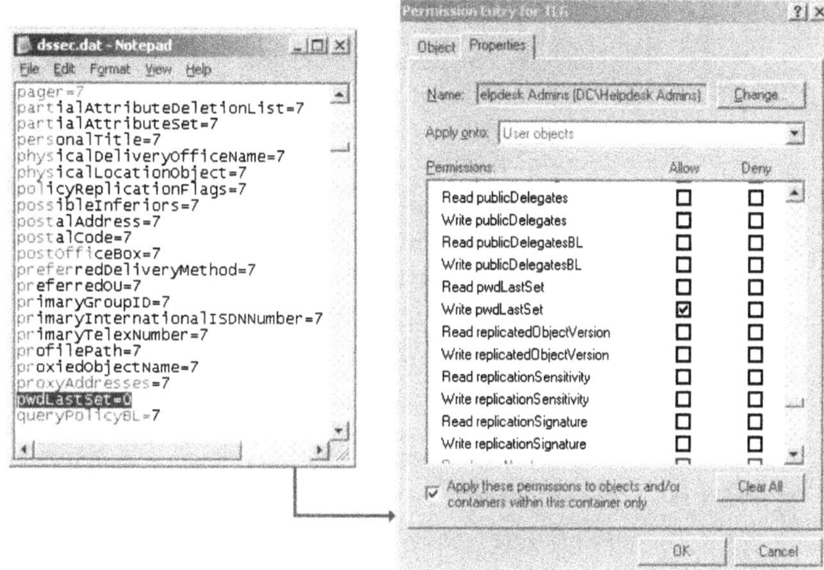

Figure 10.36 *Setting permissions for the pwdLastSet user account attribute.*

and so forth. This feature can be leveraged to reduce workload on the help-desk administrators for simple and recurring user account property changes.

To enable user self-management, Microsoft provides a special security principal called self. By default, various permissions are set for the self security principal, enabling every user to edit attributes on his or her own user account in AD. To edit the attributes that can be self-managed, change the default authorization settings (default security descriptor) for the user class object in AD. The default AD security descriptor and its properties were explained earlier in this chapter. Figure 10.37 shows the permissions that are given by default to the self security principal for the user object class. Only newly created objects will have the updated permissions if you change the default security descriptor of its object class. In Windows Server 2003 you can re-apply the permissions to the default security settings via the new "Default" button in the advanced view of the ACL editor. You can also use the support tools utility DSACLS with the /S /T switches to reset the permissions on all accounts in an OU.

Networking service management delegation scenario

Table 10.20 gives some examples of network service management–related tasks that you may want to delegate to particular administrators in your organization and how you can set these delegations up.

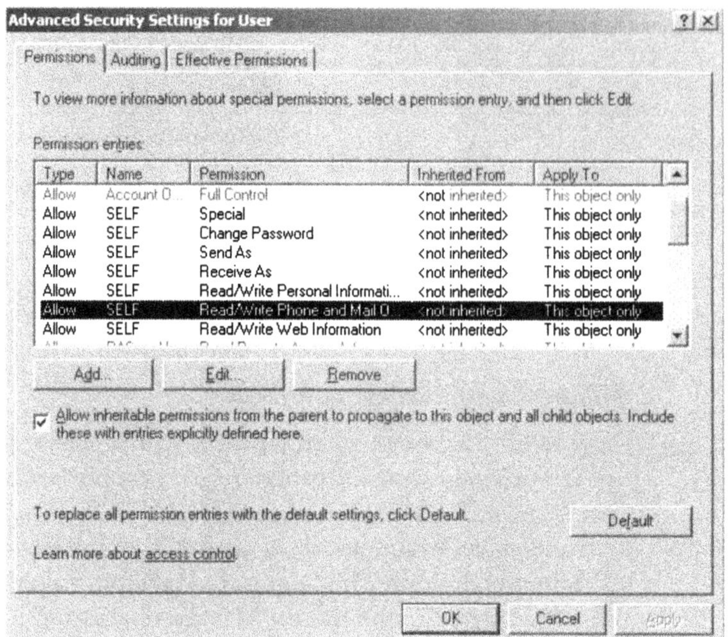

Figure 10.37 *Default permissions for self security principal*

Table 10.20 *Administrative Delegation for Network Service Management–Related Tasks*

Management Task	How to Set Up Administrative Delegation
Authorize DHCP servers	Grant special permissions to DHCP administrators on the NetServices container in the AD configuration naming context: ■ Allow Create DHCPclass objects. ■ Allow Read, Write, All Validated Writes for DHCPclass objects.
Stop, start DNS servers	Grant special permissions to DNS administrators on DNS service: ■ Read permission ■ Start, stop, and pause permission
Create DFS roots	Grant special permissions to DFS administrators on DFS-Configuration container in the AD domain naming context: ■ Allow Create ftDfs objects. ■ Allow Read, Write, All Validated Writes for ftDfs objects.

Table 10.21 *Third-Party AD Delegation Tools*

Product	More Information at:
Quest FastLane ActiveRoles	http://www.quest.com/fastlane/activeroles
Aelita Enterprise Directory Manager	http://www.aelita.com/products/edm4.htm
BindView bv-Control for Active Directory	http://www.bindview.com/Products/DirAdminMig/
NetIQ Directory Security Administrator (part of the Security Administration Suite)	http://www.netiq.com/products/admin/default.asp

Third-party AD delegation tools

Table 10.21 lists a set of third-party software products[5] that can help facilitate AD administrative delegation. All of them provide a role-based abstraction layer that is implemented on top of AD. They all include logic that translates the roles and their associated AD administration tasks into native AD access permissions. In the future, Microsoft may provide similar capabilities using the Authorization Manager that is included with Windows Server 2003. For more information on role-based authorization and the Authorization Manager, refer to Chapter 12 of this book.

10.8 Authorization tools

Table 10.22 lists the authorization troubleshooting and administration tools that are shipped with Windows Server 2003 or as part of the Windows Server 2003 resource kit or the Windows Server 2003 support tools.

More Information on Managing Windows Authorization Settings Using Scripting and WMI It is possible to automate the security descriptor configuration with scripts instead of using the ACL Editor. *Leveraging WMI Scripting* by Alain Lissoir (Digital Press, 2003) demonstrates how this can be achieved for the registry, the file system (files and folders), the WMI CIM repository, Active Directory, and Exchange 200x mailboxes. The 210 pages of WMI and ADSI security scripting techniques are dedicated to help administrators understand and automate this complex configuration. More information can be found at http://www.lissware.net.

5. A feature comparison between these products is available from http://mcpmag.com/features/article.asp?EditorialsID=359&whichpage=2&pagesize=10.

Table 10.22 *Authorization Administration and Troubleshooting Tools*

Tool	Explanation
Windows Server 2003	
cacls	A command-line tools to view and update file system ACLs.
Whoami	Can be used to look at the content of a user's access token (use the /all switch).
Resource Kit Tools	
Showpriv	A command-line tool that displays the privileges granted to users and groups.
ntrights	A command-line tool that can be used to grant or revoke Windows 2000 rights for a user or group.
permcopy	A command-line tool that copies share permissions and file ACLs from one share to another.
showacls	A command-line tool that enumerates access rights for files, folders, and trees.
subinacl	A command-line tool to transfer security information from user to user, from local or global group to group, and from domain to domain.
showmbrs	A command-line tool that shows the user names of members of a given group.
Support Tools	
Acldiag	A command-line tool that helps diagnose and troubleshoot problems with permissions on Active Directory objects.
ADSIEdit	Very useful tool to administer the permissions on AD objects.
Dsacls	A command-line tool to manage the ACLs of AD objects.
Ldp	A GUI-based tool that can display the raw content of an AD object's security descriptor (in the SDDL format).
Sidwalker	Sidwalker consists of three separate programs. Two of these, Showaccs and Sidwalk, are command-line tools for examining and changing ACEs. The third, Security Migration Editor, is MMC snap-in for editing mapping between old and new SIDs.
Sdcheck	A command-line tool that displays the security descriptor for any AD object.
xcacls	A command-line tool that can be used to set all file-system security options accessible in Windows Explorer from the command line.

11

Malicious Mobile Code Protection

In recent years, Microsoft software has been the preferred target of some infamous Trojan horses, viruses, and worms. In Windows Server 2003, Windows XP, and the .NET framework, Microsoft provides clear responses to the malicious mobile code (MMC) threats: Software Restriction Policies (SRPs) and Code Access Security (CAS). Both technologies are discussed in the context of Windows Server 2003 authorization because they both provide solutions to authorize pieces of code to execute or perform particular tasks on a Windows-rooted computer system.

11.1 Malicious mobile code protection architecture

Before Windows Server 2003, XP, and the .NET framework, Microsoft has provided individual patches and extensions to most of its end-user applications like Office and Internet Explorer to deal with some of the MMC threats. In Windows Server 2003 and XP, Microsoft takes a different approach: MMC protection is moved from the application level to the OS level. Also, in the .NET framework MS provides a solution to provide MMC protection when the code is loaded into the .NET execution engine.

On the Windows Server 2003 and XP OS level, the new MMC protection technology affects all application code running on top of the OS. This technology is known as Software Restriction Policies (SRPs), or by its code name, SAFER. In the .NET development framework, Microsoft provides a technology known as Code Access Security (CAS). Both technologies are sometimes referred to as Microsoft's new Code Authorization Layer (illustrated in Figure 11.1).

CAS is only available to applications that have been developed using the .NET development methodology and are using the .NET class libraries and

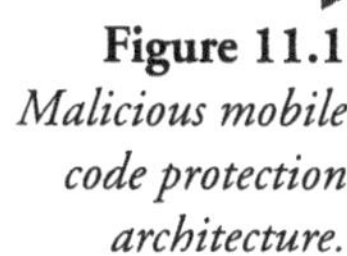

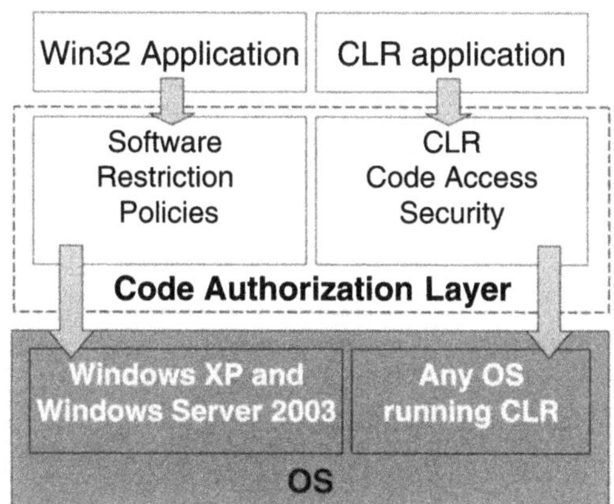

Figure 11.1 *Malicious mobile code protection architecture.*

methods. Software restriction policies can be used to protect against the execution of any executable. The SRP enforcement engine, however, is only available on Windows XP and Windows Server 2003 systems.

If you are looking for more information on how to protect your NT4 and Windows 2000 systems and legacy Microsoft applications against malicious mobile code, I advise you to regularly check the latest news on Microsoft security patches and malicious mobile code protection features on the Microsoft security Web site at http://www.microsoft.com/security. Also—and this is applicable to all Windows systems—I advise you to read the section on security patch management in chapter 18 of this book. It contains important information on how to automate the distribution of security patches in a Windows-rooted I.T. infrastructure to better protect your systems against MMC threats. For more general background on MMC, I recommend the book *Malicious Mobile Code: Virus Protection for Windows* by Roger A. Grimes (O'Reilly and Associates, 2001).

11.2 Software restriction policies

Software restriction policies allow code to be classified as either trusted or untrusted. Trusted code can be executed; untrusted code cannot. Software Restriction Policies are a powerful mechanism: No code stored on your XP Professional or Windows Server 2003 system can hide from SAFER policies—no matter where that code comes from and no matter who or what (a user, a machine, or a service) executes it. SRPs apply to any piece of code, for example, scripting code, an executable, or a Dynamic Link Library (DLL). There a couple of exceptions to this rule: SRPs do not apply to drivers or other kernel mode software, any program that runs in the security

context of the local system account and macros defined in Microsoft Office 2000 or Office XP documents.

You can use SAFER policies, for example, to prohibit an administrator from starting a Telnet session from a particular server, restrict user access to Minesweeper, or prohibit the execution of ActiveX controls that Microsoft has not signed. In large environments, such as those of terminal services Application Service Provider (ASP), you can use SAFER policies to limit the applications available to different users.

11.2.1 Managing, distributing, and enforcing SRP settings

From a management, distribution, and enforcement point of view, SAFER is tightly integrated with Windows Group Policy Object (GPO) technology, introduced in Windows 2000. To enforce Software Restriction Policies, administrators need to configure the corresponding GPO settings. Because enforcement of the SAFER settings requires the appropriate GPO client-side extension, you cannot enforce them on earlier servers and clients. They will simply ignore the SAFER policy settings.

To define a Software Restriction Policy, you first need to set one of two default security levels: Unrestricted (meaning an account can run any piece of code if it has the appropriate access rights) or Disallowed (meaning an account cannot run any code, no matter what its access rights are). If you are an administrator who knows little about the software that your users run, I recommend that you choose the Disallowed security level.

Security levels are defined in the "Security Levels" GPO container, located in the Windows Settings\Security Settings\Software Restriction Policies GPO containers (see Figure 11.2). If you are trying to define Software Restriction Policies for a particular GPO for the first time, this container will not show up. Instead, Windows displays a warning message "No Software Restriction Policies Defined." To make the container visible, right-click the "Software Restriction Policies" container and select "Create New Policies." The default security level shows a black checkbox on its icon. In the example in Figure 11.2, the default security level is set to "Disallowed."

After you set the default security level, you can create additional "rules" to refine and set exceptions to the default security level. A software restriction policy rule basically identifies a piece of software. If the default security level is set to "unrestricted," all additional rules will identify code that cannot be executed (is disallowed). If the default security level is set to "disallowed," additional rules identify code that is allowed to execute.

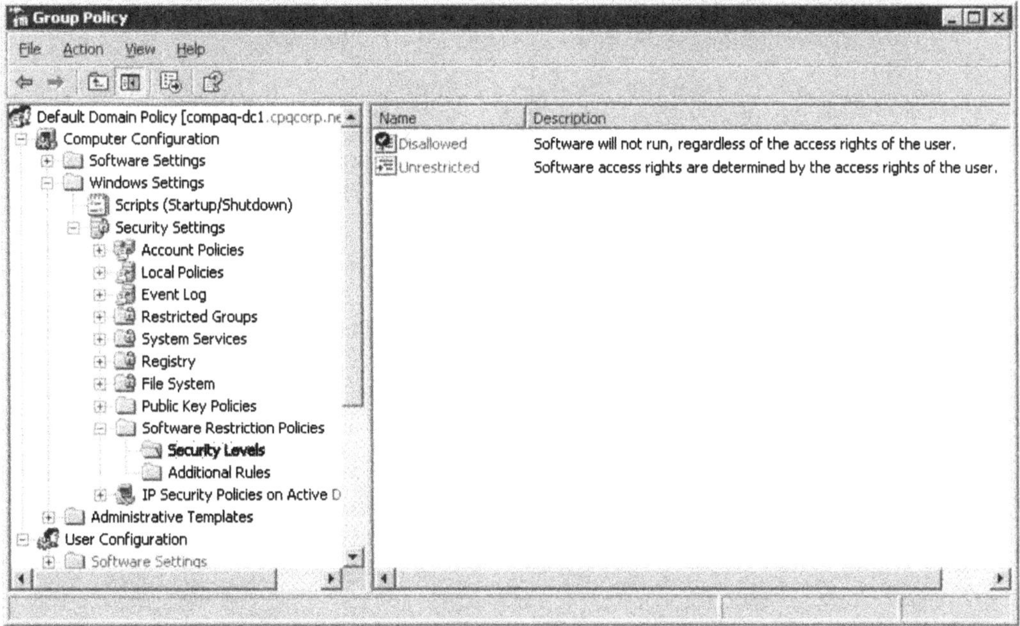

Figure 11.2 *Setting the default security level.*

Pieces of software can be identified using one of the following four rules:

1. A *hash rule* identifies code based on its hash thumbprint.
2. A *certificate rule* identifies code based on the software signing certificate that was used to sign the code.
3. A *path rule* uses the file system path to the folder where the code is stored for code identification.
4. A *zone rule* identifies code using the Internet zone of the Web site from which the code was downloaded.

You create rules by right-clicking the "Additional Rules" container (see Figure 11.2) and selecting "New Certificate Rule..." or any of the other three rules. Figure 11.3 shows how a hash rule for the Solitaire executable (Sol.exe) is defined. When the program's executable has been selected, SAFER will automatically calculate the file hash and fill in its file properties.

11.2.2 Fine-tuning SRP application

In addition to the definition of a default security level and exceptions to this default level, SAFER also allows you to specify the file types that are subject

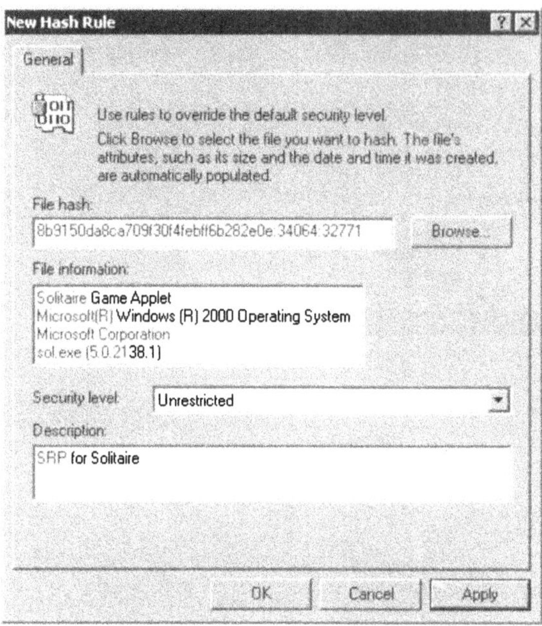

Figure 11.3 *Creating a hash rule for the Solitaire executable.*

to a particular software restriction policy, and to set special enforcement and trusted publisher rules. This is set from the "Enforcement," "Designated File Types," and "Trusted Publishers" GPO entries located in the "Software Restriction Policies" container.

By default, any SRP always applies to executables (*.EXE), Dynamic Link Libraries (*.DLL), and Visual Basic Scripts (*.VBS). In addition to this, the "Designated File Types" SRP property allows you to add or remove other file-type extensions. If you open up the "Designated File Types" dialog box for the first time (as illustrated in Figure 11.4), you will notice that—by default—it consists of a list of file types, ranging from batch files (*.BAT) to registry files (*.REG).

The additional Enforcement settings allow you to exclude dynamic link libraries (DLLs) and local administrators from the software restriction policies. Excluding DLLs from the SRP rules may be an interesting option if the default rule is set to "disallowed." If in this setup you want to give users access to a particular program, you will have to define plenty of SRP exception rules. Remember that SRP rules apply not only to program executables but also to DLLs.

The Trusted Publishers settings allow you to define who can add certificates to the "Trusted Publishers" certificate container and how a code sign-

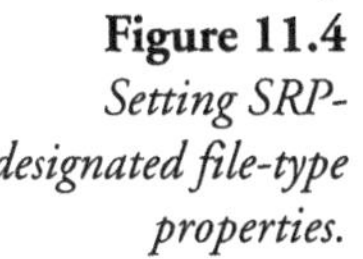

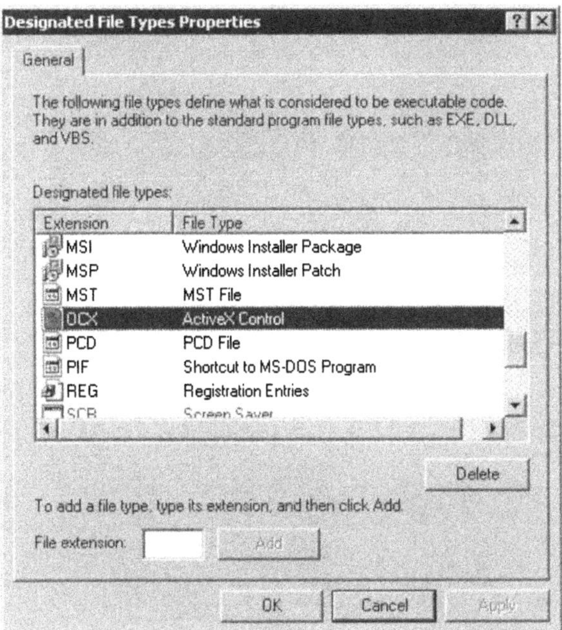

Figure 11.4 *Setting SRP-designated file-type properties.*

ing certificate is checked for revocation. The Trusted Publishers certificate container is a special certificate store container that holds the certificates of all trusted code signing entities. Accounts that are allowed to add certificates to this container indirectly decide which code is considered trustworthy on a user's machine.

11.2.3 The rules of the SRP game

As with any GPO setting, Software Restriction Policies can be configured for users and machines, at different levels of the AD hierarchy (domain, OU), and for AD sites. This means that you may end up with multiple SRP rules linked to the same piece of code or program. A rule of thumb to decide which rule will be applied is that "higher-quality" SRPs always take precedence over "lower-quality" SRPs. This means that a hash rule (which can match only a single program) will always have precedence over a path rule (which can match all programs contained in the same file system folder). This rule of thumb brings up the following order of precedence: first hash rules, then certificate rules, then path rules, and finally zone rules. If two rules have the same quality level, the most restrictive rule will apply. The latter can occur when, for example, two path rules point to the same program.

Let's illustrate this with the example given in Figure 11.5. In this example, a user named David Jagger is contained in the organizational unit (OU), "Engineering." The computer that David Jagger uses to log in to the domain is contained in the "user desktops" OU. Both the user and the computer account are defined in the "Europe" domain. In the example, the administrator of the Engineering OU wants to prohibit the members of the Engineering department from running "Solitaire" ("sol.exe"). The following sol.exe-related SRPs have been defined:

- The Europe domain has a user and computer SRP rule defined in the "European Policies" GPO. The user SRP rule allows all programs located in "%WINDIR%\System32" to be executed. The computer SRP allows the Solitaire program to run based on the "%WINDIR%\System32\sol.exe" path rule.
- The "Engineering" OU has an SRP rule defined in the "Engineering" GPO. This SRP prohibits users to run Solitaire based on a hash rule.
- The "user desktops" OU has two SRP rules defined in the "user desktops" GPO. The first SRP is a path rule that allows all programs in "%WINDIR%" to run. The second SRP prohibits Solitaire to run through the "%WINDIR%\System32\sol.exe" path rule.

What will happen if user David Jagger tries to run Solitaire? To answer this question we first must gather all SRP rules applicable to the user, its machine, and the Solitaire program. (All applicable SRP rules are listed in Figure 11.5.) Then we must classify these rules in order of precedence. Remember that the rule with the highest quality has precedence over all the others. In the scenario in Figure 11.5, the hash rule for sol.exe clearly has the highest precedence. As a consequence, David Jagger will not be able to run Solitaire. Instead, the system displays an error message stating "Windows cannot open this program because it has been prevented by a software restriction policy. For more information, open Event Viewer or contact your administrator."

The example in Figure 11.5 shows that a path rule has a lower precedence than a hash rule. Also, the path rules for "%WINDIR%/system32/sol.exe" have higher precedence then the path rules for "%WINDIR%/system32" and for "%WINDIR%." This is because the "%WINDIR%/system32/sol.exe" path points to a single file—the "%WINDIR%" path points to all files contained in %WINDIR%. Finally, you may point out that even though the two path rules for "%WINDIR%/system32/sol.exe" have the same quality level, the one that disallows Solitaire to run has the highest precedence—because it is the most restrictive SRP.

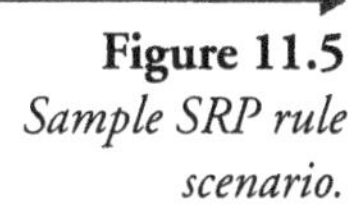

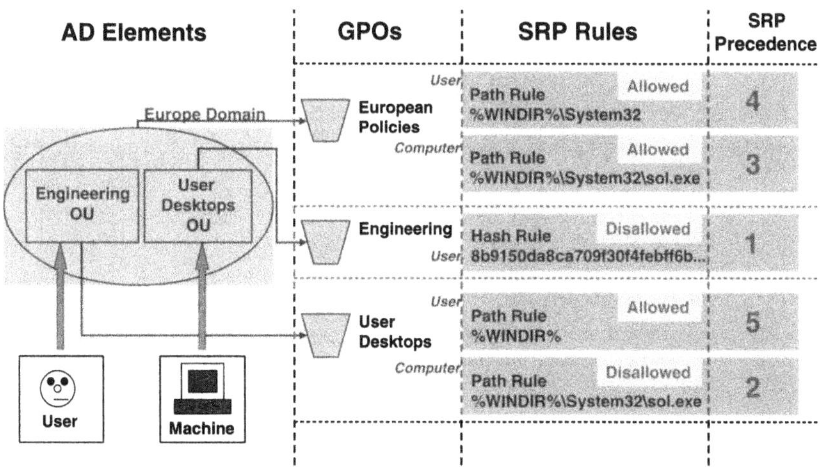

Figure 11.5 *Sample SRP rule scenario.*

SRP Event Logging Microsoft supports two ways to log SRP-related events. SRP-related events are automatically logged in the Event Viewer's System event log with an event source of "Software Restriction Policy." You can enable advanced SRP logging to a separate text file by setting the following registry value (REG_DWORD): HKEY_LOCAL_MACHINE\Software\Policies\Microsoft\Windows\Safer\CodeIdentifiers\LogFileName. To log to a file named srp.txt you can use the following command line:

```
reg.exe add "HKEY_LOCAL_MACHINE\Software\Policies\Microsoft\Windows\
Safer\CodeIdentifiers" /v LogFileName /d srp.txt
```

11.3 Code Access Security

The SAFER Software Restriction Policies (SRPs) are a huge step in the right direction in the battle against malicious mobile code; however, they are not a panacea. One of the key problems of SRP rules is that they are not granular enough. Only a complete process can be blocked—it is impossible to block a tiny portion of code executing in the context of an application process. Also, using SRPs you either disallow or allow a program to run, and you cannot restrict access to only a limited set of system resources.

The solution to this granularity problem is the Common Language Runtime (CLR) and its CAS technology. The CLR is the execution (run time) environment driving the .NET framework. CAS allows for highly granular code access control enforcement. One of the key features of CAS will be its ability to give different levels of trust to the same piece of code depending on factors such as the calling process and the machine where the code is executed. One of the interesting trust levels CAS will support is

"sandboxing"—a code isolation technology that has proven effective in the JAVA world. Unlike SAFER, MS promised to make the CLR work on non-Windows XP platforms such as Windows 98, ME, and NT.

Another fundamental feature of CAS is its code-centric access control enforcement approach. Whereas the classic Windows OS and COM+ access control models enforce the security policy based on the identity of a user, CAS uses the identity of a piece of code. Limiting a piece of code's capabilities by identifying the code and enforcing access control is currently the best way to protect against malicious mobile code execution. Because access control settings are linked to pieces of code, the engine that executes the code can enforce the settings independently of the user or service requesting access to the code.

The CAS approach also separates the definition of access control settings at development time from code execution and the application of security settings at run time. Finally, CAS also creates one of the foundations for Web services security: Applications that are possibly using components spread all over the Internet need an efficient code-centric access control enforcement mechanism.

In the following sections we focus on the administrative aspects of CAS. We explain the key CAS concepts of which every Windows Server 2003 administrator and architect should be aware. This section can also serve as an introduction to CAS for developers. It does not, however, address the programmatic nuts and bolts of CAS.

11.3.1 .NET framework concepts

The .NET term for a logical unit of code is an assembly. A .NET Framework–based application can call one or more assemblies. Developers compile assemblies into platform-independent Intermediate Language (IL). At run time, the engine that compiles and executes the assemblies—the .NET run time or the Common Language Runtime (CLR)—uses a just-in-time (JIT) compilation process to convert IL into platform-dependent native code. The CLR also includes the subsystem that enforces CAS-based access control.

Code that takes full advantage of the CLR's features (e.g., CAS, JIT compilation, .NET class libraries) is called managed code. Older Win32 COM+ code that uses the legacy COM run time environment is called unmanaged code. Although administrators cannot use the .NET Framework's CAS mechanism to control unmanaged code, they can use the Windows Server 2003 SAFER feature (explained previously) to protect against the execution of legacy malicious mobile code.

Keep in mind that an application cannot take advantage of CAS unless the developer built the application using the .NET Framework building blocks and features mentioned earlier. Also, the platform executing the application code must have the .NET Framework installed. Microsoft bundles the .NET Framework (including the CLR and CAS support) with the Windows Server 2003 Server OS and also makes it available as an add-on component for XP, Windows 2000 (requires Service Pack 2—SP2), Windows NT 4.0 (requires SP6a), Windows ME, and Windows 98. You can download the .NET Framework add-on component from the Microsoft Developer Network (MSDN) Web site at http://msdn.microsoft.com.

11.3.2 CAS concepts

CAS is built around the concept of evidence-based access control. This basically means that a piece of code is only allowed to do certain things with certain system resources after it has provided certain "evidence" to the CLR engine executing the code.

You can look at evidence as the equivalent of an identity in the classical Windows authorization model. What a piece of code is exactly allowed to do with a system's resources is nailed down in a policy. A policy links evidence to system resource permissions. These are the three key concepts of CAS: policy, evidence, and permissions. In the following sections we explore these three concepts in greater detail.

Policy

Security policies are probably the most important element of the .NET Framework's CAS. Policy evaluation is a core task of the CLR's CAS subsystem. A CAS policy links up "evidence" with "permissions;" in other words, it tells what a particular piece of code is allowed or not allowed to do. "Evidence" and "permissions" will be explained later, but let's first have a look at "policy."

In the .NET Framework, policies can be defined on four different levels. The policy levels are differentiated by (1) the persons that can define and administer the policies, (2) the assemblies to which the policies apply, and (3) the order in which they are evaluated by the CAS engine. Table 11.1 lists these four policy levels and their characteristics. In what follows I will focus on the enterprise, machine, and user policies, because typically the .NET application developer, not the systems or domain administrator, defines and configures application domain policies programmatically.

Table 11.1 *CAS Policy Types*

Policy Type	Administered By	Applies To	Evaluation Order
Enterprise	Administrator	All managed code running on machines that are part of an Active Directory domain or forest infrastructure	1
Machine	Administrator	All managed code running a specific computer	2
User	Administrator or user	All managed code running in the context of a specific user's logon session	3
Application Domain	Application Developer	All managed code part of a specific application domain	4

Evidence

Evidence equals an assembly's identity. The CLR's CAS subsystem uses an assembly's evidence and security policy to determine the permissions that the assembly receives. By default, CAS supports the evidence types listed in Table 11.2. An assembly's evidence can be based on where the assembly is located (URL, Site, Zone, or Application Directory), who created it (Publisher and Strong name), or its content (hash). You can also add your own application-specific evidence types.

Table 11.2 *CAS Evidence Types*

Evidence Type	Comments
URL	The URL or file system location from which the assembly originates. An example is http://www.compaq.com/products.
Site	The site from which the assembly originates. An example is www.compaq.com.
Zone	The zone from which the assembly originates. The zone concept is similar to the one used in Internet Explorer.
Application directory	The application's installation directory.
Hash	The cryptographic hash value of an assembly.
Authenticode digital signature	The Authenticode digital signature of the assembly.
Strong name	The strong name of the assembly. This is a special kind of digital signature. Key elements in a strong name are the assembly's name, version, and public key.

Code groups

Evidence is linked to assemblies using the concept of "code groups." A code group is a collection of assemblies that have identical evidence. Assemblies that are within the same code group receive identical permissions.

Every policy level has a code group hierarchy. In a code group hierarchy, a parent code group can have multiple child code groups. If an assembly's evidence matches the evidence of multiple code groups within the same policy level, the assembly will be a member of multiple code groups.

The .NET Framework comes with a set of predefined code groups and hierarchies (see Table 11.3), but you can also define your own. If, for example, you build a Web application for your intranet users and the application has specific CAS security requirements, you probably want to create a new child code group called "MyWebApplication" underneath the LocalIntranet_Zone code group.

Permissions and permission sets

Permissions determine how an assembly can use protected system resources or what protected operations the assembly can perform. Examples are writing to a particular registry key or accessing certain performance counters on

Table 11.3 *Predefined Code Groups and Code Group Hierarchies*

Enterprise Policy Code Groups
All_Code
Machine Policy Code Groups
All_Code
My_Computer_Zone
Microsoft_Strong_Name
ECMA_Strong_Name
LocalIntranet_Zone
Internet_Zone
Restricted_Zone
Trusted_Zone
User Policy Code Groups
All_Code

the machine that executes the code. As you can see in Table 11.4, the CLR's CAS mechanism lets you define very granular assembly permissions. Table 11.4 lists the protected system resources and operations for which you can define permissions. As with evidence and code groups, you can extend the CAS permissions and add your own application-specific permissions.

Table 11.4 *CAS Permission Resources*

Permission Resources (Permission Class Name)	Comments
Environment Variables (EnvironmentPermission)	Used to grant/deny assemblies read and/or write access to system environment variables
File Dialog (FileDialogPermission)	Used to grant/deny assemblies access to the open and/or save file dialog boxes
File IO (FileIOPermission)	Used to grant/deny assemblies read/write/append/path discovery access to files and directories
Isolated Storage File (IsolatedStorageFilePermission)	Used to grant/deny assemblies access to file-based isolated storage—can also be used to set disk quotas
Reflection (ReflectionPermission)	Used to grant/deny assemblies permissions to discover certain information about other assemblies at run time
Registry (RegistryPermission)	Used to grant/deny assemblies read, write and/or create access to registry keys
Security (SecurityPermission)	Used to grant/deny assemblies security permissions (for example, allow policy control, allow calls to unmanaged assemblies, and so forth)
User Interface (UiPermission)	Used to grant/deny assemblies access to user interface elements like Windows, events, and the clipboard
DNS (DnsPermission)	Used to grant/deny assemblies access to DNS for name resolution
Printing (PrintingPermission)	Used to grant/deny assemblies access to printers
Event Log (EventLogPermission)	Used to grant/deny assemblies browse, instrument or audit access to the event logs
Socket Access (SocketPermission)	Used to let assemblies accept or deny access to certain connections based on IP addresses, ports, TCP, or UDP use
Web Access (WebPermission)	Used to let assemblies accept or deny access to certain Web connections based on Web addresses
Performance Counter (PerformanceCounterPermission)	Used to grant/deny assemblies access to performance counters

Table 11.4 *CAS Permission Resources (continued)*

Permission Resources (Permission Class Name)	Comments
Directory Services (DirectoryServicesPermission)	Used to grant/deny assemblies browse or write access to directory service paths
Message Queue (MessageQueuePermission)	Used to grant/deny assemblies browse, peek, send, receive or administer access to message queues
Service Controller (ServiceControllerPermission)	Used to grant/deny assemblies control or browse access to services
OLE DB (OleDBPermission)	Used to grant/deny assemblies access to OLE DB providers
SQL Client (SqlClientPermission)	Used to grant/deny assemblies access to Microsoft SQL Servers using ADO.NET

A very interesting permission is the Isolated Storage File permission, which refers to a special file storage system that you can define on top of the regular file system. The permission's main characteristic is isolation: It lets an assembly store data and makes sure that the assembly cannot affect other assembly or system data.

To facilitate permissions management, permissions can be grouped into permission sets, which you can link to code groups. As for code groups, there is a set of predefined permission sets for every security policy level. Table 11.5 lists the preconfigured permission sets that come with the .NET Framework.

11.3.3 CAS policy management

A higher level of security and ease of administration rarely go hand in hand, and CAS security policy configuration is no exception. To configure the different policy levels, code groups, and permission sets, you can use the Microsoft Management Console (MMC) .NET Framework Configuration snap-in (mscorcfg.msc), or you can use the CAS Policy tool (caspol.exe), a command-line utility. The .NET Framework Configuration snap-in is available on any machine that has the .NET framework installed. The CAS policy tool comes with the .NET Framework software development kit (SDK).

An application developer can configure CAS policies and properties programmatically. Administrators can always override specific application

Table 11.5 *Preconfigured Permission Sets*

Permission Set	Comment
Nothing	No permissions
Execution	Permissions to run
Internet	Default permission set for code originating from the Internet
LocalIntranet	Default permission set for code originating from within the intranet
Everything	All permissions, with the exception of the permission to skip verification
FullTrust	Full access to all resources
SkipVerification	Grants right to bypass the verification

domain-level permissions by explicitly denying them at a higher policy level (remember the CAS policy evaluation order mentioned earlier).

If you use the .NET Framework Configuration snap-in, you will set security policies from the Runtime Security Policy container, as Figure 11.6

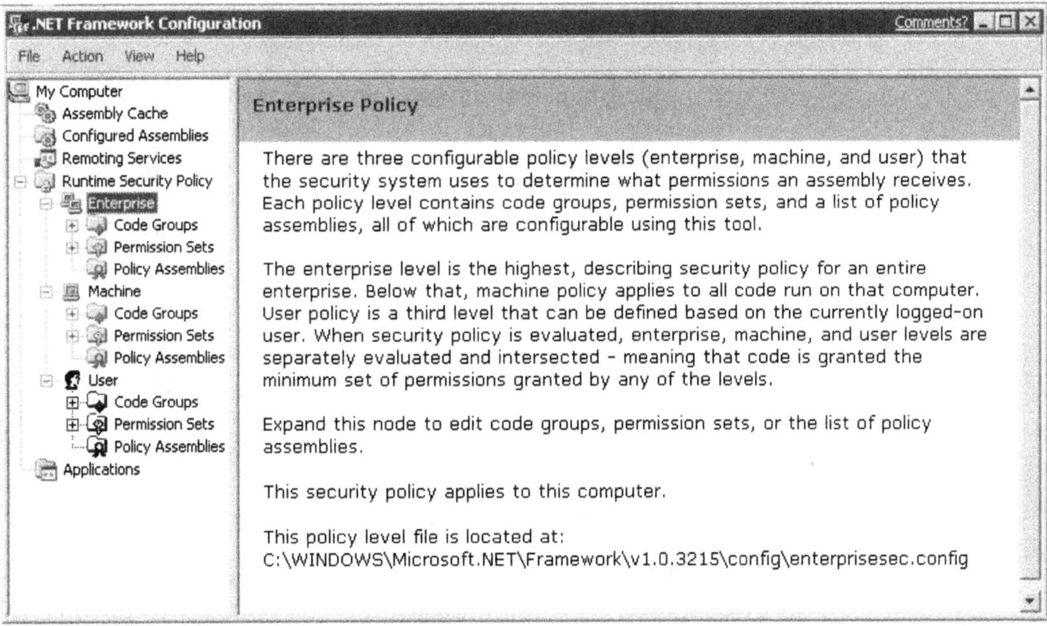

Figure 11.6 *.NET Framework Configuration tool and Security Policy containers.*

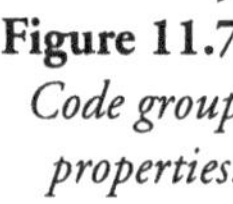

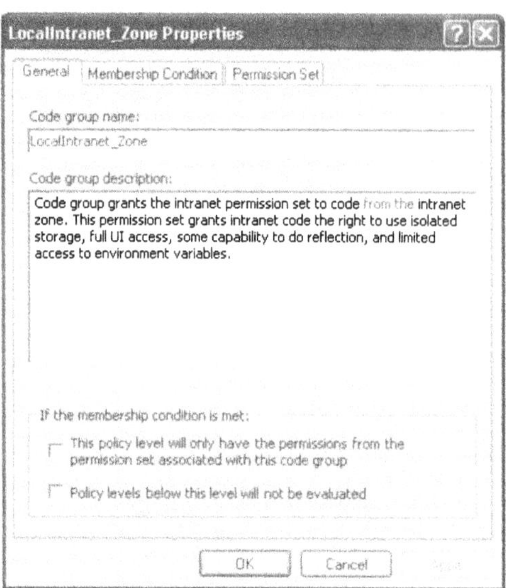

Figure 11.7 *Code group properties.*

shows. Each Runtime Security Policy container has three subcontainers: code groups, permission sets, and policy assemblies. The policy assemblies' subcontainer can contain custom code that the CLR's CAS subsystem uses to evaluate security policy—this custom code can define things such as custom CAS evidence or permissions.

To view a code group's description, right-click the code group you want to view, and open the Properties dialog box (as illustrated in Figure 11.7). Click the General tab to see a description of the code group. The second tab, "Membership Condition," shows the evidence used to uniquely identify the code group, and the third tab, "Permission Set," shows the permissions that are available to the code group.

A .NET Framework–enabled machine stores the CAS security policy configuration in XML documents. The enterprise policy XML configuration files (enterprisesec.config) and machine policy XML configuration files (security.config) are stored in the .NET run time installation directory. The user policy XML configuration file (also named security.config) is kept in the user's profile directory. The only exception to this is application domain policy definitions; they are embedded in the assemblies themselves.

Administrators can distribute new CAS security policies to the enterprise by generating a Windows Installer (.msi) file for a given security policy level. They can also change individual policy settings using caspol.exe. If administrators want to use caspol.exe to change multiple policy settings, they can bundle different calls to the tool in a script or batch file.

11.3.4 CAS policy evaluation

In this section we look in more detail at how the CAS policy settings are evaluated. Given the different policy levels and multiple code groups, this is a rather complex topic.

Figure 11.8 shows the reference code group hierarchy that we use to explain policy evaluation. In this example there is a code group hierarchy defined for the enterprise, machine, and user policy levels. The assembly that we are evaluating has the necessary evidence to make it a member of all code groups that have a dark gray rectangle. On the machine policy level, for example, our assembly is a member of the "Internet," "www.hp.com," and "www.hp.com/dev" code groups.

CAS policy evaluation happens when the assembly is loaded into the run time by a CLR component that is commonly referred to as the policy evaluator. Remember that the ultimate goal of the CAS policy evaluation is to determine the permissions a particular assembly will receive. During the policy evaluation process, the CAS policy evaluator will first evaluate the enterprise-level policies, then the machine-level policies followed by the user-level policies, and finally the application domain-level policies. Within each policy level the policy evaluator will start with evaluating the root code group and will then walk down the tree to evaluate all underlying child

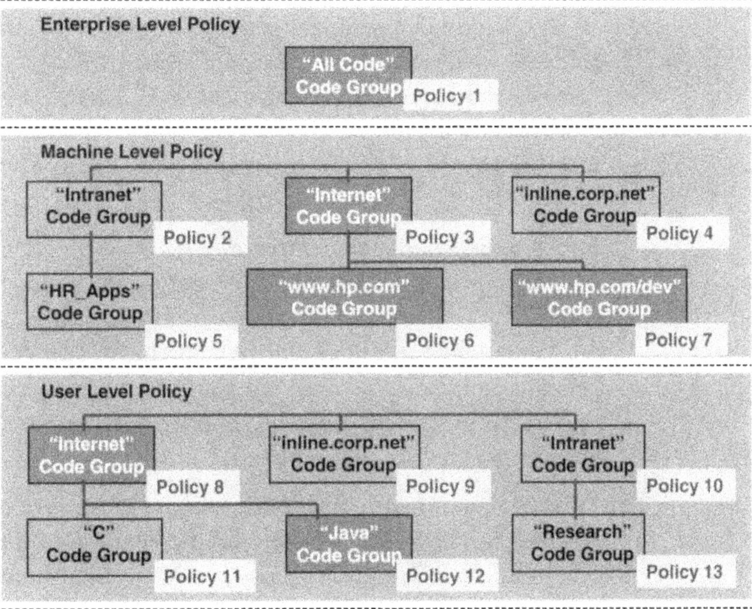

Figure 11.8 *CAS policy evaluation order.*

code groups. If an assembly is not a member of a parent code group, none of its child groups will be evaluated.

At a given policy level, the effective permissions that are granted to an assembly is the union of the permissions granted to the different code groups the assembly is a member of. In our example on the machine policy level, the permissions granted our test assembly will be the sum of the permissions granted to the "Internet," "www.hp.com," and "www.hp.com/dev" code groups.

When the CAS policy evaluator is finished evaluating permissions on the different policy levels, it takes the intersection of the permissions granted on these levels to determine the final set of permissions that will be granted to the assembly. After all, this looks relatively simple: On the policy level, the policy evaluator performs a union operation; to determine the final set of permissions it uses an intersection operation between the results of the different policy levels. All of this is summarized in Figure 11.9.

In Figure 11.9, a code group hierarchy is defined on the four CAS policy levels: enterprise, machine, user, and application domain. On each policy level the CAS engine calculates the sum of permissions granted in the different code groups that apply to the assembly. For example, on the enterprise policy level, this is the union of the permission granted to the A, B, C, and D code groups. The final set of permissions granted to the assembly is the intersection of the results of the different policy levels.

A code group's properties contain two ways to change the default policy evaluation process, as outlined in Figure 11.9. You can do so using the checkboxes located at the bottom of the "General" tab in the code group's properties (as illustrated in Figure 11.7). Their effect is illustrated in Figures 11.10 and 11.11.

The first option, *This policy level will only have the permissions from the permission set associated with this code group*, makes membership in a particular code group an assembly's primary code group membership. If the assembly is a member of other code groups located at the same policy level, the CAS policy evaluator will ignore these code groups. This option is known as the Exclusive code group attribute. At a given policy level, only a single code group can have the Exclusive attribute set. Figure 11.10 shows the effect of the Exclusive attribute.

The second option, *Policy levels below this level will not be evaluated*, limits assembly code-group–membership evaluation to the security policy level of a given code group. If you select this option, known as the LevelFinal

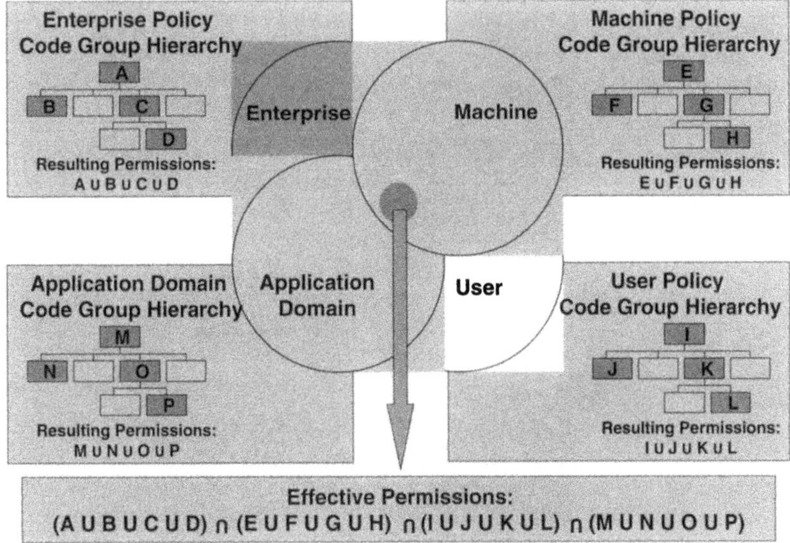

Figure 11.9 *Default CAS policy evaluation process.*

code group attribute, the CAS policy evaluator will not evaluate membership of code groups lower in the security policy hierarchy. Figure 11.11 shows the effect of the LevelFinal attribute: In this example the user policy level is ignored.

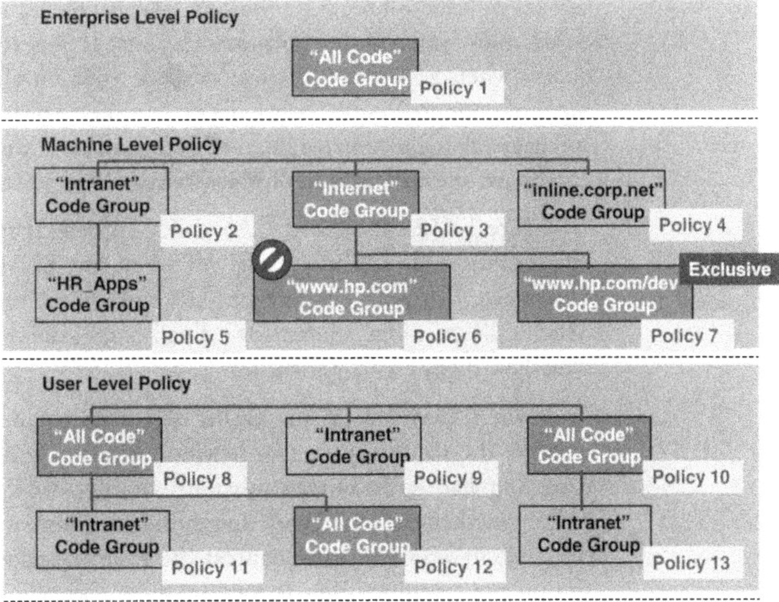

Figure 11.10 *Effect of the "Exclusive" code group attribute on CAS security policy evaluation.*

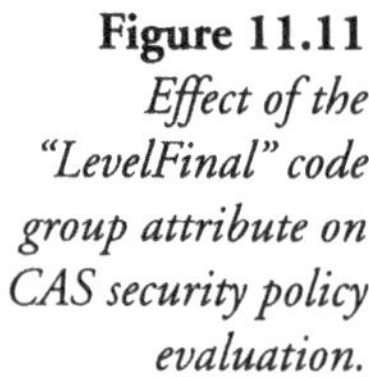

Figure 11.11 *Effect of the "LevelFinal" code group attribute on CAS security policy evaluation.*

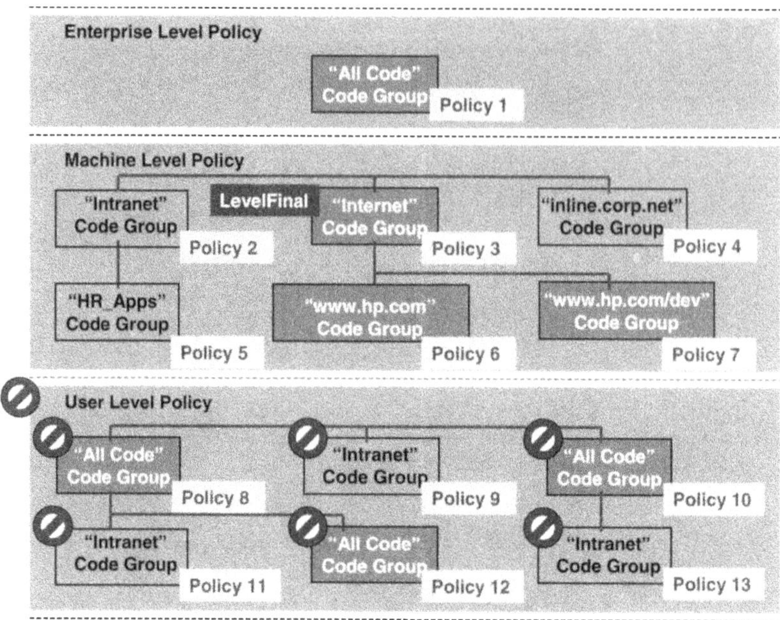

11.3.5 CAS policy enforcement

In the previous section we looked at how CAS policy is evaluated; in this section we look at how it is enforced. One of the key features of CAS policy enforcement is its ability to protect against luring attacks. A luring attack occurs when an untrusted piece of code calls on the services of another piece of code to elevate its privileges. In other words, the trusted code has privileges that the untrusted code does not have, and the untrusted code tries to get these by calling on the services of the trusted code.

Figure 11.12 shows how CAS policy enforcement works under normal circumstances. Everything starts off when assembly A1 is loaded on the CLR stack for execution. Assembly A1 calls on the services of assembly A2, which calls assembly A3; the latter finally calls assembly A4, which contains a method that needs a permission P.

In the COM+ world the COM execution engine would have checked whether the security principal in whose security context assembly A4 was executing had sufficient permissions. In the .NET world the CLR will check whether the code itself has sufficient permissions, not the security principle in whose security context the code is executing. Remember from the previous sections that thanks to code evidence we can now uniquely identify a piece of code.

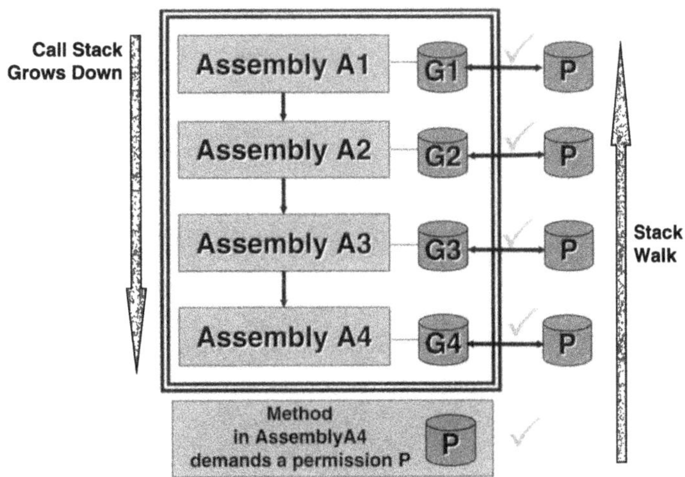

Figure 11.12 *Normal CAS stack walk behavior.*

The great thing about CAS policy enforcement is that not only will the permissions of assembly A4 be checked, but also the ones of all other assemblies that called on the services of assembly A4. This explains the CAS capability to protect against luring attacks. When assembly A4 demands a permission P, the CLR CAS subsystem will start a process that is known as a "security stack walk." During this stack walk, the CLR will check whether all calling assemblies have been granted the same permission P as requested by assembly A4. If this is not the case for one of the calling assemblies on the stack, the CLR will generate a security exception and the stack walk will terminate. To check the permissions for the calling assemblies, the CLR will let the CAS policy evaluator subsystem perform a CAS policy evaluation for all calling assemblies. The policy evaluation process was explained in detail earlier.

In the example in Figure 11.12, everything turns out fine for assembly A4: Assembly A4 itself and all the calling assemblies have the permission P, and thus assembly A4 is effectively granted permission P.

Figure 11.13 illustrates a luring attack and how it is blocked by the CLR. In the example assembly A2 is granted a set of permissions G2 that does not contain the permission P requested by assembly A4. Assembly A2 tries to elevate his or her privileges by calling on A3, who then calls on A4. Thanks to the security stack walk, we can block assembly A2's luring attack.

Developers can add certain operations to their code to modify the CLR's security stack walk behavior. These operations are methods that are defined on all the CAS permission classes and permissions sets. They are also

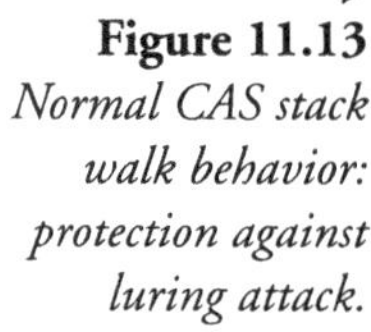

Figure 11.13 *Normal CAS stack walk behavior: protection against luring attack.*

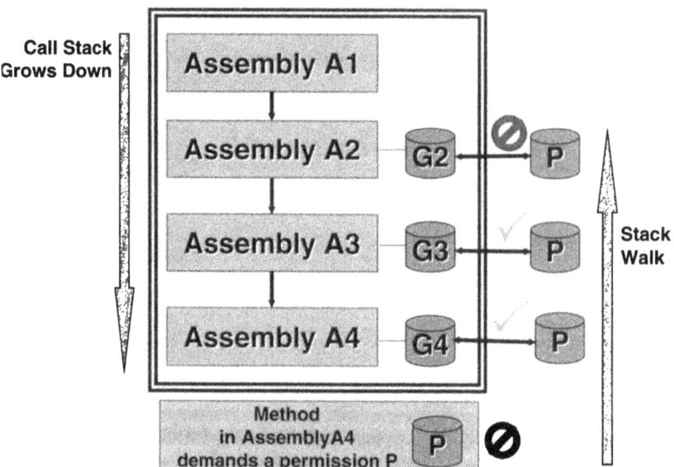

referred to as stack walk modifiers. Next we will illustrate the two most important stack walk modifiers: the Assert and Deny methods.

When the Assert method is used for a particular permission, the assembly will get this permission independently of the permissions granted to the calling assemblies. In other words, in this case the CLR is not interested in the outcome of the rest of the security stack walk. The Assert method is a dangerous option: When application developers use it, it is very important that they check the trustworthiness of the calling assemblies on the stack in their code. In the example in Figure 11.14, permission P is set to Assert in

Figure 11.14 *CAS stack walk behavior with the "Assert" stack walk modifier.*

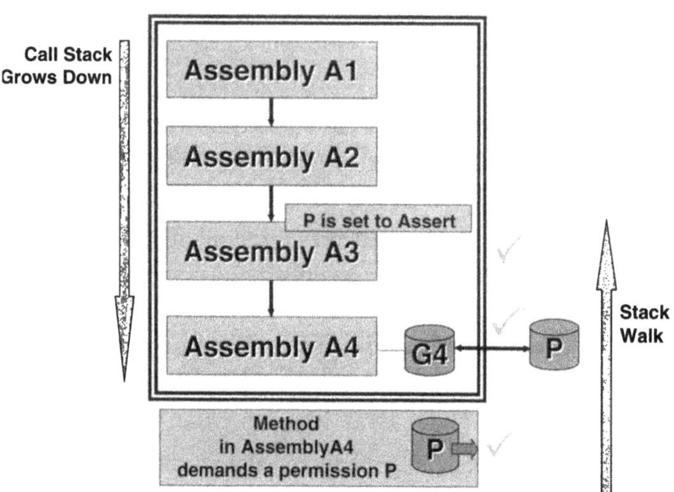

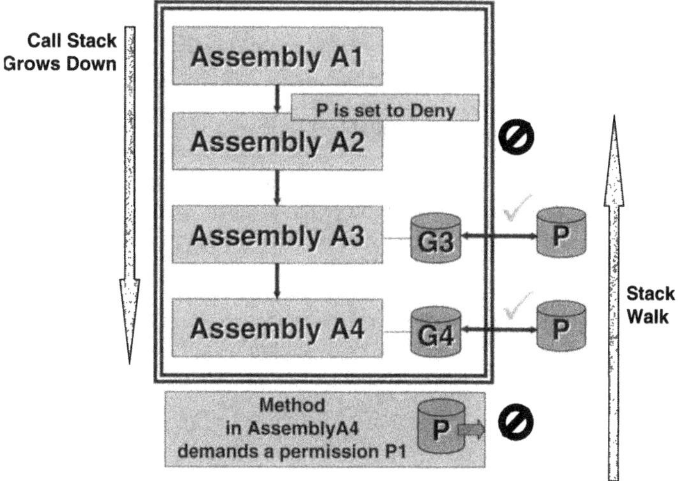

Figure 11.15 *CAS stack walk behavior with the "Deny" stack walk modifier.*

assembly A3. As a consequence the CLR will not even call on the policy evaluator to check assembly A3's permissions: It will simply terminate the stack walk and grant assembly A4 permission P.

The Deny method is the opposite of the Assert method: Whereas the use of the Assert method can terminate the stack walk with a successful outcome, the use of the Deny method can terminate the stack walk with a negative outcome or, in other words, with the generation of a security exception. In the example in Figure 11.15, permission P is set to Deny in assembly A2. As a consequence, the CLR will not even call on the policy evaluator to check assembly A2's permissions: It will simply terminate the stack walk and generate a security exception.

11.4 Comparing SRPs and CAS

Table 11.6 provides a short comparison between Software Restriction Policies (SRPs) and Code Access Security (CAS).

Here are some last words about CAS. CAS is clearly the most powerful technology of the two. It is a fundamental component of the .NET Framework that will let application developers write more-secure code, however, I hope this chapter has shown that application developers are not the only ones who need to understand this important technology: CAS will affect the tasks of any security-aware Windows architect, consultant, or administrator because configuring and fine-tuning CAS security policies is generally

Table 11.6 *SRP/CAS Comparison*

	SRPs	CAS
Important for...	Administrators, Architects	Administrators, Architects, Developers
Can be applied to...	Any file (*.exe, *.dll, *.vbs...). For executables and libraries, SRPs can be applied independently of whether the code behind them is COM+ or .NET based	Any assembly written using the .NET development framework
Can be administered by...	GPO Administrator	Forest, domain, or machine administrator, user, or developer
Level of access control enforcement	File is allowed to run or not	Very granular access control enforcement: access control can be set for individual system resources
Available on...	Windows Server 2003 and XP platforms	Any platform that has the .NET Framework installed

beyond an application developer's responsibilities. Configuring CAS security policies is complex, but it is a process with which you will want to become familiar as soon as possible. If you want to secure your .NET environment, don't miss the CAS Express.

12

New Authorization Tracks: Role-Based Access Control and Digital Rights Management

In Windows Server 2003, Microsoft is exploring some interesting new paths in the area of access control enforcement. One of them is support for role-based access control management, using a technology called the Authorization Manager and a brand-new API—the Authorization API.

A path that is at least as interesting as the previous one is the support for digital rights management (DRM). Microsoft calls their enterprise DRM solution "Rights Management Services" (RMS).

This chapter provides an introduction to both the Authorization Manager and Rights Management Services.

12.1 Role-based access control

Authorization Manager is a fundamental shift In Microsoft's way of dealing with access control enforcement and management. In the long run it will affect everyone (including architects, administrators, and developers) who is dealing with the new generation of Microsoft enterprise operating systems and the applications that are running on top of these platforms. The Authorization Manager is all about Microsoft's efforts to introduce a role-based access control model (RBAC) for applications running on top of the Windows platform.

In Windows Server 2003 Authorization Manager and its role-based access control model can be used to role-enable LOB applications. An interesting combination is using Authorization Manager together with IIS 6.0's URL-based authorization feature. So far, MS does not provide applications that are out-of-the-box role-enabled—and in that sense at the time of writing Authorization Manager is mainly developer-focused. In the years to come MS may however natively RBAC-enable other Windows applications.

12.1.1 Introducing RBAC

The concepts behind the role-based authorization model (RBAC) were created by David Ferraiolo and Richard Kuhn of the U.S. National Institute of Standards and Technology (NIST). They introduced the concept of role-based access control to the IT world in 1992 in their paper entitled "Role-Based Access Controls."

Until 1992, most platforms and applications supported either a mandatory access control model (MAC) or a discretionary access control model (DAC). These two models are specified in the U.S. Department of Defense (DoD) Trusted Computer Security Evaluation Criteria (TCSEC) that was published in 1985. Of the two, DAC is certainly the most commonly used model. It is used in many commercial OSs, including Microsoft Windows NT and Windows 2000.

In the DAC model, granting and revoking of access privileges to a resource are left to the discretion of the individual users. DAC allows users to grant or revoke access to any of the objects under their direct control (in Windows terms, objects or resources that the user owns) without the intercession of a system administrator. As such, DAC proposes a highly decentralized approach to access control management.

On the other end of the spectrum is the MAC model. MAC proposes a highly centralized access control model where a central authority grants or denies user access to resources. In the MAC model the central authority typically performs the following two key tasks:

1. It gives users a clearance level (a process that is also known as granting membership or clearing users).
2. It labels the resources with an access level for the different clearance levels (a process that is also known as associating operational sensitivities to resources).

Central control is usually very well applicable to military and government organizations. In such environments the primary concern is to prohibit the unauthorized flow of information from a higher level to a lower level in the organization.

Now that we have an idea what the MAC and DAC models are about, let's look at what the RBAC model means. In what follows I will only focus on the differences between the DAC and the RBAC models. This is simply because DAC is the model used in NT, and Microsoft so far has not provided any commercial-off-the-shelf (COTS) support for the MAC model.

As mentioned earlier, RBAC stands for role-based access control. In the RBAC model, everything centers on the organizational role of a user. Access to resources is based on the role that individual users take as part of an organization. The definition of a role takes into account the specification of an individual user's duties, responsibilities, and qualifications.

In the DAC model, access control management and enforcement is very object- and resource-centric. From an administrative point of view, it is more natural to manage access control in a role-based fashion, which is why the DAC model creates the overhead for an administrator to translate the organizational model—based on users' roles—into the object-centric model—based on access rights to resources. The role concept in the RBAC model can be thought of as a special type of access control group. Anyone familiar with NT should know the concept of a group. A role is a special group that is linked to a set of tasks that a user or a set of users can perform in the context of a particular organization and the applications that are defined in that organization. A role is also fundamentally different from a group. This is explained in the next sections and in Figure 12.1.

The key difference between a role and a group is that groups as we know them from the DAC model are only used to facilitate access control management on the resource level. They group users and take away the administrative burden to define and maintain access control for every individual user. A role, on the contrary, directly implies a set of resource access permis-

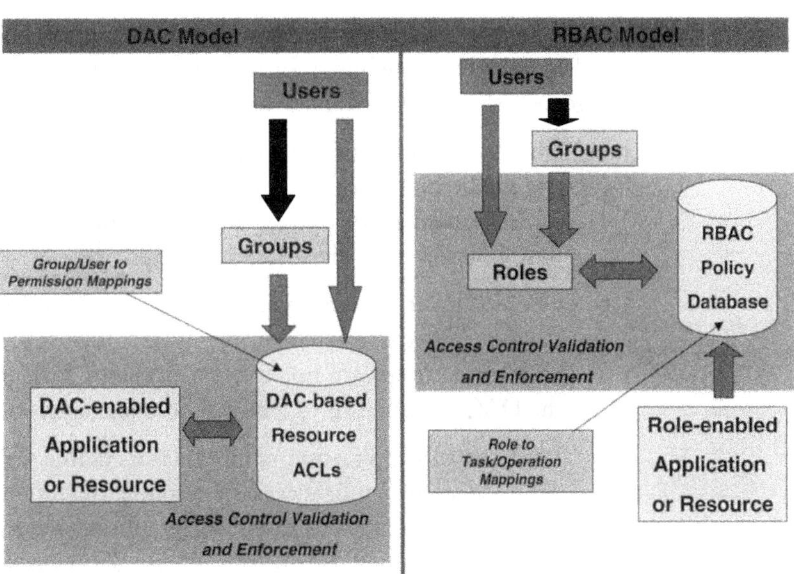

Figure 12.1 *Comparing the DAC and the RBAC models.*

sions. These permissions are based on the role definition or the role to task/operation mappings that are stored in the RBAC access control policy database. To know what tasks or operations a user is allowed to perform, it is sufficient to know his or her role. Unlike in the DAC model, there is no more need to query the access permissions of the different resources at the time of access.

Another important difference with the DAC model is the notion of centralized access control validation and enforcement in the RBAC model. In the RBAC model, role-enabled applications query the RBAC policy database or the associated access control authority to find out whether a user is allowed to perform a particular action or not. In the DAC model, access control enforcement and validation is completely decentralized and occurs on the DAC-enabled application or resource level. In NT, for example, a local machine entity known as the security reference monitor (SRM) is responsible for comparing the content of a user's access token to the entries in an Access Control List (ACL) on a resource and deciding whether a user is allowed access or not.

The reason why centralization is so attractive when it comes to access control enforcement is the following: In most organizations, resource and information security objectives support a security policy. The latter is usually defined at the highest level of the organization. To support such policies, a capability to centrally control and maintain access rights is required (or at least highly recommended).

It can also be argued that the RBAC model in general better maps to the administrative model used for resource and application access control management that is used in most organizations:

- The security administrator is responsible for enforcing the access control policy in a centralized way. Contrary to the DAC model, in the RBAC model a user cannot simply pass his or her access permissions onto other users at his or her discretion.
- The administrators managing people are responsible for adding users to roles. To facilitate role management, they can create user groups. This time groups are not used to facilitate ACL management (as in the DAC model), but to facilitate role management.
- Resource and application administrators define what a given role can do in terms of application and resource operations and tasks. They pass this information to the security administrator. The latter makes sure the appropriate role-to-operation/task mappings are stored in the access control policy database. As opposed to the DAC model,

Table 12.1 *Comparing the DAC and RBAC Access Control Models*

	Discretionary AC (DAC)	Role-Based AC (RBAC)
Focus Area	Object- and resource-centric	Organizational role-centric
Access Control Policy Storage	Decentralized access control policy storage	Centralized access control policy storage
Administrative Model	Difficult to map to administrative model used for access control management	Relatively easy to map to administrative model used for access control management

resource and application administrators should not bother about setting the appropriate ACLs on every individual resource anymore.

Table 12.1 summarizes the major differences between the DAC and RBAC models.

12.1.2 Windows Server 2003 RBAC architecture

Before digging into the Windows Server 2003 RBAC architecture, it must be said that role-based access control is not entirely new to Microsoft OSs and applications:

- The concept of user and resource "groups" that has been around since the early days of Windows NT provide role-like functionality. Nevertheless, as explained earlier, NT groups are fundamentally different from RBAC roles.
- The COM development framework also has the notion of an application-specific role. This role is very similar to the one used in the context of the Windows Server 2003 RBAC model. The key difference with RBAC roles is that COM roles can only be used in applications written using the COM and COM+ development frameworks. The Windows Server 2003 RBAC model is independent of the development framework.

It is also important to stress that the new RBAC model introduced in Windows Server 2003 will not replace all DAC models that are currently in place on the Windows platform. The two models can easily coexist. Later on, Microsoft may integrate some of the applications' DAC models into the RBAC model or even fully move applications to a RBAC model. Figure 12.2 shows the current Windows Server 2003 RBAC architecture and its major components.

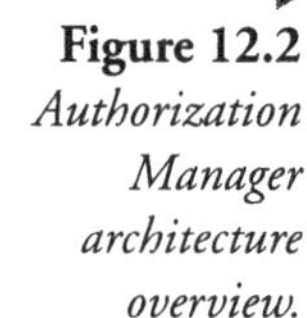

Figure 12.2 *Authorization Manager architecture overview.*

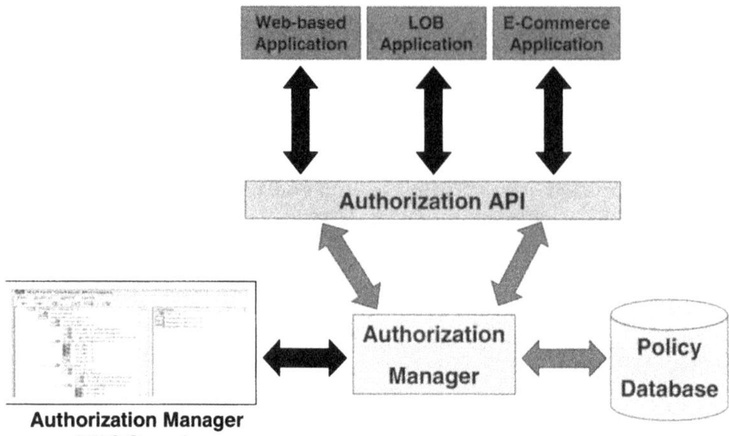

At the center of the RBAC architecture sits the Authorization Manager. The Authorization Manager is the management and decision-making engine of the RBAC system.

The authorization manager makes sure all RBAC information is properly stored in the policy database. It also provides access points to the database for applications to query the authorization policy and for administrators to manage the authorization policy.

RBAC-enabled applications query the Authorization Manager at run time to find out whether a particular user is allowed to perform a certain application-level operation or not. The Authorization Manager gives a go/no-go based on the role membership of the user and the application operation/task-to-role mapping information that is stored in the policy database. Remember that this is a fundamental change compared to the DAC model: In this model the local resource manager on the host machine makes the access control decision. RBAC-enabled applications access the authorization manager and its functions through a set of COM-based run-time interfaces. These are commonly referred to as the Authorization API (or, as its abbreviation, AuthzAPI).

The Authorization Manager's centralized access policy database can be kept either in Active Directory or in an XML file. To use AD as the access control policy store, your AD domain should be in the native Windows Server 2003 functionality level. The advantage of using AD over an XML file for storage is that you can delegate the administration of subcomponents (authorization stores, applications, and scopes—these concepts are explained later) of your access control policy to different administrators.

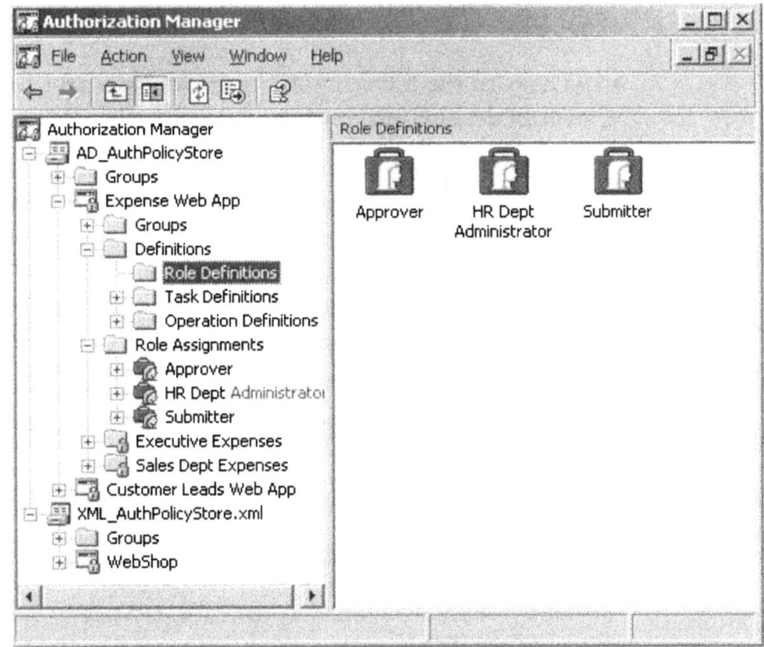

Figure 12.3 *Authorization Manager MMC snap-in (azman.msc).*

AD-based Authorization Stores are by default stored in the "Program Data" container in the AD domain naming context. As a consequence, they are replicated to every domain controller (DC) in a domain.

The primary administration interface to the authorization manager is an MMC snap-in called azman.msc, which is illustrated in Figure 12.3. In the next section I use this interface to explain the Authorization Manager's conceptual model. The snap-in supports two modes: developer mode and administrator mode. The most restricted mode is administrator mode: In this mode users can do everything except create new authorization stores, applications, or operations, and change operations, application names, or version information (these concepts are explained later). To switch between modes, use the Action\Options... menu option.

Perhaps the most important feature of Microsoft's implementation of the RBAC model is that it allows for highly flexible and dynamic access control decisions.

- The access control policy can be easily applied to application-specific objects or operations (e.g., "send a mail," "approve an expense"). The latter is a key differentiator with Microsoft's implementation of the DAC model: This model was tailored to be applied to specific objects, such as file system objects, registry objects, and database objects.

- Thanks to the following Authorization Manager features, the access control decision-making behavior can easily be changed at run time:
  - Authorization Manager supports dynamic groups whose membership can change depending on the outcome of an LDAP query that is launched at run time.
  - Authorization Manager supports authorization scripts that are executed at run time and that can be used to link access control decisions to real-time data such as the time of day, currency, and stock values.

I will come back to both dynamic groups and authorization scripts in Section 12.1.3.

Authorization Manager also supports fine-grain run-time auditing. Authorization Manager audits application initialization, client context initialization and deletion, and all access checks with pass and fail audits. Obviously, administrators can also use store-level auditing: on the AD objects (if the AD is used as policy store) and on the file-system level (if an XML file is used as policy store).

All of the this makes the Authorization Manager's access control model very well suited for line of business (LOB) applications. In such applications, access control decisions often depend on specific business logic. The latter may involve special operations or even the execution of a piece of workflow logic: Examples are querying a directory, waiting for a mail approval to come back from a manager, or querying a Web service for a currency or stock value. This richness is very distinct from the limited access control decision logic that is available in Microsoft's classical DAC model. In this model, access control decisions are simply based on the group memberships and user rights contained in users' access tokens.

12.1.3 Authorization Manager concepts

The Authorization Manager's Authorization Policy Store is made up of one or more collections of the following object types: applications, groups, roles, tasks, scopes, and bizrules. These concepts are illustrated in Figure 12.4 and explained next.

The policy store can contain the access control policies of multiple applications. In the example in Figure 12.4, it contains the access control policy for a Web-based expense application and a Web-based customer lead

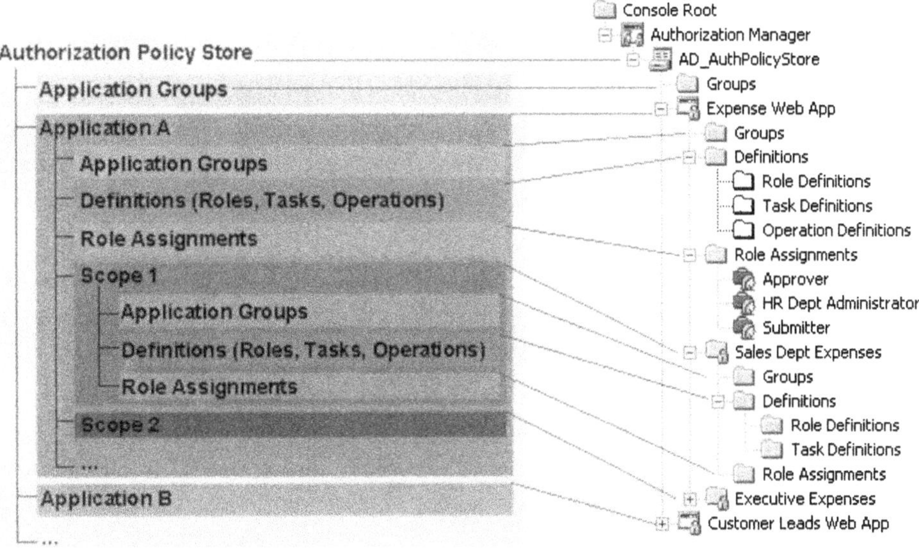

Figure 12.4 *Authorization Manager concepts.*

application. In the following examples, I will look in more detail at the access control policy elements of the Web-based expense application.

To assign users to role definitions, Authorization Manager can use Windows users and groups or Authorization Manager–specific groups. Windows users and groups have a Security Identity (SID) and exist in the Windows security database (AD). Authorization Manager–specific groups (these are also referred to as "application groups") do not have an SID and only exist within the context of an Authorization Manager Policy Store, application, or application scope. As you can see in Figure 12.4, the Groups container appears on the policy store, application container, and scope levels. There are two types of Authorization Manager–specific application groups:

1. Basic application groups have the unique property that they have both a members attribute and a nonmembers attribute. The latter allows for exceptions similar to the deny ACEs used on AD and file system objects. Both attributes can contain Windows users and groups and other Authorization Manager application groups.

2. LDAP-query application groups have the unique property that they can provide dynamic group membership. The latter is based on an LDAP-query that is launched against AD at run time.

An Authorization Manager role is defined in terms of tasks and operations:

- An operation is a low-level operation that usually only makes sense to the manager of a resource. Examples are "read user expense quotum" or "write user password." Operations can only be defined at the application level and are always identified by an operation number (which is an integer).
- Tasks are collections of operations that do make sense to the administrator of an application. Examples are "Approve Expense" or "Submit Expense." Tasks can be defined at both the application and the scope levels.

Authorization Manager supports the creation of a hierarchical role model and thus role inheritance. During the definition of a role, Authorization Manager allows for the specification of a lower-level role from which the newly created role will inherit all associated tasks and operations.

As mentioned earlier, to make the authorization process more dynamic, Authorization Manager allows for linking authorization scripts (or Bizrules, as Microsoft calls them) to tasks. Just like the LDAP queries behind dynamic application groups, Bizrules are evaluated at run time to qualify real-time information such as the time of day, currency, or stock values. They can be written in either VBscript or Jscript and are stored in the policy store along with all the other policy information.

An application access control policy can also be fine-tuned using Authorization Manager scopes. A scope is a subcollection of objects within an application's access control policy. A scope can be as simple as a file system path (for a file system–based application), an AD container (for an AD-based application), or a URL (for a Web-based application). In the example of Figure 12.4, I defined two additional scopes within the Expense Web application: one for the treatment of the sales department expenses and another for the executive expenses.

12.1.4 Authorization Manager deployment scenarios

Authorization Manager opens up many new, interesting application deployment scenarios. In what follows, we look at how Authorization Manager can enhance the security quality of multitier applications that are using the trusted application architectural model.

Two commonly used architectural models for multitier applications are the impersonation/delegation and trusted application models. The differences between the two models are summarized next. Windows Server 2003 comes with enhancements for both models. An interesting change enhancing the impersonation/delegation model are these Kerberos extensions coming with Windows Server 2003: constrained delegation and protocol transition (explained in Chapter 5).

In the impersonation/delegation model, the middle-tier application (typically a Web server application) can do one of the following:

- Generate an impersonation token that reflects the user's access control data and use this token to access back-end resources on the user's behalf.
- Forward the user's authentication token to the back-end resource. The latter is called delegation and only works when the Kerberos authentication protocol is involved in one way or another. The use of the Kerberos authentication protocol also enables multitier delegation.

The basic idea behind the impersonation/delegation model is that the user identity survives beyond the middle tier. Doing so, access control settings on back-end resources can be set using the user identity.

In the trusted application model, the user's identity does not survive beyond the middle tier. In the trusted application model, all access to back-end resources is done using the Web server or Web application's service account. The difference between the two models is illustrated in Figure 12.5.

Integrating Authorization Manager into the trusted application model has the following advantages:

- It adds the capability to perform very granular role-based access control enforcement at the Web application level.
- It provides fine-grain run-time auditing capabilities at the Web application level.

In addition to these two key advantages brought by Authorization Manager, the trusted application model obviously keeps its classic advantages:

- *Easier access control management on the back-end resource/application servers.* All access control settings can be set using a single account: the Web server or Web application's service account.
- *Support for connection pooling provides a higher level of scalability.* Connection pooling only makes sense if all connections to the back-end infrastructure run in the same user security context. Connection pooling does not add a lot of value when the impersonation/delega-

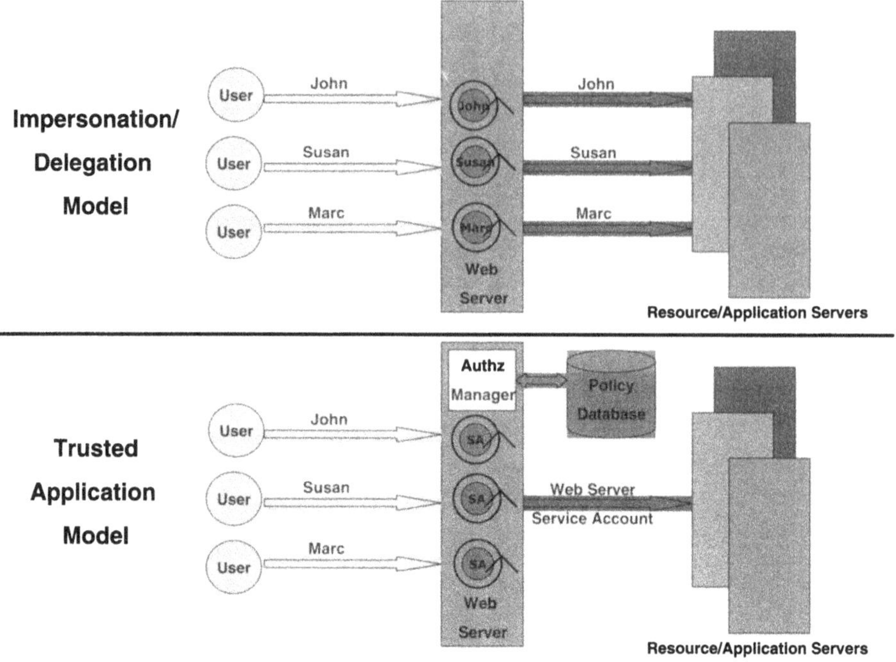

Figure 12.5 *Impersonation/delegation versus trusted application model.*

tion model is used because every connection runs in another user's security context (the context of the impersonated or delegated user).

- *Provides a controlled access point.* In the trusted application model, all user access to back-end resources occurs using the Web front end. There is no way for users to access the back-end resources using some other channel bypassing the Web front end (on the condition that the appropriate ACLs are in place on the back-end resources).

12.2 Digital rights management

The goal of this section is to provide a technical introduction to the Microsoft Rights Management (RMS). I will explain the major RMS concepts and technologies and how MS makes these collaborate to provide enterprise-level digital rights management (DRM).

Microsoft released the RMS server software as a free add-on to Windows Server 2003 late 2003. The RMS server add-on will runs only on Windows Server 2003. RMS is not the first DRM software MS ever created: Windows Media Player has included DRM features for years.

12.2.1 Why digital rights management?

The goal of any DRM software can be summarized as follows: to provide persistent integrity protection of digital media. Let's look in more detail at the different components of this goal statement.

- *Persistent Protection:* DRM protects digital information at any time and in any place. DRM access control data is attached to the digital information and cannot be bypassed. The protection is end to end: The information is protected while it is transmitted over a communication channel and when it is stored in a repository.

  This means that the level of protection offered by a DRM solution goes far beyond what is currently provided by perimeter protection–based security solutions. Everyone certainly knows these security solutions that are in use today—to name just a few, firewalls, access control lists, encryption solutions (VPN software to protect communication channels, S/MIME-based solutions to protect e-mail messages), and so forth. None of these provides persistent protection. At one point in time or at a certain location, they all leave the information unprotected; for example, when the information leaves the internal network protected by a corporate firewall, when it leaves the communication channel protected by a VPN software, when it is retrieved from a file server (protected by ACLs) and copied to another repository (a Web site, an FTP site, and so forth), or when it is unencrypted and stored to the local system drive.

- *Integrity Protection:* DRM protects digital information from unauthorized access and unauthorized modification. From a security service point of view, DRM provides integrity, confidentiality, and user data authentication services.

- *Digital Media:* DRM only applies to digital media. DRM access control information is attached in a digital format to digital data. Because of its digital roots, it cannot be applied to analog data. Microsoft uses this excellent image of a computer screen that is put on a photocopier to illustrate this point. This underlines an important shortcoming of DRM and of all security technologies. A global security solution is not just about technology, but also requires a global solution approach that, besides technology, also incorporates procedural, policy-based, and social security measures.

Two important DRM features that make DRM unique and that can be used to promote the use of DRM solutions are the following:

- *DRM provides a means of differentiating between content ownership and content possession.* In other words, just because I have a legitimate copy of the content on my computer or device does not make me the "owner" in the sense that it really belongs to me in a copyright sense.
- *DRM can provide a very fine level of granularity of access rights to digital information.* Without it you either have access to the content or you don't. But with DRM you can have the right to view, print, copy, forward, and so forth.

For many IT companies, an important driver behind the development of DRM software is the many legislative and regulatory requirements that have popped up in recent years in the area of digital information protection. Good examples are the requirements set forward by the Securities and Exchange Commission (SEC), the Healthcare Insurance Portability and Accessibility Act (HIPAA), and the Gramm-Leach-Bliley Act (GLBA—more information can be found at http://www.epic.org/privacy/glba/ and http://www.ftc.gov/privacy/glbact/). Properly implementing DRM solutions will enable organizations to better comply with these legislative and regulatory requirements.

12.2.2 RMS and XRML

In a DRM solution, the persistent protection of digital media is offered by persistent usage policies. A usage policy defines what can be done with a particular digital medium: who can do what, when this can be done, and under which conditions. Usage policies are created by the data creators or owners and remain with the data for their entire lifetime, independently of where or when the data is used or accessed.

To express these usage policies, RMS relies on the eXtensible Rights Markup Language (XrML) and more particularly on XrML licenses. An XrML license is a digital document that is linked to a digital medium. It tells the user of the medium what he or she is allowed to do with that particular medium. Linked to licenses are two key RMS processes:

- "Licensing," or the process of generating and linking licenses to digital media
- "Enforcement," or the process of ensuring that the use of the digital media adheres to the restrictions stated in the associated licenses

XrML provides a universal method for expressing licenses in a DRM environment. It is an open standard that is promoted by a company called

ContentGuard and endorsed by important IT industry players such as Microsoft and IBM. Microsoft uses XrML 1.2 in its current RMS software and plans to move to XrML version 2.0 in the next major RMS release. For more information on XrML (including the XrML version 2.0 specification), see the XrML Web site at http://www.xrml.org.

XrML is not the only DRM standard. An important competitor is the Open Digital Rights Language (ODRL)—which is very popular in the mobile world and promoted by the W3C (World Wide Web Consortium), the Open Mobile Alliance (formerly known as the WAP Forum), and companies like Nokia.

In an XrML license a usage policy is expressed in terms of trusted entities (or principals), resources (or digital media), usage rights, and usage conditions. Usage rights link certain operations on resources to trusted entities. Usage rights may be further constrained by usage conditions. A trusted entity can be a user defined in the RMS system who is allowed to read a document. It can also be a machine from which a document can be read.

A good example is a usage policy for a Word document that states that only Joe can read the document until June 2004, and that Paul is allowed to modify the document until June 2004. In this example, Joe, Paul and their respective PCs are the entitiles trusted by the RMS system. Joe's right to reaad the document and Paul's right to modify the document are examples of usage rights. These rights are further restricted by usage conditions: Joe can only read the document until June 2004; Paul can only modify it in until June 2004.

Figure 12.6 gives an example of what an XrML license looks like. This license statesthat a particular trusted entity (identified by its digital signature) can print an e-book (located at a particular URL) before December 25, 2001. The example clearly illustrates the different components of a license: trusted entity, usage right, resource, and usage condition.

The Microsoft RMS and XrML are excellent examples of solutions using hybrid cryptographic technology: They combine the power of both symmetric and asymmetric encryption technology. An XrML license contains a secured symmetric encryption key, which key is used to encrypt the digital medium the license protects. The symmetric key can only be accessed if a user is authorized to read the content of the license. Access to the content of an XrML license is secured using public and private key technology.

Figure 12.6 *XrML license example.*

```
<license>
   <grant>
      <keyHolder>                                                    Trusted Entity
         <info>
            <dsig:KeyValue>
               <dsig:RSAKeyValue>
                  <dsig:Modulus>Fa7wo6NYfmvGqy4ACSWcNmuQfbejSZx7aCibIg
                  kYswUeTCrmS0h27GJrA15SS7TYZzSfaS0xR9lZdUEF0ThO4w==
                  </dsig:Modulus>
                  <dsig:Exponent>AQABAA==</dsig:Exponent>
               </dsig:RSAKeyValue>
            </dsig:KeyValue>
         </info>
      </keyHolder>
      <cx:print/>                                                    Usage Right
      <cx:digitalWork>                                               Resource
         <cx:locator>
            <nonSecureIndirect URI="http://www.contentguard.com/sampleBook.spd"/>
         </cx:locator>
      </cx:digitalWork>
      <validityInterval>                                             Usage Condition
         <notAfter>2001-12-24T23:59:59</notAfter>
      </validityInterval>
   </grant>
</license>
```

12.2.3 RMS components

Microsoft's RMS technology consists of the following components:

- A Microsoft server-side component: the MS RMS Enrollment and Activation Web Service. This component handles the enrollment and activation of trusted RMS servers, machines, and users. It is a web service hosted and managed by Microsoft.
- *A customer server-side component:* the the RMS server (code-named "Tungsten"). This component functions as a proxy server for the enrollment and activation of RMS servers, machines, and users. It also generates WRM certificates and licenses. In the future (2004) enterprises may have to option to add a secure server appliance to the RMS server setup: this appliance will handle the RMS activation of an organization's RMS clients.

  The RMS server requires IIS 6.0 and thus only runs on top of Windows Server 2003. The RMS server engine and communication protocols are Web service–based: They make extensive use of SOAP, XML (and more particularly XrML), and SSL (HTTP over SSL) to secure the communication channels. The RMS server uses MS SQL Server 2000 with SP3 or the MS SQL Server 2000 Desktop Engine (MDSE) with SP3 to store the RMS configuration and usage policy information.
- *A client-side component:* This is a set of RMS dynamic link libraries (DLLs) and associated APIs. This component is downloadable via

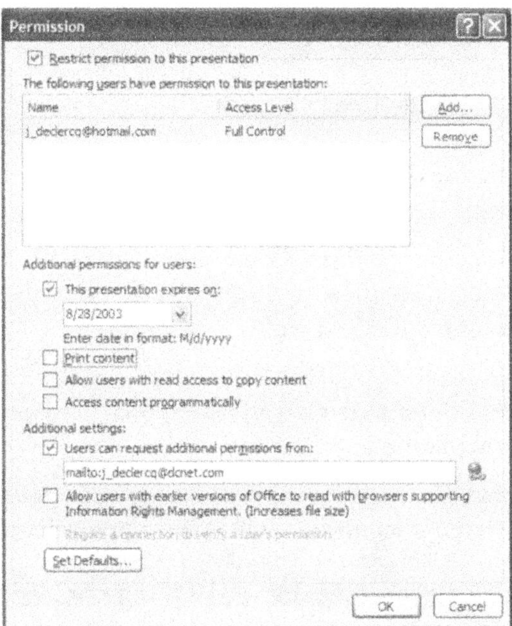

Figure 12.7 *Setting RM on PowerPoint 2003 presentation.*

Windows Update for legacy Windows platforms and will be made available in upcoming Service Packs (SPs) for MS OSs. In a first phase, Microsoft will support the following client platforms: Windows XP, Windows 2000 Service Pack 3 (and later), and Windows Server 2003.

- *RMS-enabled applications:* In order for an application to be capable of using RMS and enforce the RMS policies on the digital media with which it deals, the application must understand the RMS language. In other words, it must include extensions that allow it to talk to the RMS APIs and DLLs. All Office 2003 applications are RMS-enabled. Also, MS released an add-on to RMS-enable Internet Explorer (IE).[1] Figure 12.7 shows how you can set RMS properties on a PowerPoint 2003 presentation.

  The IE add-on, for example, allows IE to interpret rights-protected HTML files (files with *.rmh[2] extensions) and enforce the rights inside IE. Figure 12.8 shows how the look of your IE toolbar changes when you have this add-on installed. Clicking the permis-

1. Minimum supported IE version is IE 5.5.
2. rmh stands for rights-managed HTML.

Figure 12.8 *IE with RM add-on.*

sions button will bring up the RMS permissions that are linked to a particular *.rmh file.

- *An RMS server Software Development Kit (SDK):* This SDK includes tools, documentation, and sample code to enable organizations to customize the RMS server.
- *A RMS client SDK:* This SDK includes tools, documentation, and sample code to enable organizations and software vendors to RMS-enable applications.

RMS has licensing requirements for each user or device that connects to an RMS server: it requires an RMS Client Access License (CAL).

12.2.4 RMS objects: About certificates, lockboxes, licenses, revocation lists, and exclusion lists

RMS deals with the following objects: certificates, lockboxes, licenses, revocation lists, and exclusion policies. All of them are structured using XrML syntax.

Just like the certificates that we know from the Public Key Infrastructure (PKI) world, XrML certificates are used to identify trusted WRM user and machine entities. Unlike PKI certificates, they do not use an X.509 format. One of the key differences with an X.509-based certificate is that XrML certificates can also be used to securely transport private keys (and not just public keys). This is one of the X.509 deficiencies that demonstrate X.509's lack of flexibility and that explain why MS did not build on X.509 for its DRM solution.

Lockboxes are secured digital files (DLLs) that are used to securely store the private key of a RMS-enabled client machine and to provide a secure RMS execution environment on the client machine. Currently, all lockboxes are generated by the central MS RMS Activation Service. In a future RMS release, MS may provide support for an enterprise-level lockbox generation server appliance. The latter will be secured using Microsoft's Next Generation Secure Computing Base (NGSCB) technology (which was formerly known as Palladium).

Licenses are a special kind of certificate telling the users of digital data what can be done with the data, or, in other words, how they can consume the digital data. They are the most essential part of RMS: They reflect the persistent usage policies that are linked to digital data. RMS uses two types of licenses:

1. *Publishing licenses:* These are general licenses linked to digital media. They reflect the permissions as they were set by the author or the owner of the digital media. They can be generated by a RMS server or by a trusted machine possessing a Client Licensor Certificate (CLC) (explained later).

2. *Use licenses:* These are specific licenses linked to digital media. They reflect the permissions of one particular recipient or user of the digital medium. They can only be generated by an RMS server.

Revocation lists are—like certificates—very similar to the concept of a certificate revocation list (CRL) as we know it in the PKI world. It is a blacklist informing certificate users about bad certificates. A CRL tells the user of a certificate whether the certificate is still valid or still trustworthy. A certificate may end up on a CRL when its associated private key has been compromised. An exclusion policy is less restrictive than a revocation list: It only prevents entities from obtaining new licenses from a particular RMS server. Both revocation lists and exclusion policies are optional features—this is different from many PKI-enabled applications that require revocation checking.

Table 12.2 gives an overview of the concepts used in a RMS environment. The meaning of these different object types and their exact roles will become clearer in the following sections.

12.2.5 RMS information flow

Now that we have learned about the basic RMS concepts and components, let's look at how RMS information flows in a typical DRM usage example. The example in Figure 12.9 shows how an author can provide persistent protection for a document that he or she authored. This means that the author wants to make sure that only the intended recipient(s) can read the document, can forward it to other people, can print it, and so on. Note that RMS supports recipients that are outside of the organization (external) as well as recipients within the organization (internal).

Table 12.2 *WRM Objects*

WRM Object Types	Goal
Machine Certificate	■ Identifies a trusted machine. ■ Contains a unique public key for the machine. ■ Is issued by a Microsoft-hosted RMS activation web service or by an enterprise-level secure server applicance (the latter option will only be available in 2004) ■ Is distributed together with a machine lockbox.
Lockbox	■ Provides secure storage of a trusted machine's private key. ■ Provides a secure RMS execution environment on a trusted machine. ■ Consists of a set of DLLs that are stored on a trusted machine. ■ Is issued by a Microsoft-hosted RMS activation web service or by an enterprise-level secure server applicance (the latter option will only be available in 2004). ■ Is distributed together with a machine certificate.
RM Account Certificate (RAC)	■ Identifies a trusted user entity. ■ Contains a unique public-private key pair for the user. ■ Its content is secured using a machine certificate. ■ Is issued by a RMS server.
Client Licensor Certificate (CLC)	■ Identifies a trusted machine entity that is authorized to publish RMS-protected information offline (this means without contacting the RMS server). ■ A machine possessing a CLC is referred to as an offline entity. ■ Contains a unique public-private key pair for the user. ■ Its content is secured using an RAC. ■ Is issued by a RMS server
Publishing License	■ Defines the policy for obtaining a use license. ■ Contains the symmetric key used to encrypt the RMS-protected information. ■ Its content is secured using the public key of the RMS server or the offline user entity. ■ Is issued by a RMS server or an offline user entity.
Use License	■ Grants a trusted entity the permission to consume RMS-protected information as defined in the publishing license. ■ Contains the symmetric key used to encrypt the RMS-protected information. ■ Its content is secured using the public key of the RMS server or the offline user entity. ■ Is issued by a RMS server.
Revocation List	■ Names entities that are no longer trusted by the RMS system. ■ On the list entities are identified using their RMS public key.
Exclusion Policy	■ Prevents entities from obtaining new licenses from a particular RMS server. ■ Does not define an entity as "untrusted" (unlike a revocation list). ■ Exclusion can be based on a user ID, RAC, or lockbox version.

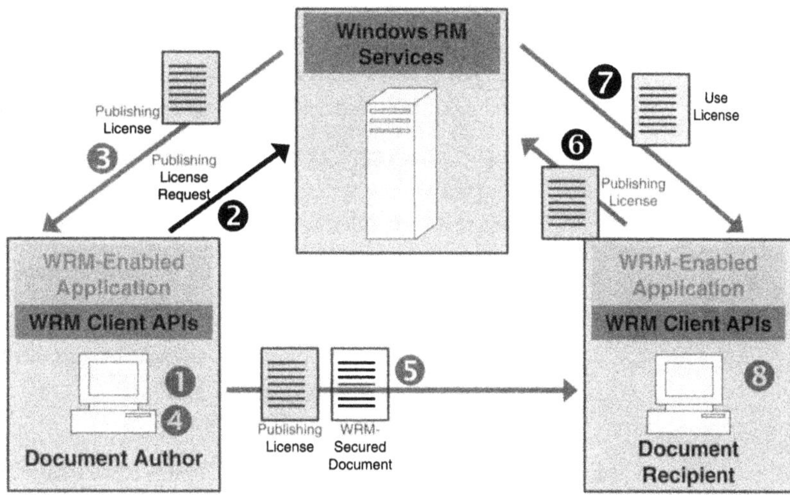

Figure 12.9 *WRM information flow.*

In this example we need the following from a RMS component point of view:

- A corporate RMS server
- This RMS server will need to communicate with the MS RMS Enrollment and Activation web services (not shown in Figure 12.9).
- A set of clients that have the RMS APIs and DLLs installed (distributed via Windows Update or a Service Pack)
- Every client must have a RMS-enabled application: In this example we would need a RMS-enabled Word application that is capable of adding RMS data to documents and enforcing RMS restrictions on documents.

A WRM-secured document exchange would include the following information exchanges between the different components:

1. The author creates a document using a RMS-enabled application (e.g., MS Word 2003) and adds a set of document usage rights and conditions. To identify recipients, the author can use the recipients' AD or MS Passport accounts. An interesting detail is that Passport accounts are not trusted by default.[3]

3. The accounts that are considered trustworthy in an RMS setup are configured on the RMS server. RMS also allows you to create RMS federations with other RMS installations or MS Passport.

2. The RMS-enabled application generates a symmetric encryption key to secure the document's content and sends it together with the usage rights and conditions to the RMS server. The latter message also contains a publishing license request.
3. The RMS server generates a publishing license: It encrypts the symmetric key with its public key. It then returns the publishing license to the RMS-enabled application.
4. The RMS-enabled application encrypts the document with the symmetric key and links the publishing license to the document.
5. The author distributes the RMS-secured document to a recipient, who receives the document and opens it using a RMS-enabled application (e.g., MS Word 2003).
6. The RMS-enabled application sends a request for a use license to the RMS server. This use license request includes the publishing license and the recipient's RMS Account Certificate (RAC). The latter is used to authenticate the recipient to the RMS server.
7. The RMS server checks the recipient's identity, validates that the recipient is authorized to read the file, and creates a use license. During this process the RMS server extracts the symmetric encryption key from the publishing license (using its private key) and reencrypts it using the recipient's public key (extracted from the recipient's RAC). The RMS server then returns the use license to the recipient's computer.
8. The RMS-enabled application renders the RMS-secured document and enforces the usage restrictions.

This example shows an online RMS information flow where the RMS client communicates in real time with a RMS server. RMS can also work in offline mode—at least to generate publishing licenses.

The offline operation mode is possible if the client's computer has been issued a Client Licensor Certificate (CLC) by the RMS server. In that case the client's computer will be capable of generating the publishing license. In this case the symmetric encryption key is stored twice in the publishing license: once encrypted with the RMS server's public key, and once encrypted with the public key held in the CLC. When the recipient gets the publishing license, it will use it to request a use license to the RMS server that issued the CLC certificate (the publishing license issued by a CLC includes a URL pointing to its issuing RMS server). Note that working in offline mode only works for generating publishing licenses: Generating use licenses requires an online RMS server.

12.2.6 RMS setup and enrollment

RMS setup and enrollment differ for the different RMS components. Table 12.3 gives an overview of the enrollment procedures. Two important setup details are the following:

1. The setup of the first RMS Server for an organization requires communication with MS RMS Enrollment Service—which is a secure Web service Microsoft that makes available on the Internet. Subsequent enterprise RMS servers are configured based on the first RMS server's configuration information. Their installation does not require additional communication with the MS Enrollment web service.

2. The setup of any RMS enabled client computer requires communication with the MS RMS Activation web service or with the enterprise-level secure activation appliance. Remember that the latter option will only be available in 2004.

Table 12.3 *RMS Enrollment Procedures*

WRM Entity	Enrollment Procedure
First RMS server	Contacts the MS RMS Enrollment web service for a RMS licensor certificate. Outcome of this enrollment process is a RMS licensor certificate.
Subsequent RMS servers	Takes existing configuration from first customer RMS server. Does not need to contact the MS RMS Enrollment web server.
Client computers	Gets RMS code (APIs and DLLs) via Windows Update or Service Pack. Contacts local RMS server for enrollment and activation. The local RMS server contacts the MS RMS Activation web service for client activation or, if an enterprise secure activation appliance is available, contacts the appliance (remember, the latter option will only be available in 2004). Outcome of this enrollment process is a RMS Machine Certificate.
Users	Requires availability of an activated RMS client computer. Talks to local RMS server for enrollment. Outcome of this enrollment process is a RMS Account Certificate (RAC).
Client computers authorized for offline publishing	Talks to local RMS server for enrollment. Outcome of this enrollment process is Client Licensor Certificate (CLC).

Microsoft claims that during the enrollment and activation processes no information is persisted on the MS RMS servers. Also, the cryptographic keys involved in these exchanges are not used in subsequent licensing operations. In other words, if MS can never decrypt information protected by an organization's RMS setup.

13

Introducing Windows Server 2003 Public Key Infrastructure

This chapter is the first chapter on Windows Server 2003 PKI in this book. In this chapter we will look at the added value of using Microsoft Windows Server 2003 PKI as the building block for advanced IT security in your organization. We will also take a closer look at all of its core components: the certificate server, the CryptoAPI, the Data Protection API, and the Active Directory.

13.1 Getting started

Reading this chapter requires a good understanding of the general concepts of cryptography (and particularly asymmetric cryptography) and public key infrastructure (PKI). Good introductions to cryptography and PKI are available in the following books:

- *Understanding Public-Key Infrastructure* by Carlisle Adams and Steve Lloyd (Macmillan, 1999).
- *Planning for PKI: Best Practices Guide for Deploying Public Key Infrastructure* by Russ Housley and Tim Polk (John Wiley, 2001).
- *PKI: Implementing and Managing E-Security* by Andrew Nash (McGraw-Hill, 2001).
- *Introduction to the Public Key Infrastructure for the Internet* by Messaoud Benantar (Prentice Hall, 2001).

13.2 A short history of Windows PKI

With the release of Windows Server 2003, Microsoft ships version 3 of its PKI software. Figure 13.1 shows a timeline of the Microsoft PKI software versions and the different NT releases.

Figure 13.1 *Microsoft Windows NT and PKI timeline.*

1993	Windows NT 3.1	-
1994	Windows NT 3.5	-
1995	Windows NT 3.51	-
1996	Windows NT4	-
1998	NT 4 Option Pack	MS CA/PKI v1
2000	Windows 2000	MS CA/PKI v2
2003	Windows Server 2003	MS CA/PKI v3
200x	Windows "Longhorn"	MS CA/PKI v4
200x	Windows "Blackcomb"	MS CA/PKI v5

Microsoft's original Certificate Authority (CA) software, which became available as part of the Windows NT 4.0 Option Pack, is a basic PKI solution that many administrators use to generate Secure Sockets Layer (SSL) or Secure Mail (S/MIME) certificates.

Windows 2000 contains an updated CA product that offers Active Directory integration capabilities, enhanced scalability, and support for multilevel PKI hierarchies. Still, the Win2K CA software lacks important features, such as granular PKI-administration capabilities (e.g., the ability to delegate permission to an administrator to approve certificate issuance for only a specific group of users), advanced certificate- and CA-configuration features (e.g., features that let you change certificate-content layout or set advanced CA-auditing options), and the ability to easily build custom PKI-enabled applications to extend and reuse the PKI platform. These shortcomings have prevented some large companies from deploying a Windows-based PKI.

The Windows Server 2003 PKI, which Microsoft has designed to work in conjunction with XP and other downlevel Windows client systems, counters most of the drawbacks of earlier Windows PKIs. The Windows Server 2003 PKI supports features such as cross-certification (as well as hierarchical certification), qualified subordination, customizable certificate templates, centralized key archiving and key recovery, user autoenrollment, and delta certificate revocation lists (CRLs). It also provides enhanced role separation, administrative delegation, and auditing options. All the new Windows Server 2003 PKI features and more are explained in greater detail in this and the next chapters.

The upcoming release of the Windows Server 2003 operating system (code-named Longhorn and Blackcomb) will contain further enhancements to Microsoft's PKI software.

13.3 Why use the Microsoft PKI software?

Version 3 of Microsoft's PKI software is more scalable, flexible, and extensible than its Windows 2000 and NT4 Option Pack predecessors. The following is a summary of the main arguments supporting the choice for Windows Server 2003 PKI over another PKI product.

- *Scalability:* Windows Server 2003 PKI software has almost unlimited scalability when it comes to the number of certificates a single CA can issue. Microsoft did tests where more than 35 million certificates were issued on a single CA—they were issued at a rate of about 60 certificates per second. An explanation for this high level of scalability can partially be found in the fact that in Windows 2000 Microsoft adapted JET Blue technology for the CA database. Another important scalability factor is the full support for multiple-level CA hierarchies, consisting of a root CA and multiple levels (up to 40) of subordinate CAs. The NT 4 Option Pack PKI software only supported two-level hierarchies.
- *Flexibility:* The Windows Server 2003 CA service can be installed in two modes: enterprise or stand-alone. Each mode is built to fit particular enterprise security needs. Compared to versions 1 and 2, the Windows Server 2003 CA service offers much more configuration options. One of the greatest features of Windows Server 2003 PKI is that an administrator has complete control over what is contained in a Windows Server 2003 certificate (through the use of editable certificate templates).
- *Interoperability:* Microsoft PKI supports the major open PKI standards: ITU-T X.509, IETF PKIX, and PKCS.[1] Windows Server 2003 PKI supports a wide range of cryptographic algorithms: RSA, DSA, RC4, AES, and so forth. A Windows Server 2003 CA can also be integrated relatively easily with PKI software from other vendors. To test specific interoperability scenarios and issues, Microsoft has been actively participating in interoperability initiatives such as the European Electronic Messaging Association's pki Challenge (more information can be found at http://www.eema.org).
- *Extensibility:* The Windows Server 2003 CA is extensible. Its policy and exit modules can be customized to meet an enterprise's specific CA needs. To meet advanced security requirements, the Windows Server 2003 CA can be linked to hardware security modules (HSM).

1. Appendix 2 gives an overview of the different Public Key Cryptography Standard (PKCS) standards.

Windows Server 2003 also comes with new facilities that can be used to easily PKI-enable an application: A good example is the support for CAPICOM.

- *Reduced TCO:* Windows Server 2003 PKI allows an organization to leverage the investments made in an enterprise AD infrastructure. Ideally, the PKI design should be run in parallel with the AD design.
- *Pricing:* An important argument that has been present since the first releases of Windows PKI and a competitive ace that Microsoft will continue to play is the low cost of the Windows PKI products. Although it is true that advanced PKI products such as Entrust and Baltimore PKI offer some interesting features that are still not available in Windows Server 2003 PKI, we should not forget that the opposite is also true: Features such as machine- and user-autoenrollment are not supported by all advanced PKI products. An interesting detail is that in this release Microsoft's CA software is only included with Windows Server 2003 Enterprise Server (formerly known as Windows 2000 Advanced Server) and Windows Server 2003 Datacenter Server.

Although the Windows Server 2003 PKI might not yet offer all the capabilities of more advanced products (like Entrust, Baltimore, or Smarttrust PKI), its affordability might make it attractive to a lot of smaller companies. Given Windows Server 2003 PKI's low cost and enhanced features, it might well be the product that brings PKI to the masses. Although Windows PKI is not a fully proven technology—an important requirement for success in enterprises with high-end security requirements—the software will probably prove itself as it matures over the years and as more organizations adopt it. In the meantime, this upgrade to the Windows PKI is worthy of serious consideration.

13.4 Windows Server 2003 PKI core components

In the following sections we look in detail at the core components of Windows Server 2003 and XP PKI: the certificate server, Active Directory, the CryptoAPI, certificates, and the Data Protection API.

13.4.1 Certificate Server

In this section we focus on the architecture of Microsoft's Certificate Server; in Chapter 16 we return to the specific configuration options of Certificate Server.

The Windows Server 2003 certificate server provides the following core services: It receives and processes certificate requests, it identifies and validates certificate requests, it issues certificates according to the security policy, it renews and revokes certificates, it publishes certificates, it creates and publishes CRLs, and it logs all certificate and CRL transactions into a log database. A brand-new function of the Windows Server 2003 CA is that it can also take care of secure private key archival.

Certificate Server architecture

The architecture of the Microsoft Certificate Server is illustrated in Figure 13.2. It is largely identical to the one that was used in the previous editions of the Certificate Server. An architectural feature not available in previous versions is that the CA database layout has been modified to let the CA cope with private key archival and recovery.

At the heart of the Windows Certificate Server sits an engine (certsrv.exe) that generates certificates and CRLs and directs the message flow between the other components. The engine communicates with three important modules: the entry, policy, and exit module.

- The *entry module* accepts PKCS10 and CMC formatted certificate requests. Its only job is to place these requests in a queue for treatment by the policy module.
- The *policy module* implements and enforces the CA policy rules as set forward by the CA administrator. It informs the CA engine about the

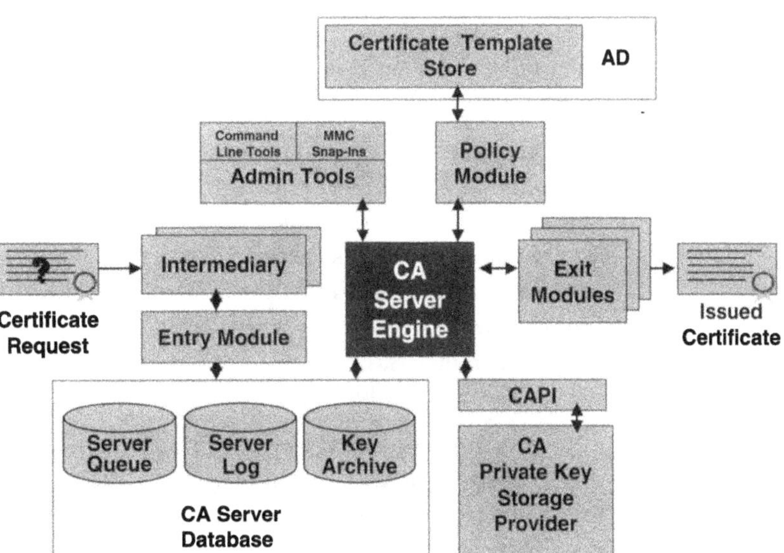

Figure 13.2 *Certificate Server architecture.*

layout of a certificate and decides if a certificate request should be issued, denied, or left pending. To make the latter decision and to retrieve certificate layout information, the policy module can call on information stored in a directory or database. Windows Server 2003 comes with a policy module (called certpdef.dll) that supports two policy types: the enterprise policy and the stand-alone policy. Details on the two policy types are discussed later in this chapter. To check out the policy module installed on your CA, look at its properties (Policy Module tab) in the Certification Authority MMC snap-in.

- The *exit module* distributes and publishes certificates, certificate chains, CRLs, and delta CRLs. The exit module can write PKI data to a file or transport it across HTTP or RPC to a remote location. The Windows Server 2003 CA can support multiple exit modules. This enables it to publish and distribute certificates, certificate chains, CRLs, and delta CRLs to different locations in parallel: LDAP directories, file shares, Web directories, or even ODBC-compliant databases. The default Windows Server 2003 CA exit module (called certxds.dll) comes with LDAP, FTP, HTTP, and SMTP support. The last protocol was not supported in the Windows 2000 CA. It allows the CA to automatically send notification messages to PKI users and administrators. To check out the exit modules installed on your CA, look at its properties (Exit Module tab) in the Certification Authority MMC snap-in.

The exit and policy modules are both customizable and replaceable. If the policy module or the exit module does not correspond to the needs of an organization, it can develop modules in C++ or Visual Basic (VB) and plug them into the CA architecture. All this is documented in the Windows Server 2003 platform SDK.

The policy and exit modules can be configured using the Certification Authority MMC snap-in or using the certutil command-line utility. Using the properties of the CA-object in the Certification Authority MMC snap-in, you can do things like add another exit module, configure X.509 certificate extensions [CRL and delta CRL distribution (CDP) and Authority Information Access (AIA) points], and configure CRL and delta CRL publication parameters. I will return to the configuration capabilities of the certutil utility later in this book.

The Certificate Server obviously has its proper database and administration interfaces. It also interacts with entities known as intermediaries to communicate with PKI clients and the CryptoAPI to access the CA private key storage provider.

- The certificate server uses a database to store certificate transactions and status information, certificates, and optionally archived private keys. The database (<CAName>.edb) is by default located in the system32\certlog folder. The Certificate Server engine communicates with its database through the certdb.dll. In the Windows 2000 release of Certificate Server, Microsoft changed its database technology to JET Blue. The same technology is used for Active Directory and the Exchange databases. This switch gave the Windows 2000 CA a scalability injection.

- Windows Server 2003 CA management is primarily done from the Certification Authority MMC snap-in. Another option is to use the certutil.exe command-line utility. Both administration tools communicate with CA engine using the certadm.dll.

- Applications that help the client in generating correctly formatted PKCS10 or CMC certificate request files are known as intermediaries or Registration Authorities (RAs). An intermediary or RA gathers user-specific and request-specific data that are required for a valid certificate request. For example, a request that is sent to a Windows Server 2003 Enterprise CA should mention a certificate template. An intermediate can add a template specification to the request. Intermediaries are bound to a specific transport protocol. Thanks to this, the CA engine does not need to deal with different transport providers.

  Examples of Windows Server 2003 intermediaries are the Web enrollment pages—an HTTP intermediary—and the MMC Certificates snap-in, which calls on the Certificate Request Wizard—an RPC intermediary. The HTTP intermediary calls on the xenroll.dll to generate private keys on the client machine and the scenroll.dll to generate private keys on a smart card. The RPC intermediary calls on the certcli.dll to perform these tasks. Examples of third-party RA software are discussed later in this chapter.

- For all cryptographic functions—including accessing and using the CA's private key—the CA calls on the CryptoAPI (CAPI). The CA's private key can be stored on hard disk or on a dedicated hardware device [such as a Hardware Security Module (HSM)].

CA installation modes

When you install a Windows Server 2003 Certificate Server, you have the following installation options: You can install it as a root or a subordinate CA, or you can install it as an enterprise (AD integrated) or stand-alone CA (non-AD integrated). Installing the Certificate Server in Enterprise mode provides full integration with Active Directory. It activates the Enterprise mode of the Windows Server 2003 CA policy module. Let's look now at what this really means and how this is different from a CA installed in stand-alone mode.

Comparing the two CA installation modes

Installation requirements To install a CA in enterprise mode, two requirements must be met:

1. The account installing the CA should be an Enterprise administrator and a domain administrator of the root domain of the AD forest.
2. The server on which the Enterprise CA is installed should be a member of a domain with a functioning AD.

If one of these two conditions is not met, the enterprise mode installation options will be grayed out during the CA installation, and you will only be able to install the CA in stand-alone mode.

To install a stand-alone CA, no AD is required; you can install it on a stand-alone server, member server, or domain controller. Also, there is no need for the account performing the installation to be an enterprise or domain administrator—local machine administrator permissions are sufficient. If you do install a stand-alone CA using enterprise administrator privileges, the CA will offer some additional features. For example, if an enterprise administrator installs it on a member server that is joined to the domain, the stand-alone CA will publish the certificates it issues to the AD.

Use of certificate templates An enterprise Certificate Server uses the certificate templates that are stored in the AD configuration naming context. Certificate templates define the content and characteristics of a certificate. Windows Server 2003 PKI supports version 2 certificate templates. Contrary to version 1 templates, version 2 templates are fully customizable. Certificate templates also provide a way to control which certificate types an enterprise CA can issue and which users can request which certificate type to an enterprise CA. Certificate templates are explained in detail in Section 13.4.4, "Certificates."

A stand-alone CA cannot use AD certificate templates. As a consequence, you cannot set which user can get which certificate type(s) from it. By default, a stand-alone CA can only issue Web authentication (SSL, TLS), e-mail protection (S/MIME), server authentication, code signing, time-stamp signing, and IPsec certificates. You can, however, modify the stand-alone CA's Web interface (to list other certificate types) or simply request other certificate types using special OID values that are stored in a certificate's Extended Key Usage (EKU) X.509 extension.

Information retrieval for certificate requests An enterprise CA retrieves user information from the AD during certificate enrollment. This information is used to populate certain certificate fields. For example, a certificate issued by an enterprise CA contains a reference to a user's user principal name (UPN) in the certificate's SubjectAltName X.509 field.

Because a stand-alone CA has no access to AD, user identification information that is required for the certificate must be filled in manually by the user on the CA's enrollment Web site.

For both enterprise and stand-alone CAs, you can change the default values that are added to a certificate request at enrollment time. You can do so by editing the certdat.inc file that is located in the %SystemRoot%\system32\certsrv directory. You can change the default values for the following certificate entries: sDefaultCompany, sDefaultOrgUnit, sDefaultLocality, sDefaultState, and sDefaultCountry.

Automated certificate enrollment support An enterprise certificate server supports automated certificate enrollment, or in short certificate autoenrollment. In Windows Server 2003, the latter feature has been extended to cover both users and machines. Automated certificate enrollment is explained in greater detail in Chapter 15.

A user who wants a certificate from a stand-alone CA has to start the enrollment process himself or herself. No automation is provided.

Certificate request approval An enterprise Certificate Server can support automatic or manual certificate request approval. Request-handling properties can be set in the properties of an enterprise CA (use the properties of the policy module) or in the properties of a version 2 certificate template (use the Issuance Requirements tab). In the first case it will apply to all certificates the CA issues, but in the second case only to one particular certificate type (as defined in the template).

The same options are available for a Windows Server 2003 stand-alone CA. The only difference is that a stand-alone CA cannot use certificate templates, and as a consequence request-handling properties cannot be set for individual certificate templates.

Certificate and CRL publication An Enterprise CA uses the Active Directory to store and publish certificates, CRLs, and delta CRLs. Each certificate published in the AD is automatically mapped to the Windows account of its requestor. The certificate is added to the multivalued usercertificate attribute of the user object. Not every certificate generated by an enterprise CA is automatically published in the AD. Examples of certificates that are not automatically published are an enrollment agent or a CTL signing certificate.

A stand-alone CA can publish the issued certificates to AD, but not automatically as a part of the certificate enrollment process. You can obviously publish the certificates manually to the AD.

Centralized key archival An enterprise CA supports centralized key archival in the CA database, a standalone CA doesn't.

Conclusion

Enterprise mode typically targets enterprise certificate users that have an AD user account and that authenticated to your AD infrastructure using the Kerberos protocol. Stand-alone mode, on the other hand, is clearly targeting external users (like extranet users) that do not have an internal Windows account.

Table 13.1 compares the default characteristics of a Windows Server 2003 stand-alone and enterprise CA.

Registration authorities

In large PKI setups, PKI users use a Registration Authority as the primary point of contact for a CA. An RA typically deals with PKI user identification and enrollment. Like its predecessors, Windows Server 2003 PKI does not include a true Registration Authority function.

Windows Server 2003 supports some limited RA functionalities through special "Enrollment agent" certificates (OID 1.3.6.1.4.1.311.20.2.1—Certificate Request Agent). Enrollment agent certificates can be used for:

- *Smart card bulk enrollment:* Administrators with a special Certificate Request Agent certificate can bulk enroll users' certificates on smart cards and act as a registration authority for smart card certificates.
- *Integration with the Exchange Key Management Server (KMS):* If your organization has implemented Exchange advanced mail security

Table 13.1 *Windows Server 2003 Stand-Alone Versus Enterprise CA*

Windows Server 2003 Stand-Alone CA	Windows Server 2003 Enterprise CA
Non-AD integrated.	AD integrated.
Extranet and Internet certificate user oriented.	Intranet certificate user oriented.
Can issue a limited set of certificate types and certificates requiring a custom OID in their EKU extension; does not support certificate templates.	Can issue all Windows Server 2003 certificates defined in the Windows Server 2003 certificate templates MMC snap-in. Supports version 1 (Windows 2000 PKI) and version 2 (Windows Server 2003 PKI) certificate templates.
User enrollment interface is Web-based. You can also use the certreq.exe command-line utility.	User enrollment can be done using a Web interface or using the MMC Certificates snap-in. Enrollment can also happen automatically using the certificate autoenrollment feature. You can also use the certreq.exe command-line utility.
Communication with the CA front-end is occurring across HTTP or HTTPs.	Communication with the CA front-end can use RPC/DCOM or HTTP/HTTPs.
User has to enter identification information manually at certificate request time.	User identification information is automatically retrieved from Active Directory.
Certificate enrollment approval happens automatic or manual. The CA has a single setting that controls this behavior for all certificate types.	Certificate enrollment approval happens automatic or manual. This behavior can be controlled globally on the CA level or per certificate type using a certificate template setting. Also, the certificate approval process can use the AD authentication and access control model through the ACLs that are set on certificate templates.
The certificate is downloaded to the user profile when it is manually retrieved from the CA Web site. By default, the CA does not publish certificates to AD.	Depending on the certificate template, the certificate is automatically downloaded to the user profile and/or published to AD.
CRL and CA certificate can be published manually to AD.	CRLs, Delta CRLs, CA, and cross-certification certificates are automatically published to AD.
Does not automatically support AD based certificate lookup and retrieval.	Supports AD-based certificate lookup and retrieval.
Can be installed on Windows Server 2003 Domain Controller, Member server, or stand-alone server (not a member of any domain).	Can be installed on Windows Server 2003 Domain Controller or Member server. No support for centralized key archival in the CA database. Supports centralized key archival in the CA database.

Table 13.2 *RA Software for Windows Server 2003 PKI*

Company Name (Web Site)	Product Name	Key Features
Alacris (http://www.alacris.ocm)	idNexus	■ Web-based RA administration interface ■ Smart card enrollment support ■ Advanced reporting capabilities
Spyrus (http://www.spyrus.com)	SignalRA	■ MMC-based RA administration interface ■ HSM support ■ Smart card and security token enrollment and management support ■ Advanced reporting capabilities ■ Dedicated audit log (SQL Server Database)

(S/MIME) in combination with Microsoft Certificate Server, the Exchange Key Management Server acts as an RA. It identifies users and passes the certificate requests to the Windows 2000 CA.

Advanced RA support for Windows Server 2003 PKI is available from third-party software vendors. Some examples are mentioned in Table 13.2, which does not provide an exhaustive list of RA software—also, it is not the goal of this book to provide a feature comparison between the different RA software products.

The reason why Microsoft did not include an RA function with the Windows Server 2003 OS probably has to do with the high level of customization that is required to fit an RA to an organization's needs. One organization may require that the RA is linked to its ERM system, another one may require smart card enrollment and life-cycle management integration, and yet another one may require integration with its building access control mechanism. Some regions also have special legal requirements for an RA function: The European Union, for example, imposes very strict rules for the implementation of an RA that is dealing with qualified certificates and certificates that are used for advanced digital signatures.

13.4.2 Active directory

A PKI uses a directory to store certificate revocation lists (CRLs), delta CRLs, user, CA, and cross-certification certificates. When setting up a Windows Server 2003 PKI, the Active Directory is an obvious directory choice. AD is the only possible directory option if you want to take advantage of some typical Window.NET AD-based PKI features (like the use of

Microsoft enterprise CAs, certificate templates, and so forth) or "easily" implement certain PKI-enabled applications (like Windows smart card logon). This does not mean that it is impossible to implement PKI-enabled applications such as Windows smart card logon using another non-Microsoft directory: When using another directory, it may simply cost more time and effort to set up and maintain the PKI-enabled application.

Windows Server 2003 PKI in general is very tightly integrated with AD. A nice example of this integration is the use group policy objects to distribute trusted CA information to Windows 2000 or Windows XP Professional workstations. As explained in the previous sections, this integration is very tight when deploying Windows Server 2003 enterprise Certificate Servers. In that case Windows Server 2003 PKI also uses AD to store CA- and PKI-related configuration information.

PKI-related AD entries

Table 13.3 shows the Windows Server 2003 PKI-specific information that is added to the Active Directory and where it is created. Compared to Windows 2000 PKI, AD contains two brand-new PKI-related containers: the KRA and OID containers. Also, Windows Server 2003 PKI comes out of box with more predefined certificate templates: 29 instead of 24 in Windows 2000 PKI. Table 13.4 shows when this information is added to the Active Directory.

Table 13.3 *Windows Server 2003 PKI Information Stored in AD*

Object Distinguished Name (DN)	Object Class	PKI-Related Attributes
CN=<*CA Name*>, CN=AIA, CN=Public Key Services, CN=Services	CertificationAuthority	AuthorirityRevocationList CaCertificate CaCertificateDN CaConnect CertificateRevocationList CrossCertificatePair DeltaRevocationList
CN=<*CA Name*>,CN=<*Servername*>, CN=CDP, CN=Public Key Services, CN=Services	CRLDistributionPoint	AuthorityRevocationList CertificateAuthorityObject CertificateRevocationList DeltaRevocationList

Table 13.3 *Windows Server 2003 PKI Information Stored in AD (continued)*

Object Distinguished Name (DN)	Object Class	PKI-Related Attributes
CN=<*Certificate Template Name*>, CN=Certificate Templates, CN=Public Key Services, CN=Services)	PKICertificateTemplate	MsPKI-Certificate-Application-Policy MsPKI-Certificate-Name-Flag MsPKI-Certificate-Policy MsPKI-Cert-Template-OID MsPKI-Enrollment-Flag MsPKI-Minimal-Key-Size MsPKI-Private-Key-Flag MsPKI-RA-Policies MsPKI-RA-Signature MsPKI-Supersede-Templates MsPKI-Template-MinorRevision MsPKI-Template-Schema-Version Pkicriticalextensions Pkidefaultcsps Pkidefaultkeyspec Pkienrollmentaccess Pkiexpireationperiod Pkiextendedkeyusage Pkikeyusage Pkimaxissuingdepth Pkioverlapperiod
CN=<*CA Name*>, CN=Certification Authorities, CN=Public Key Services, CN=Services	CertificationAuthority	AuthorityRevocationList Cacertificate CacertificateDN CaConnect Certificaterevocationlist CrossCertificatePair DeltaRevocationList
CN=<*CA Name*>, CN=Enrollment Services, CN=Public Key Services, CN=Services	PKIEnrollmentService	Cacertificate CacertificateDN Certificate Templates
CN=<*CA Name*>, CN=KRA, CN=Public Key Services, CN=Services	msPKI-PrivateKey RecoveryAgent	Usercertificate

Table 13.3 *Windows Server 2003 PKI Information Stored in AD (continued)*

Object Distinguished Name (DN)	Object Class	PKI-Related Attributes
CN=NTAuthCertificates, CN=Public Key Services, CN=Services	CertificationAuthority	AuthorityRevocationList CaCertificate CacertificateDN CaConnectCertificaterevocationlist CrossCertificatePair DeltaRevocationList
CN=<*OID Name*>, CN=OID, CN=Public Key Services, CN=Services	msPKI-Enterprise-OID	MsPKI-OID-Attribute MsPKI-OID-CPS MsPKI-OIDLocalizedName MsPKI-OID-User-Notice
Domain and Global Catalog User Object	User	UserCert (single-valued attribute) UserCertificate (multivalued attribute) UserSMIMECertificate (multivalued attribute)

Table 13.4 *Creation of PKI-Related Information in AD*

Action	Add Stand-Alone Root CA	Add Enterprise Root CA	Add Stand-Alone SubCA	Add Enterprise SubCA	Install First Enterprise CA in Forest
CA Object in AIA Container	Yes	Yes	Yes	Yes	Yes
CDP Object in CDP Container	Yes	Yes	Yes	Yes	Yes
Certificate Template Object in Certificate Templates Container	No	No	No	No	Yes
CA Object in Certification Authorities Container	Yes	Yes	No	No	Yes
Enrollment Service Object in Enrollment Services Container	Yes	Yes	Yes	Yes	Yes
KRA Object in KRA Container	Yes	Yes	Yes	Yes	Yes
CA certificate added to CACertificate Attribute of NTAuthCertificates Object	No	Yes	No	Yes	Yes
OID Object in OID Container	No	No	No	No	Yes

The official PKIX LDAP and directory schema extensions can be found in the IETF's RFC 2587 and 2256 and the Internet draft titled "Internet X.509 Public Key Infrastructure LDAP Schema and Syntaxes for PKIs." RFC 2587 describes some of the PKI subschema applicable to LDAPv2 servers. RFC 2256 describes some of the PKI-related subschema elements for LDAPv3 servers. The Internet draft supercedes both RFC2587 and RFC 2256 and provides the complete PKI subschema for LDAP v3 servers.

The AIA container contains a CA object for every CA (root or subordinate, enterprise or stand-alone CAs) that is located on a server that is a member of the Windows Server 2003 forest. Every CA object has a CaCertificate attribute holding the CA certificate and the CA certificate history. The Authority Information Access (AIA) certificate is used during certificate validation to locate CA certificates. Every certificate issued by a Windows Server 2003 enterprise CA contains an LDAP pointer to the CA object in the AD AIA container.

The CDP container is the Active Directory CRL and delta CRL Distribution Point (CDP) that allows PKI users to download the latest CRLs and delta CRLs from AD. The CDP container contains one subcontainer for every Windows Server 2003 server in the forest that has a CA installed. Every server container holds a CDP object that is named after the CA running on that server. The CDP object holds CRLs in its CertificateRevocationList attribute and delta CRLs in its DeltaRevocationList attribute. The CDP object is created independent of whether the CA is a root or a subordinate, an enterprise or a stand-alone CA. Every certificate issued by a Windows Server 2003 enterprise CA contains an LDAP CDP pointer to an AD CDP object.

The Certificate Templates container contains all certificate template definitions—both for version 1 and version 2 certificate templates. They are added to the AD's configuration naming context when the first enterprise CA is installed in the Windows Server 2003 forest. The ACL that is set on the template objects allows or disallows a user or group to enroll and/or autoenroll for a particular certificate type. Note that because a template's definition and ACL settings are part of the configuration naming context, they can be defined only once, for an entire forest.

The Certification Authorities container holds a CA object for every root enterprise or stand-alone CA in the Windows Server 2003 forest. Every CA object holds the CA certificate and certificate history in its CaCertificate attribute. The Certification Authorities container holds all CAs that are considered trust anchors for all the users in a Windows Server 2003 forest. The concept of trust anchors is explained in more detail in Chapter 14.

The Enrollment Services container contains a PKIEnrollmentService object for every CA (root or subordinate, enterprise or stand-alone CAs) in the Windows Server 2003 forest. The object is named after the CA to which it is linked. Every object's "certificate templates" attribute lists the certificate templates that a particular CA supports and for which PKI users can enroll at that CA. For a stand-alone CA this attribute is empty. The Enrollment Services container can be used by Windows PKI-enabled applications to locate a machine that is hosting a CA in a Windows Server 2003 forest. The permissions that are set on a CA's PKIEnrollmentService object are critical in order for users or machines to be able to locate a CA. If a user or machine does not have read permission on this object, it will not be able to find the CA.

The KRA container contains an msPKI-PrivateKeyRecoveryAgent object for every CA (root or subordinate, enterprise or stand-alone CAs) in the Windows Server 2003 forest. The object is named after the CA to which it is linked. Every object holds the certificates of the key recovery agents that are defined on a particular CA in its usercertificate attribute.

The NTAuthCertificates Object is used to determine which enterprise CAs in a Windows Server 2003 forest are authorized to issue smart card logon and other logon certificates. The authorized CAs' certificates are stored in the NTAuthCertificates object's CaCertificate attribute.

The OID container contains all PKI-related object identifiers (OIDs) and their characteristics that are defined in a Windows Server 2003 forest. They are added to the AD's configuration naming context when the first enterprise CA is installed in the Windows Server 2003 forest.

If a CA is removed from your Windows 2000 or Windows Server 2003 forest, the CA object in the Enrollment Services container will be removed. All of the other AD entries remain. This will make it impossible for PKI clients to request new certificates from the CA, while still giving them the ability to retrieve the CA's certificate, CRLs, and delta CRLs. If you want to remove all AD entries related to a particular CA from the AD, use the following certutil command-line command:

```
certutil -delds <CAName>
```

User certificates that an enterprise CA automatically publishes to AD are stored in a user object's multivalued "UserCertificate" (as specified in the PKIX LDAP schema extensions). User certificates stored in the AD affect the size of the AD database. The average size of one certificate is about 1,200 bytes.

Querying AD for PKI-related information

To look at the PKI and CA related entries in the AD configuration naming context of your Windows Server 2003 forest, you can use several tools:

- The certutil command-line tool with the "-v -ds" switch
- The Sites and Services MMC snap-in: All PKI-related configuration naming context entries are visible from the Public Key Services container (as illustrated in Figure 13.3).
- The ADSIEdit tool (coming with the Windows Server 2003 Support tools)
- The LDP tool (coming with the Windows Server 2003 Support tools)
- The PKIView tool (coming with the Windows Server 2003 Resource Kit): This tool can retrieve the content of the AIA, CDP, KRA, Certification Authorities, Enrollment Services, and NTAuthCertificates AD containers (as illustrated in Figure 13.4).

To query AD for user certificates, you can use the Search\For People... function available from the Windows Server 2003 or Windows XP start menu. The last tab of the user object properties is named Digital IDs and

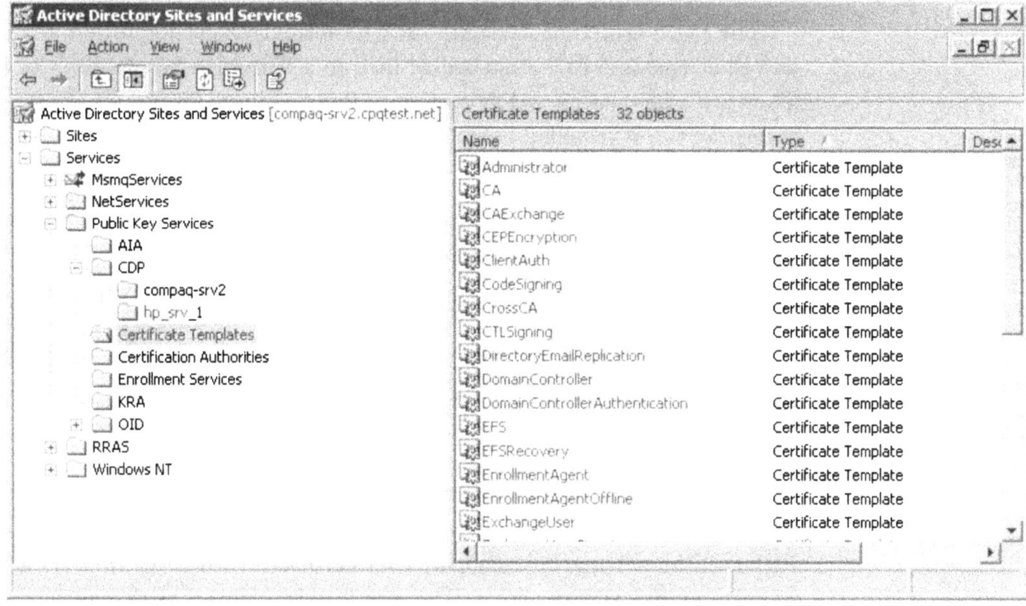

Figure 13.3 *Querying AD for PKI-related information using the Sites and Services MMC snap-in.*

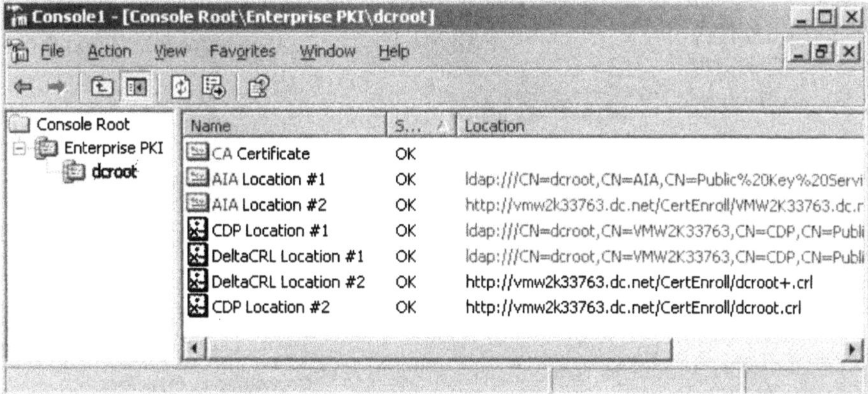

Figure 13.4 *PKIView tool.*

contains all the user certificates that are published in AD. The same interface can be used to export certificates to a file; afterward you can import the certificate-file into your personal certificate store.

13.4.3 CryptoAPI and cryptographic service providers

The CryptoAPI is an Application Programming Interface (API) that comes bundled with the Windows Server 2003 and XP operating systems. It enables programmers to add cryptography-based security services, such as authentication, confidentiality, and integrity protection, relatively easily to their applications. It also enables them to interact with certificates, private keys, and their secure storage providers. What is most important is that CryptoAPI hides the implementation details of the complex cryptographic algorithms to the programmer.

Late 2003 Microsoft released the CAPImon tool. This tool can be used to capture and display the calls PKI-enabled applications make to the CryptoAPI. The tool can be very useful for PKI troubleshooting (for example, to troubleshoot certificate chain validation or revocation checking). You can download the tool for free from the Microsoft Downloads website at http://www.microsoft.com/downloads.

CryptoAPI architecture

The CryptoAPI architecture (which is illustrated in Figure 13.5) consists of a programmatic interface, a set of software modules, and a set of pluggable Cryptographic Service Providers (CSPs). The CryptoAPI and its interfaces are fully documented in the Windows Server 2003 platform SDK.

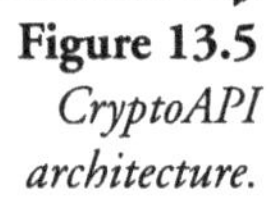

Figure 13.5 *CryptoAPI architecture.*

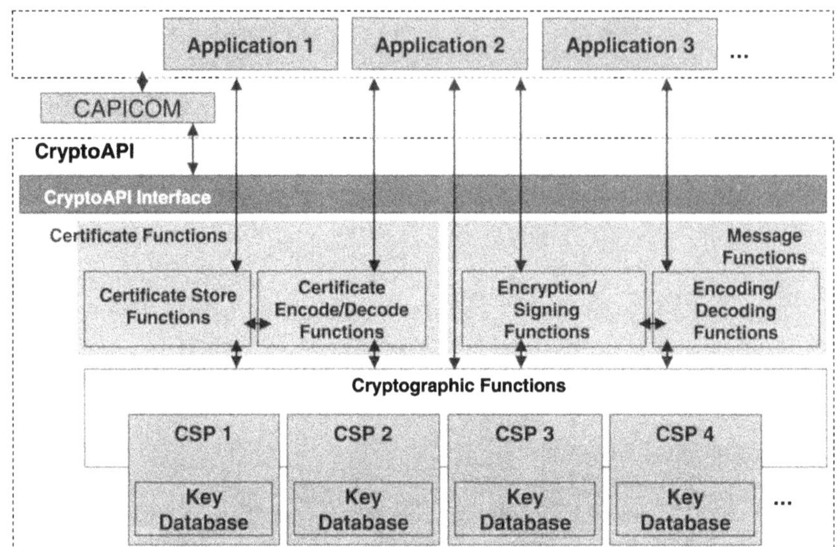

The software modules can be categorized in software modules providing certificate-related functions and others providing message-related functions:

- The modules providing message-related functions can be called to generate cryptographic keys, perform hashing, digitally sign data, or perform data encryption and decryption. They also deal with message encoding and decoding services to and from the PKCS7, PKCS10, and ASN.1 message formats.
- The modules providing certificate-related functions deal with certificate management services: They can be called to generate, manage, and validate certificates, to interact with the certificate stores, and to encode and decode certificates.

The CryptoAPI functions can also be called through CAPICOM. CAPICOM is a COM client that can perform cryptographic functions using ActiveX and COM objects. CAPICOM can be used from applications created in Visual Basic, Visual Basic Scripting Edition, or C++. CAPICOM version 2.0 includes support for the generation and verification of digital signatures, encryption and decryption of data, certificate store searching, hashing, and the AES algorithm. CAPICOM is not available from a default Windows Server 2003 installation. CAPICOM version 2.0.0.3 (cc2rinst.exe) can be downloaded from the Windows Platform SDK Redistributables Web site at http://www.microsoft.com/downloads/details.aspx?displaylang=en&familyid=860ee43a-a843-462f-abb5-ff88ea5896f6.

Cryptographic Service Providers (CSPs) are software libraries that contain implementations of cryptographic algorithms and ciphers. The use of libraries creates a pluggable architecture: Third-party vendors can plug their proper CSP in the OS and provide security services to applications.

CSPs can be implemented in both hardware and software. A hardware-based CSP implementation provides better security than a software-based implementation. This is because hardware security devices such as smart cards, security tokens, and hardware security modules (HSMs) typically offer better protection against tampering.

To embed a CSP into Windows Server 2003 or XP, it must be cryptographically signed by Microsoft. How to do this is described in the CSP Development Kit available from Microsoft.

A CSP does more than just providing the implementation of a cryptographic cipher. CryptoAPI also deals with sensitive key (session keys and private keys) storage. It stores them into key databases that are embedded in the CSPs. The CSP key database contains a key container for each user, named after the user's logon name. The key containers can be stored in the registry, on the file system, or on a smart card. The key containers can never be accessed directly: They can only be accessed through the CryptoAPI and by using the appropriate CryptoAPI functions.

CSPs located on different machines cannot directly communicate. It happens though that keys need to be exchanged between different CSPs. CryptoAPI allows sensitive keys to be exported from a CSP's key container and transported in a secure way to another CSP. You can, for example, export and import certificates and private keys between different CSP key containers using a PKCS12-formatted file. When exporting a private key to a PKCS12 file, CryptoAPI forces you to protect it using a password. This password functions as a symmetric key and provides confidentiality protection for the exported private key.

Cryptographic service providers

Table 13.4 gives an overview of the CSPs that come preinstalled with Windows Server 2003 and Windows XP. To get an overview of all CSPs available on your machine, query the following registry folder: HKEY_LOCAL_MACHINE\Software\Microsoft\Cryptography\Defaults\Provider.

Windows Server 2003 and Windows XP come preinstalled with the enhanced CSPs. The Enhanced CSPs include support for 56-bit DES, 3 DES (112-bit 2key and 168-bit 3key), 16,384-bit RSA, 128-bit RC2, and RC4. The Base CSPs only support 512-bit RSA, 40-bit RC2, and RC4. In

Windows 2000, users had to install the High Encryption Pack to get access to these CSPs. These enhanced CSPs are only available to users living in countries to which the export of strong crypto from the United States is permitted and to organizations that are on the exception list of the U.S. crypto export regulations. If you still have Windows 2000 clients, the High Encryption Pack for Windows 2000 can be downloaded from http://windowsupdate.microsoft.com. In Windows Server 2003 and XP, Microsoft also added a new CSP implementing the AES algorithm, the new U.S. standard for symmetric encryption.

Table 13.5 shows that Windows Server 2003 and XP contain both hardware and software implementations of CSPs. So far, Windows Server 2003 and XP include by default three smart card vendors' CSPs: Infineon, Gemplus, and Schlumberger.

Table 13.5 *Windows Server 2003 and XP Cryptographic Service Providers (CSPs)*

CSP Name	Description
MS Base Cryptographic Provider v1.0	Base CSP
MS Base DSS Cryptographic Provider\	Superset of the CSP in the previous row, including support for DSA and SHA
MS Base DSS and Diffie-Hellman Cryptographic Provider	Superset of the CSP in the previous row, including support for the Diffie-Hellman key agreement protocol
MS Diffie-Hellman SChannel Cryptographic Provider	SChannel CSP: used for secure Web communications using SSL/TLS
MS RSA SChannel Cryptographic Provider	
MS Enhanced Cryptographic Provider v1.0	Enhanced version of base provider: supports longer key lengths. FIPS 140-1 Level 1 compliant.
MS Enhanced DSS and Diffie-Hellman Cryptographic Provider	Enhanced version of base provider: supports longer key lengths. FIPS 140-1 Level 1 compliant.
MS Enhanced RSA and AES Cryptographic Provider	Enhanced version of base provider: supports longer key lengths and the AES algorithm for symmetric encryption. FIPS 140-1 Level 1 compliant.
MS Exchange Cryptographic Provider v1.0	Exchange-specific CSP
MS Strong Cryptographic Provider	Microsoft Strong Cryptographic Provider
Infineon SiCrypt Base Smart Card CSP	Infineon hardware CSP for smart card support
Gemplus GemSAFE Card CSP v1.0	Gemplus hardware CSP for smart card support
Schlumberger Cryptographic Service Provider	Schlumberger hardware CSP for smart card support

Microsoft received a FIPS 140-1 Level 1 security certification for the following CSPs:[2] the MS Enhanced Cryptographic Provider, the MS Enhanced DSS and Diffie-Hellman Cryptographic Provider, and the MS Enhanced RSA and AES Cryptographic Provider. If your IT environment requires a higher level of FIPS 140-1 compliance, have a look at the hardware-based private key storage solutions discussed at the end of this chapter.

13.4.4 Certificates

In this section we focus on the characteristics of the certificates that are generated by Windows Server 2003 Certification Authorities. Critical to understanding the Windows Server 2003 and XP certificate layout are certificate templates. We also look in detail at how certificates are stored on the Windows Server 2003 and XP OS platforms.

Certificate layout and viewer

A certificate's format is defined in the ITU-T X.509 version 3 standard. This standard was later adopted by the IETF in RFC 2459. A copy of the ITU standard can be downloaded from the ITU-T Web site at http://www.itu.int/ITU-T/. The RFC is available from http://www.ietf.org. Appendix 1 contains an overview of the X.509 certificate version 3 and certificate revocation list (CRL) version 2 format.

Three key tools when dealing with certificates in Windows Server 2003 and XP are the certificate viewer and the Certificate Templates and Certificates MMC snap-ins. The latter two are covered in detail in the following sections. The certificate viewer displays a certificate's content (as illustrated in Figure 13.6). The Windows default certificate viewer is automatically started when you double-click a certificate file. The first tab of the viewer shows general information such as the applications for which the certificate can be used, the subject name, the issuer name, the validity period of the certificate, and whether the certificate has a corresponding private key stored in the user's profile. The second tab shows all X.509 certificate entries: the standard fields and the critical and noncritical certificate extensions. The third tab shows the certification path and the certificate status.

Certificate templates

To let a CA cope with different certificate types, Microsoft has chosen to implement a flexible and modular architecture. The characteristics of a certificate—including the applications for which it can be used—are defined

2. More information is available at http://csrc.nist.gov/cryptval/140-1/1401val2002.htm.

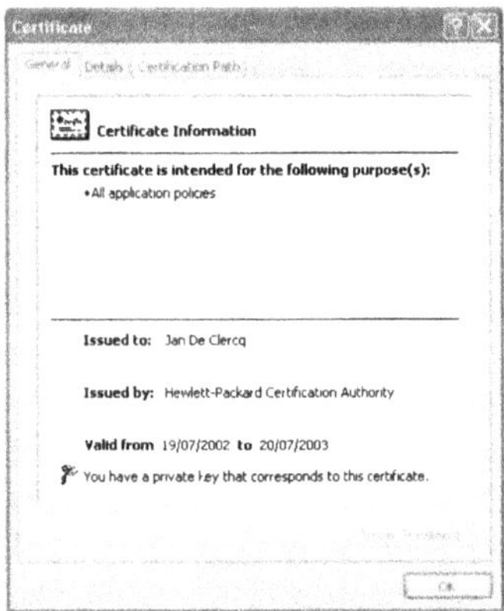

Figure 13.6 *The Windows certificate viewer.*

in a certificate template that is stored in the AD. Windows Server 2003 comes with support for version 2 certificate templates. The key difference between V1 and V2 templates is that V2 templates can be modified. Thanks to the support for V2 templates, a CA administrator can now also create its own templates, reflecting the certificate needs of the organization.

Certificate templates can also be used to define an enterprise CA's certificate issuance policy.

- You can use them to set the certificate types a CA can issue. This is done by loading the appropriate templates in the CA's policy module. To do so use the Certification Authority MMC snap-in, right-click the Certificate Templates container, and select New\Certificate Template to Issue.
- On the Windows Server 2003 AD forest level, you can use them to set which users can enroll and/or autoenroll for which certificate types. Like any other AD object, certificate templates have an ACL you can use to set which users can enroll and/or autoenroll for a particular certificate type. To set the ACLs,[3] use the Certificate Templates MMC snap-in (use the security tab in the properties of a certificate template).

Because Windows stand-alone CAs lack AD integration, you cannot use certificate templates to customize a stand-alone CA's issuance policy.

3. Certificate template ACLs can also be set from the AD Sites and Services MMC snap-in: The templates are available from the Certificate Templates container in the Public Key Services container. I recommend, however, using the Certificate Templates MMC snap-in.

To administer certificate templates in Windows Server 2003 you must be a member of the Enterprise Admins group or the Domain Admins group of the forest root domain. In Windows 2000 only members of the Domain Admins group of the root domain can administer certificate templates.

Certificate templates are stored together with their properties in the system registry of servers hosting a Windows Server 2003 CA (HKLM\Software\Microsoft\Cryptography\Certificatetemplatecache) and in the Active Directory configuration naming context (cn=certificate templates, cn=public key services, cn=services, cn=configuration).

To administer version 2 certificate templates, use the Certificate Templates MMC snap-in (illustrated in Figure 13.7). You can invoke the Certificate Templates snap-in from the Certification Authority MMC snap-in by selecting the Certificate Templates folder, right-clicking it and selecting Manage. A subset of a certificate template's definition is displayed in the MMC Certification Authority snap-in: Right-click a template in the Certificate Templates container and select properties.

Support for version 2 certificate templates requires specific AD schema extensions. This is not a problem in a native Windows Server 2003 envi-

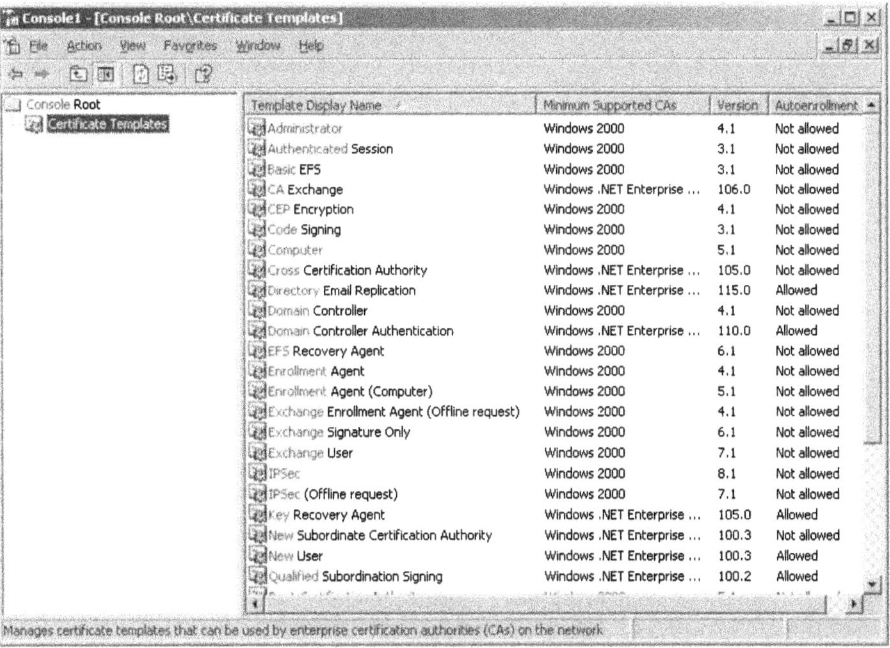

Figure 13.7 *The Windows Server 2003 Certificate Templates MMC snap-in.*

ronment where all Domain Controllers (DCs) are running the Windows Server 2003 Enterprise Server OS. If you have a mixed Windows Server 2003–Windows 2000 domain controller environment, you can extend the AD schema using the adprep.exe utility (use the /forestprep switch), which is available from the Windows Server 2003 CD. Also, in this case at least, Windows 2000 Service Pack 3 will be required on the Windows 2000 DCs. Certificates that are rooted on version 2 certificate templates can also only be issued from a Windows Server 2003 Enterprise or Datacenter edition CA installation.

From a PKI client point of view, all clients can enroll for certificates that are based on V2 templates from a CA's Web enrollment interface. Enrollment for a certificate that is based on a V2 template from the Certificates MMC snap-in can only be done from a Windows XP or Windows Server 2003 OS platform. A user running the Windows 2000 OS can only request certificates that are based on V1 templates from the Certificates MMC snap-in.

Default certificate templates

Table 13.6 lists the default certificate templates that are loaded to AD when you install the first Windows Server 2003 enterprise CA in your AD forest. For every template it lists the supported applications (in the EKU/Application Policies column), the OIDs corresponding to the different applications (in the Corresponding OIDs column), whether the corresponding certificates are automatically published in Active Directory (in the AD? column), and the certificate template version (1 or 2) (in the Version column). The names between brackets in the first column are the templates' registry names: This name sometimes differs from the template name and is interesting to know when you are requesting certificates using the certreq command-line utility.[4]

The certificate templates that are marked as offline are certificates for which the CA will not retrieve user information from the Active Directory at certificate request time. This means that the requestor has to provide the information himself. Offline templates are used for non-Windows PKI clients, like non-Microsoft IPsec clients or non-AD integrated Web servers. Because these entities do not have an AD object entry, their information cannot be retrieved from AD. Offline templates can also be very useful to deploy IPsec machine certificates to clients that are not part of a Windows domain.

4. When using the certreq command line you can reference the certificate template that must be used with the –attrib switch. For example: certreq –attrib "CertificateTemplate:CrossCA"

Table 13.6 also shows that Windows Server 2003 supports both single-use (having a single OID) and multiple-use certificates (having multiple OIDs).

Table 13.6 *Windows Server 2003 Certificate Templates*

Template Name (*Registry Name*)	EKU/Application Policies*	Corresponding OIDs	AD?	Version
Administrator (*Administrator*)	MS Trust List Signing Encrypting File System Secure E-mail Client Authentication	1.3.6.1.4.1.311.10.3.1 1.3.6.1.4.1.311.10.3.4 1.3.6.1.5.5.7.3.4 1.3.6.1.5.5.7.3.2	Y	1
Authenticated Session *(ClientAuth)*	Client Authentication	1.3.6.1.5.5.7.3.2	N	1
Basic EFS *(EFS)*	Encrypting File System	1.3.6.1.4.1.311.10.3.4	Y	1
CA Exchange *(CAExchange)*	Private Key Archival	1.3.6.1.4.1.311.21.5	N	2
CEPEncryption *(CEPEncryption)*	Certificate Request Agent	1.3.6.1.4.1.311.20.2.1	N	1
CodeSigning *(CodeSigning)*	Code Signing	1.3.6.1.5.5.7.3.3	N	1
Computer *(Machine)*	Client Authentication Server Authentication	1.3.6.1.5.5.7.3.2 1.3.6.1.5.5.7.3.1	N	1
Cross Certification Authority *(CrossCA)*	—	—	Y	2
Directory E-mail Replication *(DirectoryEmailReplication)*	Directory Service Email Replication	1.3.6.1.4.1.311.21.19	Y	2
DomainController *(DomainController)*	Client Authentication Server Authentication	1.3.6.1.5.5.7.3.2 1.3.6.1.5.5.7.3.1	Y	1
Domain Controller Authentication *(DomainControllerAuthentication)*	Client Authentication Server Authentication Smart Card Logon	1.3.6.1.5.5.7.3.2 1.3.6.1.5.5.7.3.1 1.3.6.1.4.1.311.20.2.2	N	2
EFS Recovery Agent *(EFSRecovery)*	File Recovery	1.3.6.1.4.1.311.10.3.4.1	Y	1
Enrollment Agent *(EnrollmentAgent)*	Certificate Request Agent	1.3.6.1.4.1.311.20.2.1	N	1
Enrollment Agent (Computer) *(MachineEnrollmentAgent)*	Certificate Request Agent	1.3.6.1.4.1.311.20.2.1	N	1
Exchange Enrollment Agent (Offline Request) *(EnrollmentAgentOffline)*	Certificate Request Agent	1.3.6.1.4.1.311.20.2.1	N	1
Exchange Signature Only *(ExchangeUserSignature)*	Secure E-mail	1.3.6.1.5.5.7.3.4	N	1

Table 13.6 *Windows Server 2003 Certificate Templates (continued)*

Template Name (*Registry Name*)	EKU/Application Policies*	Corresponding OIDs	AD?	Version
ExchangeUser *(ExchangeUser)*	Secure E-mail	1.3.6.1.5.5.7.3.4	N	1
IPSec *(IPSECIntermediateOnline)*	IP security IKE Intermediate	1.3.6.1.5.5.8.2.2	N	1
IPSec (Offline Request) *(IPSECIntermediateOffline)*	Certificate Request Agent	1.3.6.1.5.5.8.2.2	N	1
Key Recovery Agent *(KeyRecoveryAgent)*	Key Recovery Agent	1.3.6.1.4.1.311.21.6	N	2
RAS and IAS Server (RASAndIASServer)	Client Authentication Server Authentication	1.3.6.1.5.5.7.3.2 1.3.6.1.5.5.7.3.1	N	2
Root Certification Authority *(CA)*	—	—	N	1
Router (Offline Request) *(OfflineRouter)*	Client Authentication	1.3.6.1.5.5.7.3.2	N	1
SmartCardLogon *(SmartcardLogon)*	Client Authentication Smart Card Logon	1.3.6.1.5.5.7.3.2 1.3.6.1.4.1.311.20.2.2	N	1
SmartCardUser *(SmartcardUser)*	Secure E-mail Client Authentication Smart Card Logon	1.3.6.1.5.5.7.3.4 1.3.6.1.5.5.7.3.2 1.3.6.1.4.1.311.20.2.2	Y	1
Subordinate Certification Authority *(SubCA)*	—	—	N	1
Trust List Signing *(CTLSigning)*	Microsoft Trust List Signing	1.3.6.1.4.1.311.10.3.1	N	1
User *(User)*	Encrypting File System Secure E-mail Client Authentication	1.3.6.1.4.1.311.10.3.4 1.3.6.1.5.5.7.3.4 1.3.6.1.5.5.7.3.2	Y	1
User Signature Only *(UserSignature)*	Secure E-mail Client Authentication	1.3.6.1.5.5.7.3.4 1.3.6.1.5.5.7.3.2	Y	1
Web Server *(WebServer)*	Server Authentication	1.3.6.1.5.5.7.3.1	N	1
Workstation Authentication (Workstation)	Client Authentication	1.3.6.1.5.5.7.3.2	N	2

* The applications that a certificate supports are kept in the Extended Key Usage (EKU) certificate extension (for certificates based on V1 templates) or in the Application Policies certificate extension (for certificates based on V2 templates).

Certificate template properties

Table 13.7 provides an overview of the certificate template properties that can be administered from a template's properties dialog box in the Certificate Templates MMC snap-in. The properties dialog box is illustrated in Figure 13.8: It shows the General tab in the cross-certification authority certificate template's properties. Note that you can only modify version 2 certificate template properties. The properties of version 1 certificate templates can be viewed from the MMC snap-in, but they cannot be changed.

The meaning of the different certificate template permissions (configurable from the security tab in a template's properties) can be summarized as follows:

- The Read permission allows the template to be discovered by a user.
- The Enroll permission allows a user to enroll for a particular certificate type.
- The Full Control permission allows a user to set or modify the permissions of a template.
- The Autoenroll permission is set when a user or computer can automatically enroll for a particular certificate template.
- The Write permission allows a user to modify the properties of a certificate template.

Certificate storage

In Windows, certificates are stored in a PKI entity's personal certificate store. In the following section we go more in detail on architecture of the Windows Server 2003 and XP certificate stores. Besides certificates, an entity's certificate store can also contain Certificate Trust Lists (CTLs), Certificate Revocation Lists (CRLs), and delta CRLs. Each Windows Server 2003 and XP user, machine, and service has its proper certificate store.

Figure 13.9 illustrates the certificate store architecture. As mentioned in Section 13.4.3, one of the CryptoAPI's tasks is certificate management. CryptoAPI provides tools to attach certificates to messages and to store, retrieve, delete, list, and verify certificates.

The Windows Server 2003 and XP certificate store is divided into two abstraction layers: the logical certificate store and the physical certificate store. The purpose of this architecture is to abstract physical certificate storage from logical certificate categories. A Windows PKI user should not

Table 13.7 *Certificate Template Properties*

Certificate Template Properties Tab	Parameter	Comments
General	Template Display Name	Cannot be modified after template creation
	Minimum Supported CAs	"Windows 2000" or "Windows Server 2003, Enterprise Edition"—Cannot be modified after template creation
	Template Name	Cannot be modified after template creation
	Validity Period	Specified in years
	Renewal Period	Specified in weeks
	Publish Certificate in AD	Checkbox
	Do not automatically reenroll if a duplicate certificate exists in AD	Checkbox
Request Handling	Purpose	"Encryption," "Signature," or "Signature and encryption"
	Archive subject's encryption private key	Checkbox
	Include symmetric algorithms allowed by the subject	Checkbox
	Delete revoked or expired certificates (do not archive)	Checkbox (grayed out)
	Minimum key size	512, 1024, 2048, 4096, 8192 or 16384
	Allow private key to be exported	Checkbox
	Do the following when the subject is enrolled and when the private key associated with this certificate is used	"Enroll subject without requiring any user input," "Prompt the user during enrollment," or "Prompt the user during enrollment and require user input when the private key is used"
	CSPs to be used	"Request can use any CSP available on the subject's computer" or "Request must use one of the following CSPs"
Subject Name	"Supply in the Request" or "Build from AD information"	—
	Subject Name format	Only available if subject name is build from AD information: "Fully distinguished name" or "Common name"

Table 13.7 *Certificate Template Properties (continued)*

Certificate Template Properties Tab	Parameter	Comments
Subject Name *(cont'd.)*	Include E-mail name, DNS name, UPN, SPN	Only available if subject name is build from AD information: checkboxes
Issuance Requirements	Require CA certificate manager approval for enrollment	Checkbox
	Require a number of authorized signatures for enrollment	Checkbox
	Policy type required in signature	"Application policy," "Issuance policy," or "Both application and issuance policy"
	Application Policy	Select Application Policy
	Issuance Policy	Select Issuance Policy
	Reenrollment Criteria	"Same criteria as for enrollment" or "Valid existing certificate"
Superseded templates	Certificate templates	Select superseded templates
Extensions	Application Policies	Select Application Policy—mark extension as critical or noncritical (checkbox)
	Basic Constraints	"Do Not Allow subject to issue certificates to other CAs"—mark extension as critical or noncritical (checkbox)
	Certificate Template Information	Cannot be changed
	Enhanced Key Usage	Cannot be modified (only appears on V1 templates)
	Issuance Policies	Select Application Policy—mark extension as critical or noncritical (checkbox)
	Key Usage	Set "Encryption" or "Signature" key usages—mark extension as critical or non-critical (checkbox)
Security	—	Set full control, read, write, enroll and autoenroll permissions for individual users or groups

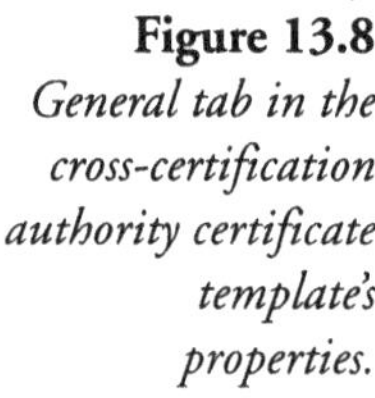

Figure 13.8
General tab in the cross-certification authority certificate template's properties.

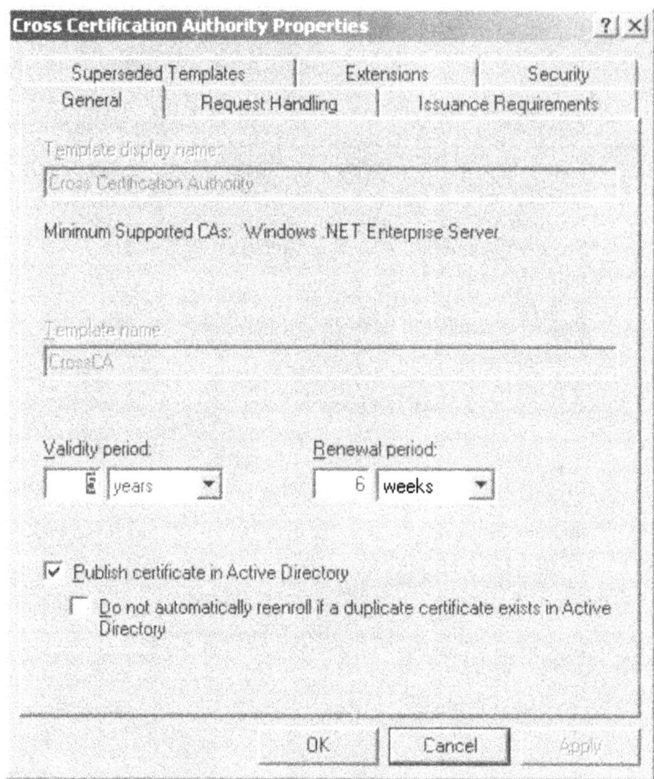

bother about where a certificate is stored physically but rather about what he or she can do with it and to what category of PKI entity it belongs. The Windows certificate store architecture provides ways to make the content of multiple physical stores visible in one logical store or, the other way around, to provide content inheritance from one physical store to multiple logical stores.

Table 13.8 and Figure 13.9 show the different logical and physical certificate containers available in Windows Server 2003 and XP. Table 13.8 also shows in which PKI entities' certificate stores these containers are available: user, machine, or service entities. The name in parentheses in the first column is the corresponding registry name for the logical store containers.

To look at the content of a user, machine, or service certificate store and its different containers, use the MMC Certificates snap-in. A user can also use the Lightweight certificate viewer. The latter is accessible from the Internet Options/Content/Certificates menu in Internet Explorer.

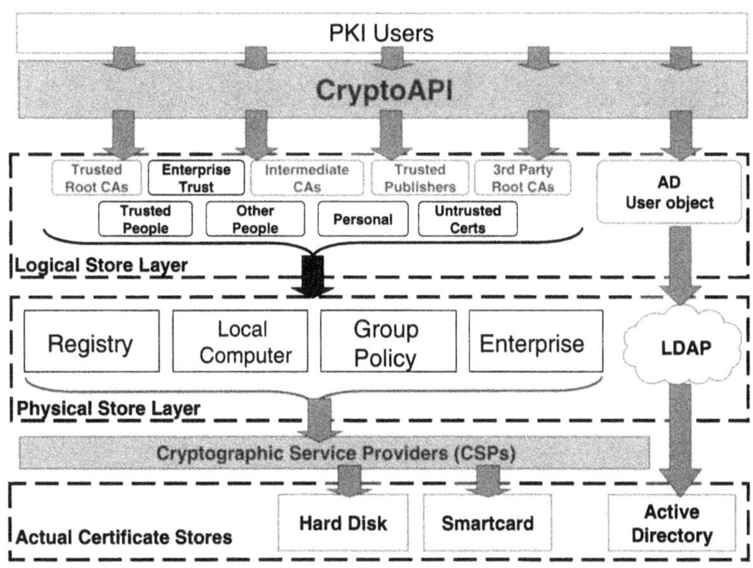

Figure 13.9 *Windows Server 2003 and XP physical and logical certificate stores.*

Table 13.8 *Logical and Physical Certificate Store Containers for User, Machine, and Service Principals*

Logical Store Containers (Registry Name)	Physical Store Containers	User (U), Machine (M), Service (S)
Personal (MY)	Registry	U, M, S
Trusted Root Certification Authorities (ROOT) (also known as the Root Store)	Registry	U, M, S
	Local Computer	U, S
	Enterprise	M
Enterprise Trust (TRUST)	Registry	U, M, S
	Group Policy	U, M
	Local Computer	U, S
	Enterprise	M
Intermediate Certification Authorities (CA)	Registry	U, M, S
	Group Policy	U, M
	Local Computer	U, S
	Enterprise	M

Table 13.8 *Logical and Physical Certificate Store Containers for User, Machine, and Service Principals (continued)*

Logical Store Containers (Registry Name)	Physical Store Containers	User (U), Machine (M), Service (S)
Active Directory User Object (USERDS)	User Certificate	U
Trusted Publishers (TRUSTEDPUBLISHER)	Registry	U, M, S
	Group Policy	U, M
	Local Computer	U, S
	Enterprise	M
Untrusted Certificates (DISALLOWED)	Registry	U, M, S
	Group Policy	U, M
	Local Computer	U, S
	Enterprise	M
Third-Party Root Certification Authorities (AUTHROOT)	Registry	U, M, S
	Group Policy	U, M
	Local Computer	U, S
	Enterprise	M
Trusted People (TRUSTEDPEOPLE)	Registry	U, M, S
	Group Policy	U, M
	Local Computer	U, S
	Enterprise	M
Certificate Enrollment Request (REQUEST)	Registry	U, M, S
SPC (SPC)	Registry	M
	Group Policy	M
	Enterprise	M

By default, the MMC snap-in only shows the logical certificate containers. If you want, you can also see the physical certificate containers. To do this, select Options in the MMC View menu, and select the Physical certificate stores checkbox. To look at the user or machine certificate store from the command prompt, you can use the certutil command-line utility: Use it with the -store switch to display the machine certificate store; with the -user -store

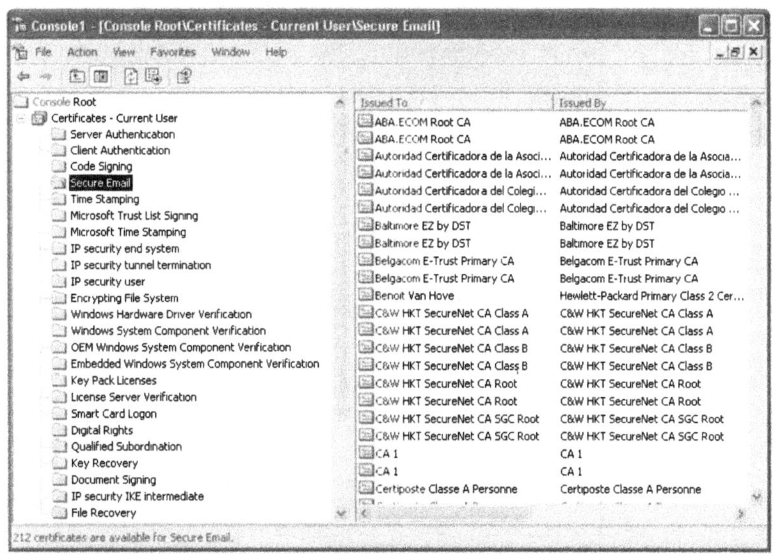

Figure 13.10 *Classifying certificates in a certificate store based on certificate purpose.*

switches to display the user certificate store; and replace the -store with –verifystore switch if you not only want to list but also to verify the certificates in a store. Certutil is only available on Windows Server 2003 platforms.

Windows Server 2003 and XP automatically archive expired and renewed certificates and their private keys in the certificate store. This happens as part of the autoenrollment process. Archiving enables a user to decrypt old documents, even if the original certificate has expired or been renewed. To look at the archived certificates that are part of an entity's certificate store, select Archived certificates in the view options of the MMC certificates snap-in. The same menu contains a checkbox to look at the certificates in an entity's certificate store, based on the purpose or application for which they can be used (as illustrated in Figure 13.10).

In the following sections we look in more detail at the physical and logical certificate store layers.

Logical certificate stores

Figure 13.11 shows the logical certificate store layer as you can view it from the Certificates MMC snap-in. Let's run through the different default[5] containers and look at their content:

- The Personal container contains the certificates that are stored in a user's profile. Certificates in this folder have their corresponding pri-

5. PKI-enabled applications may create application-specific logical certificate containers.

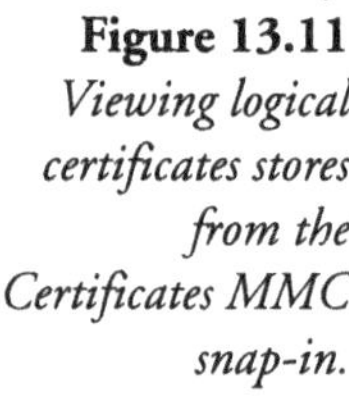

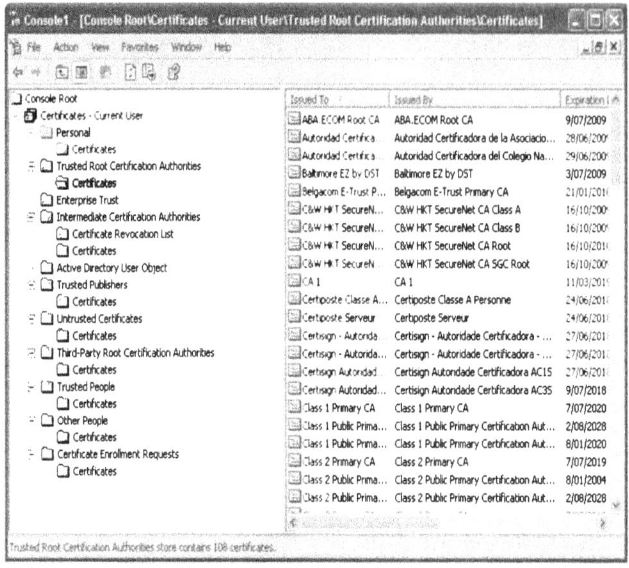

Figure 13.11 *Viewing logical certificates stores from the Certificates MMC snap-in.*

vate key stored in a secured user portion of the system registry (which is also a part of the user profile).

- The Trusted Root Certification Authorities container holds by definition only self-signed root CA certificates. In practice, however, nonroot CA certificates can also be added to this store. These CAs can be internal Windows 2000 CAs as well as CAs that are external to the company. This container is also referred to as the root store, which basically means that the certificates in this store are considered trust anchors. PKI trust and trust anchors are discussed in more detail in Chapter 14.
- The Enterprise Trust container holds Certificate Trust Lists (CTLs). CTLs are signed lists containing CA certificates. They are automatically downloaded to Windows Server 2003 or XP clients using GPOs. The CA certificates that are part of a CTL are considered trust anchors if the CTL signing certificate is valid.
- The Intermediate Certification Authorities container holds by definition only intermediate CA certificates and their CRLs and delta CRLs. Again, in practice you can also add root CA certificates to this store. These intermediate CAs can be internal Windows 2000 CAs as well as CAs external to the company. The certificates in the Intermediate Certification Authorities store are *not* trust anchors. If they are marked as trustworthy, this is because their certificate chain contains

the certificate of a CA that is kept in the Trusted Root CA or Third-Party Root CA container or in a valid CTL.

- The Active Directory User Object container holds user certificates that are published in the Active Directory. In AD certificates are stored in a user object's usercertificate attribute. This store only exists for user accounts: It does not exist for machine or service accounts.
- The Trusted Publishers container (previously known as the SPC container) holds Software Publisher Certificates. These certificates are used to verify code that was signed using the Authenticode code-signing technology.
- The Untrusted Certificates container holds certificates that are not trustworthy. The presence of this container (which did not exist in Windows 2000) is Microsoft's reaction to an incident that took place in 2001 where a malicious person obtained a certificate for Microsoft's identity.
- The Third-Party Root Certification Authorities container holds theoretically only third-party root certificates and CRLs. Again, in practice you can also add root CA certificates to this store. Like the Trusted Root Certification Authorities container, the certificates in this container are by default considered trust anchors. Unlike the Trusted Root Certification Authorities, the certificates in this container can also *not* be considered trust anchors. The latter is controlled using a Group Policy Object setting that is explained in more detail in Chapter 14.
- The Trusted People container holds certificates of people who are explicitly marked as trustworthy. These are typically self signed certificates that do not chain to a trusted root CA.
- The Other People container holds the certificates of people with whom a user shares encrypted documents such as S/MIME secured e-mail messages. It is the general cache for certificates that do chain to a trusted root CA.
- The Certificate Enrollment Requests container holds certificate request files. These files are created when a user is requesting a certificate to a stand-alone Windows 2000 CA or when an enterprise CA goes offline during a certificate enrollment request.

Knowing all this, you can perform the following operations on the level of the MMC Certificates snap-in:

- *Publish user certificates to the Active Directory.* The MMC certificates snap-in has built-in drag-and-drop functionalities. To publish one of your certificates to AD, simply pull it to the Active Directory User Object container.
- *Trust or untrust root CA certificates.* To untrust a CA certificate, simply cut it out of the Trusted Root Certification Authorities container and paste it into the Untrusted Certificates container. From a security point of view it is a best practice to move all CA entries that Microsoft put in the OS from the Trusted Root Certification Authorities to the Untrusted Certificates container, unless you implicitly trust Microsoft to embed trustworthy trust anchors in your software.

New to Windows Server 2003 is that in a domain environment the user's ability to make his or her proper root CA trust decisions can be controlled by the domain administrator: The latter is controlled using a GPO setting and is explained in more detail in Chapter 14.

Physical certificate stores

Figure 13.12 shows the physical certificate store layer as you can view it from the MMC Certificates snap-in. Let's run through the different containers and look at their content:

- The Registry container is an entity's personal certificate and CTL store. For a user it is part of the user portion of the system registry, which is part of the user's profile. The Registry container holds both certificates that have their corresponding private key stored in the user profile and others that have not. The Trusted Root Certification Authorities part of this container on the user level is also known as the user's root store. Because certificates (and private keys) are stored in the user profile, they can be made accessible from any computer the user logs on to if your environment supports roaming profiles.
- The Local Computer container holds the local machine's certificate, CRL, delta CRL, and CTL store. It is part of all users' user profiles. You may have noticed in Table 13.8 that user and service accounts have a physical local computer container for most of the logical stores. This is a very nice feature because it takes away unnecessary duplication of certificates, CRLs, and CTLs. For example, external root CA certificates should not be stored in every certificate store. They are stored once in the machine certificate store, and automatically a pointer to this store is added in every other user and service's certificate store that is logging on to that particular machine.

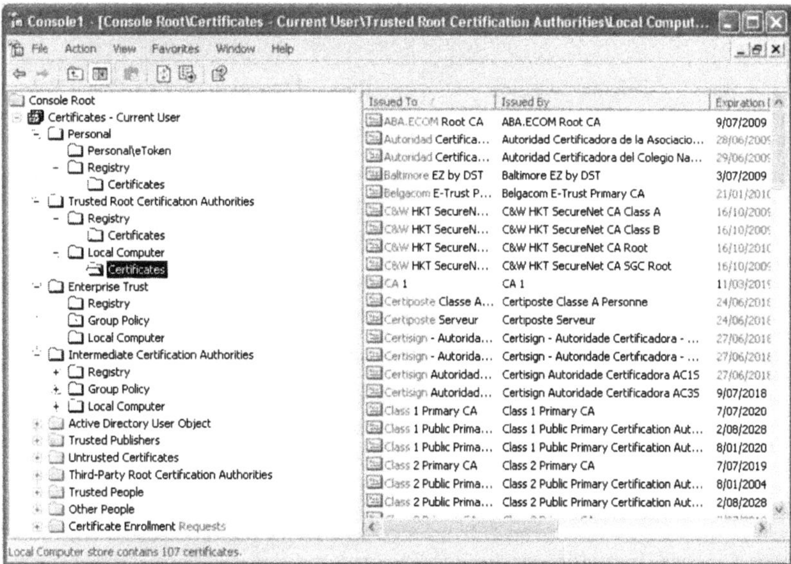

Figure 13.12 *Viewing physical certificates stores from the Certificates MMC snap-in.*

- The Group Policy container holds the certificates (Trusted Root Certification Authorities) and CTLs that are distributed using GPO settings.
- The User Certificate container holds the user certificates that are published in a user's usercertificate Active Directory attribute.
- The Enterprise container holds the certificates of root CAs that are stored in the Active Directory configuration naming context. These certificates are registered in the AD when an enterprise or root domain Administrator installs a root CA in the Windows 2000 forest.

Table 13.9 shows where the physical stores' content is originally located, where it is stored on the client side, and when it is copied from its original location to the PKI client certificate store.

Knowing all this, you can perform the following operation on the level of the MMC Certificates snap-in. You can make a CA certificate available to every user logging on to the machine. To do so, drag the certificate from the registry\certificates to the local computer\certificates physical container in the Trusted Root Certification Authorities logical container. Doing this will bring up a dialog box requesting whether you really want to add or delete a certificate to or from the Root store.

Table 13.9 *Physical Store Details*

Physical Store	Original Location	Physical Location on PKI-Client Side	Copied When?
Registry	N/A	For users: File system (user profile): %SystemDrive%\Documents and Settings\ <usename>\ApplicationData\Microsoft\ SystemCertificates\My\Certificates For machines and services, see "Local Computer" row below	N/A
Local Computer	Machine Registry	File System (machine profile): %SystemDrive%\\Documents And Settings\ All Users\Application Data\Microsoft\RSA\ MachineKeys Machine Registry: HKLM\software\Microsoft\ systemcertificates\my	PKI client performs logon from local computer
Group Policy	Sysvol and AD	Machine Registry: HKLM\software\policies\Microsoft\ systemcertificates User Registry: HKCU\software\policies\Microsoft\ usercertificates	GPO application event
User Certificate	N/A	Not physically stored on the PKI client: the certificate store contains an LDAP pointer to the certificates that are stored in AD	As part of a certificate enrollment
Enterprise	AD configuration naming context: CN=Certification Authority, CN=Public Key Services, CN=NTAuthTemplates, CN=Public Key Services	Machine Registry: HKLM\software\Microsoft\ enterprisecertificates	During the autoenrollment event

13.4.5 Private key storage

In asymmetric cryptography—on which both PKI and PKI-enabled applications (PKA) are built—access to and secure storage of the private key are critical. Because public keys are public entities, we should not bother about secure public key storage. (This does not mean you should not worry about the authenticity of the public key.) Let's look at some examples of how you could misuse someone else's private key.

- If you gain access to someone's private e-mail encryption key, you will be able to decrypt all the messages encrypted using the corresponding public key. If you get access to someone's e-mail signing key, you will be capable of signing messages on that person's behalf.
- If you gain access to a Certification Authority's private key, you become even more powerful: This will enable you to issue fraudulent certificates and make CA users believe that you are the acting trusted third party. As such, you will have succeeded in compromising the complete CA trust system.
- If you gain access to a software vendor's code-signing private key, you could sign your code with the vendor's key. Users would then, without their knowledge, download and execute your (possibly malicious) code.

Physical private key storage options

Private keys can be stored in different places. There are two main approaches to storing private keys: You can either place them on dedicated hardware devices or use software to hide them.

Software-based storage

The bulk of today's operating systems—including Windows Server 2003 and XP—and PKI-enabled applications store private key material in an encrypted format on the file system. Windows stores private keys or pointers to them (in case a hardware storage device is used) in the user's profile. They are stored in the subdirectory %UserProfile%\Application Data\Microsoft\Crypto\RSA. The security of Microsoft's private key storage on the file system is rooted on what Microsoft calls the Data Protection API (DPAPI). More details on DPAPI are provided later.

Dedicated hardware device storage

Examples of dedicated hardware devices used for private key storage are smart cards, USB tokens, and Hardware Security Modules (HSM). A smart card or USB token is used to store the private key of a user. HSMs are used to store the private keys belonging to services or machines. A good example of HSM usage is for secure CA private key storage. Table 13.10 lists some popular vendors of these hardware devices (this list does not provide a complete overview).

Table 13.10 *Hardware Devices for Private Key Storage: Solution and Vendor Overview*

Vendors	URL
Smart Card Vendors	
Gemplus	http://www.gemplus.com
Schlumberger	http://www.schlumberger.com
Oberthur	http://www.oberthurcs.com
Datakey	http://www.datakey.com
ActivCard	http://www.activcard.com
Spyrus	http://www.spyrus.com
USB Token Vendors	
eAlladin (eToken)	http://www.esafe.com
Rainbow Technologies (IKey)	http://www.rainbow.com
Spyrus	http://www.spyrus.com
Hardware Security Module Vendors	
nCipher (nShield)	http://www.ncipher.com
Rainbow Chrysalis (Luna CA)	http://www.chrysalis-its.com
Rainbow Chrysalis (Luna RA)	http://www.chrysalis-its.com
Spyrus (Lynks)	http://www.spyrus.com
Eracom (ProtectHost)	http://www.eracom-tech.com

Most dedicated hardware devices serve more goals than just secure private key storage. They can also provide secure onboard key-generation capabilities and cryptographic processing capabilities to accelerate digital signing and other cryptographic operations. A key advantage of using external devices to store encryption and signing algorithms is that the private key never makes it to the user's PC.

Neither smart cards nor USB tokens are perfect, although they have an excellent reputation for providing secure private key storage. Over the past few years, several researchers conducted successful private key chases on both types of devices. Two important details are: (1) To conduct an attack on such a device, you need very expensive and highly specialized hardware; (2) most attacks require that you uncover the chip in the device. This means that usually you cannot perform an attack without physically damaging the device. A couple of successful USB token attacks are explained in detail at http://www.atstake.com/research/reports/usb_hardware_token.pdf. For an overview of possible smart card attacks, see the Cryptography Research Web site at http://www.cryptography.com/dpa/technical/index.htm.

To protect against physical tampering with a device, there is only one better category of solutions available on the market: Hardware Security Modules (HSMs). HSMs are extremely expensive devices; that is why they are only used to protect very important keys such as Certificate Authority (CA) private keys.

When evaluating hardware devices for secure private key storage, make sure that you check compliance with important security standards such as the Common Criteria (http://www.commoncriteria.org), the U.S. government's FIPS 140-1 (http://csrc.nist.gov/cryptval/), and the U.K. government's ITsec (http://www.cesg.gov.uk/assurance/iacs/itsec/index.htm). Next we will pay special attention to the FIPS 140-1 compliance of HSM devices.

We return to smart card integration in Windows Server 2003 and XP in Chapter 17. In the following sections we look in more detail at some of the security technologies behind the HSMs supported in Windows Server 2003. The goal is not to make a competitive comparison between different HSMs but rather to facilitate understanding of the security technologies they use. We use the examples of the nCipher and Chrysalis HSM.

The nCipher Hardware Security Module The nCipher's HSM is called nShield. It can be used from many different operating systems (including NT, Windows 2000, Solaris, AIX, and HP-UX) and can protect the cryptographic keys used by a variety of applications, including Microsoft Certificate Server, the Apache Web server, Netscape's Certificate Management Server, Enterprise Server, and many others. The nShield device is available with a PCI, internal, or external SCSI connector. Figure 13.13 shows the internal SCSI connector model. nShield's front panel contains a smart card reader.

nShield's advanced key protection is built around the concept of a "security world," which provides a multilayered, secure approach to managing HSMs, valuable application keys, and backup and disaster recovery processes.

Figure 13.13
nShield device with internal SCSI connector.

From a high-level point of view, a security world (as illustrated in Figure 13.14) is made up of one or more nShield HSM modules, a set of data (cryptographic keys) maintained in the secure memory of the HSM, and a set of encrypted data stored on the hard disk of the host machine.

An nShield module and its security world's primary reason for existence are protecting cryptographic keys. This includes making sure that only the legitimate users and applications are authorized to access and use the keys.

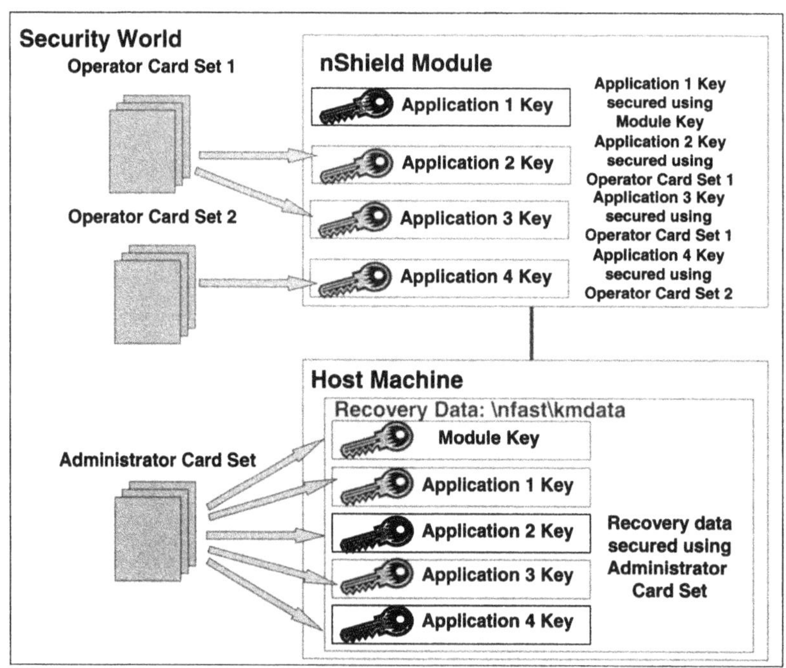

Figure 13.14
An nShield security world and its different components.

Let's first look at how a cryptographic key that is used by a particular application is securely stored in a module's security world. Such a key is referred to in the nShield documentation as an "application key." A good example of an application key would be the private key used by a Windows Certification Authority. Application keys can be stored securely in two different ways: They can be encrypted using the security world key or additionally using an operator key. This brings up two other key types: a security world key (also known as the "module key") and an operator key (this type of key is also referred to as an "operator logical token").

An operator key is not stored on the nShield module but is shared over a set of operator smart cards—also known as an operator card set (OCS). An OCS stores an operator key in a very special way: The key is never stored entirely on a single smart card (unless you have only a single card in your OCS) but in fragments that are spread across several different cards. In order to restore the operator key and thus to enable the decryption of application keys, one needs access to a predefined number of operator key fragments, each of which is stored on another operator smart card. The reason why nCipher splits operator keys is to let the access to an application key depend on the decision of more than one different person. In military terms this is known as the "missile silo" principle: A general can never decide all by himself to launch a nuclear missile; before he can do so, he needs—for example—the approval of at least one another general, the minister of defense, and the president.

nCipher calls this key fragmentation mechanism the *k*-of-*n* mechanism. The number *k* defines the number of cards that is needed to gain access to the operator key. The number *n* defines the total number of cards in the OCS. Coming back to the military example, you can look at the number *k* as the number defining how many cards are needed to authorize the decryption of an application key.

A security world may contain many different OCSs. This allows an nShield module to be shared between different applications that have different administration needs. The security world in Figure 13.2, for example, contains two OCSs. Application keys 2 and 3 are both protected by the operator key linked to OCS number 1. Application key 4 is protected by the operator key linked to OCS number 2.

A security world key (also known as the module key) is a cryptographic key that is created when the security world is created. It is stored securely on the nShield module and is used to encrypt application keys that must be available to several applications at all times—this means without needing multiple smart cards.

By default, any nShield device is FIPS 140-1 Level 2 compliant. FIPS 140-1 Level 3 compliance requires the use of a specific device type (nC4032W-xxx or nC3031S-xxx modules). It also requires you to set a configuration option during the initialization of the nShield security world. One of the most visible changes when an nShield device is FIPS 140-1 Level 3 compliant is the requirement to have an extra authorization (which can come from a card in the ACS or any OCS) before an OCS can be created or erased.

The Chrysalis Hardware Security Module Chrysalis has two HSM models that can be used in a Windows Server 2003 PKI environment: the Luna CA and Luna RA. The CA model targets advanced CA security, and the RA model targets advanced RA security. Like the nCipher nShield HSM, both of the Chrysalis models can be used from many different operating systems (including NT, Windows 2000, Solaris, Redhat Linux AIX, and HP-UX) and can protect the cryptographic keys used by a variety of applications. The Luna CA HSM requires a PCI connector. The Luna RA HSM requires a PCMCIA Type II slot. The CA device is FIPS 140-1 Level 3 compliant; the RA device is only Level 2 compliant.

In the following section we focus on the Luna CA device (illustrated in Figure 13.15). Figure 13.15 shows clockwise from the top the Luna DOCK token reader, the Luna CA cryptographic token, the color-coded PED keys, and the Luna PED authentication device. The Luna CA securely stores the cryptographic keys on the cryptographic token.

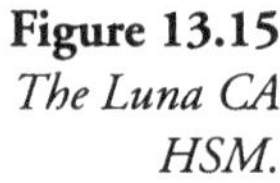

Figure 13.15
The Luna CA HSM.

The security model used by the Luna CA is very similar to the one used by the nCipher nShield device (use of a multilayered security model, support for a k-of-n key splitting mechanism, and so forth) with the following exceptions:

- A Luna CA HSM is by default FIPS 140-1 Level 3 compliant.
- For cryptographic key backup, the Luna CA uses a technique known as "Key Cloning." Luna CA backs up cryptographic keys to another cryptographic token (every Luna CA device comes by default with two tokens). nShield backs up the cryptographic keys to the hard disk of the computer host.
- To authenticate the HSM administrators, the Luna CA uses a host-independent authentication scheme. This scheme uses the Luna PIN Entry Device (PED) and a set of PED keys. PED keys are key-like security tokens that have a role identical to the smart cards used in an nShield Security World. Contrary to the nShield solution, the Luna CA's two-factor identification scheme is host-independent: the PIN associated to a PED key has to be entered on the PED. An nShield administrator enters his or her PIN in a dialog box that pops up on the screen of a possibly insecure host.

The Windows private key storage architecture

Windows 2000, Windows Server 2003, and Windows XP are using an architecture called the Data Protection API (DPAPI) to securely store private keys on a Windows computer system. In previous operating system releases, Microsoft used a technology known as the protected store. The DPAPI is explained next.

The data protection API

The DPAPI provides a password-based data protection service. In this context, data protection means that DPAPI provides data confidentiality and integrity protection services. DPAPI is bundled with the kernel of the Windows OS (its public interfaces are part of the crypt32.dll). DPAPI data decryption and encryption occur in the security context of a Windows system's local system account. Figure 13.16 shows the DPAPI key protection architecture.

The data encryption key that the DPAPI uses to securely store data is called the symmetric encryption key. The symmetric encryption key is never stored on a system—it is derived from the encryption key and the master key.

- The encryption key consists of a set of user- and/or machine-specific data that are not secret.
- Access to the symmetric session key is really based on the master key. That is why the master key is the most important key in the DPAPI. The master key is securely stored in the protect folder of a user's profile (file system path: %UserProfile%\Application Data\Microsoft\Protect\<UserSID>).

Figure 13.16 shows how the master key is protected using the master key encryption key. The latter is cryptographically derived from a user's password credentials. The cryptographic algorithms involved in this protection scheme are the 3DES (CBC mode) encryption algorithm, the SHA-1 hash function, and the Password-based Key Derivation Function (PBKDF2). The latter is described as part of the PKCS#5 standard.

DPAPI provides the following master key backup and recovery mechanisms:

- On stand-alone machines a secure backup of the user's password can be stored on a password recovery disk (PRD). This secured copy of the user's password is referred to as the recovery key. The PRD and its recovery key allow users to access a system when they forgot their password and to reset their old password to a new one. Indirectly, this system also provides a recovery mechanism to access the master key. The security of the data on the PRD is based on a public-private key–based encryption scheme.
- Domain controllers and workstations and servers that are part of a domain also store a secured copy of the master key. In this case the master key is secured using a DC's public key. This system allows DPAPI to access the master key if it cannot get to the master key encryption key.
- For every user, an encrypted copy of the user's password is stored in the credential history folder (which is a part of the user profile). In this folder the user's password is securely stored using a credential encryption key. This system allows for master key encryption key recovery when a user's password has changed and access to an old master key encryption key (encrypted with an old user password) is needed.

An important drawback of using a user's password to secure access to its protected data is that all the applications that are running in the user's security context can access all of a user's protected data. To counteract this, DPAPI allows an application to use an additional secret to protect the data.

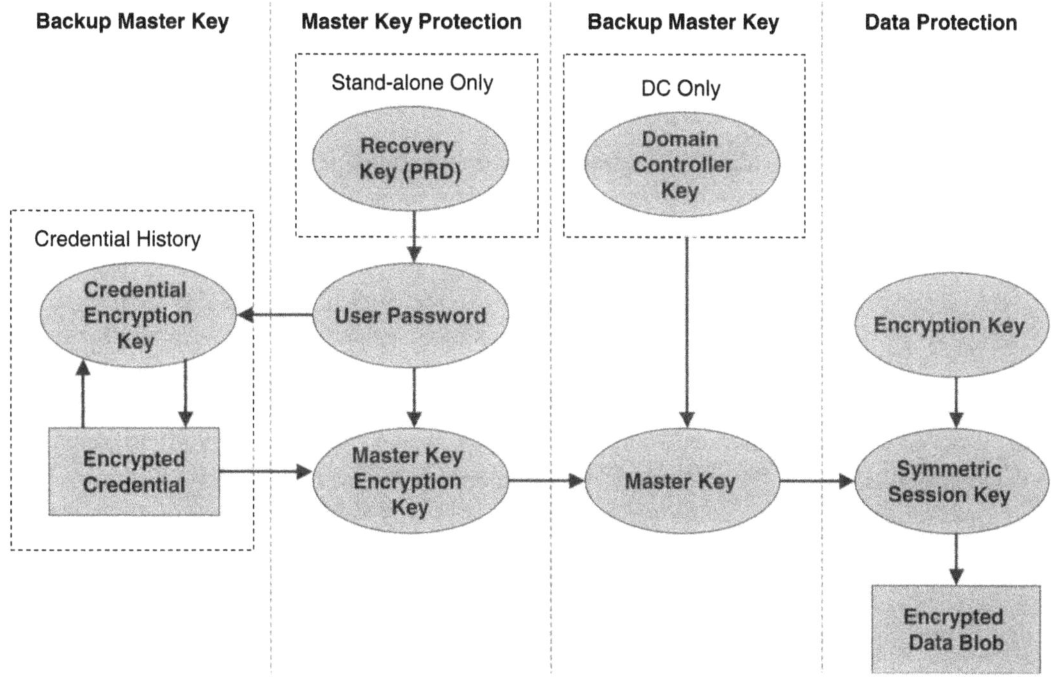

Figure 13.16 *DPAPI key protection architecture.*

The additional secret is then required to unprotect the data. In PKI terminology, this feature is referred to as strong private key protection (which is explained in a following section).

Important private key properties

Two private key properties that impact the key's security level and that are both driven by the DPAPI are whether the key is exportable and whether it has strong private key protection enabled.

Private key exportability To enable all-time data recovery and to protect against cracking attacks, private keys used for recovery of encrypted data should be backed up or exported from the Windows system and stored on some other secure medium. To make the private key exportable, the user should check Mark keys as exportable in the Advanced Certificate Request options on the Web enrollment pages. This option is only available if the certificate will be used for key exchange only. A key can also be made exportable programmatically, by setting the CRYPT_EXPORTABLE property. How to do this is explained in detail in the platform SDK. If you want more than just backup and you really want to delete the local private key (to protect against cracking attacks), don't forget to check the option to delete the private key if the export succeeds. The DPAPI also defines a CRYPT_ARCHIVABLE flag to allow a one-time export during a key archival operation.

Private key exportability is a predefined property that is set in the certificate templates that are used when requesting certificates to an Enterprise CA. The private keys of certificates for user signature, user, CTL signing, smart card user, smart card logon, enrollment agent, code signing, client authentication, and administrator are, by default, marked as nonexportable. Windows private signing keys are always marked as nonexportable. Signing keys should never be copied or stored on a medium different from the one that was used to store the private key when it was generated. This could be a serious security risk: A malicious person could export another person's private key and impersonate him or her. The private keys of EFS and EFS recovery certificates are by default exportable for data recovery reasons.

Strong private key protection In both the Web enrollment pages and the Certificate Request Wizard, a user can choose to enable strong private key protection. Strong private key protection means that the user will be prompted every time the private key is used by an application. Two levels of

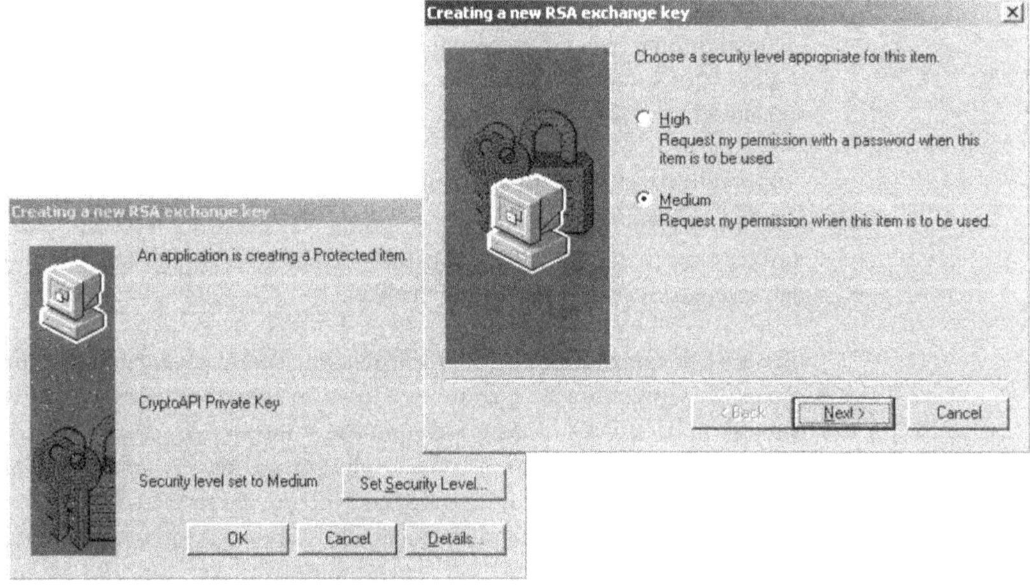

Figure 13.17 *Setting strong private key protection.*

strong private key protection can be set: high and medium (this is the default). High means that the user will, besides being prompted, also be asked to enter a password. The password is used by the DPAPI to add another security level for private key storage. Figure 13.17 shows the dialog box that pops up when you select strong private key protection.

14

Trust in Windows Server 2003 PKI

In this chapter we focus on the concept of trust in a Windows Server 2003 public key infrastructure (PKI). We will explore Windows Server 2003 PKI trust types and trust models and look at how you can define and manage PKI trust relationships in a Windows Server 2003 environment. Windows Server 2003 PKI includes some very important changes in all of these areas.

14.1 PKI is all about trust

The most fundamental question that must be answered in a PKI is: Which public keys are trustworthy? When you use the public key of Alice to provide an important security service, you want to be sure that you are really using Alice's key. The latter is easy to check when you know Alice very well: You could simply ask her. Anyhow, you usually have a lot of confidence in people you know very well. This is not true for a person (let's call him Bob) you accidentally met in some Internet newsgroup. The bigger the distance between two people, the lower the confidence level. In cases like that, trusted third parties (TTPs) can make your life much easier. A TTP may know you and Bob very well and may convince you of the trustworthiness of the other user's key. A TTP in a PKI environment is called a Certification Authority (CA).

Trust in a PKI starts off with trust in the Certification Authority. When you trust a CA, you trust every certificate it issues. Trust of the CA means that you expect that a particular CA can create legitimate certificates that uniquely bind information about an individual to a public key. You also expect that the CA—before it issues the certificate—verifies the individual's identity and checks whether his or her private key is stored securely. These expectations can be based on observations that you have made over a longer period of time. They can also be based on a rumor you heard or simply a belief you have.

The word *belief* in the previous phrase shows that trust in a PKI, in a certificate, or in a public key, is not a scientific fact; in many cases it is based on some assumption. The latter may be hard to understand for technologists used to dealing with IT logic. The ITU-T X.509 standard (paragraph 3.3.23) also uses the term *assumption* in its definition of trust: "An entity can be said to 'trust' a second entity when it (the first entity) makes the assumption that the second entity will behave exactly as the first entity expects. This trust may apply only for some specific function. The key role of trust in the authentication framework is to describe the relationship between an authenticating entity and a certification authority; an authenticating entity shall be certain that it can trust the Certification Authority to create only valid and reliable certificates."

14.2 A trust taxonomy

Trust relationships in the PKI world are very similar to trust relationships in the real world. Trust is a very complex notion that cannot be easily defined or classified. If we simplify things a bit, we can distinguish three basic types of trust relationships (they are illustrated in Figures 14.1 and 14.2): direct, third-party, and extended third-party trust relationships. Both third-party and extended third-party trust relationships are also referred to as indirect trust relationships.

In a direct or peer-to-peer trust relationship, Alice trusts user Bob's certificate, because user Alice knows Bob in person. Alice considers anything (including Bob's certificate) that she gets from Bob to be trustworthy. If the same is true the other way around, there is a mutual or bidirectional direct trust relationship between Alice and Bob. If many users had a direct trust relationship with Alice, Alice would become a trusted third party. This is what happens with Charlie in Figure 14.2.

In the context of a third-party trust relationship, there is a direct trust relationship between Alice and a third-party Charlie and also between the same third-party Charlie and Bob. If the previous two trust relationships are

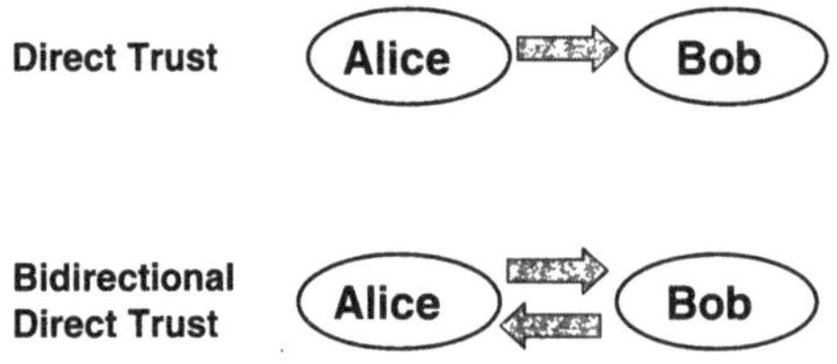

Figure 14.1 *A trust taxonomy: direct trust relationships.*

Direct Trust
Alice
Bob

Bidirectional Direct Trust
Alice
Bob

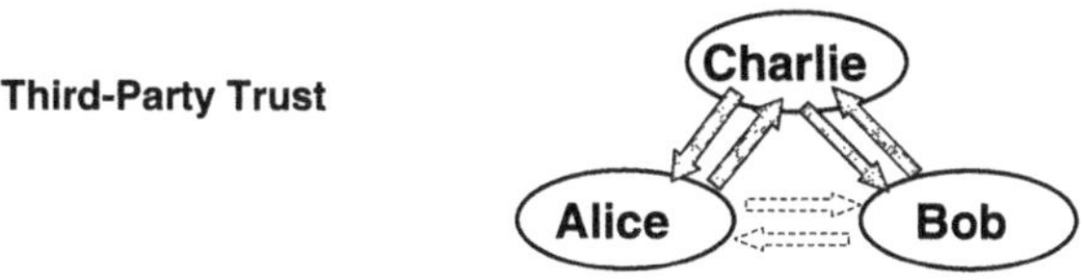

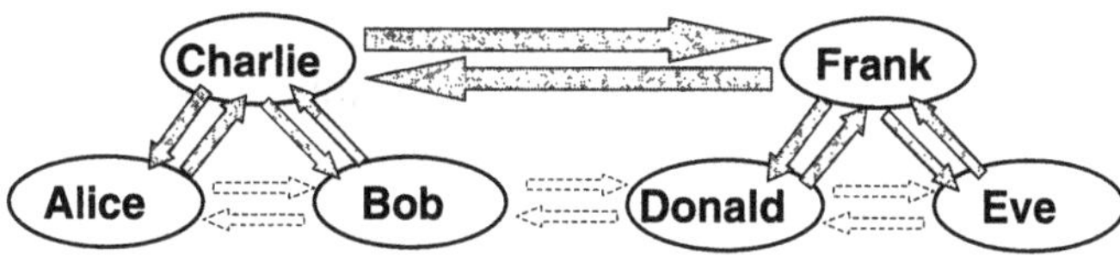

Figure 14.2 *A trust taxonomy: indirect trust relationships.*

transitive, there will be an implicit trust relationship between Alice and Bob. This is very important: A third-party trust relationship—which is an indirect trust relationship—only exists if two other direct trust relationships are transitive. Transitivity of trust relationships greatly simplifies trust management. It also reduces the number of trusts needed between entities that want to interoperate. If transitive trusts are available, the use of third-party trusts is a scalable solution for large organizations. Unfortunately, transitivity is not always available—it may also be available in a limited scope or degree, applying to only certain actions or a certain period in time.

An extended third-party trust relationship occurs when both Alice and Bob have a trust relationship with Charlie, both Donald and Eve trust Frank, and there is also a trust relationship set up between Charlie and Frank. The extended third-party trust relationship between Bob and Donald is an indirect trust that will only exist if two other third-party trust relationships are considered transitive.

14.3 PKI trust terminology

PKI trust models provide a technological framework for the management of PKI trust relationships between CAs and between CAs and PKI users. They also define the rules that are needed to discover and traverse a PKI trust path. PKI trust path traversal is a critical part of certificate validation.

A CA's trust domain defines the community or boundaries within which the CA is considered trusted. Trust domain boundaries are typically based on organizational or geographical boundaries; however, a single organization may also be split into different trust domains, following, for example, the organization's divisions or departments.

All PKI users in the CA's trust domain consider the CA a trust anchor. This is a CA in which the PKI user has a very high level of confidence. During certificate validation, the PKI software will try to discover a trust path up to the level of a trust anchor. How PKI trust path discovery and traversal exactly work in the different trust models is not covered in this chapter.

14.4 PKI trust models

In the following we will discuss the following PKI trust models: the hierarchical, networked, meshed, bridge CA, and hybrid trust models. Let's first look at why we need multiple CAs.

14.4.1 Why multiple CAs?

Before diving into the nuts and bolts of PKI trust models, let's examine why your organization may need more than a single CA. It is pretty obvious why we may need multiple CAs in an environment that's made up of different organizations, but why would we need more than one CA in a single organization?

First of all, using multiple CAs limits the negative consequences of CA private key compromise. If your organization has a single CA and its private key is compromised, everyone in your organization will be affected. If your organization hosts multiple CAs, only the entities belonging to the CA's trust domain will be affected. You may need multiple CAs for sizing, load balancing, and environmental or organizational reasons:

- Your organization may need too many certificates to be generated, issued, and maintained by a single CA.
- If many users need to get a certificate simultaneously, you may want to spread the request load by setting up multiple CAs.
- Geographical locations that are connected to a central location using a low-bandwidth link may all need their own CA.
- Your organization may need a different CA for every entity type with which it is dealing (e.g., one for partners, one for contractors, and one for employees).

Setting up multiple CAs also provides more flexibility:

- You can support applications that have different PKI security policy requirements. For example, you could have one certificate-based application dealing with large financial transactions and another with the distribution of corporate information. Both use certificates for client authentication, but the first one obviously needs a much higher level of user identification at certificate enrollment time than the second one. They also may have different backup scheme requirements and different CA key and certificate change interval requirements.

- You can map the PKI structure to the organizational structure more easily. Organizations often have departments with different PKI security policy requirements. Members of the human resources department usually must satisfy higher security requirements to get a certificate than members of the logistics department, who usually do not deal with confidential information.
- You can cope more easily with political and legal requirements. A part of your organization may require its own CA because it cannot tolerate any involvement of external people in its security-related services. The latter may also be imposed by legal requirements in certain environments.

14.4.2 Hierarchical trust model

A hierarchical trust model consists of a tree of CAs. The top of the hierarchy is a root CA—it is usually the trust anchor of the hierarchy. Within a hierarchy it is the only entity that is authorized to sign its own certificate. The self-signed root certificate makes it impossible for just anyone to pretend to be the root CA: Only the root CA knows and possesses its private key.

In a hierarchical trust model there is a clear superior-subordinate relationship between the CAs on the different hierarchical tiers. The root CA certifies the tier-1 CAs (one tier below), which in turn certify the tier-2 CAs, and so on. In a strict hierarchy every subordinate CA will only have one superior CA. The certificate issued by a superior CA to a subordinate CA is illustrated in Figure 14.3. The nonroot CAs in a hierarchical trust model are called subordinate CAs. A hierarchy can contain two types of subordinate CAs: intermediate CAs and issuing CAs. Issuing CAs issue certificates to PKI users. It is a best practice that intermediate CAs issue only subordinate CA certificates. This allows you to take intermediate CAs offline to provide an additional level of security.

The hierarchical trust model supports delegation: A superior CA can delegate part of its certificate-issuing responsibilities to a subordinate CA. That is why organizations that have a clear hierarchical structure can usually easily be mapped to a hierarchical PKI trust model.

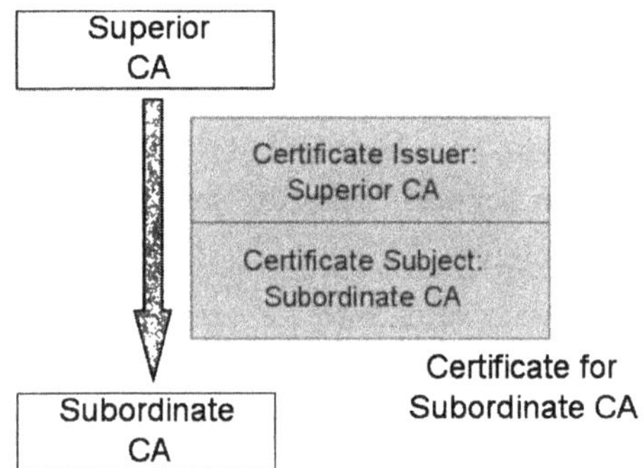

Figure 14.3 *A trust taxonomy: indirect trust relationships.*

Windows 2000, Windows Server 2003, and Windows XP PKI clients all support the trust path discovery and traversal mechanisms that are needed in a hierarchical trust model (see Figure 14.4). When validating a certificate that has been issued by a CA that is part of a hierarchical trust model, the PKI client software will try to discover a trust path that links the issuing CA to the CA trust anchor. The latter may be a root CA or another CA in the hierarchy.

When building a CA hierarchy using Windows Server 2003 PKI, you should use standa-lone CAs for the root and intermediate (every nonissuing CA). This will facilitate taking these CAs offline. The issuing CAs can be Windows Server 2003 enterprise CAs. The choice to make a CA a stand-alone or an enterprise CA is made when installing a Windows Server 2003 CA.

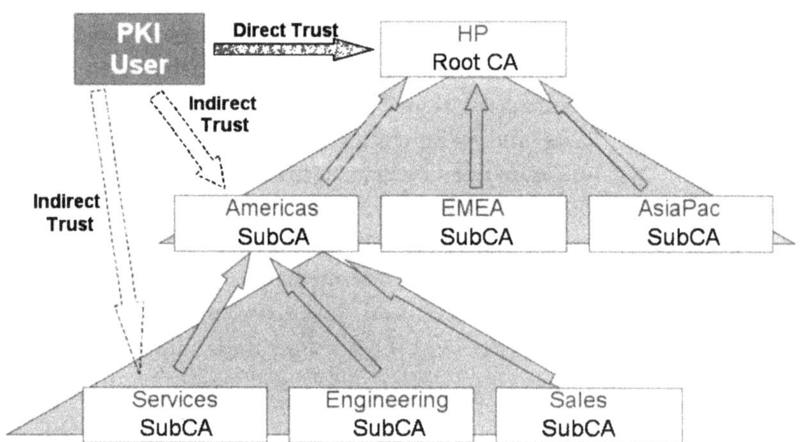

Figure 14.4 *Hierarchical trust model.*

14.4.3 Networked Trust Model

In a networked trust model (illustrated in Figure 14.5), there are no superior-subordinate relationships between the different CAs. All CAs are considered peers. The networked trust model is also known as the peer-to-peer or the distributed trust model. In a networked trust model, trust anchors differ and a single CA will typically not be the trust anchor for the entire PKI community (like was the case for a hierarchical trust model). To set up trust relationships in this peer-to-peer community, two techniques can be used: cross-certification and certificate trust lists (CTLs). Whereas Windows 2000 PKI only supported CTLs, Windows Server 2003 supports both of them.

A CTL is a signed list of trusted CA certificates that is centrally managed by a PKI administrator and distributed throughout the organization to all PKI clients. In Windows 2000 and Windows Server 2003 PKI, CTLs can have a limited validity period and their scope can also be configured to a limited amount of PKI-enabled applications. We will come back to them more extensively in Section 14.5.2.

Cross-certification simply means that a CA issues a certificate for another peer CA and also the other way around. The ITU-T X.509 standard defines cross-certification as follows: "A certification authority may be the subject of a certificate issued by another certification authority. In this case, the certificate is called a cross-certificate..." and "Cross-certificate—This is a certificate where the issuer and the subject are different CAs. CAs issue certificates to other CAs either to authorize the subject CA's existence (e.g. in a strict hierarchy) or to recognize the existence of the subject CA (e.g. in a distributed trust model). The cross-certificate structure is used for both of these."

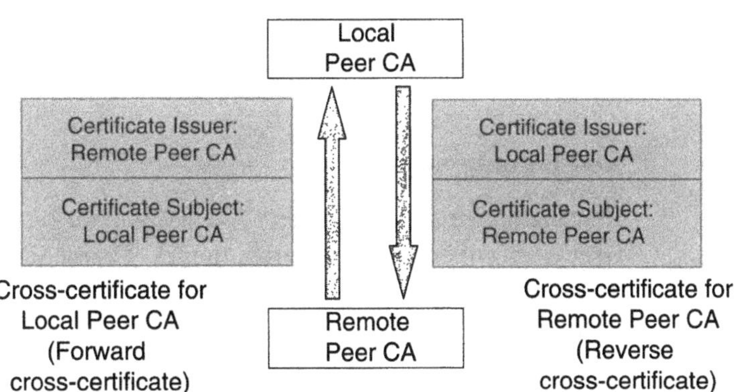

Figure 14.5 *Networked trust model.*

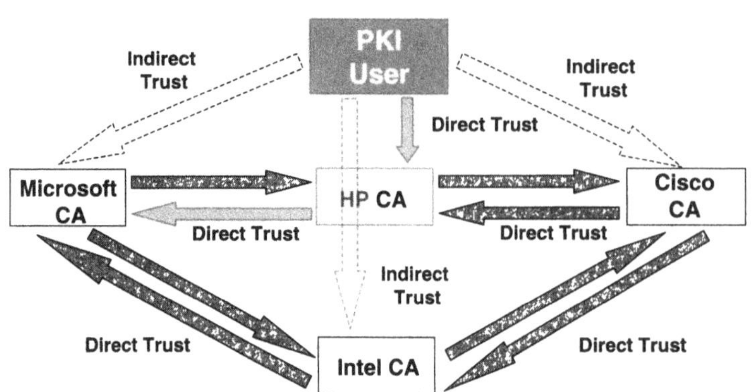

Figure 14.6 *Cross-certification CA trust relationship.*

A cross-certification trust relationship may be one-way or two-way. In a two-way trust relationship, the certificate issued by the local CA for a remote CA is called the reverse cross-certificate. The certificate issued by the remote CA for the local CA is called the forward cross-certificate. The certificates issued in a cross-certification CA trust relationship are illustrated in Figure 14.6.

Windows Server 2003 and Windows XP PKI clients all support the trust path discovery and traversal mechanisms that are needed in a networked trust model made up of several cross-certifications. These mechanisms are not available on Windows 2000 clients. When validating a certificate that has been issued by a CA that is part of a networked trust model, the PKI client software will try to discover a trust path that links the issuing CA to its local CA trust anchor. When building a networked trust model using Windows Server 2003 PKI, you can use either stand-alone or enterprise CAs.

The following two trust models, the meshed and the bridge CA trust models, can be regarded as special flavors of the networked trust model. They are both built on cross-certified CA trust relationships. Both the meshed and bridge CA trust models are supported in Windows Server 2003 PKI.

Meshed trust model

In a meshed trust model, every CA has a cross-certified trust relationship with every other CA in the trust model. This model is also known as the web of trust.

In both the networked and the meshed trust model, trust transitivity may lead to unexpected and unwanted trust relationships. Imagine that in the example in Figure 14.7 the HP CA sets up a cross-certification trust

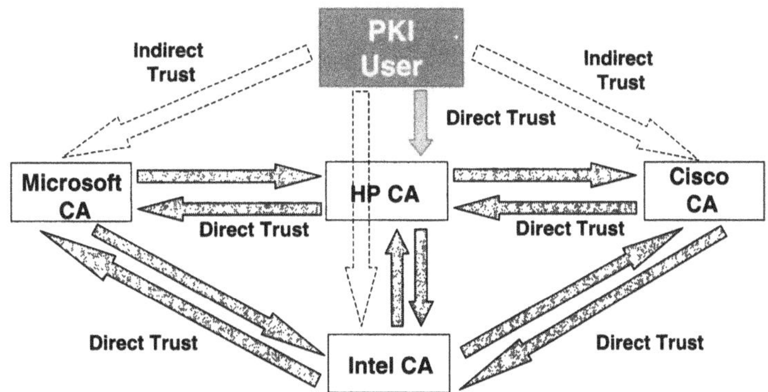

Figure 14.7 *Meshed trust model.*

with a CA from Sun. Through trust transitivity Microsoft may suddenly end up with a PKI trust relationship with Sun. This problem is sometimes referred to as the "trust cascade." To deal with this problem, you can set up constrained trust relationships. These are explained in Section 14.4.5.

Bridge trust model

In a bridge CA or hub-and-spoke trust model- all cross-certification trust relationships are centralized at a central CA, called the bridge CA. Every other CA will have a cross-certified trust relationship with the bridge CA. The bridge CA acts a sort of trust facilitator between different trust domains or organizations. Contrary to the meshed trust model, every trust domain does not need to set up a two-way cross-certification trust relationship with every other trust domain. Also contrary to the meshed trust model, a bridge CA trust model allows for centralized trust transitivity control. We will come back to this when we discuss constrained trust relationships.

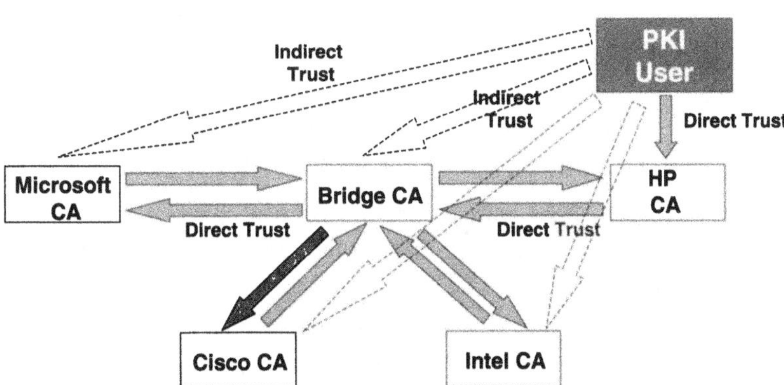

Figure 14.8 *Bridge CA trust model.*

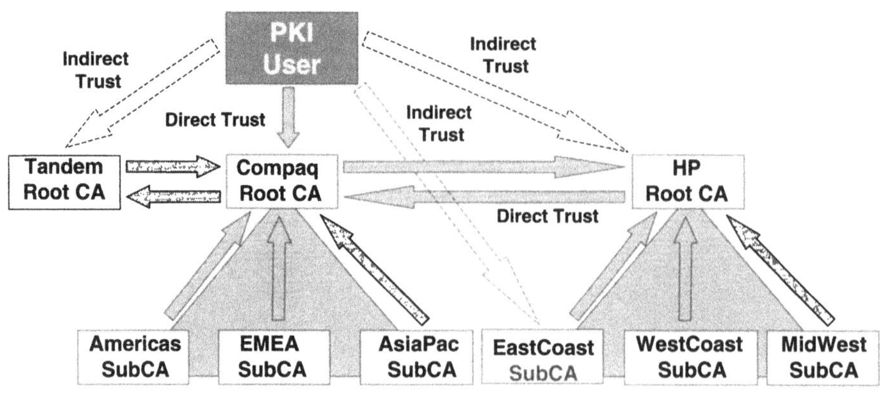

Figure 14.9 *Hybrid trust model.*

14.4.4 Hybrid trust model

In a hybrid trust model, multiple trust models are combined into a single trust model. The example in Figure 14.9 combines a networked trust model with a hierarchical trust model. The dynamic nature of modern business relationships makes it very probable that this will be the PKI trust model of the future.

14.4.5 Constrained trust models

One of the major changes in Windows Server 2003 PKI is the built-in support for constrained trust models, or "qualified subordination" as Microsoft calls it. Qualified subordination allows the CA administrator to put constraints on the trust relationship that is set up with a subordinate CA (in a hierarchical trust model) or a peer CA (in a networked trust model). This ability to qualify trust aligns PKI trust closer to real-life trust: In reality it happens only occasionally that the trust is complete and not subject to certain conditions. It is a common misunderstanding that Windows Server 2003 qualified subordination only applies to cross-certified PKI trust relationships: It is available in both hierarchical and networked trust models.

The trust constraints used in qualified subordination are defined using certificate extensions embedded in a subordinate CA's or a peer cross-certified CA's certificate. Windows Server 2003 PKI supports the following trust constraint-related certificate extensions: basic constraints, name constraints, application policies, certificate policies, policy constraints, policy mappings, application policy constraints, and application policy mappings. Table 14.1 gives an overview of the constraint types.

Table 14.1 *Certificate Constraint Extensions*

Constraint Type	Used in Which Certificates?	Supported by PKI Clients?	Supported by CA Software?	Certificate Extension Used by Microsoft
Basic Constraints	CA and end-entity certificates	Windows 2000, Windows XP, Windows Server 2003	Windows 2000, Windows Server 2003	Basic Constraints
Name Constraints	CA certificates	Windows XP, Windows Server 2003	Windows Server 2003	Name Constraints
Application Policies	CA and end-entity certificates	Windows XP, Windows Server 2003	Windows Server 2003	Application Policies
Issuance Policies	CA certificates	Windows XP, Windows Server 2003	Windows Server 2003	Certificate Policies
Application Policy Mappings	CA certificates	Windows XP, Windows Server 2003	Windows Server 2003	Application Policy Mapping
Application Policy Constraints	CA certificates	Windows XP, Windows Server 2003	Windows Server 2003	Application Policy Constraints
Issuance Policy Mappings	CA certificates	Windows XP, Windows Server 2003	Windows Server 2003	Policy Mapping
Issuance Policy Constraints	CA certificates	Windows XP, Windows Server 2003	Windows Server 2003	Policy Constraints

The name and policy constraints, policy mappings, application policy constraints, application policy mappings, and certificate policies extensions can only be added to CA certificates. Basic constraints and application policies can also be added to end-entity (user) certificates. Basic constraint extensions can be interpreted by Windows 2000, Windows Server 2003, and Windows XP PKI clients. The name, application policies, certificate policies, policy constraints, policy mappings, application policy constraints, and application policy mappings extensions can only be interpreted by Windows Server 2003 and Windows XP PKI clients. Likewise, a Windows 2000 CA only understands the basic constraint extensions; a Windows Server 2003 CA can deal with all of them. Figure 14.10 shows a certificate for a subordinate CA holding all eight new extensions as it is displayed in the Windows Server 2003 and XP certificate viewer.

More information about the certificate constraint extensions can be found in RFC 3280 (which replaces RFC 2459). With the exception of the following, Microsoft's use of the extensions is relatively in line with the content of RFC 3280. To store application policies, Microsoft uses the applica-

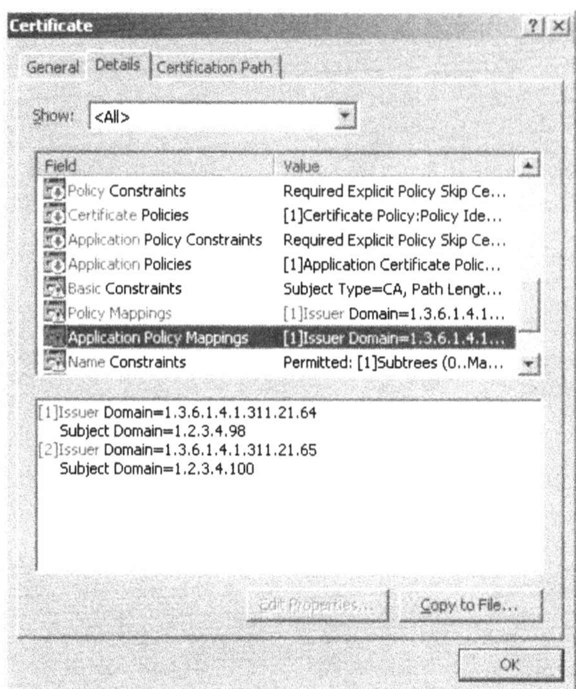

Figure 14.10 *The new constraint extensions in the certificate viewer.*

tion policies extension, which is not defined in RFC 3280—the latter recommends using the certificate policies extension for this purpose. The same is true for the application policy mappings and application policy constraints extension—RFC 3280 recommends storing the first one in the policy mappings extension and the second one in the policy constraints extension.

Basic Constraints

Basic Constraints is a certificate extension that can contain a field called "pathLenConstraint" (or path length constraint in readable format). It can only be used if the Basic Constraints "ca" field is set to true—which is only the case for a CA certificate. It gives the maximum number of nonself-issued CA certificates that may follow a certificate in a certification path and can be used to limit the length of the certificate chain.

In the hierarchical trust example in Figure 14.11 (Config 1), the administrator put a basic constraint in a subordinate CA's certificate that limits the path length to 1. As a consequence, the CA that is located one level below that CA will not be able to issue another CA certificate but only end-user certificates. We will obtain the same result when we add a path length constraint

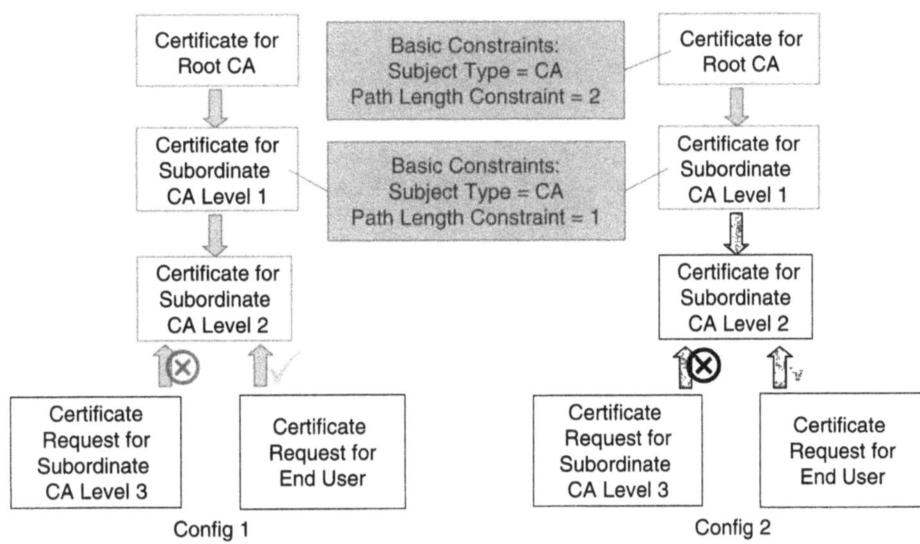

Figure 14.11 *Basic constraints—Path Length Constraint example.*

of 2 to the root CA's certificate (which is illustrated in Config 2 in Figure 14.11). In that case the PKI software will automatically add a path length constraint of 1 to all subordinate CA certificates issued by the root CA.

The Path Length Constraint provides a solution to the trust cascade problem discussed earlier. It basically provides a trust "hop count." The earlier example shows how the number of trust hops can be limited in a hierarchical PKI trust model. A Path Length Constraint can also be useful in a peer-to-peer cross-certification-based trust model. For example, in the bridge CA trust model, if the bridge CA wants to make sure that CAs cannot cross-certify with other CAs, he or she can issue them a certificate that contains a Path Length Constraint that is set to 0.

Name Constraints

A Name Constraint certificate extension can only be set in a CA certificate. It allows you to restrict the population to which a subordinate or cross-certified CA can issue certificates. You can use it to indicate a namespace within which the subject names and subject alternate names in a certificate request, or the IP addresses from which the certificate requests that were sent to a CA were issued must be located. It is kept in a CA certificate's "Name Constraints" extension. Table 14.2 gives an overview of the Name Constraint types supported by Windows Server 2003 PKI and also lists the standards defining the different name formats.

Table 14.2 *Name Constraint Types and Their Meaning*

Name Constraint Type	Meaning
DNS Names (RFC 1034 and 1035–based)	Allows you to restrict certificate issuance based on the DNS name mentioned in the certificate request.
X.500 Distinguished Names (DNs) (X.500-based)	Allows you to restrict certificate issuance based on the DN mentioned in the certificate request. Can be used to issue certificates to a limited amount of users or computer objects in Active Directory.
Uniform Resource Identifiers (URIs) (RFC 2396–based)	Allows you to restrict certificate issuance based on the URI mentioned in the certificate request. Can be used to limit the issuance of SSL Web server certificates.
E-mail and User Principal Name (UPN) (RFC 822–based)	Allows you to restrict certificate issuance based on the e-mail address or UPN mentioned in the certificate request.
IP address (RFC 791 or RFC 2460–based)	Allows you to restrict certificate issuance based on the IP address of the machine from which the certificate request was sent.

Following RFC 3280, a certificate name constraint extension indicates a namespace within which all subject names in subsequent certificates in a certification path must be located. As a consequence, a subordinate CA can only further reduce the namespace rule it received from its parent CA; it can never extend it. For example, if a subordinate CA is permitted to issue certificates for users in the research.hp.com DNS domain, it can never issue a subordinate CA certificate that permits to issue certificates for users in the hp.com DNS domain.

In the hierarchical trust example in Figure 14.12, you can notice that a name constraint can contain both exclusive and inclusive rules. During name constraint validation, exclusive rules always have precedence over inclusive rules. In the example, the root CA administrator put a name constraint in subordinate CA 1's certificate that excludes the UPN "@ibm.com" and permits the DNS names ".hp.com" and ".compaq.com." When a certificate request comes in for "joe@ibm.com," it will be rejected. If a request comes in for "webserver1.hp.com," it will be accepted. Subordinate CA 2's namespace is even more restricted: It can only issue certificates in the .compaq.com DNS namespace. As a consequence, when a request for webserver2.hp.com comes in, it will be rejected. If a request comes in for mail.compaq.com, it will be accepted.

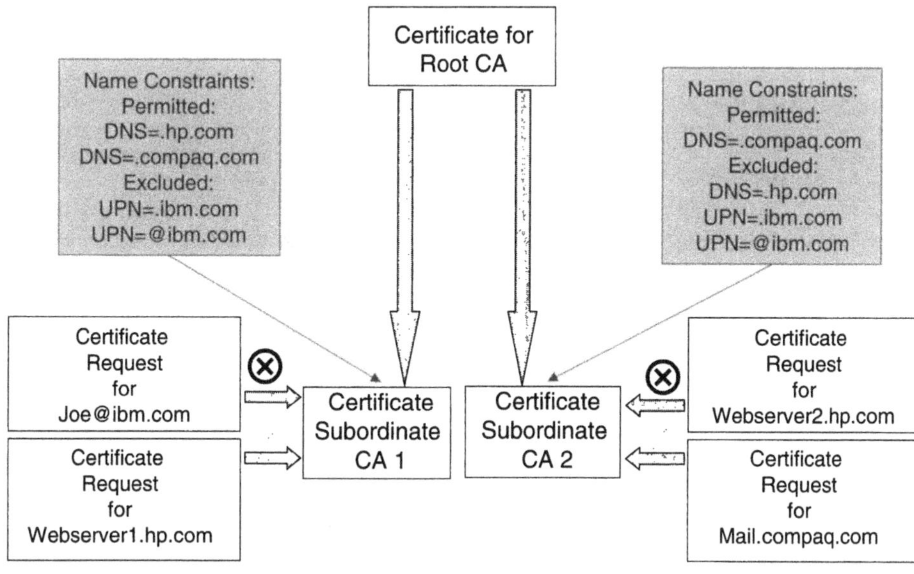

Figure 14.12 *Name Constraints example.*

Issuance policies

An issuance policy defines the conditions that were met when the certificate was issued. In a Windows Server 2003 certificate, an issuance policy is identified using its corresponding Object Identifier (OID) and is kept in a certificate's "Certificate Policies" extension.

When they are added to a CA certificate, they define the set of issuance policies that will be included in any certificate (CA or end entity) issued by that CA. By including them in the cross-certification CA certificate, you can use them to limit the trust you have in the certificates issued by a cross-certified CA. In this context the enforcement of the extension is up to the certificate chain validation logic. The latter logic is only available in Windows XP and Windows Server 2003.

When issuance policies are included in an end-entity certificate, enforcement of the policies must be done on the level of the PKI-enabled application. It must check whether it permits a certificate issued under a certain issuance policy or not. This means that the application must be intelligent enough to know which issuance policies it supports.

Windows Server 2003 PKI comes with four predefined issuance policies. Table 14.3 shows their corresponding OID and meaning. The a, b, c, d variables in the OID for the low, medium, and high assurance issuance

Table 14.3 *Predefined Windows Server 2003 PKI Issuance Policies and their Meaning*

Issuance Policy Type	Meaning
All Issuance OID: 2.5.29.32.0	Issuance policy containing all other issuance policies. This type is only used for CA certificates.
Low Assurance OID: 1.3.6.1.4.1.311.21.8.*a.b.c.d*.1.400	Certificates issued with no additional security requirements.
Medium Assurance OID: 1.3.6.1.4.1.311.21.8. *a.b.c.d*.1.401	Certificates issued with additional security requirements. A good example of such requirements is a smart card certificate requiring a face-to-face issuance process.
High Assurance OID: 1.3.6.1.4.1.311.21.8. *a.b.c.d*.1.402	Certificates issued with the utmost security requirements. A good example of such requirements is the issuance of a key recovery agent certificate that may require additional security background checks as part of the issuance process.

policies represent a randomly generated value that is unique for every Windows Server 2003 forest. You can also define your own, depending on the needs of your PKI environment or application.

Figure 14.13 shows the effect of setting issuance policies in an end-entity certificate, in this case the low assurance issuance policy (which is inherited from the issuing CA at Level 1). When the certificate is used in a PKI-enabled application requiring a high assurance issuance policy, it will be rejected. It can only be used in PKI-enabled applications requiring a low assurance issuance policy.

Application policies

An application policy limits the applications for which a certificate can be used. It can be set in both CA (hierarchical and cross-certified) and end-entity certificates. As for issuance policies, application policies are identified using the OID of the corresponding policy. They are kept in a certificate's "Application Policies" extension. Table 14.4 shows the predefined application policies of Windows Server 2003 PKI and their corresponding OIDs.

In version 2 certificates[1] generated by Windows Server 2003 CAs, application policies have exactly the same function as the Extended Key Usage (EKU) certificate extension. For downlevel compatibility, Windows Server 2003 CAs and Windows Server 2003 and XP clients can still deal with the EKU extension. Microsoft has chosen to use the application policies exten-

1. Version 2 certificates are certificates that are generated by an Enterprise CA based on a version 2 certificate template.

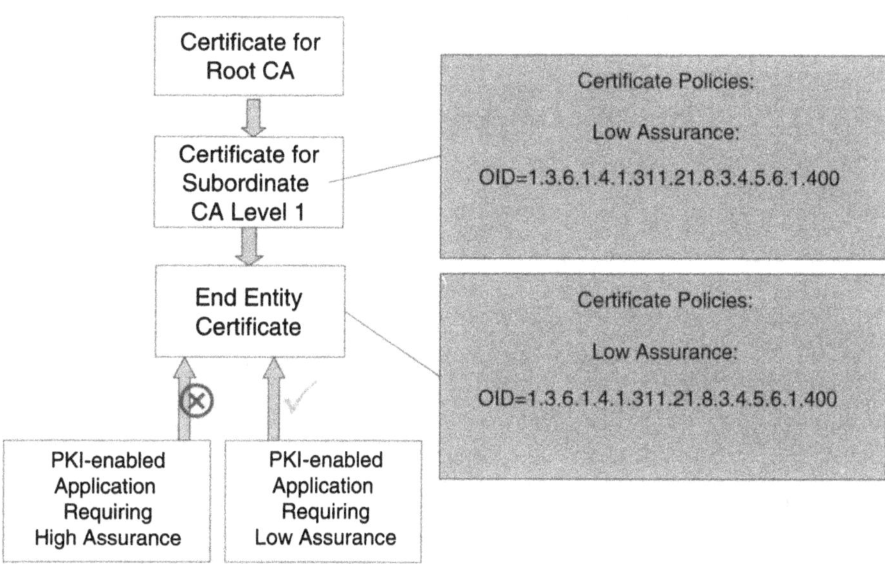

Figure 14.13 *Issuance policy example.*

Table 14.4 *Predefined Application Policy Constraints and Corresponding OIDs*

Application Policy Name	Corresponding OID
All Application Policies	1.3.6.1.4.1.311.10.12.1
Certificate Request Agent	1.3.6.1.4.1.311.20.2.1
Client Authentication	1.3.6.1.5.5.7.3.2
Code Signing	1.3.6.1.5.5.7.3.3
Digital Rights	1.3.6.1.4.1.311.10.5.1
Directory Service E-mail Replication	1.3.6.1.4.1.311.21.19
Document Signing	1.3.6.1.4.1.311.10.3.12
Embedded Windows System Component Verification	1.3.6.1.4.1.311.10.3.8
Encrypting File System	1.3.6.1.4.1.311.10.3.4
File Recovery	1.3.6.1.4.1.311.10.3.4.1
IP Security End System	1.3.6.1.5.5.7.3.5
IP Security IKE Intermediate	1.3.6.1.5.5.8.2.2
IP Security Tunnel Termination	1.3.6.1.5.5.7.3.6

Table 14.4 *Predefined Application Policy Constraints and Corresponding OIDs (continued)*

Application Policy Name	Corresponding OID
IP Security User	1.3.6.1.5.5.7.3.7
Key Pack Licenses	1.3.6.1.4.1.311.10.6.1
Key Recovery	1.3.6.1.4.1.311.10.3.11
Key Recovery Agent	1.3.6.1.4.1.311.21.6
License Server Verification	1.3.6.1.4.1.311.10.6.2
Lifetime Signing	1.3.6.1.4.1.311.10.3.13
Microsoft Time Stamping	1.3.6.1.4.1.311.10.3.2
Microsoft Trust List Signing	1.3.6.1.4.1.311.10.3.1
OEM Windows System Component Verification	1.3.6.1.4.1.311.10.3.7
Private Key Archival	1.3.6.1.4.1.311.21.5
Qualified Subordination	1.3.6.1.4.1.311.10.3.10
Root List Signer	1.3.6.1.4.1.311.10.3.9
Secure Email	1.3.6.1.5.5.7.3.4
Server Authentication	1.3.6.1.5.5.7.3.1
Smart Card Logon	1.3.6.1.4.1.311.20.2.2
Time Stamping	1.3.6.1.5.5.7.3.8
Windows Hardware Driver Verification	1.3.6.1.4.1.311.10.3.5
Windows System Component Verification	1.3.6.1.4.1.311.10.3.6

sion instead of the EKU extension because application policies can be mapped and restricted using the application policy mappings and application policy constraints certificate extensions.

Application policies can be set in both end-entity and CA certificates. If it is set in an end-entity certificate, it limits the applications for which the certificate can be used. If it is set in a CA certificate, it will be copied in all certificates (end-entity and CA) the CA issues and thus limit the applications for which those certificates can be used. In this case it will also limit the certificate types that a CA can issue. For an enterprise CA, the application policy settings even overrule the certificate templates that have been loaded in its certificate templates container. For example, if you want a sub-

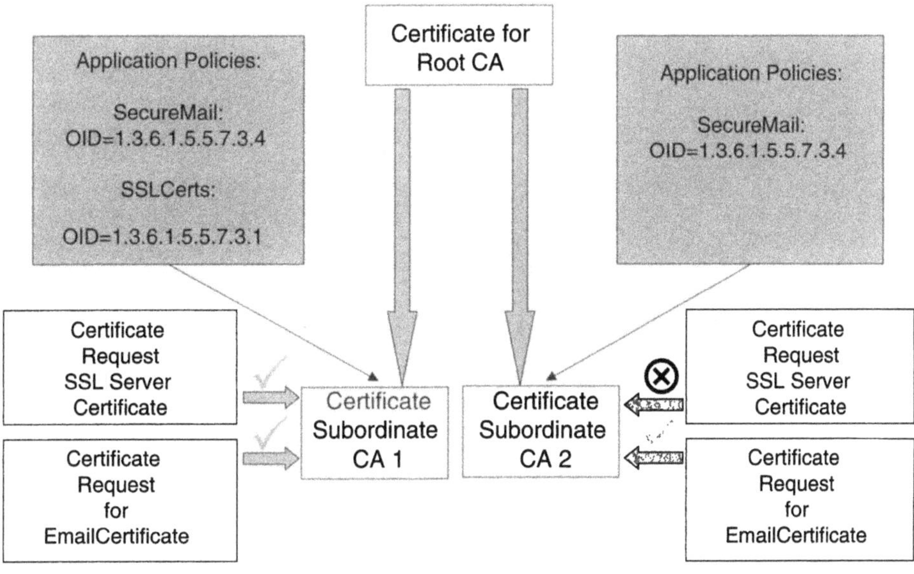

Figure 14.14 *Application policy example.*

ordinate CA to issue only user certificates, you need to make sure that you add the application policy OIDs for the Encrypting File System, Secure E-mail as well as Client authentication. The User certificate template covers all three application policies.

Application policies that are set in cross-certification certificates limit the applications for which a certificate that has the cross-certificate in its certificate chain can be used. In this case enforcement of the application policy is the certificate chain validation software's responsibility. Again, the code needed to do this validation is only available in Windows XP and Windows Server 2003.

Figure 14.14 shows the effect of setting application policies in CA certificates. In the figure an application policy has been set in the certificates of the subordinate CAs 1 and 2. Subordinate CA 1 will accept both e-mail and SSL certificate requests. Subordinate CA 2 can only issue e-mail certificates. It will reject SSL certificate requests.

Policy Mappings and Policy Constraints extension

In this section we explain two other trust constraint-related certificate extensions that are supported by Windows Server 2003 PKI: the Policy Mappings, Policy Constraints, Application Policy Mappings, and Application Policy Constraints extensions. The first two apply to issuance policies

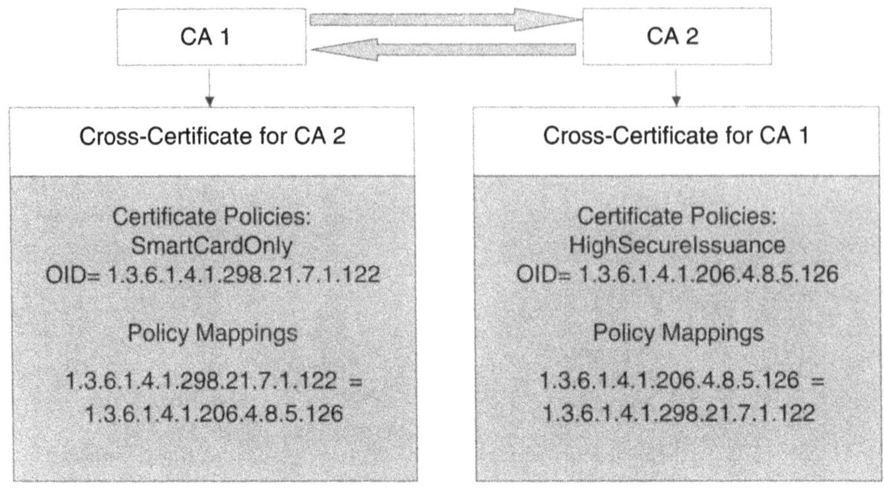

Figure 14.15 *Issuance policy mapping for cross-certified CAs example.*

and the latter two to application policies. Only the first two extensions are defined in RFC 3280.

When defining issuance and application policies in a cross-certified CA trust relationship, policy mappings must be set up between the two cross-certified CAs because the policy OID used in one CA's trust domain cannot be understood by the users of the other CA's trust domain. In the example in Figure 14.15, a policy mapping has been defined between the issuance policies of two cross-certified CAs. CA2's cross-certificate contains a mapping between the CA1 issuance policy and its proper issuance policy. CA1's cross-certificate contains a mapping between the CA2 issuance policy and its proper issuance policy.

Figure 14.16 shows the effect of defining policy mappings in a cross-certificate on the certificates trusted by a user. User 1 in the example trusts CA1. CA1 has issued a cross-certificate for CA2 containing policy mappings between its proper issuance policy called SmartCardOnly and the issuance policy of CA2 called HighSecureIssuance. When no policy mappings were defined in CA2's cross-certificate, user 1 would not trust the certificate of user 2—because it contains an unknown issuance policy. Thanks to the inclusion of a policy mapping in the cross-certificate, user 1 will trust user 2's certificate.

The Policy Constraints extensions allow you to specify how an issuance or application policy constraint that has been defined in the certificate of a particular CA will affect the validity of the certificate chain of a certificate

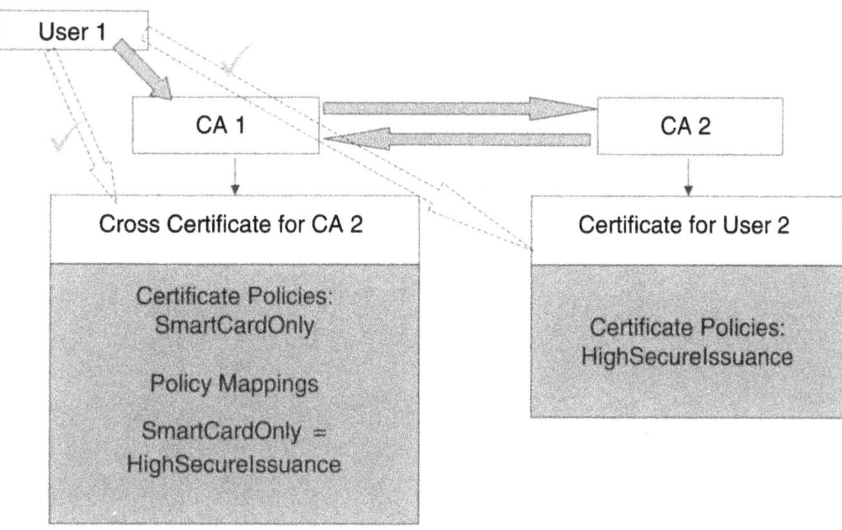

Figure 14.16 *Issuance policy mapping PKI user example.*

containing that CA certificate. In other words, it specifies how an issuance or application policy constraint that has been defined in the certificate of a particular CA affects the validity of the CA certificates that are subordinate to that CA. The latter CAs can be subordinate CAs (in a hierarchy) or cross-certified CAs (in a networked trust model).

Two types of policy constraints can be defined:

- *Require explicit policy:* This constraint specifies a number that indicates the number of layers below the CA that has the constraint in its certificate where the issuance or application policy must be defined in the subordinate CA certificate. If the application policy is not defined in the subordinate CA certificates, the certificate that has these CA certificates in its chain will be rejected.

  Figure 14.17 shows the effect of setting the Require explicit policy extension to 1 in a subordinate CA's certificate. The end entity's certificate in config 1 will be invalid because the subordinate CA that's located one level below the level 1 subordinate CA does not have the "HPpolicy" policy defined in its certificate. In config 2 the end entity's certificate will be valid because the subordinate CA at level 2 does have the "HPpolicy" policy defined.

- *Inhibit policy mapping:* This constraint specifies a number that indicates the number of layers below the CA that has the constraint in its certificate where policy mappings can be defined in the subordinate

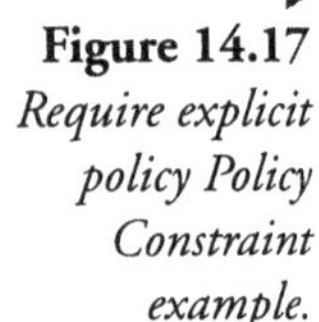

Figure 14.17 *Require explicit policy Policy Constraint example.*

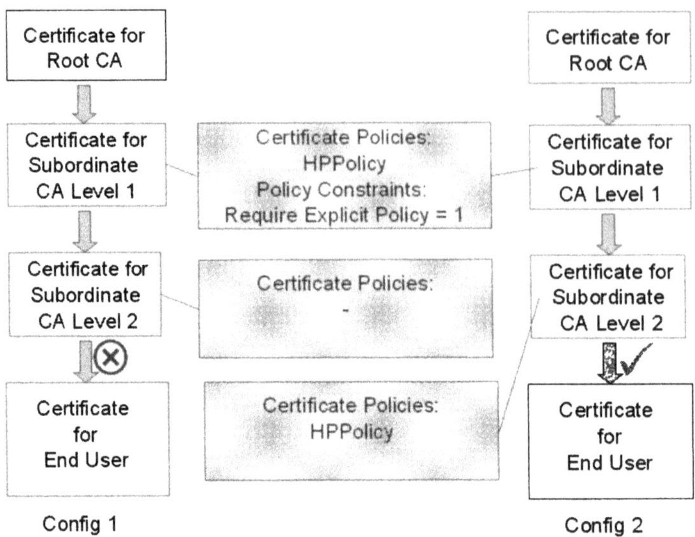

CA certificate. This means that at levels below the specified number, policy mappings will be ignored. This setting protects against unexpected trust relationships as a consequence of policy mappings.

Figure 14.18 shows the effect of setting the Inhibit policy mapping extension to 1 in a cross-certification certificate: The user will

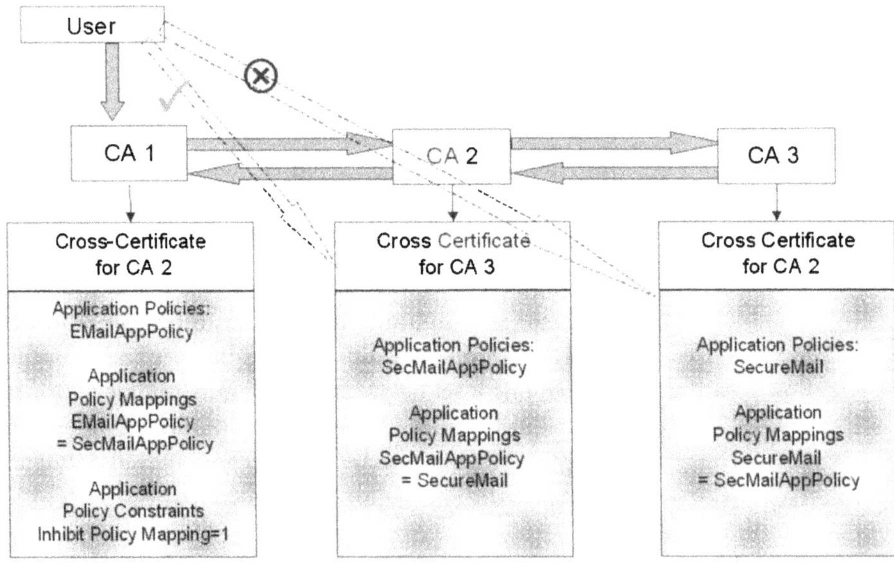

Figure 14.18 *Inhibit policy mapping Policy Constraint example.*

Table 14.5 *Which Trust Model for Which Environment: Overview*

Environment	Trust Model
Within a Single Organization (Outsourced PKI)	Hierarchical Model
Within a Single Organization (Insourced PKI)	Hierarchical Model
■ Small Organization	Hierarchical Model (one level)
■ Medium Organization	Hierarchical Model (two levels), possibly with constrained trust (Qualified Subordination)
■ Large Organization	Hierarchical Model (three levels), possibly with constrained trust (Qualified Subordination)
Between Organizations	Networked Model (including meshed and bridge CA trust models), possibly with constrained trust (Qualified Subordination) Hybrid Model, possibly with constrained trust (Qualified Subordination)

not trust the cross-certificate issued by CA3 for CA2. If the extension was set to 2, the user would trust the latter certificate. Setting Inhibit policy mapping to 1 limits the number of layers where policy mappings can be defined to 1. Although the cross-certificate issued by CA3 for CA2 contains a valid mapping, it is two layers away from the certificate where the Inhibit policy mapping restriction is set. This example shows how the Inhibit policy mapping extension can be used to deal with the trust cascade problem that was mentioned earlier in this chapter.

14.4.6 Which trust model for which environment?

Table 14.5 provides an overview of the trust models that are typically chosen for a particular environment. Table 14.5 does not provide the ultimate overview of which trust model to choose for which environment. Your organization may have valid reasons to choose a completely different trust model than the one shown in the table. Choosing a trust model is a complex problem involving many different factors.

14.5 User PKI trust management

Windows Server 2003 and Windows XP include several mechanisms to control a PKI user's trust anchors. Some of them are user-driven, and others

Table 14.6 *User PKI Trust Management Mechanisms*

Mechanism	Scope	Managed by	Management Interface or Mechanism
Machine Certificate Store	Machine	Local Administrator	MMC Certificates snap-in
User Certificate Store	User	User	MMC Certificates snap-in IE Certificates Viewer
Enterprise Trust (Certificate Trust Lists)	Depends on AD object GPO is linked to	GPO Administrator	GPO Editor
Trusted Root CAs	Depends on AD object GPO is linked to	GPO Administrator	GPO Editor or certutil.exe –dspublish RootCA" command line
NTAuth Store	Forest	Forest or Domain Administrator	certutil.exe –dspublish NTAUth" command line
Windows Update	All machines having the Root Certificate Update Service enabled	Microsoft (and Forest or Domain Administrator)	Only for subscribers to Microsoft Root Certificate Program

are local machine administrator or even domain or forest administrator-driven. The latter are obviously only available when the PKI client is a member of a Windows Server 2003 forest or domain. Table 14.6 gives an overview of the available mechanisms and their characteristics. We will discuss them all in more detail in the following sections.

14.5.1 User-centric PKI trust management

Windows Server 2003 and Windows XP both allow PKI users to make their proper trust decisions. The key to this is their certificate store and more particularly the Trusted Root Certification Authorities certificate container—also known as the root certificate store. To access the certificate store, you can use the MMC Certificates snap-in or the certificates viewer from your Internet Explorer.

All CA certificates contained in the root certificate store container are by default considered trust anchors. By default, a PKI user has complete control over which CA certificates he or she wants to add to or remove from this container. When a user tries to add a CA certificate to the root store, a dialog box will pop up asking whether he or she really wants to add this certificate to the root store (as illustrated in Figure 14.19).

Figure 14.19 *Pop-up dialog box when adding a certificate to the root certificate store.*

You will notice that on a default Windows XP and Windows Server 2003 installation, the root certificate store comes prepopulated with a set of CA certificates. This is obviously a good thing from an ease-of-use point of view because the user does not need to add all CA certificates to his or her store. From a pure security point of view, however, this is not a very sound practice: The user is relying on the trust judgment of the software vendor to decide whether a certificate is trustworthy or not. In enterprise environments it is therefore recommended to remove all prepopulated CA certificates and add only those that are considered trustworthy by the IT security department. Again, in consumer environments the prepopulated root store is a good solution if you look at it from a purely ease-of-use point of view: It takes away some of the complexity of dealing with PKI and PKA for consumers.

Windows Server 2003 comes with an important new GPO extension impacting user trust management. It allows an administrator to set whether a user is allowed to make his or her own root certificate store trust decisions and to determine which certificate store containers are considered trust anchor stores. The new settings can be accessed from the properties of the \Computer Configuration\Windows Settings\Security Settings\Public Key Policies\Trusted Root Certification Authorities GPO container and are illustrated in Figure 14.20.

To allow users to make their own trust anchor trust decisions, check the Allow users to select new root certification authorities (CAs) to trust checkbox. If you set Client computers can trust the following certificate stores to Enterprise Root Certification Authorities, only the certificates stored in the following Active Directory container will be trusted: CN=Certification Authorities, CN=Public Key Services, CN=Services, CN=Configuration, DC=<domain>,DC=<domain>. If you choose the other setting, both the certificates in the above AD container and the ones in the certificate store's "Third Party Root Certification Authorities" container will be trusted.

Figure 14.20
GPO trusted root certification authorities settings.

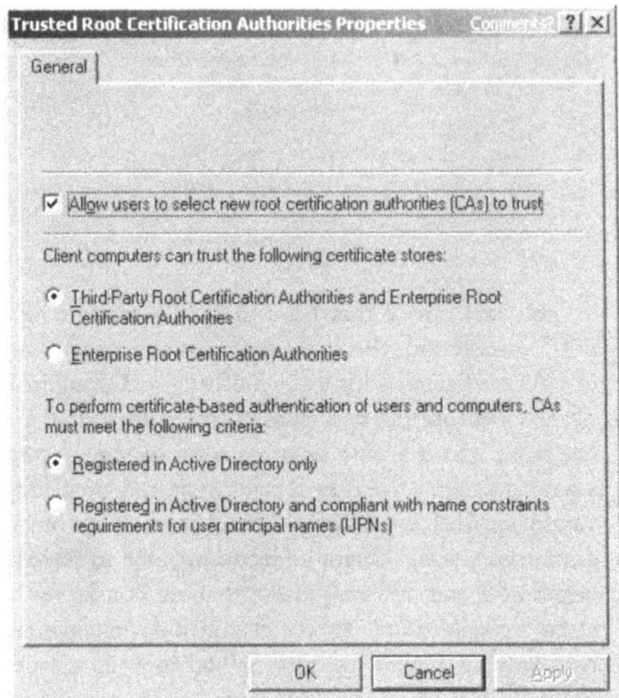

Independent of this, a user can always set for which applications or purposes it trusts a particular certificate that is stored in his or her certificate store. To access this functionality, open a certificate, go to the Details tab, click Edit Properties, select Enable only the following purposes, and then check the applications or purposes you want to trust the certificate for (as illustrated in Figure 14.21). Setting this certificate property has the same effect on applications as if the certificate contained an Extended Key Usage (EKU) or Application Policy X.509 extension.

Remember that the bulk of the trust anchor certificates in the root store are inherited from the local machine certificate store. Only the local administrator can directly modify the trust anchors on the local machine. To look at the content of a machine's certificate store, open the MMC Certificates snap-in and select local machine. To see the certificates in your personal certificate store that are inherited from the machine store, select "show physical certificate stores" in the view options of your personal certificate store. Each logical certificate container will then hold a container called "Local Computer" holding the certificates inherited from the local machine certificate store.

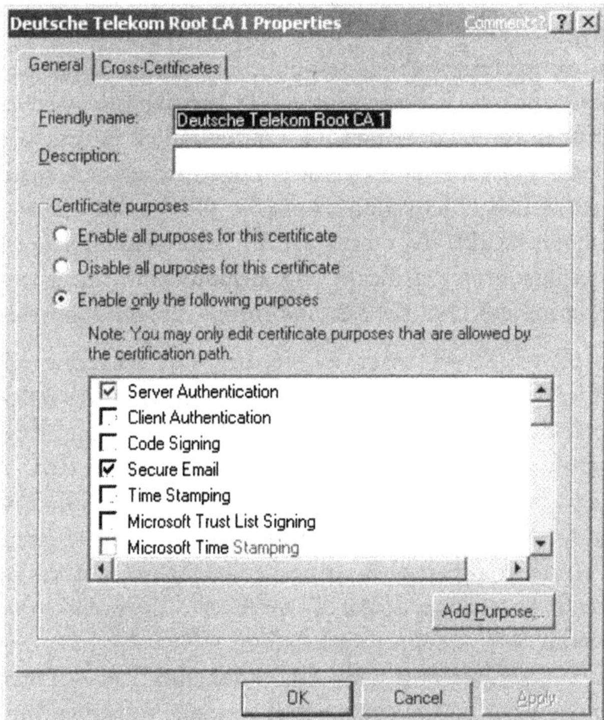

Figure 14.21 *Configuring trust settings on individual certificates.*

14.5.2 Centralized user PKI trust management

Windows Server 2003 provides three ways to control a PKI user's trust anchors in a centralized way: through a set of GPO settings, using the NTAUTH Active Directory store, and using the Windows Update service.

The following GPO settings affect a PKI user's trust anchors: "Trusted Root Certification Authorities" and "Enterprise Trust." The entries in both GPO settings are automatically downloaded to PKI clients as part of the GPO application process.

The Trusted Root Certification Authorities container is used to distribute trustworthy enterprise CA certificates to enterprise PKI users. Contrary to the other trust anchor-related GPO setting (discussed next), the trust in the CA entries in this container is unlimited (as long as the certificates have not expired).

The Enterprise Trust container contains a set of Certificate Trust Lists (CTLs), which are basically signed lists of CA certificates. The entries in a

CTL are typically CA certificates or certificates of CAs belonging to other organizations. They are only considered trust anchors if the CTL is signed using a private key whose public key certificate has been issued by another trust anchor. Contrary to the GPO setting discussed earlier, the amount of trust in the entries of a CTL can be limited in time and to a set of applications. The latter two can be specified from the Certificate Trust List Wizard, which is accessible from the GPO MMC snap-in (as illustrated in Figure 14.22). To create a CTL administrators need a CTL signing or administrator certificate. By default both members of the Enterprise Admins and Domain Admins groups can enroll for these certificate types.

The NTAUTH Active Directory store is a very special trust anchor store. It holds the CA certificates of all Windows Server 2003 Enterprise CAs and CAs that are trusted to issue Windows smart card logon certificates or any certificate that contains a client authentication EKU or application policy (e.g., for use with SSL client authentication, RAS/VPN authentication, and so forth). The NTAUTH trust anchor certificates are downloaded to every PKI client as part of the autoenrollment event. They are stored in the CaCertificate attribute of the NTAuthCertificates object that's located in the following Active Directory location: CN=Public Key Services, CN=Services, CN=Configuration, DC=,DC=<domain>, DC=<domain>. The autoenrollment event occurs when a user logs on, when you use the gpupdate utility to manually refresh the local GPOs, or during an automatic group policy refresh (which occurs every 8 hours by default).

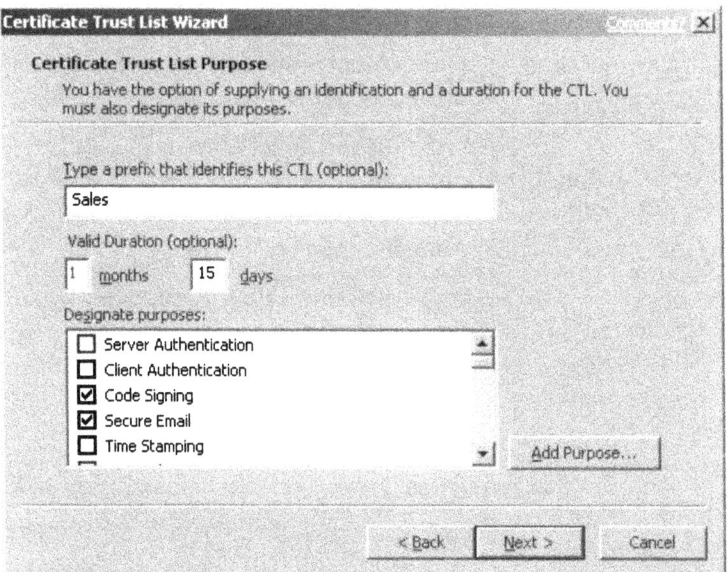

Figure 14.22 *Specifying CTL time and application trust limits.*

A third centralized user PKI trust management solution is the Root Certificate Update Service—which is an extension to Windows Update. The goal of this service is to provide a dynamic CA certificate distribution mechanism that can replace the preloaded CA certificates. The software that is required for this service to work on the client side can be installed through the Windows XP and Windows Server 2003 Update Root Certificate installation option. Behind this service there is an engine that will automatically download new root CA certificates to the Third-Party Certification Authorities container in the machine and user certificate stores. The service uses a special CTL, called the Windows Update CTL, to automatically download CA certificates when the Windows XP or Windows Server 2003 client-side certificate validation software checks the appropriate Windows Update download location. Organizations that want to distribute their CA certificate using this feature have to subscribe to the Microsoft Root Certificate Program (more information at http://www.microsoft.com/technet/security/news/rootcert.asp).

14.6 CA trust definition

In the following sections we look at how you can define PKI CA trust relationships in Windows Server 2003. We examine how to set up hierarchical, cross-certified, and constrained PKI trust relationships.

14.6.1 Defining Hierarchical Trust Relationships

A hierarchical trust relationship between a parent and a subordinate CA is defined as part of the Windows Server 2003 CA installation process. In the CA type dialog box, you can select whether the CA will be a root or a subordinate CA (as illustrated in Figure 14.23 for a stand-alone CA). For a subordinate CA you have the choice to submit the certificate request (the *.req file—which contains a PKCS#10 or CMC formatted request blob) immediately to the parent CA (if the CA is visible in AD and online) or provide it to the parent CA manually (e.g., using a floppy disk).

Figure 14.24 gives a typical hierarchical trust example: an internal PKI for HP made up of a root CA and three regonial CAs: one for the Americas, one for EMEA, and one for AsiaPac.

14.6.2 Defining cross-certified trust relationships

Contrary to a hierarchical trust relationship, a cross-certification trust relationship can be set up at any time after the CA installation. Cross-certifica-

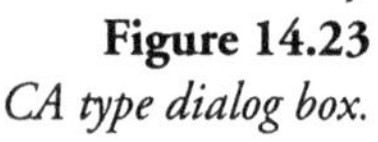

Figure 14.23
CA type dialog box.

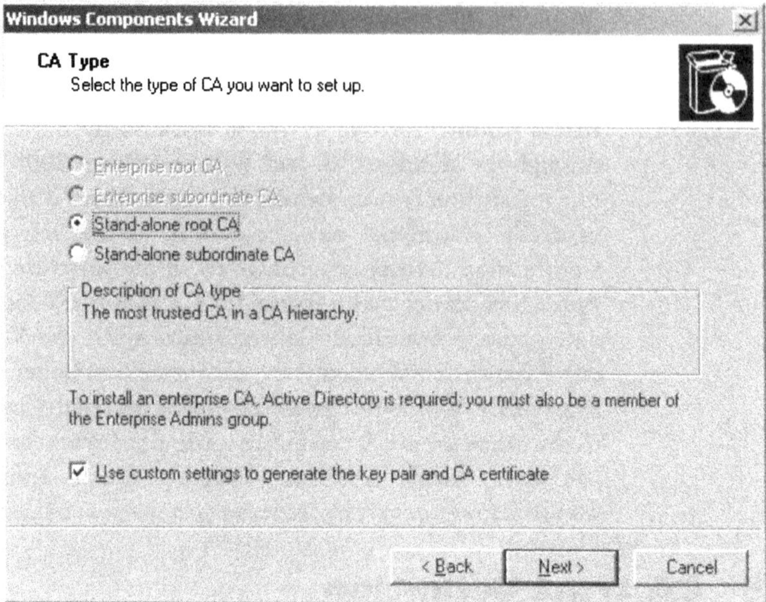

tion is typically done between the CAs of different organizations. Figure 14.25 gives an interorganizational cross-certified trust example: The Compaq CA has issued a cross-certificate to the HP CA; the HP CA does the same thing the other way around.

Figure 14.24
Hierarchical trust example.

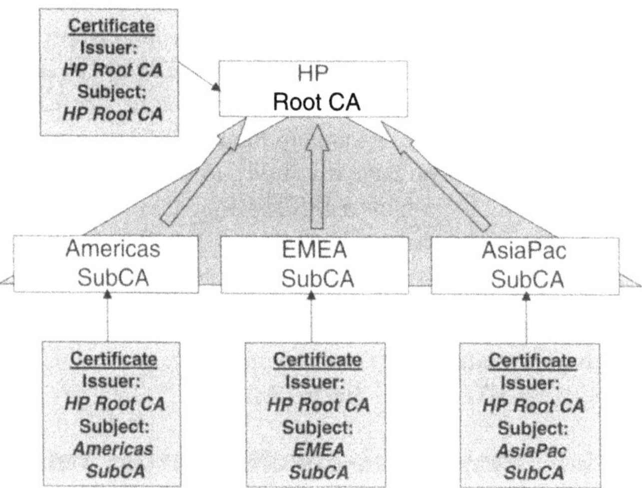

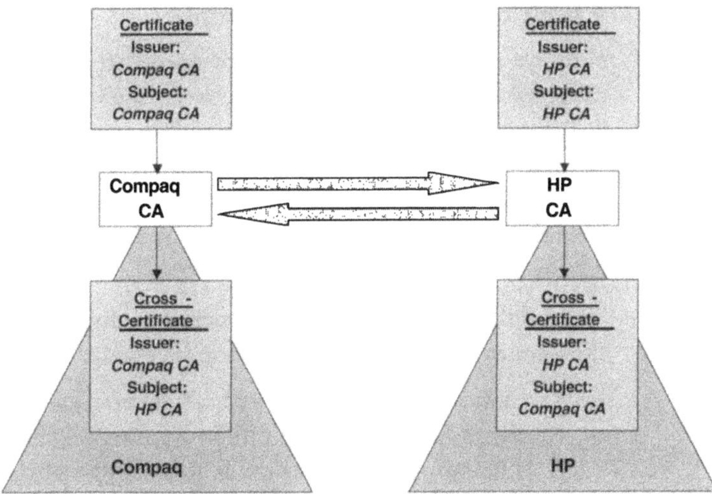

Figure 14.25 *Cross-certified trust example.*

A cross-certification trust relationship can be set up between different types of CAs: they can be enterprise or stand-alone CAs, they can be root or subordinate CAs, and so forth. Figure 14.26 gives some sample scenarios.

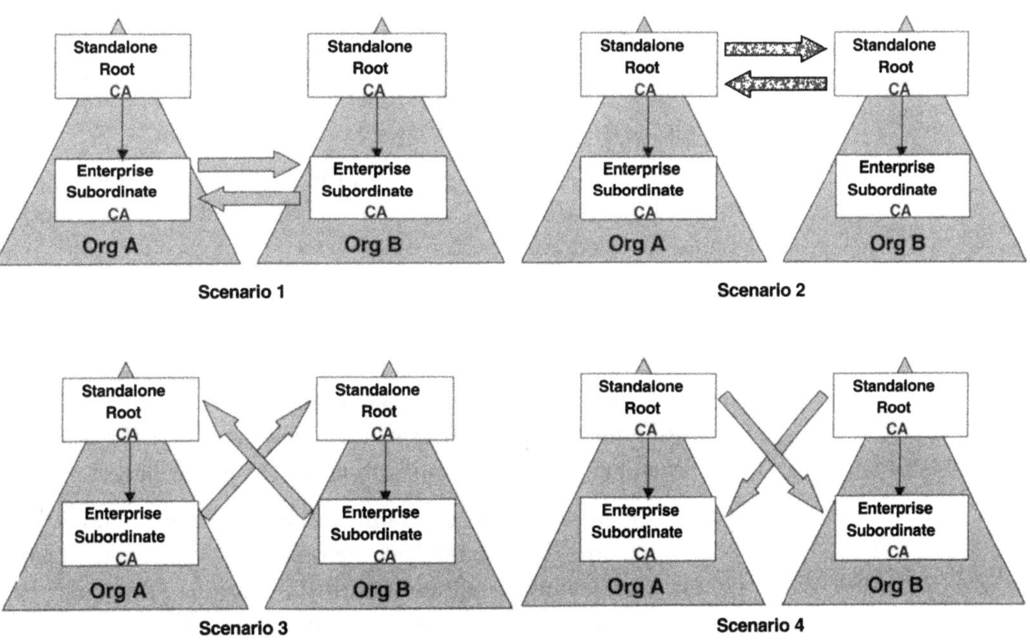

Figure 14.26 *Cross-certification scenarios.*

A basic cross-certification example

Next we discuss the different steps needed to set up a basic bidirectional cross-certified trust relationship between the Compaq CA and the HP CA of Figure 14.25. Basic in this context means without defining any trust constraints. Although the chances are relatively small that organizations will ever set up such an unconstrained trust relationship, this example will facilitate the understanding of how to set up more complex constrained cross-certified trust relationships.

In order for the HP CA to generate a cross-certification certificate for the Compaq CA, you need to do the following:

1. Obtain a copy of the Compaq CA certificate and the HP CA policy.inf file. Store these files in a folder on the HP CA computer. The policy.inf file, which is normally used to specify trust constraints, is in this case almost empty. It contains the following information:

   ```
   [Version]
   Signature= "$Windows NT$"
   ```

2. Make sure that the administrator that is generating the cross-certification request for the Compaq CA has a Qualified Subordination Signing certificate. We need this because the certificate template for a Cross Certification Authority requires the request to be signed using a certificate that has a Qualified Subordination Application Policy (as illustrated in Figure 14.27).

   The steps needed to generate a Qualified Subordination Signing certificate differ depending on whether the HP CA is a standalone or an enterprise CA:

   - If the HP CA is an enterprise CA, you will need to generate a new certificate template (Windows Server 2003 PKI, by default, does not include a template for Qualified Subordination Signing certificates) and then request a new certificate using that template. To generate a new certificate template for Qualified Subordination Signing, do the following:

     - Open the Certificate Templates MMC snap-in and duplicate the Enrollment Agent template.
     - Call the new template Qualified Subordination Signing (in the General tab) and make sure the following template properties are set:

Request Handling tab: Purpose: Signature.
Subject Name tab: Subject name format: Fully Distinguished Name/User principal name (UPN) checkbox enabled.
Issuance Requirements tab: CA certificate manager approval enabled.
Extensions tab: Remove the Certificate Request Agent Application Policy/Add the Qualified Subordination Policy.

- If the HP CA is a stand-alone CA, you can request a Qualified Subordination Signing certificate by including the Qualified Subordination OID in an advanced certificate request. To do so, initiate an advanced certificate request using the CA's Web enrollment interface (http://<server-name>/certsrv) and fill in the following OID: 1.3.6.1.4.1.311.10.3.10 in the OID box (accessible when Type of Certificate Needed\Other is selected).

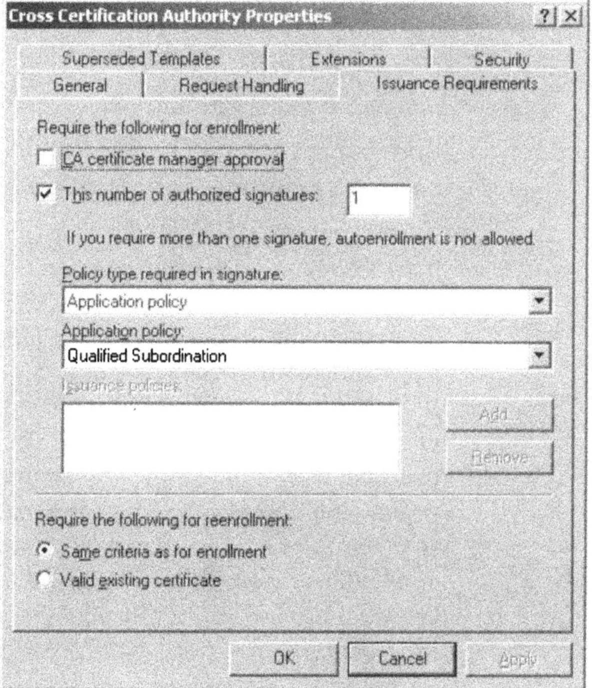

Figure 14.27 *Issuance requirements for cross-certification authority certificate.*

3. Run the following command from the folder where you copied the above files:

```
certreq.exe -policy—attrib
CertificateTemplate:CrossCA
```

   The certreq.exe utility will then:

   - Prompt you to open the Compaq CA's request file (which is the Compaq CA's certificate—this file normally has a *.cer extension) and the HP CA's policy.inf file.
   - Ask you to select a Qualified Subordination signing certificate.
   - Ask you for a name and path to save the cross-certification request (file with *.req extension).

4. To let the HP CA process the cross-certification request and generate the cross-certification certificate, perform the following steps:

   - Open the Certification Authority MMC snap-in.
   - Right-click the CA object and select All Tasks\Submit new request.
   - In the Open Request File dialog box, select the cross-certification request file that was generated in step 3, and click Open.
   - The next step is different depending on whether the HP CA is a stand-alone or an enterprise CA:
     - If the HP CA is an enterprise CA, it will generate the cross-certificate, ask for a name and path to save the cross-certificate, and publish the cross-certificate in the Active Directory Configuration Naming Context.
     - If the HP CA is a stand-alone CA, it will add the request to the pending requests queue. The CA administrator can then manually approve the request (by right-clicking the request and selecting Issue) to issue the certificate. Unlike an enterprise CA, a stand-alone CA will not automatically publish the cross-certificate in the Active Directory. The CA administrator can do this manually by first exporting the cross-certificate from the CA database (use the Issued Certificates CA container) and then using the following command line (where xcert.crt is the name of the cross-certification certificate):

```
Certutil -dspublish -f <xcert.crt> CrossCA
```

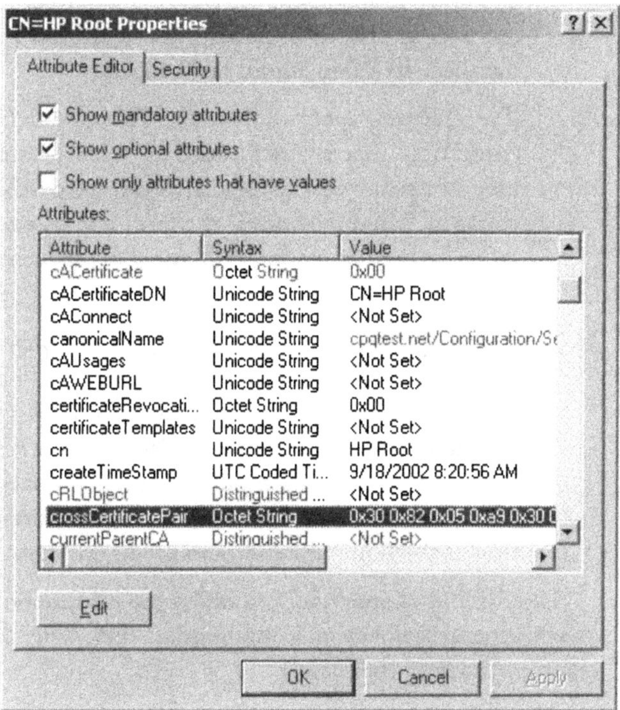

Figure 14.28 *crossCertificatePair attribute for an AD CA object (viewed using AdsiEdit).*

At the end of this process, the HP Active Directory must contain a cross-certificate for the Compaq CA. The cross-certificate is stored in the crossCertificatePair attribute of the CA object for the Compaq CA in the \Services\Public Key Services\AIA AD Configuration naming context container. You can check this using the AdsiEdit or the LDP tools. This is illustrated in Figure 14.28 using AdsiEDit for the cross-certificate of a CA called HP Root.

14.6.3 Defining trust constraints

The different PKI trust constraints available in Windows Server 2003 PKI together with their functionality were discussed extensively in Section 14.4.5. In this section we will look at how you can set them up. There are three tools we can use to define PKI trust constraints:

1. *The CAPolicy.inf configuration file.* This file is used to set the PKI trust constraints of a CA certificate together with other CA configuration settings (like CRL Distribution Points, AIAs, and so forth). The content of the file is evaluated at CA installation time

and every time the CA certificate is renewed. It must be stored in the %SystemRoot% folder of the machine where the CA is installed. Its name cannot be changed.

2. *The Policy.inf configuration file.* This file defines the PKI trust constraints that are embedded in a certificate request file. It is used as a parameter to the certreq.exe executable. Its name can be changed. This is definitely the most complete configuration tool: It can be used to configure all the different categories of PKI trust constraints (see also Table 14.2).

3. *The properties of version 2 certificate templates.* Certificate templates define the properties (including the PKI trust constraints) of certificates issued by Windows CAs. New to the version 2 certificate templates introduced in Windows Server 2003 PKI is that their content can be modified. V2 templates, however, cannot offer the same level of granularity for PKI trust constraint definition as the policy.inf and capolicy.inf configuration files.

Later in this chapter you can find more information on the syntax of the policy.inf and capolicy.inf configuration files. The chapter also contains a sample of each of the files.

Defining trust constraints using version 2 certificate templates

PKI trust constraints can be defined in the Extensions tab of a version 2 certificate template (as illustrated in Figure 14.29). Certificate templates can be administered from the Certificate Templates MMC snap-in. When setting PKI trust constraints this way, keep the following in mind:

- The extensions you set will be applied to *all* certificates that are issued using that template. The capolicy.inf and policy.inf configurations are applied to individual certificates.
- Not all PKI trust constraints discussed in this chapter can be set using V2 certificate templates. You cannot use them to set name constraints, issuance policy mappings, issuance policy constraints, application policy mappings, application policy constraints, and the basic constraint path length. Table 14.7 gives an overview of the PKI trust constraints that can be configured using V2 certificate templates.

Defining trust constraints using the CAPolicy.inf configuration file

In this section we give an example of how to set up a constrained PKI trust relationship in both a hierarchical and a networked trust model.

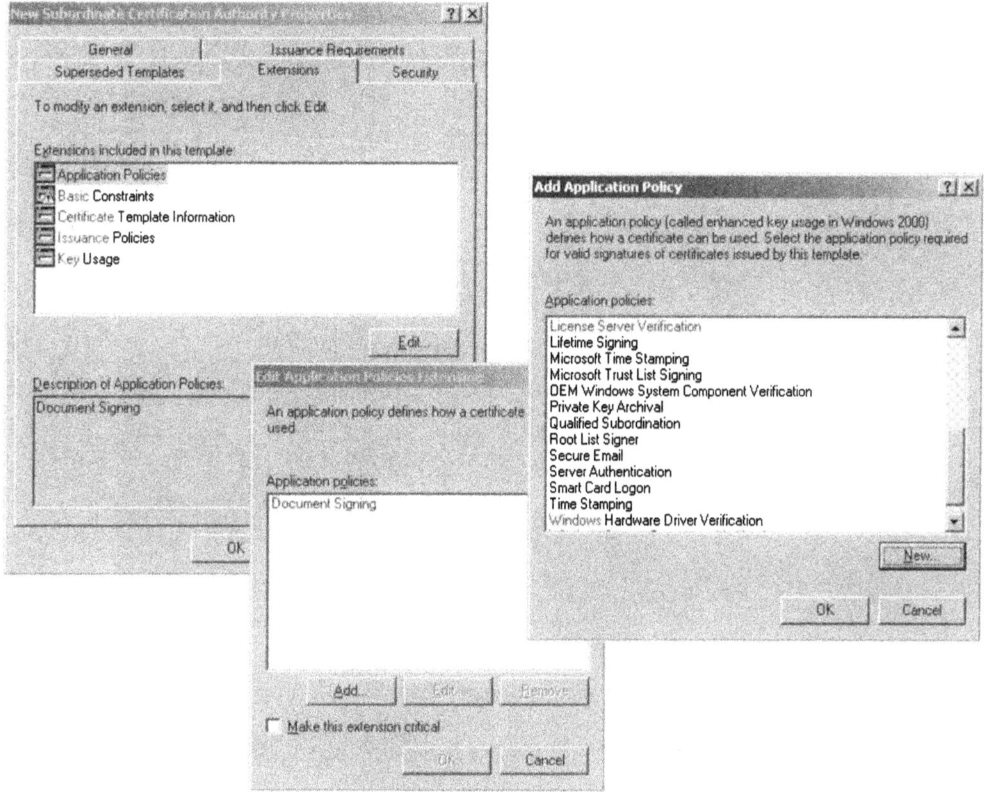

Figure 14.29 *crossCertificatePair attribute for an AD CA object (viewed using AdsiEdit).*

Table 14.7 *Overview of the PKI Trust Constraints That Can Be Configured Using the Properties of a Version 2 Certificate Template*

PKI Trust Constraint	Parameter
Issuance Policies	Criticality
	Issuance Policy Name
	Issuance Policy OID
	Issuance Policy CPS location
Application Policies	Criticality
	Application Policy Name
	Application Policy OID
Basic Constraints	Criticality
	CA certificate or End-entity Certificate

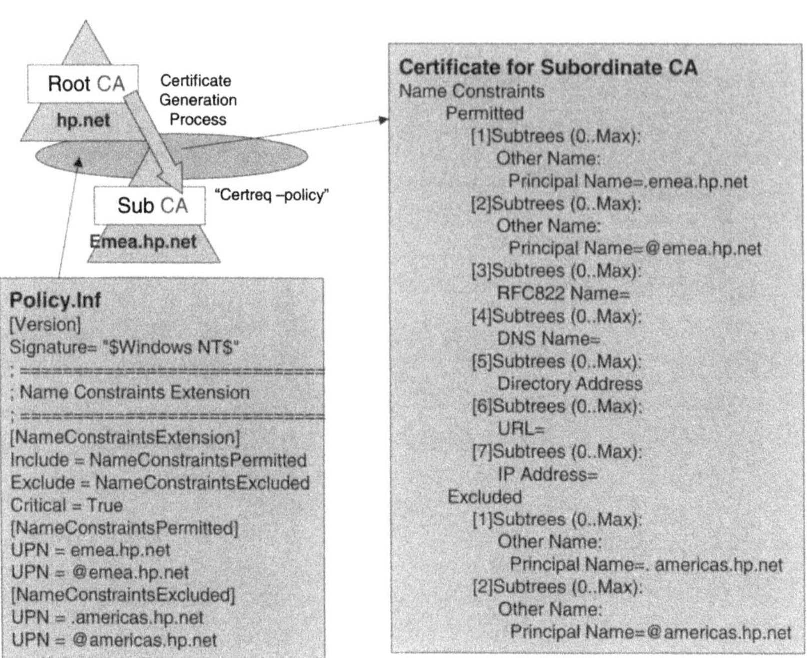

Figure 14.30 *Setting application policies on a version 2 certificate template.*

Figure 14.30 illustrates the constrained PKI trust relationship we want to set up between a root and a subordinate CA in a hierarchical trust model. This scenario shows a typical Windows Server 2003 forest environment consisting of a parent domain called hp.net and a child domain emea.hp.net. A root CA has been defined in the hp.net domain, and a subordinate CA will be defined in the emea.hp.net domain. When the CA administrator of the hp.net root CA issues the subordinate CA certificate for the CA in emea.hp.net, he or she wants to apply the following PKI trust constraint to it: It should only be capable of issuing certificates to users that have a emea.hp.net UPN extension; it should never be capable of issuing certificates to users that have an americas.hp.net UPN extension (this would be the responsibility of another CA—located in the americas child domain—which is not shown in the figure). In order to enforce this we will apply a name constraint to the subordinate CA certificate that the root CA issues to the emea.hp.net subordinate CA.

The following is a summary of the major steps you need to follow to set this up:

- During the installation of the subordinate CA for emea.hp.net, choose to save the certificate request to a file.

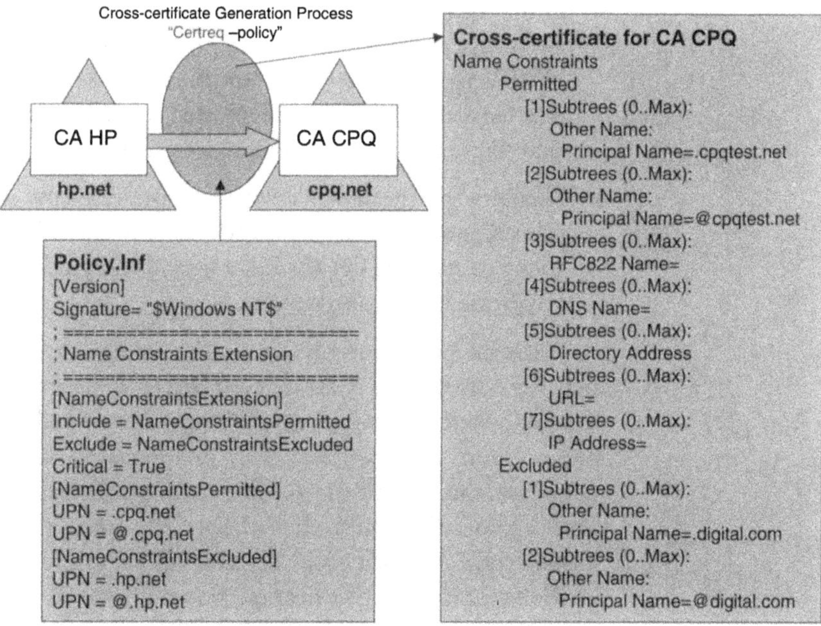

Figure 14.31 *Setting application policies on a version 2 certificate template.*

- Copy the request file to a folder on the hp.net root CA and create a policy.inf as illustrated in Figure 14.30. Note that when using name constraints, all name types (UPN, DNS, and so forth) must be included or excluded (also the ones for which you do not want to define an explicit constraint) in the policy.inf file; otherwise, all namespaces for the missing name types will by default be all included or excluded (all name types were not added in Figures 14.30 and 14.31 because of space constraints). See Section 6.3.6 for a complete policy.inf example.
- Run the following command line from the directory where both the request file and policy.inf file are located:

```
Certreq -policy
```

This command will first prompt you for the request file and the policy.inf file. Then it will ask you for a Qualified Subordination Signing certificate (for more information on how to create such a certificate see Section 14.6.2 on how to set up cross-certification), and finally it will ask you for a name and location to save the new request file (containing the policy constraints).

- In the next step, we will provide this new request file to the root CA for certification. To do so, simply open the Certification Authority MMC snap-in, right-click the CA object, and select All Tasks\Submit new request. After you have selected the request file, the CA will generate the certificate and ask you for a name and location to save it.
- Finally, copy the newly created certificate to the machine where the subordinate CA is installed and link it to the subordinate CA—when trying to start the CA service, a wizard will guide you through the CA certificate installation process.

A similar procedure can be used to set up a constrained PKI trust relationship between two CAs that are part of different organizations. This is a scenario where you would typically use a networked trust model made up of one or more cross-certified trust relationships. It is illustrated in Figure 14.31 for the organizations CPQ (Compaq) and HP (Hewlett-Packard). Both organizations have their proper AD forest (hp.net and cpq.net) and Certification Authority (CA HP and CA CPQ). If both organizations want a bidirectional cross-certification, you will have to run the above procedure twice: once on the HP CA for the CPQ CA and once on the CPQ CA for the HP CA.

Defining trust constraints using the Policy.inf configuration file

This section contains an example of how to use the CAPolicy.inf configuration file to define PKI trust constraints for a stand-alone root CA. Remember that the CAPolicy.inf file can only be used to define basic and issuance policy constraints.

Using a CAPolicy.inf to define PKI trust constraints is relatively easy. Just make sure the file contains the correct statements (the CAPolicy.inf syntax is covered in the next section) and that it is saved to the %systemroot% directory of the system where you want to install the CA. A sample is given in Figure 14.32. It contains a basic path length constraint of 1 and refers to an issuance policy called LegalPolicy.

CAPolicy.inf and Policy.inf syntax

Table 14.8 shows the syntax of the entries that are needed to define PKI trust constraints using the capolicy.inf and policy.inf configuration files.

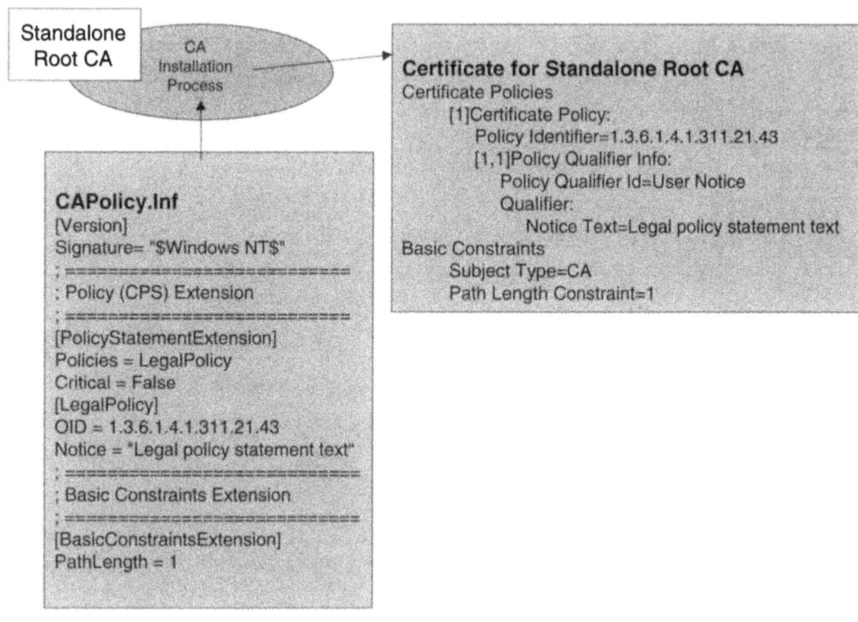

Figure 14.32 *Setting application policies on a version 2 certificate template.*

Table 14.8 *PKI Trust Constraints and Corresponding CAPolicy.inf and Policy.inf Section Header and Tags*

PKI Trust Constraint	Corresponding Section Header and Tag Syntax	
Name Constraints (Policy.inf only)	(NameConstraintsExtension)	
	Critical	Criticality of certificate extension (True or Yes = Critical)
	Include	Tag for included namespace section
	Exclude	Tag for excluded namespace section
	DNS	DNS namespace; e.g., mydomain.com or server@domain.net
	Email	Email namespace; e.g., user@domain.net
	UPN	UPN namespace; always requires two entries: one with a . and one with an @. e.g., @domain.net and .domain.net

Table 14.8 *PKI Trust Constraints and Corresponding CAPolicy.inf and Policy.inf Section Header and Tags (continued)*

PKI Trust Constraint	Corresponding Section Header and Tag Syntax	
Name Constraints (Policy.inf only) *(cont'd.)*	IPAddress	IP address namespace; e.g., 10.34.56.0,255.255.255.0 or 10.34.56.3
	URL	URL namespace; e.g., http://myserver/test.htm or file://\\myserver\tes.htm
	DirectoryName	Directory namespace; e.g., cn=company,ou=ou,s=state,c=country
Issuance Policies (Both Policy.inf and CAPolicy.inf)	(PolicyStatementExtension)	
	Policies	Tags for Issuance Policy sections
	Critical	Criticality of certificate extension (True or Yes = Critical)
	OID	Object Identifier of the Issuance Policy
	Notice	Notice text associated to Issuance Policy
	URL	URL linked to Issuance Policy (can be HTTP, FTP, or LDAP URL)
Issuance Policy Mappings (Policy.inf only)	(PolicyMappingsExtension)	
	Critical	Criticality of certificate extension (True or Yes = Critical)
	<IssuancePolicy1_OID> = <IssuancePolicy2_OID>	Issuance Policy Mapping
Issuance Policy Constraints (Policy.inf only)	(PolicyConstraintsExtension)	
	RequireExplicitPolicy	Require Explicit Policy constraint, contains a numeric value
	InhibitPolicyMapping	Inhibit policy mapping constraint, contains a numeric value
Application Policies (Policy.inf only)	(ApplicationPolicyStatementExtension)	
	Policies	Tags for Application Policy sections
	Critical	Criticality of certificate extension (True or Yes = Critical)
	OID	Object Identifier of the Application Policy
	Notice	Notice text associated to Application Policy
	URL	URL linked to Application Policy (can be HTTP, FTP, or LDAP URL)

Table 14.8 *PKI Trust Constraints and Corresponding CAPolicy.inf and Policy.inf Section Header and Tags (continued)*

PKI Trust Constraint	Corresponding Section Header and Tag Syntax	
Application Policy Mappings (Policy.inf only)	(ApplicationPolicyMappingsExtension)	
	Critical	Criticality of certificate extension (True or Yes = Critical)
	<ApplicationPolicy1_OID> = <ApplicationPolicy2_OID>	Application Policy Mapping
Application Policy Constraints (Policy.inf only)	(ApplicationPolicyConstraintsExtension)	
	RequireExplicitPolicy	Require Explicit Policy constraint , contains a numeric value
	InhibitPolicyMapping	Inhibit policy mapping constraint, contains a numeric value
Basic Constraints (Both Policy.inf and CAPolicy.inf)	(BasicConstraintExtension)	
	Critical	Criticality of certificate extension (True or Yes = Critical)
	PathLength	Path Length constraint, contains a numeric value

Sample CAPolicy.inf configuration file

The following is a sample CAPolicy.inf file. The trust constraint-related information is marked in bold.[2]

```
[Version]
Signature= "$Windows NT$"

[PolicyStatementExtension]
Policies = LegalPolicy, LimitedUsePolicy, OIDPolicy
Critical = 0

[LegalPolicy]
OID = 1.3.6.1.4.1.311.21.43
Notice = "Legal policy statement text."

[LimitedUsePolicy]
OID = 1.3.6.1.4.1.311.21.47
URL = http://http.site.com/some where/default.asp
URL = ftp://ftp.site.com/some where else/default.asp
Notice = "Limited use policy statement text."
```

2. The variables (%1...) that are used in the AuthorityInformationAccess, CRLDistributionPoint, and CrossCertificateDistributionPointsExtension fields are explained in Chapter 16.

```
URL = "ldap://ldap.site.com/some where else gain/
default.asp"

[oidpolicy]
OID = 1.3.6.1.4.1.311.21.55
[AuthorityInformationAccess]
URL = http://%1/Public/My CA.crt
URL = ftp://foo.com/Public/MyCA.crt

URL = file://\\%1\Public\My CA.crt
CriticAL = false

[CRLDistributionPoint]
URL = http://%1/Public/My CA.crl
URL = ftp://%1/Public/MyCA.crl
URL = file://\\%1\Public\My CA.crl
CriticAL = true

[CrossCertificateDistributionPointsExtension]
SyncDeltaTime = 600 ; in seconds
URL = http://%1/Public/My CCDP.crl
URL = ftp://%1/Public/MyCCDP.crl

URL = file://\\%1\Public\My CCDP.crl
CriticAL = yeS

[EnhancedKeyUsageExtension]
OID = 1.3.6.1.4.1.311.21.6 ; szOID_KP_KEY_RECOVERY_AGENTOID
= 1.3.6.1.4.1.311.10.3.9 ; szOID_ROOT_LIST_SIGNER
OID = 1.3.6.1.4.1.311.10.3.1 ; szOID_KP_CTL_USAGE_SIGNING
CriticAL = true

[BasicConstraintsExtension]
pathlength = 13
criticaL=false

[certsrv_server]
renewalkeylength=2048
RenewalValidityPeriodUnits=0x18
RenewalValidityPeriod=years
CRLPeriod = days
CRLPeriodUnits = 2
CRLDeltaPeriod = hours
CRLDeltaPeriodUnits = 4
```

Sample Policy.inf configuration file

The following is a sample Policy.inf file. The trust constraint-related information is marked in bold.

```
[Version]
Signature= "$Windows NT$"

; ============================================
; Request Attributes
; ============================================

[RequestAttributes]
CertificateTemplate = CrossCA

; ========================================
; NameConstraintsExcluded Name Constraints Extension
; ========================================
[NameConstraintsExtension]
Include = NameConstraintsPermitted
Exclude = NameConstraintsExcluded
Critical = TrUe

[NameConstraintsPermitted]
DNS = foo@domain.com
DNS = domain1.domain.com

email=me@you.com

UPN=user.domain.com
UPN=user@domain.com

; the first is an IP address, the second is an IP address
mask

ipaddress =255.255.18.172,255.255.255.0

url=http://localhost/certsrv/default.html
url=file://\\localhost\certsrv\default.html

DIRECTORYNAME = "cn=mycn,ou=myou,s=mystate,c=us"

[NameConstraintsExcluded]
; list of user defined excluded DNS names
DNS = baddomain.com

email = @baddomain.com

UPN = . baddomain.com
UPN = @baddomain.com

; the first is an IP address, the second is an IP address
mask
```

```
ipaddress =255.255.19.172,255.255.255.0

url=http://hrsrv1/public/default.html
url=file://\\hrsrv1\public\default.html

DIRECTORYNAME = "DC=baddomain,DC=com"

; ==========================================
; Policy (CPS) Extension
==========================================

[PolicyStatementExtension]
; list of user defined policies
Policies = LegalPolicy, LimitedUsePolicy, OIDPolicy
CRITICAL = FALSE

[LegalPolicy]
; each policy has OID, and zero or more Notice and URL keys
OID = 1.3.6.1.4.1.311.21.43
Notice = "Legal policy statement text"

[LimitedUsePolicy]
OID = 1.3.6.1.4.1.311.21.47
URL = http://http.site.com/folder/default.asp
URL = ftp://ftp.site.com/folder/default.asp
Notice = "Limited use policy statement text."
URL = "ldap://ldap.site.com/folder/default.asp"

[oidpolicy]
OID = 1.3.6.1.4.1.311.21.55

; ==========================================
; Policy Mapping Extension
; ==========================================

[PolicyMappingsExtension]
; list of user defined policy mappings
; first OID is Issuer Domain Policy OID
; second is Subject Domain Policy OID
; each entry maps one foreign policy OID to local
1.3.6.1.4.1.311.21.43 = 1.2.3.4.87
1.3.6.1.4.1.311.21.47 = 1.2.3.4.89
critical = yEs

; ==========================================
; Policy Constraints Extension
==========================================

[PolicyConstraintsExtension]
```

```
; consists of two optional DWORDs
RequireExplicitPolicy  = 3
InhibitPolicyMapping = 5

; ==========================================
; Application Policy (CPS) Extension
; ==========================================

[ApplicationPolicyStatementExtension]
; list of user defined policies
Policies = AppLegalPolicy, AppLimitedUsePolicy,
AppOIDPolicy
CRITICAL = FALSE

[AppLegalPolicy]
; each policy has OID, and zero or more Notice and URL keys
OID = 1.3.6.1.4.1.311.21.54
Notice = "Application Legal policy statement text"

[AppLimitedUsePolicy]
OID = 1.3.6.1.4.1.311.21.58
URL = http://http.site.com/application/default.asp
URL = ftp://ftp.site.com/application/default.asp
Notice = "Application Limited use policy statement text."
URL = "ldap://ldap.site.com/application/default.asp"
[Appoidpolicy]
OID = 1.3.6.1.4.1.311.21.66

; ==========================================
; Application Policy Mapping Extension
; ==========================================

[ApplicationPolicyMappingsExtension]
; list of user defined application policy mappings
; first OID is Issuer Domain Policy OID
; second is Subject Domain Policy OID
; each entry maps one foreign policy OID to local
1.3.6.1.4.1.311.21.54 = 1.2.3.4.98
1.3.6.1.4.1.311.21.58 = 1.2.3.4.100
critical = true

; ==========================================
; Application Policy Constraints Extension
; ==========================================

[ApplicationPolicyConstraintsExtension]
; consists of two optional DWORDs
RequireExplicitPolicy  = 6
InhibitPolicyMapping = 10
```

```
; ============================================
; Basic Constraints Extension
; ============================================

[BasicConstraintsExtension]
; Subject Type is not supported always set to CA
; maximum subordinate CA path length
PathLength = 3

[EnhancedKeyUsageExtension]
;OID = 1.3.6.1.4.1.311.21.6            ;szOID_KP_KEY_RECOVERY_
AGENT
;OID = 1.3.6.1.4.1.311.10.3.9        ; szOID_ROOT_LIST_SIGNER
;OID = 1.3.6.1.4.1.311.10.3.1        ; szOID_KP_CTL_USAGE_
SIGNING
;Entries match the [ApplicationPolicyStatementExtension]
section:
OID = 1.3.6.1.4.1.311.21.54
OID = 1.3.6.1.4.1.311.21.58
OID = 1.3.6.1.4.1.311.21.66
CriticAL = true

; ============================================
; Cross Certificate Distribution Points Extension
; ============================================

[CrossCertificateDistributionPointsExtension]
SyncDeltaTime = 24
URL = http://%1/Public/My CA.crt
URL = ftp://foo.com/Public/MyCA.crt
URL = file://\\%1\Public\My CA.crt
CriticAL = false
```

Trust constraint inheritance in hierarchical trust models

An interesting detail that was not covered so far in this chapter is whether trust constraints are inherited between the certificates of the different entities in a hierarchical trust model. Are trust constraints set in a parent CA certificate automatically copied in a subordinate CA's certificate? Also, are they copied automatically to an end-entity certificate? Table 14.9 gives an overview.

Table 14.9 *Trust Constraint Inheritance in a Hierarchical Trust Model*

Trust Constraint Type	Set in Parent CA Certificate?	Copied to Subordinate CA Certificate?	Copied to End-Entity Certificate?
Basic Constraints	Yes	Yes	No
Name Constraints	Yes	No	No
Application Policies	Yes	Yes	No
Issuance Policies	Yes	No	No
Application Policy Mappings	Yes	No	No
Application Policy Constraints	Yes	No	No
Issuance Policy Mappings	Yes	No	No
Issuance Policy Constraints	Yes	No	No

14.6.4 CA trust definition: Summary

Table 14.10 summarizes CA trust definition in Windows Server 2003 PKI: It shows when and how trust relationships are defined for the different PKI trust types. The table clearly shows that not every tool discussed previously can define all types of PKI trust constraints. Also, some of these tools cannot be used in a stand-alone CA environment and require the presence of enterprise CAs.

Table 14.10 *CA Trust Definition Overview*

PKI Trust Type	When and How Defined?	Applies to Which CAs?
Hierarchical Trust	During the CA installation process. ■ Select whether the CA will be a root or subordinate CA in the CA installation wizard.	Root and subordinate CAs in a hierarchical trust model
Cross-Certified Trust	Any time after the CA installation process. ■ Using the Policy.inf file and the certreq.exe utility (use the –policy switch)	Cross-certified CAs in a networked trust model

Table 14.10 *CA Trust Definition Overview (continued)*

PKI Trust Type	When and How Defined?	Applies to Which CAs?
Constrained Trust: Basic Constraints, Issuance Policies	During the CA installation process or at CA certificate renewal time. ■ Using the CaPolicy.inf file	Root or subordinate CAs (that are subordinate to a stand-alone CA) in a hierarchical trust model
	During the CA installation process or at CA certificate renewal time. ■ Using the properties of a V2 certificate template. The V2 template properties can only be used if the CA is subordinate to an enterprise CA. ■ Using the Policy.inf file and the certreq.exe utility (use the –policy switch)	Subordinate CAs (that are subordinate to an enterprise CA) in a hierarchical trust model
	Any time after the CA installation process. ■ Using the Policy.inf file and the certreq.exe utility (use the –policy switch)	Cross-certified CAs in a networked trust model
Constrained Trust: Application Policies	During the subordinate CA installation process or at subordinate CA certificate renewal time. ■ Using the properties of a V2 certificate template. The V2 template properties can only be used if the CA is subordinate to an enterprise CA. ■ Using the Policy.inf file and the certreq.exe utility (use the –policy switch)	Subordinate CAs (that are subordinate to an enterprise CA) in a hierarchical trust model
	Any time after the CA installation process. ■ Using the Policy.inf file and the certreq.exe utility (use the –policy switch)	Cross-certified CAs in a networked trust model
Constrained Trust: Name Constraints	As part of the subordinate CA installation process or at subordinate CA certificate renewal time. ■ Using the Policy.inf file and the certreq.exe utility (use the –policy switch)	Subordinate CAs in a hierarchical trust model
	Any time after the CA installation process. ■ Using the Policy.inf file and the certreq.exe utility (use the –policy switch)	Cross-certified CAs in a networked trust model

14.7 Summary

Trust is a fundamental concept of PKI. This chapter illustrated how the enhanced trust features of Windows Server 2003 PKI make Windows PKI both more powerful and flexible. Of course, all of this adds more complexity to PKI trust design and administration. This chapter also showed the richness of PKI when it comes to trust definition—no other security protocol or technology available today can define trust in such a granular way.

15

The Certificate Life Cycle

This chapter focuses on the Windows Server 2003 PKI certificate life cycle and its different subprocesses.

15.1 Overview of the certificate life cycle

The life of a certificate can be subdivided into three main phases in which different processes can occur. The phases are the start, issued, and end phases. The complete certificate life cycle, its different phases, and their processes are illustrated in Figure 15.1.

A very important aspect of the certificate life cycle is the degree of automation for the different processes. This is very important from an end user's ease-of-use and an administrator's ease-of-management points of view. This is the main advantage of what is called a managed PKI solution: In a managed PKI, most processes are automated. Windows 2000 PKI comes with

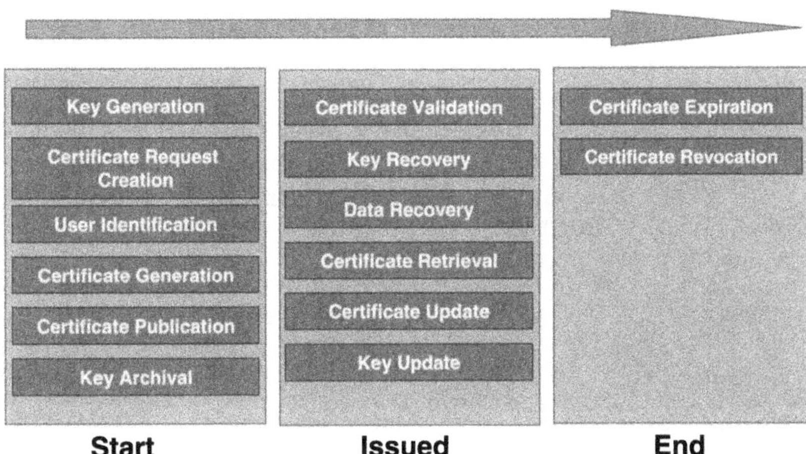

Figure 15.1 *The certificate life cycle.*

much more automation than its predecessor, Windows NT4 PKI. The degree of automation is even higher in Windows Server 2003, and that is why we can call it a true managed PKI solution.

We will run through all the certificate life cycle processes in the following sections. Some of the processes are grouped together in a single section, (e.g., certificate enrollment includes key generation, certificate request, user identification, certificate generation, certificate publishing, and encryption key archival).

15.2 Certificate enrollment

Certificate enrollment enables a user, machine, or service to participate in and use PKI-enabled applications (PKA) or processes. Certificate enrollment consists of a cycle of events: key generation, certificate request, identification, certificate generation, publishing, and encryption key archival.

Certificate enrollment can be started manually by a user or an administrator. In some PKI-enabled applications, it requires an initiative from both the user and an administrator. A good example is the scenario in which a Windows enterprise CA is issuing certificates. In this case the administrator first must authorize which users the machines can enroll for a particular certificate type. The latter can be done by setting access control permissions on the certificate templates.

In most cases, a user (whether a user, machine, or service account) initiates certificate enrollment. In Windows 2000 and Windows Server 2003, there is one exception to this rule: smart card enrollment. In this enrollment model an administrator who has a special smart card enrollment agent certificate[1] is allowed to enroll for a certificate on a user's behalf. He or she can also load the user's certificate on its smart card. We will return to smart card enrollment in the chapter on PKI-enabled applications.

For a user to enroll for a certificate from a Windows 2000 or Windows Server 2003 stand-alone CA, only enroll permission on the AD CA object is required. Before a user can enroll for a certificate from a Windows 2000 or Windows Server 2003 enterprise CA, the following conditions must be met:

- The user must have read and enroll permission on the enterprise CA level. This permission must be set on the AD CA object.

1. It is not required that the enrollment agent's proper certificate and private key are stored on a smart card for this enrollment model to work.

- The appropriate permissions must be set on the certificate template (enroll and read).
- The right certificate template must be configured on the CA.

Enrollment can also be initiated automatically for both user and machine accounts that are part of a Windows domain environment. This feature is known as certificate autoenrollment. Autoenrollment will be explained in more detail next.

In the following sections, we look in more detail at the following key elements and aspects of the Windows certificate enrollment process:

- Certificate autoenrollment
- Enrollment interfaces
- Key and certificate request generation
- Requestor identification
- Certificate generation, distribution, and publication

15.2.1 Certificate autoenrollment

Certificate autoenrollment is the Windows 2000, Windows XP, and Windows Server 2003 OS capability to automatically enroll users and machines for certificates. Windows 2000 PKI only supports certificate autoenrollment for machines and Encryption File System (EFS) user certificates. Windows Server 2003 PKI extends certificate autoenrollment to users and all certificate types, greatly enhancing the PKI's ease of use. Compared to the feature set of other PKI products on the market, certificate autoenrollment is also a unique feature that gives Windows Server 2003 PKI an important advantage over other PKI products.

Certificate autoenrollment not only handles certificate enrollment: It also automates certificate renewal and certain certificate housekeeping tasks. The latter include removing revoked certificates from a user's or machine's certificate store, or downloading the trusted root CA certificates and cross-certificates from AD.

The following are some typical examples of how certificate autoenrollment is or can be used:

- Every Windows 2000 and Windows Server 2003 domain controller automatically gets a domain controller certificate when the machine joins a domain in which an enterprise certification authority is defined.

- An administrator can set a GPO setting that automatically enrolls machines for an IPsec or SSL certificate.
- An administrator can set a GPO setting that automatically enrolls a number of users for a user or secure mail certificate.
- When the CA administrator wants to change a property (e.g., the lifetime) of a particular certificate type, he or she can duplicate the old certificate template to create a new certificate template and let the new one supersede the old one. Autoenrollment will then automatically distribute a new certificate based on the new template to the concerned PKI users.

Certificate autoenrollment for users requires extra client-side code that at the time of this writing was only bundled with XP and Windows Server 2003 clients. Autoenrollment requires both the machine and the user to be part of a Windows Active Directory domain. Also, autoenrollment properties can only be set on version 2 certificate templates. Remember that only a domain with a Windows Server 2003 schema supports version 2 templates and that only a Windows Server 2003 Enterprise Edition or Datacenter Edition AD-integrated CA can issue certificates that are based on version 2 certificate templates.

Setting up machine autoenrollment

As in Windows 2000, in Windows Server 2003 you enable machine certificate autoenrollment from the GPO Public Key Policies' Automatic Certifi-

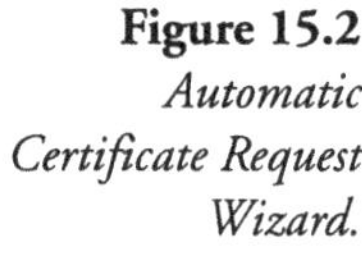

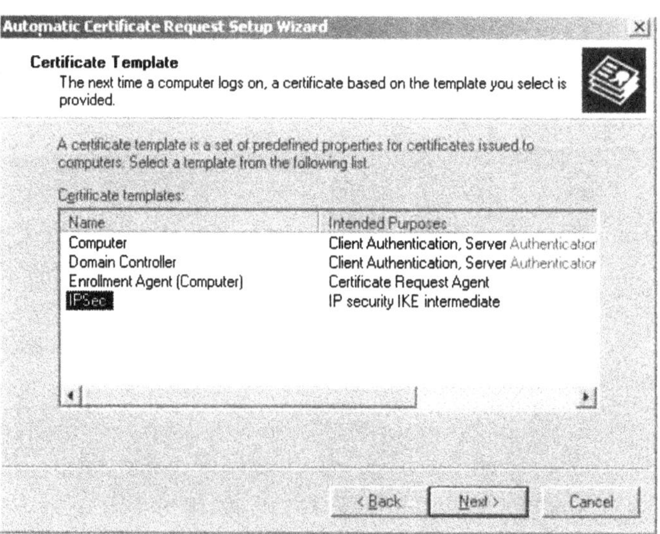

Figure 15.2 *Automatic Certificate Request Wizard.*

cate Request Settings container. If you right-click this container and select New\Automatic Certificate Request..., the Automatic Certificate Request Setup Wizard (illustrated in Figure 15.2) will start and will guide you through the machine certificate autoenrollment process.

Setting up user autoenrollment

To set up user certificate autoenrollment, you must make configuration changes in both the MMC Certificate Templates and Group Policy snap-ins.

- To enable autoenrollment at the template level, open the Certificate Templates snap-in, open the template, go to the Security tab, and set the appropriate ACL settings to give users or groups the Autoenroll permission (as illustrated in Figure 15.3(b)).

  These user autoenrollment properties can only be set on version 2 certificate templates. Only a domain with a Windows Server 2003 schema supports version 2 templates and only a Windows Server 2003 Enterprise Edition or Datacenter Edition AD-integrated CA can issue certificates that are based on version 2 certificate templates.

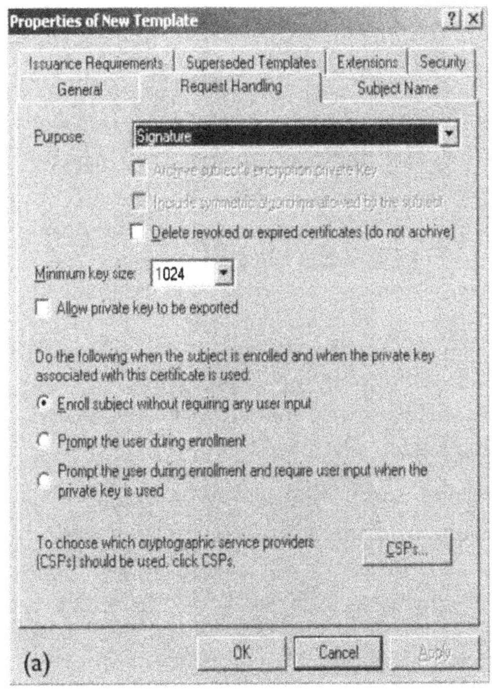

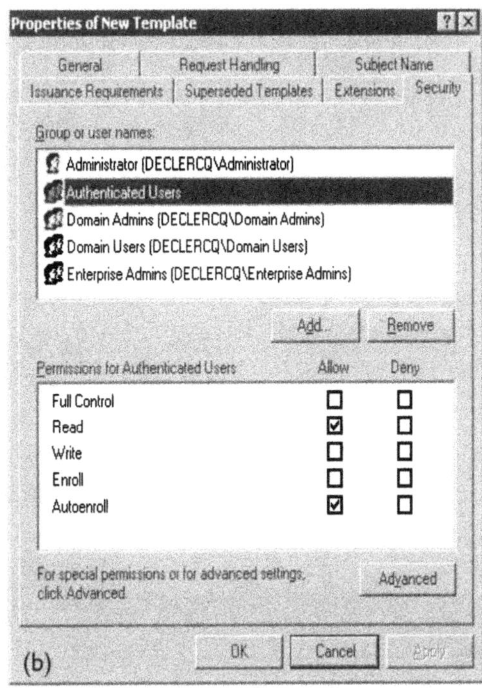

Figure 15.3 *Setting autoenrollment permissions on the certificate template level.*

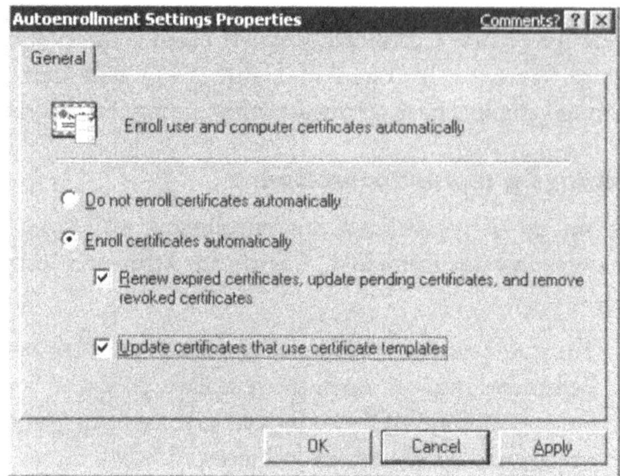

Figure 15.4 *Setting autoenrollment properties at the GPO level.*

If you want autoenrollment to occur without any user intervention, leave the default settings on the Request Handling tab unchanged (as illustrated in Figure 15.3(a)). If you want to prompt the user to start the autoenrollment process, select the "Prompt the user during enrollment" radio button. User input is required when enrolling smart card certificates.[2] Requiring user input on machine certificate templates will make machine autoenrollment fail.

- To enable autoenrollment at the GPO level, open the Group Policy snap-in, go down to Computer Configuration\Windows Settings\Security Settings\Public Key Policies, and then open the Autoenrollment Settings Properties dialog box, which is shown in Figure 15.4. In this dialog box, check the "Enroll certificates automatically" radio button and check the "Update certificates that use certificate templates" checkbox.

  If you want the autoenrollment process also to take care of certificate renewal and other certificate housekeeping tasks, make sure that you also check the "Renew expired certificates, update pending certificates, and remove revoked certificates" checkbox.

When user autoenrollment occurs and it has been set up to occur without user input, everything will happen automatically without user intervention. If it has been set up to occur with user input, a warning balloon will appear in the user's taskbar tray (illustrated in Figure 15.5). After approxi-

2. Enrolling for certificates that must be stored on a smart card requires the user to enter a smart card in the smart reader. In most cases it also requires the user to enter a PIN code.

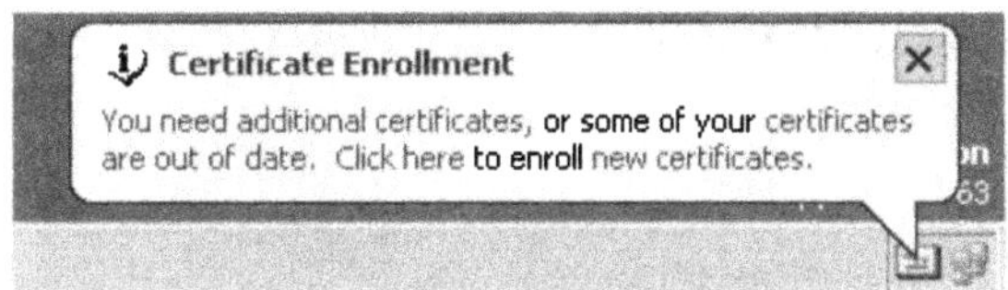

Figure 15.5 *Autoenrollment text balloon.*

mately 15 seconds, the warning balloon is replaced by a certificate icon. When the user clicks the balloon or the certificate icon, a dialog box appears and prompts the user to choose whether to start the autoenrollment process (illustrated in Figure 15.6). If the user clicks the Remind Me Later pushbutton in this dialog box, the warning balloon will reappear at the next group policy refresh interval or at the next interactive logon.

The warning balloon appears with a delay of 60 seconds after the interactive logon sequence. If you want the balloon to appear immediately after the interactive logon sequence, make the following registry hack on the user's machine. Set the HKEY_CURRENT_USER\SOFTWARE\Microsoft\Cryptography\AutoEnrollment\AEExpress registry key to value 1 (REG_DWORD).

Forcing automatic enrollment and renewal

You can force certificate enrollment to occur without waiting for the next logon or automatic GPO refresh.

- To force automatic certificate enrollment for both user and machine certificates, you can manually force a group policy update using the gpupdate.exe command-line utility. Triggering a GPO update will in turn trigger an autoenrollment event.

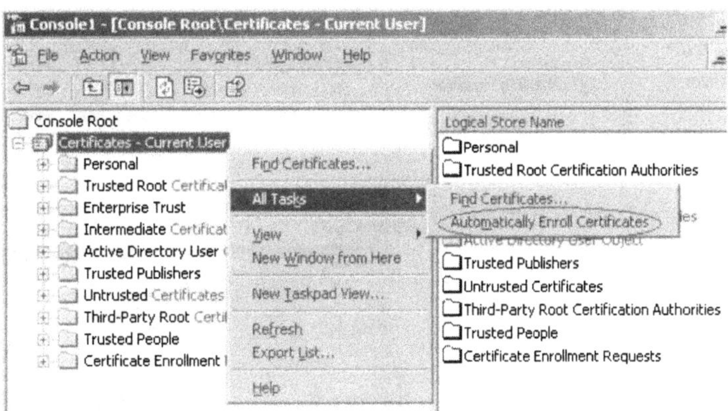

Figure 15.6 *Forcing user certificate autoenrollment.*

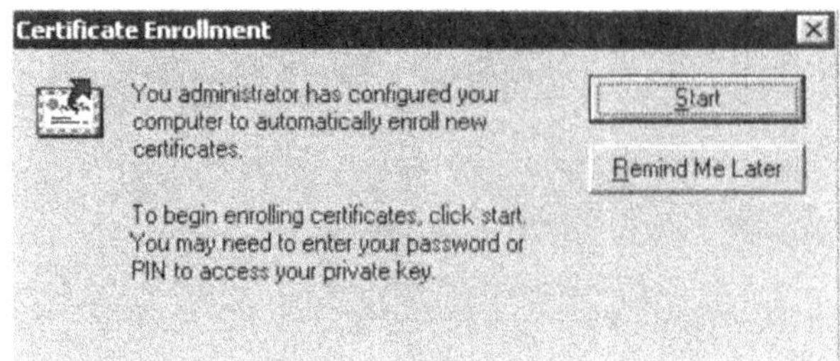

Figure 15.7 *User autoenrollment confirmation dialog box.*

- To force automatic certificate enrollment for user certificates only, open the MMC Certificates snap-in and open your personal certificates container. Then right-click the Certificates—Current User container and select All Tasks\Automatically Enroll Certificates… from the context menu (as illustrated in Figure 15.7).

You can also force renewal of specific user or machine certificate types. To do so, in the Certificate Templates MMC snap-in, right-click the template and select "Reenroll All Certificate Holders Certificate"—as illustrated in Figure 15.8. When you select this option the version number of the certificate template is increased. This version number update will actually trigger the autoenrollment event.

To manually force a download of the root CA and cross-certificates stored in AD that are downloaded as part of the autoenrollment process, you must delete the following registry key and all subordinate keys on the client machine: HKEY_LOCAL_MACHINE\SOFTWARE\Microsoft\Cryptography\AutoEnrollment\AEDirectoryCache.

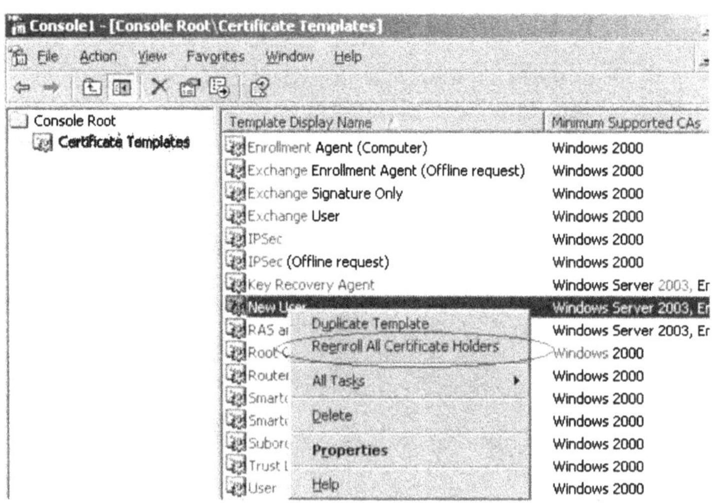

Figure 15.8 *Forcing user certificate autoenrollment.*

Advanced autoenrollment options

Next we discuss some of the advanced autoenrollment options: the requirement for certificate manager approval, the selfRA feature, the concept of superseding certificate templates, and the meaning of the "Do not automatically reenroll if a duplicate certificate exists in Active Directory" certificate template property. All of these options are only available on version 2 certificate templates.

Version 2 certificate templates have a property called "CA certificate manager approval" (on the Issuance Requirements tab—illustrated in Figure 15.9). If this property is set, CA manager approval is required before the CA will actually issue the certificate. Until the CA manager approves the request, it is added to the CA's pending requests container. This feature works in conjunction with certificate autoenrollment. The autoenrollment process will periodically check the CA for approved requests and automatically install the certificates on the client machine.

SelfRA is a new Windows Server 2003 PKI feature that allows you to set special enrollment requirements on version 2 certificate templates. It requires the presence of an existing—previously issued—certificate and its associated private key to sign a new certificate request. SelfRA is also configured from

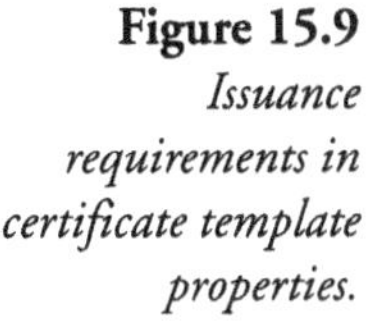

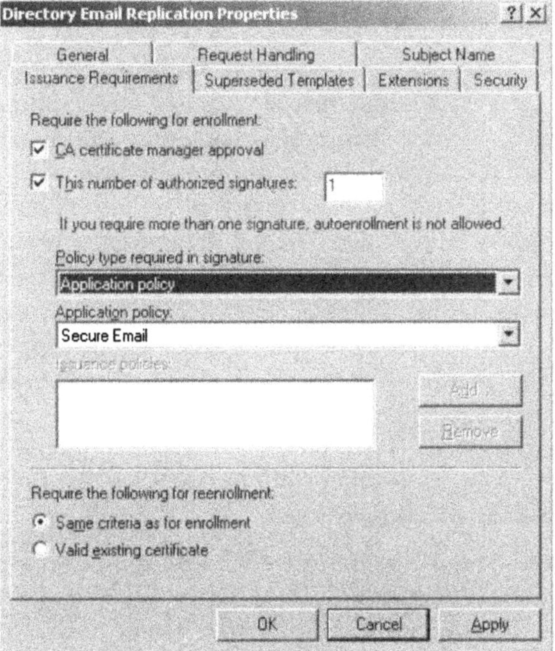

Figure 15.9 *Issuance requirements in certificate template properties.*

the Issuance Requirements tab in the certificate template properties. SelfRA can work in conjunction with autoenrollment. However, autoenrollment cannot deal with requests that require more than a single signature to authorize the enrollment request. The following selfRA-related properties can be set (they are illustrated in Figure 15.9):

- The number of signatures required to authorize the certificate request. Remember, when using autoenrollment, the number of signatures is limited to 1.
- The content of the application and/or issuance policy fields in the X.509 certificates extensions of the authorization certificate
- The requirements for automatic reenrollment: Use the same criteria as the ones used for the original enrollment (these are the ones listed in the upper part of the Issuance Requirements tab) or just check whether a valid certificate of the type mentioned in the certificate template is present in the PKI user's certificate store.

Superseding certificate templates allow CA administrators to automatically reenroll users for certain certificate types. This allows you, for example, to change a property of a particular certificate type (e.g., the lifetime or the content of an X.509 extension) by issuing a new one. To set up superseding templates, use the Superseded Templates tab in the properties of a version 2 certificate template (as illustrated in Figure 15.10).

Another very useful certificate template property related to autoenrollment is "Do not automatically reenroll if a duplicate certificate exists in Active Directory" (which is available from the General tab of a version 2 certificate template). When this property is enabled, autoenrollment will not enroll a user for a certificate, when a similar certificate exists in the AD object of the user—even if a certificate does not exist in the "My" container of the user's certificate store. In this case the autoenrollment process will query AD to determine whether the user should be enrolled. This is an interesting option for users who do not have roaming profiles and log on to multiple machines. Without this setting, these users would be automatically enrolled for a certificate on every machine to which they are logging on.

How autoenrollment works

Certificate autoenrollment (or the autoenrollment event as we call it in the following explanation) is triggered by the winlogon process. The latter is initiated every time an interactive logon is performed and every time machine- or user-based group policies are applied. By default, group poli-

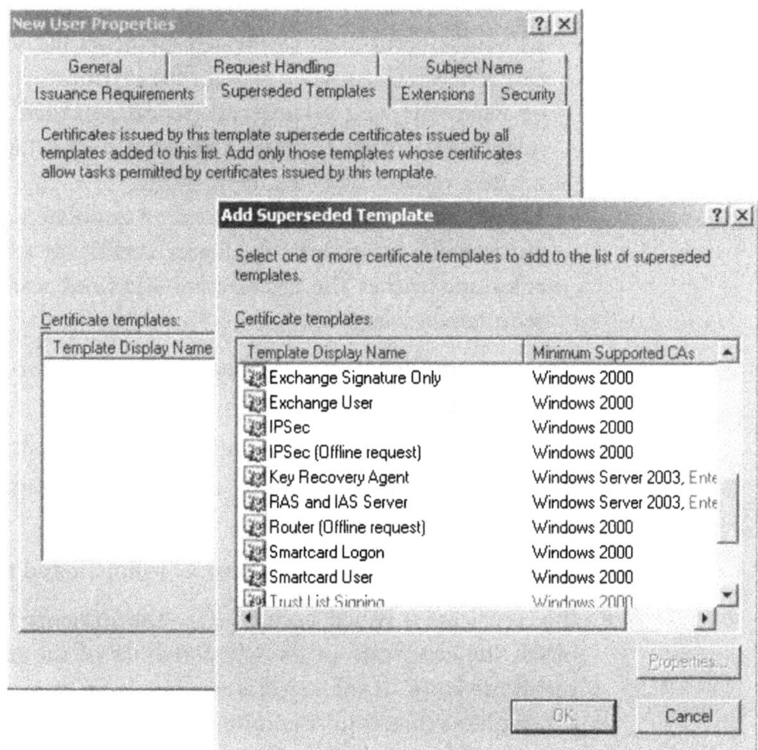

Figure 15.10 *Setting up superseding certificate templates.*

cies are applied every 8 hours. As mentioned above GPO updates can also be triggered manually. Unlocking a workstation does not trigger a certificate autoenrollment event.

Here is what happens following an autoenrollment event:

- The client OS queries AD to download the content of a set of predefined certificate stores to the local store on the client machine. These stores include the NTAuth, the trusted root CA, certificate templates and AIA (for cross-certificates) AD containers.
- The autoenrollment process processes the certificate templates, analyzes their properties, and creates a list—referred to as the requirements list—of tasks to be done during the autoerollment event. The requirements list includes:
  - Certificate *enrollment* tasks. All templates that have autoenroll and read permission set for the current machine or user will be added to the requirements list.
  - Certificate *renewal* tasks. The autoenrollment process processes the user or machine's My certificate store container to look for

expired certificates or certificates that are about to expire and will add these certificates to the requirements list. Automatic certificate renewal starts when 80% of the certificate lifetime has passed, or when the renewal interval period specified in the certificate template has been reached. The latter is specified on the General tab of a version 2 certificate template.

- Certificate enrollment tasks based on template *supersede* rules. The autoenrollment process evaluates certificate template supersede rules and makes the appropriate additions and deletions to the requirements list.

- The autoenrollment process then searches AD for an enterprise CA that can issue the certificates.
- If a CA is found, the autoenrollment process will pass the requirements list to the CA using certificate enrollment and renewal requests.
- The CA will process the certificate enrollment and renewal requests.
- If a certificate is issued from the CA, the autoenrollment process will install the certificate in the My container of the user's or machine's certificate store. If the certificate's state is set to pending (for certificate requests that require administrator approval), the autoenrollment process will save the certificate request information in the request container of the user or machine's certificate store.
- At the end of the autoenrollment process, the outcome (success or failure) of the process will be logged in the local system's application event log. If the autoenrollment failed, a summary dialog box will appear. See the following sidebar to set up verbose autoenrollment logging.
- For requests that were set to pending, the autoenrollment process will regularly query the CA to check whether the request has been approved. This will happen every time the group policies are refreshed. Autoenrollment will even retrieve pending certificates that were enrolled manually through the CA web interface.

As pointed out earlier, the autoenrollment event triggers more than just certificate autoenrollment:

- Trusted root CA certificates are downloaded from the AD-based Certification Authorities and NTAuth stores to the local machine's "Trusted Root Certification Authorities" certificate store container. The autoenrollment process doesn't download the complete NTAuth

Setting up verbose logging for certificate autoenrollment events The autoenrollment process can be configured to log more verbose information and events in the application event log by setting the AEEventLogLevel key (REG_DWORD) in the following registry containers to value 0:

- HKEY_CURRENT_USER\Software\Microsoft\Cryptography\Autoenrollment (for user autoenrollment)
- HKEY_LOCAL_MACHINE\Software\Microsoft\Cryptography\Autoenrollment (for machine autoenrollment)

store: only the deltas between the content of the user certificate and the NTAuth store are downloaded.

- Cross-certificates are downloaded from AD to the local machine certificate store. Like for trusted root CA certificates only the deltas are downloaded.
- The autoenrollment process enumerates the pending certificate requests in the request container of the user's certificate store. It downloads the certificate, once it has been issued, from the issuing CA and installs it in the user's certificate store. If the request has been pending for more than 60 days, the autoenrollment event removes it from the request container in the user's certificate store.
- The autoenrollment process also deletes expired and revoked certificates in the userCertificate attribute of the user's AD object and in the user's local certificate store. The latter only occurs if the "Delete revoked or expired certificates" property has been set on the Request Handling tab of the certificate template properties.

15.2.2 Enrollment interfaces

Both Windows 2000 and Windows Server 2003 PKI can support four different certificate enrollment interfaces: a Web interface, a GUI interface, a command prompt interface, and a scripting interface:

- Web interface: To enroll for certificates from an enterprise or a stand-alone CA using a Web browser, the user can go to the following URL: http://<CAservername>/certsrv. The latter is the default URL—you can change it using the IIS Manager MMC snap-in.
- GUI interface: A user can enroll for certificates from an enterprise CA or a stand-alone CA using the certificate request wizard (illus-

Figure 15.11 *Certificate Request Wizard.*

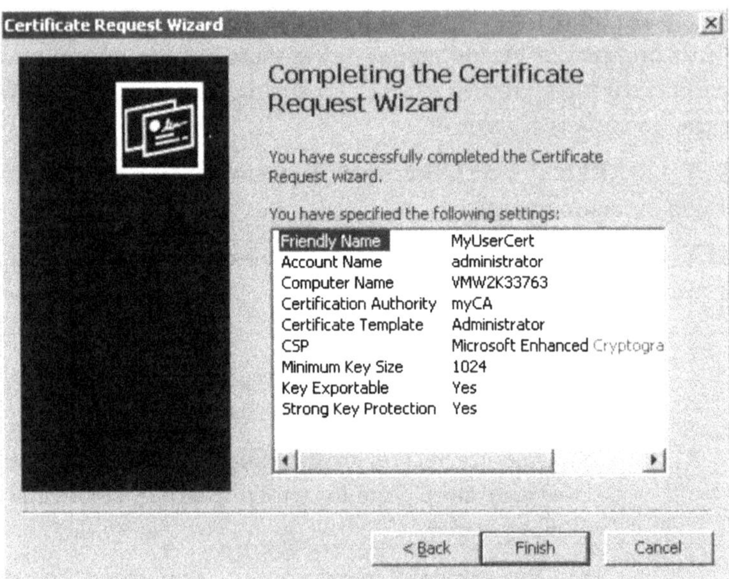

trated in Figure 15.11) that's available from the MMC Certificates snap-in. GUI-based enrollment will only work if the client-side PKI logic can find a CA object in AD and if the user's machine is joined to an AD domain. A message like the one illustrated in Figure 15.12 will be displayed.

- Command line interface: A user can enroll for certificates from an enterprise CA using the command prompt utility certreq. He or she can also use certreq to retrieve approved pending certificate requests from a CA. To do so, use the following certreq syntax:

```
CertReq [-Submit] [Options] [RequestFileIn [CertFileOut
[CertChainFileOut [FullResponseFileOut]]]]

CertReq [-Retrieve] [Options] RequestId [CertFileOut
[CertChainFileOut [FullResponseFileOut]]]
```

Figure 15.12 *Certificate Request Wizard error message.*

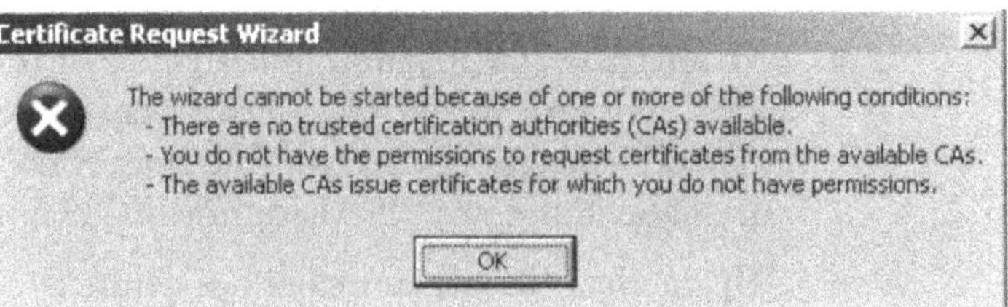

- Scripting interface: You can use CAPICOM (explained in Chapter 13) in conjunction with the xenroll.dll dynamic link library to create custom certificate enrollment interfaces. The latter is explained in more detail next.

Web based enrollment Interface

The Web based enrollment interface (illustrated in Figure 15.13) is made available through the Certificate Services Web Enrollment Support, an installation option that is selected by default when installing a CA on a server that has IIS installed. The Web server hosts the Certsrv virtual directory and application and the Certcontrol and CertEnroll virtual directories. All of them are automatically created during the Web interface installation process. You can also create the CA virtual directories manually using the certutil.exe command line tool with the -vroot switch.

The CA with which the Web interface is communicating should not necessarily be on the same machine as the Web interface itself. When

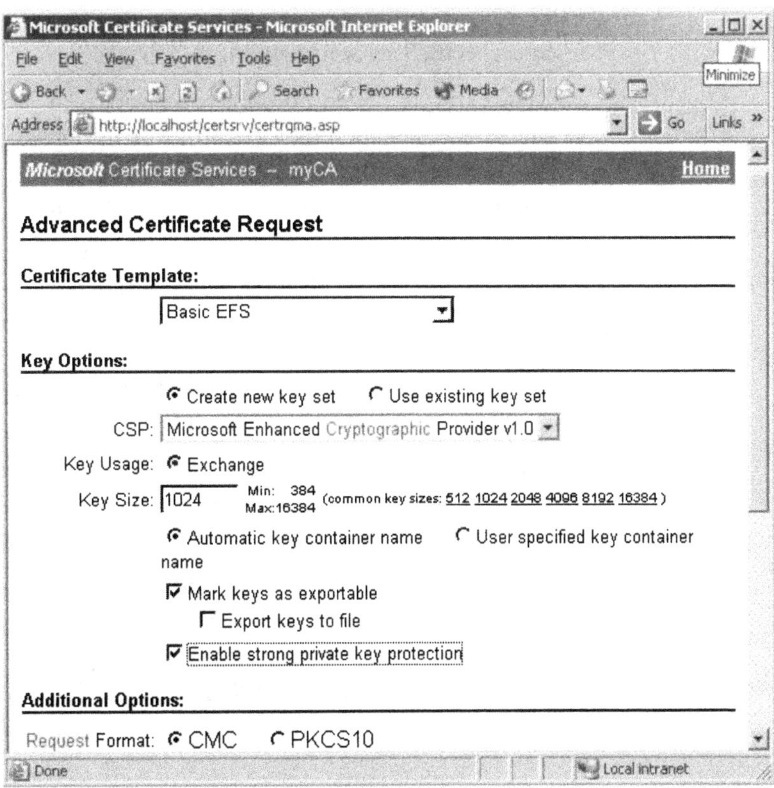

Figure 15.13 *Web enrollment interface.*

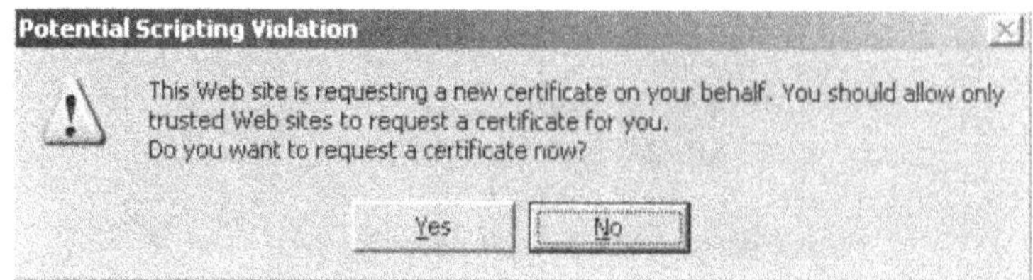

Figure 15.14 *Web enrollment warning message (following the IE enhanced security configuration).*

installing the Web interface on a server that does not have a CA installed, the installation program will prompt you for the name of a CA server to which the interface must point. This means you can deploy multiple CA Web interfaces on the same or on a different machine that are pointing to the same certificate server. This gives you an elegant way to deal with, for example, the different language requirements of your PKI clients: Just deploy one Web interface per language that you need to support.

The CA Web interface is built on ASP pages that detect the client's browser type. If they detect Internet Explorer, they will use the Certificate Enrollment Control (CEC) and its ActiveX controls (explained later). If it detects a Netscape browser it will generate a key and request through the Netscape specific KeyGen method.

When using the Web enrollment interface in Windows Server 2003, you will notice that the inclusion of the IE Enhanced Security Configuration[3] in Windows Server 2003 brings along some interesting error and warning messages (like the one illustrated in Figure 15.14).

Table 15.1 shows the certificate enrollment choices that are available from the Web interface. There are slight differences in the options available from the Web interface of a stand-alone CA and an enterprise CA.

Scripted enrollment options for custom enrollment interfaces

In case your organization has special enrollment requirements, Windows 2000 and Windows Server 2003 make it relatively easy for a developer to modify existing or to develop custom certificate enrollment interfaces.

You can use the CAPICOM automation object. CAPICOM can be used for signing enrollment requests or adding multiple signatures to a CMC-formatted enrollment request. CAPICOM is not installed by default on a Windows Server 2003 platform. You can download CAPICOM version 2.0.0.3 (cc2rinst.exe) from the Windows Platform SDK Redistributables

3. The IE Enhanced Security Configuration basically locks down the security settings of the IE Web content zones.

Table 15.1 *Windows Server 2003 CA Web Interface Options*

Windows Server 2003 CA Web Interface Options	Remarks
1. Request a certificate	
1.1 User certificate request 1.1.1 Stand-alone CA: Web browser certificate or e-mail protection certificate 1.1.2 Enterprise CA: User certificate	■ Stand-alone CA: Fill in name, e-mail, company, department, city, state, country/region (all filled in except for name e-mail) ■ Enterprise CA: Identification data retrieved automatically from AD
1.1.3 More options 1.1.3.1 Select a CSP 1.1.3.2 Enable strong private key protection 1.1.3.3 Request Format	Supported Request formats: ■ CMC or PCKS10
1.2 Advanced certificate request	
1.2.1 Create and submit a request to this CA	■ Stand-alone CA: Fill in name, e-mail, company, department, city, state, country/region (all filled in except for name e-mail) ■ Enterprise CA: Identification data retrieved automatically from AD
1.2.1.1 Certificate template	Enterprise CA only
1.2.1.2 Type of certificate needed	Stand-alone CA only Client authentication certificate... other (given OID)
1.2.1.3 Key options 1.2.1.3.1 ■ Create new key set ■ Use existing key set 1.2.1.3.2 CSP 1.2.1.3.3 Key usage (exchange) 1.2.1.3.4 Key size 1.2.1.3.5 ■ Automatic key container name ■ User specified key container name 1.2.1.3.6 Mark key as exportable ■ Export keys to file 1.2.1.3.7 Enable strong private key protection 1.2.1.3.8 Store certificate in local computer certificate store	Supported key sizes: ■ Minimum: 384 ■ Maximum: 16,384 Storing the certificate in the local computer store requires local administrator rights.

Table 15.1 *Windows Server 2003 CA Web Interface Options (continued)*

Windows Server 2003 CA Web Interface Options	Remarks
1.2.1.4 Additional options 1.2.1.4.1 Request Format 1.2.1.4.2 Hash algorithm 1.2.1.4.3 Save request to a file 1.2.1.4.4 Attributes 1.2.1.4.5 Friendly Name	Supported Request formats: ■ CMC or PCKS10 Supported Hash algorithms ■ SHA-1, MD2, MD4 or MD5
1.2.2 Submit a cert request by using a base64-encoded CMC or PKCS10 file, or submit a renewal request by using a base64-encoded PKCS7 file 1.2.2.1 Base64-encoded request 1.2.2.2 Certificate Template 1.2.2.3 Additional Attributes	
1.2.3 Request a certificate for a smart card on behalf of another user by using the smart card certificate enrollment station 1.2.3.1 Certificate Template 1.2.3.2 Certification Authority 1.2.3.3 CSP 1.2.3.4 Administrator signing certificate 1.2.3.5 User to enroll	Enterprise CA only
2. View the status of a pending certificate request	
3. Download a CA certificate, certificate chain, or CRL	
3.1 To trust certificates from this CA, install this CA certificate chain.	
3.2 To download a CA certificate, certificate chain, or CRL, select the certificate and encoding method. 3.2.1 CA certificate ■ Select CA 3.2.2 Encoding method ■ Select DER or Base64 ■ Then select: Download CA certificate Download CA certificate chain Download latest base CRL Download latest delta CRL	Downloaded files are using the following format: ■ *.cer format (for certificates) ■ *.p7b format (for certificate chains) ■ *.crl format (for CRLs and delta CRLs)

Web site at http://www.microsoft.com/downloads/details.aspx?displaylang=en&familyid=860ee43a-a843-462f-abb5-ff88ea5896f6.

Windows 2000 and Windows Server 2003 also come with two reusable software modules that can be called from any customized certificate enrollment application: the Certificate Enrollment Control (CEC) and the

Smartcard Enrollment Control (SEC). The certificate request wizard, discussed earlier, uses the CEC.

Both modules are located in the %windir%\system32\certsrv\certcontrol\x86 directory on the server side and in the %windir%\system32 directory on the client side. A client-side copy of the controls is needed to enable the module to write to the local certificate stores. The CEC and SEC are extensively documented in the Windows 2000 security platform SDK.

The SEC module (scrdenrl.dll) enables an administrator who has an enrollment agent certificate to request certificates on behalf of other users, and to store them on a smart card.

15.2.3 Key generation

Certificate enrollment starts with key generation. During the key generation process, an asymmetric key pair or a private and public key are generated. Most PKI-enabled applications use a single key pair; some use a dual key pair or even a triple key pair. Secure mail applications that are providing key recovery, for example, use a dual key pair to enable both the support for encryption key recovery and nonrepudiation services based on the user's signing key. Both services have different requirements. Nonrepudiation and digital signatures require that the access to and the use of the signing private key is strictly limited to a single user. Key recovery, on the other hand, requires the private decryption key to be archived in some centralized database. In a triple key pair model, one key pair is used to identify a user, one is used for digital signatures, and another one is used for data encryption.

Remember from Chapter 13 that once the private key has been generated it must be stored in a secure place. The latter can be a secure file system location (e.g., a DPAPI-secured part of the user profile) or in the best case a smart card.

In Windows 2000 and Windows Server 2003 the tasks of key generation, secure private key storage, and embedding the public key in a certificate request are all performed by the CEC (xenroll.dll) and SEC (scrdenrl.dll). Both modules were explained in the previous section. Certificate request generation is covered next.

15.2.4 Certificate request creation

When the public key is prepared for certification, it is embedded in a certificate request. A certificate request contains besides the public key also the identity of the certificate requestor, the location (read: certificate store) where the certificate must be published, and some other request attributes that depend on the type of CA to which the request is sent. A commonly used certificate request format that is supported in both Windows 2000 and Windows Server 2003 PKI is PKCS10, which defines the certificate request syntax. More information on PKCS10 is available from http://www.rsasecurity.com/rsalabs/pkcs/pkcs-10/index.html. Windows Server 2003 PKI also supports the CMC syntax. CMC stands for Certificate Management messages over CMS and is defined in RFC 2797 (available from http://www.ietf.org/rfc/rfc2797.txt). CMS stands for Cryptographic Message Syntax. CMS is defined in PKCS7 (more information on PKCS7 can be found at http://www.rsasecurity.com/rsalabs/pkcs/pkcs-7/index.html).

There are two ways to look at the content of a Windows 2000, Windows XP, or Windows Server 2003 certificate request as it is submitted to a CA:

- On the PKI user side: Open the Certificate Enrollment Requests certificate container in a user's certificate store. When you open a certificate request, you will see properties similar to the ones illustrated in Figure 15.15. Note that the General tab of the certificate request properties shows an integrity error.

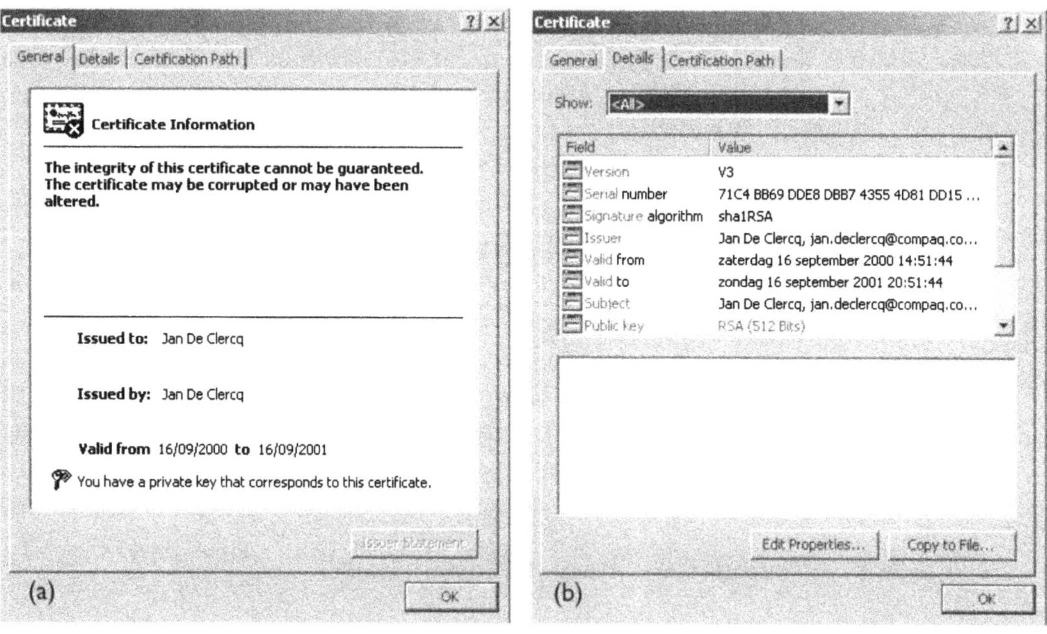

Figure 15.15 *Content of a certificate request.*

- On the CA side: Open the Pending Requests container, right-click a pending request in the right pane of the Certification Authority MMC snap-in, and select All Tasks\View Attributes/Extensions...

Windows 2000 and Windows Server 2003 also support the Simple Certificate Enrollment Protocol (SCEP), a certificate enrollment protocol developed by Verisign and Cisco. The support for SCEP enables, for example, a Cisco router to enroll for an IPsec certificate with a Windows 2000 or Windows Server 2003 CA. More information on SCEP can be found at http://www.cisco.com/warp/public/cc/pd/sqsw/tech/scep_wp.htm. The SCEP support add-on for Windows Server 2003 can be downloaded from the following URL: http://www.microsoft.com/downloads/details.aspx?displaylang=en&familyid=9f306763-d036-41d8-8860-1636411b2d01.

To enable a Windows 2000 or Windows Server 2003 CA to support SCEP, you must install the mscep.dll (an ISAPI filter) coming with the Windows 2000 or Windows Server 2003 resource kit. A detailed procedure on how to set this up is also available in the resource kit and in the Q249125 Microsoft Knowledge Base article titled "Using Certificates for Windows 2000 and Cisco IOS VPN Interoperation" that is available at http://support.microsoft.com/?kbid=249125.

15.2.5 Requestor identification

Before the certificate is actually generated by the CA, the CA will validate the certificate request (this includes the validation of the request format) and identify the requesting user. Identification is an often forgotten, critical step of certificate enrollment. Identification means that the CA will check whether the entity requesting the certificate is really the one that is mentioned in the request message and whether the requesting entity possesses the private key corresponding to the public key in the certificate request.

In Windows 2000 and Windows Server 2003, the identification method depends on the enrollment interface the PKI user uses to enroll for a certificate. When users enroll for certificates using the certificate enrollment wizard, the CA authenticates users using the Kerberos protocol. The CA will use the NTLM protocol to authenticate clients when the client does not support Kerberos or when there is no Kerberos KDC available. The NTLM authentication protocol is explained in Chapter 4; Kerberos authentication is explained in Chapter 5.

The authentication protocol that is used when enrolling through a Web interface depends on how authentication has been configured on the CA

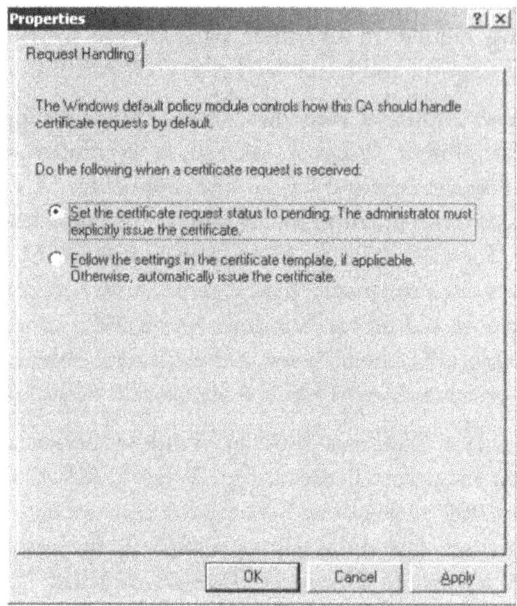

Figure 15.16 *Changing a stand-alone CA's policy properties.*

Web directory (certsrv). For more information on the IIS authentication options, see Chapter 6.

CA administrators that want to use user identification methods other than the ones that are rooted on the Windows and IIS authentication protocols can configure the Windows CA to require CA certificate manager approval before the certificate is actually issued—this means that the request will go to a pending state when it arrives at the CA. As part of the CA certificate manager approval process, the manager can then identify the user using a custom method (e.g., face-to-face identification or identification based on the user's driver's license). After the user is uniquely identified using the custom method, the manager can then manually issue the certificate. When using an enterprise CA, certificate manager approval can be configured on the certificate template level. A stand-alone CA by default puts all incoming requests in a pending state. The latter can be changed from the policy properties of the CA object (as illustrated in Figure 15.16).

15.2.6 Certificate generation

During certificate generation the CA will sign the certificate content using its private key. The content of a certificate depends on the content of the certificate request. In the case of an Enterprise CA, some of the requestor-specific data are retrieved from the Active Directory. The layout of the certificate is defined in certificate templates that the CA retrieves from the AD or the registry.

15.2.7 Certificate distribution and publication

Once a certificate has been generated, it can be distributed and published. Most PKI systems publish the certificate in a directory. In Windows 2000 and Windows Server 2003, certificate publication to AD depends on a certificate template setting.

- On version 1 certificate templates the AD publication behavior cannot be changed. For an overview of which V1 certificate templates publish certificates to AD, see "Certificate templates" in Section 13.4.4.
- On version 2 certificate templates AD publication depends on a changeable template property: Publish certificate in Active Directory. This property can be changed from the General tab of the certificate template properties (as illustrated in Figure 15.17).

To publish certificates to other locations than AD (e.g., other LDAP directories or Web sites), you can develop custom exit modules that can be plugged into the Windows CA architecture. For more information on exit modules, see Chapter 13. In case you want to do this, remember that no mat-

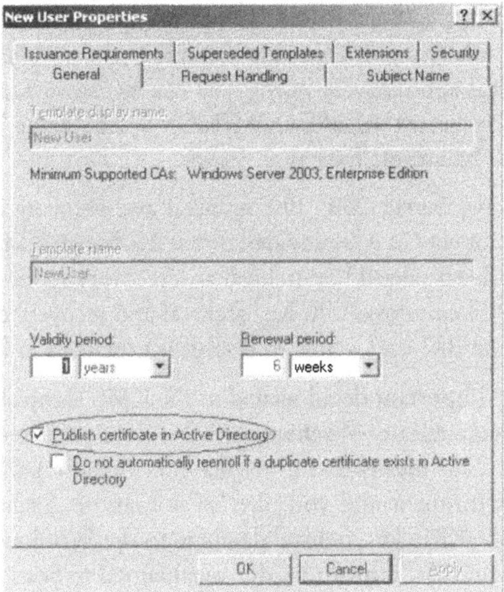

Figure 15.17 *Certificate template property for certificate AD publication.*

ter what exit modules you create and install, certificates will not be published unless the publication location is specified in the certificate request.

To distribute the certificate back to the user, a Windows enterprise CA sends a copy to the user using a CMC- or PKCS7-formatted message. Certificates returned from the CA are then automatically installed in the user's certificate store. When requesting a certificate using the Web enrollment pages, the user also has the option to store the returned certificate in the local machine's certificate store. This way the certificate becomes available to all users logging on to that system. A stand-alone CA stores the newly generated certificate on the CA's Web site, from which it can then be retrieved by the user.

An interesting detail related to certificate publication is that the machine account of the server hosting the CA must be a member of the Cert Publishers global group of every domain in the forest. Members of this group are the only ones who can write certificates to the usercertificate attribute of AD user objects.

15.3 Key archival and recovery

Key archival and recovery are PKI services that are used to recover lost, stolen, or simply unavailable private encryption keys. Encryption key archival and recovery are a key requirement in PKI-enabled applications that are dealing with persistent data. Good examples are secure mail applications.

Microsoft first introduced automatic and centralized private encryption key archival and recovery in the Key Management Service (KMS), which is part of the Secure MIME (S/MIME)–based secure mail application that ships with Microsoft Exchange Server.

Windows Server 2003 PKI archival and recovery builds on the central-database concept as it is provided by the Exchange KMS: It includes an automated and centralized key archival and recovery service with every Windows Server 2003 enterprise CA. Key archival and recovery can also be done manually by the PKI user—how to do this is explained in Section 15.3.1.

A very important detail related to the KMS archival service is that the latest Exchange release—Exchange 2003—does not come with a KMS service anymore. This means that if you have an operational KMS in an Exchange 2000 environment and you plan to migrate to Exchange 2003, you must migrate the KMS key archival database to the Windows Server 2003 CA key archival database. How to do this is explained in Section 15.3.5. Chapter 17 contains more information on the S/MIME standard for secure mail and how it can be used in a Windows Server 2003 PKI environment.

15.3.1 Manual key archival and recovery

There are different ways for a PKI user to manually back up his or her private encryption keys. The preferred and most commonly used format to store archived private keys is PKCS12. Access to and the confidentiality of a PKCS12 file's (*.pfx) content can be secured using a password. To manually back up your private keys to a PKCS12 file, you can do one of the following:

- Open your personal certificate store using the Certificates MMC snap-in. Right-click the certificate whose private key you want to manually back up and select All Tasks\Export… This action brings up the Certificate Export Wizard. Make sure that you check the "Yes, export the private key" option and that you enable strong key protection (as shown in Figure 15.18)—the latter option will make the wizard prompt you for a password to protect the PKCS12 file's content. Do not check the "Delete the private key if export is successful" option.
- From Internet Explorer: Select the Internet Options menu option from the tools menu. In the Internet Options dialog box, go to the Content tab. Click the Certificates pushbutton—this brings up the Certificates dialog box. Select the certificate whose private key you want to export and click Export… This action will also bring up the Certificate Export Wizard. Use the same options as mentioned above.

You can also archive your private encryption keys from Outlook. Outlook does not store the keys in a PKCS12 formatted file, though; it uses a

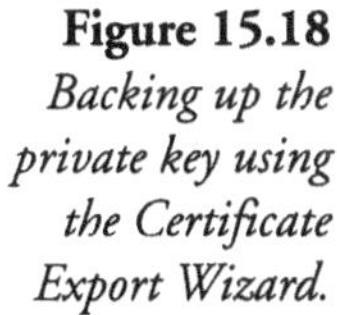

Figure 15.18 *Backing up the private key using the Certificate Export Wizard.*

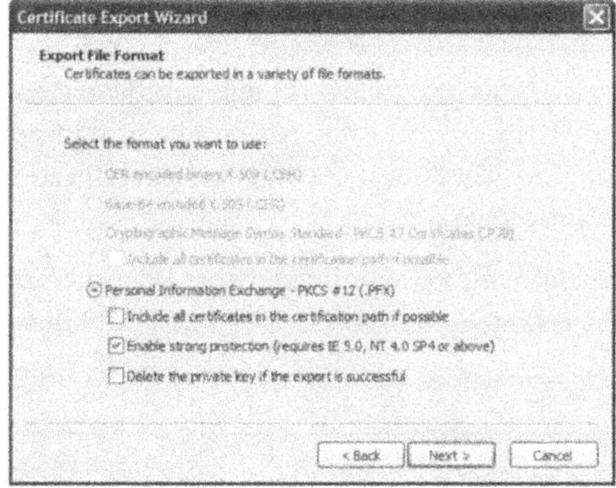

special Outlook export format (*.epf). Like PKCS12, this format can be secured using a password that is provided by the user. To export your private encryption keys from Outlook, select the Options menu option in the Tools menu and go to the Security tab. At the bottom of the Security tab, click the Import\Export pushbutton. This brings up the Import\Export Digital ID dialog box—in this box, check the "Export your Digital ID to a file" radio button. Select the Digital ID whose private key you want to export, and fill in a filename and password. Make sure that you do not check the "Delete Digital ID from system" checkbox.

The epf extension shows the historical roots of Microsoft Outlook's secure mail technology: epf stands for Entrust profile. One of the reasons why Outlook still uses this format is that it supports X.509 version 1 certificates, which were used in the early Exchange KMS implementations.

15.3.2 Automatic key archival and recovery architecture

A Windows Server 2003 CA securely stores the archived private keys in the CA database. The CA uses a symmetric 3DES key to encrypt a private key, and then uses a key recovery agent's public key to encrypt the symmetric key. A new symmetric encryption key is randomly generated for every new key archival request.

A key recovery agent (KRA) is a Windows account that has key recovery privileges. An account has those privileges if it owns a key recovery certificate and private key.[4] If more than one KRA is defined, the symmetric encryption key will be encrypted with each KRA's public key. Windows Server 2003 PKI comes with a predefined key recovery agent certificate template, so it is relatively easy to set up a key recovery certificate for a particular account.

The key archival process occurs in a completely transparent way for the PKI user. It occurs as part of the certificate enrollment process. Whether or not a private key is archived depends on a certificate template setting that will be explained next.

During a certificate enrollment that incorporates an automatic key archival, the following steps occur—Figure 15.19 illustrates this process:

4. For advanced security reasons, both the KRA certificate and private key can be stored on a smart card. This is supported in Windows Server 2003 PKI.

- The PKI client queries AD for a CA. It specifically looks for CA entries in the enrollment services container in the configuration naming context. AD returns the name and location of CA.
- The PKI client requests the CA for a copy of its CA exchange certificate.
- The CA returns the CA exchange certificate to the client.
- The PKI client validates the CA's CA exchange certificate. It verifies the signature, performs a revocation check, and validates the certificate format.
- The PKI client encrypts the private key that must be archived with the CA exchange certificate's public key. This encrypted blob is then embedded in a CMC-formatted request object and forwarded to the CA.
- The CA decrypts the encrypted private key of the client with the private key associated with the CA's exchange certificate. It then encrypts the private key with a random 3DES symmetric key.

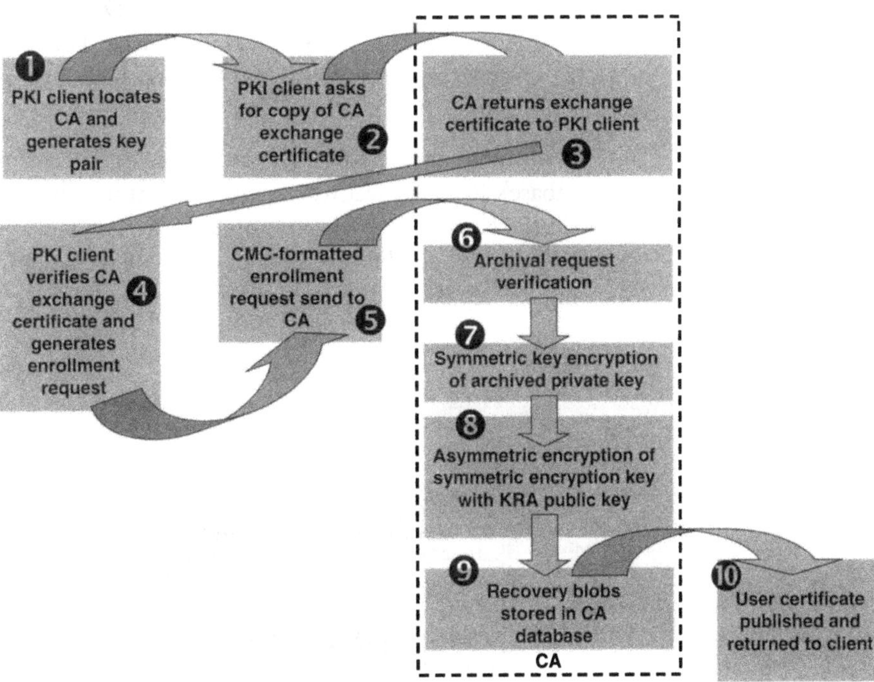

Figure 15.19 *Windows Server 2003 key archival process.*

- The CA checks whether the private key in the CMC cryptographically pairs with the public key in the certificate request. It also validates the signature on the request using the public key that comes with the request.
- Finally, the CA encrypts the symmetric key with the public keys of one or more Key Recovery Agents (KRAs) based on the CA configuration.
- The CA saves the encrypted blob containing the encrypted private key and the symmetric key encrypted with one or more KRA public keys in the CA database.
- The CA processes the certificate request. It then forwards the certificate to the user and publishes it in the directory (if this option has been set in the certificate template).

In this process the CA exchange certificate is used to provide confidentiality and integrity protection when the PKI client's private key is forwarded to the CA for archival. The CA exchange certificate's content is defined in a new certificate template coming with Windows Server 2003. A CA's CA Exchange certificate is physically stored in the attributes of the CN=<CAName>-Xchg,DC=<domainname> AD object. Its private key is stored in a secured part of the CA server's registry. For obvious security reasons, the CA exchange certificate and key pair have a very short lifetime (7 days).

The Windows Server 2003 CA stores the encrypted private key in the CA database's RawArchivedKey column and stores the encrypted symmetric key in the KeyRecoveryHashes column. You can view these columns and the rest of the CA database's schema from the command line by typing the following certutil command at the command line:

```
certutil -schema
```

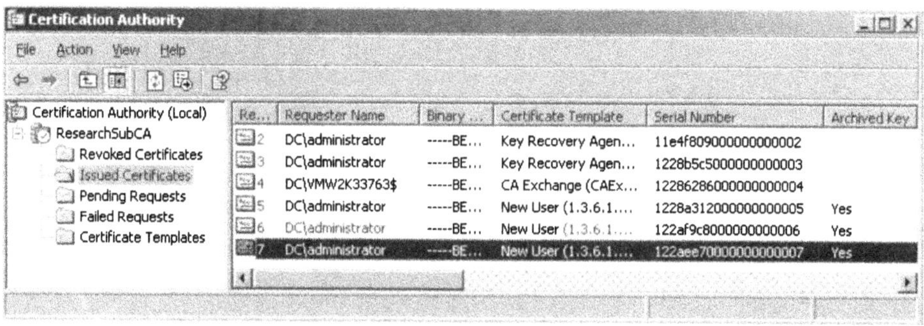

Figure 15.20 *Archived key column in CA interface.*

Whether or not the private key of a given certificate is archived in the CA database can also be seen from the CA MMC snap-in. To do so, you must change the columns that are displayed in the Issued Certificates CA container: You must add the Archived key column (as illustrated in Figure 15.20). To add this column, right-click the Issued Certificates container, then select View\Add/Remove columns… . Then add the Archived key in the available columns list.

15.3.3 Configuring automatic key archival and recovery

Configuring automatic key archival and recovery in Windows Server 2003 requires configuration changes in the CA and the certificate template properties. The changes are explained next.

To configure a CA object's key-archival settings, open the MMC Certification Authority snap-in, open the CA object's Properties dialog box, and then go to the Recovery Agents tab, which is shown in Figure 15.21. Select the Archive key checkbox to enable key recovery.

You can specify the number of KRAs you want to define in the "Number of recovery agents to use" text box. At the bottom of the Recovery

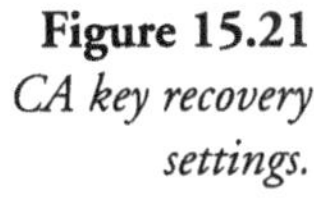

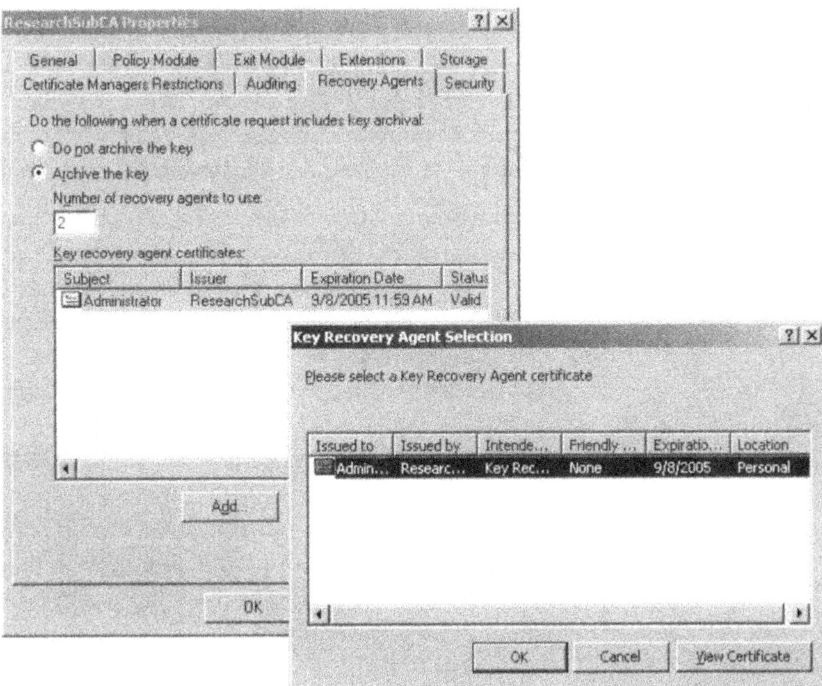

Figure 15.21
CA key recovery settings.

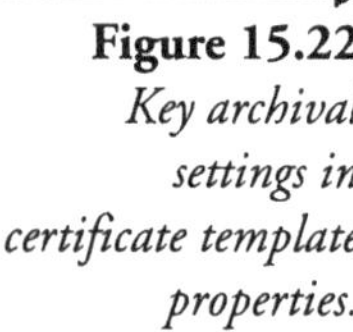

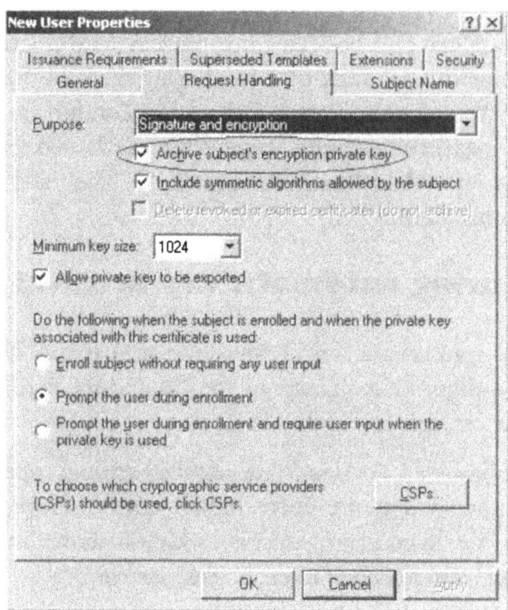

Figure 15.22 *Key archival settings in certificate template properties.*

agents tab, you can select the KRA certificates you want to use for key archival.

When you click the Add button, the CA logic will query the KRA container in the AD configuration naming context and retrieve a list of available KRA certificates. Each time you add a new KRA certificate you must restart the CA service. As long as the CA service has not been restarted, the status column of the KRA certificate will say Not Loaded.

To enable key archival at the certificate-template level, you must use the Certificate Templates MMC snap-in. To automatically archive the private key when a user requests a certificate based on a particular template, open the template, go to the Request Handling tab, and select the Archive subject's encryption private key checkbox (as illustrated in Figure 15.22). You can set the key-archival option only on version 2 certificate templates.

15.3.4 Key recovery from the CA database

A key recovery is typically initiated by a PKI or PKI-enabled application (PKA) user. Key recovery requires the intervention of at least one key recovery agent (KRA)—depending on how key archival and recovery has been configured in the CA properties.

Key recovery requires the intervention of both a certificate manager and a KRA: a certificate manager to retrieve the recovery data from the CA database and a KRA to retrieve the archived private key from the recovery data.

An archived private key can be recovered from the command line or from the Windows GUI.

A full Windows Server 2003 private key recovery sequence from the command line consists of the following steps:[5]

- The KRA identifies the user who requests a key recovery.
- The KRA writes down the user principal name (UPN), user common name (CN), account name (domain\username), SHA-1 thumbprint (hash), or serial number, of the user certificate whose private key the agent wants to recover. In this step, the most important task is to find a unique identifier for the key to be recovered. If more than one key is archived for a particular user, the safest thing is to first retrieve a list of all archived keys. This can be done using the following command:

```
Certutil -getkey <user common name, account name or UPN>
```

- Then to export the recovery data from the CA database, the KRA opens a command prompt and types

```
certutil -getkey <Unique identifier> <output file>
```

- To transform the output file to a PKCS #12 file (which will contain the recovered private key and is secured using the password "test"), the KRA types

```
certutil -p "test" -recoverkey <output file> <pkcs12
file>
```

- The KRA provides the PKCS #12 file to the appropriate user, who can then import it to his or her certificate store.

If the KRA recovered multiple keys for the same user, he or she can merge them all into a single PKCS12 file. This will facilitate the installation of the recovered keys for the user. To do so, he or she must type the following certutil command (the password used to secure the PKCS12 file is again "test"):

```
CertUtil -p "test" -MergePFX -user "<PKCS12_
File1>,<PKCS12_File2>" "<NameofCombined_PKCS12"
```

5. In this example, no role separation has been defined. Also, it uses a single KRA certificate.

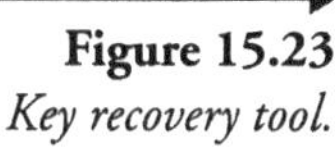

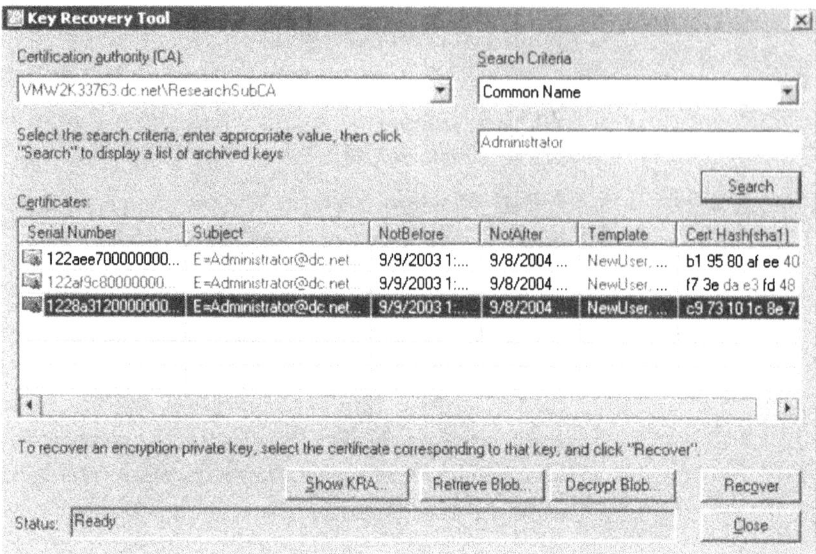

Figure 15.23
Key recovery tool.

To recover keys from the GUI, you must use the Key Recovery Tool (krt.exe) that is part of the Windows Server 2003 Resource Kit (illustrated in Figure 15.23). It offers a very convenient GUI-based way to recover keys that have been archived in the CA database.

To recover keys using the Key Recovery Tool, you must do the following:

- Select a CA from whose database you want to recover keys (in the CA drop-down box).
- Search for the archived private keys and certificates for a particular user: To do so, select a search criterion (common name, UPN, serial number, hash, or account name) in the Search Criteria drop-down box, and then fill in the user identifier and click the Search button.
- You can then:
  - Recover all archived keys at once (using the Recover button).
  - Recover a single key-certificate pair (using the retrieve Blob... and decrypt blob... buttons).

15.3.5 Migrating the exchange KMS database

As mentioned earlier, Exchange 2003 does not come with a KMS service anymore. If you have an operational KMS in an Exchange 2000 environment and you plan to migrate to Exchange 2003, you must migrate the

KMS key archival database to the Windows Server 2003 CA key archival database. This section explains how to do this.

To migrate the KMS key archival database to the Windows Server 2003 CA key archival database, you must run through the following steps:

- If you are running an Exchange 5.5 KMS, upgrade to Exchange 2000. The KMS migration process can only support an Exchange 2000 KMS database.
- Configure the Windows Server 2003 CA for key archival. How to do this has already been explained.
- Ensure that an export encryption certificate is available for KMS database migration.
- Enable the foreign certificate import option on the Windows Server 2003 CA if necessary.
- Export the Exchange KMS database's content.
- Import the Exchange KMS data into the CA's key archival database.

The export encryption certificate and its associated private key are required to secure the KMS data when they are exported from the KMS database and transported to the Windows Server 2003 CA. The export encryption certificate must be available on the KMS machine whose data you want to migrate. The certificate is a copy of the CA server's machine authentication certificate. In case the CA server does not have a machine authentication certificate, make sure it gets one before you start the KMS migration. The machine authentication certificate is stored in the CA server's local machine certificate store. To transfer it to the KMS machine, export it from the CA server using the PKCS12 format as outlined earlier and then store it in some file system folder on the KMS machine.

Importing certificates and keys that were issued by another CA into a Windows Server 2003 CA's database is only possible if you have enabled the CA to accept certificates and private keys that were issued by another CA. To enable this, use the following certutil command:

```
Certutil -setreg ca\KRAFlags +KRAF_ENABLEFOREIGN
```

To export KMS archival data, you must use the KMS Key Export Wizard that is available from the Exchange 2003 System Manager MMC snap-in. This wizard (illustrated in Figure 15.24) can be started from the properties of the Key Manager object in the Exchange 2000 System Manager: Select All Tasks\Export Users. The wizard will prompt you for the CA's

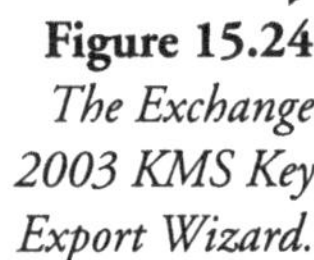

Figure 15.24 *The Exchange 2003 KMS Key Export Wizard.*

export signing certificate and will ask you for which Exchange 2000 administrative group's user keys you want to export. The wizard will by default save the export file in the %systemdrive%:\program files\exchsrvr\kmsdata directory. Locate the export file and copy it to the CA server.

The exported KMS archival data can be imported into the central CA archival database using the following certutil command:

```
Certutil -f -importKMS <Filename>
```

This command can handle files that are formatted using the Exchange KMS export format as well as *.pfx files and *.epf files. The latter two formats are used to manually archive certificate and private key data (as was explained earlier).

This certutil command is illustrated in Figure 15.25 for the import of a *.pfx archive called admin.pfx containing a manually archived certificate-private key pair.

```
C:\WINDOWS\system32\cmd.exe
C:\Documents and Settings\Administrator\Desktop>certutil -f -importKMS admin.pfx

Enter PFX password:
Key Id Hash(sha1): 04 63 34 2a 0f 0f 50 20 a9 39 4b d8 84 72 cd 0a 06 dd 6e 4b
..
Certificates with keys: 1
Certificates already imported: 1

Keys: 1
Keys updated: 1
Keys archived: 1
CertUtil: -ImportKMS command completed successfully.

C:\Documents and Settings\Administrator\Desktop>
```

Figure 15.25 *Manual CA archival database import.*

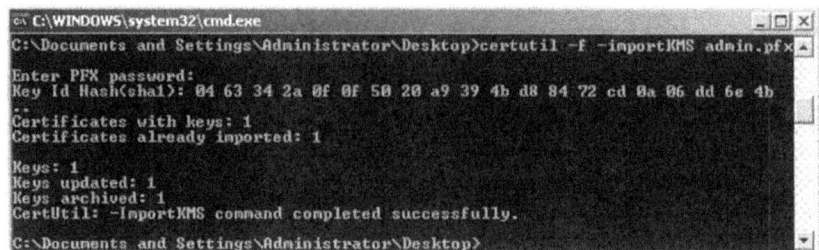

The –f switch in this command must be used if the certificate that will be injected into the database was not issued by the CA itself (which is typically the case when you are migrating a KMS key archival database). The switch stands for "issued by a foreign CA."

15.4 Data recovery

Data recovery is the PKI-related process that decrypts encrypted data following the loss of a private key. It is a service that is required when dealing with persistent data that are secured using encryption technology. The inability to decrypt data when the encryption key is lost would result in data loss. Data recovery can occur independently of user private key recovery. It can also follow key recovery.

When data recovery occurs independently of user private key recovery, a predefined set of administrators—referred to as data recovery agents—are authorized to decrypt the data. In order to make data recovery happen independently of user private key recovery, the symmetric encryption key must be available to the data recovery agents. That is why PKA using this type of data recovery typically encrypts a copy of the symmetric encryption key using the data recovery agent's public key. A good example of an application where data recovery can occur completely independent of user private key recovery is the Encryption File System (EFS) coming with Windows 2000 and Windows Server 2003. EFS is explained in more detail in Chapter 17.

Data recovery can also follow key recovery: After a user and authorized administrator gain access to the user's private key, the user can use the key to decrypt the encrypted symmetric keys that were used to encrypt the data. This is what happens in the key recovery scenarios (e.g., for S/MIME-rooted secure mail applications) that were explained in previous sections.

Keep the following in mind when you must decide upon the use of key or data recovery in a PKI:

- Data recovery is required when an organization requires access to the encrypted data independent of the user or if a policy does not allow access to private keys of users.
- Key recovery is used when the policy of an organization allows access to private keys (and possibly does not allow access to encrypted data of users).
- If access to data or private keys are not allowed, then key recovery and data recovery should not be used.

15.5 Certificate validation

Certificate validation is the process by which a PKI-enabled application finds out whether a certificate and the public key contained in it are trustworthy. During certificate validation, the following checks are performed: digital signature, trust, time, revocation, and formatting. The checks are illustrated in Figure 15.26 and explained next.

During the digital signature check, the certificate validation logic validates the digital signature that has been applied to the certificate content by the issuer of the certificate. To be able to do so, a trustworthy public key is needed. This can be the public key of the issuing CA or the public key of another CA that is part of the certificate's certificate chain. The availability of a public key is not enough to validate a signature: The public key must also be trusted. In Windows PKI, a trusted CA certificate and public key are known as a trust anchor—they are available from two specific containers in an entity's certificate store (these containers were explained in Chapter 14). The process of discovering a trusted CA certificate is done during the trust check, which is also referred to as certificate chain validation. Certificate chain validation may trigger different certificate validation loops: one for each certificate in the certificate chain. Certificate chain validation is explained in more detail later on in this chapter.

During the time check, the start-end date of the certificate are compared to the current time. One of the reasons why a certificate's lifetime is limited is to cope with the advances in computer technology. For example, every year it becomes easier to break a 512-bit key-rooted asymmetric cipher.

During the revocation check, the validation logic checks whether the certificate has been revoked. Windows 2000 and Windows Server 2003

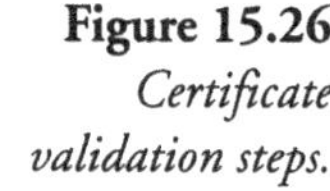

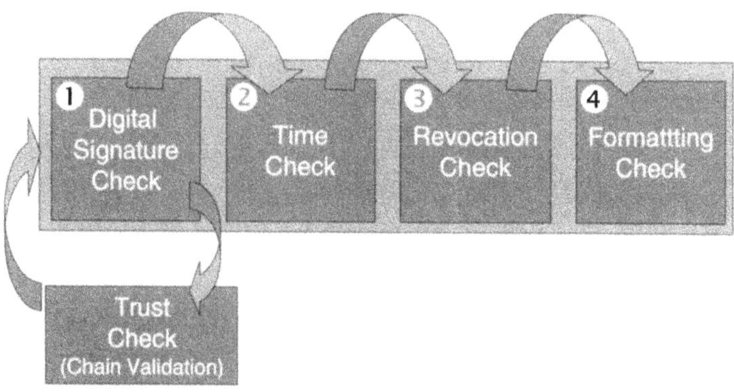

Figure 15.26 *Certificate validation steps.*

PKI support complete certificate revocation lists (CRLs) and CRL distribution points (CDPs). Windows Server 2003 PKI also supports delta CRLs. CRLs, Delta CRLs, and CDPs can provide automated certificate revocation checking. We discuss revocation in more detail in the section on certificate revocation.

During the formatting check, the format of the certificate is checked and validated. This is done according to the standard certificate format defined in the ITU-T X.509 standard. This check also includes the validation of the certificate's extensions (see also the following sidebar). Among a certificate's extensions are the basic constraints, application policy, issuance policy, and name constraints extensions that were discussed in Chapter 14. A certificate also contains a set of critical extensions that—following the X.509 standard—must be validated by every application. The validation or evaluation of the other noncritical extensions depends on the PKI application using the certificate. Most S/MIME applications, for example, will evaluate the certificate subject's RFC822 name (e.g., jan.declercq@hp.com). It will be compared to the sender entry in the header of the SMTP message. In the case of S/MIME, this check protects against impersonation or man-in-the-middle attacks. In such attacks a malicious entity reuses a user's identity. A similar check is done by most SSL implementations. SSL compares the subject's RFC822 name to the name that is contained in the URL.

Displaying a Certificate's X.509 Extensions To view the different X.509 certificate extensions, you must use the Details tab in the certificate properties (illustrated in Figure 15.27). At the top of this tab there is a drop-down box called Show that allows you to filter the X.509 field and extension data that are displayed in the bottom part of the tab. To display only the critical extensions, select Critical Extensions Only. The filter allows you to differentiate between version 1 fields only, all extensions, critical extensions only, and properties only. For most of these field types, the certificate viewer uses another icon as shown here:

- Standard X.509 fields
- X.509 extensions
- X.509 critical extensions
- Certificate properties (not X.509-based)

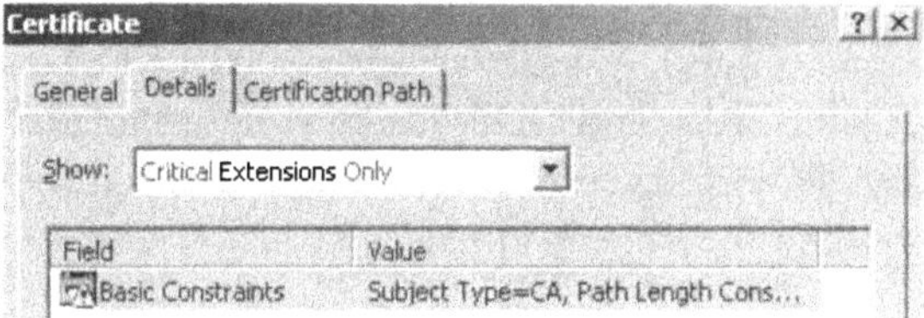

Figure 15.27 *Bringing up an X.509 certificate's critical extensions.*

15.5.1 Regular certificate chain processing

So what is a certificate chain and why do we need to process it during certificate validation? Let's try to explain this concept using the example of a hierarchical trust model.

In a hierarchical trust model, every end-entity's certificate chain consists of all CA certificates that are lying on the path between the user and the root CA of the PKI hierarchy. In a PKI hierarchy, every certificate[6] always contains a pointer to its parent or issuing CA, which is stored in the certificate issuer field. All of this is illustrated in Figure 15.28: It shows the certificate chain of a user certificate that has been issued by CA that is part of a PKI hierarchy of two levels. In the figure, certificates have been represented in a much simplified way (to provide an easy explanation): Every certificate is represented using the certificate subject and the certificate issuer. In this example, the user's certificate subject is the user; its issuer is the intermediate CA. The intermediate CA's certificate subject is the intermediate CA; it has been issued by the root CA. In a hierarchy, the root CA always has a self-signed certificate: In this case the certificate subject and issuer are identical.

During certificate validation, the certificate validation software processes a certificate's certificate chain. This process can be split into two subprocesses: chain construction and chain validation.

Chain construction

During chain construction, the certificate validation software runs through the certificate's chain until it finds a trusted CA certificate, also known as a trust anchor. In Chapter 14 we explained which CA certificates are considered trust anchors in Windows PKI. In the examples of Figure 15.29, the validation software finds a trust anchor at the root CA level (example 1) and at the intermediate CA level (example 2). When a trust anchor is found, the chain construction subprocess stops and the validation logic will switch to chain validation. In Figure 15.30 (example 3), the validation logic cannot

6. With the exception of the root CA's certificate.

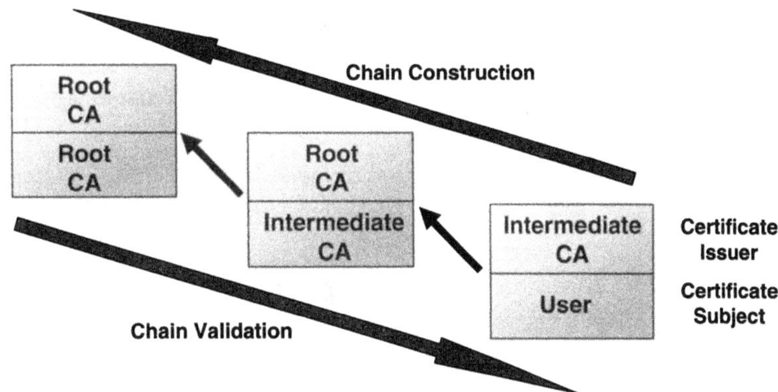

Figure 15.28 *Certificate chain processing.*

find a trust anchor. In this case, the certificate chain process stops and no decisions can be made regarding the trustworthiness of the certificate.

Chain validation

During chain validation, the certificate validation software walks the chain in the opposite direction (top-down) and validates every CA certificate that is part of the chain. In order to validate a certificate, it must be available

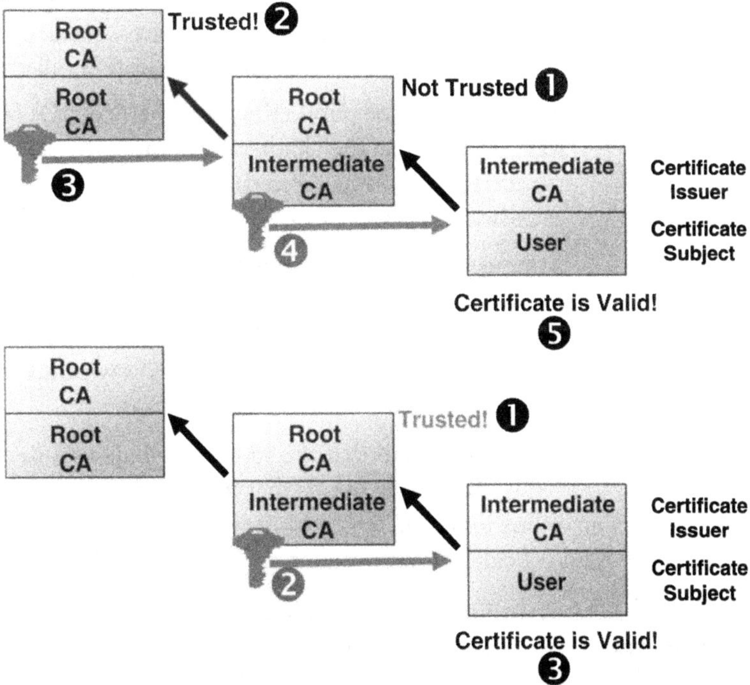

Figure 15.29 *Certificate chain processing examples 1 and 2.*

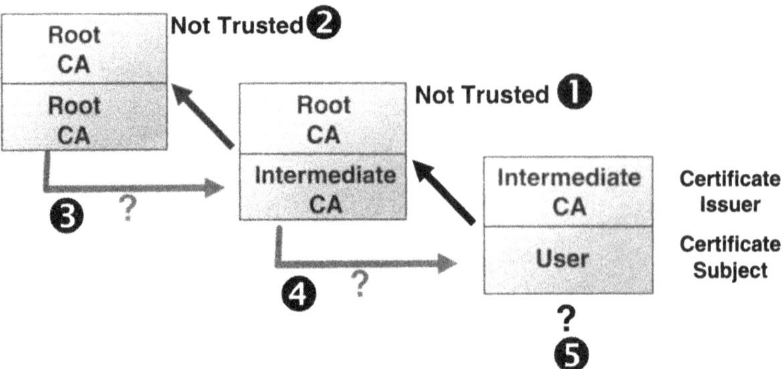

Figure 15.30 *Certificate chain processing example 3.*

locally in one of the containers of a user's certificate store (see Chapter 13). When a certificate is not available locally, the Windows PKI software will use the Authority Information Access (AIA) method that is explained next to obtain a copy of the certificate.

The identification of a CA certificate during chain validation is based on the Authority Key Identifier (AKI) field in the certificate under verification. A certificate's AKI field can contain different types of information:

- It may contain the issuer name and serial number of the issuer's certificate. In that case the chain validation logic will try to find a matching certificate using a certificate's Serial number and Subject fields. This way of identifying a certificate is called an exact match.
- It may contain the public Key identifier (KeyID) of the issuer's certificate. In that case the chain validation logic will try to find a matching certificate using a certificate's Subject Key Identifier (SKI) extension. This way of identifying a certificate is called a key match.

If the certificate under verification does not contain an AKI field, the chain validation logic will try to identify the issuing CA's certificate by matching the name in the Issuer field of the certificate under verification with the name in the Subject field. This way of identifying a certificate is called a name match.

The AIA method that the validation logic uses to obtain a local copy of the certificate simply means that it will try to download the certificate from an online location. To do this it will use a certificate's Authority Info Access (AIA) field,[7] which contains an LDAP, HTTP, or File System pointer to a

7. The content of the AIA field of the certificates a CA issues can be configured from the CA object's properties in the CA MMC snap-in. The CA certificate's proper AIA field can be configured using a capolicy.inf configuration file (as was mentioned in Chapter 14).

location where the CA's certificate is stored. If the AIA field has multiple entries, all entries will be tried out in the order that they are listed in the AIA field. All certificates that are downloaded from an AIA location will be cached in the certificate store and on the file system for future use. On the file system they are cached in the \Documents and Settings\\<*username*>\Local Settings\Temporary Internet Files folder. Note the use of the <user-name> variable in the previous file system path: the cache location is dependent on the user security context under which the calling application is running.

If the certificate is not available, certificate verification will fail. If the certificate is available, the certificate validation logic will run (for every certificate in the chain) through all of the steps that were explained earlier: time, digital signature, formatting, and revocation checking.

A certificate's certificate chain can be viewed from the certificate's properties: in the Certification Path tab. Figure 15.31 shows the certificate chain of a certificate that ends in a trusted CA certificate (Figure 15.31(a)) and another that ends in an untrusted CA certificate (Figure 15.31(b)) as they are displayed in the Windows certificate properties.

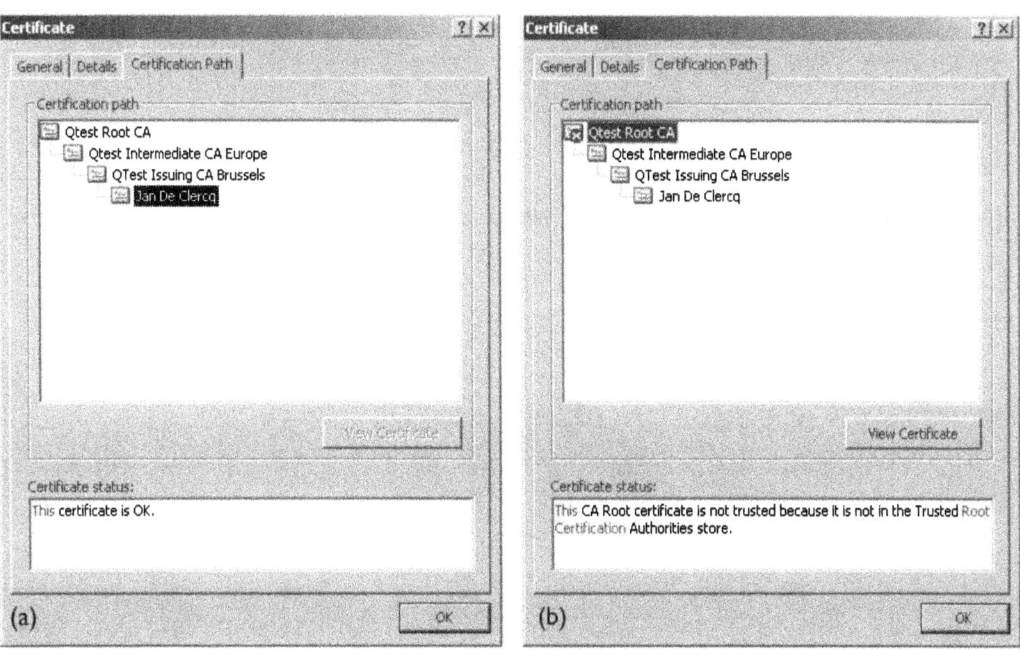

Figure 15.31 *Certificate chain viewed from the certificate properties: (a) trusted CA certificate and (b) untrusted CA certificate.*

When a user downloads a certificate using the Windows 2000 or Windows Server 2003 CA Web interface, he or she has the choice to download just the certificate or the certificate together with all of the certificates that are part of its certificate chain. This can be an interesting option for certificate validation on, for example, portable computers. All CA certificates in the certificate chain are made available on the client at once, and there is no need for the client software to download the certificates in the chain using the AIA pointers.

This section illustrates that certificates can be invalid for different reasons: expiration or other time problems, invalid signatures, unavailability of a trusted CA certificate, improper use, improper formatting, revocation, and so forth. That is why finding out the exact reason why a certificate is not valid is sometimes a tough job.

15.5.2 CTL certificate chain processing

A special case of certificate chain processing is Certificate Trust List (CTL) certificate chain processing. CTLs are signed lists of trusted root CA certificates: They can only contain self-signed root CA certificates. CTLs can be

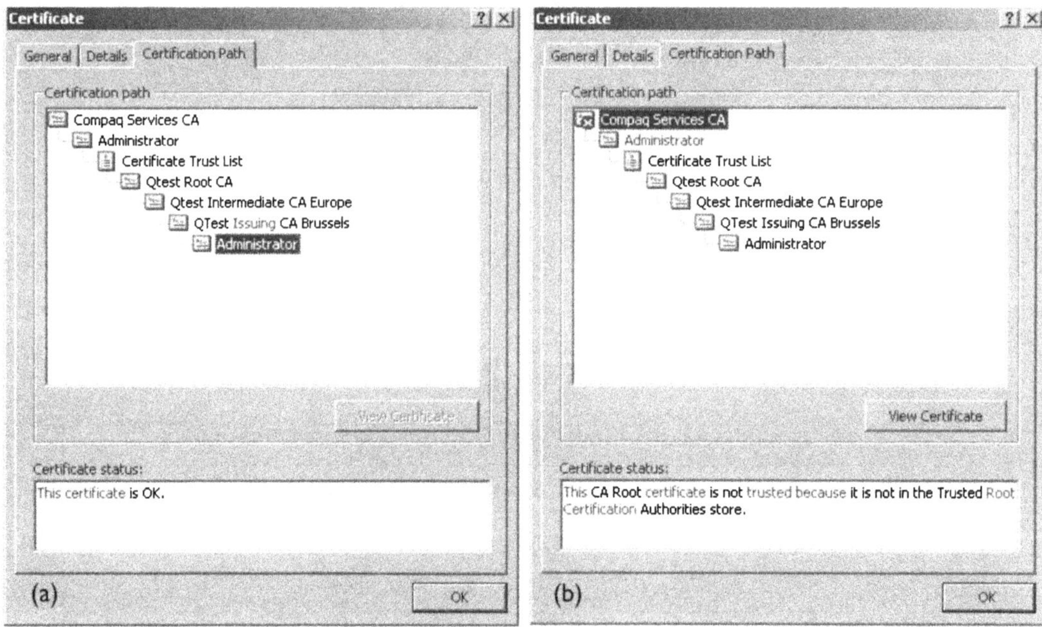

Figure 15.32 *Certificate part of a certificate chain starting of (a) a valid CTL and (b) an invalid CTL.*

defined using Windows 2000 or Windows Server 2003 GPOs and are downloaded to the Enterprise Trust container in an entity's certificate store. The Enterprise Trust container is not a trust anchor container because its content is not considered trusted by default.

In order for a CTL and its content to be trusted, the CTL signing certificate must be valid. This means that the CTL signing certificate should pass the time, digital signature, formatting, and revocation check. In order for the digital signature check to succeed, the CTL signing certificate's certificate chain should contain a certificate that is part of the Trusted Root Certification Authorities container.

Figure 15.32 shows the certificate chain of a certificate that is part of a valid CTL and one that is part of an invalid CTL as they are displayed in the Windows certificate properties.

15.5.3 Cross-certification chain processing

Cross-certification is a new Windows Server 2003 PKI trust feature. It was explained in detail in Chapter 14. Unlike CTLs, it allows for very granular PKI trust definitions between different CA entities. When setting up cross-certification between two CA entities, each CA becomes both a parent and a subordinate CA. This has interesting effects on the way certificate chain building works in a cross-certification setup.

The way that a cross-certified trust relationship shows up in the Certification Path tab of the certificate properties is illustrated in Figure 15.33. The CA trust relationships that are linked to this setup are shown on the left side of Figure 15.33. In this example, a one-way cross-certification trust is set up between OrgB and OrgA. The SubCA issues a cross-certificate to the HPCA. This will allow users in OrgB to trust a certificate named Administrator that was issued by HPCA. The users in OrgB trust the RootCA; SubCA chains to the RootCA; HPCA is cross-certified by the SubCA and the Administrator certificate was issued by HPCA.

As mentioned earlier in this chapter, cross-certificates are downloaded (just like trusted root CA certificates) to Windows PKI clients that are members of a domain at every autoenrollment event. Earlier we explained when this event occurs and how it can be manually enforced. Downloaded cross-certificates are stored in a PKI user's Intermediate Certification Authorities certificate store container.

For cross-certificates that are stored on locations other than the default AD locations, Windows XP and Windows Server 2003 allow you to define

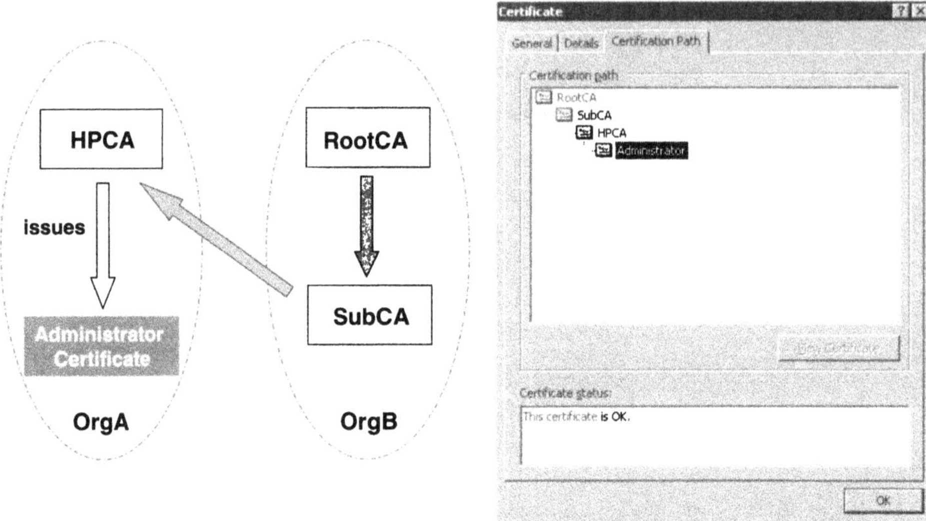

Figure 15.33 *Cross-certification example.*

additional cross-certificate download locations for each certificate that is stored in your certificate store. To do this, right-click a certificate to bring up its properties dialog box—then select the cross-certificates tab (as illustrated in Figure 15.34). This tab allows you to specify the cross-certificates download interval as well as the download URLs.

Figure 15.34 *Additional cross-certificate download locations.*

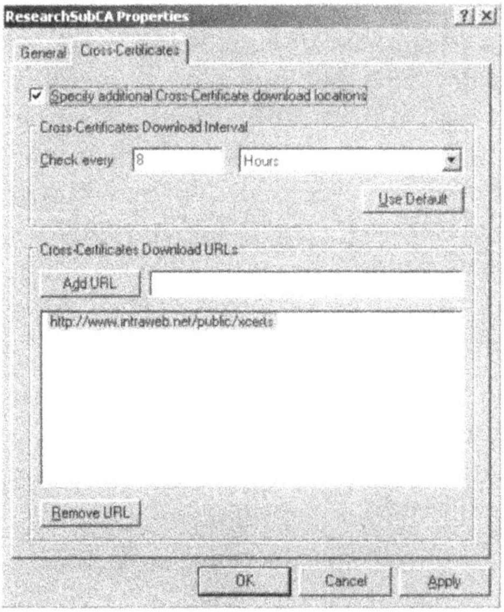

15.6 Certificate retrieval

Certificate retrieval deals with the way certificates are retrieved from a repository by a PKI user. In Windows 2000 and Windows Server 2003, certificates can be retrieved manually from any location in which the CA publishes them: from AD, a Web site, or a file share.

Windows 2000, Windows XP, and Windows Server 2003 also provide automatic retrieval of CA certificates during certificate validation. CA certificate download locations are mentioned in the Authority Information Access (AIA) certificate extension.

An interesting way for PKI users to retrieve their personal certificates from AD and store them in their local certificate store is dragging them from the Active Directory User Object to the Personal container in the Certificates MMC snap-in.

Personal certificates issued by a stand-alone CA can be retrieved from the CA's Web interface. If certificates are not downloaded from the CA's Web site within 10 days, they are purged. This default behavior can be modified by editing the certdat.inc file. By modifying the "nPendingTimeoutDays" setting in the certdat.inc file (located in the c:\winnt\system32\certsrv directory), you can set the amount of days before a certificate is purged from the stand-alone CA's Web site.

15.7 Key and certificate update

To provide better security, cryptographic keys and certificates should be updated regularly. Windows supports both manual and automatic key and certificate updating.

In Windows Server 2003, automatic certificate update is available for both machine and user accounts. Machine and user certificates that are set up for automatic enrollment will also be automatically updated when the autoenrollment event occurs.

To update your proper user keys and certificates manually, you must use the Certificates MMC snap-in. You can choose to renew an existing certificate using the same keys or using a newly generated key pair.

The manual updating of the keys and certificates of a Windows Certification Authority requires a special procedure that is discussed in Chapter 16 when we discuss CA rollover.

15.8 Certificate revocation

Some of the most important aspects in the design of a PKI are certificate revocation and, more particularly, automated revocation checking. Certificate revocation assures that a certificate's serial number is added to a blacklist (called the Certificate Revocation List [CRL]) when a PKI user's private key is compromised. It also guarantees that the revocation information is distributed to PKI clients and PKI-enabled applications (PKA) in an efficient way. Automated revocation checking is critical for PKI systems that deal with confidential and/or valuable information or transactions. Next we examine in more detail the process of revoking a certificate, Windows PKA revocation checking support, and automated revocation checking solutions.

15.8.1 Revoking a certificate

A Windows CA administrator can revoke a certificate from the Certification Authority MMC snap-in or from the command line. In the CA MMC snap-in, open the Issued Certificates container and right-click the certificate you want to revoke; then select the All Tasks\Revoke Certificate menu option. To revoke a certificate from the command line, use the following certutil command:

```
Certutil -revoke <certificate serial number> <reason code>
```

A CA administrator may have different reasons to revoke a certificate: An employee may leave the organization, there may be a compromise or suspected compromise of a user's private key, and so forth. When revoking a certificate, the CA administrator can select a revocation reason code (as illustrated in Figure 15.35). Valid revocation reason codes are unspecified, key compromise, CA compromise, change of affiliation, superseded, cease of operation, and certificate hold.

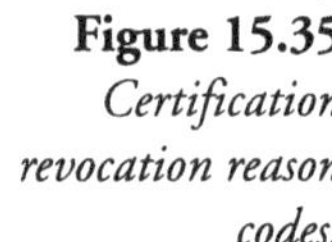

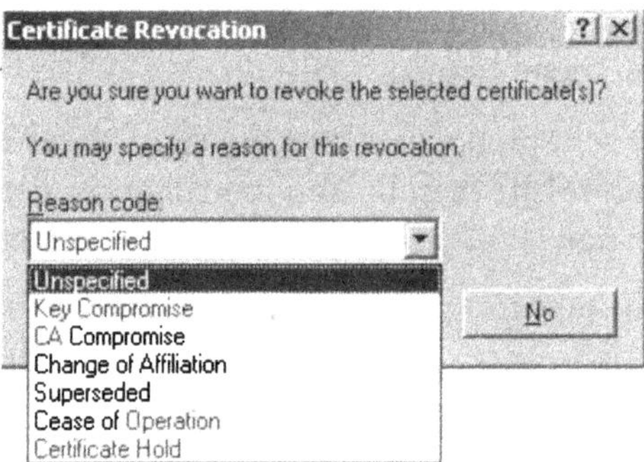

Figure 15.35 *Certification revocation reason codes.*

Table 15.2 *PKA Revocation Checking Support*

PKA	Revocation Checking Support
Internet Explorer (SSL-TLS)	Configuration option in Advanced tab of Internet Options: "Check for server certificate revocation (requires restart)."
Internet Explorer (Authenticode code signing)	Configuration option in Advanced tab of Internet Options: "Check for publisher's certificate revocation."
IIS (SSL-TLS)	IIS 5.0 and later have revocation checking enabled by default.
Outlook (S/MIME)	Enabled by default in Outlook 2002 and Outlook 2003. Can be enabled in Outlook SR1 using the registry hack outlined later.
IPsec	Not supported in Windows 2000. From Windows 2000 SP2 on, it can be enabled using the registry values outlined later.
EFS	Not supported in Windows 2000 EFS. Supported in Windows XP and Windows Server 2003 EFS when other users are added to the EFS settings of a file set up for EFS file sharing.
Smart Card Logon	The smart card logon authentication logic has revocation checking enabled by default.

15.8.2 PKA revocation checking support

Not all Windows PKI-enabled applications (PKA) automatically perform revocation checking. Also, revocation checking sometimes depends on an application-specific configuration setting. Table 15.2 provides an overview of the most commonly used Windows PKA support revocation checking.

To enable revocation checking for S/MIME in Outlook SR1, use the following registry hack: Create a REG_DWORD entry called "PolicyFlags" in the HKLM\SOFTWARE\Microsoft\Cryptography{7801ebd0-cf4b-11d0-851f-0060979387ea} registry key and set it to value 00010000.

To enable revocation checking for IPsec in Windows 2000 SP2 and later platforms, use the following registry hack: Create a REG_DWORD entry called "StrongCrlCheck" in the HKLM\System\CurrentControlSet\Services\PolicyAgent\Oakley registry key and set it to value 1 or 2. This key's values have the following meaning:

- 0: Disables CRL checking for certificate-based IPsec authentication.
- 1: Enables CRL checking and fails the validation process only if the CRL explicitly indicates that the certificate is revoked. All other failures, including when the CDP URL is unavailable, are ignored.

- 2: Enables CRL checking and fails certificate validation on any CRL check errors.

15.8.3 Automated revocation checking

In the PKI world, different models are available for automated revocation checking. Most of them, with the exception of Certificate Revocation Trees (CRTs) and the Online Certificate Status Protocol (OCSP), are based on Certificate Revocation Lists (CRLs). Examples are complete CRLs, Authority Revocation Lists (ARLs), CRL Distribution Points (CDPs), Enhanced CRLs, Delta CRLs, and Indirect CRLs. We will not discuss all of these methods, which are beyond the scope of this book. For a good overview of revocation checking methods, read the book *Understanding Public-Key Infrastructure* by Carlisle Adams and Steve Lloyd (Que, 1999).

Windows 2000 PKI supports complete CRLs and CRL Distribution Points (CDPs). Windows Server 2003 PKI adds support for Delta CRLs. Windows 2000 and Windows Server 2003 also support specific Netscape revocation extensions.

Both Windows 2000 and Windows Server 2003 publish CRLs at regular time intervals. In both environments a CA administrator can also force the publication of a new CRL (or delta CRL in Windows Server 2003). How to configure the CRL publication intervals and how to force CRL publication is explained next.

An often-heard revocation requirement is support for the Online Certificate Status Protocol (OCSP). OCSP offers real-time certificate revocation information to PKI users. The OCSP protocol is defined in RFC 2560. Neither Windows 2000 nor Windows Server 2003 support OCSP out of the box. Support can be added using third-party software from vendors such as Alacris (more information is available at http://www.alacris.com).

CRL distribution points

CRL distribution points (CDPs) offer a very convenient way to automate revocation checking. Each certificate generated by a Windows 2000 or Windows Server 2003 CA can include one or more CDP pointers. They are stored in the CRL Distribution Points X.509 certificate extension. A CDP can be a URL (HTTP or LDAP URL) or a file share. Once a certificate has been issued, its CDP pointers cannot be modified. The way CDPs work is illustrated in Figure 15.36.

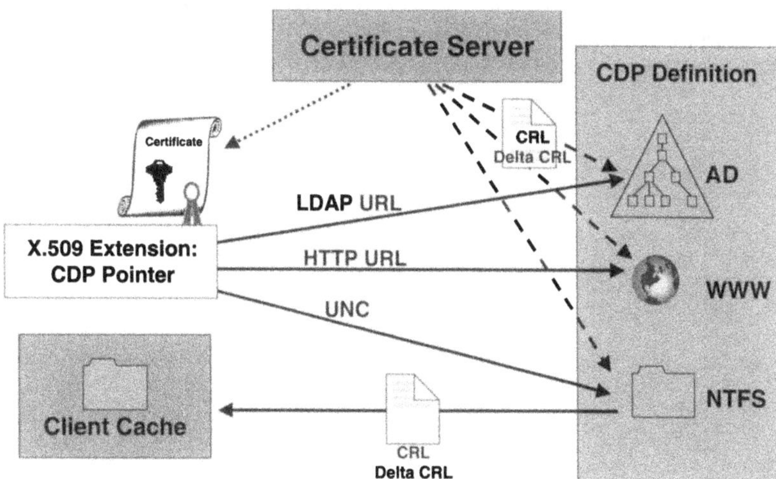

Figure 15.36 *Certificate revocation list distribution points (CDPs) operation.*

A Windows PKA that is CDP-enabled will—if it does not find a local copy of the CRL or delta CRL—check the certificate's CDPs for an up-to-date CRL or delta CRL. If a CRL or delta CRL is available from the CDPs, it will download it and cache it locally for the lifetime of the CRL or delta CRL. If a certificate does not contain any CDPs, the PKA will query the certificate's issuing CA for a CRL or delta CRL.

In order for CDPs to function correctly, not only is certificate and PKA support required, but the CA should also support them. The CA must have an exit module that can publish the CRLs or delta CRL to the appropriate file system, Web, or Active Directory CDP. By default, every Windows 2000 and Windows Server 2003 CA includes an exit module that can handle CDP publication. None of them can automatically publish CRLs or delta CRL to HTTP CDPs—you can, however, do this manually. Exit modules were explained in Chapter 13.

Besides automated revocation checking, CDPs can also increase CRL or delta CRL availability. Each certificate can contain different CDPs: If one CDP is unavailable, the PKI logic will try another CDP.

The content of the CDP fields of the certificates a CA issues can be configured in the properties of a Windows CA object from the Extension tab (as illustrated in Figure 15.37). To add a new CDP, use the Add pushbutton. The Extensions tab also contains a set of CDP-specific flags (at the bottom of the dialog box) that are explained in Table 15.3. The CA certificate's proper CDP field can be configured using a capolicy.inf configuration file (as was mentioned in Chapter 14).

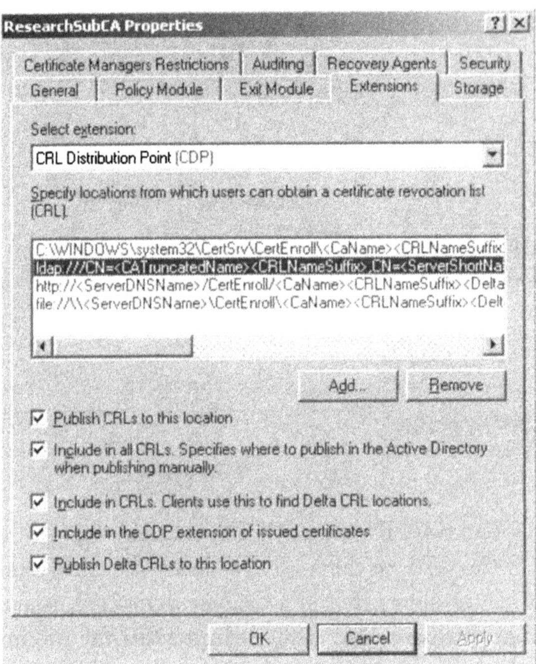

Figure 15.37 *Configuring CDPs.*

Table 15.3 *CDPs Flags*

CDP Flag	Meaning
Publish CRLs to this location	Used by the CA to determine whether to publish base CRLs to this CDP URL (not available for HTTP CDPs).
Include in all CRLs	Not used during revocation checking: Specifies where to publish in AD when manually publishing using certutil -dspublish.
Include in CRLs	Clients use this during revocation checking to find delta CRL locations from base CRLs.
Include in CDP extension of issued certificates	Clients use this during revocation checking to find base CRL locations.
Publish delta CRLs to this location	Used by the CA to determine whether to publish delta CRLs to this CDP URL (not available for HTTP CDPs).

Complete CRLs

A CRL contains a time-stamped list of revoked certificates, which is signed by a CA and made available to PKI users in a public repository. In a CRL, each revoked certificate is identified by its certificate serial number. CRLs are defined in the ITU-T X.509 standard and RFC 2459.

CRLs in their most basic format are known as complete CRLs. They are also referred to as base CRLs or full CRLs. A Windows 2000 and Windows Server 2003 CA generates a complete CRL at predefined intervals. Complete CRLs tend to be huge because revocation information accumulates in each of them. Windows CRLs support versioning, but a new version automatically inherits all revocation information from the preceding version, so a CRL becomes no smaller until a certificate expires. Also, each new CRL version causes the client to download the complete CRL, which is not an efficient use of network bandwidth. As a result, many administrators configure longer CRL lifetimes, but long CRL lifetimes reduce the revocation information's timeliness because new revocation information is not immediately available.

Testing a certificate's CDPs A very convenient way to test the CDPs embedded in a Windows X.509 certificate is the URL retrieval tool. This tool comes with the Windows Server 2003 version of the certutil.exe command line tool. To bring up the URL retrieval tool type "certutil -URL <certificate_file_name>" at the command line. This action brings up the dialog box illustrated in Figure 15.38. To retrieve the CRLs and delta CRLs, check the Retrieve CRLs radio button, then click Retrieve. Double-clicking one of the rows in the upper part of the tool brings up the CRL viewer for the selected CRL. The tool can also be used to retrieve the CA certificates mentioned in a certificates AIA field.

To limit the size of the complete CRLs in a Windows 2000 PKI environment, you can do one of these three things:

1. *Define multiple CAs.* If you define multiple CAs, with each CA having its own CRL, the size of those individual CRLs will be much smaller than the size of the CRL generated when you would have created just a single CA.

2. *Generate certificates with a short lifetime.* Windows 2000 CRLs are self-cleaning, which means that expired certificates are automatically removed from the CRL.

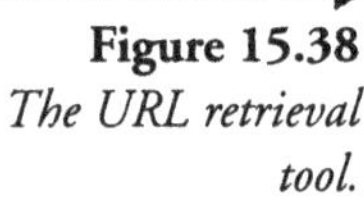

Figure 15.38
The URL retrieval tool.

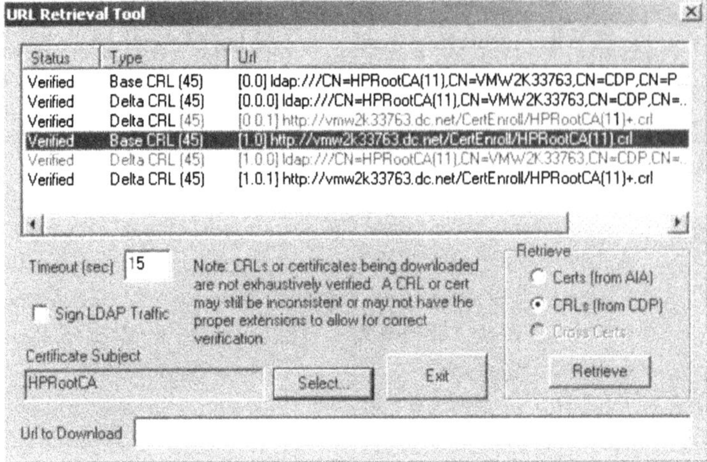

3. *Generate a new CA key pair.* Every time the CA key pair is renewed, a new CRL will be generated. The new CRL will be signed using the newly generated private key.

In Windows Server 2003, you can use delta CRLs to get around the complete CRL deficiencies. Delta CRLs are explained in the next section.

The complete CRL publication intervals can be configured from the properties of the Revoked Certificates container in the CA MMC snap-in (as Figure 15.39(a) shows). You can force a CRL publication by right-clicking the Revoked Certificates container and selecting All Tasks\Publish. This action brings up the Publish CRL dialog box requesting which type of CRL you want to manually publish: a new CRL (or complete CRL) or a delta CRL only.

To look at the content and formatting of a CRL, go to the View CRLs tab of the Revoked Certificates container properties (as illustrated in Figure 15.39(b)).

Figure 15.40(a) shows the layout of a complete CRL issued by a Windows Server 2003 CA as it shows up in the built-in CRL viewer. Notice the presence of some typical CRL extensions: Effective date, Next update, CA Version, CRL Number, Next CRL Publish, Freshest CRL, and Published CRL Locations. A list of the revoked certificates on a CRL is available from the Revocation List tab (Figure 15.40(b)).

Delta CRLs

Windows Server 2003 resolves the complete CRL problems (bandwidth impact and revocation information up-to-dateness) by introducing delta

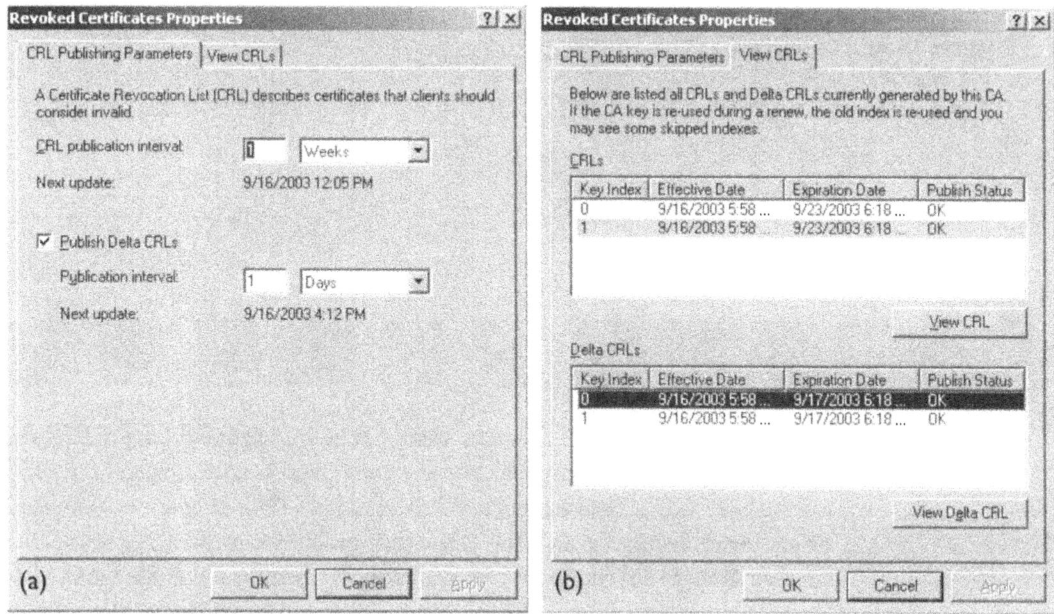

Figure 15.39 *Configuring (a) CRL publication intervals and (b) viewing CRLs.*

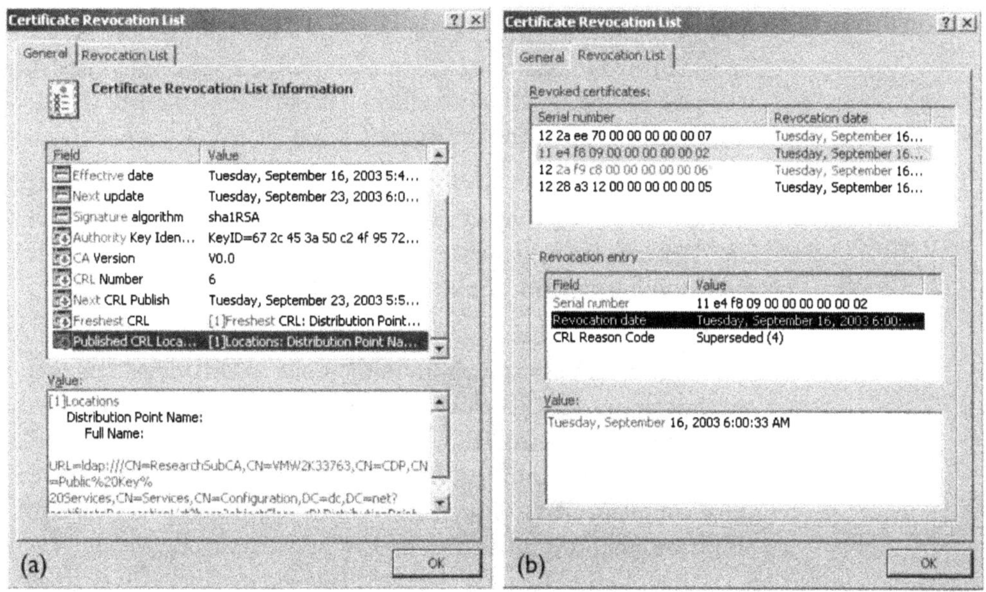

Figure 15.40 *CRL (a) layout and (b) content.*

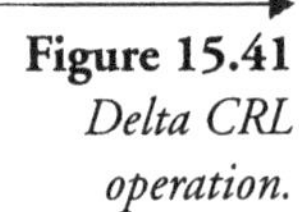

Figure 15.41 *Delta CRL operation.*

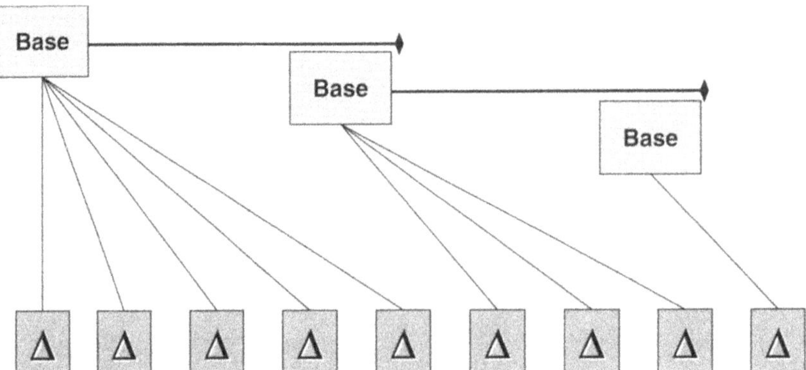

CRLs. As Figure 15.41 illustrates, delta CRLs are relatively small CRLs that contain only the revocation changes that have occurred since the most recent base CRL. Because delta CRLs are small, PKI clients can download them more regularly, and the CA can provide more accurate revocation information to its clients. Only Windows XP Professional and later Windows clients can check a certificate's validity against a delta CRL. Again, delta CRLs are not a Microsoft invention; they are defined in RFCs 2459 and 3280.

As for complete CRLs, Windows clients also cache delta CRLs. If a base CRL expires, the client retrieves a new base CRL from the CDP that is specified in the certificate. If the base CRL is valid but the cached delta CRL is expired, a Windows client retrieves only the delta CRL from the CDP mentioned in the certificate.

As for CRLs, you configure delta CRL settings and view delta CRLs' content and formatting in the CA's Revoked Certificates container's properties (illustrated in Figure 15.39). The procedure that is used for manual CRL publication also applies to manual delta CRL publication.

Figure 15.42 shows the layout of a delta CRL issued by a Windows Server 2003 CA as it shows up in the built-in CRL viewer. Notice the presence of the Delta CRL Indicator extension—indicating that this is a delta CRL, not a complete CRL. The value in the Delta CRL Indicator extension is the CRL number of the base CRL this delta must be associated with. As for a complete CRL, a list of the revoked certificates on a delta CRL is available from the Revocation List tab.

Netscape revocation extensions

Netscape is using a proprietary online certificate revocation checking method. They embed a custom extension, the netscape-revocation-url, in

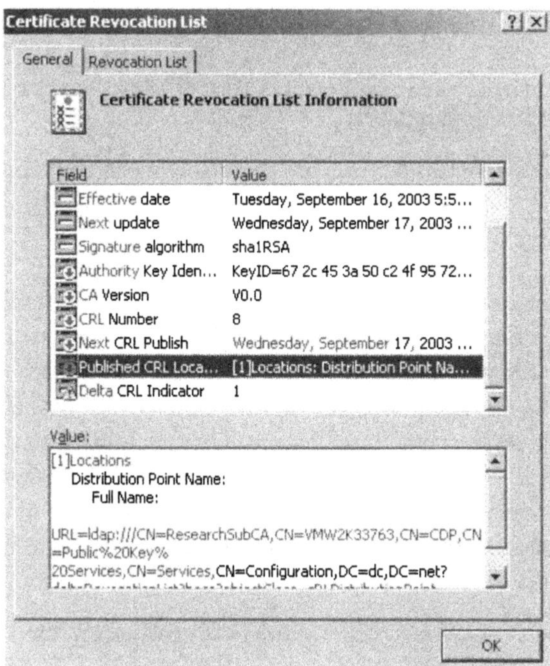

Figure 15.42
Delta CRL layout.

all their certificates. The netscape-revocation-url points to a Web page where the certificate revocation can be checked. To send the revocation checking request to the Web page, Netscape is using the HTTP GET method with a URL that is the concatenation of the netscape-revocation-url and the serial number of the certificate that needs to be checked. The response that comes back from the Web server is a document with Content-Type application/x-Netscape-revocation. It contains a single digit that is 1 if the certificate is not valid or 0 if the certificate is valid.

To enable a Windows 2000 or Windows Server 2003 to issue certificates containing this extension, use the certutil tool: certutil -setreg Policy\revocationtype +AspEnable. You also have to restart the CA service to make this change effective.

15.9 Certificate expiry and certificate lifetimes

A certificate expires at the moment in time specified in the certificate's "Valid to" field. Under normal circumstances, the issuing CA decides on the content of this field and the certificate validity period. Windows 2000 and Windows Server 2003 PKI also allow the certificate requestor to specify the validity period. This feature is disabled by default on enterprise CAs and enabled by default on stand-alone CAs. To enable this feature, use the following certutil command:

```
certutil -setreg policy\EditFlags +EDITF_
ATTRIBUTEENDDATE
```

To disable this feature, use the following certutil command:

```
certutil -setreg policy\EditFlags -EDITF_
ATTRIBUTEENDDATE
```

The certificate lifetime preferences are set differently on enterprise and stand-alone CAs. On a stand-alone CA, the certificate lifetime is set using a set of registry hacks. Both the ValidityPeriod (which can be days, weeks, months, or years) and the ValidityPeriodUnits (holds a number) key are used to set the certificate lifetime. They are located in the HKEY_LOCAL_MACHINE\SYSTEM\CurrentControlSet\Services\CertSvc\Configuration\<*CAName*> registry container. The default lifetime of certificates issued by a stand-alone CA is 1 year. To change the certificate lifetime, you can use the following script calling on the certutil command:

```
certutil -setreg ca\ValidityPeriodUnits 2
certutil -setreg ca\ValidityPeriod "Years"
net stop certsvc
net start certsvc
```

On an enterprise CA, the certificate validity period is set based on certificate template properties (from the General tab—as illustrated in Figure 15.17). The lifetime specified in version 1 certificate templates cannot be changed. The lifetime specified in version 2 certificate templates can easily be changed using the Certificate Templates MMC snap-in. Most certificate templates have 1-year lifetimes. Exceptions are the CEP Encryption, Enrollment Agent, IPsec, and Web Server templates that have 2-year lifetimes and the EFS Recovery Agent, Root CA, and Subordinate CA templates that have 5-year lifetimes.

Windows certificate lifetimes support nested validity dates. This means that a certificate can never have a lifetime that is longer than the certificate lifetime of its issuing CA. For example, if the CA's certificate is about to expire in 13 months and the default certificate lifetime is 2 years, the CA will issue certificates with a 1-year lifetime. The CA administrator should remember to renew The CA certificate early enough not to restrict the lifetime of newly generated certificates.

Within a PKI hierarchy, the lifetime of entities' certificates will differ depending on the level at which the entity is located in the hierarchy. This is because the higher the entity is in the hierarchy, the more security features will be implemented to safeguard its private key. Remember that CA private key compromise at a higher level in a hierarchy has much more impact than lower in the hierarchy. Also, consider the nesting validity dates feature of Windows PKI: Because an issuing CA's certificate is part of the certificate chain of all certificates it issues, its own CA certificate should be valid in order for any of the issued certificates to be valid. Thus the CA's certificate must under all circumstances have a lifetime that is longer than the lifetime of the certificates it issues. We will come back to this topic in the next chapter on Windows PKI design.

16

Building and Maintaining a Windows PKI

In the previous chapters we explained some of the technical nuts and bolts of Windows Server 2003 PKI. In this chapter, we look at the different steps you need to consider when planning, designing, and building a Windows-rooted PKI.

16.1 Building a PKI

Like any other IT project, a PKI project can be split into four key phases: assessment, design, implementation, and management (administration and maintenance). The phases are illustrated in Figure 16.1. A PKI project can be iterative: During the implementation phase, for example, issues may arise that require a new assessment and changes to the original design.

During the assessment phase, the current and future security requirements of an organization are analyzed. This can be done by running a security audit, performing a penetration test, or just analyzing existing processes. The assessment phase also includes a business requirement analysis.

The design phase deals with the technological and nontechnological design of the PKI solution. Nontechnological design topics include the creation of certificate policies and certification practice statements (CPS).

The implementation phase takes care of the rollout of the PKI solution, its integration with the existing IT environment, and, before the rollout, the development of customized PKI-enabled applications (PKA) or PKI software plug-ins.

Once the PKI is installed and deployed across your enterprise, you must manage and maintain it. In the management phase, you must set up the support model for the PKI (Helpdesk), PKI administrator, and user training and the management of the PKI components.

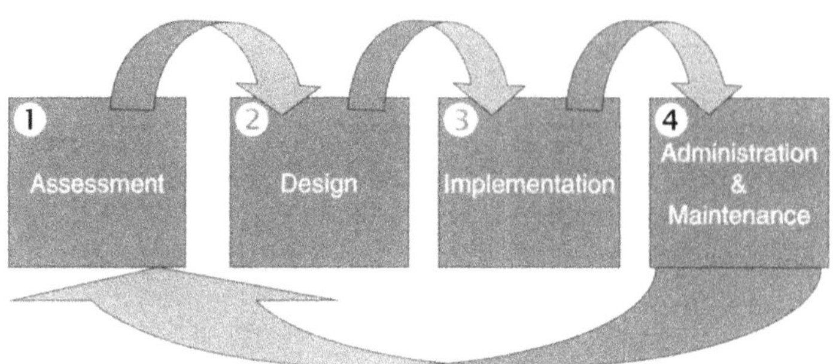

Figure 16.1 *The four major phases of a PKI project.*

16.1.1 Assessing the organizational needs for a PKI

During a PKI assessment, you must analyze your company's current and future security needs. As part of the assessment, you may need to gather some extra information. To do so, you can organize a security audit or a penetration test.

The next sections focus on three key areas of the assessment phase: the business requirement analysis, the decision on whether to insource or to outsource the PKI infrastructure, and the analysis of the applications that need PKI-based security.

Analyzing business requirements

The rollout of a PKI in an enterprise is typically driven by core business needs such as advanced security requirements for information storage and network communication. The size of the investment that a company makes in a PKI will depend on the criticality of the business problem that it wishes to resolve with it or the importance of the business processes whose security level it wants to improve by installing a PKI.

Some business security requirements do not need a certificate-based security solution and can be resolved with simpler arrangements. Also, not every certificate-based solution requires rolling out an enterprise PKI: For some solutions it is enough to buy a limited set of certificates from a commercial certification authority.

The business your organization is in may impose special requirements in the following areas:

- Availability: What level of availability does the PKI need within the organization? This affects the CAs, the CA databases, and the directories used in the PKI solution.

- Scalability: How scalable must the PKI be? Will it have to deal with rapid growth of the number of required certificates? Does planning have to take into account company mergers and acquisitions? Will more and more PKI-based applications be deployed in the future?
- Performance: PKI and its public key cryptography operations create an additional performance load for computer systems. Is this extra load acceptable? Should the existing hardware be upgraded? Should you install additional hardware that speeds up PKI operations?
- Cost: PKI products come in different flavors, with different features and in different price classes.

PKI-enabled applications

A PKI is an infrastructure, and many Windows applications can take advantage of it to provide strong security services to their users. Among these applications are networking systems, VPN systems, ERP software, document signing, and smart card–based applications.

You can build the following PKI-enabled applications (PKA) on top of a Windows PKI:

- Secure Web: You can use certificates for strong authentication using the Secure Sockets Layer (SSL) and Transport Layer Security (TLS) protocols.
- Secure mail: Signing and sealing electronic mail messages using S/MIME (Secure Multi-Purpose Internet Mail Extensions) also build on public-key cryptography.
- File system encryption: Windows 2000 and later Microsoft OSs come with the Encryption File System (EFS) extension to the NTFS version 5 file system.
- Code signing: Code signing protects against the downloading of malicious code. The Microsoft code-signing technology is known as Authenticode.
- Document signing: Document signing technology provides the capability to add a digital signature to for example a Word document. This functionality overlaps with the features provided by the Microsoft Rights Management Services discussed in Chapter 12.
- Smart card logon: Smart card logon provides strong two-factor authentication in a Windows 2000 or Windows Server 2003 domain environment.

- Virtual private networking: Windows 2000 and later Microsoft OSs support the IPsec tunneling protocol, which can use certificates to authenticate IPsec tunnel endpoints.
- Remote access authentication: The Windows 2000 and Windows Server 2003 Remote Access Service (RAS) both support the Extensible Authentication Protocol (EAP), which can deal with certificate-based TLS authentication.
- Wireless authentication: Windows Server 2003 and Windows XP support certificate-based authentication for wireless network access.
- Securing SMTP site connections: You can connect Windows 2000 and Windows Server 2003 AD sites using asynchronous SMTP connections. In that case the bridgehead domain controllers authenticate to one another using certificates. This setup also protects the confidentiality and integrity of the AD replication traffic.
- Any custom PKI-enabled application that uses CryptoAPI

Insource or outsource?

You have three choices to implement and manage a PKI: insource, outsource, or a hybrid approach. See Figure 16.2.

Insourced PKI solutions are solutions that you install, implement, administer, and maintain all by yourself. This means that your IT department must take the lead in implementing all related PKI technologies: CA hardware, CA database, RAs, directories, and the communication links

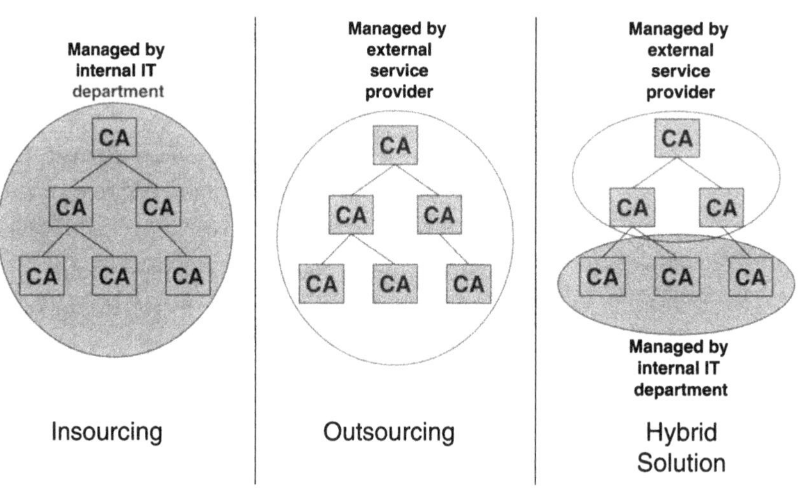

Figure 16.2 *Insourcing and outsourcing models.*

Table 16.1 *Advantages and Disadvantages of Insourcing Versus Outsourcing*

	Insourcing	Outsourcing
Pros	■ More and tighter control over certificate policy definition, certificate and key management, certificate issuance, key archival, and recovery. ■ Tighter integration options: integration with enterprise directory and in-house applications. ■ Potentially stronger trust relationships with partners because of in-house certificate policy control.	■ Leverage expertise of PKI experts. ■ Less effort for planning, design, administration, and maintenance. ■ Can be more cost-effective for a small enterprise. ■ Can be operational in a short period of time. ■ Requires less in-house expertise.
Cons	■ More expensive: cost of planning, design, administration, maintenance. ■ Requires more in-house expertise. ■ Possible complex integration and deployment. ■ Requires more time to plan, design, and deploy.	■ Less policy control and enforcement capabilities. ■ Less integration options. ■ Can be more costly for a large enterprise.

between all participating entities. This path offers you complete independence. You can create your own liability rules and security policies and can decide how to implement, administer, and maintain the PKI.

Outsourced solutions turn most of these responsibilities over to another company. The degree of outsourcing can range from a little (generating some server certificates) to a lot (outsourcing multiple CA services that are dedicated to your company). This is often the best solution for smaller companies or for those without the funds and resources required to install and maintain a proper PKI.

Hybrid solutions combine insourcing and outsourcing: Your company maintains a part of the CAs and another company maintains the rest. The CAs that are issuing certificates for applications with high security needs can, for example, be implemented and managed by the company itself. The implementation and management of CAs issuing certificates to applications with less strong security needs can then be outsourced.

Table 16.1 can help you choose between an insourced and an outsourced PKI approach.

16.1.2 Designing, planning, and implementing a windows PKI

In the following sections, we focus on the different steps you must consider when designing, planning, and implementing a Windows-rooted PKI.

With the exception of the next section, the following text focuses on the technical parts of a Windows PKI design, planning, and implementation.

PKI policy definition

An important nontechnical aspect that is often overlooked or neglected by technology-focused PKI planners is the definition of the certificate policies (CPs) and certification practice statements (CPSs). Both document categories are derived from a company's security policy (SP). This section gives an introduction to PKI policy definition, CPs, and CPSs.

CPs and CPSs help the PKI user determine the level of trust that he or she can put in the certificates that are issued by a CA that is part of the PKI. The availability of policies is critical when dealing with a PKI that is used to secure applications that are dealing with highly confidential or very valuable information. The creation of a CPS and CP is less critical when using PKI to secure applications that have less strong security requirements. In the latter case, some extra clauses regarding the use of PKI and certificates in your company that are added to the employment agreement can do.

The security policy (SP) is a high-level document that defines a set of rules regarding the availability and use of security services within an organization. It reflects an organization's business and IT strategy and provides context for an enterprise's security services. In the context of PKI, it answers high-level PKI questions such as: What applications should be secured with certificates, and what kind of security services should be offered using certificates?

A CP focuses on certificates and the CA's responsibilities regarding these certificates. It defines certificate characteristics such as certificate use, enrollment procedures, liability issues, and so on. The X.509 standard defines a CP as "a named set of rules that indicates the applicability of a certificate to a particular community and/or class of application with common security requirements." The X.509 standard can be downloaded from http://www.itu.int/rec/recommendation.asp?type=folders&lang=e&parent=T-REC-X.509.

A CP answers the following questions:

- For what applications can the certificate be used?
- How can a user enroll for the certificate?
- How are users identified when they request a certificate?
- What is a certificate's lifetime?

- How is renewal defined? Is a new key pair generated every time a certificate is renewed?
- What key lengths and ciphers are used to generate the certificate?
- Where is the private key stored? How is it protected? Can it be exported?
- What is the CA's liability when its private key is compromised?
- How should users react when they lose their private keys?

A CP is defined by a group of people within your organization that is known as the policy authority. This group should consist of representatives of the different key departments of your organization: management, legal, audit, human resources, and so forth. In most organizations, the policy authority members are also members of the group that defined the SP. This assures that the CP is in line with the SP.

The certification practice statement (CPS) translates CPs into operational procedures for CAs. Whereas a CP focuses on a certificate, a CPS focuses on a CA. Both the European Electronic Signature Standardization Initiative (EESSI) and the American Bar Association (ABA) define a CPS as "a statement of the practices that a certification authority employs in issuing certificates."

A CPS answers the following questions:

- What certificate policy or policies does the CA implement?
- What are the policies for issuing certificates? How are certificates issued? Are they issued directly to users or published into a directory? What types of certificates can the CA issue and to which users?
- Who can administer the CA? What subtasks are delegated to the different administrators?
- What are the revocation policies? How is certificate revocation handled?
- When is a certificate revoked? Where are CRLs published? How often are CRLs updated?
- How is access to the CA physically and logically secured?
- Who is responsible for backing up the CA?
- What is the quality of the CA certificate and private key? What is the lifetime of the CA keys and the certificate? What is the CA key length?

- Where and how is the CA private key stored?
- What is the procedure for CA rollover?

The CPS should be defined by members of your IT department, people who are operating and administering the IT infrastructure, and the people who defined the CP. Good examples of a CPS can be found on the Web sites of the following commercial CAs:

- Globalsign: http://www.globalsign.net/repository
- Verisign: http://www.verisign.com/repository/CPS
- Entrust.net: http://www.entrust.net/about/cps.htm

A reference to the CP and CPS to which the CA adheres are made available in the CA certificate and every certificate the CA issues. To do so, the CA embeds a unique CP Object Identifier (OID; see also the following sidebar) in its certificate's CertificatePolicies extension. This will allow the user of the certificate to reject certificates that were issued under a policy to which the user does not adhere. More detailed policy information can be added by including a URL pointer to the CPS or a short text notice in the certificate extensions.

Introducing Object Identifiers (OIDs) An OID is an object identifier. It is a string of numbers structured using a hierarchical dot notation. The OID format has been defined in the ITU X.209 standard. OIDs are maintained by the ISO standardization organization. To get an OID for your certificate policy, you must contact your local ISO naming authority.

An easy way to look up an OID assignment is available from the following Web site: http://www.alvestrand.no/objectid. This Web site also contains general OID information.

More information on CPs and CPSs is available in documents downloadable from the following Web sites:

- RFC 2527 (also known as PKIX part 4), "Internet X.509 Public Key Infrastructure Certificate Policy and Certification Practices Framework," available from http://www.ietf.org
- Entrust white paper, "Certificate Policies and Certification Practice Statements," available from http://www.entrust.com

Defining Your Topology

When designing your Windows PKI topology, you must consider the four topics outlined next. Most of them were discussed in Chapter 14.

- *Decide on the number of CAs.* Your organization may require multiple CAs for scalability, business, geographical, CA policy, or political reasons.
- *Choose a PKI trust model.* Windows Server 2003 PKI supports the hierarchical, networked, hybrid, and constrained trust models.
- *Map the trust model to the Windows domain and site model.* The PKI trust model is totally independent of the Windows domain trust model: A single CA can span multiple domains and a single domain can host multiple CAs.
- *Define relationships with external CAs or PKIs.* To provide PKI interoperability between different PKIs, Windows Server 2003 PKI supports cross-certification and Certificate Trust Lists (CTLs). No matter which of the two you use, you must always define a trust policy. Will the trust be unidirectional or bidirectional? What will be the constraints of the trust?

Specifications of the individual CAs

Certification authorities are key PKI components, so you need to spend enough time to create a detailed design for each individual CA. Part of the CA parameters are set during the installation; another part is set post installation, in the CA configuration phase. Table 16.2 shows the different installation and configuration options you must consider. Besides these installation and configuration options, you must also consider CA hardware sizing.

Table 16.2 *CA Installation and Configuration Options*

Preliminary Planning	During CA Installation	As Part of the CA Configuration
CA hardware sizing	CA role (root, subordinate—standalone, enterprise)	Revocation policy
CA architecture (exit and policy modules)	CA key and certificate properties	Supported certificate types (certificate templates)
Offline CA?	CA naming conventions	Certificate characteristics
Advanced CA private key protection (Hardware Security Module)	CA data storage locations	Enrollment policy (identification options, who can enroll for what?)
—	Reference to CPS	Recovery agent configuration
—	CA X.509 certificate extensions	CA server hardening

Preliminary planning

Before installation of a CA, you must make sure that you think about the CA hardware sizing, its architecture (are special exit and/or policy modules required?), whether the CA will be an online or offline CA, and if you will provide advanced CA private key protection. Next we will only discuss CA hardware sizing and the concept of an offline CA; the other topics were discussed in the previous PKI chapters.

CA Hardware sizing Table 16.3 provides some hardware sizing guidelines for a Windows Server 2003 CA. As far as the scalability of the Windows Server 2003 CA is concerned, Microsoft claims it is unlimited. Microsoft tested Windows Server 2003 PKI on a single four-processor, Intel-based computer, issuing more than 35 million certificates.

Offline CAs To minimize the risk of CA private key compromise, you may want to set up offline CAs. Within a certificate hierarchy, for example, it is advisable to take the nonissuing CAs (root CAs and intermediate CAs) offline. Making a CA an offline CA can include different things:

- Take it off the network.
- Protect it from the rest of the network by putting it behind a firewall or a router.
- Shut down the CA service.
- Shut down the machine hosting the CA.
- Install the CA on a stand-alone Windows server and set it up as a stand-alone CA.

Table 16.3 *CA Installation and Configuration Options*

Hardware Parameter	Comment
Processor	Is the most important CA resource. A powerful state-of-the-art CPU is strongly advised. Multiple CPUs will also enhance CA performance.
Memory	Microsoft recommendation is 512 Mb; 256 Mb is a minimum.
Disks	RAID configuration is advisable. Use separate physical disks for CA database and log files. As for the CA database size, each issued certificates takes about 16 Kb, and each archived private key takes about 4 Kb.

- Remove a CA server's hard disk and store it in a vault to which only a limited number of people have access.
- Provide strong CA private key protection by storing the CA's private key on a Hardware Security Module (HSM).

You must bring an offline CA online to issue certificates and CRLs, and every time its certificate must be renewed.

PKI users must also be able to access an offline CA's CRLs and CA certificate using CDP and AIA certificate pointers. When setting up an offline CA, you must make sure that the CDP and AIA pointers of both the CA certificate and all the certificates it issues refer to an online location. CDP and AIA configuration are explained in more detail later in this chapter.

When the offline CA is not connected to the network, you can use the following procedure to obtain a certificate for the new subordinate CA:

- During the subordinate CA installation, select "save the request to a file." The MS Certificate Services will inform you that the installation is incomplete. Put the request file (*.req) on a floppy disk and transport the floppy to the offline CA.
- Bring the offline CA online. Open the subordinate CA's request file from the offline CA, and copy the text starting with "BEGIN NEW CERTIFICATE REQUEST" and ending with "END NEW CERTIFICATE REQUEST." Paste this text into the "Submit a saved request" page (Advanced certificate request) of the offline CA's Web enrollment interface. Submit the request and save the newly generated certificate to the floppy disk. In Windows Server 2003 you can also submit a certificate request file to a CA from the CA MMC snap-in: right-click the CA object and select All Tasks\Submit new request... This action will allow you to select the certificate request file from some file system location.
- Transport the floppy to the subordinate CA. Then from the CA MMC snap-in, right-click the CA object and select "Install CA certificate." The CA certificate will be installed and the subordinate CA service will be started.

CA installation options

During CA installation, you need to think about the following CA-related parameters: the CA role (enterprise or stand-alone, root or subordinate), its keys and certificate properties, the CA naming conventions, the CA X.509

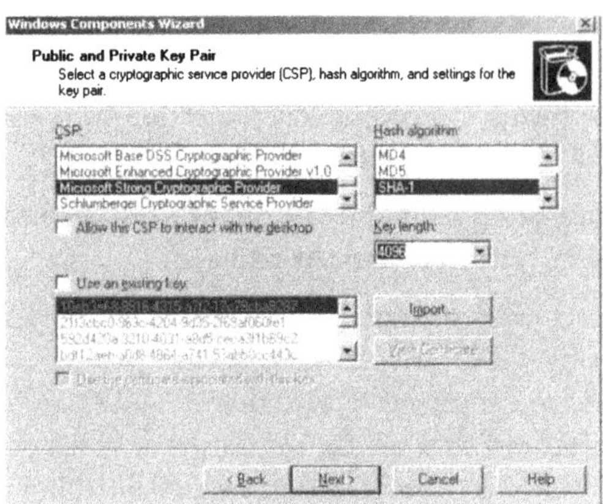

Figure 16.3 *CA key and certificate options during CA installation.*

certificate extensions, and the CA's database specifications. In the following sections we will only cover the topics that were not discussed in earlier chapters.

CA role The very first screen of the CA installation wizard will ask you whether you want to install the CA as a stand-alone or enterprise CA, or root or subordinate CA. These installation options were discussed in detail in Chapters 13 and 14.

CA keys and certificate Next during CA installation, you must choose the CA key length, the Cryptographic Service Provider (CSP), and the hash functions the CA will use for its cryptographic operations (as illustrated in Figure 16.3). This can only be done if you check the "Use custom settings to generate the key pair and CA certificate" CA installation option.

When installing a root CA, you can also set the lifetime of its certificate—this can be done from the CA identifying information screen illustrated in Figure 16.4. When installing a subordinate CA, this field says "Determined by parent CA." In that case the subordinate CA certificate's lifetime is dependent on a V2 certificate template setting (if the parent CA is an enterprise CA) or the value of registry key (if the parent CA is a stand-alone CA). How to change these settings was explained in Chapter 15.

Figure 16.4 gives an example of how the CA certificate and key lifetime and the CA key length could be defined for different CAs in a PKI hierarchy. Notice that the deeper you go in the certification hierarchy, the shorter the certificate lifetime, key lifetime, and key length become.

Level 1:
Root CA
• Standalone CA
• Key Length: 4096
• Certificate Lifetime: 20
• Renew at least every 10
Level 2:
Intermediate CAs
• Standalone CA
• Key Length: 2048
• Certificate Lifetime: 10
• Renew at least every 5
Level 3:
Issuing CAs
• Enterprise CA
• Key Length: 1024
• Certificate Lifetime: 5
• Renew at least every 2

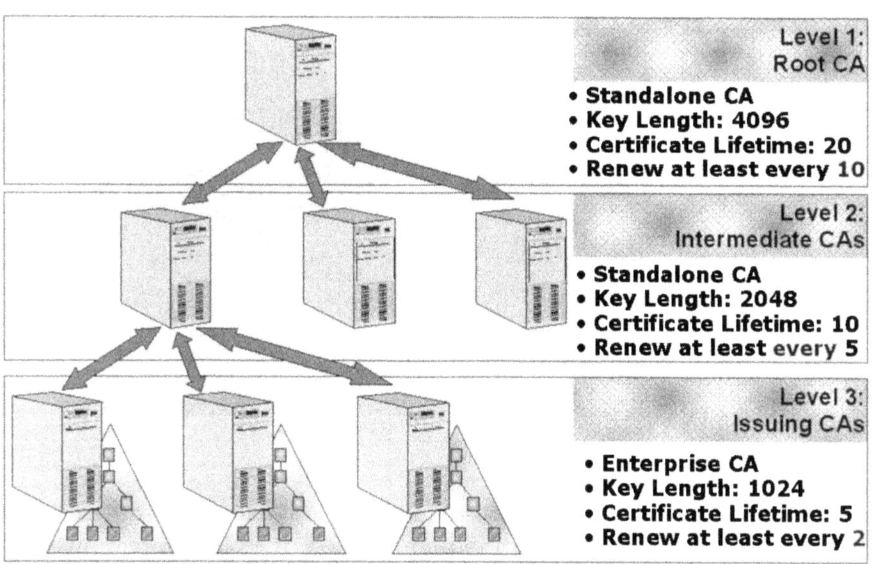

Figure 16.4 *Certificate lifetime and key length in a typical PKI hierarchy.*

A key topic to remember is that the CA is the heart of your security system, and if its private key is compromised, so is the entire PKI. Protect against attacks by choosing the longest key possible—at least 1,024 bits—and by storing the CA private key in a secure place. Secure private key storage was discussed in Chapter 13. See Figure 16.5.

Figure 16.5 *CA naming and certificate lifetime options.*

Windows Components Wizard
CA Identifying Information
Enter information to identify this CA.
Common name for this CA:
Research Root CA
Distinguished name suffix:
DC=dc,DC=net
Preview of distinguished name:
CN=Research Root CA,DC=dc,DC=net
Validity period:
5
Years
Expiration date:
9/24/2008 4:18 AM
< Back
Next >
Cancel
Help

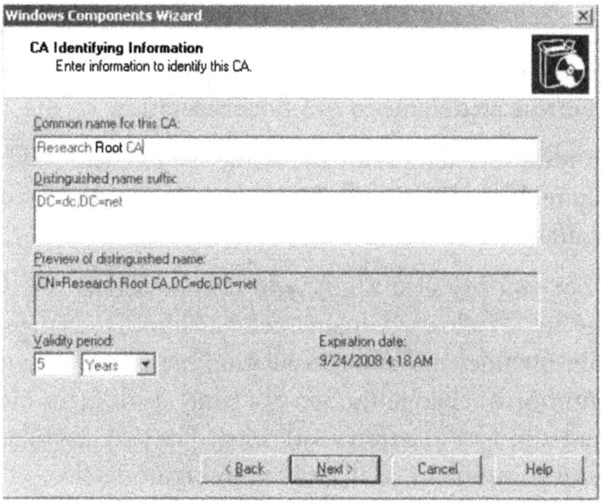

```
C:\WINDOWS\system32\cmd.exe
C:\Documents and Settings\Administrator>certutil -cainfo
Exit module count: 1
CA name: Research Root CA
Sanitized CA short name (DS name): Research Root CA
CA type: 0 -- Enterprise Root CA
    ENUM_ENTERPRISE_ROOTCA -- 0
CA cert count: 1
KRA cert count: 2
KRA cert used count: 1
CA cert[0]: 3 -- Valid
CA cert version[0]: 0 -- V0.0
CA cert verify status[0]: 0
CRL[0]: 3 -- Valid
KRA cert[0]: 3 -- Valid
KRA cert[1]: 2 -- Revoked
CRL Publish Status[0]: 0x45 (69)
    CPF_BASE -- 1
    CPF_COMPLETE -- 4
    CPF_MANUAL -- 40 (64)
Delta CRL Publish Status[0]: 0x46 (70)
    CPF_DELTA -- 2
    CPF_COMPLETE -- 4
    CPF_MANUAL -- 40 (64)
DNS Name: VMW2K33763.dc.net
Advanced Server: 1
CertUtil: -CAInfo command completed successfully.
```

Figure 16.6 *Using certutil to check the CA's sanitized names.*

CA naming conventions The CA installation wizard prompts you for the CA's identification information: the CA common name and distinguished name suffix. Make sure you agreed on the naming conventions before you start the installation. The naming choices made during installation not only affect the CA, but they are also reflected in the CA's Common Name that is stored in AD and in every certificate the CA issues.

Besides the CA's common name, Windows PKI also generates a sanitized CA name. This is the short CA name not including any non-ASCII characters and ASCII punctuation characters. It is needed for file names, key container names, and AD object names that cannot handle a CA name including special characters. Sanitized names are limited to 64 characters: If a CA's name is longer than 64, it is truncated and appended with a hash that is calculated over the truncated part. This name is also referred to as the CATruncatedName in MS documentation.

To retrieve a CA's sanitized name, run certutil with the -cainfo switch. As Figure 16.6 shows, this command also brings up other interesting CA configuration information.

Once you installed a CA, you cannot change the CA server's name or change its Windows domain membership. To change the server name or domain membership after installation, you have to uninstall the Certification Authority, change the server's name or domain membership, and then reinstall the Certification Authority. The CA installation program warns you for this problem, as illustrated in Figure 16.7.

CA database The CA installation wizard allows you to specify the location of the CA database and its log files (as illustrated in Figure 16.8). You

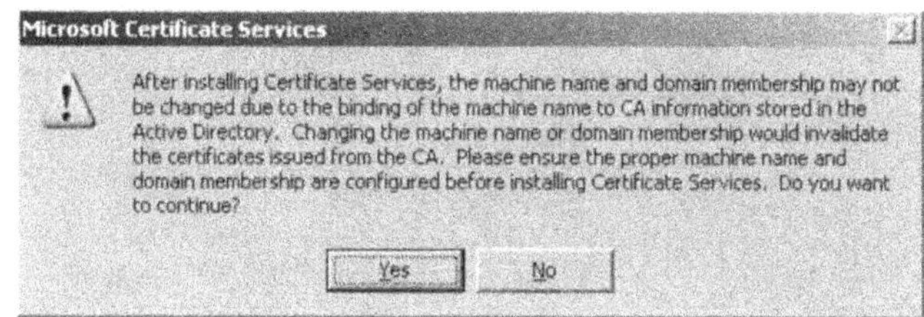

Figure 16.7 *CA installation warning.*

will also be asked whether you want to store the CA's configuration information on the file system. When you check this option, the CA installation program will copy the CA's naming information and the CA's certificate to the file system. The configuration directory is automatically shared as certconfig.

The Windows CA database is a JET Blue database. It has been designed to support an unlimited amount of certificates and is using the same database engine—the Extensible Storage Engine (esent.dll)—that is used in Exchange and the Active Directory. Just as for any other JET database, it is a best practice to split the database and its log files across different physical disk drives. By default, all CA database files are located in the certlog subdirectory of the system directory. To find out the location of your CA database files, type `certutil -databaselocations` at the command prompt or go to the Storage tab in the CA properties—available from the CA MMC snap-in. The CA database files are listed in Table 16.4.

The CA database layout used in Windows Server 2003 PKI is different from the layout that was used in previous releases. When upgrading from Windows 2000 to Windows Server 2003, the database format is automati-

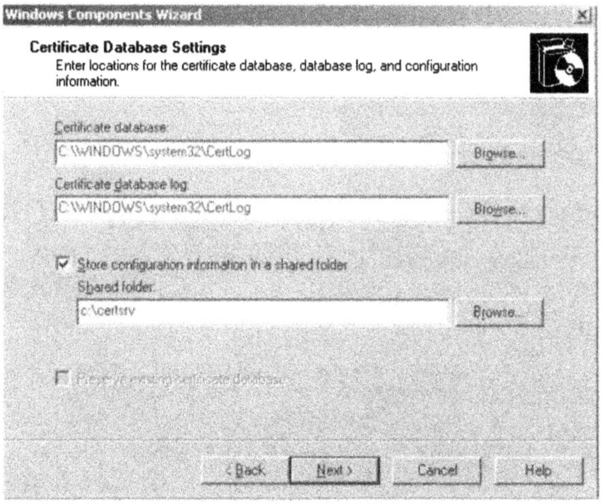

Figure 16.8 *CA database installation options.*

Table 16.4 *Windows Certificate Server Database Files*

Database File	Goal
`<CA name>.edb`	The CA store
`edb.log`	The transaction log file for the CA store
`res1.log`	Reservation log file to store transactions if disk space is exhausted
`res2.log`	Reservation log file to store transactions if disk space is exhausted
`edb.chk`	Database checkpoint file
`tmp.edb`	Temporary CA store

cally converted. You can look at the layout of the CA database by typing certutil -schema at the command prompt.

Other CA installation options: During CA installation or certificate renewal, you can also add several customized X.509 extensions and properties to the CA certificate:

- CRL Distribution Points (CDP) extensions
- Cross-certificate distribution point extensions
- Authority Information Access (AIA) extensions
- Enhanced Key Usage extensions
- Basic constraint extensions
- Issuance policy constraint extensions
- Application policy constraint extensions
- Name constraint extensions
- CA certificate renewal settings
- CRL and delta CRL validity settings

To set these certificate extensions and properties, you must create a policy statement file called capolicy.inf and store it in the Windows system directory before the installation of the CA. Chapter 14 contains a sample capolicy.inf file.

CA configuration options

Once a CA is installed, you must configure it. In this phase you must consider revocation settings, Authority Information Access (AIA) settings, policy and exit module properties, certificate template settings, delegation of administrative control, identification options, key recovery agent settings, and CA server hardening. Again, in the following sections we will not come back to the topics that were discussed extensively in the previous chapters: CA identification options, enrollment interfaces, certificate templates, and key recovery agent settings.

Revocation settings In a Windows PKI design, you must think about the following revocation-related parameters: the CRL and delta CRL lifetime and publication interval, and the number and type of CRL Distribution Points (CDPs).

All of these parameters are CA-dependent and can be configured once for each CA. If your PKI-enabled applications have different CRL or delta CRL requirements, you can install multiple CAs. For example, you can install one CA with a short publication schedule used for an application with high security requirements and another one with a longer schedule used for an application with lower security requirements.

CRL and Delta CRL Lifetime and Publication Interval The CRL and delta CRL publication intervals can be set from the properties of the Revoked Certificates container in the CA MMC snap-in or from the registry (as outlined next). In the CA MMC snap-in, automatic CRL publication cannot be disabled—this can be done for delta CRLs. Automatic CRL publication can be disabled from the registry by setting the CRLPeriodUnits parameter to 0. For delta CRLs, you must set the CRLDeltaPeriodUnits parameter to 0. When you disable automatic CRL or delta CRL publication, you must fall back to manual publication (which was explained in Chapter 15).

It is a best practice to disable delta CRL publication and set a long CRL publication interval for offline CAs. In that case, the administrative overhead or publishing CRLs and delta CRLs is not outweighed by the number of revoked certificates.

If a CA cannot publish its CRL on time, the revocation information is not updated and the old CRL will expire. Most PKI-enabled applications consider certificates invalid if the CRL has expired or is unavailable. That is why a CRL must at least be valid for the amount of time it takes for a CA recovery in case of a hardware or software failure. A 1-hour CRL publication interval is very likely not enough to perform a complete CA hardware and software restoration. This also explains why you must bring an offline CA online at regular intervals for CRL publication. See also the following sidebar on "Publishing the CRL of an Offline CA."

In Windows PKI, the CRL lifetime and publication interval are, although closely related, not the same. The CRL lifetime is derived from the publication interval and is by default 10% longer than the publication interval. This allows Windows PKI to deal with the replication delay of CRLs that are published in AD. The CRL overlap can be set in the registry of a CA server using the CRLOverlapPeriod, CRLOverlapUnits, and Clockskewminutes parameters. These parameters are located in the HKEY_LOCAL_MACHINE\SYSTEM\CurrentControlSet\Services\CertSvc\Configuration\<CA Name>\ registry container.

The following example illustrates the use of the parameters. Imagine you must deal with an AD replication delay of 4 hours. To deal with this delay, you can set the CRL overlap period to 5 hours. The following are the registry settings you would use in this example. They result in a CRL lifetime of 1 week, 5 hours, and 10 minutes. This is the sum of the CRLPeriod, CRLOverlapPeriod, and Clockskewminutes parameters. The CRL will be published every week, as specified in the CRLPeriod and CRLPeriodUnits parameters.

```
CRLPeriod              REG_SZ = Weeks
CRLPeriodUnits         REG_DWORD = 1
CRLOverlapPeriod       REG_SZ = Hours
CRLOverlapUnits        REG_DWORD = 5
ClockSkewMinutes       REG_DWORD = a

CRLDeltaPeriod         REG_SZ = Days
CRLDeltaPeriodUnits    REG_DWORD = 1
CRLDeltaOverlapPeriod  REG_SZ = Minutes
CRLDeltaOverlapUnits   REG_DWORD = 0
```

Setting the CRLOverlapUnits parameter in the registry to 0 activates the default algorithm—CRL lifetime is 10% longer than the publication interval—for the calculation of the CRL overlap. The same is true for delta CRLs. In this example, the default algorithm has been activated for delta CRLs.

CRL Distribution Points Windows PKI supports three CDP types: LDAP, file system, and HTTP-based CDPs. CDPs are used for both CRL and delta CRL distribution. For CRL downloads within your AD infrastructure, LDAP CDPs are the best choice. If you share PKI-enabled applications and certificates with external entities that do not have access to your AD, or with entities that are not using a Windows operating system, consider alternative CDP locations such as Web pages. In that case you use HTTP-based CDPs. Make sure that these CDPs do not reveal internal namespaces to the external entities.

Publishing the CRL of an Offline CA The following is a procedure for publishing the CRL of an offline CA:

- Bring the offline CA online.
- Start the CA MMC snap-in and publish the CRL to the local file system.
- Copy the CRL to a floppy disk or another removable medium.
- Shut down the CA.
- Publish the CRL at the different CDPs.

  For file system and HTTP CDPs, copy the CRL from the floppy disk or other removable medium to the appropriate file system location.

  For LDAP CDPs, copy the CRL to the file system, then use certutil together with the -dspublish switch to publish the CRL to AD.

To ensure revocation information redundancy and to make CRLs available through more than one location, it is a best practice to define multiple CDP types (LDAP, HTTP, and so forth). An AD-rooted LDAP CDP automatically provides redundancy (but only on the AD level) because the CRL is replicated in the AD to all domain controllers in the forest. Also, an LDAP CDP refers to a location in the AD configuration naming context, which is available on all AD DCs. To provide the same level of redundancy with HTTP CDPs, add a virtual Web server name pointing to several physical Web servers to the CDP.

Root CA certificates must have an empty CDP. The CDP point is always defined by the certificate issuer (because this is also the entity that is issuing the CRL). Because the root's certificate issuer is the root CA itself, it does not make sense to include a CDP in the root CA certificate.

The CDPs of an offline CA must point to a location different from the server hosting the offline CA. Otherwise, users would never be able to download an offline CA's CRLs.

To make these CDP changes to a root CA's and an offline CA's certificate, you must define the CDP settings in a capolicy.inf configuration file and make this file available on the CA machine during the CA installation. The capolicy.inf file and how to use it were explained in Chapter 14.

The CDPs of the certificates a CA issues are configured in the Extensions tab of the CA properties dialog box, which is available from the CA

Table 16.5 *Replaceable Parameter Syntax*

Text String Variable	Number Variable	Value
`<ServerDNSName>`	%1	DNS name of CA
`<ServerShortName>`	%2	NetBIOS name of CA
`<CaName>`	%3	Name of CA
`<CertificateName>`	%4	Certificate Name
`<ConfigurationContainer>`	%6	Location of AD configuration container
`<CaTruncatedName>`	%7	Sanitized name of CA
`<CRLNameSuffix>`	%8	CRL base file name and renewal extension
`<DeltaCRLAllowed>`	%9	Substitutes Delta CRL name suffix for CRL name suffix
`<CDPObjectClass>`	%10	Used in LDAP URLs for CDP extension
`<CAObjectClass>`	%11	Used in LDAP URLs for AIA extension

MMC snap-in. You can also change these settings from the command line using the following certutil commands:

```
certutil -setreg CA\CRLPublicationURLs "<list of CDPs>"
```

To define CDPs, you can use text string variables that are formatted using the replaceable parameter syntax. Microsoft added these variables to make the life of a CA administrator easier. The variables are also referred to as replacement tokens and are defined in Table 16.5.

In Windows Server 2003 PKI, Microsoft offers a new interface (illustrated in Figure 16.9) that facilitates the creation of CDPs using the replacement tokens. In the registry, these tokens are translated into number variables. The number variables must be used when you are using the replacement tokens in a capolicy.inf configuration file or in a batch file. The same tokens can be used for AIA and cross-certificate distribution point definition.

If an offline CA is not connected to the network and you provide an AD-rooted CDP, you must manually change the value of the %6 replacement token. The %6 replacement token holds the location of the AD configuration container. You can do so by typing:

```
certutil.exe -setreg ca\DSConfigDN <path to AD
configuration naming context>
```

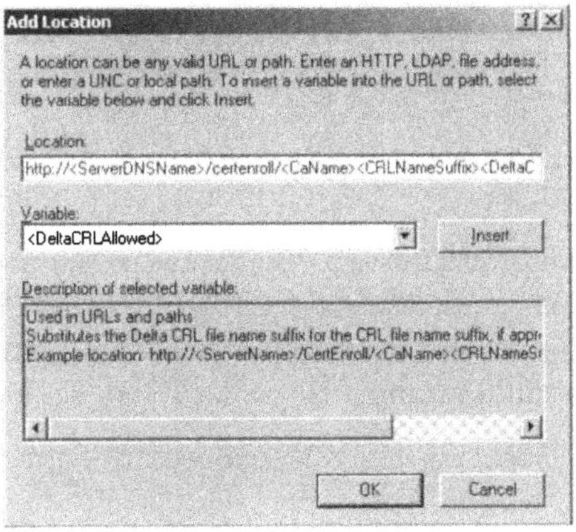

Figure 16.9 *Defining CDPs using the replaceable parameter syntax.*

For example:

```
certutil.exe -setreg ca\
DSConfigDN CN=Configuration,DC=mydomain,DC=com
```

The following are examples of an LDAP, file system, and HTTP CDP as they are defined in the CA properties (using the replaceable parameter syntax) and how these will show up in the CDP certificate extension of a certificate issued by a CA named ResearchCA located on a machine called myserver. The HTTP CDP is published on a Web server called mywebserver.mydomain.net:

```
Ldap:///
CN:<CATruncatedName><CRLNameSuffix>,CN=<ServerShortName>
,CN=CDP,CN=Public Key
Services,CN=Services,<ConfigurationContainer>,<CDPObject
Class>
```

will show up as:

```
URL=ldap:///
CN=ResearchCA,CN=Myserver,CN=CDP,CN=Public%20Key%20Servi
ces,CN=Services,CN=Configuration,DC=mydomain,DC=net?cert
ificateRevocationList?base?objectClass=cRLDistributionPo
int
```

```
File://\\<ServerDNSName>\CertEnroll\
<CaName><CRLNameSuffix><DeltaCRLAllowed>.crl
```

will show up as:

```
URL=file://\\mywebserver.mydomain.net/CertEnroll/
ResearchCA.crl
```

```
Http://<ServerDNSName>/CertEnroll/
<CaName><CRLNameSuffix><DeltaCRLAllowed>.crl
```

will show up as:

```
URL=http://mywebserver.mydomain.net/CertEnroll/
ResearchCA.crl
```

Other revocation-related settings By default, a Windows CA automatically removes expired certificates from a CRL. In some PKA scenarios, it is desirable to maintain expired certificates on the CRL. To do so, you can use the following certutil command:

```
certutil -setreg ca\CRLFlags +CRLF_PUBLISH_EXPIRED_CERT_
CRLS
```

By default, a Windows CA maintains expired CRLs in the CA database and in the AD. This is a best practice for long-term validation and auditing purposes. You can remove expired CRLs from the CA database by using the certutil command listed below. This only applies to the very last CRL the CA publishes for a given CA certificate.

```
certutil -setreg ca\CRLFlags + CRLF_DELETE_EXPIRED_CRLS
```

Authority information access settings A certificate's Authority Information Access (AIA) fields hold pointers to storage locations for CA certificates. As explained in Chapter 15, they play an important role in the certificate validation process.

For the certificates a CA issues, the AIA settings are—like the CDP settings—configured from the Extensions tab in the CA properties, available from the CA MMC snap-in (illustrated in Figure 16.10). You can also use the following certutil command line:

```
certutil -setreg CA\CACertPublicationURLs "<list of
AIAs>"
```

As for CDPs, you can specify the AIA settings in a CA's proper certificate in the capolicy.inf file; how to do this was explained in Chapter 14. In any case, when configuring AIA settings, you can also use the replaceable parameter syntax and the replacement tokens as they were defined earlier.

As for CDPs, the AIAs of the certificates an offline CA issues must point to a location different from the server hosting the offline CA. Otherwise, users would never be able to download an offline CA's certificate. If the offline CA is not connected to the network and you provide an AD-rooted

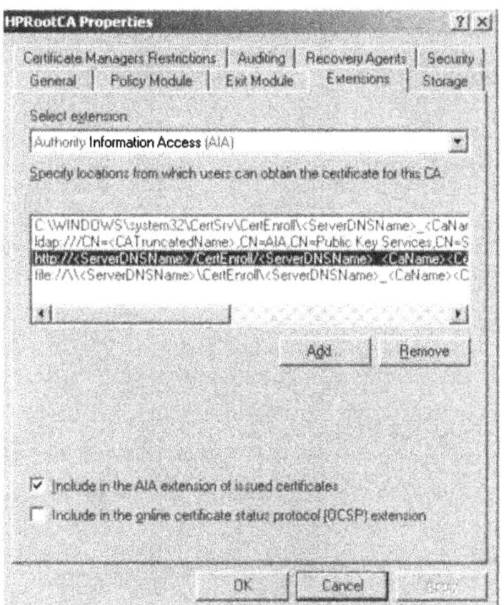

Figure 16.10 *Configuring AIAs from the CA properties.*

AIA, make sure you change the value of the %6 replacement token (location of the AD configuration container) by typing:

```
certutil.exe -setreg ca\DSConfigDN <path to AD
configuration naming context>
```

For example:

```
certutil.exe -setreg ca\
DSConfigDN CN=Configuration,DC=mydomain,DC=com
```

An AIA storage location can hold more than a single CA certificate. An LDAP-rooted AIA storage location can be used to download all CA certificates available from the AIA at once. This is because in the AD, AIA CA certificates are stored in a multivalued attribute called caCertificate of a CA object. When dealing with an HTTP-rooted or file system–rooted AIA storage location, only a single CA certificate can be downloaded at once. This is because HTTP and file system AIA pointers must point to individual CA certificates—they always end in a .cer or .crt certificate extension.

Other certificate characteristics The bulk of the certificate characteristics (with the exception of the CDP and AIA extension) can be configured from the Certificate Templates MMC snap-in. Remember that this is only true for version 2 certificate templates. Certificate templates and their properties were covered in Chapter 13.

Two very important certificate characteristics are the certificate lifetime and renewal period. When planning for these characteristics, you must consider the following:

- The trust your organization has in the certificate subjects: If you are issuing certificates to users of your corporate extranet, the certificate lifetime should be shorter than when you are issuing certificates to users of your corporate intranet. Generally, the level of trust that an organization has in its internal users is higher than the level of trust it has in the external users of the corporate IT infrastructure.
- Certificate lifetime impacts the number of certificate renewal requests that are sent across your network. In environments with limited network bandwidth (e.g., when users in a remote site are connecting to a CA across a slow WAN), this can be a reason to lengthen certificates' lifetimes.

CA administrative delegation and role separation Windows Server 2003 PKI provides a role-based administration model. Also, it allows for role and task separation between the different CA administrators. As will be explained next, this role-based model piggybacks on the Windows access control model (permissions and user rights). This new administration model is in line with the role definitions defined in version 1.0 of Certificate Issuing and Management Components (CIMC) Family of Protection Profiles. The latter can be downloaded from http://csrc.nist.gov/pki/documents/CIMC_PP_20011031.pdf.

To assign a PKI role to a user or group, you must assign the role's corresponding security permissions or user rights to the user or group. Permissions can be set from the Security tab in the properties of the CA object (accessible from the CA MMC snap-in), as illustrated in Figure 16.11.[1] User rights can be set from the GPO MMC snap-in. Table 16.6 shows the administrative roles and their associated permissions/user rights available in Windows Server 2003 PKI. Table 16.7 shows the tasks associated with every administrative role.

On a default Windows Server 2003 CA installation, the CA roles are assigned and modified by local administrators on a stand-alone machine or Enterprise Admins and Domain Admins when the CA is part of a domain.

CA Administrators have the Manage CA and Issue and Manage Certificates permissions on the CA object. Local administrators, Enterprise

1. The Security tab shows a simplified view of the ACL editor; there is no advanced view (which was available for a Windows 2000 CA).

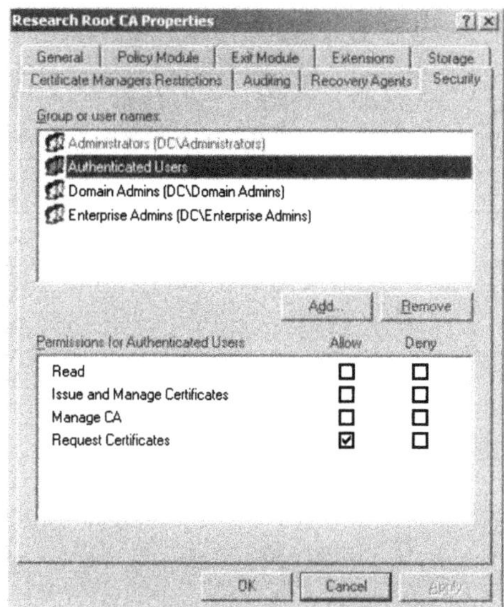

Figure 16.11 *Setting CA object permissions.*

Admins, and Domain Admins are CA Administrators by default on an Enterprise CA. Only local administrators are CA Administrators by default on a stand-alone CA. If the stand-alone CA is joined to an AD domain, the Domain Admins are also CA Administrators.

Table 16.6 *Windows Server 2003 PKI Administrative Roles*

Administrative Role (CIMC Equivalent)	Associated Permissions—User Rights	Meaning
CA Administrator	Manage CA permission	Configure and maintain the CA. This includes the ability to assign all other CA roles and renew the CA certificate.
Certificate Manager (Officer)	Issue and manage Certificates CA permission	Approve certificate enrollment and revocation requests.
Backup Operator (Operator)	Back up files and directories and restore files and directories user rights	Perform system backup and recovery.
Auditor (Auditor)	Manage auditing and security log user right	Configure, view, and maintain audit logs.
Enrollees	Request Certificates CA permission	Enrollees are clients who are authorized to request certificates from the CA.
Read	Read CA permission	Allows an entity to read records from the CA database.

Table 16.7 *Windows Server 2003 PKI Administrative Roles and Associated Tasks*

Activity	Local Admin	CA Admin	Cert Manager	Backup Operator	Auditor
Install CA	X	—	—	—	—
Configure policy and exit module	—	X	—	—	—
Stop and start the Certificate Services service	—	X	—	X (only stop)	—
Configure extensions	—	X	—	—	—
Configure roles	—	X	—	—	—
Renew CA keys and certificates	X	—	—	—	—
Define key recovery agents	—	X	—	—	—
Configure Certificate Managers restrictions	—	X	—	—	—
Delete single row in database	—	X	—	—	—
Delete multiple rows in database	X	—	—	—	—
Enable role separation	X	—	—	—	—
Issue and approve certificates	—	—	X	—	—
Deny certificates	—	—	X	—	—
Revoke certificates	—	—	X	—	—
Reactivate certificates placed on hold	—	—	X	—	—
Enable, publish, or configure CRL schedule	—	X	—	—	—
Recover archived key*	—	—	X	—	—
Configure audit parameters	—	—	—	—	X
Audit logs	—	—	—	—	X
Back up system	—	—	—	X	—
Restore system	—	—	—	X	—
Read CA database	X	X	X	—	X
Read CA configuration information	X	X	X	X	X

* Extracting the recovery blob from the CA database requires certificate manager privileges. Decrypting the blob and extracting the private key require a Key Recovery Agent (KRA) certificate; see also Chapter 15.

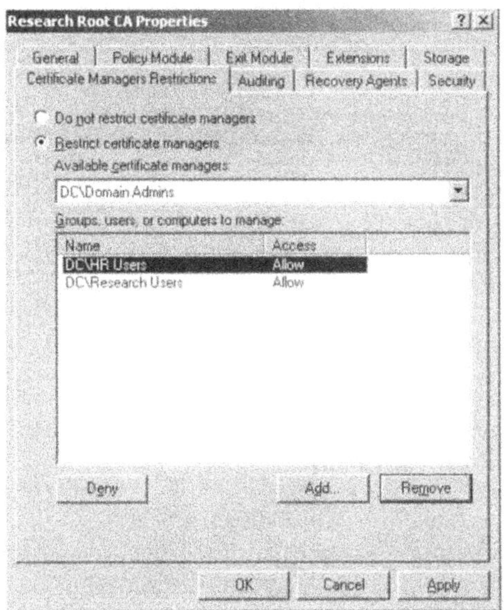

Figure 16.12 *Assigning certificate managers restrictions.*

The local administrator will always have full control of the CA system and cannot be blocked from taking control of the CA. Local administrator privileges are also required for tasks like CA key and certificate renewal, enabling role separation, and so forth.

Certificate Managers are the accounts that have been assigned the Issue and Manage Certificates permission in the security properties of the CA object. Certificate Manager roles can be fine-tuned from the CA MMC snap-in: You can restrict which users and/or groups' certificates that a Certificate Manager group can manage. To do so, open the properties of the CA object, and then go to the Certificate Managers Restrictions tab (as illustrated in Figure 16.12).

The Backup Operator role is based on the system backup user right. A CA Backup Operator has the ability to stop the CA service but not start it. The Auditor role is based on the system audit user right. By default, the local system administrator has these user rights.

The Enrollee role is based on the Request Certificates permission on the CA object. The Read role is based on the Read permission on the CA object. See Table 16.7

Windows Server 2003 PKI also allows for strict role separation between the different administrative roles. If role separation is enabled, a user can only be assigned to a single role. If a user is assigned to multiple roles and attempts to perform a CA administrative operation, the operation will be denied. To enable role separation, type the following commands at the command line:

```
certutil -setreg ca\RoleSeparationEnabled 1
net stop certsvc
net start certsvc
```

To disable role separation, type the following:

```
certutil -delreg ca\RoleSeparationEnabled
net stop certsvc
net start certsvc
```

To see whether role separation is enabled, type the following:

```
certutil -getreg ca\RoleSeparationEnabled
```

CA server hardening A CA's private key is the most critical element of PKI security. If a root or intermediate CA's private key is compromised, the entire or part of your PKI-trust infrastructure falls down. The security level provided for a CA's private key will also have an important impact on the amount of trust people have in the CA. This is why it is so important to store the CA's private key securely, to keep root and intermediate CAs offline, and to harden your CA server by boosting its physical, logical, communications, and organizational security.

- Physical security: Install Certificate Servers on computers that are located in secure areas with physical access control and adequate protection against fire, power loss, and other disasters.
- Logical security: In a Windows Server 2003 environment, logical security depends on the quality of the operating system's authentication, access control, and auditing system.
    - You can provide high-quality authentication by equipping all servers with smart-card readers, which provide two-factor authentication.
    - You can implement strict access control settings on all of the CA server's resources. You must lock down the server wherever possible and not install any unneeded services or software components. A good resource for Windows Server 2003 hardening is the Windows Server 2003 Security Guide available from the Microsoft Web site.
    - You can use the built-in Windows and CA auditing system and the Security Configuration and Analysis (SCA) tool to audit the

security- and PKI-related events on Windows Server 2003 machines.

- Communications security: To provide communications security for the CAs (issuing CAs or other online CAs) connected to your production network, you can install them on a separate subnet or behind a dedicated firewall or router that filters all non-PKI related traffic.
- Organizational security: Make the CA administrators and operators aware of the important security role of the CA. Convince them that this is not an ordinary file and print server but a server that is used to secure the rest of your corporate IT environment.

CA fault tolerance

Neither Windows 2000 PKI nor Windows Server 2003 PKI supports CA service or database clustering. Also, a Windows 2000 or Windows Server 2003 machine can only host a single CA instance.

Certificate enrollment fault tolerance is provided when using multiple enterprise CAs in an AD environment. AD-enabled PKI clients can query the AD to find out about the location of an enterprise CA and can contact another enterprise CA when one is not available.

Revocation checking fault tolerance can be provided by making sure that you can always—independent of the CA's availability—issue a new CRL and make it available to your PKA and PKI clients. In Windows PKI, this is possible thanks to a feature known as CRL resigning.

CRL resigning allows you to issue a new CRL using the old CRL provided you have access to a copy of the CA's private key. A CA's private key can be exported using the Certification Authority Backup Wizard, which can be accessed by right-clicking the CA object in the CA MMC snap-in and then selecting All Tasks\Back up CA. In the wizard, make sure that you select the "Private key and CA certificate" option (as illustrated in Figure 16.13). The wizard will save the exported private key and certificate in a PKCS#12-formatted file (*.p12). The old CRL can always be retrieved from a CDP. To resign an old CRL, use the following certutil command:

```
certutil -sign <old CRL name> <resigned CRL name>
```

Defining public key policy settings (GPO)

Windows Server 2003 GPO objects include the following PKI-related entries: Encrypting File System, Automatic Certificate Request Settings,

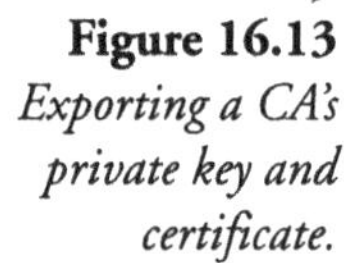

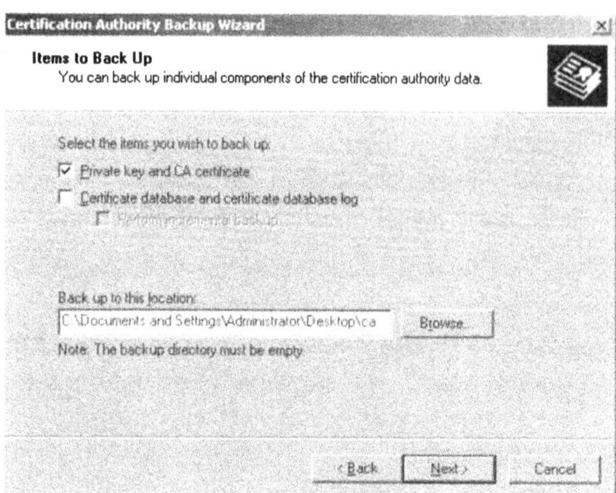

Figure 16.13 *Exporting a CA's private key and certificate.*

Trusted Root Certification Authorities, Enterprise Trust, and Autoenrollment Settings. They are located in the Windows Settings\Security Settings\Public Key Policies GPO container.

The Encrypting File System GPO container is used to define accounts that have the ability to recover encrypted EFS data. The Automatic Certificate Request container is used to define machine certificate autoenrollment settings. The Trusted Root Certification Authorities container is used to distribute trusted root CA certificates to clients. The Enterprise Trust container is used to define Certificate Trust Lists (CTLs). The Autoenrollment object is used to define user autoenrollment settings.

Table 16.8 shows on which GPO level (domain, site, OU, or local) and for which GPO portion (user or computer) the PKI-related GPO settings are available. GPO settings that are defined on the machine level are shared with all users logging on to that machine and all services running on it.

16.2 Maintaining a PKI

In this section we focus on key Windows Server 2003 PKI maintenance tasks: CA backup and restore, rollover, and auditing.

16.2.1 CA backup and restore

As for any other critical component in your IT infrastructure, it is very important to have solid backup-restore procedures for your CA, its configuration, and its database. Windows Server 2003 comes with three tools you can use to back up and restore CA configuration data: the Windows backup

Table 16.8 *PKI-Related GPO Settings*

	GPO Level	User GPO Portion	Machine GPO Portion
Encrypting File System	Domain	—	X
	Site	—	X
	OU	—	X
	Local	—	X
Automatic Certificate Request	Domain	—	X
	Site	—	X
	OU	—	X
	Local	—	—
Trusted Root CAs	Domain	—	X
	Site	—	X
	OU	—	X
	Local	—	—
Enterprise Trust	Domain	X	X
	Site	X	X
	OU	X	X
	Local	—	—
Autoenrollment	Domain	X	X
	Site	X	X
	OU	X	X
	Local	—	—

and restore wizard, the CA-specific backup and restore utility, and the IIS configuration backup and restore utility.

The Windows backup and restore wizard is available from the Windows Server 2003 Accessories\System Tools start menu option. It can be used to back up the CA data at the file system level listed in Table 16.9, as well as the CA configuration data stored in the system registry and the AD. To back up the registry data, you must check the System State option in the wizard (as illustrated in Figure 16.14).

Table 16.9 *CA File System Level Data*

CA Data	Notes
CA Database directory	Default: <%windir%>\system32\certlog
CA Web directory	Default: <%windir%>\system32\certsrv
CA Configuration directory	Only available if explicitly created during CA installation (shared as certconfig)

The CA-specific backup-restore utility is available from the CA MMC snap-in and from the command prompt (using the certutil utility). The CA-specific backup-restore utility can backup and restore the CA database and the CA private key and certificate, which are exported to a PKCS#12-formatted file. The certutil CA backup and restore-related switches and their meaning are explained in Table 16.10. For more information, type certutil /? at the command line.

Before starting the CA-specific backup utility, make sure you have prepared a separate backup medium or at least a separate folder, different from the CA configuration folder on the CA server. Also, the backup will fail if the folder you are using is not empty. The CA database can be backed up incrementally. An incremental backup can be saved at the same location as a full backup. When doing a CA database, restore from a full backup and a set of incremental backups, and never restart the CA service if not all incre-

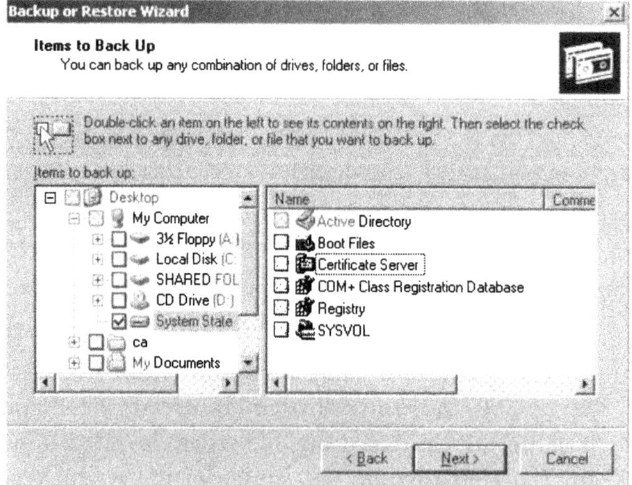

Figure 16.14 *Backing up the system state and CA configuration data using the backup wizard.*

Table 16.10 *Certutil CA Backup and Restore-Related Switches*

Certutil CA Backup and Restore Switches	Meaning
`certutil -backup` `certutil -restore`	Backs up or restores the CA database, certificate and private key.
`certutil -backupDB` `certutil -restoreDB`	Backs up or restores the CA database.
`certutil -backupKey` `certutil -restoreKey`	Backs up or restores the CA certificate and private key.

mental backups have been restored. If you do so, you will lose all of the changes starting from the last incremental backup you restored.

You can use the IIS configuration backup and restore utility to backup and restore the CA Web enrollment interface configuration settings. To start this utility, open the Internet Information Services Manager, right-click the Web server computer object, and select All Tasks\Backup\Restore Configuration. To back up and restore the CA-related Web directories, you must rely on the Windows backup and restore wizard.

16.2.2 CA rollover

In PKI terminology, CA certificate rollover is the process of generating a new CA certificate. A CA's certificate may be renewed for different reasons:

- Extend the CA lifetime
- Change the CA's public-private key pair
- Change the CA's key size
- Change CA certificate properties
- The CA's private key has been compromised
- CRL partitioning

To renew a CA certificate, you must run the renew CA certificate wizard (illustrated in Figure 16.15). It is accessible by right-clicking the CA object in the CA MMC snap-in, and selecting All Tasks\Renew CA Certificate. The wizard prompts you to reuse the same key pair or generate a new one. It brings up different dialog boxes depending on whether you are dealing with a root CA or a subordinate CA.

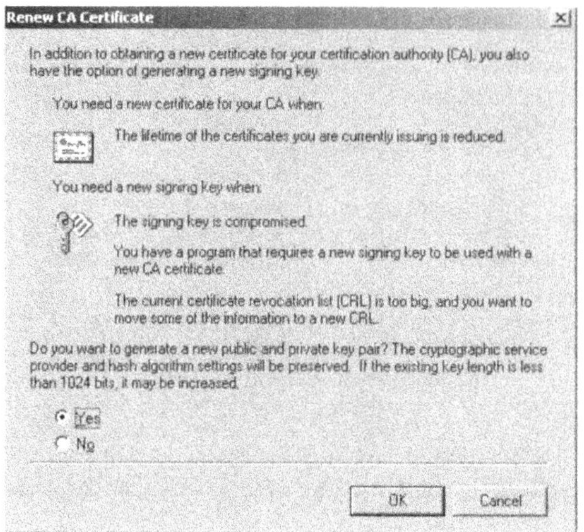

Figure 16.15 *Renew CA certificate wizard.*

Changing the CA's key size and other CA certificate properties at CA certificate renewal time can be done by specifying these parameters in a capolicy.inf configuration file and making this file available when the renewal process occurs (as was explained in Chapter 14).

When a new key pair is generated together with CA certificate renewal, the CA will generate a brand-new base CRL the next time the CRL is published. "Brand-new" means that this new CRL will not contain any of the revoked certificates contained in the previous CRL. This makes it possible to partition a CA's base CRLs because a CRL is signed with a CA's private key. When the private key is renewed, it will only be used to sign CRLs containing certificates revoked after the key renewal date. As long as the old CA keys are valid, the CA will also keep on publishing their associated CRLs. This explains why after CA certificate and key pair renewal a CA may publish multiple CRLs every time CRL publishing occurs.

Certificate renewal affects the version number of the CA's certificate, which is stored in a CA certificate's CA Version extension. Renewal without generating a new key pair will only affect the first part (the part before the dot) of the CA certificate's version number. Renewing with generating a new key pair will affect the complete CA version number: It will change both the part before and after the dot. Another way to distinguish between renewal and reissuing on the level of the CA certificate properties is the following: Reissuing will generate a new subject key identifier field.

The number of times a CA's certificate has been renewed and the content of the CA certificates can be seen from the General tab of the CA

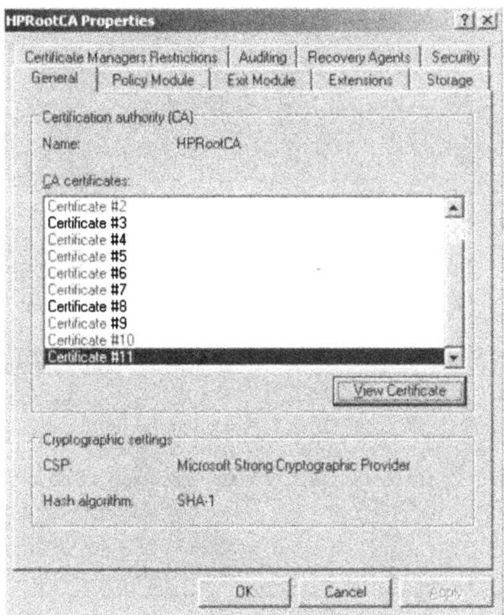

Figure 16.16 *CA properties: CA certificates.*

object's properties in the CA MMC snap-in (as illustrated in Figure 16.16). In the example of Figure 16.13, the CA certificate was renewed 10 times.

16.2.3 CA auditing

Windows Server 2003 PKI comes with interesting new CA auditing capabilities. You can enable auditing for the event groups illustrated in Table 16.11. All events are logged into the local system's security event log. CA auditing depends on object access auditing, which can be enabled from the GPO MMC or Local Security Settings MMC snap-in. To fine-tune CA auditing, go to the auditing tab (illustrated in Figure 16.17) in the properties of the CA object (accessible from the CA MMC snap-in). Table 16.12 shows the most important Certificate Services Event IDs.

Table 16.11 *CA Audit Categories*

CA Audit Category	Includes
Back up and restore the CA database	■ Backup CA database ■ Restore CA database
Change CA security settings	■ Configure CA administration roles ■ Configure Certificate Manager restrictions ■ Configure CA auditing

Table 16.11 *CA Audit Categories (continued)*

CA Audit Category	Includes
Change CA configuration	■ Add/Remove templates to the CA ■ Configure CRL publication schedule ■ Modify policy module configuration ■ Modify exit module configuration ■ Configure CRL Distribution Points (CDP) ■ Configure Authority Information Access (AIA) ■ Change policy module ■ Change Exit Module ■ Configure Key Archival and Recovery
Issue and manage certificate requests	■ Incoming certificate requests ■ Certificate issuance ■ Certificate import ■ Deletion of rows in the CA database
Revoke certificates and publish CRLs	■ Certificate revocation ■ CRL publication
Store and retrieve archived keys	■ Archival of keys ■ Retrieval of archived keys
Start and stop Certificate Services	■ Starting Certificate Services ■ Stopping Certificate Services

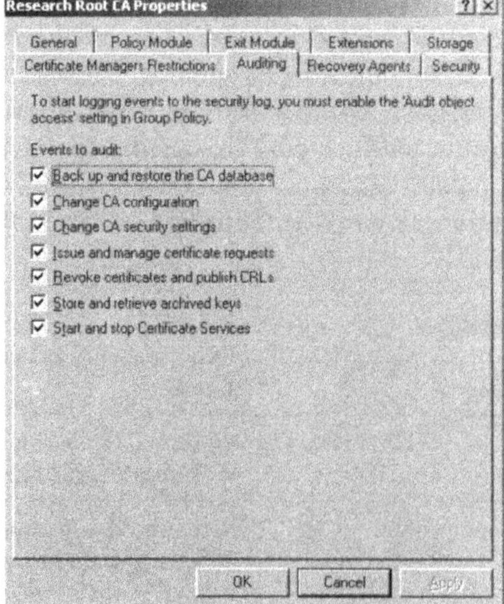

Figure 16.17 *CA auditing settings.*

Table 16.12 *Certificate Services Event IDs*

Event ID	Meaning
772	The certificate manager denied a pending certificate request
773	Certificate Services received a resubmitted certificate request
774	Certificate Services revoked a certificate
775	Certificate Services received a request to publish the CRL
776	Certificate Services published the CRL
777	A certificate request extension changed
778	One or more certificate request attributes changed
779	Certificate Services received a request to shut down
780	Certificate Services backup started
781	Certificate Services backup completed
782	Certificate Services restore started
783	Certificate Services restore completed
784	Certificate Services started
785	Certificate Services stopped
786	The security permissions for Certificate Services changed
787	Certificate Services retrieved an archived key
788	Certificate Services imported a certificate into its database
789	The audit filter for Certificate Services changed
790	Certificate Services received a certificate request
791	Certificate Services approved a certificate request and issued a certificate
792	Certificate Services denied a certificate request
793	Certificate Services set the status of a certificate request to pending
794	The certificate manager settings for Certificate Services changed
795	A configuration entry changed in Certificate Services
796	A property of Certificate Services changed
797	Certificate Services archived a key
798	Certificate Services imported and archived a key

Table 16.12 *Certificate Services Event IDs (continued)*

Event ID	Meaning
799	Certificate Services published the CA certificate to Active Directory
800	One or more rows has been deleted from the certificate database
801	Role separation enabled

16.3 Administration and troubleshooting tools

The primary administration and troubleshooting interfaces in a Windows Server 2003 PKI are the Certification Authority and Certificate Templates MMC snap-ins. Windows Server 2003 PKI also comes with a set of interesting command-line utilities: certutil (switches are listed in Table 16.13) and certreq (switches are listed in Table 16.14). The functionality of the dsstore utility that was coming with Windows 2000 PKI has now been merged into the certutil utility. The Windows Server 2003 Resource Kit includes the PKI Health (based on the pkiview.dll) and the Key Recovery (krt.exe) utilities.

Table 16.13 *Important Certutil Switches*

Goal	Certutil Switch
Display CA configuration information	`-dump`
Retrieve CA certificate	`-ca.cert`
Retrieve CA certificate chain	`-ca.chain`
Revoke certificates	`-revoke`
Publish certificates or CRLs to AD	`-dspublish`
Publish the CRL or delta CRL	`-CRL`
Check certificate, CRL, or certificate chain validity	`-verify`
Deny pending certificate request	`-deny`
Set attributes on pending certificate requests	`-setattributes`
Verify a key set	`-verifykeys`
Decode or encode base 64	`-decode` `-encode`

Table 16.13 *Important Certutil Switches (continued)*

Goal	Certutil Switch
Shut down the CA server	-shutdown
Display the CA database schema	-schema
Verify CRL or certificate URLs (CDP, AIA)	-url
Merge *.pfx files	-mergepfx
Backup and restore CA keys and database	-backup -restore -backupDB -restoreDB -backupKey -restoreKey
Display CA database locations	-databaselocations
Display certificates in the machine certificate store	-store
Display certificates in the machine certificate store and verifies certificates and private keys	-verifystore
Display certificates in the user certificate store	-user -store
Display error code message text	-error
Import certificates into the database	-importcert
Set, display, delete CA registry settings	-setreg -getreg -delreg
Create or remove CA Web virtual roots and file shares	-vroot
Retrieve archived private key recovery blob	-getkey
Recover archived private key	-recoverkey

Table 16.14 *Important Certreq Switches*

Goal	Certreq Switch
Submit a certificate request to a CA	-submit
Retrieve certificates, that were set to pending, from the CA	-retrieve
Create a cross-certification or qualified subordination certificate request	-policy

17

Windows Server 2003 PKI-enabled Applications

In the previous chapters we introduced Windows Server 2003 PKI. In this chapter we focus on three applications that can leverage your PKI investment: the Encrypting File System (EFS), S/MIME for secure messaging, and smart card–enabled applications. Windows Server 2003 obviously supports many other PKI-enabled applications, some of which were covered in previous chapters (such as SSL/TLS for secure Web communications); others are out of the scope of this book (these include communication security solutions like IPsec, wireless authentication using 802.1x, and EAP-TLS).

One of the key messages you should remember from the previous chapters is that a PKI is an infrastructure, of which multiple applications can take advantage to provide strong public key cryptography–based security to their users.

17.1 Encrypting File System

The disclosure of confidential information to unauthorized parties is a serious threat from which any organization should be protected. The Encrypting File System (EFS), a feature of the Windows 2000, XP, and Windows Server 2003 NTFS version 5 file systems, provides file system–level encryption of files and folders stored on NTFS volumes. Before Windows 2000, NT users had to use the products of other vendors to implement an encryption solution.

17.1.1 The end user EFS experience

As in Windows 2000, Windows XP and Windows Server 2003 NTFS files and folders can be encrypted manually by checking the "Encrypt contents to secure data" box in the advanced properties or by choosing the Encrypt command on a file or folder's shortcut menu. If you set the encryption attribute on the folder level, newly created files in the folder will be automatically encrypted. Unless you check the "Apply changes to this folder, subfolders, and files" checkbox, files that already existed in the folder before the encryption attribute was set will not be encrypted. The same is true for decryption.

The Encrypt/Decrypt shortcut context menu option for the Windows Explorer is disabled by default. To enable it, add the EncryptionContextMenu value with REG_DWORD data value 1 to the HKEY_LOCAL_MACHINE\Software\Microsoft\Windows\CurrentVersion\Explorer\Advanced registry key.

The cipher.exe tool can be used to automate and enforce encryption from the command prompt. You can include it in a user's logon or logoff script or in a machine's startup or shutdown script. In a Windows 2000 and Windows Server 2003 environment, you can automatically distribute these scripts throughout the enterprise using GPOs. Table 17.1 lists some sample cipher commands and their effect.

When using EFS, do not forget that the account that can encrypt data is not restricted to the owner of the data. In order to encrypt a file, you don't need file or folder ownership, but you need at least read/write permission to the file or folder.

Table 17.1 *Cipher Switches*

Command	Effect
Cipher /E /A /I <path>	Encrypts all files and subfolders in the specified file system path and ignores possible errors.
Cipher /D /A /I <path>	Decrypts all files and subfolders in the specified file system path and ignores possible errors.
Cipher /E /A <path>/*.txt <path>/*.bat	Encrypts all txt and bat files in the specified file system paths.
Cipher /E /A /F <path>/*.*	Forces the encryption of all files in the specified file system path. Files that were encrypted previously are reencrypted.
Cipher <path>	Shows the EFS status (U or E) of all files and/or folders in the specified file system path.
Cipher /U	Updates all DDF and DRF fields of encrypted files to reflect the latest user encryption key and the latest recovery agent recovery keys.

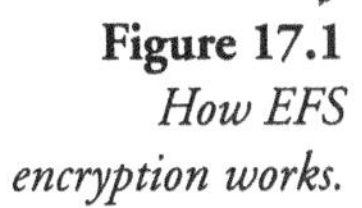

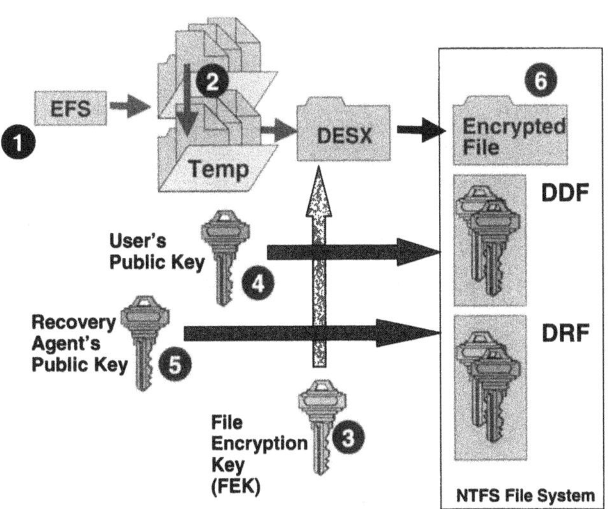

Figure 17.1 *How EFS encryption works.*

17.1.2 EFS internals

The software technology behind EFS is a good example of a hybrid cryptographic solution combining the power of both asymmetric and symmetric ciphers. EFS uses a symmetric cipher (AES)[1] to perform the bulk encryption and an asymmetric cipher (RSA) to provide secure storage of the bulk encryption key. The bulk encryption key is known as the File Encryption Key (FEK). The EFS operation is illustrated in Figures 17.1 and 17.2.

Figure 17.1 illustrates an EFS encryption operation:

1. The EFS service opens the file for exclusive access.
2. The file data are copied to a temporary file for recovery purposes.
3. A file encryption key (FEK) is randomly generated and used to encrypt the file data blocks using a symmetric key cipher (in this example DESX).
4. A data decryption field (DDF) is created containing the FEK encrypted with the user's public key.
5. A data recovery field (DRF) is created containing the FEK, this time encrypted using the recovery agent's public key (this operation is done for every recovery agent).

1. In Windows 2000 EFS used DESX for bulk encryption.

6. The EFS service writes the encrypted data, along with the DDF and DRF, back to the file.
7. The temporary file is deleted from disk.

Figure 17.2 illustrates an EFS decryption operation:

1. When an application accesses an encrypted file, NTFS recognizes the file was encrypted and sends a request to the EFS driver.
2. The EFS driver retrieves the DDF and passes it to the LSA.
3. The LSA decrypts the DDF with the user's private key to obtain the File Encryption Key (FEK).
4. The LSA passes the FEK back to the EFS driver.
5. The EFS driver uses the FEK to decrypt the file.
6. The EFS driver returns the decrypted data to NTFS, which then sends the data to the requesting application.

The processes behind EFS decryption and EFS recovery are identical. The only thing that is different is the private key used to do the decryption of the FEK. For decryption, the data owner's private key is used (as illustrated in Figure 17.2). For recovery, the data recovery agent's private key is used.

The encrypted FEK is stored along with every encrypted file or folder, in the NTFS $EFS attribute. The $EFS attribute is stored in a file's Logged Tool Stream attribute ($Logged_Utility_Stream). Changes to this attribute are logged in the NTFS change log. EFS encrypts an NTFS file's content,

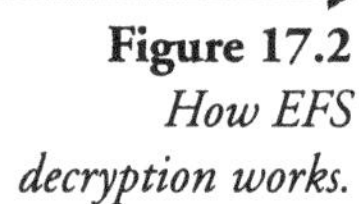

Figure 17.2
How EFS decryption works.

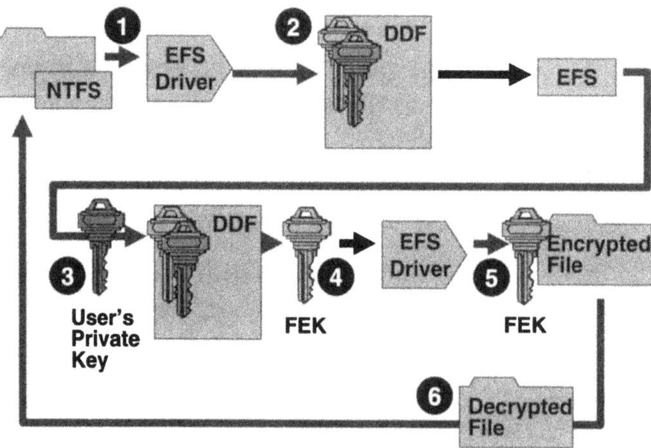

contained in the unnamed "$data" stream, but also every additional NTFS file stream. For more information on NTFS file streams, see the following sidebar.

EFS stores multiple encrypted versions of the FEK: one for the account that encrypted the information and one for every recovery agent. The first is stored in the Data Decryption Field (DDF) and the latter is stored in the Data Recovery Field (DRF). DDF and DRF are also known as key rings.

Both the DDF and DRF can contain different key entries. The DDF can contain different user decryption key entries (in Windows 2000 the DDF can only contain a single decryption key). The DRF can contain different recovery agent key entries.

NTFS File Streams NTFS file streams are also referred to as alternate data streams. An NTFS file always includes a default data stream, the $DATA stream, which includes the file's content. Every NTFS file can also have alternate data streams that Windows Explorer cannot see and that attackers can therefore use to hide malicious information or code on your system. The main reason why Microsoft included the alternate data stream capabilities in NTFS was to enable a Windows NT system to act as a file server for Macintosh clients. The Mac OS uses a similar feature, resource forks, to store file metadata (e.g., date and time information).

To set up an alternate data stream, type the following at the command prompt:

```
echo top secret > file.txt:stream1
```

This command adds an alternate data stream called stream1 to the file.txt file. To display stream1's contents, type the following at the command prompt:

```
more < file.txt:stream1
```

NTFS alternate data streams are dangerous. You do not want a malicious person to hide anything on any of your organization's core systems (e.g., file servers, Web servers, domain controllers). The first level of protection you should use is the NTFS access control settings. If attackers cannot access a file, they cannot create alternate data streams. If a malicious person manages to bypass the permissions you have set, you will need special tools to detect the existence of alternate data streams. System-integrity-checking software, such as the Tripwire integrity checker, can detect any changes (e.g., the addition of or changes to alternate data streams) that occur on a system. More information about the Tripwire is available from http://www.tripwiresecurity.com. To find out whether files have alternate data streams, you can use the Streams command-prompt utility, which is free and available at the Sysinternals Web site: http://www.sysinternals.com/ntw2k/source/misc.shtml#streams.

DDFs and DRFs contain, besides the encrypted bulk encryption key, information that facilitates the lookup of the account's private key that is needed for the decryption of the FEK:

- The account's distinguished name
- The CSP (Cryptographic Service Provider) used for encryption/decryption
- The location that the CSP uses to store the certificates (certificate store container)
- The certificate thumbprint

To retrieve a private key from a user's private key store, the Local Security Authority (LSA) will pass the certificate's thumbprint and certificate store to the CSP. The $EFS file attribute (containing a file's DDFs and DRFs) also contains a checksum that is used by the EFS system to detect integrity changes on the DDF and DRF level. This protects against tampering with the EFS data on the file system level.

To look at the content of the DDF and DRF fields, you can use the efsinfo or the efsdump tools. The first one comes with the Windows Server 2003 operating system. The latter is available from the sysinternals Web site at http://www.sysinternals.com. Efsdump displays the contents of the DDF and DRF key rings. For each entry, it shows the account name and the Subject's Distinguished Name. With efsinfo you can do the same and even more. Two interesting efsinfo switches are /C and /Y. The /C switch displays the certificate thumbprints of the encryption and recovery certificates, referred to in the DDF and DRF rings. The /Y switch displays the thumbprint of a user's local EFS certificate. To look at both the DDF and DRF fields and the associated certificate thumbprints, use efsinfo /u /r /c <filename> (as illustrated in Figure 17.3).

All EFS operations (encryption, decryption, and recovery) are fault tolerant and are logged. During an EFS operation, a hidden log file (named efs0.log) is created in the hidden system volume information folder. Besides

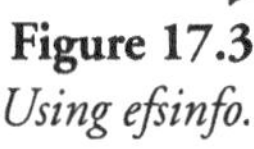

Figure 17.3
Using efsinfo.

```
C:\WINDOWS\system32\cmd.exe
C:\>efsinfo /u /r /c c:\amtg

c:\

AMTG: Encrypted
  Users who can decrypt:
    DC\administrator [Administrator(Administrator@dc.net)]
    Certificate thumbprint: CF12 1A6E 65B3 84EB 5C90 6B57 3BB7 B636 FB23 1C52
  No recovery agent found.

C:\>
```

a log file the EFS system also creates a temporary backup of the file being encrypted in the file's directory (named efs0.tmp). If your system crashes during an EFS encryption operation, the EFS operation will be rolled back and the original, possibly corrupted, file will be replaced with the backup file. To look at what is happening behind the scene on the file system level when using EFS, you can use sysinternals' Filemon tool (available from their Web site).

For obvious security reasons, the FEK is never paged to disk. However, some applications dealing with an encrypted file might copy some of the cleartext to the paging file. Because the paging file is a system file and thus cannot be encrypted, Microsoft advises users to clear the paging file at system shutdown. This can be automated by setting the GPO setting "Clear virtual memory page file when system shuts down."

The generation of a private-public key pair and a special EFS certificate happens transparently. When the users check the encrypted property, choose the encrypt option in the context menu, or encrypt a file or folder using the cipher command prompt tool, the system will automatically generate a private-public key pair and send a public key certification request to a Windows 2000 or Windows Server 2003 enterprise Certification Authority (CA). If no CA is available, a self-signed certificate will be generated by a CSP on the local machine. This enables EFS to function even in the absence of a CA.

Once the EFS certificate is created or downloaded to the local certificate store, a reference to it (the certificate hash) is put in HKEY_CURRENT_USER\Software\Microsoft\Windows NT\CurrentVersion\EFS\CurrentKeys\CertificateHash. This value can be retrieved from the registry using the efsinfo tool with the /Y switch.

The following certificate templates can be used for EFS operations: user, administrator, and basic EFS. EFS certificates can be issued by a Windows 2000 or Windows Server 2003 stand-alone or enterprise CA. EFS certificates can also be generated by third-party non-Windows CAs. How to do this is explained in the Microsoft Knowledge Base article Q273856, available from http://support.microsoft.com/default.aspx?scid=kb;en-us;273856.

Just like any other personal certificate, EFS certificates (and with them the EFS public keys) and EFS private keys are stored in the user's profile. More information on the storage of certificates and private keys can be found in Chapter 13. Even though theoretically EFS certificates and private keys can be stored on a smart card, EFS cannot access them when they are stored on a smart card. This is because EFS is hard coded to only use the

Microsoft Base, Enhanced or Strong Cryptographic Service Providers (CSPs —see Chapter 13).

17.1.3 EFS data recovery

A key feature of EFS is its ability to recover encrypted files or folders, when a user's private key is lost or becomes inaccessible. Loss of private keys can occur because of hardware or software problems on a user's computer. EFS data recovery can also be useful when an employee leaves the company, when his or her account and profile are deleted, or when access is needed to files previously encrypted by that employee.

Besides EFS data recovery the Windows Server 2003 CA can also EFS key recovery: this feature was explained in Chapter 15.

EFS data recovery means that a Windows account, known as the recovery agent, other than the original account that encrypted the data, can decrypt the FEK and recover the user's data. The recovery agent can recover a file if his or her public key was used to encrypt the FEK and the resulting encrypted FEK is part of the encrypted file's NTFS $EFS attribute; in other words, when the account was defined as a recovery agent on the moment the file was encrypted. A recovery agent needs to have a special key pair and a special certificate (an EFS recovery certificate) before the EFS encryption process takes place.

EFS recovery agents can be defined on the domain, site, organizational unit, or local machine level. You use the Windows 2000 or Windows Server 2003 group policy object (GPO) Encrypting File System entry to define them. This entry is located in the Security Settings\Public Key Policies container. The EFS GPO entry contains the EFS recovery certificates of Windows accounts that are designated as recovery agents by the GPO administrator. To facilitate the life of administrators, Microsoft provides a wizard to set the recovery agents (which is illustrated in Figure 17.4). In the wizard, the recovery certificates can be downloaded from the Active Directory or can be imported in *.cer format. You must publish the certificates manually to AD to make them available from AD; the Windows CA does not automatically publish them in AD.

EFS recovery certificates have File Recovery (OID 1.3.6.1.4.1.311.10.3.4.1) in the Enhanced Key Usage field. They can be generated by an enterprise or a stand-alone CA. They can even be generated without the intervention of any CA: The recovery certificates that are generated on a stand-alone machine are self-signed recovery certificates for the local administrator generated by the local machine. To manually generate a self-

Figure 17.4 *Setting up an EFS recovery agent using GPOs.*

signed EFS recovery agent certificate and private key on a Windows XP or Windows Server 2003 stand-alone machine, use the cipher command with the /r switch.

Enabling EFS recovery does not necessarily require a CA. However, within an AD environment, the use of a CA for the generation of EFS recovery certificates will offer more flexibility and centralized control over EFS recovery:

- An organization can provide EFS recovery privileges (in the form of an EFS recovery certificate) to specific administrator accounts.
- An organization can control the validity of an administrator's EFS recovery privilege because it has control over the lifetime and revocation status of EFS recovery certificates.

In Windows 2000 EFS, the default recovery agent is the administrator account. On a stand-alone machine, this is the local administrator account. On a machine member of a domain, it is the domain administrator. It is a best practice to change the default domain recovery account administrator to some other account. Windows Server 2003 EFS contains some important changes regarding EFS recovery are explained next.

The EFS recovery GPO settings are downloaded to the machine at startup, at the predefined GPO update interval, or when GPO application is enforced. Changes in the policy's content are not applied immediately to every encrypted file or folder in the policy scope. EFS will enforce and apply the change the first time it is used following the policy change.

Remember that to define a new DRF, EFS needs access to the FEK, which is only available at decryption time.

This explains why you must always archive the private keys and certificates of old recovery agents. Doing so, you will always be able to access any encrypted file, even those that have not been opened since an EFS recovery policy change occurred. To archive a recovery agent's private key and certificate, export them using the certificate export wizard. To find out which archived keying material you should use for a recovery, use the efsinfo tool with the /C switch to retrieve the recovery agent's certificate thumbprint from the encrypted file.

Special care must be taken of the place where the archived recovery agent private keys are stored. They should be protected from unauthorized access. Anyone possessing the recovery private key can read any encrypted file or folder within the EFS recovery policy scope. A best practice is to put the private key on a floppy disk or on a smart card and lock it in a safe. Also, when requesting a recovery certificate using the CA Web interface, be sure to check "Enable strong private key protection" in the advanced request settings to provide another level of software protection.

Besides archiving the recovery agent's private key, you should also delete it from the local system. "Delete the private key if export is successful" is an option that can be set in the certificate export wizard. The reason to do this is related to a fundamental security principle: Encryption keys should never be stored near the files they secure. This is a must-do for stand-alone machines; it is less critical for machines in a domain, where the recovery agent's private key is almost certainly located on another machine. In mid-1999 a hacker found this weakness and received lots of press attention. A less secure alternative is to use a dedicated highly secure workstation, preferably off the network, that has a local copy of the recovery private key and that is only used for EFS recovery.

The preferred procedure to recover an encrypted file is the following: Let the user back up the file using NTbackup or any third party backup solution that uses the NTBackup APIs (this is the only way that an encrypted file can be exported from a Windows system without decrypting it). Let him or her send it to a recovery agent using a secure channel. Let the recovery agent do the recovery, and let the recovery agent send the decrypted file back to the user, once more using a secure channel. A secure channel can be created by delivering the file out of band using a floppy, by copying it to a share across a VPN tunnel, or by sending it using a secured S/MIME mail message. Another way, less secure and thus less preferred, is to use a dedicated machine to perform the recovery of encrypted files.

17.1.4 Windows 2000 EFS: The bad and the ugly

Windows 2000 EFS is far from perfect from a security point of view when it is used on a stand-alone machine. Stand-alone in this context means a machine that is not a member of a Windows domain. Hackers have created tools to reset the user password of user accounts stored in a machine's local security database. These tools even work when the syskey cryptographic SAM protection feature is enabled. If you succeed in obtaining a user's credentials, you can obviously also access its encrypted files. If you get access to a local administrator's account, you can access all locally encrypted files of all users. This is because by default in Windows 2000, the local administrator is the EFS recovery agent. A very popular tool in this area is the ntpasswd tool, which can be downloaded from http://home.eunet.no/~pnordahl/ntpasswd. This attack can be countered by using syskey encryption in an operation mode where the system key is not stored on the Windows system itself (this is mode 2 or 3).

Windows 2000 EFS also lacks several interesting features. A good example is EFS's inability to let users share encrypted files with other users. The absence of these features together with the security issues made many enterprises choose solutions from other vendors to provide file encryption on their file servers, user desktops, and laptops. Popular examples are the solutions from F-Secure, SafeBoot, Utimaco, and Pointsec. In Windows XP and Windows Server 2003, Microsoft tries to remedy the obstacles encountered in Windows 2000 EFS.

17.1.5 New EFS features

The following sections provide an overview of the new features in Windows XP and Windows Server 2003 EFS.

EFS file sharing

Perhaps the most visible change to Windows XP and Windows Server 2003 EFS is the support for EFS file sharing. It enables users to share encrypted files with other users. From an administration point of view, things would certainly have been much simpler if Microsoft had let users share their encrypted files with Windows groups. Because EFS relies on X.509-based certificates that by definition honor the principle of individual accountability, this is impossible. EFS file sharing only applies to NTFS files, not to NTFS folders.

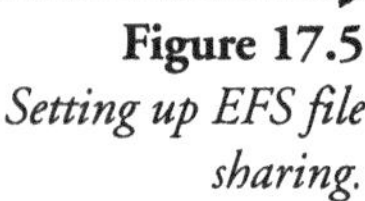

Figure 17.5
Setting up EFS file sharing.

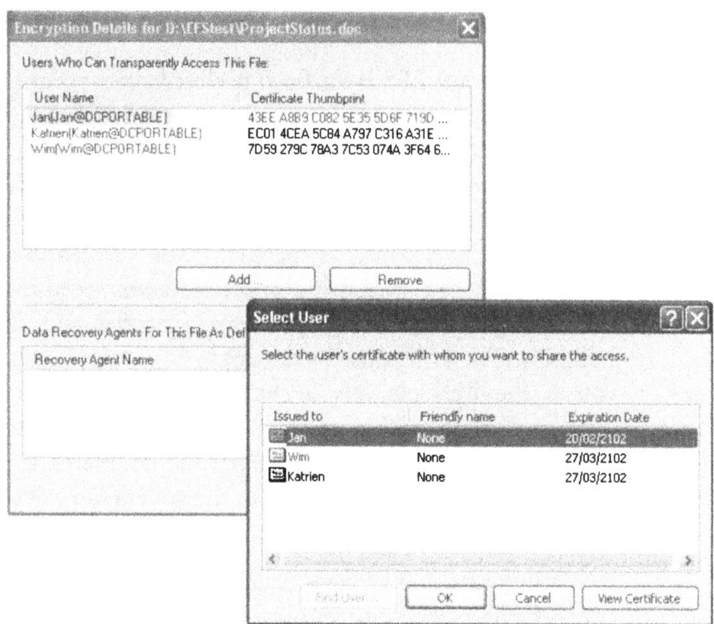

EFS file sharing is enabled in a file's advanced properties. Before you can share an encrypted file, it must be encrypted. If a file is encrypted, you will notice that the Details button in the file's advanced properties becomes available. Pushing this button brings up the dialog box illustrated in Figure 17.5, allowing you to share an encrypted file with other users. In Figure 17.5, you can see that the projectstatus.doc file is encrypted and shared between users Jan, Katrien, and Wim. The sharing of an EFS encrypted file is not an explicit privilege of the user account that encrypted the file and shared it with another user. In the example of Figure 17.5, Jan may have encrypted the file and decided to share it with Katrien. Katrien on her turn may then have decided to share it with Wim.

Let's look now at how EFS determines whether a user is authorized to change a file's EFS sharing properties and with whom he or she can share the file. To change a file's EFS sharing properties, you need at least write permission to the file. To share a file with another user, you need access to that user's EFS encryption certificate. From the Select User dialog box (illustrated in Figure 17.5), you can access the user certificates stored in the Other People and Trusted People certificate containers of your certificate store.[2] If your machine is a member of a Windows Active Directory–based

2. The Trusted People certificate store container is used for self-signed certificates that do not chain to a trusted root CA. The other people certificate store container is the general cache for certificates that do chain to a trusted root CA.

domain, you will notice that the Find User... pushbutton also lights up. Pushing this button lets you access the EFS user certificates published in Active Directory. If you want to share encrypted files with people whose EFS certificate is not available in one of the above repositories, you can always import it manually into your certificate store.

To better understand how EFS file sharing really works, it is worth looking at the cryptographic nuts and bolts of EFS file sharing. When a user shares an encrypted file with another user, an extra Data Decryption Field (DDF) is added to the file's EFS-related NTFS file streams. At no point in the EFS file sharing process is the file itself decrypted. When Jan decided to share a file he previously encrypted with Katrien, EFS will decrypt Jan's DDF with Jan's private key in order to retrieve the File Encryption Key (FEK). The EFS system will then encrypt the FEK using Katrien's public key and add the resulting DDF to the file's EFS-related NTFS file streams.

Before a user may be added to the list of users who can access an encrypted file, the EFS software validates the user's certificate. This happens when a user's certificate is selected (as illustrated in Figure 17.5). During the validation, the EFS software will perform a complete certificate chain validation. This includes a trust and certificate revocation check for all certificates included in a user's EFS certificate chain.

Web folder and WebDAV integration

An important Windows 2000 EFS design limitation surfaces when EFS is used to protect the confidentiality of files stored on file servers. The key problem here is that files are always decrypted locally on the file server and then transmitted in the clear to the user workstation. This setup also requires the file server to be trusted for delegation and to have access to a local copy of the user profile. The latter are consequences of the fact that EFS needs access to a user's private key (which is stored in the user profile) in order to decrypt an encrypted EFS file.

Windows XP and the Windows Server 2003 Web server (IIS 6.0) come with an interesting alternative for the use of EFS on file servers. In Windows XP and Windows Server 2003, Microsoft embedded support for the transport of EFS metadata using the WebDAV protocol. WebDAV stands for Web Distributed Authoring and Versioning. It is an extension of the HTTP 1.1 protocol that allows for file metadata to be transported together with the file across an HTTP connection. Support for the WebDAV protocol has been available on the client side from Internet Explorer 5.0 (through the Web Authoring Components) and on the server side from IIS 5.0 on.

The WebDAV support makes Web folders a worthy alternative to file shares for the use of EFS on file servers. That is also why Microsoft strongly recommends the Web folder solution instead of file shares for remote storage of encrypted data on file servers. The combination of EFS file sharing, Web folders, and WebDAV makes the Windows Server 2003 platform a very interesting option for the setup of secure file servers. Table 17.2 compares the features of using file shares for remote EFS operations versus those of using Web folders.

Setting up a Web folder is relatively easy. Open up the properties of the file, select the Web Sharing tab, and click "Share this folder" (as illustrated in Figure 17.6).

Table 17.2 *Comparison Between the Features of Remote EFS Operations on File Shares and Web Folders*

Remote EFS Operations On...	**...File Shares**	**...Web Folders**
Where does EFS encryption/decryption occur?	Files are encrypted and decrypted on the file server.	Files are encrypted and decrypted on the user machine.
Are the files secured during transmission over the network?	Files are sent in the clear over the network connection.	Files remain encrypted while being sent over the network connection.
What technology is or can be used to secure the transmission of the files over the network?	Requires IPsec to secure the file transfer between file server and user machine.	Does not require IPsec to secure the file transfer; relies on the WebDAV EFS extensions to securely transmit the file.
Must the file server be "trusted for delegation"?	Requires file server to be "trusted for delegation."	Does not require file server to be "trusted for delegation."
Does the solution require a copy of the user profile on the file server?	Requires availability of user profile on the file server (local or roaming profile).	Does not require availability of user profile on the file server.
Where does EFS file sharing authorization process for users take place?	EFS checks for other user certificates on the file server and/or in Active Directory.	EFS checks for other user certificates on the local machine and/or in Active Directory.
What file transport protocol/method is used?	File sharing uses SMB. SMB supports streaming and block by block writeback, which is much more efficient and performs better than HTTP-based downloading.	Web folder-based sharing uses HTTP. HTTP requires the entire file be uploaded or downloaded before an application can have access to it.

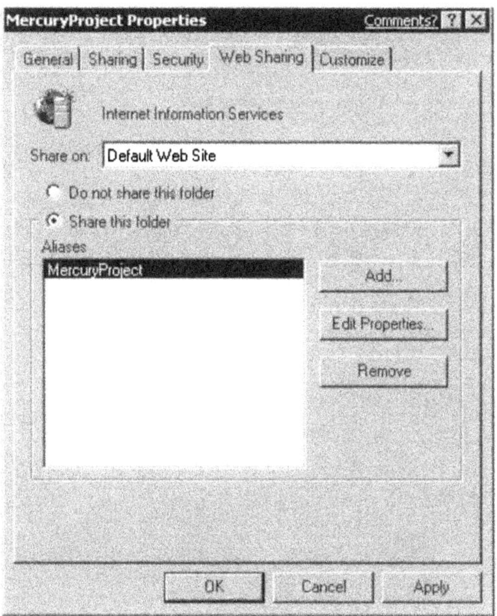

Figure 17.6 *Setting up a Web folder.*

Offline files and folders EFS support

Windows 2000 introduced the concept of offline files and folders. It enables users to access files and folders on network shares even when the user's machine is disconnected from the network. To do so, the offline files and folders system keeps a local copy of the files and folders shared on the remote machine and—even more importantly—keeps the remote and local copy of the data synchronized. All offline files and folders are stored in a Client-Side Cache (CSC) database, which is located in the hidden %systemroot%/CSC folder. In Windows 2000, offline files and folders do not preserve their EFS encryption attributes when they are copied to the local machine. Also, in Windows 2000 it was not possible to encrypt the CSC database.

From Windows XP and Windows Server 2003 onward, the EFS encryption attributes are preserved when a remote file or folder is made available offline. Also, the local client-side cache database can be encrypted.

To enable the encryption or the client-side cache database, open up My Computer or Explorer, and select Folder Options from the Tools menu. On the Offline Files tab, first enable offline files by checking the "Enable offline files" checkbox, then check the "Encrypt offline files to secure data" check-

Figure 17.7 *Enabling EFS encryption for offline files and folders.*

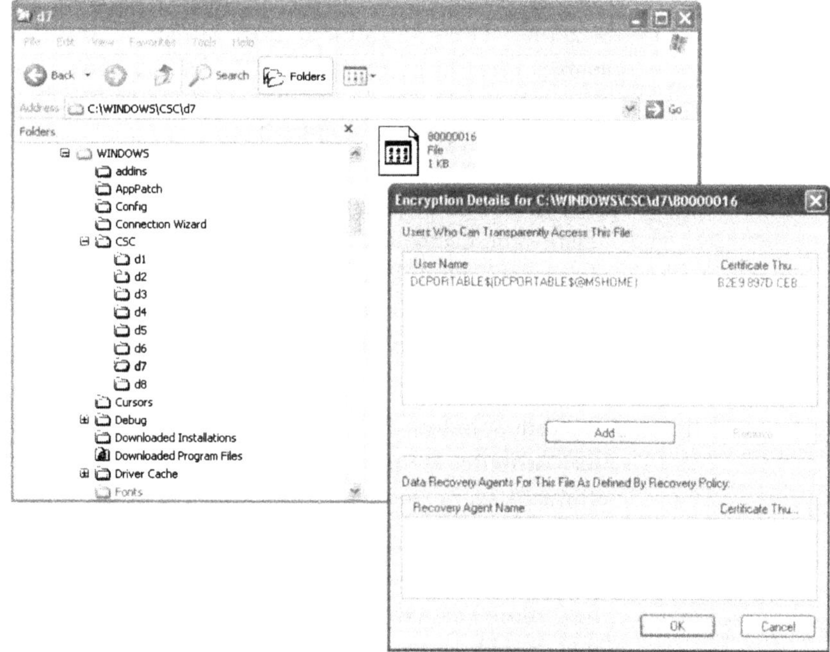

Figure 17.8 *Viewing the encryption details on the offline files and folders CSC database.*

box (as illustrated in Figure 17.7). When setting this option, the offline files in the CSC database will be encrypted using a self-signed EFS certificate issued to <local_machinename>$ (as illustrated in Figure 17.8).

Preservation of the EFS encryption settings happens automatically when making a file or folder available offline. This is done by right-clicking the original file on the remote share and selecting "Make Available Offline." An important detail is that offline files and folders functionality is not available when the XP "Fast User Switching" feature is enabled.

Cryptographic changes

Windows XP and Windows Server 2003 can both be configured to use the 3DES algorithm for EFS encryption and decryption operations. 3DES is compliant with the U.S. Federal Information Processing Security Standards (FIPS) 140-1 Level 1. The default encryption algorithm used by EFS in Windows 2000 and XP is DESX. The default encryption algorithm used in Windows XP Service Pack 1 and Windows Server 2003 is AES with a 256-bit key. Even after setting up Windows 2000, Windows Server 2003 and Windows XP to use 3DES, DESX or AES support (depending on the platform) is not lost. The platforms are still able to process files previously encrypted with DESX or AES.

There are two ways to configure EFS to support 3DES instead of DESX. A first way is to use a new Group Policy Object (GPO) setting called "System Cryptography: Use FIPS compliant algorithms for encryption." This setting will affect not only the encryption-decryption operations of EFS but also of other Windows security solutions such as IPsec. The GPO setting is located in the Computer configuration\Windows Settings\Security Settings\Local Policies\Security Options GPO container. The second way is based on a registry hack and makes the use of 3DES available only to EFS. To do so, create the AlgorithmID (REG_DWORD) registry value in the HKEY_LOCAL_MACHINE\Software\Microsoft\Windows NT\CurrentVersion\EFS registry key and set it to 0x6603.

Windows Server 2003 also supports the specification of larger default RSA key sizes for keys that are generated for EFS. The default key size used in Windows XP and Windows Server 2003 is 1024 bits. In Windows Server 2003 the default size can be changed by setting the following registry key (REG_DWORD):

HKEY_LOCAL_MACHINE\Software\Microsoft\Windows NT\CurrentVersion\EFS\RSAKeyLength. The range of this key is 1024 to 16384.

Disabling EFS

In Windows Server 2003, the use of EFS can be disabled using a GPO setting that is available from the properties of the Encrypting File System GPO container. To disable the use of EFS for the users in a domain, site, or OU, or on a local machine, uncheck "Allow users to encrypt files using Encrypting File System (EFS)." This setting only works for Windows XP and later machines.

As in Windows 2000, if you want to disable EFS on the file or folder level, you can still do the following in Windows XP and Windows Server 2003:

- To disable EFS on the file level, set the system attribute.
- To disable EFS on the folder level, set the system attribute or create a special entry in the folder's desktop.ini file: Add disable=1 in the (Encryption) section.

EFS recovery changes

As explained earlier, a unique feature of EFS is its support for data recovery and the facility for designated administrator accounts to decrypt user data. Some organizations, however, do not want an encryption solution that has recovery capabilities. This may be because of advanced confidentiality requirements or because organizations simply do not trust the EFS recovery feature.

That is why in Windows XP and Windows Server 2003, Microsoft has implemented EFS recovery slightly differently. In both operating systems EFS can function without the requirement of having an EFS recovery agent defined (as was the case in Windows 2000). Also, by default, Windows XP and Windows Server 2003 stand-alone machines and Windows Server 2003 domains do not have any recovery agents defined. In Windows 2000, the local administrator account was the default local recovery agent, and the domain administrator was the default domain recovery agent. This new EFS recovery option can be enabled from the GPO MMC snap-in by right-clicking the Encrypting File System container and selecting "Do Not Require Data Recovery Agents." This is illustrated in Figure 17.9 for Windows Server 2003; most of these options are also available for Windows XP. An option that is not available in XP is the Create Data Recovery Agent option. Contrary to the Add Data Recovery Agent option, this option does not use the recovery agent wizard. Instead, it automatically requests and installs an EFS recovery certificate for the currently logged-on user.

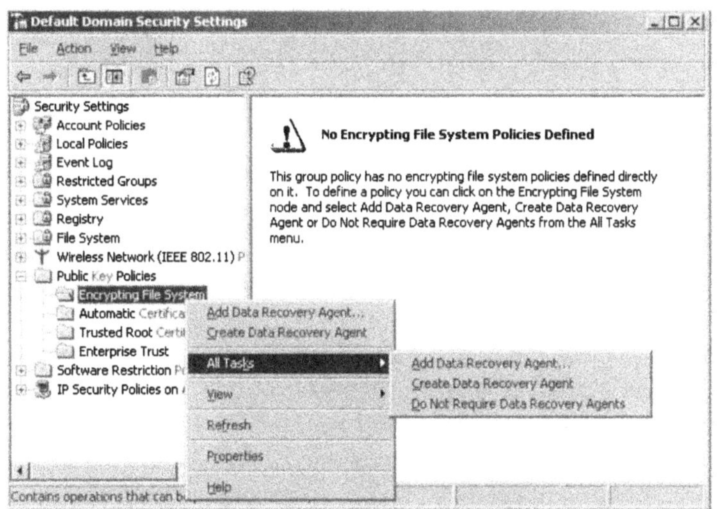

Figure 17.9 *Define an EFS data recovery policy.*

To enable all of these EFS recovery changes, Microsoft has changed the key hierarchy that it uses to protect the EFS private encryption keys in Windows XP and Windows Server 2003.[3] EFS private keys are stored in a user's profile and are cryptographically protected using a key called the master key. The master key is securely stored using a key that is derived from a user's credentials. Like private keys, master keys are stored in a user's profile. By default, Windows XP and Windows Server 2003 also provide another level of cryptographic protection for security information such as private keys: the syskey option.

All this means that when a user changes his or her password, the master key has to be decrypted and reencrypted using the new key derived from the user's new credentials. If the latter does not occur, the user loses access to his or her master key. Things can get problematic here when a user forgets his or her password and an administrator has to force a reset of the user password. From an EFS point of view, this basically means that a user's master key and at the same time his or her private keys become inaccessible, and thus previously encrypted EFS data cannot be decrypted anymore. From a security point of view, this is also good, because it means that tools such as ntpasswd that force a password reset for a local account become worthless when one wants to access the account's encrypted EFS data.

3. This is related to the introduction of the Data Protection API (DPAPI—see Chapter 13) for key protection in Windows XP and Windows Server 2003.

To remedy the problem of a user forgetting his or her password and losing access to his or her EFS data, Microsoft provides three solutions in XP: a Password Reset Disk (PRD), a backup of the EFS private key and certificate, and EFS recovery agents. The latter two options are really nothing new because they already existed in Windows 2000. A brand-new solution in XP to let a user deal with a lost password is the Password Reset Disk (PRD). However, as explained in the next section, this solution must be handled with extreme care. If you do not use it properly, it will not resolve the problem of losing access to your EFS data.

17.1.6 The challenge of authorized EFS recovery

A Password Reset Disk first and foremost allows a user to reset his or her password on a local machine without having to call on the local administrator. Indirectly it also protects a user from losing access to his or her encrypted files on a stand-alone computer because he or she forgot a password. Always remember that a PRD only works for the local accounts on a single machine. It does not work for global domain accounts, and the same PRD cannot be used on different machines. Because the PRD is the key to resetting the user's password, the user should always keep it in a secure place so that nobody else except for the user can obtain it.

A PRD can be created from the User account properties in the control panel "User Accounts" applet. To start the PRD Forgotten Password wizard, you must click "Prevent a forgotten password" (as illustrated in Figure 17.10). The wizard will then guide you through the rest of the PRD generation process.

What is behind this PRD from a cryptographic point of view? When a PRD is created, XP first creates a public-private key pair and a self-signed certificate. The PRD logic then encrypts the user's actual password using the newly generated public key and stores the result of this encryption in the HKEY_LOCAL_MACHINE\Security\Recovery\<user SID> registry key. Finally, the PRD logic exports the private key to a floppy disk and deletes it from the local system.

When you enter a wrong password on the XP logon screen, XP will prompt you "Did you forget your password? You can use your password reset disk." Clicking this phrase will start up the Password Reset wizard, which will then guide you through the rest of the password reset process. During this process you will simply be requested to enter a new password and to supply the PRD floppy disk. Behind the scenes, XP will then retrieve your PRD private key from the PRD floppy disk and use it to decrypt the

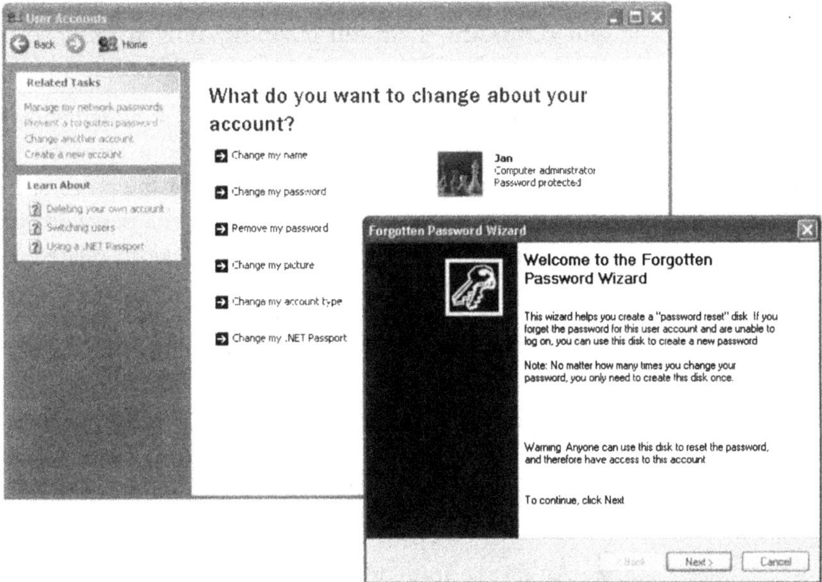

Figure 17.10 *Starting up the Forgotten Password wizard.*

encrypted copy of your password on the local machine. The fact that you have supplied the correct PRD floppy proves to the system that your request to reset your password is authentic. Given this old password, it can then derive the key that is used to secure the master key. The master key can then give the EFS system access to your private keys, and finally you regain access to your encrypted files. Because the user's password is changed during this process, the user's master key also has to be decrypted and reencrypted using the new key derived from the user's new credentials. The latter two processes happen automatically when you run the Password Reset wizard.

When using a PRD, you must take care that you update the PRD every time you change your password. Updating of the PRD happens exactly the same way as you create an initial PRD. Why is it so important that you update the PRD in this scenario? If you do not, you will lose access to your EFS encrypted files the next time you run the Password Reset wizard! The problem is that when you change your password, your master key is reencrypted using a new key derived from this new password. If you do not update your PRD, the PRD's private key will unlock an old set of credentials when it is run. The key derived from this old set of credentials will not succeed in decrypting the master key that is now encrypted with the new credentials.

A similar problem occurs when a local administrator resets your password. However, in this case it is of no use to update the PRD. The only remedy to the latter problem is to import a copy of your EFS private key and certificate. This will obviously only work if you previously created a backup of the EFS private key and certificate.

All of this is illustrated in Table 17.3, which shows the effect of several user and administrator password-related actions on (a) the password hash stored in the local security database, (b) the password stored in the secured PRD recovery registry folder, and (c) the password used to secure a user's master key. In Table 17.3, different password-related actions occur one after the other:

- At **T1** the user runs the Forgotten Password wizard to create a PRD. At that moment his password is set to A.
- At **T2** the user forgets about his or her A password. To remedy the problem he or she runs the Password Reset wizard from the logon screen using the PRD. In the Password Reset wizard the user resets his or her password to B.
- At **T3** the local administrator performs a password reset on the user account's password from the Control Panel. He or she sets the user password to C.
- At **T4** the user imports his or her previously backed up EFS private key and certificate into his or her personal private key and certificate store.
- AT **T5** the user performs a password reset from the Control Panel. The user changes his or her password from C to D.
- At **T6** the user runs the Forgotten Password wizard to update the password reset information on the PRD.

The problems that will make it impossible to access your encrypted EFS data occur at T3 and T5 (they are marked in bold):

- At **T3** the administrator resets the user password. As a consequence, the password hash stored in the local security database and the password used to secure the user's master key become out of sync and the user's EFS data become inaccessible. The user corrects this situation in **T4** by importing his or her previously exported EFS private key and certificate.
- At **T5** the user resets his or her password without doing an update of the PRD. As a consequence, the password stored in the PRD recovery registry folder and the one used to secure the user's master key are out of sync. The user corrects this situation in **T6** by updating the PRD.

From the above, we can conclude that XP adds two EFS best practices:

1. Always export a copy of your EFS private key and certificate to a floppy disk.
2. It is absolutely necessary to update the PRD after your credentials have been updated.

From what you have read so far, you may conclude that Windows XP EFS now provides perfect protection against unauthorized EFS data access. This is not completely true. Even though XP uses a different key hierarchy to protect the EFS private keys and it comes by default with an empty EFS recovery policy, the risk still exists that a hacker can exploit the EFS recovery capabilities to get access to EFS encrypted data on a stand-alone machine.

Table 17.3 *Password Change Scenarios and Their Effect on (a) the Password Hash Stored in the Local Security Database, (b) the Password Stored in the PRD Recovery Registry Folder, and (c) the Password Used to Secure the User's Master Key*

Timing	Action	User Password	(a) Password Hash Stored in Local Security Database	(b) Password Stored in Secured PRD Recovery Registry Folder	(c) Password Used to Secure User's Master Key
T1	User Runs "Forgotten Password" Wizard (Creates PRD)	A	A	A	A
T2	User Runs "Password Reset" Wizard from Logon Screen	B	B	B	B
T3	Administrator Resets Password from Control Panel "User Accounts"	C	C	B	B
T4	User Imports EFS Private Key and Certificate from Backup	C	C	B	C
T5	User Resets Password from Control Panel "User Accounts"	D	D	B	D
T6	User Runs "Forgotten Password" Wizard (Updates PRD)	D	D	D	D

A hacker can still use a tool such as ntpasswd (more information is available at http://home.eunet.no/~pnordahl/ntpasswd) to reset a local administrator account's password and gain administrator access to a stand-alone system. If you have administrator access, you can define an EFS recovery policy. The hacker could add the administrator account to the recovery policy. Because Windows automatically updates all EFS recovery information anytime an encrypted file is accessed, from that moment on all encrypted files that are accessed will have an EFS data recovery field (DRF) holding the recovery account of the administrator account. As mentioned earlier in this chapter tools like ntpasswd can be neutralized by using syskey protection (in mode 2 or 3).

17.1.7 EFS alternatives

Even though EFS should be used carefully (as explained earlier), it is a very good solution for desktop encryption. Table 17.4 shows some EFS alternatives.

The products in Table 17.4 can be categorized in file system level encryption solutions, file and folder level encryption solutions, and disk encryption solutions. EFS is a good example of a file system level encryption solution. The solutions differ in the way they protect the encryption keys, the level on which the encryption and decryption take place, the sup-

Table 17.4 *File Encryption Products*

Company	Product Name
Utimaco	Safeguard Easy
Fsecure	FileCrypto
Entrust	Entelligence File Plug-in
PGP	PGP
WinMagic	Securedoc
PC Guardian	Encryption Plus Hard Disk Encryption Plus Folders
SafeBoot	SafeBoot
Pointsec	Pointsec File Encryption

port for single or multiuser access, and the way they implement recovery of the encryption keys:

- An encryption key may be protected with another symmetric key or with a public key.
- The encryption key may be stored on the computer system or on some special device (smart card or token).
- Recovery keys may be stored with every file (decentralized) or in a central database.
- Encryption/decryption can happen on the disk level, on the file- or folder-level, or on the file system level.
- Some encryption systems are single-user oriented, whereas others can give multiple users access to the encrypted files.

17.2 Secure mail using S/MIME

In this section we look at how Microsoft has built S/MIME support into Exchange 2003, Outlook Web Access, Outlook Express 6.0, and Outlook 2003, and how this support can be integrated with Windows Server 2003 PKI.

17.2.1 S/MIME basics

Secure MIME (S/MIME) is an Internet standard for secure messaging. It can add data authentication, confidentiality, nonrepudiation, and integrity protection to MIME-formatted messages. The IETF standardized S/MIME version 3.0 in RFCs 2632 through 2634.

From a cryptographic point of view, S/MIME is an excellent example of a hybrid cryptographic solution. The basic S/MIME operation is illustrated in Figure 17.11. In a typical S/MIME scenario, Alice wants to send a secure message to Bob. Secure in this context means guaranteeing confidentiality, integrity, data authentication, and nonrepudiation.

The S/MIME exchange illustrated in Figure 17.11 can be split into six steps, as follows:

- Step 1: Alice creates a digital signature for the message using her private key.
- Step 2: Alice encrypts the message using a bulk encryption key.

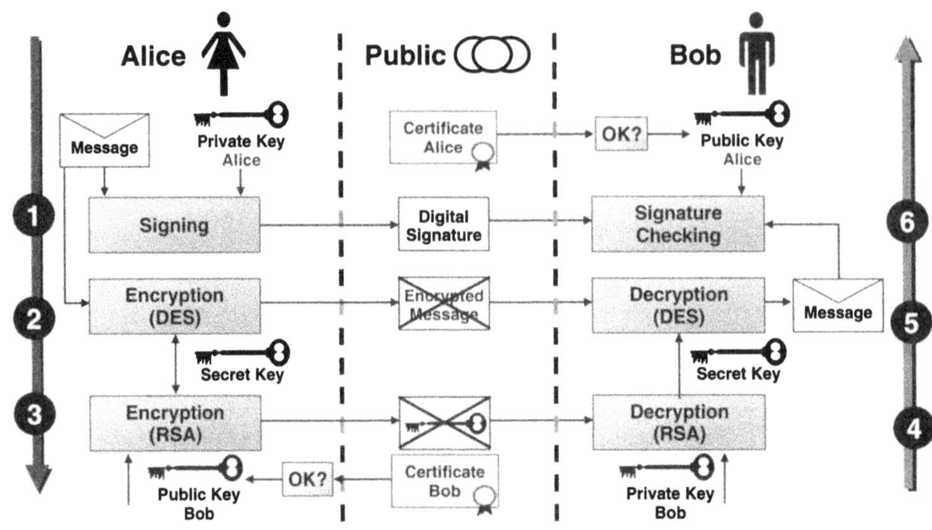

Figure 17.11 *Basic S/MIME operation.*

- Step 3: To create a secure channel protecting the confidentiality of the encryption key, Alice encrypts the encryption key with the public key of Bob. This results in a lockbox.
- Step 4: Bob decrypts the lockbox using his private key. This results in the bulk encryption key.
- Step 5: Using the bulk encryption key, Bob decrypts the message. This gives Bob the readable message.
- Step 6: Bob verifies the authenticity and integrity of the message by verifying the digital signature using Alice's public key.

S/MIME builds on MIME. Thanks to MIME, which the IETF defined in RFCs 2045 through 2049, the body of a mail message can contain data types other than just flat ASCII. An Internet mail message typically consists of a message header, which contains sender and recipient information, and an optional message body. You can use MIME to add nontextual objects, such as images, audio, formatted text, and Microsoft Word documents, to messages. MIME terminology refers to a data type as a content type. A multipart content type lets you embed different content types into a single message body. In a multipart body, boundaries mark the beginning and end of each content type.

S/MIME provides security extensions that let MIME entities encapsulate security objects, such as digital signatures and encrypted message blobs.

Table 17.5 *S/MIME Content Types and Services*

MIME Content Type	MIME Subtype	S/MIME Type	S/MIME Service	Attachment Extension
Application	pkcs7-MIME	Signed data Enveloped data	Guarantees data integrity, data authentication, and nonrepudiation. Uses opaque signing. Guarantees data confidentiality.	.p7m .p7m
Multipart	signed	N/A	Guarantees data integrity, data authentication, and nonrepudiation. Uses clear signing.	N/A
Application	pkcs7-signature	N/A	N/A	.p7s

To do so, S/MIME adds new MIME content types that provide data confidentiality, integrity protection, nonrepudiation, and authentication services. These content types are called application/pkcs7-MIME, multipart/signed, and application/pkcs7-signature. The MIME content type provides information about the type of data a message carries in its MIME attachments. By doing so, an application (in this case, the mail client's S/MIME logic) can know how it must process the MIME data before it displays them to a user.

As Table 17.5 shows, the S/MIME attachment's extension differs depending on the S/MIME service the content type provides. The MIME header specifies the name of the MIME attachment. Some mail clients, such as clients of non-S/MIME-enabled systems or early versions of S/MIME, need the attachment to recognize a message's S/MIME content. Other mail clients rely completely on the content-type information in the message header to identify MIME entities. S/MIME secures only the message body. Header information must remain unencrypted for messages to relay successfully across gateways on the path between sender and recipient.

17.2.2 Exchange Server S/MIME support

From version 4 onward, Microsoft Exchange Server has included the Advanced Security subsystem to let users secure their mail messages using S/MIME. Microsoft built Advanced Security around the optional Key Management Service (KMS). This is still true for Exchange 2000, but is not true anymore for Exchange 2003. In Exchange 2003, the KMS functionality has been merged into the Windows Server 2003 Certification Authority (CA).

In its early days, the KMS was a CA, an RA, and also the entity taking care of key archival and recovery. From Exchange 5.5 Service Pack 1 onward, you can outsource the KMS CA functionality to a Windows CA. In Exchange 2003, the CA and archival and recovery functions have been moved to the Windows Server 2003 CA. From Exchange 2000 onward, Exchange's S/MIME functionality is also tightly integrated with AD. AD stores user certificates and certificate revocation lists (CRLs).

Exchange Advanced Security has always included a key recovery feature that lets you recover copies of users' lost or deleted encryption keys. In Exchange Advanced Security, key recovery is server-oriented. The KMS database contains copies of each Advanced Security–enabled user's current and previous private encryption keys. In an Exchange 2003 environment, the key recovery function is provided by the Windows Server 2003 CA. This was explained in Chapter 15. This chapter also included information on how to migrate encryption keys from the KMS database to the CA database.

The presence of a key recovery system explains why Exchange KMS and S/MIME in general use a dual-key-pair system. In a dual-key-pair system, users have one key pair for encryption operations and another pair for signing operations. Exchange Advanced Security and S/MIME could not guarantee trustworthy digital signature services if they used a single key pair and stored the pair's private key in a central database for key recovery purposes. Digital signatures require that only users can access their private signing keys (otherwise, anyone could impersonate the user). Therefore, Exchange Server stores the signing pair's private key only on the client side. Note that not all S/MIME product vendors support the dual-key-pair system.

Because the KMS does not exist anymore in Exchange 2003, there is very little you can configure when setting up S/MIME for your mail clients. In the properties of a mailbox store, there is a checkbox that says "Clients support S/MIME signatures." This checkbox must be checked if you want to enable your clients to use S/MIME (the checkbox is enabled by default). This configuration option is illustrated in Figure 17.12.

17.2.3 Microsoft mail client S/MIME support

Both the full-blown Outlook mail client and Outlook Express have offered S/MIME support for quite some time. Brand-new to Exchange 2003 is the S/MIME support for Outlook Web Access (OWA). Outlook 2003 is the latest version of Microsoft's full-blown mail client. Outlook Express 6.0 is a lightweight Internet-oriented mail client that Microsoft distributes together

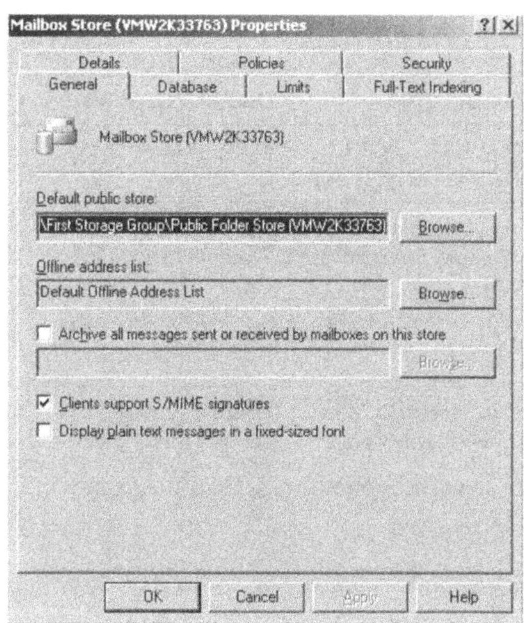

Figure 17.12 *S/MIME configuration in Exchange 2003.*

with Internet Explorer (IE) 6.0. You can connect Outlook Express 6.0 to Exchange 2003, Exchange 2000, or Exchange Server 5.5 through SMTP and POP3 or IMAP4, and you can connect it to a directory through LDAP. OWA allows for HTTP-based mail access from a browser—the OWA Web pages and logic are included with the Exchange 2003 code. Table 17.6 gives an overview of the Microsoft mail clients' main S/MIME features.

Of the three mail clients, Outlook 2003 is certainly the most complete when it comes to S/MIME functionality. It comes with support for some of the S/MIME enhanced security services (explained later) and includes easy-to-use digital ID management features. For example, from Outlook 2003 you can publish your digital ID (certificate) to the Exchange Global Address List (the Global Catalog) and request a new digital ID with an online CA.

When you click the Get a Digital ID... button in the Outlook 2003 Security Options, Outlook redirects you to the Office Marketplace Web site. From there you can, for example, request a digital ID with the United States Postal Services (USPS). To publish your personal certificates to the GAL, go to Tools, Options, Security Options, and select Publish to GAL... To disable this feature, change the Registry setting HKEY_LOCAL_MACHINE\SOFTWARE\Microsoft\Office\11.0\Outlook\Security\PublishToGalDisabled (REG_DWORD) to 1. Table 17.7 gives an overview of

Table 17.6 *Outlook Client S/MIME Features*

	Outlook 2003	Outlook Express 6.0	Outlook Web Access
Mail Connectivity Protocol	MAPI/RPC, POP3, IMAP4, SMTP, HTTP	POP3, IMAP4, SMTP	HTTP
Encryption key recovery	Yes (if combined with a Windows Server 2003 CA)	Yes (if combined with a Windows Server 2003 CA)	Yes (if combined with a Windows Server 2003 CA)
CRL Distribution Point (CDP) support	Yes	Yes	Yes
Private key storage	Data Protection API, optional Syskey protection	Data Protection API, optional Syskey protection	Data Protection API, optional Syskey protection
Support for clear and opaque signing	Yes	Yes	No, only clear signing
Support for secure receipts	Yes	No	No
Support for security labels	Yes	No	No
Certificate Provider	KMS, internal CA, commercial CA	Internal CA, commercial CA	Internal CA, commercial CA
Certificate renewal	Can be automated (if using Windows Server 2003 and XP user autoenrollment)	Can be automated (if using Windows Server 2003 and XP user autoenrollment)	Can be automated (if using Windows Server 2003 and XP user autoenrollment)
LDAP support	Yes	Yes	No

other Outlook 2003 S/MIME settings that can be controlled through registry settings. All of the settings are located in the HKEY_LOCAL_MACHINE\SOFTWARE\Microsoft\Office\11.0\Outlook\Security registry folder.

Exchange 2003 adds S/MIME capabilities to OWA. To use S/MIME in OWA, you must run IE 6 with Service Pack 1 or later. You enable OWA support in the configuration options of your OWA client. When you enable it, an ActiveX control providing the S/MIME logic will be downloaded from the OWA server to your client. You must be a power user or local administrator to install the control. If you are using OWA from different machines, you will have to enable it (and download the ActiveX control) on every machine (as illustrated in Figure 17.13). When one user has

Table 17.7 *Outlook 2003 S/MIME-Related Registry Settings*

Setting	Type – Value	Meaning
AlwaysEncrypt	REG_DWORD – 0,1	When set to 1, all outgoing messages are encrypted; corresponds to Encrypt message content and attachments GUI checkbox.
AlwaysSign	REG_DWORD – 0,1	When set to 1, all outgoing messages are signed; corresponds to Add digital signature to this message GUI checkbox.
ClearSign	REG_DWORD – 0,1	When set to 1, clear signing is used for all outgoing messages, corresponds to Send this message as cleartext signed GUI checkbox.
RequestSecureReceipt	REG_DWORD – 0,1	When set to 1, secure receipts are requested for all outgoing messages, corresponds to Request S/MIME receipt for this message GUI checkbox.

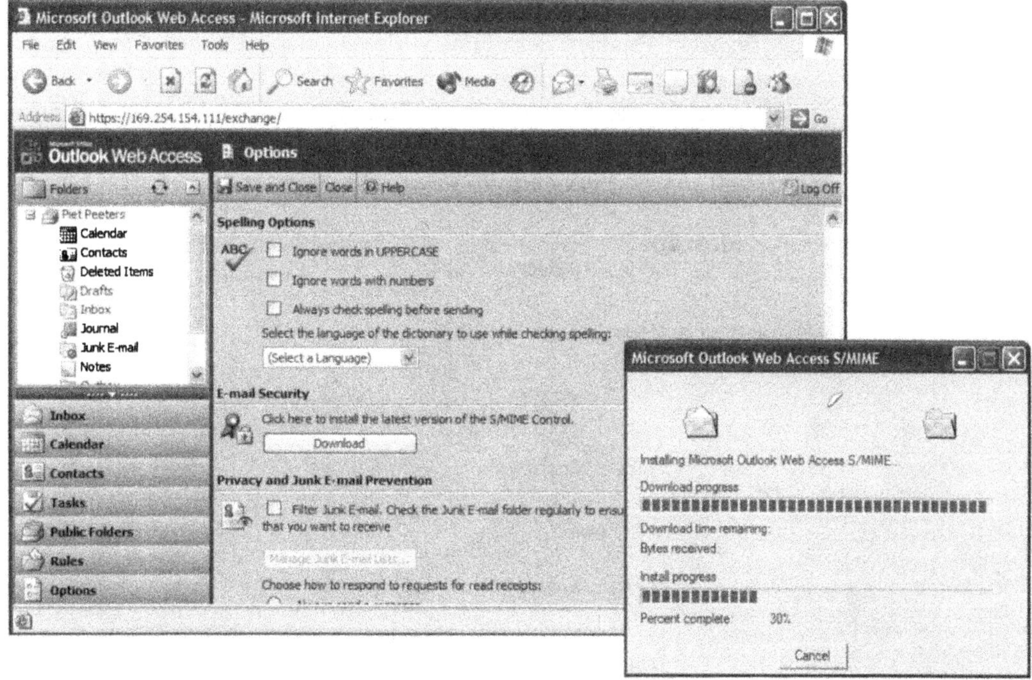

Figure 17.13 *Setting up OWA S/MIME support.*

downloaded the control to, for example, a kiosk machine, it will be available to all users of that machine. OWA users can obtain S/MIME certificates in exactly the same way as when they are using Outlook 2003 or Outlook Express 6.0: All of the certificate enrollment methods described in Chapter 15 also apply to OWA S/MIME. Once users have enabled their OWA client to use S/MIME, the OWA interface and message properties will be extended to add digital signatures and encrypt the message content. A very nice feature of the OWA S/MIME support is that all certificate-related processing (such as revocation checking) is done on the Exchange 2003 server side. By default, all OWA traffic occurs over a secured HTTP over SSL communication channel (https).

17.2.4 Clear and opaque signing

As Table 17.5 showed, you can use the application/pkcs7-MIME content type or a combination of the multipart/signed and the application/pkcs7-signature content types to sign a message body. Each application implements a different signature type: clear or opaque. These two signature types let S/MIME-enabled and non-S/MIME-enabled mail clients exchange signed messages. A clear signed message separates the digital signature from the signed data. An opaque signed message binds the signature and the message in one binary file. Figure 17.14 illustrates the difference between a clear and an opaque signed S/MIME message.

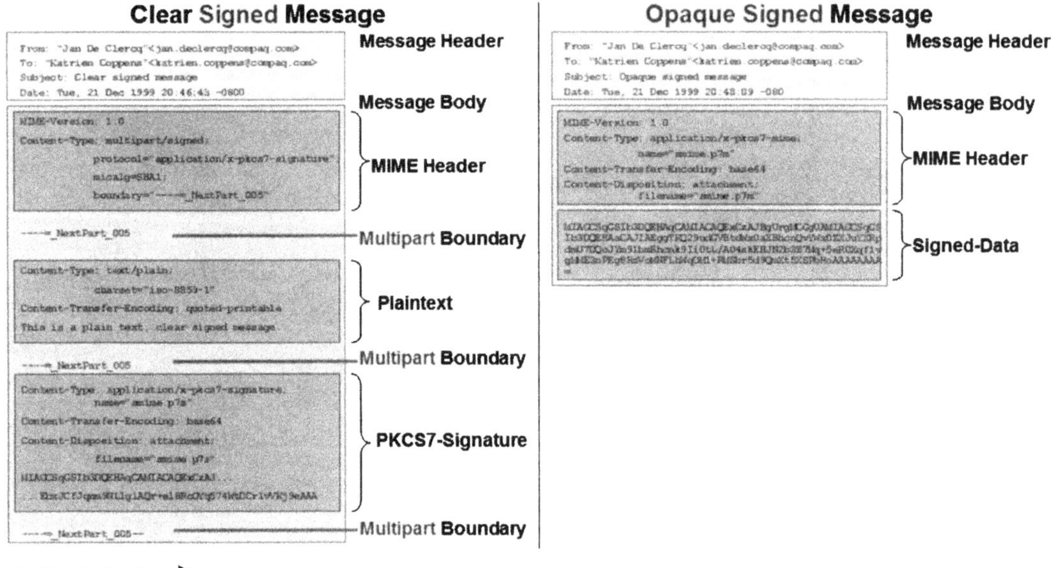

Figure 17.14 *Clear versus opaque S/MIME signing.*

Both S/MIME-enabled and non-S/MIME-enabled mail clients can read clear signed messages. Opaque signed messages can only be read by S/MIME-enabled mail clients. Opaque signed messages have an important advantage over clear signed messages because intermediate gateways cannot change the hidden plaintext section of an opaque signed message's MIME body.

When you send S/MIME clear signed messages from a MAPI mail client (Outlook 2003) to an SMTP-MIME mail client (Outlook Express), the sending client uses MAPI rules to format the message. An SMTP gateway will transform the message to MIME format. The transformation also changes the plaintext part of the message, which causes the receiving client's signature check to return an invalid outcome, as if an intrusion had occurred. This invalidation error occurs less often in Exchange 2000 and Exchange 2003 than in Exchange Server 5.5. The Exchange 2000 and Exchange 2003 streaming database stores native MIME messages, so Exchange 2000 and Exchange 2003 transform MIME messages to MAPI messages only when absolutely necessary (e.g., when a MAPI client wants to read a MIME-formatted message).

As a rule of thumb, send clear signed messages when you do not know the recipient's S/MIME capabilities. Send opaque signed messages to S/MIME-enabled clients or when sending messages from a native MAPI client through SMTP or X.400 gateways (e.g., messages between two MAPI clients across an SMTP site link, messages from a MAPI client to an IMAP4/SMTP client).

You can select either signing method in Outlook 2003 and Outlook Express 6.0. In Outlook 2003, you set the method in the message options or in the global security options (as illustrated in Figure 17.15). In Outlook Express 6.0, you set the signing method in the mail client's Advanced Security options (as illustrated in Figure 17.16). Outlook Web Access only supports clear signing.

17.2.5 Enhanced Security Services

RFC 2634 specifies four optional security service extensions, also known as Enhanced Security Services (ESS), for S/MIME. These services include secure receipts and security labels. Microsoft supports some of these extensions in Outlook 2003 and Outlook Express 6.0. The extensions were first introduced in SR1a for Outlook 2000.

Secure receipts (which you should not confuse with Outlook's delivery receipts or read receipts) provide "nonrepudiation of reading," giving you

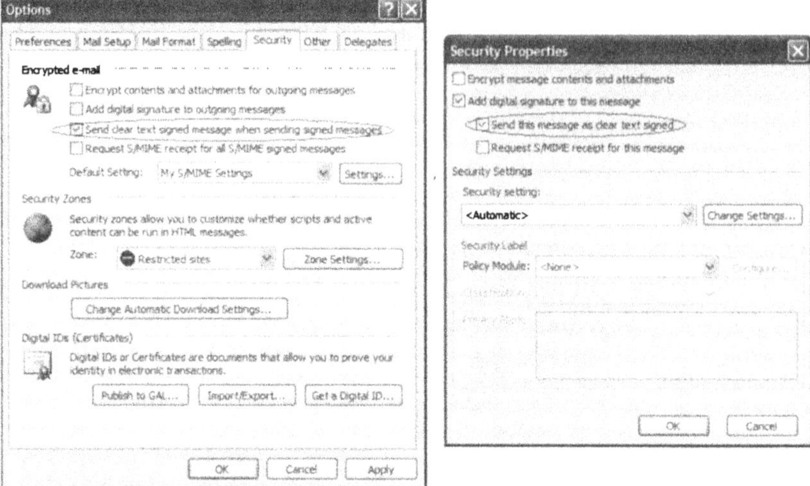

Figure 17.15 *Setting opaque and clear signing message properties in Outlook 2003.*

cryptographic proof that the intended recipient has read and verified a signed message. A secure receipt is signed, meaning that when you receive a message and reply to it using a signed or secure receipt, you sign the receipt using a private key. You cannot deny having done so because only you can access and use it. A secure receipt takes three steps in its travels. First, you generate and send a message, specifying a secure receipt. Next, the recipient responds to the secure receipt request. Finally, you receive the secure receipt.

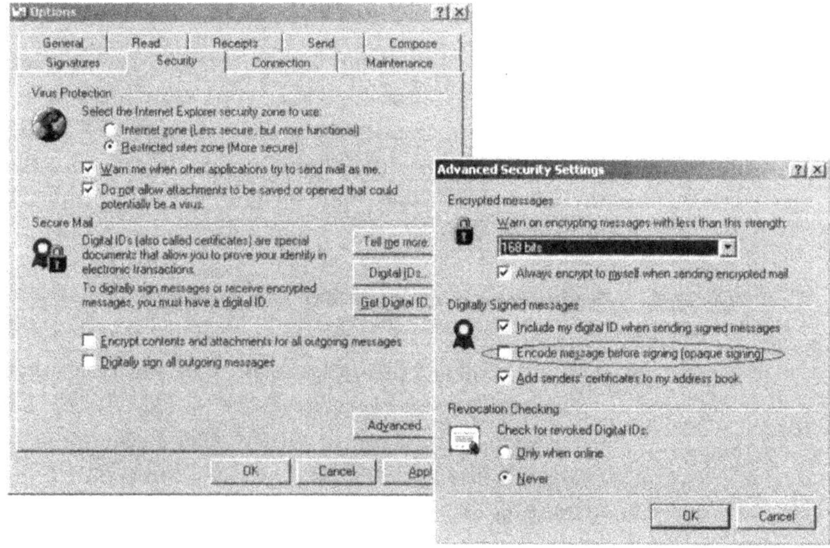

Figure 17.16 *Setting opaque and clear signing message properties in Outlook Express 6.0.*

You can set the secure receipt request for signed only or signed and encrypted messages. The message can be clear or opaque signed. You cannot make secure receipts receiver-dependent—if you set "Request S/MIME receipt for this message," it applies to all recipients. Also, secure receipts always return to the message's sender; it is not possible to set another return mailbox. You can make secure receipts the default by checking the "Request S/MIME receipt for all S/MIME signed messages" box in Outlook's security options.

By default, Outlook 2003 automatically sends a secure receipt when you open the message and when the system can cryptographically verify the message signature. If you add the Registry value HKEY_LOCAL_MACHINE\SOFTWARE\Microsoft\Office\11.0\Outlook\Security\RespondToReceiptRequests (REG_DWORD) and set it to 1, Outlook prompts you before sending a secure receipt: "A request has been made to send an S/MIME receipt when the message has been verified. Do you want to send an S/MIME receipt?"

To verify a secure receipt—to cryptographically verify the receipt's signature and instruct Outlook to check the receipt's content against the original—you must open the receipt. If the original message is not in the Sent Items folder, Outlook prompts you to find it. If you cannot find the original message, the secure receipt verification fails. If verification succeeds, Outlook 2003 automatically adds tracking information to the original message, as Figure 17.17 shows. Tracking information enables easy and centralized receipt status checking.

A security label, a kind of tagging system for e-mail messages, defines a message content's sensitivity. As with secure receipts, you can set security labels on signed messages. The power of the security label feature lies in its ability to restrict a user's access to a mail message, which is a standard requirement for messaging systems in military environments. The military,

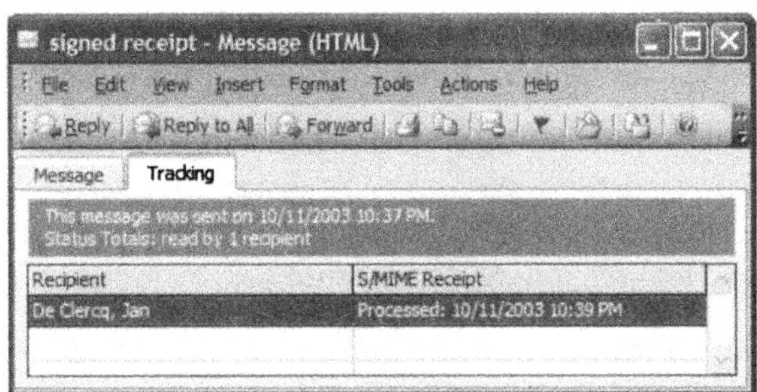

Figure 17.17 *S/MIME signed receipt tracking information.*

which does not want a sergeant—even if that sergeant is a system administrator—to have access to a general's mail, conceived of many of the concepts that RFC 2634 defines and SR1a implements.

In Outlook 2003, Microsoft provides a UI that lets you attach security labels to the messages you send. In addition to the UI, you need two things to implement security labels: (1) security policy modules, which define the classification levels, and (2) client-side logic, which enforces the security labels based on a user's classification level. Because security policies differ for each organization, Microsoft does not provide the logic for security labels out of the box. Microsoft provides a sample policy and a policy module design document in the MS Office SDK.

17.2.6 S/MIME and other SMTP security aspects

When you are planning for a complete SMTP security solution, you should look after more than just an S/MIME implementation. You must also think about content blocking, virus scanning, user blocking, and mail archiving:

- Content blocking deals with policy enforcement on mail content. Exchange 2003 comes with important new SPAM-blocking functionality. Content blocking support can also be found in products from companies such as Tumbleweed and Symantec.
- User blocking enables you to define rules on the SMTP gateway level to determine to which internal or external recipients users can send mail messages and from which internal or external senders users can receive mail messages. This functionality is also included in Exchange 2003. Products offering content blocking typically also provide advanced user-blocking functionalities.
- Virus protection (AV) software scans mail messages for viruses. A best practice is to provide virus scanning on different levels and to use different scanning engines (remember the principle of defense in depth). Numerous AV products are available that can integrate with Exchange 2003 and Outlook 2003 (Symantec, McAfee, and Antigen).
- Mail archiving copies every incoming and outgoing message into a special archival repository. Archiving is a legal requirement in many companies. Archival solutions for Exchange are available from companies such as Ixos, CommVault, KVS, and Essential.

An important detail to keep in mind is that end-to-end encryption and AV/content scanning are mutually exclusive. You can, however, combine the three security requirements by implementing encryption on the gateway level. This means that a message will be scanned for viruses and on content before it is encrypted, and vice versa for incoming messages. Products that can offer S/MIME functionality on the gateway level are available from companies such as Tumbleweed and ZipLip.

17.3 Leveraging smart cards and USB tokens for PKI-enabled applications

Windows 2000, Windows XP, and Windows Server 2003 can support both smart cards and USB tokens. Although these two device types have a different form factor and typically use a different computer connection interface, they both offer the same service: secure hardware-based PKI credential (private keys and certificates) storage.

Unfortunately, not every Windows PKI-enabled application supports smart card or USB token credential storage. As of this writing, the following Windows PKI-enabled applications are natively capable of dealing with smart card–enabled or USB token–based credentials:

- Secure mail using S/MIME from the Outlook mail client
- Smart card logon to a Windows Server 2003 domain (interactive logon)
- Smart card logon to Windows Server 2003 from the Windows Server 2003 Terminal Services client
- Smart card logon to a Windows Server 2003 domain using remote access
- Client authentication from Internet Explorer in SSL/TLS-based secure Web scenarios

Windows Server 2003 includes important enhancements to the way Windows administrators can use smart cards and USB tokens. Administrators can now access their credentials stored on a smart card or a USB token when running the dcpromo.exe command (to install AD), the net.exe commands, and the runas.exe command (to switch between different security identities), and when using terminal services.

Next we focus on the built-in Windows 2003 and Windows XP smart card and USB token support, Windows Server 2003 smart card logon, and third-party software that you can use to extend the Windows smart card or USB token management capabilities on the Windows Server 2003 platform. Unless mentioned otherwise, in the following sections "smart card" refers to both smart cards and USB tokens.

For a broader introduction to smart cards and USB tokens, refer to the following books:

- *Smart Card Security and Applications* by Mike Hendry, Artech House, 2001.
- *Authentication: From Passwords to Public Keys* by Richard E. Smith, Addison-Wesley, 2002.
- *Smart Cards: The Developer's Toolkit* by Tim Jurgensen and Scott Guthery, Prentice Hall, 2002.

17.3.1 Windows Server 2003 and Windows XP smart card support

For a complete list of all the smart card readers and USB tokens that are compatible with Windows 2003 and Windows XP, refer to the Windows Hardware Compatibility List (HCL), available from http://www.microsoft.com/windows/catalog/ for Windows XP and http://www.microsoft.com/windows/catalog/server/ for Windows Server 2003. All Windows Server 2003 and Windows XP compatible smart card readers support the PC/SC smart card interface. More information on the PC/SC smart card interface standard is available from http://www.pcscworkgroup.com/.

Out-of-the-box Windows Server 2003 supports smart cards from Gemplus, Infineon, and Schlumberger. The support for smart cards depends on the availability of a driver and a smart card Cryptographic Service Provider (CSP).[4] Both software components enable the operating system to communicate with the card for credential storage, cryptographic, and configuration operations. Smart cards and USB tokens from other vendors (ActivCard, Datakey, eAlladin, and Spyrus) are supported if you add the appropriate drivers and CSPs.

Most smart cards and tokens come with special management software allowing you to configure different card or token properties such as the PIN code. When you associate a PIN code with a smart card, you bind the card to the entities knowing the PIN code—a process that is known as smart card personalization. Most management software also allows you to set the number of bad PIN entry attempts after which the card is locked.

4. CSPs and CryptoAPI were explained in Chapter 13 of this book.

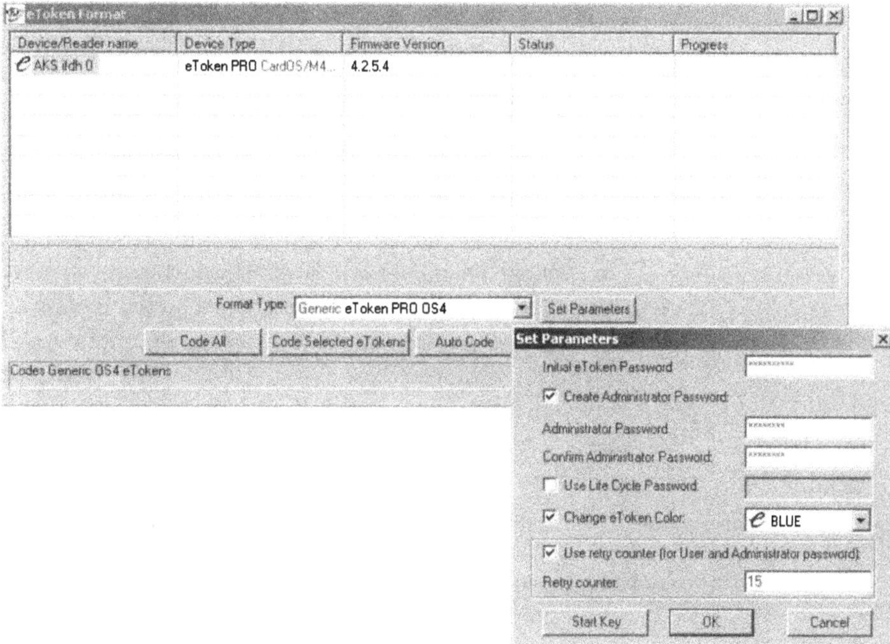

Figure 17.18 *eAlladin eToken Format utility.*

Figure 17.18 shows the token management utility eToken Format, which is made available by eAlladin together with its eToken USB tokens.

17.3.2 Enrolling for smart card-based credentials

In a Windows Server 2003 environment, a user can enroll for smart card credentials (certificates and private keys), provided he or she has the appropriate permissions on the smart card certificate templates and provided the templates are available on the CA. To enroll for smart card credentials, a user can use any of the enrollment methods mentioned in Chapter 15.

Windows Server 2003 comes with two default smart card-related certificate templates: smart card user and smart card logon. Besides SSL/TLS client authentication and smart card logon, the smart card user template offers support for secure e-mail. Smart card certificates are visible in a user's certificate store. When a smart card is plugged in, CryptoAPI will automatically copy the smart card certificates to the user's certificate store. CryptoAPI will only propagate the first certificate on the smart card to the user MY certificate store container. It's up to the Cryptographic Service Providers (CSPs) to propagate other certificates stored on the smart card.

An alternative is to let the user certificates and private keys be loaded centrally by an administrator with a special enrollment agent certificate. This is what Microsoft calls enrollment using a smart card enrollment station. Given the importance of smart card enrollment from a security point of view and given the difficulty of the user certificate enrollment procedure in general, the use of a smart card enrollment station is the preferred way to enroll users for smart card–based credentials in a corporate environment.

The smart card enrollment station interface is Web-based (it is illustrated in Figure 17.19). It is accessible from the default certificate server Web interface (provided that you are using an enterprise CA) by selecting the "Request a certificate for a smart card on behalf of another user by using the smart card certificate enrollment" option (which is available from the advanced certificate request menu option). Only administrators who have an enrollment agent certificate in their personal certificate store can request smart card certificates on behalf of another user. Smart card certificate

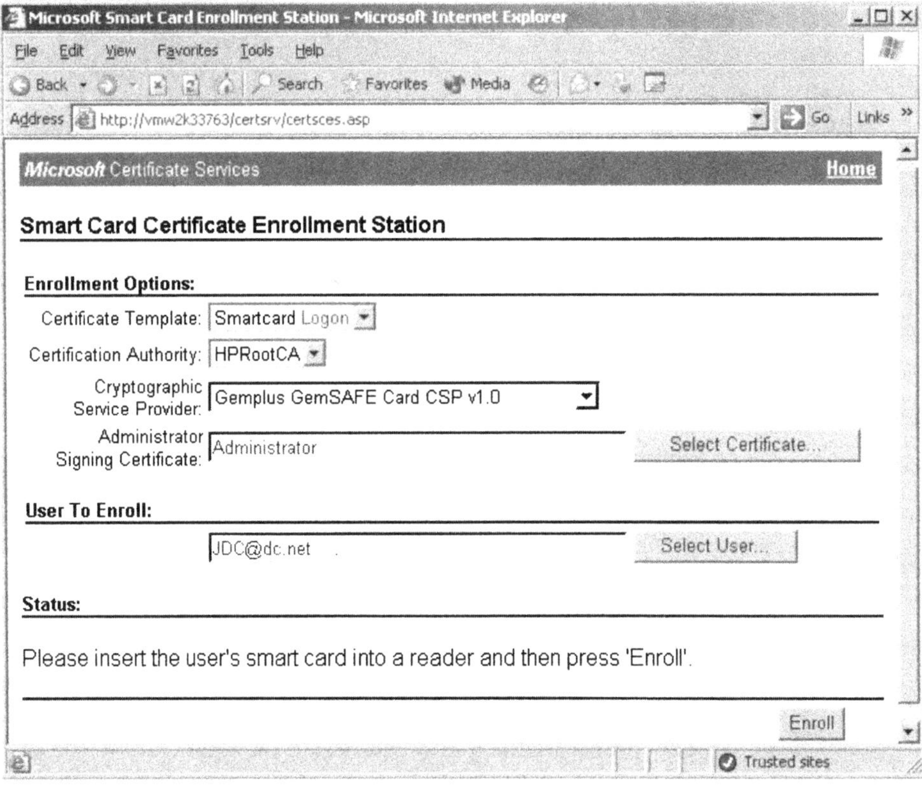

Figure 17.19 *Smart card certificate enrollment station interface.*

requests are signed using the enrollment agent's private key. The CA validates the requests using the enrollment agent's corresponding public key. If you check the access control settings on the enrollment agent certificate template, you will notice that by default only domain and enterprise administrators can enroll for an enrollment agent certificate.

By now it should be clear that enrollment agent certificates and smart card enrollment stations should be handled with extreme caution. An administrator with an enrollment agent certificate can impersonate anyone in the corporate network. He or she is the one generating smart card credentials, so he or she can also use them on behalf of a user to log on. If someone succeeds in logging on to an enrollment station using an administrator's credentials, he or she can do even more harm. He or she can request smart card certificates on behalf of anyone in the organization and impersonate anyone on machines where a smart card reader is available. That is why it is advisable to install a smart card enrollment station on a dedicated highly secured machine, limit the number of enrollment agent administrators, use a special CA to issue smart card certificates, implement strict access control settings on the enrollment agent certificate templates, and write special security policies regulating the use of enrollment agent certificates and smart card enrollment stations.

17.3.3 Smart card logon

Smart card logon in Windows 2000 and Windows Server 2003 is based on an extension to the Kerberos protocol, called PKINIT, which stands for use of Public Key technology for Initial authentication. The details of PKINIT were explained in Chapter 5 on Kerberos. Remember that in PKINIT all occurrences of the hashed password in the initial Kerberos authentication sequences are replaced by a user's public and private keys.

The use of smart cards for identification offers the following advantages:

- Smart cards offer a user identification alternative that is much stronger than plain password identification. Smart card logon is based on two-factor authentication: It combines knowledge (of an alphanumeric PIN code) and possession (of the smart card).
- Smart card logon is more difficult to break. The smart card logon sequence relies on asymmetric keying material instead of symmetric crypto-based hashed passwords.
- Smart cards offer secure and tamper-resistant credential storage. The user's credentials (private keys and certificates) never leave the card.

Theoretically, all critical calculations involving the private key also occur only on the card itself.

- Smart cards can provide roaming of credentials. A user can log on and have access to his or her credentials from every system that has a smart card reader installed.

Installing a smart card reader on a Windows 2000, Windows XP, or Windows Server 2003 machine will change the GINA (the screen that pops up when you press <CTRL>-<ALT>-<DEL>), as illustrated in Figure 17.20 for Windows Server 2003.

The easiest way to set up smart card logon is to use a Windows enterprise CA. An enterprise CA automates most of the enrollment-related tasks, such as publishing the certificate to AD and linking it to the user's Windows account. Smart card logon certificates can also be issued by third-party CAs (e.g., an Entrust or Baltimore CA). How to do this is explained in the Microsoft Knowledge Base article Q281245 available from http://support.microsoft.com/default.aspx?scid=kb;en-us;281245. In order for a smart card logon to work, both the domain controller, validating the smart card authentication request, and the user, logging on using a smart card, must have valid certificates. Valid means that both certificates must chain up to a trusted CA and that none of the certificates in the domain controller's or the user's certificate chains should be revoked. In order to check for revocation, the CRLs must be available and valid. For more information on certificate validation, please refer to Chapter 15.

A nice feature of smart card logon in Windows 2000, Windows XP, and Windows Server 2003 is that OS behavior for smart card removal can be set. The smart card removal behavior can be configured in the machine Security Options of the Domain, Site, OU, and Local Computer GPO objects at the following location: Computer Configuration\

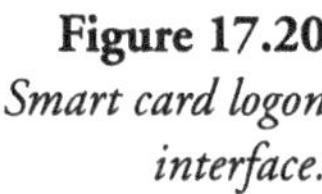

Figure 17.20
Smart card logon interface.

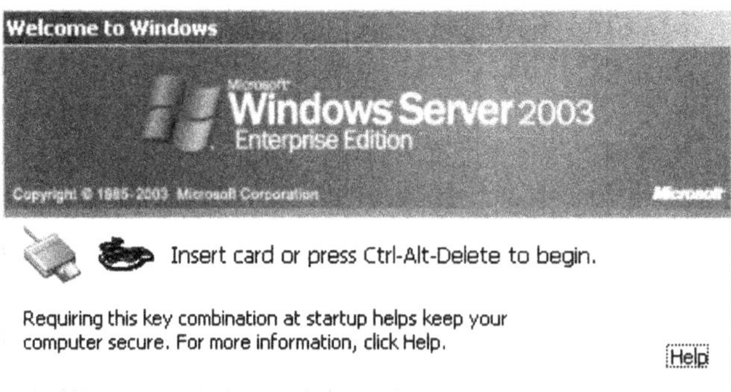

Windows Settings\Security Settings\Local Policies\Security Options. The values that can be set are No Action, Lock Workstation, and Force Logoff.

Windows 2000 and Windows Server 2003 also allow an administrator to force the use of a smart card for interactive logon. By default, a user who has a smart card can still log on using his or her password. To do so, check the "Smart card is required for interactive logon" box in the user object account properties or set the "interactive logon: Require smart card" security option in the computer portion of the GPO security settings.

17.3.4 Smart card management systems

For many large enterprises, the built-in Windows 2000 and Windows Server 2003 smart card management features are not enough. They are looking for advanced smart card and token management capabilities, such as:

- Assigning smart cards or tokens to users. In a Windows environment this means linking the smart card or token (and not just the PKI credentials) to an AD user account.
- Keeping track of the smart card or token content and usage.
- Defining which PKI-enabled applications can be used with a user's smart card or token.
- Handling lost smart cards or tokens.
- Formatting or reformatting smart cards or tokens.

Table 17.8 provides an overview of software vendors selling smart card management system software.

Table 17.8 *Smart Card Management Software*

Vendor	Product	URL
ActivCard	ActivCard Identity Management System (AIMS)	http://www.activcard.com
Alacris	idNexus Smart Card Management Module	http://www.alacris.com
BellID	ANDiS	http://www.bellid.com
CardBase	Mascot	http://www.cardbase.com
Datakey	Card Management System (CMS)	http://www.datakey.com
eAlladin	Token Management System (TMS)	http://www.ealladin.com
Intercede	Edefice	http://www.intercede.co.uk

18

Windows Server 2003 Security Management

Security management is a critical security service that guarantees that the security settings and software on computer platforms and security infrastructure servers can be configured and maintained in an easy and coherent way. The security configuration together with the software that's allowed to run on a computer system are defined in a security policy. Computer platforms can become trusted platforms if the security policy is audited—this means checked for compliance by a trusted entity—at regular intervals. This is the goal of security-related auditing.

In what follows, we discuss how Microsoft supports security management in Windows Server 2003 in the following three key areas: security policy management, security patch management, and security-related auditing. This chapter specifically focuses on Microsoft security management solutions. A deeper coverage of third-party (non-Microsoft) security management solutions is beyond the scope of this book.

18.1 Security policy management

The security policy for a computer platform defines all security-related configuration settings for that platform. It includes all the configuration settings listed in Figure 18.1. As Figure 18.1 shows, Microsoft does not offer a single tool to deal with the configuration all security-related settings. Most of the settings can be configured using Group Policy Object (GPO) settings; others can be configured though the Security Configuration Editor; and some cannot be configured using a Microsoft security policy configuration tool.

Next we introduce the security policy life cycle. The other sections contain an overview of the different security policy management tools available in the Windows Server 2003 and Windows XP platforms. We discuss

<table>
<tr><td>File ACLs</td><td>Registry ACLs</td><td>AD ACLs</td><td>Share ACLs</td><td>AV settings</td><td>Port/IPSec settings</td></tr>
<tr><td>User rights</td><td>Security options</td><td>ISAPI filters</td><td>Services</td><td>Audit settings</td><td>Browser security</td></tr>
<tr><td>Zone security</td><td colspan="2">Group membership, account policies</td><td>Trusted certificates</td><td>Patch levels</td><td>Software lockdown</td></tr>
<tr><td>EFS settings</td><td colspan="2">App security (Office macro, IE, etc.)</td><td colspan="2">Server settings (TS, DHCP, DNS, etc.)</td><td>Password policy</td></tr>
</table>

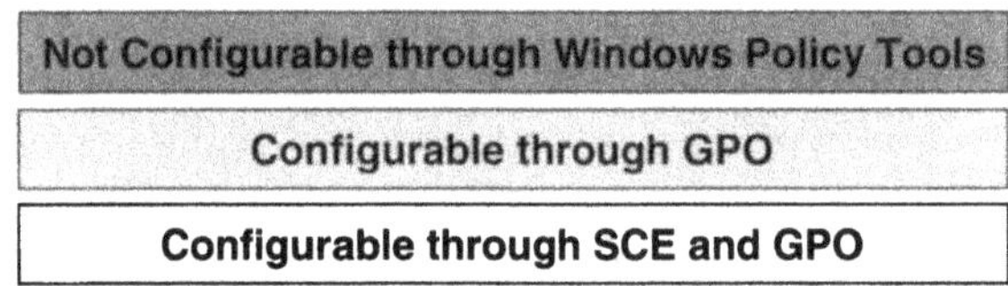

Figure 18.1 *Coverage of security-related configuration settings by Windows security policy management tools.*

Group Policy Objects (GPOs), the Security Configuration Editor and Analysis tool (SCE-SCA), the Security Configuration Wizard (SCW), and the Microsoft Baseline Security Analyzer (MBSA). We also look at third-party security policy management tools that can supplement the Microsoft tools.

18.1.1 The security policy life cycle

The life cycle of a Windows security policy can be split into several different phases:

- Policy creation: During this phase, security administrators define the security configuration of a Windows platform. Typically, a different security policy is defined for each machine type in the enterprise: workstations, file servers, and mail servers.
- Analysis: During this phase, security administrators validate the security configuration of a Windows platform against the settings defined in the security policy.
- Enforcement: During this phase, the security settings defined in the security policy are enforced on the different Windows platforms.
- Reporting: This phase deals with the generation of security policy compliance reports.

- Monitoring: This phase deals with the generation of real-time alerts when a machine's security settings are changed.

18.1.2 Group Policy and Group Policy Objects

Group Policy refers to a group of software technologies that allow centralized configuration and change management of user and computer environments. Through its tight integration with Active Directory, Group Policy Objects (GPOs) are highly scalable and extensible. Microsoft introduced Group Policy in Windows 2000.

Group Policy covers six major system management areas: registry setting management, software deployment, folder redirection, scripts, software restriction policy, and security settings management. Software restriction policies were added in Windows Server 2003 (and discussed in detail in Chapter 11).

The basic unit of Group Policy is a Group Policy Object (GPO), a collection of policy configuration settings that can be linked to an Active Directory container (a domain, site, or OU) or to a local machine. The latter GPO type is referred to as a Local GPO (LGPO). The administrative interface for GPO management is the MMC Group Policy snap-in, also known as the Group Policy Editor (GPE), which is illustrated in Figure 18.2.

Windows 2000 and Windows Server 2003 come with two predefined GPOs: the default domain controllers and the default domain policy GPO.

- The default Domain Policy GPO is the GPO that is automatically applied to every user and computer object in a Windows 2000 or Windows Server 2003 domain. It is linked to an AD domain object. The default domain policy is the only policy that can be used to control the security settings (password quality, account lockout, and so forth) of AD account objects (also known as global accounts)
- The default Domain Controllers GPO is the GPO that is automatically applied to every Windows 2000 and Windows Server 2003 domain controller. It is linked to the Domain Controllers Organizational Unit (OU) container.

Next we briefly introduce the major GPO changes in Windows Server 2003. Afterward we look at how you can use GPOs for security policy management. For more information on GPOs and GPO settings and to learn more about the GPO design and the GPO application process, see the information contained in the Microsoft Technet library or Chapter 7 of my previous book, *Mission-Critical Active Directory*.

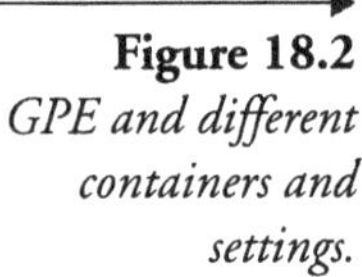

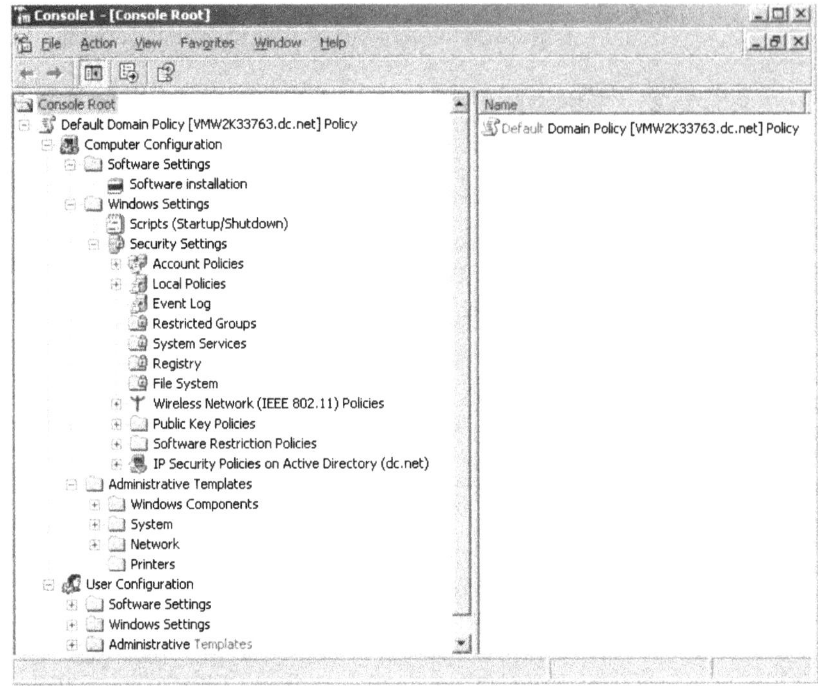

Figure 18.2 *GPE and different containers and settings.*

Key Windows Server 2003 Group Policy changes

Windows Server 2003 includes important GPO enhancements that improve administrators' ability to design, manage, and troubleshoot GPOs. The following sections provide an overview of the key enhancements. We will not come back to software restriction policies, which were covered extensively in Chapter 11.

Group Policy Management Console

The Group Policy Management Console (GPMC) provides a unified view (illustrated in Figure 18.3) of GPOs, sites, domains, and OUs in an enterprise and can be used to manage either Windows Server 2003 or Windows 2000 domains. Because GPMC supports the new forest trust type, administrators can use it to manage GPOs in multiple forests from a single console. Until the release of GPMC, enterprises had to look at third-party tools to obtain a unified Group Policy management interface. A good example is FullArmor's FAZAM 2000 software.

GPMC comes with an HTML-based reporting feature and provides GPO backup, restore, and copy support. GPMC also provides a set of

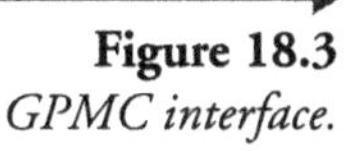

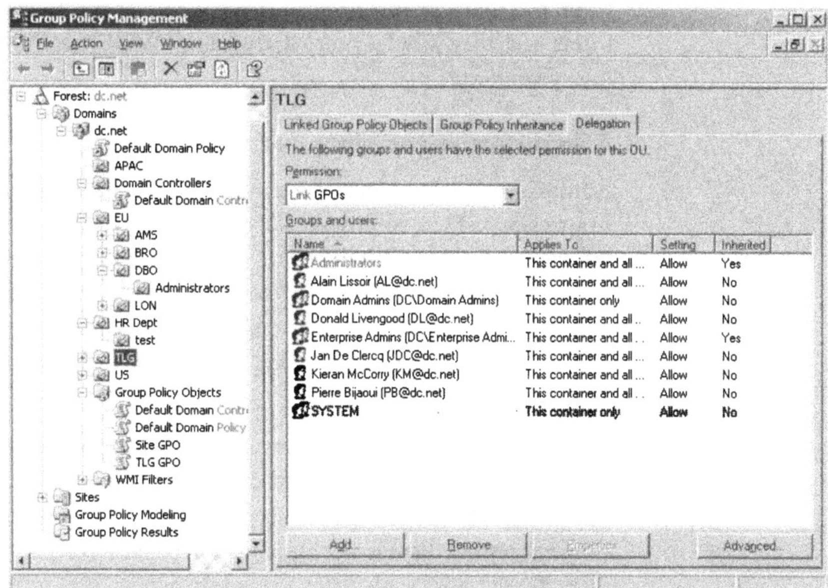

Figure 18.3
GPMC interface.

scripts that can be used to automate GPO operations at the command line. Among its most powerful features are GPO results and modeling support. GPMC exposes the Resultant Set of Policy (RSoP) data. RSoP makes it easy for administrators to determine the resulting set of policies for a user or computer in both actual and what-if scenarios.

GPMC runs on Windows XP Professional SP1 and Windows Server 2003. In Windows XP Professional, you must have Service Pack 1 and the .NET Framework installed before installing the GPMC. The tool can be downloaded from the Microsoft downloads Web site.

WMI filters

Windows 2000 supports a GPO feature, known as GPO filtering, that allows you to define to which users and computers a GPO will be applied. This can be done by modifying the permissions on the GPO. In Windows XP and Windows Server 2003, Microsoft adds an additional filtering mechanism based on the Windows Management Instrumentation (WMI) interface.

A WMI GPO filter lets you dynamically determine the application scope of a GPO based the on properties of the target computer or user. You can, for example, create a WMI filter that only applies the GPO if the target computer is running Windows XP Service Pack 1. When using a WMI filter, the GPO is only applied if the result of the WMI query is true. WMI filters use the WMI Query Language (WQL), a WMI-specific SQL-like query language.

Administrative template changes

Administrative templates drive the configuration of Windows registry settings using GPOs. Windows Server 2003 provides a great deal of additional information about the different registry settings: Every setting now comes with an explain text. The text contains information about OS requirements and details about the effect of enabling or disabling the setting. The explain text is visible from the Extended GPO view or by double-clicking a setting and going to the Explain tab.

Not every administrative template setting can be applied to every Windows version. Windows Server 2003 GPO includes new features to expose this template versioning system in the interface. Under the hood, this versioning system builds on the supported keyword in administrative template files (*.adm). To filter the administrative template settings based on the Windows version requirements, right-click an administrative templates container, and then in the View menu, select Filtering (as illustrated in Figure 18.4).

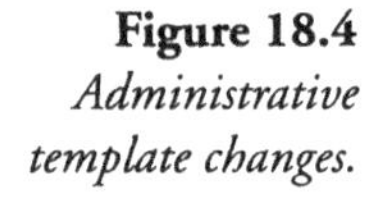

Figure 18.4 *Administrative template changes.*

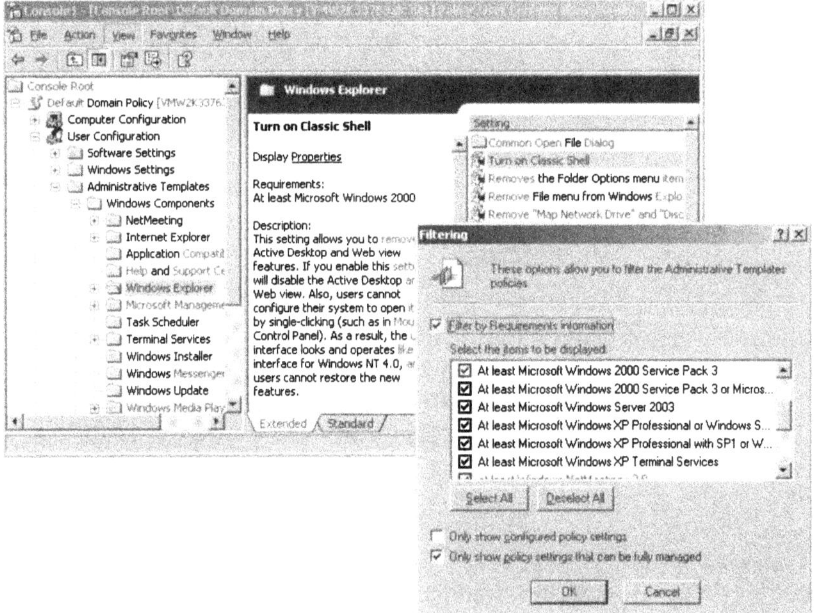

Command-line support

Administrators can now refresh policy settings from the command line using gpup*date, which replaces the Windows 2000 secedit /refreshpolicy.

Windows Server 2003 includes a new tool called dcgpofix.exe to restore the default domain and the default domain controllers GPOs to their original state—meaning their default state after a fresh Windows Server 2003 installation.

Using GPOs for security policy management

The GPO security policy management portion includes configuration options for the following security policy areas (Table 18.1 contains an overview):

- Account policies to configure password, account lockout, and Kerberos settings.
- Local policies to configure auditing, user rights, and security options.
- Event log settings to configure the properties of the application, system, and security logs.
- Restricted group settings to configure the membership of security sensitive groups.
- System services settings to configure security and startup settings for services.
- Registry settings to configure security permissions on registry keys.
- File system settings to configure security permissions on files and folders.
- Wireless network settings to configure wireless network access policies.
- Public key policies to configure EFS recovery agents, trusted root CAs, user and machine certificate autoenrollment settings, and Certificate Trust Lists (CTLs).
- Software restriction policies to configure malicious mobile code protection rules.
- IP security policies to configure IPsec-related settings.

All of these settings can be configured from the Windows Settings\Security Settings GPO container (as illustrated in Figure 18.2). To configure local security policy settings on member servers, workstations, and stand-alone machines, you must use the local security policy settings MMC snap-in (illustrated in Figure 18.5). The wireless network settings and software restriction policies settings are new to Windows Server 2003. Only the soft-

Table 18.1 *GPO Security Settings Containers and Equivalent NT4 Administration Tool*

GPO Security Settings Subcontainer (Windows 2000, Windows XP, and Windows Server 2003)	Equivalent NT4 Administration Tool (NT4)
Account policies	
Password policy	User manager => Policy/Account Policy
Account lockout	User manager => Policy/Account Policy
Kerberos policy*	N/A
Local policies	
Audit policy	User manager => Policy/Audit Policy
User rights assignment	User manager => Policy/User Rights
Security options	N/A
Event log*	Event Viewer => Log/Event Log Settings
Restricted groups*	N/A
System services*	Control Panel => Services
Registry	N/A
File system*	N/A
Wireless network policies*	N/A
Public key policies	N/A
Encrypting File System	N/A
Automatic Certificate Request Settings*	N/A
Trusted Root Certification Authorities*	N/A
Enterprise Trust*	N/A
Software restriction policies	N/A
IP security policies	N/A

* Not configurable on workstations, member servers, and stand-alone machines.

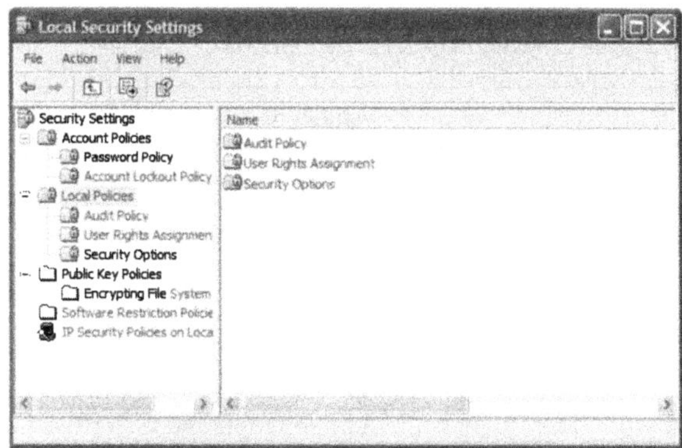

Figure 18.5 *Local security policy configuration tool.*

ware restriction policies and public key policies can be configured in both the user- and machine-portion of the GPOs; the other settings can only be configured in the machine-portion of the GPO.

In the GPO security policy management portion, Microsoft brought together the configuration of several security settings that before, in NT4, were spread across different administration tools. Table 18.1 gives an overview of the different security setting categories configurable through the Windows 2000, Windows XP, and Windows Server 2003 GPO security settings and their NT4 administration tool counterpart.

The Account policies in the GPO security policy management container deserve a bit more explanation. Account policies can refer to local accounts or domain accounts. Account policies for domain accounts can only be set in the Default Domain Policy. This means that password, account lockout, and Kerberos policies for domain accounts can only be defined once: on the domain level using the Default Domain Policy. Account policies that are set in other GPOs will not affect the domain account policy but local account policies. Local account policies means policies linked to accounts stored in the SAM (the local security database).

A very interesting category of GPO security settings is the Security Options, located in the Local Policies container. Windows Server 2003 comes with a lot of additional Security Options; they are listed in Table 18.2. I strongly advise you to look closely at these new security options. Administrators can also add additional security-related registry configuration settings to the Security Options. How to do this is explained in the Microsoft Knowledge Base article Q214752.

GPO security policy management is closely related to the Security Configuration Editor and Analysis tool (SCE/SCA), which is discussed later in

Table 18.2 *New Windows Server 2003 Security Options*

Security Option	Values
Guest account status	Enabled/Disabled
Limit local account use of blank passwords to console logon only	Enabled/Disabled
Allow undock without having to log on	Enabled/Disabled
Allowed to format and eject removable media	Administrators/Administrators and Power Users/ Administrators and Interactive Users
LDAP server signing requirements:	None/Require Signing
Refuse machine account password changes	Enabled/Disabled
Maximum machine account password age	x days
Require strong (Windows 2000 or later) session key	Enabled/Disabled
Require domain controller authentication to unlock workstation	Enabled/Disabled
Require smart card	Enabled/Disabled
Allow anonymous SID/Name translation	Enabled/Disabled
Do not allow anonymous enumeration of SAM accounts	Enabled/Disabled
Do not allow anonymous enumeration of SAM accounts and shares	Enabled/Disabled
Administrator account status	Enabled/Disabled
Do not allow storage of credentials or .NET Passports for network authentication	Enabled/Disabled
Let Everyone permissions apply to anonymous users	Enabled/Disabled
Remotely accessible registry paths	Names of registry paths
Remotely accessible registry paths and subpaths	Names of registry paths and subpaths
Restrict anonymous access to Named Pipes and Shares	Enabled/Disabled
Shares that can be accessed anonymously	share names
Sharing and security model for local accounts	Classic: local users authenticate as themselves / Guest: local users authenticate as Guest
Do not store LAN Manager hash value on next password change	Enabled/Disabled

Table 18.2 *New Windows Server 2003 Security Options (continued)*

Security Option	Values
LDAP client signing requirements	None/Negotiate Signing/Require Signing
Minimum Session Security for NTLM SSP-based (including secure RPC) clients	Require message integrity/Require message confidentiality/Require NTLMv2 session security/Require 128-bit encryption
Minimum Session Security for NTLM SSP-based (including secure RPC) servers	Require message integrity/Require message confidentiality/Require NTLMv2 session security/Require 128-bit encryption
Allow automatic administrative logon	Enabled/Disabled
Use Certificate rules on Windows executables for SRPs	Enabled/Disabled
Force strong key protection for user keys stored on the computer	User input is not required when new keys are stored and used/User is prompted when the key is first used/User must enter password each time they use a key
Use FIPS compliant algorithms for encryption, hashing, signing	Enabled/Disabled
Default owners for object created by members of the Administrators group	Administrators group/Object creator
Allow floppy copy and access to all drives and all folders	Enabled/Disabled
Require case-insensitivity for non-Windows subsystems	Enabled/Disabled
Optional subsystems	Subsystem names (Posix)

this chapter. GPOs complement the SCE/SCA by making it possible to enforce security policy settings on the domain, OU, and site level. Both the SCA and GPO security management use the same client-side extensions for security policy enforcement: the scecli.dll on Windows client platforms and the scesrv.dll on Windows servers. Both also use the same local security configuration database: secedit.sdb.

Both the GPO- and SCE-rooted security policy management support security configuration templates (*.inf files). These are security configuration-specific templates that can be easily exchanged between different GPOs and machines. The templates are stored in the %systemdrive%\winnt\security\templates directory. Like the administrative templates used for registry configuration (*.adm), the security configuration templates are customizable. To edit security configuration templates, you use a plaintext

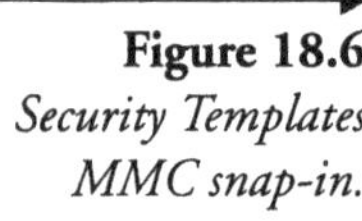

Figure 18.6
Security Templates MMC snap-in.

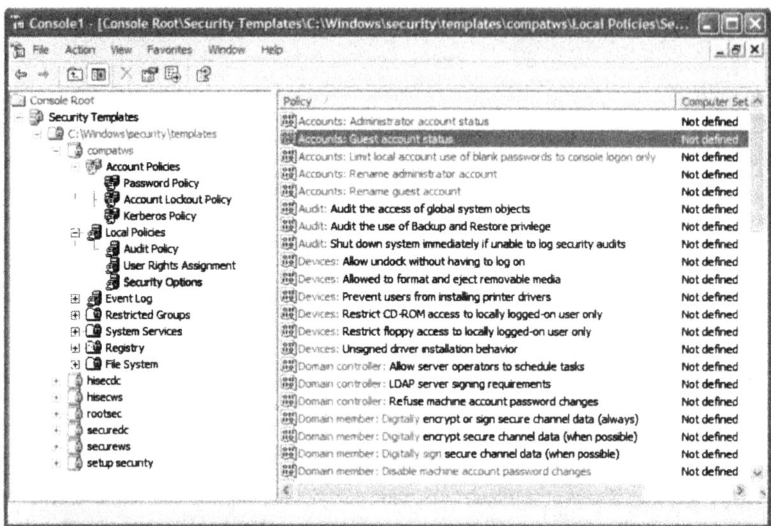

editor (like Notepad) or the Security Templates MMC snap-in, illustrated in Figure 18.6.

Microsoft provides two basic categories of security configuration templates: default and incremental security templates:

- Default security templates contain the default Windows security settings, as they are applied to a Windows system during a normal installation.
- Incremental security templates define higher or lower security levels; they can be used to bring a machine from the default security level to a higher or lower security level. The compatws.inf template, for example, loosens security on a Windows machine to allow applications to write to more registry keys. The hisecdc.inf template, on the other hand, tightens the security of a Windows domain controller. An incremental template should never be applied without first applying a default template. Microsoft defines three levels: compatible, secure, and high secure.

Each of these categories contains specific templates for a Windows workstation, server, and domain controller. The security configuration templates available in Windows are listed in Table 18.3.

To load a template in the GPO interface, right-click the security settings container and select import policy (as illustrated in Figure 18.7). The security settings are the only GPO settings that can be copy-pasted or imported-

Table 18.3 *Windows XP and Windows Server 2003 Security Templates*

Security Template Category	Template Name	Meaning
Default templates	DC security.inf	The default template for a Windows domain controller
	Setup security.inf	The default template for a Windows workstation
Incremental templates	Compatws.inf	Compatible incremental template for a Windows workstation. Relaxes security settings to deal with noncertified applications.
	Rootsec.inf	Applies default root permissions introduced in Windows XP to the OS partition and propagates them to child objects that are inheriting from the root.
	Securedc.inf	Secure incremental template for a Windows domain controller
	Securews.inf	Secure incremental template for a Windows workstation
	Hisecdc.inf	High Secure incremental template for a Windows domain controller
	Hisecws.inf	High Secure incremental template for a Window workstation

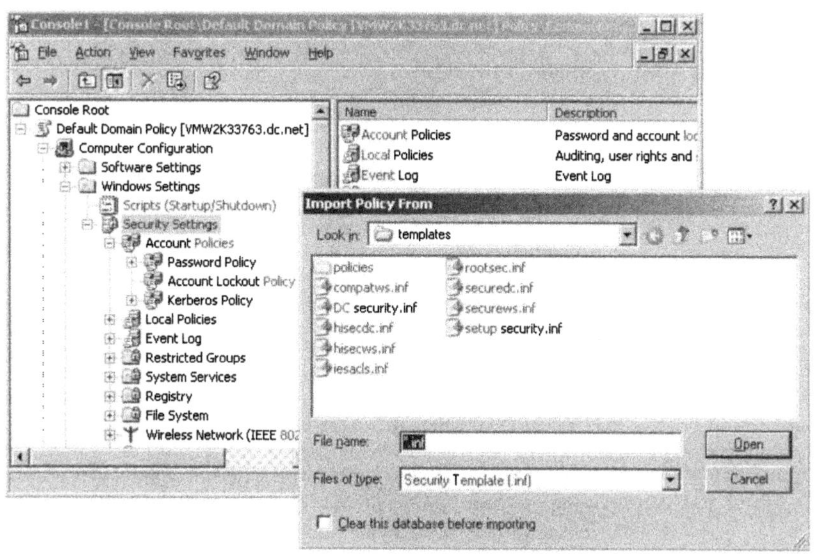

Figure 18.7 *Importing security templates for a GPO's security settings.*

exported between different GPOs.To export the security settings defined in a GPO, you must use the secedit tool with the /export switch.

18.1.3 Security Configuration Editor

The Security Configuration Editor and Analysis (SCA) tool can be used to edit and analyze the security settings on a Windows 2000, Windows XP, or Windows Server 2003 computer. SCA was introduced in SP4 for NT4; an updated version is provided with Windows 2000, Windows XP, and Windows Server 2003.

Using the SCA, an administrator can validate a computer's security settings against the values defined in a security template. He or she can also enforce the settings following the values defined in a security template. The security templates used by SCA are the ones used by the GPO security policy management section; they were explained in the previous section.

Like the GPO security policy management section, SCA uses the secedit.sdb security database. The SCA engine can be run from the Security Configuration and Analysis MMC snap-in or from the command prompt, using the secedit executable. Table 18.4 shows the secedit switches. Note that the secedit /refreshpolicy switch that was available in Windows 2000 to refresh GPOs has been replaced in Windows Server 2003 by the gpupdate tool.

Table 18.4 *Secedit Switches*

Secedit Switch	Meaning
`/analyze`	Analyze the security settings on a computer against the values defined in a security template.
`/configure`	Configure the security settings on a computer based on the values defined in a security template.
`/export`	Export security settings stored in secedit database.
`/import`	Import a security template into the secedit database.
`/validate`	Validate the syntax of a security template.
`/generaterollback`	Generate a rollback template with respect to a particular security template. When applying a security template to a computer, you have the option of creating a rollback template which, when applied, resets the security settings to the values before the configuration template was applied.

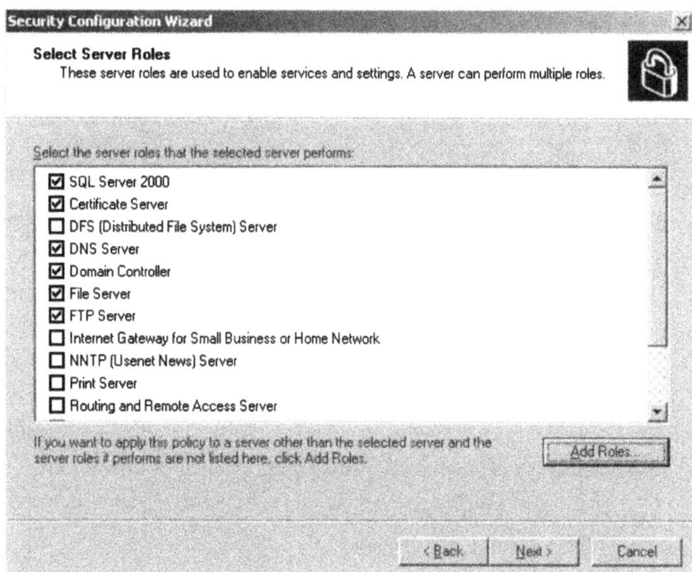

Figure 18.8 *Security Configuration Wizard.*

18.1.4 Security Configuration Wizard

The Security Configuration Wizard (SCW or secwiz.exe) allows administrators to easily create a baseline security policy for a Windows server based on the server's organizational role. SCW does not provide a complete Windows security policy coverage: instead it focuses on the network-related security policy settings. These include service configuration, and TCP and UDP port usage. The goal of the SCW is to help maximize the security of Windows server systems without sacrificing their required functionality. Microsoft refers to the SCW as a policy authoring tool, whose primary goal is to reduce the Windows attack surface.

The SCW constructs XML-formatted security policies for their different types of servers. These policies can be applied directly to a server using the wizard, or they can be transformed[1] into native scripts or security templates (*.inf) that can then be deployed on individual machines or via Group Policy. The SCW is linked to a database that's referred to as the SCW knowledge base. It is made up of different xml-formatted files. These files are stored in the %windir%/security/ssr/KBs folder (ssr refers to the initial name of the tool: secure server roles) and hold the preferred security policy

1. At the time of writing, the tool to transform the SCW's XML files to an *.inf file was not yet available.

configuration settings for different server roles. If you want you can add your own SCW knowledge base extensions.

Microsoft makes the Security Configuration Wizard (see Figure 18.8) available as a part of Service Pack 1 (SP1) for Windows Server 2003. SCW supports Windows 2000 and Windows Server 2003.

18.1.5 Microsoft Baseline Security Analyzer

You can use the Microsoft Baseline Security Analyzer (MBSA- mbsa.exe) tool to perform a security scan on NT4 and later Windows systems. The tool can be installed on any Windows 2000 or later system. Although the MBSA tool cannot be installed on an NT4 system, it can be run against an NT4 system that has at least NT4 Service Pack 4 installed. The tool's installation program (an *.msi file) can be downloaded for free from the Microsoft Web site. At the time of writing the latest MBSA release was version 1.1.1.

MBSA is a tool that can be run from both the Windows GUI and the command prompt (mbsacli.exe). It can analyze both the local and remote systems. It can scan for common security misconfigurations in the following products: Windows NT 4.0, Windows 2000, Windows XP, Windows Server 2003, Internet Information Server (IIS) 4.0, 5.0, and 6.0 SQL Server 7.0 and 2000, Internet Explorer (IE) 5.01 and later, and Office 2000 and XP. MBSA can also scan for missing security patches for Windows NT 4.0, Windows 2000, Windows XP, Windows Server 2003, IIS 4.0, 5.0 and 6.0, SQL Server 7.0 and 2000, Exchange 5.5 and 2000, IE 5.01 and later, and Windows Media Player 6.4 and later. Once a system is analyzed using MBSA, you must use other tools to deploy missing patches to the system (as explained in Section 18.2). More information on the MBSA tool is available in the following Microsoft Knowledge Base article: http://support.microsoft.com/default.aspx?scid=kb;en-us;q320454.

Running a security check against a system using the tool is as simple as starting the tool by double-clicking the desktop shortcut, clicking "Scan a computer," entering the IP address of the computer you want to scan, selecting the scan options (check for Windows vulnerabilities, weak passwords, IIS vulnerabilities, and so forth), and clicking "Start scan." Figure 18.9 shows a report as it is automatically generated by the MBSA tool at the end of a security scan. The MBSA reports are stored in an XML format in the %userprofile%\Securityscans file system folder. To run MBSA, the user must have local administrator access to the computer.

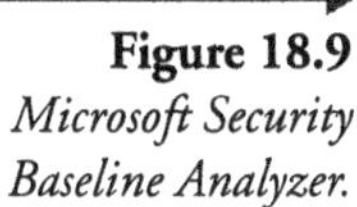

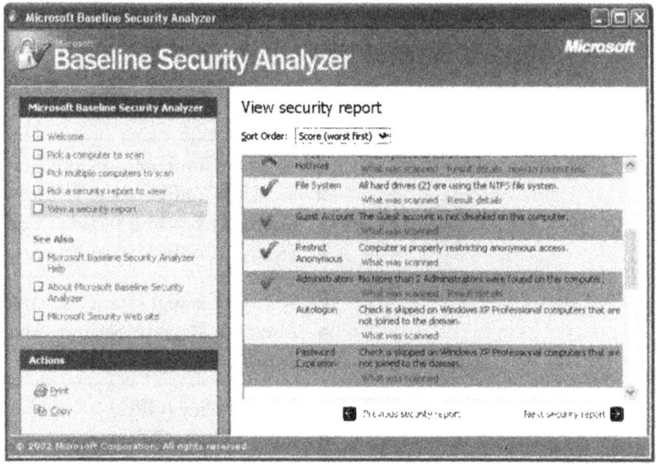

Figure 18.9 *Microsoft Security Baseline Analyzer.*

18.1.6 Third-party security policy management tools

Microsoft currently lacks the tools to centralize security policy management and to provide advanced management features such as real-time alerting. Table 18.5 provides a nonexhaustive overview of other third-party management tools that can provide such functionality for the Windows platform.

18.1.7 Security policy management: Overview

Table 18.6 provides an overview of the security policy management tools explained previously and the security policy life cycle phases for which they can be used. A fundamental engine that is called on for most of the security

Table 18.5 *Third-Party Security Policy Management Tools (Nonexhaustive)*

Third-Party Tool	More Information Is Available At...
Bindview Policy Compliance Center, Bindview Bv-Control	http://www.bindview.com/Products/PolicyComp/index.cfm
HP Openview Security Management	http://www.openview.hp.com
NetIQ VigilEnt Policy and Compliance Management	http://www.netiq.com/solutions/security/policy.asp

Table 18.6 *Security Policy Management: Overview*

Security Policy Life Cycle Phase	Tools
Policy Creation	■ Security Configuration and Analysis (SCA) tool ■ Security Configuration Wizard (SCW) ■ Microsoft Baseline Security Analyzer (MBSA) ■ Security Configuration Engine and database
Analysis	■ Security Configuration and Analysis tool (SCA) ■ Microsoft Baseline Security Analyzer (MBSA) ■ Security Configuration Engine and database
Enforcement	■ Group Policy (GPO) ■ Local Security Policy tool ■ Security Configuration Wizard (SCW) ■ Security Configuration Engine and database
Reporting	■ Security Configuration and Analysis tool (SCA) ■ Microsoft Baseline Security Analyzer (MBSA) ■ Security Configuration Engine and database
Monitoring	■ Third-party tools (NetIQ, Bindview, HP Openview)

policy life cycle phases is the security configuration engine and database. This engine and database are available on every Windows 2000, Windows XP, and Windows Server 2003 installation.

18.2 Security patch management

Keeping your systems up-to-date from a security patch point of view is a critical security requirement. Microsoft provides several tools to help with efficient security patch management: the Microsoft Baseline Security Analyzer (MBSA), Windows Update, the Software Update Services (SUS), SUS Feature Pack for SMS 2.0, and the qchain tool. All tools are discussed in more detail next.

All of these tools rely on the Security Patch Bulletin Catalog (mssecure.xml) to decide upon which security patches are already installed and which patches are required on a system. Every time a patch is installed, all of the tools call on hfnetchk.exe (explained below) to download the latest version of mssecure.xml from the Microsoft Web site.

18.2.1 Microsoft Baseline Security Analyzer

The Microsoft Baseline Security Analyzer (MBSA) was discussed earlier in Section 18.1.5. It also provides security patch scanning functionality. When starting a scan from the MBSA GUI, you have the option to check for security updates (as illustrated in Figure 18.10). When running MBSA from the command line (using mbsacli.exe), you must use the /hf switch to scan a machine's security patch status. Once a system is analyzed using MBSA, you must use other tools to deploy the missing patches to the system. To do so, you can use one of the tools explained next.

The command-line version of MBSA (mbsacli.exe) builds on an earlier MS scan tool, HFnetchk.exe, for its security patch management functionality. HFnetchk.exe is also known as the hotfix network checker. This tool was developed for Microsoft by a company called Shavlik. Microsoft does not provide updates to HFnetchk anymore; however, an up-to-date version of the tool can be downloaded from the Shavlik Web site at http://www.shavlik.com. Shavlik also provides an advanced version of the HFnetchk tool, called HFnetchkPro. This is a GUI tool that allows for the distribution and installation of missing security patches after an HFnetchk scan (something that cannot be done with MBSA).

MBSA can be integrated with the Microsoft Software Update Services (SUS)—SUS is explained in more detail in Section 18.2.3. This means that MBSA can check the enterprise SUS server for security updates instead of going to the Microsoft Web site. MBSA will automatically call upon the enterprise SUS server when its location has been configured in the system

Figure 18.10 *Checking for security updates from the MBSA.*

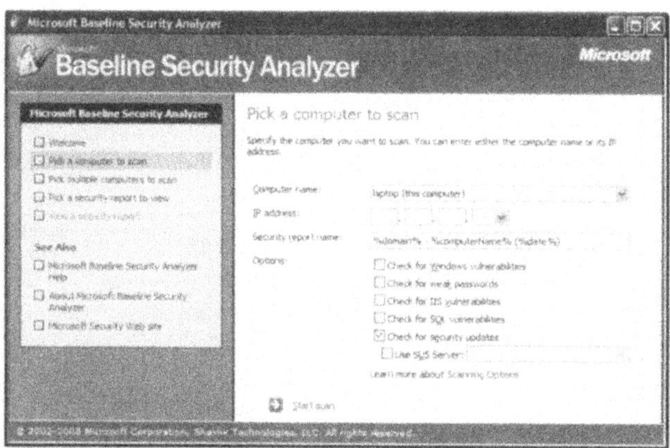

registry (this can be done using GPOs; see SUS section below). You can also force MBSA to go to a particular SUS server by typing the following at the command line:

```
Mbsacli.exe /hf /sus "http://<SUS_server_FQDN>".
```

The key difference with using MBSA without SUS is that SUS-rooted MBSA scans will only include enterprise-level approved security updates as they are available on the SUS server rather than all available updates available on the Windows Web site.

MBSA is also compatible with the SMS SUS feature pack (explained in Section 18.2.4). SMS can be used to push mbsacli.exe to all clients and perform a local security patch scan. SMS can then distribute all missing security patches to the clients.

18.2.2 Windows Update

The Windows Update service allows Windows 98, Windows 2000, Windows Me, Windows XP, and Windows Server 2003 users to easily download and install the latest Microsoft security patches. User can manually initiate a Windows Update sequence by selecting Windows Update from the Windows Start Menu, by going to the http://windowsupdate.microsoft.com URL in Internet Explorer or by running wupdmgr.exe from the command line. Windows Update will then connect to the Microsoft Windows Update Web site (illustrated in Figure 18.11) on the Internet. On this Web site, users must run through a set of steps to update their system: Initiate a scan

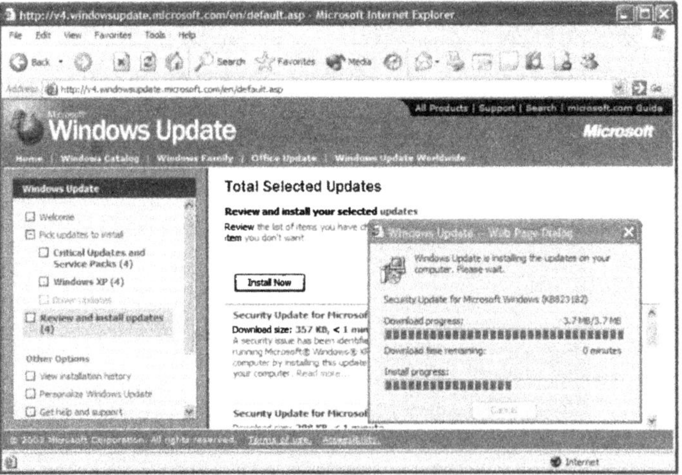

Figure 18.11
Windows Update.

(by clicking "Scan for updates"), pick the updates to install, review them, and then install the updates. Windows Update provides a patch classification system: Users must make sure they always install at least the critical patches.

Because Windows Update is a Web-based tool, it can only work if the following conditions are met:

- Internet Explorer must support cookies. IE cookie-related behavior is configured from the Privacy tab in the IE Internet Options.
- Internet Explore must allow ActiveX controls. IE ActiveX-related behavior is configured in the IE Security Zone properties.
- The user initiating a Windows Update sequence must be a member of the local Administrators group.

Windows Update can also be configured to run automatically at predefined intervals. This feature is referred to as automatic patch updating and is only available on Windows 2000 Service Pack 3 and later, Windows XP, and Windows Server 2003 systems. Automatic patch updating can be configured in different ways:

- From the properties of the My Computer object in Windows XP, Windows 2000, and Windows Server 2003. These properties are also accessible from the System Control Panel applet.
- From the Automatic Updates Control Panel applet in Windows 2000 Service Pack 3 or later
- From the system registry
- From the GPO settings (as illustrated in Figure 18.12) in Windows Server 2000 and Windows Server 2003

In all four cases, you have the option to enable or disable automatic patch updating. If you enable it, the Windows Update can notify users for both patch download and install, notify only for install, or automatically perform both the patch download and install.

To configure automatic updates from the registry (e.g., in non-AD environments), use the keys listed in Table 18.7. These keys are all located in the HKEY_LOCAL_MACHINE\Software\Policies\Microsoft\Windows\WindowsUpdate registry container. When automatic update has been configured for notification when installing only (AUOptions value 3), a dialog box similar to the one in Figure 18.13 will be presented to the user.

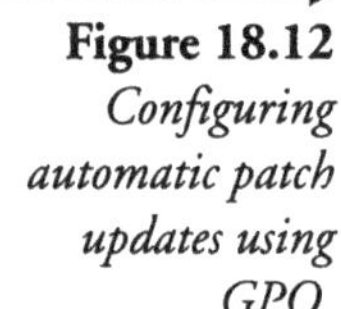

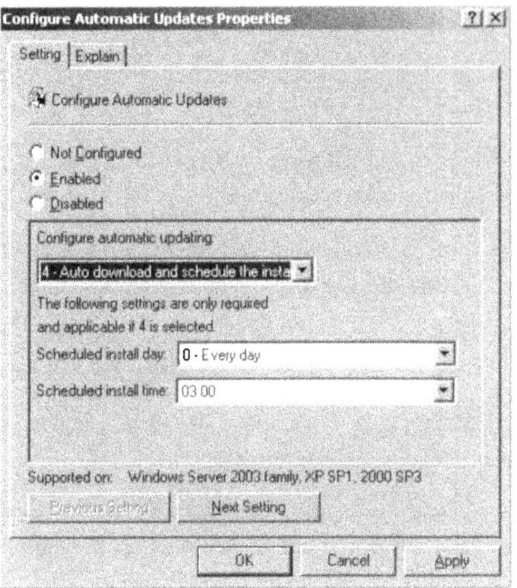

Figure 18.12 *Configuring automatic patch updates using GPO.*

18.2.3 Software Update Services

Software Update Services (SUS) builds on the Windows Update service. It gives enterprise administrators the ability to provide Windows Update–based security patch services in a controlled and secure manner. SUS can be used to set up an enterprise Windows Update server from which internal

Table 18.7 *Automatic Update Registry Keys*

Registry Key	Values and Meaning
NoAutoUpdate (REG_DWORD)	1: Automatic updates are enabled.
AUOptions (REG_DWORD)	2: Notify for download and install 3: Notify for install only 4: Automatically perform download and install following a predefined schedule
ScheduledInstallDay (REG_DWORD)	Specifies day for scheduled automatic update. 0 means every day, 1 means Sunday, . . . , 7 means Saturday.
ScheduledInstallTime(REG_DWORD)	Specifies time for scheduled automatic update. Holds a value ranging from 0 to 23.

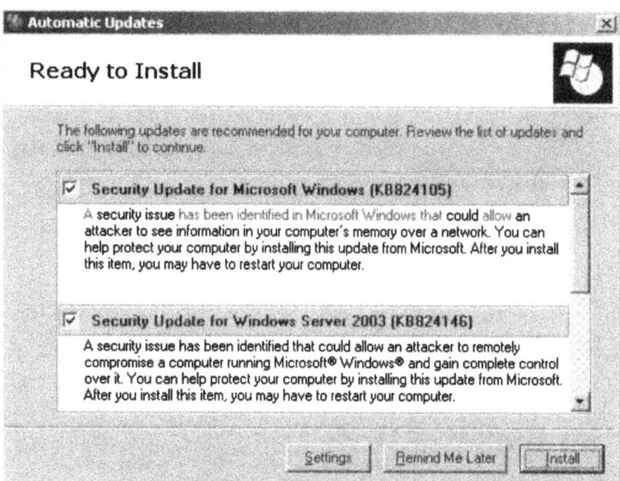

Figure 18.13 *Automatic updates dialog box.*

Windows clients can download the latest patches. To receive security patch updates, the internal Windows Update server obviously links up to the MS Windows Update infrastructure.

The SUS software is a free download available from http://www.microsoft.com/downloads/recommended/susserver. SUS requires IE 5.5 or later, IIS 5.0 or IIS 6.0, Windows 2000, or Windows Server 2003 and cannot be installed on a domain controller. It can distribute patches to Windows 2000, Windows XP, and Windows Server 2003 platforms.

SUS configuration and administration options are accessible from the SUS Administration Web page (http://<SUSServerName>/susadmin). To set configuration options, click the Set Options hyperlink (illustrated in Figure 18.14). To update the SUS server patch data, click the Synchronize Server hyperlink.

SUS also provides a security patch staging solution: It allows the SUS administrator to define which security patches are approved for distribution to its Windows clients. To approve patches, click the Approve Updates hyperlink on the SUS Administration Web page. Unlike the SUS Feature Pack for SMS 2.0 (explained next), SUS cannot define which client gets which updates. Every client that connects to the SUS server gets all approved security patches.

The SUS server used by a Windows client can be configured using GPO settings (Computer Configuration\Administrative Templates\Windows Components\Windows Update\Specify intranet Microsoft update

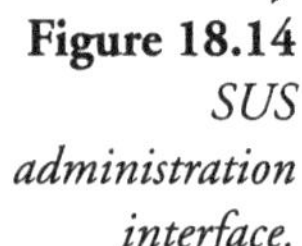

Figure 18.14 *SUS administration interface.*

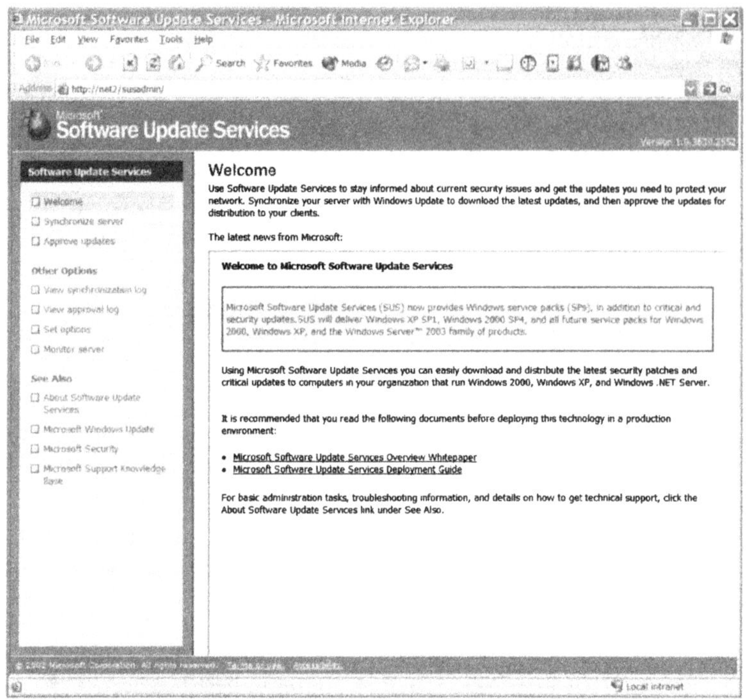

service location). In non-AD environments, you can configure the Windows clients' SUS server using the registry keys illustrated in Table 18.8. These keys are all located in the HKEY_LOCAL_MACHINE\Software\Policies\Microsoft\Windows\WindowsUpdate registry container.

18.2.4 SUS Feature Pack for SMS 2.0

The SMS Software Update Services (SUS) Feature Pack is Microsoft's most advanced security patch management tool. It provides the ability to determine security patch status, distribute patches, install patches, and generate

Table 18.8 *SUS Client Registry Keys*

Registry Key	Values and Meaning
UseWUServer (REG_DWORD)	1: use a SUS server
WUServer (REG_SZ)	Contains URL of SUS server
WUStatusServer (REG_SZ)	Contains URL of SUS statistics server

reports on the patch status. Unlike any of the other patch management tools discussed so far, the SMS SUS Feature Pack allows an administrator to identify and target specific computers for security patch updates. For example, it allows for the deployment of a specific set of patches to a subset of the machines in an enterprise.

SMS SUS Feature Pack also provides security patch update facilities for Windows platforms other than Windows XP, Windows 2000, and Windows Server 2003. Unlike SUS, SMS can also distribute and install service packs (SPs). Microsoft recommends using SMS and the SMS SUS Feature Pack when distributing patches to more than 5,000 computers. The SUS Feature Pack is specifically made for SMS version 2.0 Service Pack 3 or later. The complete Feature Pack's functionality will be an integral part of the SMS 2003 release.

The SMS SUS Feature Pack consists of four major components: the Security Update Inventory tool (uses MBSA 1.1), the MS Office Inventory tool, the Distribute Software Updates wizard, the Software Updates Installation Agent and the SMS Web Reporting tool. The SUS Feature Pack can be downloaded for free from http://www.microsoft.com/smserver/downloads/20/featurepacks/suspack/. This URL also includes pointers to the SUS Feature Pack deployment guide.

18.2.5 Qchain

Qchain allows you to install multiple security patches in a single installation run. This eliminates the need for several system reboots. Qchain works for NT 4.0, Windows 2000, Windows XP, and Windows Server 2003. The tool evaluates all of the patch components (DLLs, executables, and so forth) and makes sure that only the most recent versions of the components are installed. The following is a sample batch file script that can be used to install two security patches using qchain:

```
@echo off
setlocal
set PATHTOFIXES=c:\systemfixes
%PATHTOFIXES%\Q123456_w2k_sp1_x86.exe -z -m
%PATHTOFIXES%\Q123457_w2k_sp1_x86.exe -z -m
%PATHTOFIXES%\qchain.exe
```

In this command the –z switch prevents reboots, and the –m switch enables unattended installation. More information on the tool is available in MS Knowledge Base article Q296861.

Table 18.9 *Third-Party Security Patch Management Software*

Company	Product	URL
Altiris, Inc.	Altiris Patch Management	http://www.altiris.com
BigFix, Inc.	BigFix Patch Manager	http://www.bigfix.com
BMC Software	Patrol	http://www.bmc.com/patrol
Computer Associates	Unicenter	http://www.ca.com/unicenter
Configuresoft, Inc.	Security Update Manager	http://www.configuresoft.com
Ecora, Inc.	Ecora Patch Manager	http://www.ecora.com
GFI Software, Ltd.	GFI LANguard Network Security Scanner	http://www.gfi.com
Gravity Storm Software, LLC	Service Pack Manager 2000	http://www.securitybastion.com
Hewlett-Packard	Openview	http://openview.hp.com
IBM	Tivoli	http://www.ibm.com/tivoli
LANDesk Software, Ltd	LANDesk Patch Manager	http://www.landesk.com
Novadigm, Inc.	Radia Patch Manager	http://www.novadigm.com
PatchLink Corp.	PatchLink Update	http://www.patchlink.com
Shavlik Technologies	HFNetChk Pro	http://www.shavlik.com
St. Bernard Software	UpdateExpert	http://www.stbernard.com

18.2.6 Third-party security patch management tools

Table 18.9 gives an overview of third-party security patch management tools. It is beyond the goals of this book to cover these products in more detail.

18.3 Security-related auditing

The auditing system of an operating system keeps track of all activities that occur on a computer system. It gathers not only security-related information, but also application- and system service-related information.

18.3.1 The Event Viewer and the Event Logs

When discussing auditing in Windows Server 2003, we must address two topics: Event Logs and the Event Viewer. Windows Server 2003 gathers all events in Event Log files. By default, these files (*.evt) are located in the <%systemdirectory%>\config\ subdirectory. The default log files are named Appevent.evt, Secevent.evt, Sysevent.evt, ntds.evt, dnsevent.evt, and ntfrs.evt. The Event Logs are governed and fed by a system's Local Security Authority (LSA); see Chapter 2 for information on the LSA.

The Event Viewer is Windows' primary Event Log viewer. The Event Viewer also allows you to filter the Event Logs and display only certain categories of events. For every Event Log entry, the Event Viewer shows an event description, the account that caused the event, the event type (warning, error, or information), the event ID, the source of the event (originating service), and the date and time of the event. From a troubleshooting point of view, the event description and the event ID are the most important fields. The event ID allows you to uniquely identify the event so you can, for example, look up its meaning in the Microsoft Knowledge Base. Earlier chapters of this book contain examples of event IDs related to specific security processes. For example, for logon-related event IDs, see Chapter 4.

You may have some difficulty locating the Event Viewer in the Windows 2000, Windows XP, and Windows Server 2003 interface. It is now integrated with the Computer Management MMC snap-in. You can also view it from the Event Viewer MMC snap-in. As in NT4, you can launch the event viewer from the command prompt by typing eventvwr.

Compared to its NT4 predecessor, the Event Viewer has been extended: It includes a set of new folders to gather auditing information related to OS core services such as the Directory Service, the DNS Service, and the File Replication Service. Also, the description portion of the events has been extended, facilitating troubleshooting. Some events even include an HTTP pointer to the Microsoft online support site. Last but not least, the event logs can now also be accessed using a WMI (Windows Management Instrumentation) management interface.

Like NT4, the Event Viewer includes an application (to log application-specific information), security (to log security events), and system log (to log system-related events). The application log entries are fixed and set by the application developer. The system log entries are fixed as well and set by the OS. By default, no security entries are logged. The security entries that are logged can be configured by an administrator, as is explained in the next section. An important exception to this in Windows Server 2003 is domain controllers: They now have security auditing enabled by default for successful account logon and logon events.

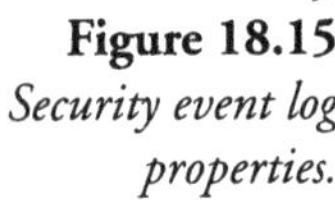

Figure 18.15 *Security event log properties.*

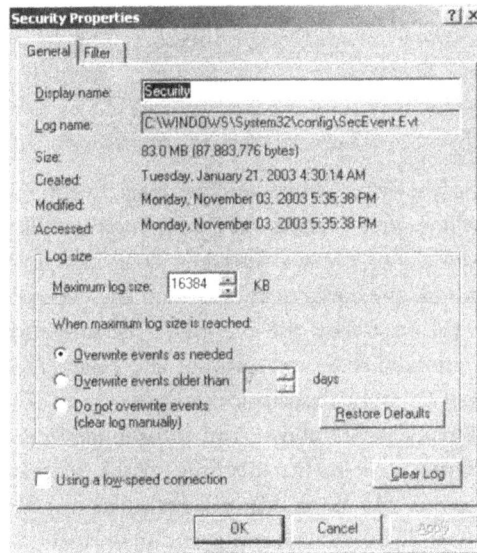

The Windows Server 2003 Event Log files have, like their NT4 and Windows 2000 predecessors, a limited size. In Windows Server 2003, the default log file size has been increased to 32 Mb; In earlier Windows versions (including Windows 2000 and Windows XP), this was 512 Kb. The maximum log size has been increased to 4 Gb. The size of a log file can be set per individual event viewer container, as illustrated in Figure 18.15 for the Security event log container. Because all event logs are permanently kept open in system memory, the practical maximum log file size limit is around 300 Mb.

To cope with this limited size, different retention policies can be set per individual container:

- Overwrite events as needed: When this option is set, the oldest events will automatically be overwritten with newer events when the log file fills up. Keeping in mind the above practical log file size limit (300 Mb each), "overwrite events as needed" is the recommended retention policy. This is not true for systems that have the crashonauditfail security policy option enabled (this option is explained below).
- Overwrite events older than X days: When this option is set, only events older than X days will be overwritten. If all events older than X days are overwritten, no more events are logged. Logging will start again from the moment some older events expire (or reach the X days limit).

- Do not overwrite events: When this option is set, no events are overwritten. When the log is full, logging stops. Logging can only be started again by manually clearing the logs.

A critical event log file is the security log. To read and clear the security logs of a Windows system of a Windows system, a user must have the "Manage auditing and security log" user right (SeSecurityPrivilege). By default, this privilege is given only to members of the Administrator group. To write to the security log, you must have the "Generate security audits" user right (SeAuditPrivilege). In addition to using these two user rights, you can also modify the access control permissions on the security event log file (secevent.evt) to better protect against unauthorized access to the security event log.

Both the Security Configuration and Analysis (SCA) tool and the security portion of the Windows Server 2003 GPOs include important event logging-related configuration settings. The settings are listed in Table 18.10, together with their corresponding registry entry. The first four settings can be set for the application, security, and system log and are set from the Event Log container in the Security Settings. The last three can be set from the Security Options in the Security Settings' Local Policies container. Table 18.11 lists the recommended values for these settings for Windows Server 2003 Domain Controllers and Member Servers.

Table 18.10 *Event Logging-Related Registry Hacks*

Setting	Registry Entry:
	HKLM\System\CurrentControlSet\Services\Eventlog\<log name>
Maximum log size	MaxSize (REG_DWORD)
Restrict local guests group from accessing log	RestrictGuestAccess (REG_DWORD)
Retain log	Retention (REG_DWORD)
Retention method for log	Retention (REG_DWORD)
	HKLM\System\CurrentControlSet\Control\LSA
Audit: Audit the access of global system objects	Auditbaseobjects (REG_DWORD)
Audit: Audit the use of Backup and Restore privilege	Fullprivilegeauditing (REG_BINARY)
Audit: Shut down system immediately if unable to log security audits	CrashOnAuditFail (REG_DWORD):

Table 18.11 *Event Logging-Related Registry Hacks Recommended Settings*

Setting	Recommendation for Domain Controllers	Recommendation for Member Servers
Maximum log size	32 Mb for System, Application, and Security logs; make sure that no log data are lost by backing up the log files at regular intervals	16,384 Kb for System, Application, and Security logs; make sure that no log data are lost by backing up the log files at regular intervals
Restrict local guests group from accessing log	Enabled for System, Application, and Security logs	Enabled for System, Application, and Security logs
Retain log (Retention method for log)	Overwrite as needed for System, Application and Security logs.	Overwrite as needed for System, Application and Security logs.
Audit: Audit the access of global system objects	Disabled	Disabled
Audit: Audit the use of Backup and Restore privilege	Enabled	Disabled
Audit: Shut down system immediately if unable to log security audits	Depends on importance of AD data	Disabled

RestrictGuestAccess and CrashOnAuditFail are two critical parameters from a security point of view. RestrictGuestAccess prohibits members of the Guests group to view the information in one of the event log containers.

CrashOnAuditFail prevents that unauthorized actions can occur when they cannot be logged in the security log. When it is enabled, Windows will crash the computer if it is unable to write an event to the event logs. The system crash occurs as a blue screen that contains a STOP error code and displays {Audit Failed} along with a description of why the audit failed. When the computer crashes, the CrashOnAuditFail value is automatically changed from 1 to 2 and the type of CrashOnAuditFail registry entry is changed from REG_DWORD to REG_NONE. After a CrashOnAudit-Fail-initiated crash, only a local administrator or a member of the Domain Admins group can log in. Before other users are allowed to log back in, the CrashOnAuditFail registry value must be deleted and readded to the system registry as a REG_DWORD with a value of either 0 or 1.

18.3.2 Setting up security-related auditing

The security auditing system in Windows Server 2003 is very closely related to the access control system. Like access control settings, auditing settings can be set on individual objects and are stored in an object's security descriptor. Each time an object is accessed, its auditing settings are checked to see whether this type of access needs to be audited. Next we will focus on how to set up security-related auditing in Windows Server 2003.

To set up security event logging, you must define a security audit policy and set auditing properties for several event categories on the object level. Once set up, Windows will log the security-related events to the security container of the Event Viewer. To look at the content of this container, you must be a local administrator on the system.

A Windows Server 2003 audit policy defines which categories of audit events will be recorded in a computer's local security log. It is defined through Group Policy Object settings on the domain, site, or OU level. You can find the audit policy in the GPO computer configuration, underneath Windows Settings\Security Settings\Local Policies\Audit Policy. You can also set the audit policy locally using the Local Security Policy configuration tool.

Table 18.12 shows the event categories that can be logged. For all categories, you can set auditing for both successful and failed attempts. Table 18.13

Table 18.12 *Audit Policy Categories*

Audit Policy Category	Meaning
Audit Account Logon Events	Monitors logon attempts against a Windows security database (SAM or AD).
Audit Account Management	Monitors creation, deletion, and modification of security principals (user, computer, and group accounts).
Audit Directory Service Access	Monitors administrative access to AD objects in the configuration and schema naming contexts. The domain naming context is covered by the "Audit Account Management" category.
Audit Logon Events	Logs events at the machine where the authentication takes place. During an interactive logon this is at the local computer. During a network login, this is at the machine where the resource is located.
Audit Object Access	Monitors access to all objects that have a system ACL (SACL).
Audit Policy Change	Logs events for audit policy changes.
Audit Privilege Use	Logs events when a security principal exercises a user right.
Audit Process Tracking	Logs events for attempts to create and end processes.
Audit System Events	Logs events for changes to the computer's operating environment. This includes changing the system time, clearing the security event log, and shutting down the computer.

Table 18.13 *Recommended Audit Policy for Domain Controllers and Members Servers*

Audit Policy Category	Domain Controller Configuration	Member Server Configuration
Audit Account Logon Events	Success, Failure	Success, Failure
Audit Account Management	Success, Failure	Success, Failure
Audit Directory Service Access	Failure	Failure
Audit Logon Events	Success, Failure	Success, Failure
Audit Object Access	Success, Failure	Success, Failure
Audit Policy Change	Success, Failure	Success, Failure
Audit Privilege Use	Failure	Not enabled
Audit Process Tracking	Not enabled	Not enabled
Audit System Events	Success, Failure	Success, Failure

shows the recommended audit settings for Windows Server 2003 domain controllers and member servers.

To set up auditing on the object level, right-click the object and select properties; then open up the Security tab, click Advanced, and select the Auditing tab. You will see that you can set up auditing based on the account or group performing an action and the type of action being performed (as

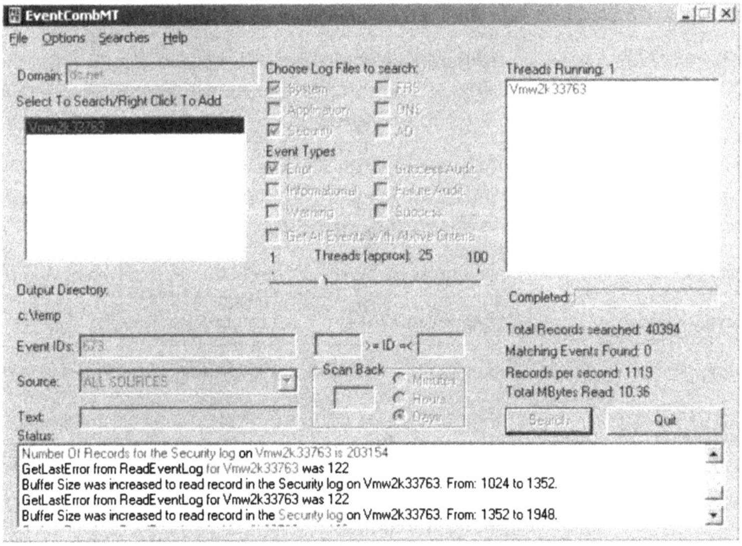

Figure 18.16 *The eventcombmt tool.*

illustrated in Figure 18.16). As with authorization, Microsoft included some important object auditing changes in Windows 2000 and Windows Server 2003:

- Windows 2000 and Windows Server 2003 permit a much finer granularity for object and property auditing than NT4. Just as with access control, auditing settings can be defined based on object types and object properties.
- Windows 2000 and Windows Server 2003 include the capability to define auditing setting inheritance between parent and child objects.
- The object auditing administration interface has been extended to reflect the changes mentioned previously and is integrated with the new ACL editor.

18.3.3 Event log-related tools

To archive the log file content, you can rely on your standard backup utility. To make sure that no log entries are lost, you must align the log settings described earlier with the archival procedure. To dump the content of the event log, you can use command-line tools such as Microsoft's dumpel.exe or Systinternals' psloglist.exe. The first one can be downloaded from the MS Downloads Web site. The second one is available from the Sysinternals Web site. The following dumpel command will dump all events in the security log on a server named Myserver to a file named security.xls:

```
dumpel -f security.xls -s myserver -l security
```

Dumpel can also filter out certain event types when it dumps the event log content. For example, to filter out event ID 528 in the above example, type:

```
dumpel -f security.xls -s myserver -l security -e 528
```

A great resource kit tool to query the local and remote event logs is the eventcombmt.exe (illustrated in Figure 18.17) Resource Kit utility. It allows an administrator to look for occurrences of a single event ID, multiple event IDs, a range of event IDs, specific event types or sources, or a specific event message text. The eventcombmt tool drops the results of its query in the eventcombmt.txt file in a system's temporary folder.

A brand-new tool is the Microsoft Audit Collection System (MACS), which provides a security log collection service. MACS facilitates role separation between Windows system administrators and IT system auditors. Before MACS, Microsoft customers had to turn to products like Sentry or

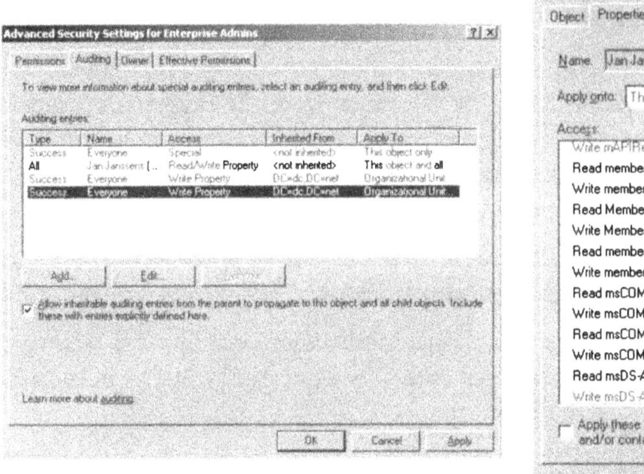

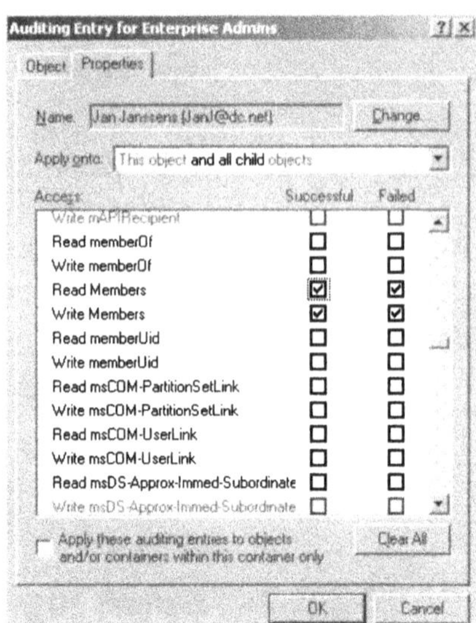

Figure 18.17 *Setting up auditing.*

Microsoft MOM to provide this kind of functionality. MACS is made up of a client (the MACS agent) and a server component (the MACS collector). The MACS server stores the security log data in a SQL Server or MSDE database. Transport of the log data happens in a secure way. MACS agents locate the MACS collector using a DNS SRV record (named _adtserver). Here MACS agents can authenticate to the MACS collector using Kerberos or SSL (in non-domain environments). MACS provides an API that can be used by application developers to build host-based intrusion detection systems (IDSs). MACS is an add-on service to Windows Server 2003. The first release of the service will be made available as a free Web download; later releases may be integrated with the Microsoft Operations Manager (MOM). At the time of writing, MACS was planned to run on Windows 2000, Windows XP, and Windows Server 2003.

The ITU-T X.509 Standard for Certificate and CRL Formats

These tables list and explain the different fields that make up an X.509 certificate and CRL. More detailed information can be found in the ITU-T X.509 Recommendation (version 03/2000), which can be downloaded from the ITU Web site at www.itu.int.

Table A.1 *X.509 Certificate Format*

X.509 Field Name	Field Meaning	X.509 Version/Optional-Required/ Criticality for Extensions
Version	X.509 version of the encoded certificate	V1 Required
SerialNumber	Unique serial number of the certificate. The serial number together with the issuer name identify a unique certificate.	V1 Required
Signature	Contains the algorithm identifier for the algorithm and hash function used by the CA when signing the certificate.	V1 Required
Issuer	Identifies the entity that has signed and issued the certificate.	V1 Required
Validity	Start and end date of the certificate or the time interval during which the CA warrants that it will maintain status information of the certificate.	V1 Required
Subject	Identifies the entity associated with the public key found in the subject public key field.	V1 Required
SubjectPublicKeyInfo	Carries public key being certified and identifies the algorithm of which the public key is an instance.	V1 Required

Table A.1 *X.509 Certificate Format (continued)*

X.509 Field Name	Field Meaning	X.509 Version/Optional-Required/ Criticality for Extensions
IssuerUniqueIdentifer	Used to uniquely identify an issuer in case of a name reuse.	V2 Optional
SubjectUniqueIdentifier	Used to uniquely identify a subject in case of a name reuse.	V2 Optional
Extensions	Allows addition of new fields to the certificate structure.	V3 Optional
AuthorityKeyIdentifier	Identifies public key to be used for certificate signature verification.	V3 Optional—always Noncritical
SubjectKeyIdentifier	Identifies public key being certified .	V3 Optional—always Noncritical
KeyUsage	Identifies purpose for which the certified public key is used.	V3 Optional—Critical or Non-critical
PrivateKeyUsagePeriod	Indicates period of use of private key corresponding to certified public key.	V3 Optional—always Noncritical
Certificate Policies	Identifies certificate policies, recognized by issuing CA, that apply to this certificate.	V3 Optional—Critical or Non-critical
PolicyMappings	For CA certificates only: Maps certificate policy defined in one domain to policy in another domain.	V3 Optional—always Noncritical
SubjectAltName	Alternative names for the certificate subject.	V3 Optional—Critical or Non-critical
IssuerAltName	Alternative names for the certificate issuer.	V3 Optional—Critical or Non-critical
SubjectDirectoryAttributes	Lists directory attributes for the certificate subject.	V3 Optional—always Noncritical
BasicConstraints	"CA" field: Can public key listed in this certificate be used to verify other certificates? "PathLengthConstraint" field: Maximum number of certificates that can follow this certificate in certification path.	V3 Optional—Critical or Non-critical
NameConstraints	Indicates name space within which all subject names in subsequent certificates in a certification path shall be located.	V3 Optional—Critical or Non-critical

Table A.1 *X.509 Certificate Format (continued)*

X.509 Field Name	Field Meaning	X.509 Version/Optional-Required/ Criticality for Extensions
PolicyConstraints	Specifies constraints that may require explicit certificate policy identification or inhibit policy mapping for the remainder of the certification path.	V3 Optional—Critical or Non-critical
InhibitAnyPolicy	Specifies that any-policy is not considered an explicit match for other certificate policies.	V3 Optional—Critical or Non-critical
CRLDistributionPoints	Identifies CRL Distribution Point to which a certificate user should refer to ascertain if the certificate has been revoked.	V3 Optional—Critical or Non-critical
Signature	Digital signature on certificate content.	V1 Required

Table A.2 *x.509 CRL Format*

X.509 Field Name	Field Meaning	X.509 version/Optional-Required/ Criticality for Extensions
Version	X.509 version of the encoded CRL.	Optional
Signature	Contains the algorithm identifier for the algorithm and hash function used by the CA when signing the CRL.	Required
Issuer	Identifies the entity that has signed and issued the CRL.	Required
ThisUpdate	Indicates the issue date of the CRL.	Required
NextUpdate	Indicates the date by which the next CRL will be issued.	Optional
RevokedCertificates	Lists the revoked certificates.	Optional
UserCertificate	Serial number of the revoked certificate.	Required
Revocationdate	Specifies date on which revocation occurred.	Required
CRLentryExtensions	Used to provide additional information on single CRL entries.	Optional—V2 only
ReasonCode	Identifies reason for certificate revocation	Optional—always Noncritical

Table A.2 *x.509 CRL Format (continued)*

X.509 Field Name	Field Meaning	X.509 version/Optional-Required/ Criticality for Extensions
HoldInstructionCode	Provides a registered instruction identifier indicating the action to be taken after encountering a certificate that has been placed on hold.	Optional—always Noncritical
Invaliditydate	Provides date on which it is suspected that the private key was compromised.	Optional—always Noncritical
CertificateIssuer	Allows a CRL to include entries from more than one certificate issuer.	Optional—always Critical
CrlExtensions	Used to provide additional information on the whole CRL.	Optional—V2 only
AuthorityKeyIdentifier	Provides a means to identify the public key that is needed to validate the CRL signature.	Optional—always Noncritical
IssuerAltName	Allows additional name forms to be associated with the CRL issuer.	Optional—Critical or Noncritical
CRLNumber	Increasing sequence number for each CRL issued by the CRL issuer.	Optional—always Noncritical
deltaCRLIndicator	Identifies a CRL as a delta CRL,	Optional—always Critical
IssuingDistributionPoint	Identifies the CRL distribution point for a CRL and indicates whether the CRL covers revocation for end entity certificates only, CA certificates only, or a limited set of reason codes.	Optional—always Critical
FreshestCRL	Identifies how to obtain delta CRL information for the base CRL containing the extension.	Optional—always Noncritical
SignatureValue	Digital signature on CRL content.	Required

B

PKCS Standards

PKCS #1: RSA Encryption Standard

PKCS #2: Integrated in PKCS#1

PKCS #3: Diffie-Hellman Key-Agreement Standard

PKCS #4: Integrated in PKCS#1

PKCS #5: Password-Based Encryption Standard (PBE)

PKCS #6: Extended-Certificate Syntax Standard

PKCS #7: Cryptographic Message Syntax Standard

PKCS #8: Private-Key Information Syntax Standard

PKCS #9: Defines Selected Attribute Types for use in other PKCS standards

PKCS #10: Certification Request Syntax Standard

PKCS #11: Cryptographic Token Interface Standard

PKCS #12: Personal Information Exchange Syntax Standard

PKCS #13: Elliptic Curve Cryptography Standard

PKCS #14: Pseudo Random Number Generation

PKCS #15: Cryptographic Token Information Format Standard

Index

www.ingramcontent.com/pod-product-compliance
Lightning Source LLC
Chambersburg PA
CBHW080337220326
41598CB00030B/4530

* 9 7 8 1 5 5 5 5 8 2 8 3 8 *